European Politics in Transition

European Politics in Transition

FIFTH EDITION

Mark Kesselman
Columbia University

Joel Krieger
Wellesley College

Christopher S. Allen
University of Georgia

Stephen Hellman
York University

David Ost
Hobart & William Smith Colleges

George Ross
Brandeis University

Houghton Mifflin Company   Boston   New York

MK—for Rasil and Romen Basu
JK—for Lyn and Patrick Dougherty

Publisher: Charles Hartford
Sponsoring Editor: Katherine Meisenheimer
Development Editor: Fran Gay
Editorial Assistant: Kristen Craib
Senior Project Editor: Bob Greiner
Editorial Assistant: Robert Woo
Senior Art and Design Coordinator: Jill Haber
Senior Photo Editor: Jennifer Meyer Dare
Senior Composition Buyer: Sarah Ambrose
Senior Manufacturing Coordinator: Marie Barnes
Senior Marketing Manager: Nicola Poser

Cover Photo:
European Parliament in Strasbourg, France.
Photographs © Vincent Kessler/Reuters/Corbis.

Printed in the U.S.A.

Library of Congress Catalog Number: 2004117527

ISBN: 0-618-43295-7

1 2 3 4 5 6 7 8 9-MP-09 08 07 06 05

Brief Contents

Contents

Part III: Britain   133

JOEL KRIEGER

Part IV: France   213

MARK KESSELMAN

Part V: Germany   301

CHRISTOPHER S. ALLEN

Part VI: Italy   401

STEPHEN HELLMAN

Part VII: East-Central Europe in Transition   497

DAVID OST

Maps

Preface

For several editions of *European Politics in Transition* colleagues have warned us that sooner or later the title would outlive its usefulness. But Europe has once again proven these friendly admonitions premature! From a Europe of six prosperous West European countries at the founding of the European Economic Community (EEC) in 1958 to a mélange of twenty-five diverse polities tilting east and heading south today, Europe has been transformed—and the end is still not in sight, as illustrated by the decision in 2004 to open negotiations with Turkey over membership in the European Union (EU). Europe remains a moving target, as the institutional, cultural, constitutional, and geographical dimensions of the continent—and the Union—remain in flux, and dramatically so. Who knows what other changes teachers and students of European politics will have to absorb in the coming months and years?

This context of fast-paced and in some cases historic changes has inspired the work of all the contributors to the fifth edition of *European Politics in Transition*. Like any text in comparative politics, *European Politics in Transition* looks to bring politics alive for students and provide the wherewithal for instructors to come to terms with the protean patterns of continuity as well as change in the institutions and processes of government within—and across—the countries that comprise our case studies.

This edition of *European Politics in Transition* reflects several significant developments:

- In substantive terms, we address the consequences of globalization in a more focused way than in the fourth edition.

- We analyze the historic constitution-building developments in the EU and consider the implications of enlargement for European integration from the perspective of the fifteen members of the EU in the West as well as from the perspective of the new members to the East.

- We highlight even more than in past editions the centrality of the EU for the domestic politics of our country studies. Four of the five chapters of the country treatments include a subsection on the EU, thus providing clear comparative analysis of the interplay of domestic and European politics and policies. We identify the EU as the last historical juncture in the first chapter of each country section; in the second chapter, we provide a subsection on European integration; the third chapter emphasizes the European dimensions of governance and policy-making; and the fifth chapter includes the challenges of European integration.

- We address the consequences of the terrorist attack on the United States on September 11, 2001, and the subsequent war on terrorism for political institutions, processes, and policies in each country case study.

- We consider the repercussions of these developments—as well as the war in Iraq and its aftermath—on relations with the United States.

- We highlight issues involving immigration and the challenges posed by growing ethnic and religious diversity.

We are happy to reassure instructors, however, that when it comes to the organization and design of the text, there is far more continuity than change! As in previous editions, the fifth edition begins with an Introduction, which provides a general framework for the rest of the text. Then, given the extraordinary significance of enlargement and constitution-building within the EU, as in the fourth edition we open this edition with a comprehensive and timely section on the EU. Moreover, the country sections provide running analyses of the interplay between the EU and national politics.

As in the fourth edition of *European Politics in Transition*, we organize our treatment within the same framework for analyzing continuity and change that is used in *Introduction to Comparative Politics* (Houghton Mifflin, 3rd edition, 2004), an introductory comparative text that we co-edit with William Joseph. A distinctive feature of both books is our application of four comparative themes to frame the analysis and presentation of each country study. We explain the themes in the Introduction, and present an intriguing puzzle for each theme to stimulate student reactions and encourage them to extract a variety of "solutions" as they work through the country studies. These themes focus attention on the continuities and contrasts described in the text:

- **A World of States** highlights the importance of state formation and the changing dynamics of interstate relations, transnational processes, and globalization for understanding domestic political developments.

- **Governing the Economy** analyzes state strategies for promoting economic competitiveness and stresses the effects of globalization on domestic policies and political outcomes.
- **The Democratic Idea** examines the challenges posed by citizens' demands for greater control and participation in governance and highlights the gaps everywhere between theory and practice.
- **The Politics of Collective Identities** considers the political consequences of race, ethnicity, gender, religion, and nationality, the problems of social exclusion, and the challenges of governance.

Instructors who have previously used *European Politics in Transition* will find that this edition both reflects the approach we have developed in earlier editions and involves a top-to-bottom updating and refinement of our coverage to reflect epochal developments and scholarship of the past few years. As always, the contributors and editors have done everything we can to provide timely, engaging, and authoritative analysis of European politics and EU developments, as they unfold, and to locate these developments within firm institutional and historical contexts.

We have been fortunate to receive excellent advice from many colleagues, including Paul R. Abramson, Michigan State University; Mark Croatti, George Washington University; Ronald A. Francisco, University of Kansas; Sylvia Maier, Georgia Institute of Technology; and Bumba Mukherjee, New York University. We are grateful to the superb staff at Houghton Mifflin Company, including Katherine Meisenheimer, Frances Gay, Bob Greiner, and Robert Woo.

M. K.
J. K.

European Politics in Transition

P A R T

I

Introduction

Mark Kesselman/Joel Krieger

The whirl of daily newspaper headlines and television news broadcasts flattens events and makes it difficult to distinguish between issues that are of more important and enduring significance as opposed to those that may be hard to recall in a month. Consider early 2004. Amid the myriad events occurring in Europe, four, described here in chronological order, may eventually be regarded as involving substantial changes in contemporary European politics:

1. *March 11, 2004.* Tragically, Europe experienced its own version of 9/11 when, during the morning rush hour on March 11, 2004, in Madrid, Spain, nearly two hundred commuters were killed and hundreds more were injured by two powerful bomb attacks on rail lines. The terrorist assault, probably in retaliation for Spain's partnership with the United States during the invasion of Iraq in 2003, was on a far smaller scale than the assaults of 9/11/01 on the World Trade Center in New York and the Pentagon in Washington, D.C. (Along with the British government of Prime Minister Tony Blair, the Spanish government of José María Aznar was the United States's closest ally during the second Iraq war.) Moreover, unlike the United States, Europe had been the site of numerous internationally based terrorist attacks, and the Madrid bombings did not produce a cataclysm in Spanish politics comparable to what occurred in U.S. politics following the events of 9/11. However, an immediate result was that the incumbent Spanish government, which had strongly supported the United States, was voted out of office in parliamentary elections held days after the bombings. Yet in a key respect 3/11 resembled 9/11: both sent a loud signal that there is no sanctuary from terrorism.

2. *May 1, 2004.* The European Union (EU) is an organization of states in Europe that promotes political and economic integration as well as increased foreign and security policy cooperation among its members. Among the international organizations in the world today, such as the United Nations, the International Monetary Fund, and the World Trade Organization, the EU ranks as the one with the broadest regulatory scope and most extensive powers over the citizens, organizations, and states that are part of the organization. For this reason, it has been called a quasi-state. First known as the European Economic Community, it was established in 1957, not long after World War II, in reaction to the horrific violence and destruction of that war (the second world war in less than three decades). Its aim was to promote economic cooperation among its members as a way to prevent another cycle of interstate violence on the European continent.

The EU initially included only six member states of continental Western Europe on a quite narrow basis: EU member states agreed to reduce tariffs on imports of raw materials, notably coal and iron, from other EU member states. From 1957 until 1995, the organization grew from six to fifteen members; it changed its name in 1994 to the European Union. The difference in designation reflected the fact that the EU has substantially broadened and deepened the scope of its activities. As we will describe in Part 2, the EU now regulates a vast array of activities, and its key institutions—the European Commission, the European Central Bank, and the European Court of Justice—have far-reaching powers over member states. From a small, narrowly focused organization, the EU has evolved into a quasistate. Indeed, in June 2004, final details were hammered out for a draft constitution for the EU. If and when it is formally ratified, the constitution will specify the EU's institutional architecture and operating procedures. The result would be to create order and simplify the many thousands of EU treaty commitments, regulations, and directives that have accumulated since the EU's creation.

What is the significance of May 1, 2004, the date opening this description of the EU? The answer is that, on that day, the EU nearly doubled in size, from fifteen to twenty-five member states. Moreover, the region of Europe in which the new member states are located is also enormously significant. Until 2004, the EU was a club of relatively wealthy states from Western Europe, stretching from southern Europe (Greece, Italy, Spain, and Portugal) to northern Europe (Germany, Sweden, and Denmark). The states that joined in 2004 were predominantly located in Eastern and Central Europe, such as Poland, the Czech Republic, and Hungary. These states are quite poor and were successors to the communist regimes that ruled in the halfcentury after World War II.

There are immense challenges ahead both for the new member states and for the EU in "digesting" the change. On the one hand, because EU membership requires member states to comply with a vast array of demanding economic and political directives, the new members will be busy reorganizing their legislation, policies, and activities. In some cases, these changes will impose substantial economic hardship on the citizens of these countries. On the other hand, the EU faces a daunting task in harmonizing policies that apply to states of vastly different levels of economic and political development. Yet, whatever the outcome, the fact that the EU undertook this substantial expansion signifies that Europe is undergoing an extraordinary evolution that remakes not only the map delineating geographic boundaries but also Europe's political, economic, and social landscape.

3. *Mid-May, 2004.* Soon after the accession of the ten new states to the EU, the Organisation for Economic Co-operation (OECD) issued its semiannual economic report analyzing the world economy. The OECD is an organization of wealthy industrialized countries focusing on providing economic analysis and advice to the thirty member states of the organization. The headline in the World Business section of the *New York Times* on May 12, 2004, stated that the OECD "Says Europe Is Lagging in Global Recovery." The article described the report's major finding: "The United States and Asia are leaving Europe behind in an accelerating, but uneven global economic recovery."[1]

Europe has been among the wealthiest regions in the world for centuries, and it continues to enjoy great prosperity. Moreover, European states provide their citizens with extensive assistance to counteract life's hazards, including nearly free medical care, extensive unemployment insurance, decent pensions, paid maternity (and in some cases paternity) leave, low-cost university education for those who pass stiff high school graduation exams, and on and on.

During the glory years following the reconstruction from damage from World War II, Europe seemed to have it all. It had found the secret of combining both economic growth and efficiency along with social equity (provided by the extensive social provisions just described). Yet, as the OECD report released in May 2004 describes, Europe has at least temporarily stumbled. Not only is growth lagging, both compared with past performance and relative to that of other regions in the world, but the crisis of the welfare state is a familiar theme in virtually every European country. In brief, Europe has gone from having its cake and eating it—that is, growth with equity—to having less of both.

4. *June 10–13, 2004.* This date registers the impact of the three earlier developments. On June 10–13, elections were held throughout the member states of the EU to select members of the European Parliament (the EP), the assembly that meets in Strasbourg, France, and is the representative institution of the European Union. Three results of these elections are worthy of notice—and troubling.

- The elections occurred at a highly auspicious moment: just after the enlargement of the EU and as the final details of the EU constitution were being negotiated. Yet relatively few citizens bothered to turn out to elect representatives to the EP. Abstentions hit record levels. Turnout was just over 50 percent in the fifteen states that were members of the EU prior to the accession of the ten new entrants. However, when viewed from the perspective of Eastern and Central Europe, Western Europe appeared to be a model of civic participation. For, in the ten states just acceding to membership in the EU—an achievement that was feted as historic throughout the region—voting turnout was barely 40 percent; it was a dismal 20 percent in Poland, the largest of the new members of the EU! The fact that voters throughout Europe paid so little attention to the elections bodes badly for the EU project.

- Those voters who did come to the polls tended to vote against candidates to the EP associated with incumbent national governments. There were nationally specific reasons for voters expressing displeasure with their national leaders: British voters were punishing Prime Minister Tony Blair for his close partnership with the United States during the second Iraq war; French and German voters were opposing their incumbent governments' support of welfare state retrenchment (note that in 2004 a left-leaning government sat in Germany and a conservative one governed France); and Italian voters were registering their opposition to Prime Minister Berlusconi's high-handed style of governing and corruption scandals that considerably exceeded the norm, even for past Italian governments—which are not known for their squeaky-clean records! But the consistent pattern of opposing governments that have supported the deepening of European integration seems to unite voters across the continent and across the political spectrum. This raises unsettling questions about the future of Europe.

- The last point is highlighted by a third salient feature of the elections: a significantly larger proportion of voters throughout the continent chose candidates from parties openly opposed to the EU. Whether it was the UK Independence Party (UKIP) in Britain or what the French dub "sovereignist," or nationalist, parties—those that champion the defense of national sovereignty against what they regard as the illegitimate and oppressive hand of the EU—substantial minorities of voters openly rejected the form that European integration has been taking in recent years. This discontented group is a reminder that the EU has produced costs as well as benefits for Europeans.

"It was the best of times; it was the worst of times." We borrow the famous opening line of Charles Dickens's *A Tale of Two Cities,* set in London and Paris during the French Revolution in the late eighteenth century, to describe the tumultuous character of the current transition in European politics. In a manner reminiscent of the period of violent revolutions in Dickens's time, the European continent is apparently, as it was when Dickens wrote, at the close of one era and the beginning of another.

Does Europe comprise, as it has for centuries, discrete sovereign states, animated by national identities and interests? Or have processes of European integration inaugurated more than a half-century ago produced a European Union that is a genuinely transnational polity? More than ever before, students of European politics must weigh and evaluate both propositions, for each captures important truths about contemporary Europe. Considered side by side, they identify the current transition in European politics marked by the challenges of overlapping jurisdictions, multilevel governance, negotiated sovereignties, and even the shifting boundaries of what is meant by Europe.

Of course, there is far more at play in Europe than tensions between nation-states and the EU. The revolutions of 1989 in Eastern and Central Europe marked the disintegration of much of the communist world. When the Berlin Wall, which divided East and West in both physical and symbolic terms, was dismantled brick by brick in November 1989, the architecture of Europe was forever altered. Within a year, Germany was unified after nearly a half-century of cold war division, and by the end of 1991 the Soviet Union had splintered into fifteen troubled republics. The destruction of the wall, resulting from the pent-up pressures for change originating in the East, opened the floodgates between East and West Berlin, East and West Germany, and Eastern and Western Europe. The result was a massive movement of ideas, commodities, capital, technology, and people. Immediately, the people of East-Central Europe faced rapid and often disorienting dual transitions to market economies and democratic polities. These transitions, swiftly followed by the accession to EU membership of many of the former communist states in East and Central Europe—literally unthinkable until the 1990s—are fundamentally redefining the political geography and the identity of Europe.

By highlighting the importance of Europe's recently redrawn boundaries, we do not mean to imply that the process is complete. The EU does not comprise numerous states in Eastern Europe. Most were formerly part of the Soviet empire. Although they hope to join the EU, their application for membership has not yet been accepted because EU members consider that their political and economic performance does not qualify them for membership in the select club. Two states should be singled out for particular notice. One is the biggest and most powerful state of them all: Russia, which straddles Europe and Asia. Probably because cold war divisions have not entirely disappeared, there is no imminent prospect that Russia will seek membership in the EU or that, if it does, its application would be approved. The second state is Turkey, which also straddles Europe and Asia. In contrast with Russia, Turkey has ardently pursued the dream of joining the EU. However, until 2004, it had consistently been turned away. The stated reason is that Turkey is

not a sufficiently authentic democracy to qualify for membership in an organization that puts a premium on democratic governance. However, a more troublesome reason is that Turkey would be the first predominantly non-Christian country to join; indeed, although it is an increasingly secular country, nearly all of Turkey's almost 70 million people are Muslim. This is an important reason why many EU members oppose Turkey's application, for the xenophobia directed at Muslims and the association of Christianity with European identity seem to create hurdles for Turkish membership that are higher than those faced by other countries seeking admission. In 2004, the EU Commission agreed to open negotiations with Turkey over Turkey joining the EU. The decision has significant ramifications for the meaning of Europe as well as for Turkey's future. Thus, despite the enormous changes that have occurred toward enlarging and integrating member states in the EU, Europe remains an unfinished story in key respects.

Although much remains unresolved, the wall dividing Europe has come down in intellectual terms, and the patterns of development and questions we ask about East and West are more similar than they were before. Without neglecting the distinctive historical and institutional legacies of the nations of East-Central Europe, we can now—perhaps for the first time since the early twentieth century—consider some critical common themes. We can study the political causes and consequences of changes in economic performance and investigate in each country the growing demands for political participation by those who do not consider themselves adequately represented through the formal channels of government. We can consider the ebb and flow of xenophobic and hypernationalistic movements. And we can study the complex interplay of international and domestic politics within a context of increasing global interdependence, European integration, and the post-9/11 and post-3/11 shadow of terrorism. Indeed, we have just sketched out the four key themes that frame our discussion of

European politics in transition, at the level of each country we analyze and at the level of the EU: the interaction of states within the international order; the role of states in economic management; the challenges resulting from demands for more participation, transparency, and accountability facing the transitional democracies of East-Central Europe, the durable democracies of Western Europe, and the EU itself; and the political impact of diverse sources of social identity and group attachments.

What Makes Europe . . . Europe?

This book is about the politics of Europe, a politics shaped by specific country-by-country as well as regional histories, cultures, political systems, and institutional genealogies. The countries of EU Europe share important similarities in levels of development and long-standing democratic traditions with the United States and other capitalist democracies, such as Canada, Japan, and Australia. Yet there is both a quite distinctive European model of political governance and social policy, and significant country-by-country variations. Similarly, the countries of East-Central Europe share some common experiences and challenges with transitional democracies in other parts of the world, such as Argentina or Nigeria, but the challenges they face are compounded by their need to develop democracy and the market economy at the same time; few other transitional democracies in regions outside East-Central Europe must confront a nearly half-century legacy of command economies. Moreover, the postsocialist pathways that these countries follow are highly influenced by specific national trajectories.[2]

European Politics in Transition investigates both the whole and the parts: European politics at a critical juncture in the geographical and political-institutional integration of the region and the different ways specific countries have addressed common challenges such as competitiveness, integration, democratization, social di-

versity, EU membership or exclusion, terrorism, and relations with the one remaining superpower across the Atlantic Ocean. Before undertaking the systematic study of European politics, we need to clarify some important issues concerning the meaning and practice of democracy, the organization of the economy, and the cultural context.

What Is the Meaning—or, Rather, Meanings—of Democracy?

As with many other important concepts, debate over the meaning of democracy is contentious. The wide popularity of the term conceals some important ambiguities, and we can identify contending positions on many key issues regarding the very definition. Should democracy be defined solely on the basis of the procedures used to select top governmental officeholders? That is, for a political system to qualify as democratic, is it sufficient that occupants of the highest offices of the state be selected on the basis of free, fair elections in which opposing parties are allowed to organize to present candidates and all citizens are entitled to cast a vote for a contending party? Or must there be respect for citizens' civil liberties (including rights of free expression, dissent, and privacy), regardless of what a democratically elected government might desire? What is the relationship between religious practice and the exercise of political power? To what extent must all citizens be guaranteed certain minimum economic and social rights and resources in a democratic regime, as distinct from political and civil rights (such as the right to vote and criticize the government)? Otherwise put, what is the relationship between democracy defined in purely procedural terms and democracy defined as a system that provides an adequate level of resources and promotes substantive equalities?

Despite intense debates about the meaning(s) of democracy, a rough consensus has emerged among practitioners and students of comparative politics, or "comparativists," about the minimum required for a regime to qualify as democratic. Generally, the following conditions must obtain:

- Selection to the highest public offices is on the basis of free and fair elections. For an election to qualify as fair, votes must be counted accurately, with the winning candidate(s) selected according to preexisting rules that determine the kind of plurality or majority required to gain electoral victory.

- All citizens possess civil and political rights—the right to participate and vote in elections periodically held to select key state officeholders—and civil liberties—the rights of free assembly, conscience, privacy, and expression, including the right to criticize the government.

- Political parties are free to organize, present candidates for public office, and compete in elections.

- The opposition party or parties—those not represented in government—enjoy adequate rights of contestation—that is, the right to organize and to criticize the incumbent government.

- The elected government develops policy according to specified procedures that provide for due process and the accountability of elected executives (at the next election, through judicial action, and, in parliamentary systems, to parliament).

- The political system contains a judiciary with powers independent of the executive and legislature, charged with protecting citizens' civil rights and liberties from violation by government and other citizens, as well as with ensuring that governmental officials respect constitutionally specified procedures.

Although these six points make a useful checklist of the essential elements of a democracy, several qualifications should be added. First, this definition does not claim that electoral outcomes are always (or possibly even often) rational, equitable, or wise. Democracy specifies a set of procedures for making decisions, but it does not guarantee the wisdom of the outcome. Indeed, as we discuss below, in the fourth qualification to the checklist, we believe that political outcomes

in all democracies, in respect to both elections to office and the decisions of officeholders, are systematically and importantly influenced by economic inequalities that limit the ideal of "one person, one vote."

Second, no government has ever fully lived up to democratic standards. All democratic governments at various points in their histories have violated them to a greater or lesser extent. For example, Britain retained a system of plural votes for certain citizens until after World War II; French women did not gain the right to vote until 1945.

Third, the way that the constituent elements of democracy on the checklist are interpreted and implemented is often debatable and sometimes becomes a contentious political issue. For example, in the 1990s, and again in 2004, there was intense controversy in France about whether Muslim girls should be permitted to wear a headscarf, which signifies adherence to Islam, to public school. On the one hand, many public officials and citizens wanted to prohibit girls from wearing the scarf on the grounds that France is a secular state and that prominently displaying the scarf constitutes proselytizing in public schools and symbolizes girls' subordinate status. On the other hand, defenders of the practice argued that Muslim girls were simply exercising their fundamental right of self-expression.

Fourth, economic inequalities load the political deck. Wealthy citizens, powerful interest groups, and business firms can use their substantial resources to increase their chances of winning an election or influencing public policy. This creates a tension in all democracies, to a greater or lesser degree, between the formal political procedures (such as voting), in which all are equal, and the actual situation, in which the affluent are, in novelist George Orwell's famous phrase from the satirical novel *Animal Farm*, "more equal" than others because of their ability to have greater political influence.

The tension between citizens' economic inequalities and their equal right to participate in the choice of elected officials and governmental policies—that is, the tension between "one person, one vote" and "one euro, one vote"—is found in all European democracies and is typically a source of intense political division. Opposing political coalitions advocate very different governmental policies that reflect the interests of their distinctive socioeconomic constituencies. Three key areas of policy difference involve the following issues:

- *The distribution of tax burdens.* Although all governments levy taxes on citizens and businesses to support government activities, who pays how much is often a source of intense political debate.
- *Governmental economic priorities.* Should economic policy be directed above all toward restraining inflation (a particular concern for the affluent or elderly, since inflation threatens to reduce the value of their assets and savings) or toward reducing unemployment (which traditionally has harmed working people the most)?
- *The extent of governmental spending for social programs.* How much can and should be spent on the public provision of job training, unemployment compensation, old-age pensions, assistance to the needy, and other programs that are part of what is commonly called the welfare state?

Finally, although all democracies share the six key elements outlined above, democracies vary widely in their political institutions. A common classification of democracies is based on differing relationships between the executive and the legislature. In presidential systems, such as in the United States, the chief executive (the president) and the national legislature are chosen in separate elections, and there is a sharp separation of powers between the executive branch and the legislature. This system is actually an unusual form of democracy. Most of the world's democracies (including Britain, Germany, and Italy) have parliamentary governments in which executive and legislative powers are fused rather than separated: the chief executive (whether called prime minister, chancellor, or president)

and the cabinet are chosen from the legislature and generally are the leaders of the dominant party in parliament.

The formal and informal rules of the game for reaching and exercising power are very different in presidential and parliamentary systems. In presidential systems, members of the legislature jealously preserve their autonomy. Because the legislature is elected separately from the president, it is constitutionally authorized to set its own agenda, initiate policy proposals, and defy presidential directives. Presidents have resources that they can deploy more or less effectively to persuade the legislature to go along, but even when the same party controls both the presidency and the legislature, the key word is *persuade.*

In parliamentary systems, the legislature may serve as a forum for dramatic policy debate, but it represents neither an independent source of policy initiatives nor a decisive obstacle that prevents the government from legislating its own proposals. On rare occasions, a rebellion within the ranks of the majority party (or coalition) in parliament brings down the cabinet—that is, forces the chief executive to resign. However, one can count such examples on one hand in post–World War II Britain and Germany. The fact that this happens all the time in Italy suggests the value of comparing particular systems, as we do in this book, rather than engaging in generalizations about political systems.

"So what?" you may ask in response to this discussion of political institutions. Good question![3] Ponder what difference the type of system makes as you study parliamentary and presidential systems in this book. And note how rare presidential systems are—a point that may surprise those who think that the U.S. presidential system is typical.

The distinction between presidential and parliamentary systems does not exhaust the range of institutional variation within industrial democracies. You will discover that France's hybrid semipresidential system is quite different from both. France has a dual executive, with both a directly elected president and an appointed prime minister. As you will learn, these differences raise the kinds of questions that are at the heart of comparative politics: How do different political institutions and procedures embody the same democratic values? What consequences do these differences have for the effectiveness of government and the distribution of resources?

Debates about political institutions involve central questions about relations among social groups, for the way that power is organized affects the structure of political conflicts and coalitions and the outcome of governmental decisions and policies. Nor are debates regarding the choice of the appropriate manner of organizing state institutions ever fully settled. Britain, the nation with the longest parliamentary democratic tradition (it is centuries old), has recently experienced renewed controversy regarding the distribution of powers between levels of government, as well as the extent of autonomy appropriate for the constituent units of the United Kingdom (which comprises Scotland, Wales, and Northern Ireland, as well as England). In France, reforms since the 1980s have decentralized political power to regional and local governments, thereby significantly reducing France's centuries-old pattern of state dominance. In East-Central Europe, citizens and political elites evaluate presidential and parliamentary models as they craft new democratic regimes.

What Economic System for Democracy? Capitalism, Socialism, and Democracy

A long-standing political debate involves the question of whether a democratic political system must be associated with a capitalist organization of the economy. To sketch the context broadly, one can identify two ways to organize modern economic life. In a capitalist system, production is organized within the framework of voluntary (market) exchanges between private participants. The bulk of economic decisions—notably, what goods will be produced, by what methods, and by

whom—are private, that is, they are made by private individuals (not public officials) who own and control productive assets. Their decisions are based on the goal of reaping the highest possible profits from selling goods in the market. In a socialist system of production, by contrast, key decisions concerning the organization of the economy are considered public, not private. They are made by elected representatives, state planners, and administrators, as well as workers who produce goods (in the case of the self-managed firm).

Many scholars contend that democratic political institutions cannot flourish unless the economy is organized within a capitalist framework. They believe that democracy requires leaving substantial power in the hands of individual citizens, and citizens cannot have this requisite power if government makes the key decisions involving the organization of production, exchange, and consumption. In this view, public control of the economy is both inefficient and tyrannical. On the other hand, those on the other side of this debate assert that for a system to be democratic, it is not sufficient for democratic procedures to apply in the political sphere; there must also be a significant measure of democratic decision making within the economy. The distinguished democratic theorist Robert Dahl explains why. Private "ownership and control [of business firms] contribute to the creation of great differences among citizens in wealth, income, status, skills, information, control over information and propaganda, [and] access to political leaders. . . . Differences like these help in turn to generate significant inequalities among citizens in their capacities for participating as political equals in *governing the state.*"[4] In this view, democracy is crippled when some of the most important decisions affecting the character of the entire society are made by affluent citizens and private business firms that are not democratically chosen or accountable.

The relationship among capitalism, socialism, and democracy is an issue of vital importance.[5] When reading about individual countries in this book, consider how political movements and governments have addressed the question of whether capitalism is a necessary condition for democracy, an impediment—or both.

Although the political and scholarly debate on the relationship of capitalism, socialism, and democracy has not been fully settled, all the countries covered in *European Politics in Transition*, as well as other democracies throughout the world, have capitalist economies. Moreover, you will discover that the countries in this book exhibit a broadly similar relationship between democratic political institutions and capitalist economic institutions. In all stable democracies, there is quite extensive state intervention in the economy alongside extensive market competition by privately owned and controlled firms. The characteristic situation has often been called a mixed economy and was described by political scientist Adam Przeworski as a system "that relies on [state] regulated markets to allocate resources and on the state to assure a minimum of material welfare for everyone."[6]

Within the broadly similar context of a mixed economy, however, we find extensive variation from one democratic country to the next regarding the precise balance between state regulation and free markets. Some of the major political conflicts in democratic regimes—both the long-standing durable regimes in Western Europe and the transitional democracies of East-Central Europe—concern the extent and priorities of state economic intervention, in particular, the optimum trade-offs among a variety of desirable goals: high employment, low inflation, economic growth, provision of welfare, international competitiveness, and so forth. For each country, we discuss the form that these conflicts have taken. Look for the range of policy differences in this arena, consider what difference they make for citizens in these countries, and develop your own position on the most desirable form of political economy.

The Cultural Context

Are there particular historical and cultural requisites of democracy? Comparativists have long debated whether democracy requires specific cultural orientations. In an important contribution on this question, *Making Democracy Work*, political scientist Robert Putnam and his coauthors document the energetic and effective way that Italians in the north used newly created regional governments to improve their situation; by contrast, Italians in the south were less able to exploit the possibilities created by the regional form.[7] What made democracy work better in the north? Putnam suggests there was more abundant *social capital* in the north, that is, a greater capacity by northerners to coordinate their efforts to work for the common good. In the south, in contrast, citizens were less likely to combine their energies to make the new regional governments an instrument for economic and social advancement; in other words, social capital was lacking. Putnam claims that a key to why social capital was more prevalent in the north is that northerners were more likely than southerners to trust their fellow citizens in engaging in common public pursuits.

Can we extend Putnam's argument to the global scale? Are some cultures more hospitable to the kind of trust and pragmatic compromises that are essential for democracy to work? Or, as Sidney Tarrow, a sympathetic critic, charged, does Putnam mistake effect for cause? Tarrow suggests that the greater extent of trust and social capital in the north was no accident; it was nurtured by Italian state policies favoring the region.[8] The debate between Putnam and Tarrow in part hinges on the question of which is more important in explaining effective political and economic performance: state policies or political-cultural attitudes. Consider this question as you read about the democratic performance of the countries that comprise *European Politics in Transition*.

A somewhat different question about the cultural base of democracy is whether, for democracy to flourish, there must first be broad agreement or consensus on the democratic rules of the game, notably democratic procedures and the acceptance of the electoral verdict even for those on the losing side. In *The Civic*

Culture, a contemporary classic in comparative politics, Gabriel Almond and Sidney Verba claimed, by comparing the distribution of political attitudes in five nations, that citizens in democratic regimes are more likely than citizens in authoritarian regimes to trust government and accept the values of both participating in government and accepting directives from their government.[9] In a rejoinder to this approach, Dankwart Rustow countered, "The basis of democracy is not maximum consensus. It is the tenuous middle ground between imposed uniformity (such as would lead to some sort of tyranny) and implacable hostility (of a kind that would disrupt the community in civil war or secession). There must be a conscious adoption of democratic rules, but they must not be so much believed in as applied, first perhaps from necessity and gradually from habit. The very operation of these rules will enlarge the area of consensus step-by-step as democracy moves down its crowded agenda."[10] Consider the applicability of these two quite distinct claims to each country study and particularly to the case studies of East-Central Europe, where the development of democratic civic cultures remains an abiding challenge.

The Framework: Four Themes

This book seeks to go beyond "textbook" understandings. However important, politics in the narrow sense of governmental institutions and formal political processes (that is, politics as "how a bill becomes a law") is only part of a far more complex story, which encompasses not only political parties, voting behavior, and the institutions of government, but also the emergence of powerful forces in society, as well as the interaction of international and domestic factors. Within European nations, politics has always involved social movements—from the English Chartists and popular movements on the Continent in the 1830s and 1840s, who demanded rights of political participation and democracy (some of which

still have not been achieved), to Green parties in many contemporary Western European nations that struggle for women's rights, nuclear disarmament, and ecological concerns. European politics also involves class conflicts between working people and the financial and business elites, conflicts that force the state to intervene in the economy by regulating market forces, managing industrial disputes through political negotiations, and affecting how the wealth of society is divided among competing social groups. European politics today involves regional, ethnic, racial, and gender divisions, as well as the politics of the EU and relations between Eastern and Western Europe, within a context of intensified global interdependence, the ever-present influence of the United States, and the ominous threat of transnational terrorist networks.

To make sense of the large volume of information presented in *European Politics in Transition,* we structure our study of European politics around four core themes that we believe are central for understanding the transition that European politics is experiencing now:

1. The interaction of states within the international order
2. The role of states in economic management
3. The particular challenges facing European democracies and the pressures for more democracy
4. The political impact of diverse sources of social identity, including class, gender, ethnicity, and religion

These four themes provide a framework for organizing the extensive information on political institutions, processes, conflicts, policy, and changes that we present in the country chapters. The themes help explain continuities and contrasts among countries. We will also suggest a way that each theme highlights some puzzle in comparative politics that helps to illuminate our understanding of European politics.

Before we introduce the themes, we offer several warnings. First, our four themes cannot possibly capture all of the infinitely varied experience of politics throughout the world. The framework of *European Politics in Transition* provides a guide to understanding many features of contemporary comparative politics. But we urge students (and rely on instructors!), who through study and experience know the politics of the United States and many other countries, to challenge and augment our interpretations. Second, we want to note that a textbook builds from existing theory but does not construct or test new hypotheses, which is the goal of original scholarly studies. The themes are intended to crystallize some of the most significant findings in the field of scholarly literature on contemporary European politics. Although these themes can usefully be applied to politics anywhere in the world, they serve here as an analytical tool to reveal both the specificity of national experiences and the distinctiveness of a European model of politics.

Theme One: A World of States

The theme that we call *a world of states* highlights the fact that since the beginning of the modern era several centuries ago, states have been the primary actors on the world stage. Although international organizations and private actors like transnational corporations play a crucial role, since the seventeenth century it has been state officials who send armies to conquer other states and territories, states whose legal codes make it possible for business firms to operate within their borders and beyond, and states that regulate, through immigration law and border police, the movement of people across borders. Courses in international relations focus primarily on interaction among states or other cross-border transactions. In *European Politics in Transition*, we emphasize a key feature of the international arena: the impact on a state's domestic political institutions and processes of its relative success or failure in competing economically and politically with other states.

No state, even the most powerful, such as the United States, is unaffected by influences origi-

nating outside its borders. Today a host of processes associated with *globalization* underscore the heightened importance of intensified cross-national influences. The terms *globalization* or *the global era* are frequently applied as general catchphrases to identify the growing depth, extent, and diversity of cross-border connections that are a key feature of the contemporary world. Discussions of globalization often begin with accounts of economic activities, including the reorganization of production and the global redistribution of the workforce (the "global factory") and the increased extent and intensity of international trade, finance, and foreign direct investment. Globalization involves the movement of peoples due to migration, employment, business, and educational opportunities.

The term *globalization* links a highly diverse set of changes. Consider the attacks in the United States on September 11, 2001. The hijackers were members of Al Qaeda, a thoroughly transnational network that recruits throughout the world and has cells in many continents. The hijackers trained and lived in locations thousands of miles apart. They communicated by cell phone and courier, transferred funds through a sophisticated system linking international banks and traditional moneychangers based in bazaars. Similarly, the network that bombed the Madrid railroads on March 11, 2004, was composed of members from many countries, and the planning and execution of the attack required intricate transnational cooperation.

Globalization includes other profound changes that are less visible but equally significant. For example, new applications of information technology (such as the Internet and CNN) blur the traditional distinction between what is around the world and what is around the block, thereby instantly transforming cultures, and eroding the boundaries between the local and global. These technologies make instantaneous communication possible, link producers and contractors, headquarters, branch plants, and suppliers in "real time" anywhere in the world. Employees may be rooted in time and place, but employers can shop for what will bring them the greatest advantages in a global labor market. Employees who have an apparently secure job today may be unemployed tomorrow as employers downsize or move their operations offshore. But job destruction in one region may be offset by job creation elsewhere.

Globalization forges new forms of international governance, from the European Union to the World Trade Organization. And as described above, international terror networks can strike anywhere—from New York to Bali to Madrid. In an attempt to regulate and stabilize the myriad international flows, an alphabet soup of international organizations—NATO, the UN, IMF, WTO, OECD, NAFTA, to name but a few—has been enlisted. And globalization also involves grassroots movements from around the world that challenge the construction of globalization "from above." The first such challenge occurred when the World Trade Organization sponsored a meeting of government ministers in Seattle in 1999 that was disrupted by thousands of protesters. Ever since, conferences called to develop rules for global commerce have been the site of demonstrations by coalitions of environmental, labor-based, and community activists from around the world.[11] Thus, to Seattle, one can add the names of cities around the world—Washington, D.C., Prague, Nice, Davos, Genoa, Miami, and Cancún—where activists have assembled to protest the activity of international financial and intergovernmental institutions.

The varied elements of globalization erode the ability of even the strongest countries to control their destinies. No state can guarantee economic and life-cycle security for its citizens. None can preserve pristine "national models" of economic governance—or distinctly national cultures, values, understandings of the world, or narratives that define a people and forge their unity. None is safe from violence targeting its citizens, public officials, institutions, and territory justified in the name of transcendent religious or political principles.

In the brave new world in which we live, countries face a host of challenges from above and below. The capacities of states to control domestic outcomes and assert sovereignty are compromised by regional and global technological and market forces, as well as growing security concerns. Countries are simultaneously assaulted by ethnic, nationalist, and religious challenges that often involve both internal and external components. The challenge of democratic self-government is heightened when many of the decisions that fundamentally affect citizens' lives are made by organizations located far outside a country's borders.

Today, in the early years of the twenty-first century, nations are experiencing intense pressures from an expanding and increasingly complex mix of external influences. In every country, politics and policymaking are affected by influences that come from outside its borders. But international political and economic influences do not have the same impact in all countries, and some states help shape the institutional form and policy of international organizations in which they participate.[12] It is likely that the more advantaged a state is—as measured by such factors as level of economic development, military power, and resource base—the more it will shape the global order. Conversely, the policies of less advantaged countries are more extensively shaped by other states, international organizations, and broader international constraints.

When states pool their political and economic resources, they can leverage their influence in the international setting. Perhaps the foremost example in the world today is the EU, to which all the countries analyzed in this book belong. As Part II, devoted to the EU, describes, it has been no easy matter for former rivals like France, Britain, and Germany to delegate key decisions to EU institutions. A further daunting challenge that confronts the EU and its member states is to "digest" the ten new countries (eight from East-Central Europe as well as Cyprus and Malta) that joined the EU in 2004. The EU fits uneasily in a world of states, but international organizations like the EU (along with the North American Free Trade Association, the World Trade Organization, and others) are increasingly important actors in world politics.

The theme we identify as *a world of states* includes a second important focus: similarities and contrasts among countries in how they formed as states and how their states are presently organized. We study the ways that states developed historically, diverse patterns in the organization of political institutions, the processes—and limits—of democratization, the ability of the state to control social groups in society and sustain power, and the state's economic management strategies and capacities. We observe how state formation and the position in the international order of states are linked. For example, compared with other states, the British state had (and continues to have) a less developed capacity to steer British industry. The state was less concerned with the competitiveness of the British domestic manufacturing industry because of the commanding position within international finance enjoyed by the private financial institutions comprising the City of London (London's financial district, equivalent to Wall Street in New York). Moreover, the vast scope of Britain's colonial empire meant that trade with the colonies could sustain the British economy. Consequently, the British state intervened less extensively, and private firms were allowed to develop in a freer fashion than was the case for France and Germany.

A Puzzle: To What Extent Do States Still Remain the Basic Building Blocks of Political Life? Increasingly, the politics and policies of states are shaped by external actors as well as by the more impersonal forces of globalization. At the same time, many states face increasingly restive constituencies that challenge the power and legitimacy of central states. In reading the analysis of the EU, the four country case studies, and the section on East-Central Europe, try to assess what impact pressures from both above and below have had on the role of the state in carrying out its basic functions and in its rela-

tionship to its citizens. What is the relationship between member states and the EU?

Theme Two: Governing the Economy

The success of states in maintaining their authority is greatly affected by their ability to ensure that an adequate volume of goods and services is produced to satisfy the needs of their populations. Certainly the inability of the Soviet economic system to meet this challenge was an important reason for the rejection of communism and the disintegration of the Soviet Union. Conversely, the relatively great political stability of the wealthy industrialized nations described in this book is closely linked to their superior economic performance. How a country organizes production and exchange—that is, *governs the economy*—is one of the key elements in its overall pattern of development. Countries differ widely in how successful they are in competing with other countries that offer similar products in international markets, and in the relative importance of market forces versus government control of the economy.

An important goal in the contemporary world is to achieve durable economic development. Effective economic performance is near the top of every country's political agenda. The term *political economy* refers to how governments affect economic performance—and how economic performance affects a country's political processes. We accord great importance to political economy in *European Politics in Transition* because we believe that politics in all countries is deeply influenced by the relationship between government and the economy.

Two Puzzles: What Factors Foster Successful Economic Performance? And What Exactly Is Successful Economic Performance? These are questions that students of political economy have long pondered—and to which there are no easy answers. Consider the apparently straightforward question of whether states that intervene more vigorously to manage the economy outperform states with less developed capacities for economic management. France developed an extensive array of financial and industrial management tools in the post–World War II period. This directive approach was often praised as a means to promote vigorous economic modernization and growth. British policymakers tried (quite unsuccessfully) to copy French planning institutions. Through unification, Germany's social market economy—a complex interplay of laissez-faire and extremely sophisticated state-centered policies (which formed a very different policy from France's state-centered approach)—created an economy that was the envy of the world. Yet in recent years, Britain's less-is-more approach to governing the economy has been quite successful, while key elements of the French and German models of economic governance have been eliminated in response to economic and political challenges. Indeed, with the disappearance of some of the more distinctive features of French and German economic governance, a frequent topic of discussion among European specialists is whether a convergence is occurring in the economic policies of European countries. There is general agreement both that some of the most important features differentiating economic governance have been dismantled, yet that there remain significant contrasts in the varieties of European capitalism (to paraphrase the title of an important study of the question).[13] In reading the country studies as well as the analysis of East-Central Europe, try to decide what stance of the state is most likely to produce economic success, what kinds of contrasts exist across countries, whether countries are becoming more similar in their approach to governing the economy, and what accounts for these outcomes.

Before resolving the problem of how to achieve maximum economic performance, one must first decide how one knows it when one sees it—and the meaning of economic success is not self-evident. The conventional measure of economic success is the rate at which a country's gross domestic product (GDP) grows—that is, economic growth. While certainly useful for many purposes, this measure is quite crude and even misleading. For one thing, the GDP growth does not reflect changes in the size of a country's population. A rapidly increasing population may produce a larger GDP at the same time that the average income of each person in the population—that is, per capita income—shrinks (and, thus, people are worse off). Further, measuring economic success by GDP ignores the social value of the products that are produced. GDP lumps together the value of tobacco products along with the value of medical care required to treat the diseases caused by tobacco use. A classic illustration of the pitfalls in this measure is the story of the man who reduced the size of national income by marrying his housekeeper. What other measures of economic success are available? One possible yardstick is the United Nations Development Program's Human Development Index (HDI), a composite of qualitative measures like life expectancy along with per capita income and other quantitative measures of equity and well being.

European states have historically prided themselves on giving priority not only to economic growth and efficiency but also to social equity. The European model of social welfare allocates generous public expenditures to providing adequate replacement income during periods of sickness, unemployment, or old age. Yet, to highlight that there may not be easy answers, the OECD report summarized above criticized European governments for devoting too many resources to social purposes and not giving sufficient priority to policies facilitating economic growth and efficiency.

When reading the country sections, ponder the question of how to measure economic performance in alternative ways to the standard measure of gross domestic product. Doing so will alert you to the importance of the interaction between politics and economics, for the way that a country organizes the production and distribution of its resources fundamentally affects its economic performance and social equity.

Theme Three: The Democratic Idea

Our comparative studies indicate a surprising level of complexity in the apparently simple theme of the *democratic idea.* We focus first on the near universality of the claim that citizens should exercise substantial control over the decisions that their states and governments make. Especially since the collapse of Soviet communism, democracy has no viable contender as a legitimate basis for organizing political power in the contemporary world. (Perhaps nationalism, especially when fused with religion, might be considered an alternative, but even many forms of religious nationalism claim to be based in democracy.)

In discussing the democratic idea, we focus second on the diverse sources of support for democracy. Democracy has proved appealing for many reasons. In some historical settings, it may represent a standoff or equilibrium among political contenders for power, in which no one group can gain sufficient strength to control outcomes alone.[14] Democracy may appeal to many people in authoritarian settings because states having democratic regimes often rank among the world's most stable, affluent, and cohesive countries. Another important source of support for democracy is the widespread popular desire for dignity and equality. Even when dictatorial regimes provide some of the benefits often associated with democratic regimes—for example, sponsoring development or using ideological appeals to garner popular support—intense pressures for democracy remain. Although authoritarian governments can suppress demands for democratic participation for a long period, our discussion of East-Central Europe in this book provides abundant evidence that the domestic and, in recent years, international costs of doing so are high.

Third, we emphasize the potential fragility of transitions from authoritarian to democratic rule. That popular movements and leaders of moderate factions within authoritarian regimes often overthrow undemocratic regimes and force

the holding of elections does not mean that democratic institutions will endure. As our case studies of Poland, Hungary, and the Czech and Slovak Republics demonstrate, a wide gulf exists between a *transition* to democracy and the *consolidation* of democracy. Historically, powerful groups have often opposed democratic institutions because they fear that democracy will threaten their privilege, whereas disadvantaged groups may oppose the democratic process because they see it as unresponsive to their deeply felt grievances. As a result, reversals of democratic regimes have occurred in the past and will doubtless occur in the future. The country studies in *European Politics in Transition* do not support a philosophy of history or theory of political development that sees a single (democratic) end point toward which all countries will eventually converge. One important analytical work, published in the early phase of the most recent democratic wave, captured the fragility of the process of democratization in its title: *Transitions from Authoritarian Rule: Tentative Conclusions About Uncertain Democracies.*[15] The difficulty in maintaining democracy once established is captured in the observation that it is easier for a country to hold its first democratic election than its second. The fact that the democratic idea is so powerful does not mean that all countries will adopt or preserve democratic institutions.

Moreover, even when democracy has become relatively secure, we do not believe that it can be achieved in any country once and for all. Indeed, our *democratic idea* theme suggests the incompleteness of democratic agendas even in countries (several of which are included in this book) with the longest and most developed experiences of representative democracy. In virtually every democracy in recent years, many citizens have turned against the state when their living standards were threatened by high unemployment and economic stagnation. Social movements have targeted the state's actions or inactions in such varied spheres as environmental regulation, reproductive rights, and race or ethnic relations. Comparative studies confirm that the democratic idea fuels political conflicts even in long-established democracies because there is invariably a gap, even in the most egalitarian and longest-lived democracies, between democratic ideals and the actual functioning of democratic political institutions. Witness, for example, the extensive degree of economic and political inequality in Britain, France, and Germany, countries classified as among the most democratic in the world. Nor do challenges to democracy originate only with contentious movements: public officials in even the most stable democracies have violated democratic procedures by engaging in corruption and using illegal force against citizens.

In order to analyze more deeply the underpinnings of democratic stability, *European Politics in Transition* confines its attention to countries with extensive democratic traditions. With the exception of states in East-Central Europe, which adopted democratic institutions after the collapse of communism in 1989, all the countries surveyed in this book have been democratic for longer than a half-century.

A Puzzle: Does Democracy Enhance or Endanger Stability? Comparativists often debate whether democratic institutions contribute to political stability or, on the contrary, to political disorder. On the one hand, democracy by its very nature encourages political opposition. One of its defining characteristics is that competition is legitimate among those who aspire to gain high political office, as well as among groups and parties defending different programs. Political life in democracies is often turbulent and unpredictable. On the other hand, the fact that political opposition and competition are legitimate in democracies paradoxically has the effect of promoting acceptance of the state even among opponents of a given government. Because opposition movements are free to express their opposition in democratic regimes, the result is greater political stability. Evidence for this claim has been provided by an important study comparing democratic and authoritarian regimes, which finds that economic disruptions are much

less destabilizing for democracies.[16] In reading the country studies in this book, look for stabilizing and destabilizing consequences of democratic institutions and the particular challenges that long-standing democracies face.

Theme Four: The Politics of Collective Identity

How do individuals understand who they are in political terms, and on what basis do people form groups to advance common political aims? In other words, what are the sources of group attachments, or *collective political identity?* At one point, social scientists thought they knew. It was generally held that age-old loyalties of ethnicity, religious affiliation, race, gender, and locality were being dissolved by economic, political, and cultural modernization. Comparativists thought that class solidarities based on the shared experience of work or economic position more broadly had become the most important source of collective identity. And it was believed that as countries became politically modern or mature, groups would pragmatically pursue their economic interests in ways that were not politically destabilizing. We now know that the formation and interplay of politically relevant collective identities are far more complex and uncertain.

In the industrial democracies, the importance of identities based on class membership has declined, although class and material sources of collective political identity remain significant in political competition and economic organization. In contrast, contrary to earlier predictions in social science, in many countries nonclass identities—affiliations that develop from a sense of belonging to particular groups based on language, religion, ethnicity, race, nationality, or gender—have assumed growing significance.

The politics of collective political identity involves struggles to define which groups will be full participants in the political community and which ones will be marginalized. It also involves a constant tug of war over the relative power and influence—both symbolic and material—among groups. Issues of inclusion and priority remain pivotal in many countries, and are constantly changing as a result of immigration, ideological changes, and changing geopolitics. Thus, to cite an example dividing many European countries, recently there have been intense controversies involving the relationship of Muslim minorities to the wider community. One reason that conflict around the issue of collective identities can be so intense is that political leaders in the state and in opposition movements often seek to mobilize support by sharpening ethnic, religious, racial, or regional rivalries.

A Puzzle: Can You Split the Difference When It Comes to Identity Politics? Once identity demands are placed on the political agenda, to what extent can governments depolarize them by distributing resources in a way that redresses the grievances of the minority or politically weaker identity groups? Collective identities operate at the level of symbols, attitudes, values, and beliefs and at the level of material resources. However, the contrast between material- and nonmaterial-based identities and demands should not be exaggerated. In practice, most groups are animated both by feelings of loyalty and solidarity *and* by the desire to obtain material benefits for their members. But the analytical distinction between material and nonmaterial demands remains useful, and it is worth considering whether the nonmaterial aspects of the politics of collective identities make political disputes over ethnicity, religion, language, or nationality especially divisive and difficult to resolve.

In a situation of extreme scarcity, it may prove well-nigh impossible to find any compromise among groups, even when their conflicts revolve only around clashing material interests. But if at least a moderate level of resources is available, such conflicts may be easier to resolve because groups can "split the difference" and get a share of resources that they find at least minimally adequate. This process, which refers to who gets what, or how resources are distributed, is called *distributional politics*. However, the demands of

ethnic, religious, and nationalist movements may be difficult to satisfy by a distributional style of politics precisely because the group demands more than merely a larger share of the economic pie. The distributional style may be quite ineffectual when, for example, a religious group demands that its religious values be imposed on the whole society—or, for that matter, that it be allowed to engage in practices either prohibited by law or widely regarded as illegitimate. A good example is provided by the controversy in French politics involving whether to prohibit Muslim girls from wearing headscarves in school. Similarly, can the difference be split when a dominant linguistic group insists that a single language be used in education and government throughout the country? In such cases, political conflict tends to assume an all-or-nothing quality. The country studies in this book examine a wide range of conflicts involving collective identities. It will be interesting (and possibly troubling) to ponder whether and under what conditions such conflicts are subject to the normal give-and-take of political bargaining.

These four themes provide our analytic framework. With the four themes in mind, we can now discuss some of the common features and issues explored in the country studies that comprise *European Transitions in Politics*, as well as how the text is organized.

European Politics in Transition: Critical Junctures

European political systems are dynamic, not frozen. They respond to complex challenges and are shaped by preexisting institutional and cultural legacies, by battles lost and won, and by the challenges of everyday life as it is experienced—and understood—by ordinary citizens, who make a host of messy demands on their governments. In this section we look at some of the major stages and turning points in European political development.

Industrialization, State Formation, and the Great Divide

For several decades following World War II, it was common for students, scholars, and policy-makers to think of two Europes: East and West. The meanings we attach to the political arrangements for any part of the globe emerge historically. The words we use are not neutral and have important political and ideological implications. For example, expressions like *First World*, which refers to Western Europe, Japan, and the United States, and *Third World*, which refers to the less economically developed states of Latin America, Africa, and Asia, may intentionally or unintentionally reflect a Eurocentrism in which the economically and politically dominant West is given pride of place. And terms like *Western Europe* and *Eastern Europe* are as much political and ideological as they are geographical. In this case, the terms were linked to the cold war divide that pitted the United States against the Soviet Union, each allied with European states.

When we look at the evolution of modern European societies, we see two fundamentally transformative processes at work: the emergence of the modern state and the advent of developed capitalism linked to the Industrial Revolution. Absolutist states emerged in Europe during the sixteenth century. Monarchies with firm, centralized authority replaced the more localized and personal administration of power that characterized the large number of small principalities, city-states, leagues, and so on scattered throughout medieval Europe. The introduction of permanent bureaucracies, codified laws, national taxes, and standing armies heralded the arrival of the first modern European states. In the competition between the widely varied political units of the time, victory went to monarchs who devised more efficient methods of governing—bureaucracies—and more productive economies.[17]

By the eighteenth century, new economic developments associated with capitalist industrialization began to clash with states' increasingly archaic monarchical forms. Although bitter feuds between landowners and monarchs were not uncommon, absolutist regimes were generally linked by economic, military, and political ties to the traditional landholding aristocracy. With the Industrial Revolution, the owners of manufacturing enterprises, the bourgeoisie, increasingly gained economic prominence and political influence. A growing incompatibility between old state forms and new economic demands fostered revolutionary upheavals—often violent, as in the French Revolution of 1789; sometimes less violent, as occurred in eighteenth-century Britain (although Barrington Moore's classic study emphasized how Britain's peaceful incrementalism in later periods was facilitated by the violence that occurred at an earlier period—in the Glorious Revolution of 1688).[18] The outcome of eighteenth-century struggles was often the development of more modern constitutional forms of the state. Industrialization and state formation were closely linked historical phenomena and developed in tandem.

Another point is crucial to an understanding of both the history of European societies and the organization of this book. Until the Russian Revolution in 1917 and the subsequent post–World War II division of Europe, Europe was not divided into East and West. In earlier centuries, absolutist states in Central or Eastern Europe—Austria, Prussia, and Russia—existed alongside similarly centralized bureaucracies in France, Spain, and England. (The situation in Eastern Europe was complicated by the breakup of the great multinational empires, notably the Ottoman and Austro-Hungarian empires, and the creation of a host of small new nation-states after World War I.)

With the Russian Revolution and the emergence of socialist states in Eastern and Central Europe in the aftermath of World War II, a great divide split Europe into East and West. The iron curtain that divided the continent, in the words of British Prime Minister Winston Churchill, was linked to the global campaign waged by the United

States and the Soviet Union to win allies and se-cure geopolitical and ideological dominance. For over half a century, profound differences in politi-cal and economic processes separated the capitalist democracies of Western Europe from the socialist regimes of Eastern Europe.

The passing of communism in East-Central Europe in the 1990s has created new geopolitical territories—or rather, it has restored the situation that prevailed until the Russian Revolution of 1917. Yet the risk of new and bitter divisions within Europe also exists because the same process of widening the EU means that while some states will be admitted, others will be excluded. The most notable example was the repeated rejection prior to 2004 of Turkey's application for EU member-ship. But other countries that have been left stand-ing, hat in hand, at the entrance to the EU include Macedonia, Romania, and Ukraine.

To understand the current transition in Eu-rope, a useful historical baseline is the period fol-lowing World War II. This was when the framework was established that at first regulated political conflict for a generation and then itself proved the source of new challenges beginning in the late 1960s whose result was to press for-ward the agenda of European integration.

Our account centers on Western Europe, the major focus of *European Politics in Transition.* We also consider briefly the evolution of East-Central Europe. In the West, the key domestic political tension involved the balance between private market forces as opposed to state control over the economy. Linked to the question of states versus markets was the issue of expanding democratic rights, political participation, and so-cial equity.

The solution fashioned after World War II, which set the stage for an unprecedented period of prosperity and political stability, involved the widespread application of a newly formulated theory of economic management (known as Keynesianism, which we discuss below) and the extension of the welfare state. The new political formula called for cooperation among the state, organized labor, and organized capital around the quest for economic growth as a way to re-solve the problem of class conflict. During a mo-ment that some thought would last forever, it appeared that economic growth organized within a capitalist framework was not only com-patible with but depended on steadily expanding democratic participation and state-mandated so-cial benefits.

Postwar stability declined when the social and economic bases of the postwar settlement crum-bled. Gradually cooperation among classes gave way to conflict, new non-class-based social ac-tors grew more assertive, and the possibility and desirability of linking economic growth, welfare state expansion, and democratic participation were challenged. This is the story that we now recount in fuller detail.

World War II and the Emergence of the European Model

The years following World War II represented a period of rapid economic growth in Western Eu-rope, sustained by secure and widely popular regimes. In Germany and Italy, the Christian Democrats ruled throughout the period, and in Britain, Labour and Conservative governments shared a mainstream consensus. In contrast to the economic depression and social instability of the interwar period, the years following World War II reflected an unusual degree of social har-mony. (These observations must be qualified in the case of southern Europe, as we discuss later in this section.)

During this period, many scholars and politi-cal elites believed that intense social, economic, and political conflicts were a thing of the past. Sociologist Daniel Bell described "the end of ide-ology" and the waning of ideological passions; political sociologist Seymour Martin Lipset pro-claimed that the fundamental problems of in-dustrial society had been solved. In brief, economic growth seemed to provide the solvent for reducing class antagonisms. Rather than the major economic classes struggling to enlarge their share of a static economic pie, or to gain control of the pie, the new approach (that we dub the postwar settlement) postulated that all groups should cooperate to increase the size of the pie—and thereby achieve the gains deriving from economic expansion. To change metaphors, another common observation during this period was that a rising (economic) tide lifted all boats. Given rapidly rising standards of living, the more radical social movements seeking fundamental change in the organization of society and control of economic resources appeared outmoded. "The performance of capitalism since the end of the Second World War has been so unexpectedly dazzling," wrote an observer in 1965, that "it is hard for us to believe that the bleak and squalid system which we knew could, in so short a time, have adapted itself without some covert process of total destruction and regeneration to achieve so many desired objectives."[19]

Although class conflicts persisted in Europe, especially in southern Europe (Italy and France among our studies), the general trend was toward a consensus on the value of state regulation of market forces. The most common approach, often described as *neocorporatism*, involved direct negotiations over prices or incomes between representatives of labor unions and organizations composed of business firms, with the coordination and guidance of the state. A key shift was that the state persuaded organized labor to moderate its demands for substantial wage gains, autonomy, and control of the workplace in exchange for attractive benefits, including full employment, stable prices, welfare programs, and steady wage increases. And the state also persuaded employers to recognize the legitimacy of labor unions, both in representing workers at the workplace and in participating in decisions about the entire economy. The understandings and arrangements of the postwar settlement helped to end the era of strife associated with the transition to an industrial capitalist order.

The postwar settlement was linked to changes within technology and the organization of production and consumption—what some scholars have termed a shift to a *Fordist system* of mass production and consumption. The American industrialist Henry Ford lent his name to the two key elements of Fordism because he was among the first to introduce the new techniques. In the realm of production, Ford pioneered in reducing the cost of producing that quintessential consumer durable—the automobile. The secret was to simplify production by introducing fewer parts (often interchangeable from one model to another) that were brought together to produce the finished automobile through assembly-line methods that divided the work into repetitive, simple operations. By standardizing the production process and the skills that workers needed, Ford was able to lower the cost of automobiles dramatically.

Fordist production techniques not only affected the way that goods were produced—that is, by mass production—but also facilitated the growth of mass consumption. This occurred because applying Fordist techniques widely in industrial production brought the cost of goods within reach of large numbers of consumers. Further, because assembly-line work was so repellent, Ford was forced to pay workers more than the prevailing wage. The indirect result was that, thanks to the greater purchasing power enjoyed by workers at Ford and other large firms, the potential market for goods—automobiles and other mass-produced consumer durables—dramatically expanded. The social consequence of Fordism was to swell the ranks of semiskilled manual-industry workers, a group that came to rank as one of the largest in the societies of Western Europe. The fact that these workers and their families enjoyed some of the material benefits of industrial production, especially when the postwar settlement integrated them into political arrangements, cemented their loyalty to the established regime.

With the benefit of hindsight, particularly in light of renewed political conflict since the late 1960s, it becomes evident that the harmony of the postwar settlement derived from an unusual set of circumstances. Wartime destruction exhausted political passions and placed a premium on cooperation within and among the states of Europe to rebuild their shattered economies and achieve a takeoff into the era of mass production. At the same time, the division of global influence between the United States and the Soviet Union reduced the possibility of pan-European unity and placed the states of Western Europe in a situation of economic and military dependence on the United States. *Pax Americana* meant that Western European nations lacked the material means to challenge the United States's leadership, even as the perceived threat of a Soviet military invasion quelled potential political conflicts.

U.S. military, political, and economic intervention promoted European recovery and was also directed toward preventing the emergence of radical regimes in Western Europe. Nevertheless, despite the aims of some policymakers in the United States, convergence between U.S. and European political systems was limited because historical differences between the two regions were too strong to be overridden. Two factors were particularly important: the difference in the configuration of class forces in Western Europe and the role of the state. European workers were more conscious of their class affiliations and often defined their lives in terms of their participation in political parties and in party- and class-linked subcultures that provided strong bonds of friendship and community. European workers were likely to organize along class lines in the political sphere and support a range of parties—labor, social democratic, socialist, communist—that sought to extend state control over the private market system as well as expanded social provision. Although most such parties were not radical, they did energetically seek to extend state-provided social services in ways that widened the gap separating Europe and the United States.

Moreover, not all workers and worker-supported parties were enthusiastic participants in the postwar settlement. Notably, Communist parties in France and Italy (among the largest parties in the country) were fundamentally, and quite openly, opposed to the entire capitalist system. Thus, contrary to the U.S. experience, political party cleavages within European politics reflected to a considerable extent class divisions dating from the emergence of industrial capitalism in the nineteenth century. In contrast to the United States, a fundamental axiom of European political life involved the continued conflict between working people (organized through trade unions and socialist parties of one variety or another) and the propertied classes (manufacturing elites and those linked to the world of finance, organized through business associations and bourgeois parties). If the gulf between classes diminished, it remained a central source of partisan conflict.

The role of the state—the bureaucracy, parliament, and the entire range of national governmental institutions—was far greater in Western Europe than in the United States. In Europe, the state provided substantial welfare benefits, directed fiscal and monetary policy, regulated industrial relations, and engaged in extensive efforts to sponsor industrial growth and restructure failing industries. In the postwar period, states throughout Western Europe extended their activities in the economic and social welfare spheres. For example, in many countries, a wave of nationalization of industry after the war resulted in state-owned enterprises controlling basic industries like steel, energy, and air and rail transport.

Therefore, the social harmony of the 1950s and 1960s did not lead to an Americanization of Western European politics. Rather, the two factors that most clearly distinguished Europe from the United States—party mobilization along class lines and activist state institutions—produced a special (Western) European model of politics that was more statist than what occurred in the United States, albeit unmistakably capitalist.

The process of constructing political harmony involved negotiating a set of nationally specific arrangements in each of the Western

European countries, in which a wide array of state, business, trade union, and political party elites participated.[20] It was at this time that the welfare state was consolidated, high levels of employment were achieved, anticapitalist forces were marginalized, and an unusual degree of social, industrial, and political consent for mainstream and reformist policies was secured.

Both the nature of political participation and the character of the economic system underwent significant changes as the European model emerged after World War II and developed in the intervening half-century or more. Although contemporary European politics involves fundamental changes in the agreements that were negotiated in the 1940s and 1950s, the postwar settlement remains a critical juncture of great importance. Indeed, the agenda for European integration partially transferred the logic of the postwar settlement—negotiations over distributive politics sustained by a normative appeal to common fates—from the national to the EU level. Two major challenges involve whether the growth of EU institutions and policies throughout Western Europe can achieve the same result as occurred in the postwar settlement and (perhaps even more daunting) whether the same process can be extended by the eastward expansion of the EU.

The Transformation of Political Parties.

Political parties played a key role in organizing political participation and consent within the emergent European model. However, as parties were transformed in the process of organizing and sustaining the postwar consensus, they also eventually destabilized its social basis, thereby weakening its underlying foundations.

The structure and behavior of political parties were transformed as parties with explicit organizational and ideological links to the working classes, on the one hand, and parties linked historically to the interests of economic elites on the other competed by appealing to broader constituencies. As an alternative to more adversarial ideological appeals, parties of both the left and the right often sought to generate broad-based electoral support. They did so by representing themselves to the electorate not as the party of the working class or the economic elite, but as the best modernizing party—the one that could master technological change and guide the national economy in a complex system of international interdependence. (One scholar termed this a shift from class-based, ideological, mass parties to "catch-all" parties that sought to "catch" support from voters of diverse social classes.)[21]

As parties in the 1960s began seeking interclass support on election day and became less concerned with mobilizing stable subcultures around class-based issues, class identities began to erode relative to nonclass forms of self-identification, including region, age, and religion. Social movements based on these and other non-class-based factors also erupted on the scene beginning in the 1960s to further supplant citizens' class identities.

A New Political Framework.

The new political framework that developed in Western European nations after World War II involved a tacit alliance between the organized working class and large-scale business, an arrangement that had not existed in the past and would crumble by the 1970s. Under the guidance of the state, the two groups cooperated in a manner that stimulated economic growth, political moderation, and social harmony. While states intervened extensively to regulate the economies and ensure nearly full employment, higher wages, and expanded social welfare provision, the working class was asked to accept as its part of the bargain severe limits on both its industrial and political demands.

Political scientist Adam Przeworski has elaborated a theoretical model that helps illuminate the conditions for the emergence and functioning of the postwar settlement. The political arrangements organizing this model are known as social democracy, in which a center-left party closely allied with the labor movement controls the government to orient state policy along the lines described here. According to the social democratic model that Przeworski elaborates (and which is a formalized model of what existed in considerable measure in practice in the postwar period), the working class must be sufficiently organized, cohesive, and centralized to act in a unified, disciplined manner, and workers must gain a reasonable assurance from business and the state that they will receive a steady stream of benefits, including high employment levels, regular wage increases, and generous welfare state benefits. In return, the organized working class, through its leaders within the trade union and socialist party spheres, finds it worthwhile to moderate demands in ways that enable business to carry on profitable activities.[22]

Working-class moderation had several elements. In contrast to a past marked by intense class conflict, workers came to accept the prerogatives of capitalist control in the overall organization of the economy and within the production process. In effect, demands for annual wage increases and welfare state programs became a substitute for the satisfaction of demands that were more threatening to capitalist production (for example, workers' control over the pace, content, and conditions of work or over investment decisions, industrial policy, and technological innovations).

The model specifies that business must also accept constraints for the new agreement to work. Business firms must renounce the arbitrary exercise of their power in the workplace and political sphere, accept the legitimacy of unions, and provide workers with high levels of wages and employment. Finally, for the agreement to succeed, the state must do its part—for example, by vigorously pursuing policies aiming to maximize employment levels, price stability, social equity, and economic growth. More generally, the state must appear to be a neutral arbiter serving the general interest, rather than siding unduly with either employers or workers. If the state were seen as favoring business interests, workers would protest rather than cooperate; if

the state were seen as favoring workers' interests, capitalists would refuse to invest (what has been dubbed a capital strike), and economic stagnation would result.

In Przeworski's model, the postwar settlement pattern of class relations appears to represent a situation of positive-sum cooperation, in which citizens from both major classes, as well as other groups, gain from mutual cooperation and restraint. In fact, however, the appearance of universal benefit was misleading. Not all classes and social forces gained from the creation of the new, rationalized capitalist order. Although industrial workers (whether in blue-collar or office positions) began to enjoy the benefits of the consumer society, they continued to be subjected to the harsh conditions of industrial labor. Given a shortage of labor, owing to rapid economic expansion, millions of immigrant workers were recruited to northern Europe from southern Europe (Portugal, Spain, Italy, Greece, and Turkey) and Eastern Europe (especially Poland and Yugoslavia), as well as from Africa and Asia. Immigrant workers were assigned the most menial positions and received low wages and meager welfare benefits. They were denied citizenship rights and were subjected to discrimination in housing and educational opportunities. Women also received fewer benefits from the new order as a result of their unequal position in employment, in the domestic sphere, and in welfare state provisions.

Labor Movements, Social Democracy, and Western European Politics. The reforms, which resulted from the cross-class and cross-party political settlements that ushered in the postwar order of European politics, were first set in place in the 1950s. However, important political and economic differences generally divided the capitalist democracies in Western Europe by a north-south dimension: the nations of northern Europe (represented in this book by Britain and Germany) and those of southern Europe (represented by France, a mixed case, and Italy).

Workers in northern Europe were more likely to gain citizenship rights early and to be included within the dominant system. In West Germany (but not in Britain), labor unions were more unified, and workers gained greater benefits from the system. As a result, they were more likely to be moderate in their political stance. In contrast to southern Europe, working-class elements were not excluded from the decision-making process, nor did they remain hostile to the existing economic and political order in significant numbers. Indeed, social democratic governments in northern Europe were in the vanguard, sponsoring most of the major policy innovations that composed the postwar settlement. Then, moderate conservative governments elsewhere emulated these reforms.

Labor movements in southern Europe were divided internally by ideological and religious differences that found expression in rival national confederations engaging in bidding wars for members at the workplace, firm, and industry levels. National union leaders had neither the authority nor the mandate to negotiate with business representatives and the state, and rank-and-file workers often refused to abide by any agreements that were struck. Business was likely to be opposed to unions on ideological grounds, and, in any event, unions could not, and were not inclined to, offer management the kinds of benefits that unions routinely provided in northern Europe. Thus, the working class was relatively excluded from the ongoing economic order, which strengthened its tendency toward oppositional values and protest activity.

This comparison of labor movement dynamics in northern and southern Europe finds an important parallel in workers' political activity. For example, in the two northern European nations covered in this book, Britain and Germany, two-thirds or more of all workers were unified in a single socialist party, and these parties were either the first or second most powerful in their respective party system. The British Labour Party and the West German Social Democratic Party alternated as the governing party with center-right parties and played crucial roles in promoting progressive reforms. These social democratic parties made a vital contribution to forging the class compromise that prevailed in northern Europe. Within social democracy, the state provided more expansive welfare benefits, tax laws were more progressive so that income inequalities were somewhat narrowed, and state policies placed a higher priority on full employment.

In southern Europe, workers divided their support about equally among communist, socialist, and more conservative Christian democratic parties. As a result, the right governed in these countries, although sometimes in complex and unstable coalitions. This circumstance reinforced workers' exclusion from the political community and also fostered more conservative state policies.

France is a mixed case in our analysis of the north-south split regarding the postwar settlement. Although it industrialized rapidly after World War II, and thus in this respect converged with northern Europe, its political and cultural patterns—notably a high degree of ideological conflict, labor militancy, and political fragmentation—were reminiscent of southern Europe.

Despite important differences in the way that political conflict was structured in the various Western European nations and the north-south split that we have identified, there was a broad convergence in the policies sponsored by the major Western European governments. The rapid industrialization associated with the postwar settlement fueled the expansion of housing, education, old-age pensions, and unemployment insurance. Far more than in the United States, Western European governments shared major responsibility for providing all citizens with basic services, including housing, medical care, and old-age pensions. The means varied through time and from country to country. By the late 1950s, the European Economic Community (EEC), forerunner of the EU, which provided for lower tariffs and a harmonization of economic policies among member states, provided additional impetus toward convergence.

Nonetheless, national differences persisted as a result of variations in historical evolution, political culture and institutions, and the specific balance among social forces and political parties. In the country sections of this book, we review the particular policy orientation adopted by each state. Nevertheless, there were some common elements on the postwar policy agenda of all the Western European states covered in the book.

Economic Regulation and the Keynesian Welfare State. Within the economic realm, the state engaged in ambitious efforts to achieve the goals of full employment, growth, economic modernization, and assistance to export-based industries. The European model of economic regulation, as it informally came to be known, involved vigorous state intervention with the twin aims of maximizing economic growth *and* ensuring that the fruits of economic growth would be diffused throughout the population. Two key terms can be suggested to summarize the policy mix: *Keynesian economics* and *the welfare state.* Taken together, the policy package is sometimes referred to as the *Keynesian welfare state.*

Keynesian economics was inspired by the distinguished English economist John Maynard Keynes. His work centered around understanding the causes of the Great Depression of the 1930s, when the industrialized economies of Europe and North America stagnated, living standards plummeted, and unemployment soared to unprecedented levels, reaching as high as 20 percent. Keynes sought to devise policies to end the depression and prevent the recurrence of future depressions. Rather than accepting fiscal orthodoxy, which stipulated that governments should cut spending when times were hard, Keynes advocated precisely opposite policies. According to Keynes, when governments cut spending, which orthodox economics claimed was necessary for governments to live within their reduced means, this *further* reduced demand, thereby contributing to the downward spiral of dwindling demand

and investment. On the contrary, Keynes claimed, governments should boost spending during hard times—thereby countering the "natural" movement of the business cycle—in order to bolster demand and stimulate new investment. (This is why Keynes's economic recommendation is often called *countercyclical* demand management.) In brief, he posited that a more vigorous, activist government stance would reverse the trend toward stagnation and provoke upward growth.

Keynes's name is also associated with the welfare state, the second leg of the new policy orientation that developed during the Great Depression and following World War II. He argued that the provision of welfare service, that is, an expanded welfare state, provided an ideal outlet for the additional government spending. Prior to the 1930s, government spending for the most part was devoted to defense, the maintenance of internal order (police), and education. Keynes argued that a desirable way to increase government spending during economic downturns was to redistribute resources to those most in need—the unemployed, sick, and economically dependent members of society. The term *welfare state* refers to the series of programs that transfer funds to citizens to meet social needs (transfer payments, such as unemployment insurance, pensions, and family allowances) or involve direct government provision of goods or social services (housing, medical care, job training, and the like). The origins of such programs lie earlier than the Great Depression. However, it was during the 1930s, and especially after World War II, that the welfare state expanded to alter the political economies of European countries fundamentally.

Modernization of Political Institutions. After World War II, power shifted from parliamentary to executive institutions within the state. This shift involved two elements. First, the balance of power within the state shifted from parliament to the bureaucracy. The decline of legislative bodies was justified by the presumed need for speed and cohesion in policymaking. Parliamentary institutions are designed to represent diverse interests and promote debate among options, but they move quite slowly and are fragmented. The executive, on the other hand, is organized to act decisively in order to implement decisions effectively. Second, there was a shift of decision-making power within the executive. On the one hand, with the state involved in more far-flung activities, power gravitated upward, with prime ministers and their staffs exercising greater power of oversight and control over their cabinet associates and line agencies. On the other hand, because of the state's increased involvement in macroeconomic and policy activities, economic ministries gained greatly increased influence in the day-to-day administration of governmental policy.

The European Model: Crises, Variations, and Challenges

Through the late 1960s, the European model we have described prevailed (with variations from nation to nation) throughout Western Europe as governments successfully managed economic and welfare policies and the major social classes maintained their modernizing alliance with the state. For the most part, the central trade-off of the national postwar settlements held: governmental steering mechanisms fostered full employment and economic growth, while increased social and welfare expenditures helped purchase relative social harmony and labor peace. The tension between democracy (now meaning participation through interest associations and cross-class political parties) and capitalism (now meaning politically regulated "modern capitalism" with extensive public holdings) was reduced—some thought forever.

Suddenly, and virtually without warning, this social harmony shattered, and a new era of political uncertainties began. The critical juncture unfolded in two stages. It was succeeded in the 1990s by a whole new era in European politics.

Stage One—From the Late 1960s Through the Mid-1970s: The Price of Success. In a way, the renewal of political conflict was rooted in the process of economic growth itself, which generated a host of political tensions that had been obscured by the strong grip of organized labor, capital, and the state. With state regulation aimed at forcing the pace of economic growth rather than reducing its damaging social consequences, the balance of costs and benefits shifted. Urban sprawl, traffic jams, and congestion became common. Forests were destroyed and rivers poisoned by industrial pollution. Migrants from rural areas and "guest workers," the euphemism for immigrant workers, jammed into hastily constructed blocks of high-rise flats that began to ring older central cities.

Women were drawn into the paid labor force in high numbers as a result of a tight labor market and an increase in clerical and governmental service positions, but they were recruited to poorly paid, subordinate positions. Economic growth was achieved in part through the introduction of new technology, which displaced skilled workers and posed threats to workers' health and safety.

The rapid expansion of the educated, urban middle class helped spark the early phase of militant protest. Many university students were radicalized by opposition to the U.S. military action in Vietnam as well as to the rigid authority patterns they encountered closer to home in their universities, political parties, and families. Many sought nontraditional goals: they wanted production to be democratically organized, resisted the traditional demands of marriage and career paths, and were the first to warn of environmental dangers from corporate abuses.

Political scientist Ronald Inglehart has coined the term *postmaterialism* to describe the values espoused by many educated youths in the postwar generation.[23] He discerns an intense generational cleavage created by the very different conditions under which prewar and postwar generations reached political maturity. Those born before World War II craved material and physical security because this was what they most lacked as a result of the Great Depression and military cataclysm. In contrast, Europeans born after the war were raised in a period of relative material security linked to the postwar settlement. They were more likely to be highly educated and to have the confidence born of expecting to gain stable and well-paid jobs.

Rather than expressing satisfaction and political quiescence, the postwar generations took their material advantages for granted and developed higher expectations. They resented, more than their parents did, being forced to submit to hierarchy, whether, for working-class youth, the tedium and mindlessness that characterized assembly-line production jobs, or, for middle-class youth, the tedium of the rigid hierarchies they encountered in corporations, universities, and government. Postwar youths were more likely than their elders to reject the human and physical costs of military confrontation and economic growth. They sought to pursue nonmaterial goals, including self-expression, a sense of community, and autonomy. Because they were less integrated within established institutions, they were inclined to express their frustration through unruly protest.

But we should beware of assuming that the rebellion of the late 1960s was confined to the new middle class. A key element contributing to the outbreak of protest in the late 1960s, which scholars often overlook in their fascination with new sources of opposition, was the rebellion of the industrial core of the working class. As the pace of economic change increased, workers were forced to endure intensified work tempos, increased occupational hazards, and tedious work.

In order to understand the 1960s rebellion, we need to appreciate how it represented a confluence of diverse sources, somewhat in the manner of "the perfect storm" described in Sebastian Junger's book (and later film) of that name. That is, although there were some common grievances linking the diverse groups that protested in the 1960s, the sources were also quite diverse. "The movement" was a sprawling coalition of industrial workers; newly militant white-collar working classes; urban, educated middle-class youth; and women and nonwhites neglected by traditional unions and leftist parties.

In the late 1960s and 1970s, there was a massive and unexpected eruption of what one study termed the "resurgence of class conflict in Western Europe." The most dramatic instance occurred in France in May 1968, when nearly half of all French workers, students, professionals, and civil servants staged the largest general strike in history. In Italy, during the "hot autumn" of 1969, workers and allied groups waged widespread grassroots struggles, outside established political party or legislative channels, for workplace control, political influence, and provision of social necessities like healthcare and housing. In Sweden, industrial relations became far more conflictual in the 1970s than previously and culminated in a general strike/lockout in May 1980.

A "crisis of governability" accompanied increasing electoral volatility. At the same time, increasingly influential political ideas and campaigns emerged outside and against conventional parties from the New Left and New Right: the women's movement; both neofascist and antiracist responses to immigration; nuclear disarmament agitation; environmental protest; and taxpayers' revolt.

If economic growth had continued unabated in the 1970s, social harmony might have been restored. However, the slowdown of Western Europe's economies reinforced the crisis of the postwar settlement. Many causes contributed to the continued erosion and replacement of the postwar settlement, and each made it more difficult for governments to maintain popular support.

Changes within the organization of production further contributed to the erosion of the postwar settlement. Fordism began to be an inefficient way to produce in the new era of the microelectronic revolution. As production shifted from mass-produced goods to diverse and often smaller-scale production strategies and to service-based industries, the semiskilled (often male) industrial working class began to shrink as a proportion of the employed population. On the one hand, this fragmented the working population, complicating neocorporatist bargaining based on unified social actors. On the other hand, technological change brought about new collective identities, based on new skills and social groups newly involved in production; for example, the number of female workers expanded rapidly. These changes were difficult to accommodate within the framework of privileged institutionalized bargaining with the state by the representatives of labor and business (neocorporatism) associated with the European model.

Western Europe was affected by the wider recession that began with the sharp increase in oil prices in 1973–1974. The cost of petroleum exports by the oil-producing developing countries grew at the expense of the industrialized nations of the West. The extremely high levels of popular support for the welfare state in Western Europe meant that most governments were unable to reduce welfare state benefits significantly. Meanwhile, trade union power limited labor market adjustments, and the increasingly global scale of production encouraged an outflow of investment from flagging Western European economies.

More generally, increasing economic integration meant that national governments were less able to regulate their domestic economies. In general, though with notable exceptions (among the larger European nations, West Germany was especially dynamic), Western Europe suffered a decline in international competitiveness. The result was higher rates of unemployment and inflation, slower productivity growth, and meager increases in living standards. The golden years of the postwar settlement were over.

Stage Two—From the Mid-1970s to the Mid-1980s: Experimentation and a Rightward Turn.
Provoked by the political protest and poor economic performance that began in the late 1960s, a relatively brief phase of political experimentation occurred from the 1970s to the mid-1980s, when governments of the left and right promising new departures were elected in many Western European nations. Initially, political momentum took a leftward turn. For example, northern European regimes devised mechanisms enabling workers to participate in decisions regarding technology change and occupational health and safety. In France, the Socialist government of François Mitterrand, elected in 1981, substantially expanded the nationalized industrial and financial sectors.

Political momentum soon shifted toward the right as constraints deriving from the international economy and the opposition of conservative domestic forces brought a halt to radical reforms. Although no Western European government was highly successful in either mobilizing political support or promoting successful economic performance, the left failed utterly to develop a new beginning—especially when measured against the high expectations created by the election of radical reformist socialist regimes in France, Spain, and Greece.

If the postwar settlement was intimately associated with social democracy, the 1980s were an opportunity for a conservative counterattack. For example, in Britain the Conservative government of Margaret Thatcher mounted a massive and quite successful assault on the power of labor unions and privatized both public housing facilities and nationalized industrial firms. Equally significant, it fostered important changes in British political culture, enhancing support for initiative and entrepreneurship at the expense of collectivity. Rightist coalitions promising tax reductions were elected in Denmark, Norway, and elsewhere, often replacing social democratic incumbents.

The uncertainty, loss of confidence, instability, and general decline that prevailed in Western Europe in the early 1980s was captured by the pungent term *Eurosclerosis*, which began to be heard at the time. Europe had lost its bearings following the long period of postwar reconstruction and growth, and where the drifting was destined to stop, nobody knew. Yet since the late 1980s and 1990s, there has been a revitalization of Europe, amid new issues, problems, and challenges.

From the 1990s to the Twenty-First Century: A New European Model?

Sometime in the 1980s, the vitality disappeared from the European model that was inspired by the postwar settlement of social democratic mixed economies and national policy models. Although significant elements of the European model remain—Europe's welfare state sector remains far more extensive than its counterpart in the United States—a new model of politics has emerged since the 1990s, the product of both a renewal of the process of European integration and a distinctive new domestic policy mix pursued by governments that reject Keynesian economic policies. The present period is also marked by the reinvigoration and expansion of the EU, an intensification of economic globalization, the ever-present menace of terrorism, and the unrivaled power of the United States that often—as in the run-up to the second war in Iraq or in perpetual trade disputes at the WTO—creates friction with European allies. We are now living through a critical juncture in European political development of historic proportions.

From State to Market to the Third Way. Across the political spectrum, there has been a significant shift in expectations about the role of the state in economic management. Unions have lost power, and middle-class politics is ascendant. The state continues to play an important role in the new political economy, but the role consists of activity to bolster rather than curtail the operation of markets. The dominant tendency in Western European politics currently seems to be a powerful backlash against the principles of compromise and the balance of

public and private power that were presupposed by the postwar settlement and the welfare state. There is general agreement on lowering taxes, reducing state economic intervention, and relying more on market forces to shape socioeconomic outcomes (an orientation widely referred to as *neoliberalism*). Although many of the state steering mechanisms and welfare programs put in place during the postwar settlement have survived, the momentum for expanding political regulation of the marketplace is gone; instead, the dominant tendency is for welfare state retrenchment and the reinvigoration of private market forces wherever politically feasible.

This shift toward neoliberalism does not sweep other political concerns off the board. Many of the concerns that began to undermine the postwar settlement in the late 1960s, including environmental and other quality-of-life matters, the demand for autonomy and community, and opposition to intrusive public and private bureaucracies, continue to fuel social and political movements. And conservative parties are often less suited than left-of-center ones to respond effectively to these new issues on the policy agenda. In fact, it has become increasingly difficult to define left and right in traditional pro-market or pro-state terms.

Into the breach, a new policy orientation emerged in Europe as center-left politicians and parties, led by Britain's Tony Blair, with Germany's Gerhard Schröder a powerful ally, tried to go "beyond left and right." This *third way* attempts to transcend distributional politics, which it considers unsuited to an era of intensified global competition, and combine the best of traditional appeals of left and right: the social justice concerns of classic social democracy with reliance on the economic dynamism of the right.[24] Ralf Dahrendorf, a distinguished observer of European affairs, has commented, "In fact, the Third Way debate has become the only game in town—the only hint at new directions for Europe's politics in a confused multitude of trends and ideas."[25]

To be sure, the arrival of a new political orientation that challenges and significantly recasts the European model does not mean the eradication of the old model. Class and occupational boundaries remain politically important, albeit sometimes in unusual ways. For example, as jobs become scarce, an important cleavage pits those occupying stable jobs against those with precarious employment or none at all. As private sector jobs become unstable, an important cleavage pits private sector workers against public sector workers, who usually enjoy the security of lifetime employment. At the same time, the waning of long-standing debates between socialists and conservatives means neither the end of political ideologies nor the consecration of a centrist consensus. Witness the rise of new forces, groups, and parties that challenge the established order. Without wishing to equate them, we observe other orientations that have gained increased importance: the environmental movements and their political expression (the Greens are now solidly represented in the European Parliament), plus anti-immigrant xenophobic forces in virtually every country. Thus, although the third way may not be the only game in town, it casts a long shadow over Europe.

Old States and the New Europe. When the Treaty of Rome created the European Economic Community in 1957, many scholars confidently predicted the steady growth of European economic and political integration. Despite steps in this direction, the path was far more tortuous than many expected. Indeed, the economic turbulence beginning in the mid-1970s brought the process to a crashing halt as European states became more concerned with protecting their domestic economies than with cooperating on a European-wide level. By the early 1980s, this produced the Eurosclerosis alluded to earlier.

The same forces that drove domestic political change in the 1980s also impelled political leaders and prominent business executives to cast their lot with a strengthened EU. When French president François Mitterrand reluctantly concluded in 1983 that France could not achieve domestic reflation on its own, he decided to join forces with German chancellor Helmut Kohl in a joint effort to revive France and Germany's ailing economies through increased European economic cooperation. In so doing, the leaders of Western Europe's two major states, along with prominent business leaders and officials in the EU, rescued the EU from stagnation. When the Maastricht Treaty on European Union was ratified in 1993, a new era began in Western European politics. Maastricht deepened economic integration; incorporated some aspects of foreign relations, defense policy, and policing; and addressed the endemic demands for greater internal democracy. The regulatory and institutional changes in the framework of the EU since the early 1990s range from specific provisions expanding the organization's scope—which mandate the free movement of commodities, capital, technology, and labor—to infrastructural concerns of standardizing technical production norms and redrafting labor and other codes, as well as unresolved issues, such as the Social Charter to enhance workplace and social rights. The creation of the European Central Bank; the launching of the euro in 1999, a common currency that has replaced the national currency of twelve of the fifteen states that comprised the EU before the latest enlargement of the EU to the east; the Growth and Stability Pact negotiated in 1997 (and now on life support as key members breach its spending limits); the expansion of the EU in 2004; and provisional agreement on a European Constitution, also in 2004, are landmarks along the route of the EU's renaissance in the last two decades.

Henceforth, the story of the domestic politics of Western European countries cannot be told without paying close attention to the vastly increased importance of the EU. Other transnational influences associated with globalization have also become more powerful—for example, volatile capital flows in an era of international financial deregulation. After a close look at the evolution of the EU in Part II, we highlight in the rest of the book the many ways that EU institutions have shaped the domestic political economies of member states.

The EU is not only a source of economic progress and political optimism. It has become a target for popular discontent by streamlining European economies, standardizing production norms, and ending state subsidies for domestic producers, as well as imposing harsh convergence criteria that involve pursuing austerity policies. The situation since the deepening of the EU has been described as the New Europe. It is very much a mixed blessing: on the one hand, a revival of Europe's economic fortunes; on the other hand, widening divisions between European citizens who are winners and losers depending on education, training, and occupation. The shift in power toward the EU has also limited the capacity of the member states to regulate their own economies and societies, increased tensions over the definition of citizenship and national identity, and produced a "democratic deficit"—concerns over citizen control and institutional transparency and accountability—at the level of EU institutions. It is not yet clear what the outcome of this important transition in European politics will be. Moreover, beyond the future of the EU loom even larger issues: the declining specificity of national political and economic processes, the future of the nation-states of Europe, the relationship between Western and Eastern Europe, the identity of Europeans, and the integration of Europe in the global economy and political order.

Whatever the future of the EU and the larger issues it inspires, it is quite clear that the current transition in European politics is intertwined with the emergence of the EU as a transnational polity to rival the importance of the countries whose political systems we study.

September 11, Iraq, the Old and New Europe, March 11, and Beyond. The most recent chapter in the unfinished story of European politics in transition began on the fateful morning of September 11, 2001, when four planes hijacked by Al Qaeda militants were transformed into bombs and used to attack strategic targets in the United States. Initially, most Europeans shared Americans' sense of shock, grief, and outrage. Numerous European states provided military assistance, including troops or supplies, during the United Nations–authorized attack led by the United States on the Taliban regime in Afghanistan, the base of Al Qaeda operations. However, international support turned to opposition the following fall as the United States began preparations to invade Iraq. The overwhelming majority of Europeans opposed the U.S. invasion, and the three Western European governments supporting the action—Britain, Italy, and Spain—paid dearly. British prime minister Tony Blair never recovered the popularity that he had enjoyed until his passionate support for the United States; Italian prime minister Silvio Berlusconi also suffered a steep loss of support; and the pro-U.S. Spanish government was turned out of office in the 2004 parliamentary elections.

The situation was very different in East-Central Europe, where most governments supported the U.S. military action in Iraq. One reason advanced was that the post-communist regimes in the region were recompensing the United States for contributing in the 1980s to the demise of communist dictatorships. As opposed to most countries in Western Europe, Poland and other countries in East-Central Europe contributed military assistance and political support to the United States.

So sharp was this cleavage that, in the diplomatic campaign by the United States to win support for the war in Iraq that was to be launched in March 2003, U.S. Secretary of Defense Donald Rumsfeld distinguished between what he called the "new Europe" and the "old Europe." Rumsfeld suggested that the center of gravity in Europe had shifted east, toward the states preparing to join the EU, whom he implied represented the wave of the future. The old Europe—notably France and Germany, whose leaders and populations firmly opposed an invasion of Iraq—were, in Rumsfeld's view, facing resolutely backward in history.

Our story has now returned to the events in 2004 that opened this chapter: March 11, and the Madrid railway bombing; May 1, and the accession of ten new member states to the EU; mid-May, and the story of Europe's lagging economic recovery; and June 10–13, when European citizens expressed their displeasure with their own incumbent governments and, indirectly, the EU. Perhaps we can best capture the (uncertain) meaning of the present transition in the words of the casino croupier: "round and round it goes; and where it stops, nobody knows."

Conclusion

European politics is in transition from a stable postwar past to an uncertain future; from a set of conflicts dominated by class-based politics to a more complex political dynamic defined by both centrist and more radical versions of a politics beyond left and right; and from a situation of national autonomy to a web of European integration and an international order fraught with danger.

Europe faces a host of stresses and unanswered questions, including how to reconcile regional and ethnic diversity with national unity, national cultural differences with the evolving EU, a strengthened Western European Union with the attempt to preserve national governmental autonomy, persistent (and often disappointed) demands for economic growth with concerns about inequality and unemployment as well as environmental and social costs, and how to participate in the U.S.-sponsored war on terrorism without becoming a junior partner in actions that many Europeans oppose.

European Politics in Transition seeks to understand the historical, economic, social, and institutional forces that have shaped the transition to the New Europe. Directly following this Introduction, we provide a comprehensive analysis of developments in the EU. We then closely examine the major Western European nations: Britain, France, Germany, and Italy. We analyze more briefly Poland, Hungary, and the Czech and Slovak Republics (and consider Yugoslavia), the most important nations in East-Central Europe.

In each country study, we begin with a description of the historical legacy of state formation, which continues to have a significant impact on political forces and policies, and a broad overview of contemporary political institutions and challenges. In the second chapter in each part, we analyze the historically specific features of both the postwar settlement and the shift since the 1970s toward the more market-oriented political economy. The third chapter in each part analyzes institutions of policy formation and implementation: the government and executive generally, public and semipublic agencies, local government, and the judiciary. The fourth chapter in each part analyzes institutions of political representation, notably legislatures, political parties and elections, modes of organizing interests, and contentious movements. The last chapter in each country part focuses on the current transition: new political forces, cleavages, and policies; the impact of the EU; and likely directions of change. The influences of the EU on domestic politics and policy are thoroughly integrated into each country study.

It is quite a challenge to understand the political systems and changing dynamics of contemporary Europe. We hope that the timely information and thematic focus of European politics in transition will both prepare and inspire you to explore further the endlessly fascinating terrain of European politics.

Notes

1. *New York Times,* May 12, 2004, Section W1.

2. For a superb study of this issue, see David Stark and Laszlo Bruszt, *Postsocialist Pathways: Transforming Politics and Property in East Central Europe* (Cambridge: Cambridge University Press, 1998).

3. For attempts to answer this question, see Alfred Stepan and Cindy Skach, "Constitutional Frameworks and Democratic Consolidation: Parliamentarism Versus Presidentialism," *World Politics* 46, no. 1 (October 1993): 1–22, and Juan J. Linz and Arturo Valenzuela, eds., *The Failure of Presidential Democracy* (Baltimore: Johns Hopkins University Press, 1994).

4. Robert A. Dahl, *A Preface to Economic Democracy* (Berkeley and Los Angeles: University of California Press, 1985), pp. 54–55 (emphasis in the original).

5. For a classic discussion of this issue, see Charles Lindblom, *Politics and Markets: The World's Political Economic Systems* (New York: Basic Books, 1977).

6. Adam Przeworski, *Democracy and the Market: Political and Economic Reforms in Eastern Europe and Latin America* (Cambridge: Cambridge University Press, 1991), p. xi.

7. Robert Putnam, with Robert Leonardi and Raffaella Y. Nanetti, *Making Democracy Work: Civic Traditions in Modern Italy* (Princeton, N.J.: Princeton University Press, 1992).

8. Sidney Tarrow, "Making Social Science Work Across Space and Time: A Critical Reflection on Robert Putnam's *Making Democracy Work,*" *American Political Science Review* 90, no. 2 (1996): 389–399.

9. Gabriel Almond and Sidney Verba, *The Civic Culture: Political Attitudes and Democracy in Five Nations* (Boston: Little, Brown, 1963). See also Gabriel Almond and Sidney Verba, eds., *The Civic Culture Revisited* (Boston: Little, Brown, 1980).

10. Dankwart Rustow, "Transitions to Democracy: Toward a Dynamic Model," *Comparative Politics* 2, no. 3 (April 1970): 363.

11. For recent descriptions by sympathetic participant-observers, see John Cavanagh and Jerry Mander, eds., *Alternatives to Economic Globalization: A Better World Is Possible* (San Francisco: Berrett-Koehler, 2004), and Robin Broad, ed., *Global Backlash: Citizen Initiatives for a Just World Economy* (Lanham, Md.: Rowman & Littlefield, 2002). For a spirited defense of globalization, see Jagdish Bhagwati, *In Defense of Globalization* (New York: Oxford University Press, 2004).

12. For a superb analysis, see Saskia Sassen, "The State and Globalization," in Rodney Bruce Hall and Thomas J. Biersteker, eds., *The Emergence of Private Authority in Global Governance* (Cambridge: Cambridge University Press, 2002), chap. 5.

13. Peter A. Hall and David Soskice, eds., *Varieties of Capitalism: The Institutional Foundations of Comparative Advantage* (New York: Oxford University Press, 2001). Also see Herbert Kitschelt, Peter Lange, Gary Marks, and John D. Stephens, eds., *Continuity and Change in Contemporary Capitalism* (Cambridge: Cambridge University Press, 1999).

14. This view was first put forward in Dankwart Rustow's classic article, "Transitions to Democracy . . . ," reprinted in Lisa Anderson, ed., *Transitions to Democracy* (New York: Columbia University Press, 1999). More recently, it has been developed by Dietrich Rueschemeyer, Evelyne Huber Stephens, and John D. Stephens, *Capitalist Development and Democracy* (Chicago: University of Chicago Press, 1992), and Adam Przeworski, *Democracy and the Market.*

15. Guillermo O'Donnell and Philippe C. Schmitter, *Transitions from Authoritarian Rule: Tentative Conclusions About Uncertain Democracies* (Baltimore: Johns Hopkins University Press, 1986).

16. Adam Przeworski et al., *Democracy and Development: Political Institutions and Well-Being in the World, 1950–1990* (Cambridge: Cambridge University Press, 2000), chap. 4. For a classic statement of the opposing view, see Samuel Huntington, *Political Order in Changing Societies* (New Haven, Conn.: Yale University Press, 1968).

17. Perry Anderson, *Lineages of the Absolutist State* (London: New Left Books, 1974); Douglass North, *Structure and Change in Economic History* (New York: Norton, 1981); Hendrick Spruyt, *The Sovereign State and Its Competitors: An Analysis of Systems Change* (Princeton, N.J.: Princeton University Press, 1994); and Charles Tilly, *Coercion, Capital and*

European States, A.D. 990–1992 (Cambridge, Mass.: Blackwell, 1993).

18. Barrington Moore Jr., *The Social Origins of Dictatorship and Democracy* (Boston: Beacon Press, 1966).

19. Andrew Shonfield, *Modern Capitalism: The Changing Balance of Public and Private Power* (Oxford: Oxford University Press, 1980), p. 3.

20. The general process has been exquisitely described by Claus Offe, *Contradictions of the Welfare State* (Cambridge, Mass.: MIT Press, 1984), chap. 8 and *passim*.

21. Otto Kirchheimer, "The Transformation of the Western European Party Systems," in Joseph LaPalombara and Myron Weiner, eds., *Political Parties and Political Development* (Princeton, N.J.: Princeton University Press, 1966), chap. 6.

22. Adam Przeworski, *Capitalism and Social Democracy* (New York: Cambridge University Press, 1985).

23. See Ronald Inglehart, *The Silent Revolution: Changing Values and Political Styles Among Western Publics* (Princeton, N.J.: Princeton University Press, 1977), *Culture Shift in Advanced Industrial Society* (Princeton, N.J.: Princeton University Press, 1990), and *Modernization and Postmodernization: Cultural, Economic, and Political Change in 43 Societies* (Princeton, N.J.: Princeton University Press, 1997).

24. For the classic statement of this approach, see Anthony Giddens, *The Third Way: The Renewal of Social Democracy* (Cambridge: Polity Press, 1998).

25. Ralf Dahrendorf, "The Third Way and Liberty: An Authoritarian Streak in Europe's New Center," *Foreign Affairs* 78, no. 5 (September–October 1999): 13.

Part I Bibliography

Anderson, Perry. *Lineages of the Absolutist State.* London: New Left Books, 1974.

Berger, Suzanne, ed. *Organizing Interests in Western Europe: Pluralism, Corporatism, and the Transformation of Politics.* Cambridge: Cambridge University Press, 1981.

Dalton, Russell J., and Manfred Kuechler, eds. *Challenging the Political Order: New Social and Political Movements in Western Democracies.* New York: Oxford University Press, 1990.

Esping-Andersen, Gøsta. *Social Foundations of Post-Industrial Economies.* New York: Oxford University Press, 1999.

Hall, Peter A., ed. *The Political Power of Economic Ideas.* Princeton, N.J.: Princeton University Press, 1989.

Hall, Peter A., and David Soskice, eds. *Varieties of Capitalism: The Institutional Foundations of Comparative Advantage.* New York: Oxford University Press, 2001.

Hobsbawm, Eric. *The Age of Extremes: The Short Twentieth Century, 1914–1991.* New York: Vintage Books, 1994.

Hollingsworth, J. Rogers, and Robert Boyer, eds. *Contemporary Capitalism: The Embeddedness of Institutions.* New York: Cambridge University Press, 1997.

Hollingsworth, J. R., Philippe C. Schmitter, and Wolfgang Streeck, eds. *Governing Capitalist Economies: Performance and Control of Economic Sectors.* New York: Oxford University Press, 1994.

Huber, Evelyne, and John D. Stephens, *Development and Crisis of the Welfare State: Parties and Policies in Global Markets.* Chicago: University of Chicago Press, 2001.

Inglehart, Ronald. *Culture Shift in Advanced Industrial Society.* Princeton, N.J.: Princeton University Press, 1990.

Katzenstein, Peter J. *Small States in World Markets.* Ithaca, N.Y.: Cornell University Press, 1985.

Kitschelt, Herbert. *The Transformation of European Social Democracy.* Cambridge: Cambridge University Press, 1994.

Kitschelt, Herbert, Peter Lange, Gary Marks, and John D. Stephens, eds. *Continuity and Change in Con-*

temporary Capitalism. Cambridge: Cambridge University Press, 1999.

Laver, Michael, and Norman Schofield. *Multiparty Government: The Politics of Coalition in Europe.* Oxford: Oxford University Press, 1990.

Lichbach, Mark Irving, and Alan S. Zuckerman, eds. *Comparative Politics: Rationality, Culture, and Structure.* New York: Cambridge University Press, 1997.

Marglin, Stephen A., and Juliet R. Schor. *The Golden Age of Capitalism: Reinterpreting the Postwar Experience.* New York: Oxford University Press, 1990.

Martin, Andrew, et al. *The Brave New World of European Unions: European Trade Unions at the Millennium.* New York: Berghahn, 1999.

Moore, Barrington, Jr. *The Social Origins of Dictatorship and Democracy.* Boston: Beacon Press, 1966.

Offe, Claus. *Contradictions of the Welfare State.* Cambridge, Mass.: MIT Press, 1984.

Putnam, Robert D., with Robert Leonardi and Raffaella Y. Nanetti. *Making Democracy Work: Civic Traditions in Modern Italy.* Princeton, N.J.: Princeton University Press, 1992.

Rueschemeyer, Dietrich, Evelyne Huber Stephens, and John D. Stephens. *Capitalist Development and Democracy.* Chicago: University of Chicago Press, 1992.

Schmidt, Vivien A. *The Futures of European Capitalism.* New York: Oxford University Press, 2002.

Shonfield, Andrew. *Modern Capitalism: The Changing Balance of Private and Public Power.* Oxford: Oxford University Press, 1980.

Stark, David, and Laszlo Bruszt. *Postsocialist Pathways: Transforming Politics and Property in East Central Europe.* Cambridge: Cambridge University Press, 1998.

Swank, Duane. *Global Capital, Political Institutions, and Policy Change in Developed Welfare States.* Cambridge: Cambridge University Press, 2002.

Tarrow, Sidney. *Power in Movement: Social Movements and Contentious Politics.* New York: Cambridge University Press, 1998.

Tilly, Charles. *Coercion, Capital and European States, A.D. 990–1992.* Cambridge, Mass.: Blackwell, 1993.

P A R T

II

The European Union and the Future of European Politics

George Ross

CHAPTER

1

The Coming of a European System

On May 9, 1950, in a gilded, elegant room in the Quai d'Orsay, France's Ministry for Foreign Affairs, Foreign Minister Robert Schuman proposed that France and Germany, and any other democratic nation in Western Europe that wanted to join them, establish a "community" to regulate and govern the coal and steel industries across national borders. If one knew nothing about European history, a proposal for a European Coal and Steel Community (ECSC) might have seemed dry and technical. But France and Germany had been at war or preparing for it for most of the first half of the twentieth century, and their landscapes were dotted with memorials and cemeteries reminding them of the costs to millions of citizens. Iron and steel, at that point, were the keys both to national economic success and to war-making power. The first few sentences of Schuman's declaration spoke to the deep issues.

> World peace cannot be safeguarded without creative efforts at the level of the dangers that menace it. The contribution that an organized and vital Europe can bring to civilization is indispensable to the maintenance of peaceful relations. By championing the idea of a United Europe over the last twenty years, France has always sought to serve the cause of peace. Europe was not built and we had war. . . . Europe will not be made all at once, nor will it be made in a single holistic construction: it will be built by concrete achievements that will create solidarity in facts. Assembling European nations demands first that the secular opposition between France and Germany be eliminated. The actions that are undertaken

ought therefore first to involve France and Germany.[1]

Robert Schuman was a devout Catholic and Christian Democrat, who since his death has been repeatedly proposed for sainthood. He came from Lorraine, a steel-making area that had been the object of battles between France and Germany for decades. His German counterpart, the chancellor of the new German Federal Republic, Konrad Adenauer, was also a devout Catholic and Christian Democrat and had been mayor of Cologne before Hitler sent him to Buchenwald prison. Both knew the historic significance of what they had agreed. France and Germany were quickly joined by Italy, Belgium, the Netherlands, and Luxembourg to make up the original six countries that began the long march toward today's European Union.

Schuman had been persuaded to present his plan by Jean Monnet, justly considered a founding father of the current EU. Monnet, the son of a Cognac dealer, was a transnational networker and "fixer" of genius. During World War I, while still a young man, he had helped organize supply chains from North America to Britain and France. Then, after serving briefly as assistant secretary-general of the League of Nations, he entered private transatlantic business, where he made friends with the elite of Wall Street lawyers and bankers—Stimson, Acheson, Harriman, McCloy, and the Dulles brothers—who would dominate post–World War II American foreign policy. When World War II broke out, Monnet became the intermediary to President Roosevelt for arranging arms and financial aid to the French and by 1943 was the key link between Americans and the nascent French government in Algiers.

When the war ended, Monnet devised France's economic planning process, putting him at the heart of operations associated with the Marshall Plan, the program of foreign assistance undertaken by the United States to facilitate European recovery from the devastating war. It was in this role, in the interstices of American high cold war politics, that Monnet, never elected to anything, devised the Schuman Plan. With Schuman he also structured the clever way in which the plan was proposed. At that point the French government was an unruly coalition of different parties jostling for power. Monnet and Schuman thus circulated the plan beforehand only to the ministers they knew would be favorable to the idea. Once they knew they had a majority, they then rushed the plan through the government and shortly thereafter announced it publicly. The public announcement of the plan was followed almost immediately by German approval, locking in success before any real debate happened. This would not be the last time that Europe would progress through stealth.

The ECSC might have been a footnote in history had not in 1958, with the Treaty of Rome, the same six nations agreed to create the European Economic Community (EEC) to construct a "common market." By 1995 the EEC had become a European Union (EU) of fifteen, covering virtually all Europe west of cold war dividing lines.* On May 1, 2004, the EU accepted eight new Central and Eastern European members (along with Cyprus and Malta), with others in the membership queue, effectively ending Europe's cold war division. The result has been a new Euro-level

system of democratic politics often coordinating, sometimes complementing, and in a few areas superseding those of its members. European integration is clearly one of the few international political success stories of our era.

More than fifty years after the ECSC, today's European Union has promoted a unified economy out of separate national models, stimulated European growth, and transformed Europe into a major power in today's globalizing world. EU Europe is the largest exporter and importer on the planet, a center of economic dynamism, and a zone of unprecedented prosperity. For decades it has also been a zone of peace and an unquestionable asset to world peace. Finally, the EU has played a central role in consecrating and consolidating democracy, first in immediate postwar Western Europe, later in the former Mediterranean dictatorships, and most recently in the former Soviet bloc. EU Europe now stretches eastward from the Atlantic to Belarus, Ukraine, Russia, and Turkey, if candidates Romania and Bulgaria are included. From north to south, it extends from Arctic regions to the Mediterranean, excluding only Norway and the Balkans. All told, the EU has 450 million well-educated citizens, producers, and consumers.

The EU challenges received knowledge in political science. It is an organization of states, but is not itself a state. It is an "international organization," yet simultaneously a transnational polity whose laws and decisions constrain its members' sovereignty. The EU is a unique combination of federalism and intergovernmentalism. There is no EU government, no majority, no opposition, and no real "we the people." Instead, the EU is composed of many peoples in many societies with different national identities and languages who cooperate in harmony.

*The EU has been officially called the EEC (the European Economic Community, from 1957 to 1965); the EC (for European Communities) after the 1965 "Merger Treaty" that brought the EEC, ECSC, and Euratom (the European Atomic Energy Authority—see Chapter 2) under one institutional roof; and the European Union, after the Maastricht Treaty was ratified in 1993. Simplifying, with full knowledge of the anachronisms that result, we will use EU throughout.

Steps to Europe

European integration has been a cumulation of steps, each taken in response to large challenges, often coming from the international state system. Over time, the process has transformed the EU from a problem-solving arena of last resort to a place where European nation-states brainstorm, anticipate, and act in what they have increasingly understood to be their common interests.

The EU originated in a world of European states that had become unlivable. The European continent had been for centuries the site of bloody wars whose terrifying costs reached their peak in the first half of the twentieth century. With new military technologies and ways of mobilizing populations, the practice of European states pursuing their national interests became mutual suicide. In World War I (1914–1918), millions were killed and maimed in trench warfare over minuscule plots of land chewed to bits by artillery shells and polluted by poison gas. The interwar years, between 1918 and 1939, were a time of wild economic instability whose cycles culminated in the collapse of the international financial system and the Great Depression. The economic disruption fed antidemocratic political extremism. At this point Hitler and the German National Socialists and Stalin and the Soviet Communists each conceived their very different plans for uniting Europe. Civil war in Spain cost tens of thousands of lives and left the Spanish people under a repressive regime. Italian fascism moved from disaster to disaster. Seen from the 1930s, the future of democracy in Europe and the world was perilous.

Fine-Tuning the "Golden Age"

World War II, the culmination of a terrible half-century, cost tens of millions of lives. The Nazis killed untold numbers that they deemed undesirable, including six million Jews in the Holocaust. Populations were moved against their wills. Innocent civilians were routinely bombarded from the sky and incinerated, as in the terrifying firebombing of German cities by the Allies. Nuclear weapons, developed first by Europeans and Americans, were not used in Europe only because their development came too late.

This gigantic human catastrophe ultimately brought down Fascist regimes in Germany and Italy (those in Spain and Portugal persisted into the 1970s).

Europe in 1945 was at a turning point. The war had diminished the appeal of illiberal regimes, with the important exception of Stalinist communism. In many countries resistance forces brought democratic ideals and social reform to power. The United States, Britain, France, and the Soviet Union jointly occupied a conquered Germany, tried Nazi war criminals (most notably at Nuremberg), and reflected about preventing anything like Nazism ever recurring. Economically, Europe was prostrate. Cities, factories, and transportation networks lay in ruins, and money to reconstruct them was unavailable since European treasuries were empty.

The cold war was what prodded Western Europeans toward integration. The USSR and the United States, wartime allies, quickly became enemies, arming to the teeth to create a bipolar standoff that lasted more than four decades. Initially dependent on the United States for financial support (through the Marshall Plan), Western Europeans found themselves barred from old habits of inter-European conflict. One alternative was integration. For the ECSC "six," integration began in 1950 and culminated in the 1957 Treaty of Rome that established the European Economic Community.

The EU had the good fortune of starting amidst an unprecedented rush of prosperity, a "Golden Age." Keynesianism, an economic policy that managed demand to promote maximum employment of resources, helped bring an Americanized system of mass production and consumerism into being. Full employment, once a dream, briefly became a reasonable goal. States redistributed new wealth through expanded social programs, often backed by broad political coalitions that brought the representation of groups long excluded. These "postwar settlements" underpinned the first widespread triumph of representative democracy in Western Europe's history. The EEC, or Common

Market—the major product of the 1957 Treaties of Rome—supplemented Western Europe's thriving national economies, fine-tuning the Golden Age subject to the guidance of EEC member states. Its customs-free area created a larger trading space, so that the burgeoning industrial "national champions" of many of its members could export more. Its Common Agricultural Policy (CAP) stimulated the modernization of agriculture. Finally, the EEC's common external tariff established a buffer against the harsh winds of the international market and the economic power of the United States.

Major international change in the 1970s, this time economic, provided new stimuli for further integration but also created challenges that stalled integration for a decade. EEC members—nine after the United Kingdom, Denmark, and Ireland joined in 1973—responded to oil shocks and "stagflation" (the previously unknown combination of high inflation combined with low growth) in policy disarray. Some continued Keynesian techniques; others turned to monetarism (controlling the money supply to limit inflation); still others, like Britain after 1979, attacked labor organizations to lower wages. Policy divergence was dangerous in a customs-free area, particularly in an international context of currency fluctuation stimulated by the end of the U.S.-sponsored Bretton Woods system (a system to stabilize exchange rates through the U.S. dollar, plus institutions like the International Monetary Fund [IMF] and the World Bank to stabilize trade cycles). By the later 1970s the Common Market was itself threatened and the postwar settlements it had coexisted with were under siege. There were innovations, like the European Monetary System (EMS), but in general "Eurosclerosis," an inability to move forward, was the rule.

Challenges of Globalization and a Post–Cold War World

It took until 1985, with globalization on the horizon, for the EU to find new energy. Golden Age growth disappeared, EU Europe lost competitiveness, and high unemployment returned. EU member states, who might have gone their own ways, instead agreed to "complete the single market" by the end of 1992, a program designed to create a Europe-wide "single economic space" through new market liberalization. The culmination was the 1991 Maastricht Treaty on European Union (ratified in 1993). At Maastricht, EU members agreed to an Economic and Monetary Union (EMU) that would eventually create a unified European monetary policy, a European Central Bank to run it, and a single European currency, the euro. Maastricht also proposed a new common foreign and security policy and new collaboration in "justice and home affairs." The EU appeared revitalized.

The international setting changed dramatically yet again, however, setting up the contemporary period. The end of the cold war and the collapse of the Soviet empire changed the EU's security situation and created the new issue of integrating the ex-Communist East. At practically the same time, the consolidation of an international economic policy shift from Keynesianism to an anti-inflationary quest for price stability, hastened in Europe by the coming of EMU, obliged new outlooks. In these new economic circumstances, the single-market program failed to live up to promises of renewed economic growth. Instead, 1992 saw the beginning of deep recession lasting until 1997 and unemployment above 10 percent across much of the EU. The semiskilled manufacturing jobs that had expanded with postwar prosperity disappeared by the hundreds of thousands.

Economic change led people to question their own governments and the EU itself. Simultaneously, growing public awareness of the EU's significance collided with recognition that people had not been fully consulted about the steps creating it. From the beginning, the "Monnet method" involved promoting integration by stealth, sometimes short-circuiting national democratic processes. By the 1990s many EU citizens had concluded that there was a "democratic deficit." On top of this, the economic convergence demanded by movement to EMU was more of a strain than anyone had anticipated. The deep recession that began in 1992 made matters vastly worse, threatening the survival of the EMS itself. Ironically, it was the German government, more than anyone else, that stood solidly behind the process, reassuring those who had feared that a unified Germany might move away from the EU. EMU success meant that integration went forward.

Enlargement: Puzzles Within Puzzles

Big puzzles remained, however. What was the EU to do with the ex-Communist countries of Central and Eastern Europe (CEECs)? The EU initially lacked the resources to confront the issue, even if it quickly set up aid programs and negotiated agreements for freer trade, in the process encouraging CEEC aspirations to eventual EU membership. By the second half of the 1990s, however, the EU had begun to move toward full incorporation of the CEECs. Admitting new members meant organizing new trans-European economic interdependencies, helping the CEECs to modernize, and underwriting the consolidation of democracy where it had fragile indigenous roots. Perhaps because of the magnitude of these responsibilities, many in the EU were wary and ambivalent. Still, ten new members joined on May 1, 2004, with several others in the wings.

EU institutions had been designed in the 1950s for six members. Fifty years later, with a vastly expanded EU mandate and twenty-five members, they needed reform lest they stop working altogether. The issue of reconfiguring institutional structures thus was high on the EU's agenda, beginning in the later 1990s. The Nice and Laeken European Councils, one year apart in 2000–2001, focused on what to do, and Laeken decided to convene a "European Convention," meant to encourage the widest possible discussion of Europe's future in 2002. There were a host of complicated questions on the convention table, however. Was the EU meant primarily for "market building," as some member

states maintained? Or was market building meant as a launching pad for the broader unification of Europe? Moreover, a great debate on institutions could not avoid confronting outstanding issues of democratic legitimacy.

The end of the cold war upset Europe's cold war security certainties as well. Maastricht had proposed the creation of a common EU foreign and security policy and hinted at the eventuality of a European-level defense capability. Some key member states were quite uninterested in these matters. Violence in the Balkans, eventually necessitating taking American intervention, underscored these issues, however, and prompted small new steps, more in defense matters than in foreign policy. The EU thus began to create a rapid-reaction force and invested in logistic and intelligence support for it, with the United States protesting every step of the way through the North Atlantic Treaty Organization (NATO). The Amsterdam Treaty (1997) established a more efficient way of representing the EU to third parties. Questions remained, however. How would Europe confront potential new security problems in its own backyard? What would be the division of labor between NATO and Europe in any such confrontations?

Lurking in these interconnected puzzles were questions about the EU's position in the world and, in particular, its relationship with the United States. The United States had facilitated the founding of the EU. The end of the cold war, however, occurred when Europe was becoming an economic region as large as the United States, suggesting a "rebalancing" of economic power and the possibility of growing rivalry, particularly in trade conflicts. Europe's larger footprint in a globalizing world implied that the EU would eventually need to define its interests in areas well beyond its own European neighborhood, perhaps challenging the cold war division of labor between the United States and Europe. For decades the United States had grown accustomed to primacy, however. The stage was set for difficulties about the post-9/11 American "war on terror" and Iraq.

Euro-Politics and European Politics in Transition

Euro-politics became more significant in part at the expense of European national politics, making the EU one of the bigger reasons for the transition of national politics in Europe that other chapters in this volume will discuss. Five decades of economic integration, more recently in an enveloping context of globalization, have significantly constrained the political autonomy of EU members. As the EU probes into political realms and as globalization progresses, shrinking national sovereignty has become ever more significant. EU-wide open-market structures have transferred decision making from national governments to markets. Regulatory responsibilities have shifted from individual nations to the EU. The EU has taken over monetary policy, arguably the most important dimension of contemporary economic policymaking. Finally, parts of foreign relations and defense policy, plus some issues of citizenship, immigration, and policing, have migrated toward the EU. In all, for European nations, gains from European integration have come at real costs. "European politics in transition" happens, in large part, in nation-states. But neither local nor national actors can do what they used to do, partly because of Euro-politics. Euro-politics is itself multileveled, however, and localities, regions, and national governments spend more and more time engaged at European levels. The result has enormously complicated flows of information to citizens, making democratic public life harder to organize and understand. Euro-politics is still a construction site, however. Can Europe handle the challenges that it presently faces? Will Europe be an effective or an ineffective way of coping with globalization? Is European integration worth the price of undermining national communities and arrangements that once provided European peoples with security and optimism? Can European institutions and political processes be made more democratic? If national loyalties and identities are eroded, where and how can loyalties and identities be relocated? In the following chapters we will try to answer these many questions, first exploring the history of European integration in greater detail, next discussing EU institutions and policymaking, and finally the challenges that the European Union, and its member states, now face.

Note

1. First paragraph of the Schuman declaration of May 9, 1950, GR translation, from Joël Boudant and Max Gounelle, *Les grandes dates de l'Europe communautaire* (Paris: Larousse, 1989), pp. 14–15.

CHAPTER

2

Politics and Economics in the Making of the European Union

Immanuel Kant wrote about European integration in 1789. Saint Simon speculated about it in France only slightly later. In 1849, Victor Hugo presided over a Congress of the Friends of Peace calling for a United States of Europe. Would-be conquerors—Napoleon, Hitler, Stalin—and those desirous of frustrating their conquests, had their own notions of European unity. The bloodbath in World War I prompted more urgent reflections. In the 1920s, Count Koudenhove-Kalergi, a Central European aristocrat, mobilized a substantial pan-Europe movement. A Benelux customs union nearly came into being in the 1920s. In 1929, French prime minister Aristide Briand made an eloquent plea for European federalization to the League of Nations. The rise of fascism closed debate, and it took the massive geopolitical changes after 1945 to open it again.

A New Europe Born of the Cold War, 1950–1970

The emergence of the United States as a superpower was a huge geopolitical shift. The cold war, structured around U.S.-Soviet confrontation, was a second. These changes in the balance of international power were what set the stage for Europeans to begin integration. As victory approached in World War II, the United States was more concerned with establishing a viable postwar international trading regime than with regional integration. U.S. leadership reconstructed the capitalist world's financial underpinnings. The Bretton Woods system—named

after the New Hampshire hotel where the deals were struck in 1944—involved U.S. commitment to make the dollar a global reserve currency backed by gold. The United States was also decisive in founding a World Bank to provide development funding; an International Monetary Fund (IMF) to allow individual trading nations to run occasional payment deficits and police the trading system; and the General Agreement on Tariffs and Trade (GATT), a multilateral organization to promote free trade (succeeded by the World Trade Organization, or WTO, in 1995). The United States clearly was willing to serve as the trustee of the international trading system, an essential gesture in reconstructing market economies after the Great Depression and the Second World War.

Western Europeans were flat broke, faced huge rebuilding tasks, and had little to trade and no money to pay for what they bought. The United States, worried about European political stability and the functioning of the international market, stepped in to offer the Marshall Plan (1947), which established the United States as financier of European recovery and made billions of dollars available to reconstruct European economies, provided only that the Europeans talk to each other about putting the money to good use.[1] For Western Europe, the Marshall Plan promoted greater economic coordination, in particular through the Organization for European Economic Cooperation (OEEC, today the Organization for Economic Cooperation and Development—OECD, a leading think tank about economic issues).[2] The Western Europeans used Marshall Plan aid for national goals that they themselves defined. Well invested, the funds provided a solid foundation for Western European modernization along the consumerist lines that the United States had already pioneered. It also allowed Western European nations the financial space to consolidate social reforms instituted in the wake of the war. Finally, it solidified their attachment to the United States.

Soviet intentions for postwar Europe soon became clear. By 1947, in its Central and Eastern sphere of influence, the USSR had set about establishing "popular democracies," which were neither democratic nor popular, but dominated by local Communists mimicking Soviet ways and backed by Soviet troops. European geography—Paris was only a few hundred miles from a million Soviet troops—together with the power of Communists in some Western European electorates, nourished American fear that a Soviet westward offensive would be difficult to stop. The outbreak of the cold war, a four-decade-long standoff between the United States and the Soviet Union, thus coincided with the Marshall Plan.

Cold war rearmament was the immediate geopolitical background for European integration. The United States first committed to the most massive peacetime military buildup in American history, then persuaded and financed Western European nations to follow. Founded in 1949, the North Atlantic Treaty Organization (NATO) stationed American troops and materiel throughout Europe in position to block any offensive from the East. Europeans and other allies were expected to do their part, integrated under a unified NATO command structure. NATO formalized the hegemony of American military power in Western Europe. Western European defenses subsequently had to focus on NATO tasks and subordinate their own European rivalries. This was of critical importance since it meant that as long as the cold war went on, armed conflict among Western Europeans, the global scourge of the first half of the twentieth century, was off the agenda. As part of their plans, the Americans wanted to include the Germans in the new alliance. This meant a shift from punishing to rehabilitating Germany, leading to a new German polity in 1949—the Federal Republic of Germany—carved out of the American, British, and French occupation zones. The Soviet zone, in turn, became the German Democratic Republic (GDR), consolidating a division of Germany that would last until 1990. The Americans also wanted to arm the new West Germany, now the front line of anti-Soviet defense.

These changes happened during a widespread debate about European integration. Everyone agreed that Europe should end its habit of staging horrific wars. But postwar penury, which meant that European economies had to be nationally coordinated through price controls, rationing, and wage limitations, made large-scale transnational economic integration difficult. Moreover, the different ideas about European integration were hard to conciliate. *Federalists* wanted supranational institutions and even talked of a United States of Europe. *Intergovernmentalists* sought cooperative arrangements that preserved national sovereignty. There were also differing visions about what should be integrated and where to start.

A customs union of the Netherlands, Belgium, and Luxembourg (Benelux), opened in 1948, was one early success.[3] Failures and dead ends were more common, however. The French and Italians discussed a customs union in 1947, but the French parliament refused to ratify it. France, Italy, Belgium, the Netherlands, and Luxembourg tried to negotiate a customs union and failed. In 1949–1950, the United Kingdom and Scandinavian countries failed to agree on a free trade zone (UNISCAN). The most spectacular setback occurred at the Hague 1948 Congress of Europe, where delegates from sixteen European countries debated almost everything to an impasse. There were some results. The Council of Europe, founded in 1949, created a Court of Justice that would subsequently play an important role in advancing human rights in Europe.

Integrating a Europe of Postwar Settlements

The first breakthrough was the European Coal and Steel Community (ECSC) in 1950, emerging from Europe's biggest chronic problem, French-German relations. The French, overrun by the Germans three times in seventy-five years, had initially hoped to fragment post-Nazi Germany and neutralize its heavy industrial areas. The French steel industry in Lorraine, rich in iron ore but poor in coal, needed coking coal, however. The closest source was the Ruhr, so negotiations for an International Ruhr Authority began in 1947. It happened that the high French official working on the Ruhr problem was Jean Monnet, then head of French economic planning.[4] In the face of strong American pressure for new French policy on Germany, Monnet proposed an ECSC to integrate the French and German coal and steel industries, as we discussed in Chapter 1. The "original six," including Luxembourg, the Netherlands, Belgium, and Italy, signed the ECSC treaty in 1951, with the community officially created in July 1952. The British stood aside, refusing even to negotiate, and its then Labour government announced that "a political federation limited to Western Europe is not compatible with our Commonwealth ties, our obligations as a member of the wider Atlantic alliance, or as a world power."

Behind Monnet's ideas was "functionalist" reasoning.[5] Integration would be doomed were it to depend on resolving a huge range of matters in one giant transaction. Success was more likely were it to be founded on transnational approaches to sectoral problems. Given the interdependencies of modern economies, sectoral integration was likely to "spill over" into new areas. Coal and steel were a good place to begin, and the United States was exerting enormous pressure to normalize French-German relations. Both Germany and France knew that the United States would eventually impose its own solution, giving each an interest in negotiating their own agreement before that. French public opinion would accept normalization only if arrangements neutralized threats from Germany's heavy industries of war. German industrial interests wanted a new deal that could open markets. Both sides also faced concern about overproduction in coal and steel. The ECSC would end national subsidies and barriers to trade in coal and steel. More important historically, its Monnet-designed institutions became the model for later steps in integration.

Advocates of integration then tried to adapt the "Monnet method" to other areas, most often failing. French and Dutch proposals in 1950 for Europeanizing agriculture never got off the ground. Another French proposal for a European transport authority was dropped. A multilateral proposal to establish a European Political Community (focused on foreign affairs) was never agreed. Then in 1952 came a Monnet-French proposal for a new European Defense Community (EDC) that sought to capitalize on felt need to find acceptable ways for the Germans to rearm, a prospect that frightened most non-German Europeans. The United States wanted German integration into NATO. Monnet's EDC, in contrast, proposed a transnational European army containing German troops. EDC collapsed when the French themselves refused in 1954 to ratify it in parliament.[6]

The goals of European integration remained, however. Experiences accumulated on the ground with agreements like the Benelux customs union and "common market." Belgian minister of foreign affairs Paul-Henri Spaak then seized on the idea of a broader Common Market, earlier proposed by Dutch foreign minister Johan Beyen, and traveled throughout Europe to enlist other leaders. The Beyen-Spaak approach, more ambitious than the minimalist "free trade area" favored by the British, proposed common policies and supranational institutions. A conference in Messina, Italy, in June 1955 was the turning point. Led by Spaak and other Benelux politicians, the ECSC six announced their commitment to create a European Common Market, Euratom (a European atomic energy agency), plus harmonization of European social policies. Spaak prepared more proposals, and his report of May 1956 suggested "a European Common Market . . . [leading to] a vast zone with a common economic policy." The two Treaties of Rome in 1957 were the result, officially founding the European Economic Community (EEC) and Euratom.

Underlying agreement were again bargains between France and Germany. The French wanted Euratom, Monnet's proposal, and were much less enthusiastic about the Common Market. Their rejection of the EDC made them feel obligated to accept an EEC with safeguards rather than blocking it, however. German chancellor Konrad Adenauer believed that a Common Market would help the German economy and grant the Federal Republic more sovereignty and legitimacy. The Germans most wanted trade liberalization in industrial products. The French agreed to this only in exchange for a common agricultural policy giving them preferential access to other EEC markets and entry for tropical products from colonies and ex-colonies. The French also feared building a Common Market prior to a harmonization of wages and social protection programs and imposed further conditions. The British were again conspicuous by their absence, disagreeing with supranationality and skeptical that the EEC proposals would actually ever happen. This time, they mounted a counteroffensive, organizing a European Free Trade Association (EFTA) in 1959 that included the Scandinavian countries, Iceland, Portugal, Switzerland, and Austria. EFTA involved free internal trade, but no common external trade barriers or policies.

The Preamble to the Rome EEC Treaty promised "foundations of an ever-closer union among the peoples of Europe." Article 2 stated that

> The Community shall have as its task, by establishing a Common Market and economic community and by progressively approximating the economic policies of Member States, to promote throughout the Community a harmonious and balanced development of economic activities, a continuous and balanced

expansion, an increase in stability, an accelerated rise in living standards, and closer relations between the States belonging to it.[7]

The Common Market, the core of the new EEC, involved staged removal of direct and indirect barriers to trade and common trading rules to abolish "obstacles to freedom of movement for persons, services and capital," all behind a common external tariff and a common commercial policy toward third countries. The EEC Treaty's other objectives included common policies in agriculture, transport, a "system ensuring that competition in the Common Market is not distorted," and procedures for coordinating economic policy and controlling balance of payments disequilibria. Member states would be obligated to harmonize their legal systems on Common Market matters. There were also provisions for a European Social Fund, a European Investment Bank to promote development in less prosperous regions, and association arrangements for overseas ex-colonies and territories.[8]

Excepting internal tariff liberalization, which was set out in detail, the EEC Treaty was a "framework agreement" that pronounced general purposes but left actual programs to be worked out following a fixed schedule. Elaborating the EEC's substance therefore remained after Rome. The signatories' hope was that the Common Market would eventually lead to a single economy. The logics of market liberation and rule making then might "spill over" toward political unity—a functionalist vision that foresaw contagion from the common "lower" politics of trade and markets into the "high politics" of federalism and foreign policy. Where Rome did not delegate sovereignty explicitly to the EEC, however, nations remained sovereign.

The Rome Treaty proposed that the EEC's institutions be modeled on those of the ECSC, as follows:

- An appointed European Commission, sited in Brussels, acquired exclusive power to propose policy (as well as duties to implement and safeguard the treaty).

- A Council of Ministers, which voted Commission proposals up or down, was the EEC "legislature." It represented each national government and was coordinated by a presidency that rotated among members every six months.
- A European Court of Justice (ECJ), located in Luxembourg, would entertain litigation in those areas—mainly trade related—where the Rome Treaty granted EEC laws precedence over national statutes and precedents.
- A European Parliament (EP), located in Strasbourg, was composed of members appointed from national parliaments.

The European Commission was meant as the binding element, as central strategic planner and activist for the integration process. Implementation of programs was almost always left to national governments, which were to be exhaustively consulted before any proposals were advanced. In the right circumstances and as long as it could find suitable treaty provisions allowing action and political support from member states, the Commission could try to propose changes. Indeed, Monnet's view was that the Commission should to be a motor to expand the EEC's mandate over time. The Council of Ministers, the EEC legislature, decided according to rules spelled out in the treaty. Initially, most important decisions were to be taken unanimously, but once the Common Market had been established, there was to be a change to "qualified majority voting" (QMV), a way of weighting member state votes by size. This meant that as time went on, member states could be outvoted on significant matters. The European Parliament initially had very little power, and few people cared what it did. It was "consulted" on certain matters. It could debate an annual report that the Commission was required to submit. And, although it never did so, it could also dismiss the Commission on a vote of censure (requiring a two-thirds vote among at least half of the total number of sitting members of the European Parliament—MEPs), and it could bring action against other EEC institutions before the ECJ for "failure to act." Finally, it could pose questions to which the Commission was obliged to respond, a process that eventually became a regular "question time." In all, this "Monnet" or "Community" institutional method—the French term often used is *engrénage* (literally "getting caught in the gears")—was meant to create a way of being federalist without frightening too many people. The founders wanted ways to bypass the reticence about integration that would be expressed if peoples were actually asked. Europeans would overwhelmingly approve the new arrangements once their benefits had become clear.

EEC institutions were an open-ended experiment, defined in general terms by the Rome Treaty, with the scope of action left to trial, error, and struggle. Since the Commission would have to carve space from member states' prerogatives, the plan was a recipe for difficulties between it and the Council of Ministers. The Council's opacity—from the beginning it hid behind a shroud of diplomacy—made it simultaneously vulnerable to challenge over democratic legitimacy and open to member states' politicians seeking to circumvent and constrain their own national political lives through Euro-level decisions. The initial impotence of the European Parliament founded a dynamic of agitation for increased power in the name of diminishing the "democratic deficit." The European Court of Justice, the final major institution set up by the Rome Treaty, was charged with ensuring that "in the interpretation and application of this Treaty the law is observed." In practice, this provision allowed the Court to make European law through interpretation and the accumulation of jurisprudence, creating another open scenario. Finally, in a Europe of nations without any "we the people," the EEC was bound to have problems of democratic legitimacy and accountability.

First Years: A Common Market at the Service of National Political Economies

The EEC floated on buoyant economic conditions in its early years. Western European populations began to grow rapidly. Emulating the

American model of consumerism and mass production with a proliferation of new houses, roads, and schools, Europeans began to taste the joys of cars, household appliances, seaside holidays and television. By the 1960s, the peak boom decade, average growth in EEC member states was an impressive 5+ percent annually, and trade internal to the EEC grew even faster.[9] Paradoxically, however, the foundation of the EEC coincided with a moment when European societies were more deeply "nationalized" than ever before, following the solidification of democratic institutions, new commitments to social justice and redistribution of wealth, and, above all, economic change. With a larger economic pie to distribute, national political economies acquired a wider range of "stakeholders"—groups with strong interests. Capitalists, politicians, civil servants, and interest groups of all kinds, including labor, conservatives, socialists, young, and old, all perceived the new national order as the primary setting for achieving their goals.

In fact, European integration began successfully precisely because redesigning national social and economic models was the order of the day. EEC Europe served multiple national purposes. The Germans needed it to rebuild self-respect after the Nazi era. Others hoped it could keep the Germans in their place. The French sought to use it to implement grandiose foreign policy goals. The Italians wanted regional development funding and an external stimulus for modernization. The Benelux countries and Germany wanted it for the broader markets it brought. Smaller countries anticipated that the supranationality in EEC institutions could protect them against larger states. Everyone needed the United States's military presence because of the cold war, and the United States was happy to see Europeans coordinating their actions.

Coexistence between European integration and national dynamism was not always easy, however. EEC insiders quietly hoped that integrationist activists in Brussels, particularly in the Commission, would rapidly "Europeanize" even more. However, some national leaders had

little desire to see the EEC's mandate enlarged or its supranationality expanded. The customs union came into being faster than expected. The EEC quickly became a player in important international trade negotiations, in particular GATT, which the United States mobilized to make sure that the EEC did not become a protectionist "fortress Europe." The Common Agricultural Policy (CAP) was, in contrast, a contentious arena. The Commission, backed by the Dutch and Italians, proposed a strong, economically liberal program that was junked because it threatened French and German agricultural subsidy systems. The outcome was a scheme of price supports for agricultural goods, protecting EEC farmers from market pressures and governed by logrolling between farmers' organizations and national agricultural ministers at the expense of EEC taxpayers and consumers. Dealing was difficult in some other areas as well. Commission attempts to promote common transport, regional, and industrial policies were blocked, for example, despite the explicit intentions of the Rome Treaty.

President Charles de Gaulle of France became the symbol of member states' insistence on having the last word. His first intervention concerned British candidacy for membership in 1961. The British wanted exceptions to the Common Market, and de Gaulle disliked their "special relationship" with the United States, but everyone but the French agreed. Then in January 1963, de Gaulle vetoed the result and denounced the United Kingdom for seeking to make the EEC into a "free trade area" and a servant of Anglo-American goals.[10] The Commission became de Gaulle's next major target. A firm French nationalist and opponent of European integration prior to 1958, de Gaulle changed his mind once in power. France needed Europe economically, and the right kind of EEC could help the French acquire new international power. But de Gaulle wanted an intergovernmental "Europe of nations" without supranational institutions. When Walter Hallstein, first Commission president, sought to use the budgetary ambiguities of the Rome Treaty to finance the CAP, negotiations about this issue stalled, and the French refused to participate further. In September 1965, the French actually withdrew from the Council of Ministers, paralyzing decision making and sparking the "empty chair" episode.

The treaties proposed that after January 1966 the Council might decide certain matters by qualified majority, meaning that a nation might be outvoted. De Gaulle reasoned that, with a qualified majority, "France . . . would be exposed to having its hands forced in almost any economic matter, hence social and often even political." De Gaulle imposed the "Luxembourg Compromise" of January 1966, and Council unanimity became the norm. Hopes that the Commission would be an effective advocate of ever-greater integration were thus dashed. From this point, no matter what measure the Commission proposed, the Council could stop it unless all governments agreed.[11]

De Gaulle spoke first for France, but his words reflected deeper realities. The Common Market began at the high point of Europe's postwar boom. During this period, before globalization eroded the capacity of states, each national government developed a set of strategies for governing the economy, including welfare states, subsidies for industry, regulated credit, pump priming to stimulate demand, and sometimes outright planning. Profoundly national development models established limits on Europeanization. European integration was a very important supplement, however. The customs-free zone brought substantial increase in inter-EEC trade in goods (from 1960 to 1970, EC internal trade rose from less than 40 percent to nearly 60 percent of total member state trade), which stimulated greater economic growth. The EEC, which saw to the fairness of internal European trade, provided tools that its member states could shape and control. The common external tariff provided some protection from the harsh winds of open international trade, making the EEC simultaneously a buffer against and a sub-

system within the U.S.-coordinated Bretton Woods system. The Common Market thus was handmaiden to continental Europe's postwar boom, a useful tool in some policy areas, but an unwelcome intrusion in others. The further economic Europeanization that the Rome Treaty had proposed—free movement of capital, for example—was not in the cards, because it would have undercut key components of different national models.

Preparing for Globalization? Crisis and Renewal, 1970–1989

After de Gaulle's 1969 resignation, leaders found new energy for the European project. The 1969 Hague Summit concluded that progress might be possible toward the single European economic space that the Rome Treaty had foreseen. The summit also set out plans to "widen" the EEC to the British, Danish, Irish, and Norwegians and to "deepen" it by giving the Community larger budgetary powers, some foreign policy coordination ("European political cooperation"), and to create economic and monetary union (EMU).

The EEC expanded from six to nine members in 1973, when the British, Irish, and Danes joined (Norway also negotiated entrance, but its people voted against it in a referendum), beginning growth to today's twenty-five (see Table 2.1). It also gained new financial autonomy by acquiring its "own resources." To this point the EEC had depended on direct funding from member states' budgets. Direct revenues from agricultural levies, import duties, and a percentage of national value-added taxes gave it greater breathing space and autonomy, even though the EEC budget remained very small. There were also ambitious plans for regional development (through the creation of the European Regional Development Fund—ERDF) and social policy.

Harder times were coming, however. The first enlargement did not go smoothly, with the British proving particularly troublesome. The United Kingdom paid too high a price to get in,

Table 2.1   EU Enlargement, 1957–2004

Members		Accession Year
Belgium	Italy	1957
France	Luxembourg	
Germany	Netherlands	
Denmark		1973
Ireland		
United Kingdom		
Greece		1981
Portugal		1986
Spain		
Austria		1995
Finland		
Sweden		
Czech Republic	Lithuania	2004
Cyprus	Malta	
Estonia	Poland	
Hungary	Slovakia	
Latvia	Slovenia	

CAP administrators to realign price supports repeatedly and creating a new source of tension. In the meantime, the agricultural policy had become a system of perverse incentives to overpricing, overproduction, and international dumping.

Member states had to renege on their pledge to reach full economic and monetary union by 1980, largely because of the oil shocks of 1973 and 1979. Dependent on imported oil denominated in U.S. dollars, Europe had to deal with rapidly rising oil prices that fueled an already dangerously inflationary economic environment.[12] Unions pushed for higher wages, companies for higher prices, and governments for more revenues. Efforts to fine-tune policies to cope with these new problems revealed a perplexing "stagflation"—simultaneous inflation and sluggish growth. Growth levels declined (as Table 2.2 shows), unemployment rose (Table 2.3), state spending on social programs was constrained, and public finances were more precarious. Profit margins and investment levels declined, and European industry began to lose

becoming a "net contributor" to the EEC budget to finance a CAP from which British agriculture received little. Monetary policy then turned into a nightmare. The United States, threatened by import vulnerability and chronic trade deficits, decided to end the Bretton Woods dollar/gold standard, meaning that henceforth the dollar and other currencies would "float" against each other, resulting in fluctuating exchange rates fed by speculation in currency markets. The new system was treacherous for the EEC with its multiplicity of currencies, making it difficult for European actors to forecast, dampening enthusiasm, slowing trade growth, and tempting member state governments to use monetary revaluation as a trading weapon. The CAP, based on a price support system to provide adequate incomes to farmers, had to confront capriciously changing prices in different countries, forcing

Table 2.2   EEC Economic Growth Rates, 1960–1984 (in percent)

	1960–1967	1968–1973	1974–1979	1980–1984
Belgium	4.7	5.2	2.3	1.5
France	5.7	5.6	2.8	2.7
Germany	4.5	5.0	2.4	1.0
Italy	5.7	4.9	3.5	1.9
Luxembourg	2.8	6.1	1.3	2.1
Netherlands	5.2	5.5	2.6	0.7
Denmark	4.8	4.0	2.0	1.7
Ireland	3.9	5.4	5.0	2.6
United Kingdom	3.2	3.4	1.6	0.8

Source: Loukas Tsoukalis, *The New European Economy*, 2nd ed. (London: Oxford University Press, 1993), Table 2.1, p. 22.

Table 2.3   Average EEC Unemployment Rates, 1960–1984 (in percent)

	1960–1967	1968–1973	1974–1979	1980–1984
Belgium	2.1	2.3	5.7	12.1
France	1.5	2.6	4.7	8.5
Germany	0.8	0.8	2.8	5.5
Italy	4.8	5.8	6.7	9.5
Luxembourg	0.0	0.0	0.4	1.4
Netherlands	0.7	1.2	3.1	9.4
Denmark	1.6	1.4	5.5	9.9
Ireland	4.9	5.6	7.6	12.7
United Kingdom	1.5	2.5	4.2	10.5

Source: Tsoukalis, *New European Economy,* Table 2.2, p. 23.

competitive advantage. By the later 1970s the EEC had begun a downward spiral.

Responses to these challenges were not lacking, primarily through informal intergovernmental dealmaking and policy overtures. Some results were significant. Informal summits of heads of state and government, convened at least once in each Council presidency, became a new institution, the European Council (fully integrated into EC treaties in 1987), combining high-level strategic guidance with a forum to decide large issues that other European institutions had been unable to resolve.[13] In 1974 this new European Council introduced direct elections to the European Parliament, held for the first time in 1979. The European Parliament also gained some budgetary power through the creation of "own resources" for European institutions, plus the right to reject the budget as a whole.

The most significant innovation was the European Monetary System (EMS). As in many critical junctures in the evolution of EU policy, breakthrough occurred out of hard bargaining and shared interests of the Germans and the French, this time in dealings between French president Valéry Giscard d'Estaing and German

chancellor Helmut Schmidt in 1978–1979.[14] All EEC members belonged to EMS, and the EEC Monetary Committee (central bankers from each country) played a key administrative role. But membership in the EMS Exchange Rate Mechanism (ERM) was voluntary, and included only those countries willing to accept the ERM's monetary constraints (the British, for example, did not join until 1990). ERM participants had to keep the value of their currency within a "narrow band" of reference (± 2.5 percent) tied to a weighted "basket" of all member currencies. EMS included mechanisms for market intervention to help threatened currencies stay in the narrow band, along with methods for revaluing the ERM currencies against one another when the need arose.[15] EMS would prove to be a significant link between the EC's 1970s crisis and the renewal of integration in the later 1980s.

EMS notwithstanding, European integration in the early 1980s was endangered by the divergent policy responses to crisis of member states. Germany, the one success story, restructured its economy in a context of stable prices. In the early 1980s, however, it coexisted with a new Socialist administration in France that was dead set on statist, inflationary policies. Thatcherite neoliberalism in Britain went its own way, while in the United States, Reagan and the Federal Reserve Bank provoked the deepest international recession since the 1930s. Internally, the EEC was paralyzed by budget disputes in which British governments petulantly demanded their money back. When others resisted, the British resolved to prevent them from doing anything else.[16] The EEC was still alive, but the body was not stirring much.

Renewing by Liberalizing? To "1992"

In the mid-1980s an extraordinary turnaround began in which the European Commission briefly came alive, a development that followed from the realization by European elites that postwar settlements were in serious trouble. Europe's comeback became part of a new strategy to diminish the role of national states, reinvigorate market relationships, and create a new regional economic bloc around a newly opened European market, all designed to confront the threatening international market environment that we now call globalization.

The failure of the French left precipitated the renewal. Socialist François Mitterrand, elected president of France in May 1981, brought a program to reinvigorate and deepen the French postwar settlement, involving new nationalization, statist planning, new power for unions and workers, an expanded welfare state, and Keynesian economic stimulation. The program rapidly ran into difficulties. From the outset in 1981, France's inflation level had been much higher than Germany's (13.4 percent vs. 6.3 percent), and the new Keynesianism fueled this disparity while other Europeans, led by the Germans, pursued price stabilization. Pressure on the franc led to three EMS devaluations, with the Germans each time insisting on French policy changes. By the winter of 1982–1983, the French faced a dramatic choice between leaving EMS and doing major damage to European integration, or finding an entirely different domestic strategy. Since the Gaullist 1960s, the French had believed that domestic *dirigisme* (statist economic steering) was compatible with European integration, but these events were a turning point toward divorce between the two elements.

Mitterrand decided to stay in the EMS in March 1983, shifting to a strategy of renewed European integration. The most important immediate result was that the economic policies of major EU members converged to a point where new common action was plausible. The French presidency of the EU in the first half of 1984 began the renewal of European integration, quickly resolving the issues underlying "Europessimism." At the Fontainebleau European Council in June, for example, a French and German "good cop, bad cop" tactic settled the "British check" problem by a partial budgetary rebate.[17] Spanish and Portuguese accession to the EU, which had

been held up by the Greeks (who, having joined the EU in 1981, were using the new enlargement to seek "side-payments" from EU members), was also reopened. Finally, Jacques Delors, former French minister of finances and one of the architects of the French policy shift, was appointed as new president of the European Commission.

One week after taking office in 1985, Delors asked the European Parliament, "Is it presumptuous to announce . . . a decision to remove all the borders inside Europe from here to 1992 . . . ?" The first step was a White Paper on Completing the Internal Market, quickly labeled the "1992" program, that listed nearly three hundred measures to unify the EU's still largely separate national markets into an "area without internal boundaries in which the free movement of goods, persons, services and capital is ensured." Internal border posts would come down, and cross-border formalities would be simplified. Common European product norms and standards would be developed. Value-added and excise taxation, obstacles to cross-border trade, would be harmonized. The White Paper also included a detailed timetable of single-market legislation over two consecutive Commission terms (eight years) leading to "1992."

The Milan European Council of June 1985 agreed to call an "intergovernmental conference" (IGC) to modify the Rome Treaties to facilitate implementation of the White Paper's proposals. This was the first major reconsideration of the EU treaties since 1957, resulting in the Single European Act (SEA, ratified in 1987).[18] The SEA's most important contribution linked completing the single market to qualified majority (QMV) for most White Paper areas. Only the most sensitive single-market matters (fiscal policy, border controls, issues concerning the movement of people, and workers' rights) would still require unanimity. Because member states could henceforth be outvoted, the SEA linked new QMV to an extension of Parliament's amending power in a new "cooperation procedure." In QMV matters the Parliament could henceforth propose amendments that other EU institutions had to approve or reject. The SEA also expanded the areas in which the EU could act legally to include regional development policy ("economic and social cohesion"), research and technological development, and environmental policy. Finally, the SEA consecrated the European Council and European Political Cooperation (foreign policy coordination) in the treaty and foresaw further monetary integration.

Thus was European integration relaunched. The "1992" slogan simplified complex measures and generated public interest and enthusiasm. The White Paper played carefully to broader political realities with its liberalizing, deregulatory, "supply-side" vocabulary. The SEA made forward movement easier. The Germans, facing rising unemployment, hoped to profit from new trade. The French saw "1992" as an indirect way of enhancing their diplomatic power. The British, opposed to granting new sovereignty to the Community, favored liberalization and deregulation in principle. Business supported the White Paper because of its liberal nature. Economic policy elites were sensitive to the Commission's efforts to argue for "1992" through the Cecchini Report on the "costs of non-Europe" that outlined what EU members would lose without "1992." Finding enthusiasm from organized labor was more problematic because the single market threatened jobs and might facilitate "social dumping" in which corporations relocated in areas with lower social overhead costs. The Commission thus promised new "social dialogue" between Euro-level "social partners" (invoking another clause in the new SEA). The European Parliament was also a supporter, partly because of the new cooperation procedure. The most important source of support for the new policies was good economic luck, however, an upturn in European economies.

The Commission immediately tried to cash in on its new prestige to promote more change.[19]

The EU faced a big budgetary crisis, designing and funding new regional development policies, and chronic financial bleeding from the CAP. The Commission combined these three problems into a single "Delors budgetary package" involving a five-year commitment to a greatly enlarged Community budget that would give the Commission more latitude and avoid annual money fights. The package also proposed CAP reforms (cost stabilization mechanisms and a five-year program for "capping" spending). The "reform of the structural funds," a response to new Southern members who otherwise risked falling further behind because of the single market, brought substantial European-level commitment to redistributing resources between richer and poorer member states, with regional aid doubling from 1988 to 1992 and rising to 25 percent of Community spending.

Proposals for economic and monetary union were next. In June 1988, Delors persuaded the European Council to make him chair of a top-level committee of central bankers to bring forth new EMU proposals.[20] EMU could reduce transaction costs, prod restructuring of Europe's financial industries, and make intra-European factor costs more transparent. Wages would then better reflect national productivity, bring national budgetary and fiscal policies closer to economic fundamentals, and provide member state governments a good pretext for "exogenizing" reforms. In international terms, EMU's single currency could, in time, become a reserve currency to rival the dollar. Finally, EMU would be a giant step for European integration.

The Delors Committee report set out outlines for EMU that would eventually prevail—an independent European Central Bank committed to price stability, a gradual three-stage approach, and careful policies about convergence.[21] The Delors Report then came to the European Council at Madrid in June 1989, when everyone but the United Kingdom approved convening another intergovernmental conference to put EMU into the treaties.

Globalization and Uncertainty: From Maastricht to Enlargement

In early 1989, EU Europe was protected by NATO and American power. "Western" Europe was made up of twelve wealthy EU members and a few others, mostly members of the European Free Trade Association (EFTA), with the credentials to be EU members (which they would become in 1995). To the East was "existing socialism," appallingly inefficient and oppressive, but walled off by Soviet power. These arrangements had persisted for so long that they were presumed eternal. Unexpectedly, the Berlin Wall came down in November 1989, bringing on the collapse of existing socialism, including the Soviet Union, and the end of the cold war. Europe's map and agenda changed. Nineteen eighty-nine was thus a moment of joy for Europe, but with it came difficult political puzzles. Since 1985 EU Europe had begun "deepening," moving decisively toward genuine economic union, a single economy and a single currency, with initiatives for political union on the horizon. The end of the cold war threatened this "deepening" by raising the issue of "widening" simultaneously.

The first new step was German unification. The Commission took the lead in welcoming German unification and making the five ex-GDR *Länder* part of the EU, even though British prime minister Margaret Thatcher and French president François Mitterrand were both more cautious. The wisdom of this course seemed self-evident. A Germany anchored at the center of the EC was the foundation stone of the Community's future. It was essential to enhance the commitment of the Federal Republic, rapidly becoming the EU's dominant member, to the Community's future. The next step would be to find ways to give ex-socialist societies of Central and Eastern Europe help in modernizing and democratizing. Up to 1989, the EU's major regional concern had been "north-south" integration to the west of the "iron curtain." After 1989, "East-West" matters came onto the table.

Maastricht and Beyond

Much of the "deepening" begun in 1985 had been conceived in the light of globalization. Indeed, practically every speech that Jacques Delors made during this period insisted that Europe faced an urgent choice between economic survival or decline, reconfiguring its ways of doing things or getting swamped from outside.[22] The EMU proposals for a federalized monetary policy and a single currency would complete transition to a single, more vital, economic space capable of new leadership as globalization proceeded.

Reaching a deal on EMU at Maastricht was relatively easy. The 1989 Delors Report had set out a clear program, while the unequal balance of power between Germany and France previewed the ways in which final differences would be resolved. The Germans, asked to give up their most important national symbol and source of European monetary power, the deutsche mark, insisted that EMU provide iron-clad guarantees of price stability and financial responsibility. The British opposed EMU altogether, but were neutralized early on by an opt-out formula, which they and the Danes exercised. The Spanish, seeking more north-south redistribution, won a Cohesion Fund that applied to its "Club Med" colleagues as well (the term "Club Med," after the French holiday resorts, included Spain, Greece, Portugal, and Ireland, the latter two not "Med" at all).

The first Franco-German difference was about "convergence criteria" to guide policy alignment of potential EMU members to final passage to EMU. The French supported the idea, but not in its final harsh terms. The German Bundesbank wanted to exclude profligate EU member states. Convergence targets were thus set for national budget deficits (3 percent of GDP), longer-term debt (60 percent of GDP), inflation, interest rates, and currency stability within EMS tied to an average of best results across the EU. The timing of EMU phase-in was the second issue. The Delors Committee proposed that stage 2 of EMU would establish a European Central Bank (ECB) to "apprentice" for final EMU, whose date was tentatively set for 1997. The Germans, feeling the economic pinch of unification, insisted on softening stage 2 to become a "European Monetary Institute" to "monitor" convergence toward stage 3. The French also wanted an "economic government" to set Community economic policy, but the Germans refused, hence an EMU that would be more monetary than economic. The Germans also insisted upon complete independence for the proposed European Central Bank, plus strong statutory commitment to price stability. Deciding the timing of stage 3, when the new ECB would come into existence to prepare the single currency, was left until the last minute. The final compromise set a first possible date for January 1997, when a majority of states would have to be eligible, and a second date, January 1999, when EMU would begin no matter how many members were ready. This lone French victory on EMU at Maastricht may have been what ensured that EMU would actually happen.

IGC negotiations on "political union" were another story. The idea of discussing political union—a common foreign and security policy, greater democratization, more efficient institutions, and coherence among monetary, economic, and political action—had emerged only in spring 1990 on German insistence, leaving little time for preparation. The talks brought out predictable disagreements between "federalists" and "intergovernmentalists," and those who desired political integration and those who wanted none of it. French ambition to coordinate EU foreign and defense policies ran up against member state disunity about the end of the cold war, accentuated by the first Gulf War. The proposed "common foreign and security policy" (CFSP) divided pro-NATO "Atlanticists" from those who desired independent European positions and a more robust military capability as a counterweight to the United States. Such fundamental differences made for very tentative language and unwieldy decision rules, and the results were more declarations of intent than firm positions. On "justice and home affairs," di-

rections were set to extend the "Schengen" arrangements for opening borders that had earlier been struck between some EU states. There would also be a "Europol" coordinating police information and action to offset the security problems created by open internal borders, minimal standards for EU citizenship, and provisions to reach common approaches on immigration policy and political asylum. The most significant political union result was "codecision," allowing the European Parliament equal weight to the Council on most Community legislation. Unfortunately, codecision was encased in cumbersome procedures. The Parliament also acquired the right to vote proposed Commission presidents. Finally, Maastricht proposed two new institutions, a "Committee of the Regions" and an ombudsman, plus a strengthened Court of Auditors.

The Treaty on European Union revealed deep disagreement about the architecture of European integration. Advocates of a federalist tree in which everything was connected to a common trunk (the Community) remained at odds with those favoring a Greek temple in which three separate "pillars" would be topped by a connecting pediment/preamble. The "templars" won. Maastricht's CFSP and JHA (justice and home affairs), close to the heart of remaining member state sovereignty, became separate intergovernmental entities rather than "community" pillars. The "European Union" (EU) encompassed the entire temple, becoming an entity much greater than the Community, as illustrated in Figure 2.1.

After Maastricht: Trials of a Price Stability Regime

Maastricht was meant to hasten monetary and political integration, but the world dictated otherwise. The GATT Uruguay Round negotiations came to a head just after Maastricht. Without CAP reform, the Uruguay Round, the first time GATT had discussed agriculture, could not be successfully concluded. Business interests wanted more trade liberalization and the extension of

Pillar	Community Pillar 1	Pillar 2	Pillar 3
Content	• European Community • European Coal and Steel Community • Euratom (Titles II, III, and IV of the Maastricht Treaty)	Common Foreign and Security Policy (CFSP)	Cooperation in matters of justice and internal affairs (policing transnational crime, migration)
Principle of Governance	Community method Commission importance ECJ jurisprudence	Intergovernmental Council importance National jurisprudence	Intergovernmental Council importance National jurisprudence

Common Pediment
Common Principles and Objectives
Articles A through F of the Maastricht Treaty
Key Actor for Strategy and Coordination: European Council

Figure 2.1

The Maastricht Temple

multilateral agreements to services, intellectual property, and foreign direct investment, making it hard for farmers to resist CAP changes.[23] CAP reform, tied to the development of a second Delors budgetary package, would begin shifting from price supports toward "set-asides" (deficiency payments) in which farmers would be paid not to produce, roughly the way the United States subsidized its farmers. This could eventually limit the EU's surplus dumping on the international market, a key goal of those pressuring the EU. To keep farmers from rebelling, however, the new CAP would cost as much to taxpayers as the old one. With CAP reform achieved, the second Delors budgetary package could then be concluded. This debate demonstrated growing reluctance by richer countries to underwrite solidarity and cohesion and, more generally, to finance the EU, an ominous sign.

Ratifying Maastricht uncovered a well of public opposition. The Danes, always reluctant

integrators, particularly on political matters, voted no in an early 1992 referendum. Success in an Irish referendum (69 percent to 31 percent) was minor solace. The day after the Danish vote, French president Mitterrand announced a French referendum for September 1992, in the hope of restoring the momentum of integration. France's "petit oui"—51 percent yes, 49 percent no—saved, but hardly endorsed, Maastricht. The old issue of "democratic deficit," public suspicion that decisions were being made by elites in mysterious ways, had come alive again.

A precipitous economic downturn that began in early 1992 helped stimulate new public skepticism about the EU. Growth again stagnated, as it had prior to 1985. Unemployment, the most salient issue in member state politics, shot up, as Table 2.4 shows. Downturn came on top of the employment-reducing effects of the "1992" program. Then, beginning in summer 1992, fluctuations of the German deutsche mark and the

Table 2.4 EU Unemployment Rates 1975–2002

| | *Excluding East Germany* | | | | | *Including Eastern Germany* | | | | | | |
	1975	1985	1990	1991	1992	1993	1994	1995	1996	1997	1998	2002
Total Unemployed (millions)	5	14.8	12	12.7	13.6	17.76	18.47	17.85	18.16	17.93	16.95	
Unemployment Rate (percent)	3.7	9.9	7.7	8.1	8.2	10.7	11.1	10.8	10.8	10.6	10.0	7.7

Source: European Commission, *Employment in Europe*, various years.

U.S. dollar weakened most EMS currencies, largely because the German Bundesbank overshot its tightening of German monetary policy.[24] ERM members then had to push up interest rates, making countercyclical stimulation nearly impossible. Major ERM realignment might have stopped the problems quickly, but few wanted to do this in the middle of the French referendum campaign. Indeed, policymakers, with their eyes on EMU, had come to see the ERM as a proto-EMU with fixed exchange rates (the ERM had not been realigned since 1987).

One result was an explosion of currency speculation that began on "Black Wednesday," September 16, 1992, when the British pound sterling left the ERM, followed by the Italian lira, while the Spanish peseta was devalued and the Spanish, Portuguese, and Irish reintroduced exchange controls.[25] Subsequently, the currencies of Finland, Sweden, and Norway, three EFTA candidates for EU membership, cut loose their pegs to EMS. In January 1993, the Irish pound was devalued. In the wake of the French referendum the franc also fell under siege, initially saved by huge German-French intervention efforts. The EMS crisis threatened the credibility and implementation of EMU.

Amidst all this, the quiet way in which the "1992" period ended on January 1, 1993, spoke volumes. The single market had not really been completed. There were delays in value-added tax realignment, opening up public procurement, liberalizing energy markets, reconfiguring fi-nancial markets, and transposing important legislation. The failure to remove airport passport controls by the target date was visible evidence that free movement of people lagged behind the three other EU freedoms.

The Delors Commission tried to retake the initiative in late 1993, a year from the end of its term, with a new White Paper on Growth, Competitiveness, and Employment. Unemployment, which had been rising over trade cycles, had no "miracle cure." The European economy's growth rate had been shrinking over decades, investment declining, and the EU's competitive position worsening. The single market had helped, but not enough, partly because the rest of the world, facing the same challenges, had also responded intelligently. The White Paper proposed a new approach to employment policy to meet the daunting challenges of globalization. "Creating as favorable an environment as possible for company competitiveness" was essential, particularly in the advanced-technology areas. Member states should also promote flexible small and medium-sized industries and accelerate the building of "trans-European networks" (TENs) in infrastructure (particularly telecommunications) to push Europe toward the "information society," where new comparative advantage might be found. One key phrase was that "the new model of European society calls for less passive and more active solidarity." There should be a negotiated, decentralized, and constantly evolving "European social pact" in which "new gains in productivity would essentially be applied to forward-looking investments and to the creation of jobs." Wage growth should be below productivity gains to allow job-creating investments. It was fundamental to promote solidarity across generations and regions and struggle against poverty and social exclusion. Most important, however, national employment systems needed to be made more flexible, "beginning with commitment to lifelong education." More active labor market policies would encourage mobility. The cost of lower-skilled labor could be reduced by lowering payroll taxes. Unemployment compensation needed an overhaul to enhance incentives to reenter the labor market.

The White Paper was serious and prescient, but, in contrast to 1985, member states no longer had enough goodwill and sufficient political capital to invest further in European integration. In addition, the EU had accepted three new ex-EFTA applicants for 1995, Austria, Sweden, and Finland (the Norwegians rejected membership in a referendum for the second time), all with their own ideas, making the EU equation even more complicated.

There were even reasons to worry about EMU—opinion polls in France, Germany, and elsewhere turned sharply against the EU and EMU. The Germans worried about the reliability of eventual EMU partners—in particular, Italy and Spain, both prone to financial laxity. Everyone, including the Germans, fell behind in preparing EMU because of the recession. The deadline for deciding who could join was spring 1998, based on the accounts for 1997, leaving little time and enhancing the danger of short-term, one-off approaches to the convergence criteria, including creative accounting. In response, the Germans insisted on the Stability and Growth Pact (SGP, incorporated into the treaties at Amsterdam in 1997) to remain in force after January 1999, confirming strict limits on member state public finances under EMU, including a 3 percent maximum budget deficit, implying ordinary deficits of 1 percent

to create reserve capacities, enforced by "excessive deficit" warnings from the Commission and, ultimately, large financial penalties for miscreants.[26]

German worries were well founded. In the brief period before final EMU membership was decided, the Italians, with a budget deficit of 7.7 percent and cumulated debt of 124 percent (vs. the target 60 percent) in 1995, looked hopeless. The bulk of Italian effort was a "Eurotax" to raise government revenues, plus clever manipulations of interest rates on government bonds and some privatization. On the general debt-level issue, the Italians anticipated general fudging, since the Belgians had the same problem and they were necessary for EMU. The Spanish deficit in 1995 of 6.6 percent led the Commission to threaten suspension of regional development payments, but the 1996 budgetary exercise turned out better, with the new Aznar government benefiting from a drop in interest rates connected to convergence. Renewed Spanish growth and astute austerity measures brought Spain into line. The French, without whom there could not have been an EMU, trod their Gallic path. Faced with a deficit of 5+ percent in 1995, President Chirac reneged on extravagant, mildly anti-EMU, campaign promises to pump up the economy. The French shifted pension fund assets in France Telecom to the revenue side of the national budget, provoking soul searching in the Commission about book cooking. Even the German government proposed at the last minute to revalue the Bundesbank's stock of gold, but this was disallowed domestically. Despite all this, on May 3, 1998, the heads of state and government declared eleven member states eligible for EMU (the Greeks would make it twelve in 2000). Wim Duisenberg, a Dutchman, became the ECB's first president. Unhappy with this, the French insisted on a deal in which Duisenberg would be succeeded after four years by Jean-Claude Trichet, a French Central banker.

Frankfurt, We Have a Problem: Launching the Euro

The final arrival of EMU on January 1, 1999, and the introduction of euro notes and coins three years later, in January 2002, were well prepared. Creating the new ECB, ECSB, and locking eleven currencies together went seamlessly. Then, to everyone's great relief, economic growth resumed in 1998–1999, and, for the first time in what must have seemed like ages, unemployment began to decline. Worry that the new ECB might nip new growth in the bud to prove its devotion to price stability was assuaged when the bank produced a surprisingly accommodating monetary policy. The major initial criticism of the ECB was that it had problems communicating, causing confusion in markets.

Prior to 1999, experts had predicted that the euro would start strong and even appreciate versus the dollar. The opposite occurred, however. Between January 1999, when it was valued at $1.18, and autumn 2000, the euro fell over 25 percent. Amidst hand-wringing about credibility, the indignity of a "weak currency" and "undervaluing," the euro's decline actually provided a stimulus to new "euroland" growth by pumping up exports (in particular to the United States). The euro also proved successful as an alternative currency denomination for a wide range of corporate and governmental bond issues, a sign pointing toward midrange "legs" as a reserve currency.

The euro's initial slide raised the issue of international exchange-range management with the dollar. A stable international monetary environment was in everyone's interest, but producing such an environment was only partly up to the ECB. The U.S. dollar devalued, beginning in 2002, and the euro rose rapidly, to $1.30 in 2004. The costs of this for euroland were great, including the return of recession and high unemployment. The ECB also abandoned its initial accommodating stance and turned to overdriven insistence on price stability, making it almost impossible for member states to use countercyclical measures. Instead of knuckling under, by 2004 six member states, including France, Germany, and Italy, had exceeded the 3 percent deficit criterion that Romano Prodi, then Commission president, had publicly called "stupid." EMU's "one size fits all" monetary policy was troublesome as well. The ECB's initial policies, for example, worked well for France and Germany, who needed new growth, but also heated up the smaller economies of Ireland and Portugal, obliging their governments to adjust. The same thing happened to France and Germany in 2003–2004, with much greater effect on broader European economic health, when relatively high interest rates inhibited government policies and private investment.

EMU brought the institutionalization in Europe of an international shift from Keynesian to anti-inflationary price stability policies and intensified Europe's problems of low growth and high unemployment. The ECB, like the German Bundesbank before it, resolutely denied any responsibility for these problems, blaming them instead on selfish market actors and imprudent governments who needed to take "structural reform" much more seriously. In short, the ECB's first years revealed a bank that was determined to promote the Americanization of European social and regulatory policies.

By the Amsterdam Treaty in 1997, unacceptably high levels of unemployment, in part attributable to EMU convergence, had nourished public rejection of hard neoliberalism and brought several new center-left governments to power. This facilitated the inclusion of an "employment title" and employment policy clauses in the Amsterdam Treaty, giving the EU legal prerogatives and duties to "contribute to a high level of employment by encouraging cooperation between member states."

The European Employment Strategy (EES), which started in 1997, was designed to promote coordination among member states toward common goals while leaving each to choose its own approaches. The first thing that occurred in the new procedure was when the European Council announced annual Employment Guidelines for member states. During the EES's first five years these were derived from the goals of promoting employability (skills and labor market participation); entrepreneurship (encouraging business start-ups); adaptability (new flexibility); and equal opportunities (creating conditions for greater female labor market participation). Next, each member state drew up a national action plan (NAP) projecting how it would put these guidelines into practice. The Commission and the Council reviewed these NAPs annually and drew up a Joint Employment Report for the European Council, while the Commission also submitted a proposal for revising the guidelines for the year to come. The Council of Ministers, by qualified majority, could issue country-specific recommendations.[27]

This process was the first experiment with what was later named the "open method of coordination" (OMC). The EES takes a range of European economic policy goals and social policy instruments into consideration, in particular the European Social Fund, and utilizes "management by objectives" techniques, creating and using new statistical bases, setting targets, benchmarking best practices, and then reviewing achievements comparatively (including "naming and shaming" by the Commission). It recognizes that national social models differ and encourages actors in each model to design their own paths toward common targets. Finally, the EES enjoins national social partners to work together to produce and implement the NAPs.

The European employment strategy on its own was underequipped to produce major change, however. Increasing the EU employment rate was very difficult without leverage over demand for labor, a factor at least as important for employment levels as the supply-side matters to which the employment strategy had been largely confined. Addressing the demand

side would involve making demands on monetary policy, a forbidden encroachment into the ECB's domain. There may be another side to the story, however. In the words of the Belgian minister for social affairs, "An effective Open Method of Co-ordination is more than an intelligently managed learning process and a defensive instrument. If we handle it judiciously, open co-ordination is an offensive method that allows us to concretely define a 'social Europe' and to firmly anchor it into the European co-operation process as a common good."[28] The larger consecration of OMC by the Lisbon Summit in 2000 spread its use to broader social policy areas, in particular to pensions and antipoverty policies ("social exclusion" in EU jargon).

"Common" Foreign and Defense Policy After the Cold War

The cold war left little room for autonomous European foreign political and military power. Yet the successes of European integration after 1985 enhanced the EU's power in the world, particularly in economic matters. The end of the cold war created a very new situation, however, and it took a while for Europe to take its full measure. The British and the Germans remained prepared to confront a Soviet invasion long after the Soviet Union had ceased existing. The French, who had invested vast sums in an independent nuclear deterrent to provide a backbone for an independent European anti-Soviet force that never happened, found themselves with sophisticated nuclear weapons aimed at newly friendly CEEC countries. The Italians, Spanish, and others with lesser international ambitions faced analogous situations. EU member states had to do something to update their security outlooks, if only to avoid looking foolish within NATO.

In 1991, for the first time since 1945, armed conflict broke out in Europe when the Yugoslav Federation began to disintegrate. Belgrade responded to declarations of independence by Slovenia and Croatia with armed force. Its efforts in Slovenia fizzled in ten days, but protracted warfare began in Croatia in July 1991. The major problem for the EU was that the French were pro-Serb and the Germans pro-Croat. Thus an EU-organized peace conference in September 1991 did not prevent the Germans from recognizing Croatia and Slovenia in January 1992, even though the Union did mediate a cease-fire. But when Bosnia-Herzegovina declared independence, the Serbs sent in the troops, and ethnic cleansing began. Attempts at EU-UN mediation (including the Vance-Owen Plan of 1993) failed.

The Union's fecklessness in the face of extreme Serbian brutality was humiliating. Euro-posturing—solemn statements, high-powered delegations, economic sanctions, attempts at mediation, flattering diplomacy, and more—fell short first in Croatia, then in Bosnia, and later in Kosovo. EU policy was both incoherent and without convincing power, and it took tough American diplomatic brokerage at Dayton to impose a new status quo in Bosnia. Dayton was followed by hard European work providing peacekeeping forces on the ground, but the humiliation stung.[29] The Americans had "assets" to present credible threats, and this allowed them to call the shots. The Europeans had few assets and could not call the shots, even in their own backyard.

Between Bosnia and Kosovo, the EU slowly began to move toward collective foreign policy and defense capability. The wordings and decision rules on a common foreign and security policy (CFSP) in the Maastricht Treaty were changed, and "flexibility" became a theoretical possibility because of new clauses on "constructive abstention" (later termed "reinforced cooperation") and a "Mr. CFSP" was created and appointed. Quite as important, the "Petersberg" tasks (set out in 1992 to define possible new military activities) were included in the treaty, opening to humanitarian intervention, peacekeeping, and regional crisis management. This did not yet amount to much, however.

In 1993–1994, NATO, reviewing its positions, opened to the possibility of a new "European pillar" and recognized the need for "Combined Joint Task Forces" ("coalitions of the willing" for crisis management) and a "European Strategic Defense Initiative" (ESDI). In certain circumstances NATO also would make its assets available to Europeans. During the same period, key EU member states began to review their defense positions. The French ended conscription in 1995, began building a professional army, and rejoined parts of the NATO planning apparatus.[30] French experts agreed with an earlier British defense review that building rapid-response capacities was the central challenge. EU crisis management implied European actions that might not engage the United States, however. Would the United States allow Europe to use NATO assets if it disapproved of European goals? The Amsterdam Treaty sketched out a European role that, if not separate from NATO, might be semiautonomous, but it took an unexpected initiative by new British prime minister Tony Blair to move forward. After taking office the New Labour government did another defense review that shocked Blair about the low level of European preparation for new crisis management tasks.[31] He brought his shock to the European Council in fall 1998, declaring that the European defense situation was "unacceptable" and marked by "weakness and confusion." Then, in December, Blair and Chirac made a "Joint Declaration on European Defense" in St. Malo that advocated rapid implementation of Amsterdam CFSP provisions, particularly in defense policy, to give the "Union . . . the capacity for autonomous action, backed up by credible military forces, the means to decide to use them, and a readiness to do so."[32]

EU momentum was enhanced after the United States called, and fired, most of NATO's shots in Kosovo. Europeans were unable to contribute much to the American bombing offensive, partly because their equipment was not modern enough—some planes could not fly at night and others could not fly at all. They had few of the high-technology tools—smart bombs, satellite-directed guidance systems—that were the heart of the effort. And they were completely dependent on Americans for intelligence, command and communications, and airlift capacity. After the Americans had directed and starred in the military production, Europeans then paid for the less spectacular jobs like reconstruction, humanitarian assistance, occupying troops, and policing on the ground.

Kosovo led the June 1999 Cologne European Council to new decisions. Policy structures would be built within the CFSP pillar, and alternative options such as developing the autonomy of the Western European Union (WEU), the exclusive focus on ESDI within NATO, or the establishment of a fourth pillar within the EU were dismissed.[33] Six months later the Helsinki European Council committed to a rapid-reaction force of between fifty and sixty thousand, "capable of the full range of Petersberg tasks," which could be deployed within sixty days and sustained for a year (implying double the number of troops in readiness) by 2003. The Council of Ministers would set up new structures for political and strategic control over these forces, eventually bringing uniformed soldiers into the Council building in Brussels. Most important, the "European Council underlines its determination to develop an autonomous capacity to take decisions and, where NATO as a whole is not engaged, to launch and conduct EU-led military operations in response to international crises. This process will avoid unnecessary duplication and does not imply the creation of a European army."[34]

The EU thus appeared set on building a new defense identity to combine the military and nonmilitary dimensions of crisis management. Increasing levels of defense spending were needed for Europeans to achieve autonomy, including expensive satellites, intelligence systems, smart weapons, airlift capacity, independent planning capacities, and new command and control systems. In times of budgetary stringency, such money was hard to find. Increased coordination of the European defense industry was a necessity, but achieving it was a compli-

cated and uncertain process. The United States had reasons to salute a new "European pillar" in NATO, but a genuinely autonomous European defense operation was less to its taste. As a French commentator noted, Americans and Europeans "indulge in incompatible dreams. The U.S. wants to be number one, while minimizing the cost to the lives of its soldiers or to its economy. Europeans want to keep the U.S. as the ultimate insurance policy as they evolve towards a common identity."[35] The meanings of these incompatible dreams became clearer after the terrorist attacks of September 11, 2001, on the World Trade Center and the Pentagon (discussed in Chapter 5).

"Western" Europe Embraces the Rest of Europe? Enlarging the Union

Not even the most prescient of experts foresaw the abrupt end of the cold war, and few had any idea of what would happen in the countries of Central and Eastern Europe (CEECs) once their subordination to the Soviet Union ended. None of these ex-Communist societies knew how to run an efficient, competitive market system or how to combine it with democracy and the rule of law. Leaders knew that the EU had responsibilities for guiding the CEECs toward Western social and economic models, but few had clear ideas how to do so. But the end of the cold war opened opportunities for spreading democracy and markets across the entire European continent for the first time in history.

Enlargement already had a history. In the 1970s, three new members from EFTA (the United Kingdom, Ireland, and Denmark) joined the original six, followed in the 1980s by Greece, Spain, and Portugal, three countries that had lived under authoritarian regimes. In the mid-1990s, Austria, Finland, and Sweden joined. Lessons were learned in growing from six to fifteen. First, the EU had responsibilities to help nurture prospective members toward prosperity and stable democracy. Next, new members had to accept the Europe that earlier members had created. This nonnegotiable stipulation meant conforming to an *acquis communautaire,* the body of rights and obligations that bound all member states and that included not only the treaties but also all of the institutional, legal, and procedural obligations accumulated over the EU's history. As the EU had developed, the *acquis* grew to the point where in 2004 it had thirty-one chapters (the headings are listed in Table 2.5) and was over 80,000 pages long. The more Europe integrated, the more this integrated Europe stretched into every nook and cranny of governance and social organization. Enlarging the EU to the east thus involved imposing Western European standards and making sure that they were observed. Most CEECs had limited recent experience with Western-style democracy, state-of-the-art complex market economies in an open international economy, up-to-date administrative and judicial practices, and the other accoutrements of life that existing EU members took for granted.

The EU had begun helping the CEECs at the 1989 G7 Summit in Paris, even before the Berlin Wall came down, taking on the job of coordinating and delivering G24 help to Poland and Hungary (originally food and humanitarian aid, including that coming from outside the EU). The new PHARE program (a French acronym for Pologne-Hongrie: Assistance pour la Restructuration des Économies) eventually extended to infrastructure investment; assistance to business; education, training, and research aid; and funding for environmental protection (including nuclear safety and agricultural restructuring) and became the EU's major instrument to give help to all CEECs. The EU also helped found the European Bank for Reconstruction and Development (EBRD) to funnel private investment to the CEECs.[36]

Beginning in 1990, the Union negotiated "association agreements" (quickly renamed "Europe Agreements"), first with Poland and Hungary, and then with other CEECs, to prepare "a new pattern of relationships in Europe."

Table 2.5　The Chapters of the *Acquis Communautaire, 2004*

1. Free Movement of Goods
2. Free Movement of Persons
3. Free Movement of Services
4. Free Movement of Capital
5. Company Law
6. Competition Policy
7. Agriculture
8. Fisheries
9. Transport
10. Taxation
11. EMU
12. Statistics
13. Social and Employment Policy
14. Energy
15. Industrial Policy
16. Small and Medium-Sized Undertakings
17. Science and Research
18. Education and Vocational Training
19. Telecommunications and Information Technologies
20. Culture and Audiovisual Policy
21. Regional Policy
22. Environment
23. Consumers and Health Protection
24. Justice and Home Affairs
25. Customs Union
26. External Relations
27. CFSP
28. Financial Control
29. Financial and Budgetary Provisions
30. Institutions
31. Miscellaneous

Source: EU Commission, *Enlargement of the European Union: An Historic Opportunity* (Luxembourg: 2003), p. 27.

Europe agreements included cooperation on foreign policy matters; trade agreements aimed at building a free trade area; and economic, cultural, and financial help, plus the beginning of alignment of legislation on key market matters (primarily competition rules and intellectual property). The Europe Agreements did not point the CEECs clearly toward eventual EU membership, however, and some EU members were unwilling to open up markets to CEEC trade in areas where the CEECs might be competitive.

The 1993 Copenhagen European Council was a turning point, declaring that the EU was willing "conditionally" to accept eventual new memberships provided applicants met four criteria:

- Stable institutions (guarantee of democracy, the rule of law, human rights, minority rights)
- A functioning market economy and capacity to cope with competitive pressures inside the EU.
- The ability to adopt the *acquis communautaire*
- Plus the proviso that the EU had the capacity to absorb new members without endangering ongoing integration

The 1994 Essen European Council then set out a detailed "pre-accession strategy," scheduled regular enlargement meetings, and began preparations for integrating the CEECs into the single market. Essen also promised policies supporting the CEECs on infrastructure, environmental policy, CFSP, justice and home affairs, and other key matters. By this point Poland and Hungary had already applied for membership. The 1995 Madrid European Council asked the Commission to prepare "opinions" on possible candidates (the first strong step to enlargement) as soon as it had completed a study on the effects of enlargement on existing EU policies (particularly on the CAP and the structural funds) and on budgetary implications. Madrid then proposed that new accession negotiations begin six months after the Amsterdam IGC ended. The ten "associated" candidates, eight CEECs plus Malta and Cyprus, had all officially applied for membership by mid-1996.

The 1997 Amsterdam Treaty was called to work reforms allowing EU institutions to weather the new enlargement. It led instead to an inadequate compromise avoiding the most important reform issues, postponed to yet another IGC in 2000. That the EU's decision-making machinery was not working well had been obvious for some time, and Amsterdam's failure underlined this. Member states were unwilling to begin serious institutional reform until enlargement was truly at hand.

The enlargement process was nonetheless underway. The Commission's long and important report titled *Agenda 2000* opined that none of ten CEECs had yet fulfilled the Copenhagen criteria, but that the Czech Republic, Estonia, Hungary, Poland, and Slovenia were within reach, and recommended that negotiations with them be opened. The Luxembourg European Council in 1997 decided that formal negotiations should open with all ten candidates, with the first five and Cyprus to begin detailed "screening" discussions with the Commission while the second five would proceed in a slower way. *Agenda 2000* also outlined proposals for a new budgetary package with substantial pre-accession funding for candidate countries. Agreement was difficult at Berlin in 1999, but the new package projected spending on enlargement to rise from 3 percent of the budget in 2000 to nearly 20 percent by 2006. The Helsinki European Council in 1999 recommended the full accession negotiations be started with the slower five, henceforth called the "Helsinki Group."

The Council of Ministers formally negotiated enlargement treaties, but the Commission did the bulk of pre-accession work under the guidance of the Council presidency. Commission "opinions," vetted by the Council, officially began the accession process. Getting CEECs to conform to the *acquis communautaire*, chapter by chapter, was the toughest work, with the Commission reporting progress annually in "scorecards." The negotiations were often asymmetrical. Receiving full CAP funding had been a big incentive for many CEECs to apply, particularly Poland, but Western CAP beneficiaries were unwilling either to give up their own benefits or to contribute more to the EU's budget to provide comparable benefits for new members. The inevitable consequence, after acrimonious discussion, was a transition period for phasing in the full CAP. Free movement of people was restricted when Germany and Austria demanded that it be restricted.[37] The structural funds were another sticking point. *Agenda 2000* had foreseen that member states, particularly the "net contributors," would not be in the mood to increase regional development spending to help the CEECs and projected cutbacks for the EU15 in exchange for accession aid to the CEECs, leading to changed structural fund goals and prorated payoffs to EU members who stood to lose.[38]

Many EU15 member states were hesitant about enlargement. Despite this, on May 1, 2004, the EU acquired ten new members, Poland, Hungary, the Czech Republic, Slovakia, Slovenia, Estonia, Latvia, Lithuania, Cyprus, and

Malta. Together they brought 150 million new citizens into the Union. Bulgaria and Romania were left aside until 2007 (or longer, depending on when they conformed to the *acquis*). Debate raged around the prospects for Turkey, long an applicant, but whose membership was certain to be pushed as far off as the EU's dignity allowed. Turkey, with a larger population than Germany, would immediately become very powerful in EU politics after accession. It was also Islamic and geographically mainly located in Asia Minor.

Almost all of these new members were poorer and less developed than their Western colleagues, and many were quite small, as Table 2.6 shows. Almost all were nonetheless economically dynamic, and as an aggregate, the new ten were growing faster economically than the EU15. They also tended to be more liberal, less attached to the Western European social model, and more pro-American than most Western European member states. To the degree to which some CEECs are different from Western European EU members, the internal balance of the EU

Table 2.6   Enlargement 2004

Country	Population/millions	GDP Growth 2001 (percent)	GDP per inhabitant as percent of EU average 2001	Inflation Rate 2001
Cyprus	0.8	4	80	2
Czech Republic	10.2	3.3	57	4.5
Estonia	1.4	5	42	5.6
Hungary	10.2	3.8	51	9.1
Latvia	2.4	7.7	33	2.5
Lithuania	3.5	5.9	38	1.3
Malta	0.4	−0.8	55	2.5
Poland	38.6	1.1	40	5.3
Slovakia	5.4	3.3	48	10.8
Slovenia	2.0	3	69	8.6

will change, with consequences for future EU decision making. There is some danger that as the costs of membership become clearer, public enthusiasm for the EU in both the new member states and the EU15 will wane further. Enlargement also changes the external borders of the EU, bringing new neighbors (Ukraine, Russia, Belarus) and new issues about security and immigration. Bringing 150 million more people into the EU and raising their living standards to EU levels will take time, patience, and expense. Success will nonetheless consolidate a prosperous and democratic European continent.

Open Futures?

Maastricht began a fifteen-year period of institutional reform. The Maastricht negotiators themselves asked for another IGC in five years to review the workings of their Treaty. The 1997 Amsterdam Treaty presented a portrait of a cautious and conflicted EU. According to one participant, "Many governments did not want to reform anything in depth."[39] In the foreign policy area, decisions were deferred on extended Community trade competence to services and intellectual property. CFSP structures were strengthened with the creation of a planning staff, an early warning unit, and, most important, a high representative for the CFSP—Mr./Madame CFSP—who would also serve as secretary-general of the Council of Ministers.[40] For CFSP decision rules the European Council henceforth could define common European strategies unanimously, and the Council could then implement them with QMV. When neither common strategies nor Council decisions existed, however, CFSP decisions had to be unanimous. This was softened by a new provision allowing "constructive abstention" on CFSP matters. Rather than simply blocking things, dissenters could thus opt out of a particular decision provided only that the total of abstentions was not more than one-third. Another innovation was incorporation of the Petersberg tasks. In

matters of "freedom, security, and justice" (the renamed "third pillar") Amsterdam enunciated conditions under which member states might be disciplined (even suspended) for infringing basic principles of democracy, human rights, and the rule of law. It also included new language about racial and gender discrimination and data privacy. Commitment to a "zone" of freedom, security, and justice demonstrated clear new concern for incorporating human rights into the EU treaties. Finally, Amsterdam proposed a five-year shift on free circulation of persons, including immigration and asylum policies, to the Community pillar. The third pillar remained intergovernmental on criminal justice and policing—including Europol, a new agency for police cooperation foreseen by Maastricht and whose birth had been difficult.

The most interesting breakthroughs in the Amsterdam Treaty were in social policy, a matter that had not been on the agenda at all. One change was the promotion of the Maastricht Social Protocol to full treaty status because of New Labour's willingness to sign on. The Social Protocol had created an ingenious procedure for promoting Euro-level "social dialogue" between the "social partners" (unions and employers). Even without the British, these had led to "negotiated legislation" (i.e., agreements then given the force of law by Council decision) on parental leave and "atypical" employment, important pieces of the Social Charter Action Program. As discussed earlier, Amsterdam's real innovation was to introduce a new clause into the treaty committing the Union to achieve a "high level of employment" to be implemented by the development of a "coordinated strategy," which turned very quickly at Luxembourg into the beginnings of the European Employment Strategy.

Amsterdam was least successful at institutional reform, but if institutions were not reformed, the large influx of new members could paralyze both Commission and Council. Rather than confronting these issues, however, the Amsterdam negotiators instead called for yet another IGC beginning in 1999, the fourth since

1985, which culminated in the Nice Treaty of 2000. The French presidency, which chaired the final negotiations, was a political mess, however, because of cohabitation and the imminence of French presidential elections in 2002. Neither President Chirac nor Lionel Jospin, the prime minister, were willing to risk much, and in addition, the presidency was badly prepared because everything had to go through two different and mutually hostile staffs. The Nice Treaty backed away from any serious expansion of QMV voting on key issues like taxation and cultural and social policy. It did adopt a Community Charter of Fundamental Rights, pending yet another IGC in 2004. The charter projected changes in the composition of the Commission after enlargement—in particular, removing the second commissioner from the larger member states in the hope of avoiding ineffectiveness and stalemate. It decided how many members each of the member states would have in Parliament after enlargement. Most importantly, it set out controversial new voting rules in the Council of Ministers. The result, after a bitter fight between smaller and larger members, was a reweighting of voting in favor of larger members, based on a complicated new "dual majority" formula for QMV that took into account actual votes and population size. No one was

happy with the results, and the Nice Treaty was even rejected by the Irish in a referendum in 2002, but only after the Laeken European Council in fall 2001 had called a European Convention to reconsider all outstanding constitutional issues. The Convention and its consequences are discussed in Chapter 4.

Jacques Delors, who knew his EU history, was fond of describing European integration as "a few years of success, more years of crisis and many more years of stagnation." European successes had invariably been followed by disagreement, then by long moments of relative paralysis. The renewal after 1985 had happened after European integration's worst crisis. The end of the post-1985 forward movement left European integration in another crisis. Maastricht and the end of the cold war had cooled enthusiasm for integration, but both had also left urgent matters on the table that compelled Europe to move forward despite itself. The programming of the Amsterdam follow-up to Maastricht was one good example of this. It did not complete the necessary business and called for another IGC. Given the mess that was Nice, there had to be yet another IGC in 2004. By 2004 enlargement had been achieved, and that process created its own new puzzles. Huge uncertainty remained about how everything would turn out.

Notes

1. The USSR and its Eastern European satellite countries were initially invited but refused.

2. On the general circumstances surrounding the Marshall Plan, see Alan Milward, *The Reconstruction of Western Europe, 1945–1951* (London: Methuen, 1984).

3. Pierre Gerbet, "The Origins: Early Attempts and the Emergence of the Six (1945–1952)," in Roy Pryce, ed., *The Dynamics of European Union* (London: Croom Helm, 1987), pp. 40–44.

4. See François Duchêne, *Jean Monnet: The First Statesman of Interdependence* (New York: Norton, 1994).

5. For theory of European integration, see Brent F. Nelsen and Alexander C-G. Stubb, eds., *The European Union: Readings on the Theory and Practice of European Integration*, 2nd ed. (Boulder: Lynne Rienner, 1998), Pt. 2.

6. The American option prevailed, and in October 1954 the Paris Agreements were signed, creating the Western European Union (WEU), admitting the Germans to NATO, and resolving outstanding Franco-German disputes over the Saar. Then a four-power treaty (France, the United States, the United Kingdom, and Germany) granted the new German Republic full sovereignty.

7. The EEC Treaty, along with the ECSC, Euratom, and the Single European Act (1987) are found in EC, *Treaties Establishing the European Communities* (Luxembourg: EC, 1987), Article 2, p. 125.

8. Ibid., Article 3.

9. Loukas Tsoukalis, *The New European Economy*, 2nd ed. (London: Oxford University Press, 1993), chap. 2.

10. Miriam Camps, *Britain and the European Community 1955–1963* (Oxford: Oxford University Press, 1964), and Stephen George, *An Awkward Partner: Britain in the European Community* (Oxford: Clarendon Press, 1990).

11. One further small change was the negotiation of a treaty in 1965 (entering into effect in 1967) that fused the executives of the three European Communities into one. The Brussels Commission thus became the Commission of the ECSC and Euratom, hence the "Commission of the European Communit(ies)."

12. In the wake of new warfare in the Middle East, OPEC (the Organization of Petroleum Exporting Countries, dominated by Middle-Eastern oil-producing nations), which had for years seen its revenues decline in consequence of Western inflation, doubled their oil prices. A second oil shock, in 1979, had similar effects.

13. See Simon Bulmer and Wolfgang Wessels, *The European Council* (Basingstoke: Macmillan, 1987).

14. EMS was a "two-speed" affair, including only some EC members (not Britain, for example).

15. Revaluation occurred twenty-six times between 1979 and 1999 (when EMU came into existence), and many think that it should have occurred even more often.

16. Margaret Thatcher's *The Downing Street Years* (New York: HarperCollins, 1993) contains trenchant discussions of the "British Check" issue. See chap. XVIII in particular.

17. Ibid., pp. 537–541.

18. The SEA was *single* because there is only one text and to remind member states that it was to be ratified in an all-or-nothing way, and not because of the single market.

19. Delors and his team used the metaphor of "Russian Dolls" when discussing their approach. See George Ross, *Jacques Delors and European Integration* (New York: Oxford University Press, 1995).

20. Delors had earlier been instrumental (despite Thatcher) in inserting language favorable to new monetary initiatives into the Single European Act.

21. Bundesbank president Karl-Otto Pöhl suggested his own EMU program in June 1990. Membership would be restricted to the strong-currency countries of the Dmark zone and France.

22. Jacques Delors's *Mémoires* (Paris: Plon, 2004) are an essential source on this period.

23. On the GATT Uruguay Round negotiations, which ended in 1993, see Hugo Paemen and Alexandra Bensk, *From GATT to the Uruguay Round* (Leuven: Leuven University Press, 1995).

24. David Marsh, *The Bundesbank: The Bank That Rules Europe* (London: Heinemann, 1992) provides a shrewd overview of the "Buba's" position. See also John Goodman, *Monetary Sovereignty: The Politics of Central Banking in Western Europe* (Ithaca: Cornell University Press, 1992).

25. *The Financial Times,* December 11, 1992.

26. In situations where recessions were serious, the Council of Ministers could behave more flexibly.

27. The EES was evaluated after its first five years. As a result, the Commission proposed restructuring it around three objectives: achieving full employment, raising quality and productivity at work, and promoting cohesion and inclusive labor markets.

28. J. Pakaslahti and P. Pochet, *The Social Dimension of the Changing European Union* (Brussels: OSE, 2003), p. 133.

29. See Fraser Cameron, *The Common Foreign and Security Policy of the European Union* (Sheffield: Sheffield Academic Press, 1999), pp. 50–55, and Anthony Forster and William Wallace, "Common Foreign and Security Policy," in Helen Wallace and William Wallace, *Policy-Making in the European Union* (Oxford: Oxford University Press, 2000).

30. The Germans were behind, ended their review only in 1999, and while ending conscription was politically impossible, reflected on the new situation otherwise in similar ways to those of the French and British.

31. Anthony Forster and William Wallace, "Common Foreign and Security Policy," in Wallace and Wallace (2000), p. 484.

32. Cameron, p. 78.

33. Cameron, p. 79. NATO, at its fiftieth-anniversary festival, had earlier given its blessing

to a strengthened European security and defense policy.

34. Presidency Conclusions, Helsinki European Council, December 10–11, 1999, Title II.

35. Dominique Moisi, "What Transatlantic Future," in Werner Weidenfeld, ed., *Creating Partnership: The Future of Transatlantic Relations* (Gutersloh: Bertelsmann Foundation, 1997), p. 99.

36. For a subtle and thorough review of enlargement matters, see Elrich Sedelmeier and Helen Wallace, "Eastern Enlargement: Strategy of Second Thoughts?" in Wallace and Wallace (2000).

37. On the current state of the CAP, see Elmar Rieger, "The Common Agricultural Policy: Politics Against Markets," in Wallace and Wallace (2000).

38. The expression is from Brigid Laffan and Michael Shackleton, "The Budget: Who Gets What, When and How," in Wallace and Wallace (2000).

39. Franklin Dehousse, *Amsterdam: The Making of a Treaty* (London: Kogan Page, 1999).

40. Javier Solana, former Spanish foreign minister and secretary-general of NATO, was appointed the first high representative in 1999.

C H A P T E R

3

European Union Institutions

The heart of the European Union (EU) is a thicket of utilitarian, unattractive office buildings around the Rond Point Schuman in Brussels. The architecture of this "European quarter" reflects the EU's history. In the 1960s, the Common Market having been successfully launched, the European Commission moved into the Berlaymont, a huge glass-faced, X-shaped ultramodern building. Commissioners were on the top floor, with grand views over Brussels, while the Commission's administrative divisions, or DGs (directorates general), lived on the lower floors. The leitmotif of this grand design was to make everyone accessible to everyone else. The Council of Ministers' headquarters next door, on unpleasant, windswept Rue de la Loi, was small, symbolizing that the Council's work was mainly done in the member states. The Commission gained power in the 1980s and progressively colonized the entire area, decentralizing the DGs and lobbies into dull new buildings.

In June 1991, in the middle of the Maastricht negotiations, the Commission learned that the Berlaymont was polluted with asbestos and ordered it evacuated. Commissioners and their staffs went up the street to the more modest Breydel building, while administrative services dispersed all over Brussels. The Berlaymont sat derelict through the 1990s while building czars debated whether to demolish or rebuild and, more important, where to get money to do either. Immediately opposite the empty Berlaymont—covered by white plastic wrap as if pop artists had taken over—a new Council headquarters was built, large and pompous, redolent of a mausoleum. If buildings talked, this new edifice would have announced the Commission's decline and the Council ever more in charge. Towering on the near horizon, however, was a bulky concrete and glass object that resembled a gigantic beer barrel, the new Brussels home of the European Parliament, whose star also rose in the 1990s. For the Parliament, however, nothing was ever simple, and several hundred kilometers away, in Strasbourg, another large and costly new glass-covered home was also being built for it.[1]

The Institutional "Triangle"

The EU is a complex of organizations built around nation-states. While not a sovereign entity, it does exercise some measure of sovereignty. It is young and changing, and the balance of power among its institutions has varied over time. Dense and complex, the EU is basically a triangle of institutions, the Commission, the Council of Ministers, and the European Parliament. The European Council of heads of state and government, a general strategist for the Union, stands above the three pillars and this "triangle." Finally, because the EU is a community of law, this triangle operates within a body of jurisprudence from the European Court of Justice (ECJ).

The European Commission

The Rome treaties gave the European Commission (EC) three major prerogatives:[2]

- Exclusive right to propose Community legislation in the form of regulations, directives, and recommendations

- Oversight over the implementation of Community policy, monitoring member state transposition of EU law into national statute

- "Guardian" of the treaties, seeing to it that European law is observed and, if need be, bringing member states and private bodies before the ECJ

It has acquired an important fourth role, as representative of the EU internationally, particularly on all-important trade issues, and it has consistently had a fifth, de facto, role as a collective of activists to reflect upon and agitate for the future of European integration.

The Commission has specific policy competencies in which it behaves like a partial federal government. It administers EU competition (antitrust) policies, for example, to maintain a level playing field across the single market, policing state subsidies to industry, mergers and acquisitions, and the emergence of monopoly market power. The Commission administers the Common Agricultural Policy (CAP), regulating Europe's hugely expensive and complex agricultural operations. It has a major role in European environmental policy. It regulates workplace health and safety across the Union. It administers, and to some extent designs, the structural funds for developing poorer regions. It has a significant architectural role in European-level research and development strategies and programs. It draws up the basic EU budget. Besides representing the Union externally in trade matters, it also represents member states in some international organizations, and has diplomatic delegations in many countries.[3]

After the 1995 enlargement of the Union to fifteen member states, the Commission had twenty members, two for each large member state (Germany, France, Italy, the United Kingdom, and Spain) and one each for smaller ones. Maastricht set commissioners' terms at five years to coincide with the electoral life of the European Parliament. The 2004 eastern enlargement left the Commission, temporarily, at twenty-five members, one from each member state, to rise with new members until 2014, when its size will be limited to two-thirds of member states and commissioners will be appointed by "equal rotation," meaning that for the first time some member states will be without commissioners for five-year periods. The president of the Commission is nominated by the European Council and must be approved by the Parliament. The Parliament also scrutinizes the qualifications of all newly nominated commissioners and, although it cannot block appointment of specific commissioners, it may withhold approval of the entire Commission.

The Commission proper (i.e., the group of commissioners) is organized as a college, a collective in which each commissioner, whatever his or her particular policy tasks, participates in all key decisions. The Commission president has few of the powers of appointment, policy direction, and arbitration of a prime minister. His influence, such as it may be, comes from "presiding" over the Commissions, coordination, agenda-setting, and chairing (aided by the Commission's general secretariat and legal services, which report to him).[4] There are two vice presidents who stand in when the president is absent. Commissioners are all required to swear (Article 157 EEC) "to be completely independent in the performance of their duties [and to] neither seek nor take instructions from any government or from any other body." The president assigns each commissioner a portfolio of precise tasks before he or she enters office, as illustrated in Table 3.1, involving the political supervision of one or several of the Commission's "services" (DGs). Commissioners do not have ministerial powers over their services, however. Their supervisory

Table 3.1   The Prodi Commission, 2000–2004: Commissioners and Portfolios

Name (country)	Portfolio
Romano Prodi (Italy)	President
Neil Kinnock (United Kingdom)	Vice president, Administrative Reform
Loyola de Palacio (Spain)	Vice president, Relations with the European Parliament, Transport and Energy
Mario Monti (Italy)	Competition
Franz Fischler (Austria)	Agriculture, Rural Development, and Fisheries
Erkki Liikanen (Finland)	Enterprise and Information Society
Frits Bolkestein (Netherlands)	Internal Market
Philippe Busquin (Belgium)	Research
Pedro Solbes Mira (Spain)	Economic and Monetary Affairs
Poul Nielson (Denmark)	Development and Humanitarian Aid
Günter Verheugen (Germany)	Enlargement
Chris Patten (United Kingdom)	External Relations
Pascal Lamy (France)	Trade
David Byrne (Ireland)	Health and Consumer Protection
Michel Barnier (France)	Regional Policy and IGC
Viviane Reding (Luxembourg)	Education and Culture
Michaele Schreyer (Germany)	Budget
Margot Wallström (Sweden)	Environment
Antonio Vitorino (Portugal)	Justice and Home Affairs
Anna Diamantopoulou (Greece)	Employment and Social Affairs

tasks are undertaken in accordance with programmatic lines to which the entire Commission has agreed.

The Commission meets every Wednesday, three times a month in Brussels and once in Strasbourg to be present at the Parliament's monthly plenary sessions. It usually takes off the month of August, when governments shut down across Europe. Commission decisions are taken after collective debate, to which each commissioner is expected to contribute. Broad participation in debate is the heart of the college method. Ministers in classic governments argue briefs related to their ministry, participate in other areas only as informed spectators, and are subject ultimately to "arbitration" by the head of government. As members of a college, commissioners participate in all decisions, and their influence depends on their ability to do so effectively. Collegiality is designed to produce consensus, and the Commission votes only when there is no consensus.

Commissioners are assisted by "cabinets," or personal staffs, composed of a half-dozen ambitious operatives that do the legwork necessitated by collegial organization. Part of the cabinet serves as an intelligence gatherer on the entire range of issues on the Commission floor while another works more closely with services pertinent to the commissioner's portfolio and substitutes for the commissioner at policy preparation meetings before each Wednesday's full college meeting. The cabinet system, borrowed from French and Belgian practices, has always been controversial because it inserts a layer of fixers and operators between commissioners and their administrative services, even though it is difficult to see how the Commission could function as a college without something equivalent. Cabinet service has become the best way for Commission civil servants to rise rapidly in the ranks.

Despite its mythical reputation as an unstoppable "Brussels bureaucracy," the Commission administration is small, barely twenty thousand people, the size of the staff of a mid-sized European city. From this total there are six thousand A-grade officers, the real "Eurocrats," as the press calls them. The national distribution of A-level posts is carefully observed, with some jobs regularly allocated to particular countries. Each service is headed by a general director, ranked "A-1, " the Commission's highest administrative post. A-level Commission jobs are coveted because they are interesting compared with most national civil service jobs, well paid, and exempt from national taxes (although the EU itself taxes them).[5] A-levels are recruited primarily through an annual European-wide competition in which there are thousands of applicants. The Commission is obligated to translate all official documents and provide simultaneous translation into all EU languages, nineteen as of 2004. This alone requires thousands of translators and interpreters. The workaday languages of the Commission—English, French, and German— are used in the processes of hammering out official documents.[6] The remainder of the Commission's personnel provide clerical and other support services, including thousands of jobs for Belgian locals paid well above going rates in the local labor market.

The Commission is an organization with the mission of advancing the cause of European integration. At those—relatively rare—moments when it has relative power in the EU institutional triangle, the Commission is thus a hotbed of commitment, hard work, and energy. During bad moments, when the Commission's role is limited, it can be full of demoralized grumbling, as hierarchical and inflexible as any national civil service in ways that demotivate second-level officials, whose jobs become dull and whose careers are blocked. Of course, like any complex administration, the Commission is subdivided by functional divisions, which always have a tendency to become feudal and self-contained. Moreover, because it is multinational, the Commission has national cliques, clans, and rumor-mills similar to other international organizations. The Commission is a political as well as an administrative organ, and the political affiliations of the people within it matter.

The Commission's most important job is to conceive initiatives and see them enacted. The Commission rarely proposes de novo, however. In most cases it translates the desires of others and the requirements of international agreements into specific proposals.[7] The Commission spends much time sounding out and consulting politicians, national ministries, and other Euro-level institutions. Commissions are aided, in institutionalized ways, by several thousand advisory, management, and regulatory committees made up of member state civil servants, governed by codified rules called "comitology." The Commission is also the object of intense lobbying from a wide range of interest groups. Finally, the actual implementation of most Community measures is left to member state administrations, monitored by the Commission.

The Commission can initiate proposals only in areas allowed by the treaties. Originally, its prerogatives were primarily sectoral, including the CAP, competition law, common external trade policies (the administration of tariffs, and bi- and multilateral trade negotiations, including the GATT). The 1985 White Paper on Completing the Internal Market extended its "proposition force" role by making it responsible for producing the legislative measures for the "1992" program. The Single Act also gave the Community expanded competencies in "economic and social cohesion" (regional redistribution policy), environmental policy, and research and development. In more routine areas, the Commission prepares the annual Community budget for submission to the Parliament and Council of Ministers and, since the first "package," a pluri-annual budgetary program.

Maastricht clarified and changed Community and Commission prerogatives. Its Article 3 defined twenty policy areas (Table 3.2) where the Community could act (meaning where the Commission had the power of proposal), either exclusively or concurrently with member states. Many of these were traditional, sometimes with the scope of Community action expanded, but there were several new areas, including public health, education and training, and consumer protection. Maastricht also included a new article (3B) that consecrated "subsidiarity," decreeing that the Commission and Community should act only, even where the treaty did allow, where objectives could not be achieved by the member states themselves.[8]

Table 3.2   Areas for Community Action—The Maastricht List

1. Elimination of customs duties and quantitative restrictions on goods trade among member states, as well as other equivalent practices

2. Common external trade policy

3. An internal market with free circulation of goods, people, services, and capital

4. Measures to promote the entrance of and free circulation within the internal market, eventually including visa policies

5. Common policies in agriculture and fishing

6. Common transport policies

7. Competition law—although most, excepting large mergers and acquisitions cases, decentralized to member states in 2004

8. Rapprochement of national legislations for the functioning of the Common Market

9. Social policy involving the European Social Fund

10. Reinforcement of economic and social cohesion (regional policy)

11. Environmental policy

12. Enhancing the competitiveness of Community industry

13. Promotion of technological research and development

14. Encouragement of "trans-European networks" (in telecommunications, transport, and energy)

15. Contributing to a high level of public health

16. Contributing to quality education and training as the flowering of member state culture

17. Policies of development aid

18. Association with overseas territories (mainly colonies) to help trade and pursue efforts at economic and social development in common with them

19. Contributing to the enhancement of consumer protection

20. Measures in the areas of energy, civil defense, and tourism

Maastricht also reconfigured Community prerogatives in "common policy" areas. Economic and social cohesion became a "fundamental mission," meaning, in legal terms, that all EU policy areas were to integrate commitment to regional development. Environmental policy, also promoted to become a fundamental mission (as was, later, equality of opportunities between women and men), was henceforth to be decided by qualified majority decision making in all but a few areas. The treaty also established a Cohesion Fund to compensate poorer countries for the costs of Community environmental policy and the "Trans-European Networks" (TENs)—new Community-wide public works projects in transport, telecommunications, and energy infrastructure established by Maastricht. The Maastricht Treaty also broadened the scope of Community research and development policies beyond science and technology to areas such as health and the environment. Finally, Maastricht added a "social protocol"—originally signed only by eleven member states, with the British opting out (they opted in at Amsterdam in 1997)—which allowed new space for social policy.

The 1997 Amsterdam Treaty beefed up provisions enjoining equal treatment between men and women in the workplace and obliged such matters to be "mainstreamed" through all EU activities. In practice, this meant that all Community activities were supposed to consider environmental, regional, and equal opportunity concerns—a tall order! Amsterdam also reinforced consumer protection powers. Finally, it programmed the five-year shift of some tasks related to justice and home affairs (the "third pillar"—free movement of persons, immigration and external border control, asylum law) into the Community pillar and the Commission's orbit. For the five-year transition period (until 2003), the Council was charged with designing new rules in these areas (excepting asylum and immigration, where the five-year period does not apply), deciding by unanimity, and the Commission would then administer these rules. Thereafter, any new decisions would be made by qualified majority voting (QMV). The grandiloquent rubric of this shift—"establishing an area of freedom, security and justice in five years"— probably contributed to the Community charter of basic rights accepted at the otherwise inglorious Nice European Council in 2001 and included in the European Convention's draft constitutional treaty in 2003. The 2004 Constitutional Treaty, unratified and thus unimplemented at time of writing, enshrined QMV and codecision as the Union's normal method, expanded the areas covered by QMV (leaving matters of taxation, social policy, and the common foreign and security policy [CFSP] unanimous, however), and, in so doing, eliminated Maastricht's intergovernmental pillars.

The Commission has been more and less powerful depending upon the particular moment of EU history. Its moments of great significance as agenda-shaper have followed ambitious "grand bargains" by member states that set out general vectors for change in "framework" ways and

then left the Commission to fill in specific contents. The Commission thus had a moment of frenetic activity and power proposing legislation immediately after the Treaty of Rome, for example, until it went too far and drew down the wrath of de Gaulle. The "1992" White Paper and the SEA allowed the Commission to rise to what may have been the zenith of its powers until the aftermath of Maastricht in the early 1990s, when it annually proposed more legislation than national governments and moved omnivorously into new policy areas. Since Maastricht, public opinion and the member states have halted growth in Commission power.

The Commission's future is likely to be different from its past, however. Enlargement has obliged change and institutional reconfiguration. Twenty-five members and counting from 2004 to 2014 likely means that traditional methods—in particular, appointment of two commissioners by larger member states—cannot continue. Moreover, there are not enough significant jobs to spread around thirty commissioners and such a large group will make collegial functioning difficult. After 2014, when the Commission will have one-third fewer members than the number of member states and membership shared over time by a system of rotation, the consequences for the roles of the Commission are difficult to foresee, and they will likely coincide with broader political changes as well.

The Council of Ministers

In its first official portrait, the Council of Ministers was the EU's exclusive legislator, deciding alone on proposals from the Commission, usually after the Parliament had been consulted. Since Maastricht, the Council has "codecided" with Parliament on Community issues, while continuing as sole legislator in the intergovernmental pillars on CFSP and justice and home affairs. When the 2004 Constitutional Treaty is ratified, QMV and codecision with Parliament will become the default decision mechanism, and the pillar structure will disappear. The Council is composed of ministers empowered by their governments to decide European issues, and it is where member states, the fundamental actors of the EU, express their preferences. It has six major jobs, the most important of which is passing European laws. Since monetary integration, it also tries annually to coordinate the economic policies of member states through the production of broad economic policy guidelines (BEPG). In addition, it concludes international agreements for the EU, approves the EU budget (with the Parliament), and, until ratification of the 2004 changes, decides issues by unanimity in the intergovernmental CFSP and justice and home affairs pillars.

There are in practice nine different Councils, whose membership varies with the issues discussed, as listed in Table 3.3. This multiplicity of different Councils, all functioning as the Council of Ministers, creates coordination problems that are not always well resolved. The sheer number of official Council meetings, well over a hundred per year, means that the Council is more or less permanently in session.

The Council's evolving decision rules have added complexity. The Rome Treaty foresaw three different voting systems—unanimity,

---

Table 3.3   Councils Within the Council

General Affairs and External Relations—Foreign Minister (coordinating council)

Economic and Financial Affairs (ECOFIN)

Justice and Home Affairs ("third pillar" on citizenship and internal security)

Employment, Social Policy, Health, and Consumer Affairs

Competitiveness (internal market, industry, and research)

Transport, Telecommunications, and Energy

Agriculture and Fisheries

Environment

Education, Youth, and Culture

---

qualified majority voting, and simple majority—depending on the issue area. The Luxembourg Compromise narrowed things to unanimity on almost anything important. The SEA, however, applied QMV across a wide range of matters, including almost everything involved in completing the single market. Maastricht, Amsterdam, and the 2001 Nice Treaty slowly extended QMV, but not completely. QMV, or weighted majority voting, distributes voting power in accordance with the relative size of different member states, as shown in Table 3.4.

After the enlargement of 1995, a total of 62 votes (71.3 percent of population) was needed to pass a measure under QMV. Agreement of two large and two smaller member states could become a "blocking minority" of twenty-six. After a great deal of difficulty, created by the Nice Treaty, the 2004 Constitutional Treaty settled on a new "double majority" formula that would reflect both votes and population, such that a reweighted QMV involved a 55 percent majority of member states representing 65 percent of the population, while a blocking minority had to include four member states representing 35 percent.

The Council does not deliberate and decide alone any more than does the Commission. Its most important helper is COREPER (a French acronym for Committee of Permanent Representatives), whose members the *Financial Times* once called "the men who run Europe."[9] The "permanent representatives" are member state ambassadors to the EU, their deputies and top staff, the member states' Brussels front line. They do much of the hard work that ultimately shapes Council decisions, refining and vetting matters for the Council much as cabinets do for the Commission. As they work through proposals, they hammer out as much consensus as possible ("point A" matters) leaving ministers to broker the remaining disagreements (15–20 percent "point B" matters). Permanent representatives in Brussels are veterans with long EU-level careers who have total mastery of EU lore, networks, and methods.[10] The initial sorting of deci-

Table 3.4   Voting Weights in QMV vs. Population and GDP Prior to 2004 Treaty

Member State	QMV Votes Prior to November 2004	Population (millions)	% EU GNP
France	10	57.5	18.1
Germany	10	80.9	28.0
Italy	10	56.0	14.0
United Kingdom	10	58	13.9
Spain	8	30.1	6.6
Netherlands	5		
Belgium	5	10.1	3.1
Greece	5	10.3	1.2
Portugal	5	9.9	1.2
Denmark	3	5.2	2.0
Ireland	3	3.6	0.7
Finland	3	5.1	1.3
Austria and Sweden	4		
Luxembourg	2	0.4	0.2

sions for COREPER is done in 150–200 lower-level working committees governed by the rules of "comitology" and using thousands of national civil servants and experts.[11] COREPER also coordinates and staffs a number of high-level functional committees, including the Political Committee (involving member state and Commission foreign policy "political directors" from European Political Cooperation) that prepares the work of the General Affairs Council and, since Maastricht, CFSP. The K4 Committee coordinates a range of justice and home affairs matters.[12]

The actual deliberations of the Council of Ministers have always been shrouded in mystery. Only its outcomes are announced to the public, with the internal processes by which they have been reached screened out. Minutes are not circulated, even in summary form. Rising worries about Europe's legitimacy in the 1990s led to largely cosmetic efforts to clarify some of this mystery. There have been a few television broadcasts showing parts of Council proceedings. On certain matters the Council has allowed its votes to be known, although the Council usually strives for consensus rather than voting at all. Since 1995, the media, after complicated legal proceedings, can get more detail. The inside knowledge gleaned thus far has been limited, however, in part because much of the Council's work is done in bilateral and multilateral discussions between member states before anything reaches the Council room. The 2004 Constitutional Treaty has clauses on transparency and rights to information that may open up the Council, however.

The Council has been coordinated and organized by a presidency that rotates among member states every six months in an agreed-upon order.[13] The Council, with its many levels and arenas, needs help from the presidency to work coherently. The presidency also oversees

Council-Commission relationships. Because the prerogatives of the European Parliament have grown through cooperation and codecision, the presidency now coordinates demanding and sometimes intense Council-Parliament interactions, including the "conciliation committees" where codecision plays itself out, and the submission of the Council's annual program to the Parliament. The presidency also presides over and prepares European Council summits. In all such activities the member state holding the presidency can play an important role as power broker and package builder among member states, as the Belgians did in 2002 by proposing the European Convention to change the EU treaties. Finally, the presidency has traditionally spoken for the EU externally on foreign policy matters (excepting trade). For foreign policy activity, the acting presidency has been aided by the previous and next presidency, the so-called troika.[14] The development of CFSP and JHA broadened the presidency's foreign policy role while establishing a new place for "Mr. Common Foreign and Security Policy."

An effective presidency can exercise considerable power. French and German presidencies in the 1980s were critical in regenerating the momentum for integration, for example. British presidencies, in contrast, have brought caution. Smaller members can be "big" presidents as well. Tiny Luxembourg, for example, presided over the most difficult negotiations for the Single European Act and the Maastricht Treaty; Belgium, with its strong pro-integrationist sentiments, has likewise been important; and the Portuguese presidency in the first half of 2000 was particularly innovative. The rotating Council presidency has not always been the most effective of EU institutions, however. Discontinuities in leadership, bad national preparation, lack of resources, and occasional ineptitude have often disrupted the flow of business. This is why the 2004 Constitutional Treaty foresees the appointment of a European Council president for a two-and-one-half-year (once renewable) term to replace it.

The Council of Ministers relies on a secretariat of two thousand people (a scant three hundred A-level administrators, plus legal linguists, translators, and secretaries). The organization of the Council secretariat is different from the Commission's, with a staff for the secretary-general, legal services, and seven general directorates. The Council secretary-general, who has his own large cabinet, is a very important person. The Council secretariat provides services and continuity to the rotating Council presidency—one of the primary reasons why the presidencies of small countries have been able to work. The secretariat is responsible for accurate translation of all official EU actions into all official languages—hence the importance of "legal linguists" who are experts in legal translation. The Amsterdam Treaty enhanced the stature and power of the Council secretariat by establishing a high representative for foreign policy (the first "Mr. CFSP" was Javier Solana) who is also the official Council secretary-general, although an associate secretary-general actually runs the office.

The European Council came into being in 1974 as an institutionalization of the summit meetings of EU heads of state and government. The Maastricht Treaty consecrated it formally as the body that gives the European Union the impulse it needs and defines its general direction. The European Council meets twice during each six-month Council presidency. It is prepared by the sitting Council presidency with the help of the Council secretariat and settles important outstanding issues and strategizes the EU's future. Its meetings are exclusive. Only presidents or prime ministers and one other minister (usually the foreign minister), the Council secretary-general, and the Commission president and secretary-general are allowed in the room—a total of thirty-three people in the EU15. This relative intimacy was designed to facilitate frank and open discussion and produce clarification of what is possible from an agenda that has been narrowed to the most important outstanding matters. During the actual European Council, which is brief—usually two days—legions of civil servants and technicians deploy in meeting rooms, hotels, and other places within the reach of cellular phones to provide proposals, wording, and discussion when needed. The actual negotiating begins with a visit from the president of the European Parliament, who makes a declaration and then leaves. Then issue after issue is discussed, with easy ones resolved quickly and harder ones saved until later. After the second session is a working lunch where the leaders separate from their foreign ministers to begin confronting the most difficult problems, while the foreign ministers expedite the rest. If important matters remain, as they almost always do, the last few hours of any European Council are very intense. The final report of each European Council—the so-called Presidency Conclusions—reflects the agenda for the meeting. It contains comments about international events, instructions about policy initiatives for the Commission and Council to take up, and pronouncements on larger issues of the EU's future.[15] The importance of the European Council is clear from a partial list of its most important recent conclusions (Table 3.5).

From the early 1990s to the present, the balance of EU power has tipped toward intergovernmental bodies, primarily at the expense of the Commission. This shift occurred partly because of exhaustion at the end of the Delors period and the weaknesses of subsequent Commission presidents. The main reason, however, is that the progress of integration has foregrounded matters like foreign policy, defense, immigration, policing, internal security, and EU enlargement, which all fall very close to the heart of national sovereignty. With this shifting balance, the agendas of the EU's intergovernmental institutions—the Council of Ministers in particular—have become more complicated and weighty. The result has been increased difficulty in resolving problems. One result has been to pass decision-making tasks upward so that the European Council is now the default decision maker for the EU. As a result, the more the Council of Ministers dodges bullets, the more bullets the European Council must bite. The danger in this is that the European Council conducts a very brief meeting in which many things must be done. Some of the proposals in the 2004 Constitutional Treaty were designed to remedy this, but only time will tell if they actually will.

The European Parliament: 750 Characters in Search of an Author?

The European Parliament (EP) began as the successor to the European Coal and Steel Community (ECSC) assembly, composed of unelected members appointed by member state governments with little power.[16] The Parliament has since evolved slowly into an influential institution. Since 1979 the Parliament has been directly elected.[17] Table 3.6 shows how seats in the European Parliament have been allocated among member states prior to and after the 2004 enlargement.

Candidates to the EP run on national party tickets. Once elected, national party groups then form European-level family coalitions. The Socialists, who have created the transnational Party of European Socialists, and the Christian Democrats (who now include the British Conservatives), grouped in the European Peoples' Party, have long been by far the two largest EP groups.[18] Until 1999 the Socialists were larger, but the balance shifted slightly in the 1999 elections, and the shift was confirmed in 2004. The Socialist–Christian Democrat EP pivot is important since it faithfully reflects the center of gravity of continental European party politics prior to the 2004 enlargement and could be found at work in other EU institutions, underlining general commitment in the EU15 to "social market" economies. Both the Social Democrats and Christian Democrats accept that there can be no substitute for market mechanisms, but both reject hard-line neoliberalism, advocating that markets should make *all* important decisions. This picture may become more complicated in the first Parliament after the 2004 enlargement,

Table 3.5   Major Conclusions of Recent European Councils

European Council	Product(s)
Fontainebleau, 1984	Solved "British check" issue; expansion to Spain and Portugal unlocked; appointment of Jacques Delors
Milan, 1985	Approved "1992" White Paper; decided intergovernmental conference to modify treaty
Brussels, 1987	Adopted first Delors budgetary package (reform of structural funds)
Madrid, 1989	Accepted Delors report on EMU; discussed Social Charter
Dublin, 1990	Decided German reunification within the EU
Rome, 1990	Opened two IGCs (EMU and political union)
Maastricht, 1991	Maastricht Treaty
Edinburgh, 1992	Adopted second Delors budgetary package; negotiated ways to allow Denmark to hold second Maastricht referendum; decided to negotiate enlargement to four European Free Trade Association countries
Brussels, 1993	Discussed White Paper on Growth, Competitiveness, and Employment
Brussels, 1994	Designation of Jacques Santer as president of Commission
Essen, 1994	Discussed Commission paper on enlargement to Central and Eastern European countries
Madrid, 1995	Decided date to proceed to final EMU stage; named new European currency the euro
Turin, 1996	Opened IGC to review Maastricht
Dublin, 1996	Proposed EMU Stability and Growth Pact
Amsterdam, 1997	Final negotiations on Amsterdam Treaty
Luxembourg, 1997	Start of Amsterdam employment policy processes
Cologne, 1998	Wide-ranging discussions on European Strategic Defense Program
Helsinki, 1999	Adopted "Headline Goal" on creation of European rapid-reaction force by 2003
Berlin, 1999	Approved Agenda 2000 budgetary package to facilitate enlargement
Lisbon, 2000	Industrial policy summit on "information economy"
Nice, 2000	End of IGC to reform EU institutions for enlargement; Nice Treaty
Laeken, 2001	Call for the European convention
Brussels, 2003	Ten accession countries signed treaty to join EU on May 1, 2004
Brussels, 2004	Reached agreement on new Constitutional Treaty derived from Convention

however. The weight of the ten new members in the enlarged Parliament will not be huge, but it is likely to reflect considerably less commitment to the (Western) "European Model of Society."

Elections to the EP are held every five years, since 1999 by some system of proportional rep-resentation. They have consistently been second-order national elections, understood and strate-gized by politicians as important indicators of the relative strength of national political forces rather than events about the EU. As a result, when European issues are discussed during Euro-

Table 3.6   European Parliament, Seats per Country as of Nice Treaty, 2001* (alphabetical order according to country's name in its own language)

Country	Seats 1999–2004	2004–2007	2007	Country	Seats 1999–2004	2004–2007	2007
Belgium	25	24	24	Lithuania	—	13	13
Bulgaria	—	—	18	Luxembourg	6	6	6
Cyprus	—	6	6	Malta	—	5	5
Czech Republic	—	24	24	Netherlands	31	27	27
Denmark	16	14	14	Austria	21	18	18
Germany	99	99	99	Poland	—	54	54
Greece	25	24	24	Portugal	25	24	24
Spain	64	54	54	Romania	—	—	36
Estonia	—	6	6	Slovakia	—	14	14
France	87	78	78	Slovenia	—	7	7
Hungary	—	24	24	Finland	16	14	14
Ireland	15	13	13	Sweden	22	19	19
Italy	87	78	78	United Kingdom	87	78	78
Latvia	—	9	9	TOTAL	626	732	786

*The 2004 Constitutional Treaty, when implemented, will cap the size of Parliament at 750.

parliamentary campaigns, they tend to be proxies for national political conflicts and concerns.[19] This subordination of Euro-parliamentary electoral politics to the issues and rhythms of national political life intensified in the 1990s.

The Parliament elects its own president and executive bureau for two-and-one-half-year periods. The president presides over parliamentary sessions, participates in periodic interinstitutional discussions with Commission and Council counterparts, and addresses member state leaders at European Council summits. The bulk of Parliament's hard work is done by seventeen permanent committees, which produce detailed, thoughtful reports in their functional areas, often made even more interesting by the degree of political consensus that has tended to prevail about what Europe should be.[20] The centrality of the committees has also made them the logical target for the enormous army of lobbyists that the EU has acquired.

The importance of committee business is part of the explanation for the strange spectacle that visitors to parliamentary sessions often witness. Ushered into the gallery of the EP's postmodern "hemicycles" in Strasbourg or Paris, visitors most often see a vast room nearly devoid of human presence. There may be a staff person here and there, someone presiding on the dais, and several seemingly lost members of the European Parliament (MEPs) randomly distributed around the room, either speaking because their turn has come (after which they tend to leave) or waiting for the president to recognize them. Visitors who happen in at a key moment may see a momentary flood of MEPs to their seats for a scheduled vote. At these moments, disconnected in time from any relevant debate, votes on many different matters are taken electronically. After the MEPs have pushed their buttons the required number of times and the results are tallied, which happens immediately on an electronic scoreboard, the flood retreats. The room looks like a real parliamentary assembly only when it is being addressed by commissioners, the Commission and Council presidents, who report and answer questions regularly; prime ministers; heads of state; and other visiting dignitaries.

The Parliament originally had only consultative power, with legislation proposed by the Commission that the Council would decide after considering Parliament's opinion. This odd constitution of a legislative body without de facto legislative power created a parliamentary lobby for correcting the Community's "democratic deficit."[21] Considerable growth in Parliament's powers has been one consequence of this. In the 1970s, it acquired deliberative powers in the establishment of the Community's annual budget, making it an important object for lobbying and allowing it to intervene indirectly in important policy areas. The Parliament also discovered that it could delay decisions, because time limits for delivering its consultative opinions were vague. Then, in 1987, the SEA instituted a "cooperation procedure" for most single-market legislation, allowing Parliament to propose amendments and be taken seriously. Maastricht, Amsterdam, Nice 2001, and Brussels 2004 brought the invention and refinement of "codecision." All these different powers still officially coexist, although Brussels 2004 designated codecision as the normal legislative process.

The cooperation procedure created a process with two legislative readings that established mechanisms for Parliament to propose amendments that then had to be taken into official consideration by the other triangle institutions. The procedure endowed Parliament with its first substantial legislative powers, giving it new influence over both the Commission and Council, both of which were to develop new attitudes about the Parliament.

The Parliament gained new powers to reject legislation, shared with the Council, with Maastricht's "codecision" procedure, in effect since 1993. Codecision should be understood literally,

in the sense that Parliament and the Council actually "codecide" on Commission proposals as if they were two separate legislative houses. The process set out at Maastricht was exceedingly complex, however, with as many as twenty-two different ways to make decisions. Amsterdam simplified and clarified the process (see Table 3.7). In essence, Parliament and the Council each read and discuss proposals twice. If they do not agree, matters go to a "conciliation committee" composed of equal numbers from the Council and Parliament. If and when the committee agrees, the measure is sent back to Council and Parliament for adoption in a "third reading."

Table 3.7   Overview of Codecision Process

First Reading

1. Commission proposes ▶

   -Parliament gives its initial opinion.

   -Council prepares its Common Position.

Second Reading

2a. Parliament approves ▶ The measure passes

or

2b. Parliament proposes amendments to common position or makes statement of intent to reject (three months' time limit + one month extension)

if 2b, then

Third Reading

3. Conciliation committee (half from Council, half from Parliament) convened to seek agreed-upon joint text (six weeks) ▶

   -The measure passes if joint text agreed.

 or

   -If Council reverts to Common Position and Parliament votes it down by absolute majority within six weeks, the measure fails.

or

   -Passage if Parliament fails to vote or fails to vote it down within six weeks.

Parliament also has the power to "assent" to Council proposals on applications from prospective new members, important international treaties, specific tasks of the European Central Bank (ECB), changes to the statutes of the ECB/European System of Central Banks, multiyear programs in the Structural and Cohesion Funds, and uniform electoral procedures for the European Parliament. Maastricht also gave the Parliament power to constitute temporary committees of inquiry, receive petitions, and name an EU ombudsman. In addition, the Rome Treaty granted Parliament the right to bring the Commission and Council to the ECJ if they did not act in areas in which the treaty enjoined them to do so. At a later point it also acquired the right to go to court over infringement of its own powers by Council actions. The Parliament has significant budgetary powers. Finally, Maastricht also enhanced Parliament's oversight of the Commission, in particular its prerogative of approving the appointment of a new Commission and being consulted about new Commission presidents. Brussels 2004 transformed this "consultation about" to "election of" the president, although only after Council recommendation of a name. Extending the Commission's term from four to five years to coincide with the parliamentary term was yet another Maastricht effort to make the Commission more responsive to Parliament.

The most striking aspect of the European Parliament's history is its steady acquisition of power, in large part because of the chronic problems of legitimacy that European integration has created. Applying rough-and-ready standards of democratic responsibility and participation, decisions of major import to the lives of EU member state citizens could not legitimately be made through multilateral diplomatic negotiations and an unelected Commission. The transformation of an appointed European Assembly without real power into today's "codecider" was the chosen way to confront this dilemma. Since European national polities were parliamentary democracies, it was logical to approach the "democratic

deficit" issue by progressively endowing a European Parliament with real power. The process has been prodded forward energetically by the Parliament itself, which has arguably been more effective lobbying for its own position than as a parliamentary body. There is no reason to assume that this dynamic will not continue. Council QMV, correlated with codecision, has been progressively extended until officially named the normal legislative procedure, even though there remain significant exceptions.

In the medium term, however, growing parliamentary power and influence are bound to uncover other dimensions of the EU's "democratic deficit."[22] The low participation rate and public dissatisfaction shown in the 2004 EP elections, discussed in Chapter 5, are signals of this. The absence of a substantial Euro-level political culture among European citizens—excepting, of course, Europeanized elite groups—is fundamental. The reasons why this absence persists are very complex. Notwithstanding, there are some ways in which innovation at the European level could facilitate change. Parliaments traditionally become effective when their deliberations connect with the pursuit of specific platforms. This happens when they deliberate the proposals of governments that have sought specific mandates for their programs. Some form of Euro-level government and opposition structure would give Euro-parliamentary debate the clarity that it presently lacks. It would also help promote the development of the genuine Euro-level parties and coalitions that would be better armed to bring European issues to European citizens without being obscured by today's mediation through national politics. Such developments are not yet on the agenda, however.

The European Court of Justice

Europeans are a people of the law, and European integration is ultimately a legal construct. The sources of this construct are the various treaties that have constituted the EU over the years and that bind member states.

Legislation and administrative implementation of the treaties by EU institutions follow from this "treaty base." The result is that today European law is superior to, and supersedes, member state law.[23] The European Court of Justice (ECJ), born in the European Coal and Steel Community Treaty, has been the major institutional actor in making this happen, and ECJ case rulings have provided sinews and ligaments for the new Europe, as Table 3.8 shows.

The ECJ sits in Luxembourg and is presently composed of fifteen justices and nine advocates-general. Each judge is named for a six-year term by member state governments, with half the Court renewed every three years. The justices elect their president for a three-year term. Advocates-general review cases to provide legal opinion to the judges but do not rule on fundamental legal matters. The Court can sit in plenary sessions when it wishes, but must do so when dealing with matters brought by a Community institution or member state. Otherwise, it subdivides its work among six "chambers" (of three and five judges each), with the possibility that any one may send matters to the full Court. The ECJ's decisions are binding on member states and their citizens. The huge workload of the Court led to the establishment of a Tribunal of First Instance (composed of fifteen judges, again with six-year terms) by the SEA, primarily to decide complex matters of fact in litigation brought by individuals and companies (actions for annulment and complaints of failure to act, actions for damages, actions by Community staff against institutions). Decisions concerning questions of law (and not of fact) can be appealed from this court to the full ECJ. (See Figure 3.1.)

Table 3.8   Significant Decisions of the European Court of Justice

Decision	Importance
Van Gend and Loos, 1963	Ruled that the Community constituted a new legal order of international law derived from the willing limitations of sovereignty by member states whose subjects were member states and their nationals.
Costa v. ENE, 1964	Central in establishing the supremacy of EU law itself.
Van Duyn v. Home Office, 1974	Gave individuals the same right to take employment in another member state as nationals of that state, a landmark ruling about the free movement of people.
Defrenne v. Sabena, 1976	Based upon Article 119 of the Rome Treaty, which enjoined equal treatment of men and women in employment, the case opened up the EU to a wide range of social policy initiatives and further rulings with major consequences in attenuating gender discrimination in EU labor markets.
Vereniging Bond van Adverteerders v. the Netherlands State, 1988	Obliged member states to open up national telecommunications services to competition, an important step in the liberalization of service provision.
Cassis de Dijon, 1979	Perhaps the most famous of the Court's recent cases, it decreed that member states must base their acceptance of EU goods from other member states on the principle of mutual recognition, thus assuming that all member states have reasonable product standards. This ruling, which allowed the EU to avoid unending negotiations to harmonize product standards, was of huge significance to the single-market program.

**Governments of the member states appoint
15 judges and 6 advocates-general by common accord for six-year terms**

COURT OF JUSTICE
Full Court—15 judges
2 chambers of 5 judges, 4 chambers of 3 judges

TYPE OF PROCEEDING

Actions for failure to fulfill obligations under treaties (Commission or member state v. member state)

Actions for annulment (against Council or Commission)

Actions on grounds of failure to act (against Council or Commission)

Claims for damages against the Community

References from national courts for preliminary rulings to clarify the meaning and scope of Community law

Opinions

COURT OF FIRST INSTANCE
12 judges

Direct action by natural and legal persons (except anti-dumping cases), staff cases, actions under ECSC treaty, ancillary actions for damages

Figure 3.1   European Court of Justice

Recourse to the ECJ can happen in many ways. The most significant route has been via the "preliminary ruling" procedure. A national court presented with a case about the legality of European law forwards the case for preliminary ruling to the ECJ, and with ECJ advice the national court then settles the case in question. National courts may also ask the ECJ outright whether a specific national statute conforms to EU law. Anyone, whether a European institution, government, or individual, can ask the court to rule on the legality of European legislation and other measures within a two-month time limit in so-called "annulment proceedings." Next, the Commission or a member state can ask the ECJ to decide if another member state has failed to fulfill its EU legal obligations ("treaty infringement proceeding"). Member states, other EU institutions, or individuals may also bring cases against a particular institution for "failure to act" when it ought to have done so under EU treaties. Cases for damages against Community institutions may be considered as well. Member states and EU institutions may also ask for rulings on the compatibility of international agreements with EU law. Recourse to the ECJ, which has handed down thousands of decisions since the days of the ECSC, has increased with the growing salience of European integration for member states and individuals. The Court's rulings have also become central in the evolution of European integration, often serving as policy and political switch-points.

Another effort to give Europeans a sense that there was more to European integration than economics came when Maastricht introduced "European citizenship."[24] All citizens of member states became citizens of the EU with the right to move about and live in any member state (subject to exceptions, mainly concerning work). European Union citizens living outside their own country can vote and be elected in municipal elections in their country of residence and in elections to the European Parliament. Every EU citizen is entitled to full diplomatic protection from any member state embassy and consulate. EU citizens also acquired rights to petition the European Parliament and a new ombudsman/mediator. These clauses on European citizenship clearly bore the potential for considerable elaboration and expansion as precedents for new legislation and future litigation.

Newer Institutions

The Economic and Monetary Union (EMU) was by far the most important product of the Maastricht Treaty. Its workings, officially part of the Maastricht Community pillar, are generally independent of the "Community method." The key EMU institution is the European Central Bank (ECB, set up in 1998 and located in Frankfurt), sitting atop a European System of European Central Banks. The ECB is simultaneously the most federal and least democratic of EU institutions. It is run by a governing council, an executive council, and a general council and works closely with national central banks, themselves made independent following Maastricht. The ECB's central task is to manage the euro and determine the course of EMU monetary policy. The ECB has complete autonomy in its allotted monetary policy sphere, as befits the desires of member states for a completely independent central banking system, and is statutorily forbidden from seeking or accepting instructions from any other institution. The president of the Council and one Commission member participate, without a vote, on the bank's governing board. National finance ministers and the Council have limited prerogatives otherwise.

The key decisions that the ECB makes about monetary policy have indirectly become the fundaments of euro-zone economic policy. Despite French desires to produce something quite different, the EMU that emerged from Maastricht looked like the German Bundesbank writ large, devoted exclusively to the pursuit of price stability, as the severe convergence criteria used to prepare membership in the 1990s demonstrated. More generally, monetary policy, central in the general economic policies of all EU countries, is made by unelected central bankers. Whether the EMU system proves effective or not, its independence provides significant issues for democratic accountability.

The institutional complexes of the second and third Maastricht pillars were both intergovernmental, involving state-to-state negotiations. They were thus built on different foundations from those of the Community pillar and will last until the ratification of the 2004 Constitutional Treaty. The second pillar, encompassing the common foreign and security policy (CFSP), grew out of a notion, unequally shared among EU members, that the time was ripe to transform the existing system of European political cooperation (EPC) on foreign policy matters into a confederal foreign and defense policy. EPC was a longstanding system of information sharing and exchanging views (including a network for sending diplomatic ciphers) that aimed at foreign policy coordination without infringing upon member states' national autonomy.[25] The products of EPC were usually solemn declarations about world problems. The idea of CFSP was to expand EPC into arrangements that would bind member states in some areas of foreign policy and, in the last analysis, defense as well. CFSP was EPC plus a new possibility of "joint action." The key change was the introduction of—particularly unwieldy—ways to operationalize joint actions through the pooling of sovereignty for specified foreign policy purposes. But the procedures from Maastricht were so complicated that, if obliged to follow them to the letter, the EU would rarely have been able to agree on principles, and then only on relatively harmless issues. Even with agreement about the desirability of joint action on something significant, the procedures were so daunting that the EU would arrive on the scene too late to do much. The CFSP was thus initially more of a declaration of intent that the EU would eventually enter into the foreign policy area than it was an immediately practical set of policies.* It was not surprising, therefore, that the EU's foreign policy after Maastricht was generally ineffective. Yugoslavia provides the major, and most damaging, case, although there have been others—Rwanda, for example. Maastricht's vision of common European defense removed an important taboo, but the consequences were small until the end of the 1990s, when new Franco-British leadership began processes leading to the establishment of the new rapid-reaction force supported by new materiel (see Chapter 2).[26]

Maastricht's "third pillar," justice and home affairs (JHA), was also initially inchoate. This pillar was deemed necessary because of the problems that removing internal borders and allowing the free movement of people inside the EU had created. Asylum and immigration policy, rules about external borders and customs cooperation, judicial and police cooperation, fraud, and the free circulation of criminals were high on the problem list. JHA had roots in the 1985 Schengen declaration by France, Germany, and the Benelux countries, which allowed removal of internal border controls between signatories. Schengen itself was adopted by most other EU members, excepting Denmark, the United Kingdom, and Ireland, then formalized as an EU "legal convention" in 1990. Some transnational cooperation among police forces also preceded

Maastricht through the so-called Trevi group, which Maastricht's Title VI sought to formalize. This then opened paths to broader cooperation by specifying questions of common interest, including asylum policy, rules for external border controls, immigration, the fight against drugs, policies against international fraud and terrorism, and judicial, police, and customs cooperation. Because matters like internal security and crime control are fundamentally national, Maastricht's third pillar became intergovernmental.

Progress on Pillar 3 was halting until the Amsterdam Treaty, however, when the Schengen *acquis*—with which few were really familiar—was finally inserted into the treaties. Schengen's apparatus, including information-circulating techniques and agreements about transnational surveillance and police pursuit, has been difficult to generalize, however. The issues dealt with by national ministers of the interior include information and matters that member states have always been very reluctant to disclose, let alone share with others. Moreover, some EU members doubted others' reliability in upholding deals, in particular because of the growing political salience of issues concerning immigration. By 1996, free circulation of individuals inside the single market had begun in only seven out of fifteen member states. Difficult discussions went on about immigration policy and on a common (more restrictive) asylum policy. The establishment of Europol—an organization to centralize police information and exchanges, proposed by the Germans—stalled in disagreements among member states. JHA was clearly needed, but national interior ministries—often very reclusive, secretive, and self-protecting—were not eager to do much in response.

Amsterdam decided to shift parts of the third pillar, particularly those dealing with migration, immigration, and related policies, into Pillar 1 and made subject to the "Community Method." Policing and related judicial matters remained intergovernmental, but what they entailed was rewritten. Thus, in 1999, the Commission established a new directorate-general for JHA. Transfer

*The EU has observed elections, engaged in some regulation of goods that can be used for both civilian and military purposes plus antipersonnel mines, decreed sanctions on egregious international miscreants, and sent out humanitarian and other aid packages to ex-Yugoslavia and Palestine.

of migration competencies was to be completed within five years, decided by unanimity in the Council. In the meantime, the Commission had to build up its knowledge and processes, and the ongoing important issues had to be dealt with. In general, JHA matters, whether—eventually—transferred to Pillar 1 or continued on an intergovernmental basis, remained murky; interministerial cooperation was halting; and governments were either reticent, confused, or both,

about what to do. September 11, 2001, came as a wake-up call, at least on the policing and intelligence side.[27]

EMU, CFSP, and European defense are all new matters, works in progress that are changing rapidly in form and content. Chapter 5 focuses on the key evolutionary processes for the EU in the first years of the new millennium and returns to these works in progress in their unfolding, sometimes quite surprising, detail.*

*There are other European institutions of lesser importance. For example, a Court of Auditors scrutinizes financial operations, reviews EU accounts, and evaluates financial and budgetary management. There is also an Economic and Social Committee (ECOSOC), which must be consulted by the Commission and Council on economic and social issues (even though ECOSOC's opinions have no binding effect). ECOSOC is composed of appointed delegates from national labor movements, employers, profes-

sionals, and consumer organizations; it meets ten times a year in plenary and more often in specialized subgroups and is an essential sounding board for EU institutions concerning the likely reception of new policies by organized interests. Finally, Maastricht established a new Committee of Regions along the ECOSOC model. Its purposes are similar, directed toward regionalizing consciousness of the EU and creating more direct linkages between regional actors and EU institutions.

Notes

1. Each MEP had offices, faxes, and computers in two different places, between which he or she had to travel several times a month. Committees and party groups met in Brussels. Strasbourg was mainly where the Parliament met in plenary session. A fleet of trucks transported parliamentary files and other materials from Brussels to Strasbourg and back each month.

2. The enormous and indispensable EU website is at http://europa.eu.int.

3. The web address for the European Union in the United States is www.eurunion.org.

4. The Amsterdam Treaty introduced a new clause (Article 163 EEC) that "the Commission shall work under the political guidance of the President," but it is too soon to know what difference this has made.

5. An A-1 official with longevity can earn up to 15,000 euros monthly, roughly $200,000 annually, at present exchange rates.

6. For a long time French was predominant, partly because the Commission was designed and built by the French and the Belgians. Since the mid-1990s, however, English has made advances. German is rarely used.

7. One observer, a former member of Jacques Delors's personal staff, calculated that in the very busy year of 1991 only 6 percent of the Commission's proposals came from the Commission's own initiatives (a similar count in 1998 estimated 5 to 10 percent). Twenty-eight percent were linked to international agreements; 21 percent followed requests from the Council and/or member states; 17 percent modified existing texts or were needed because of ECJ decisions; 12 percent resulted from general framework programs approved by the Council (research and development, for example); 8 percent were obligatory under the treaty (setting agricultural prices, among other things); and 8 percent originated from requests from firms, particularly concerning trade practices (requests for antidumping actions, for example). The 1991 statistics are from Fabrice Fries, *Les Grands Débats Européens* (Paris: Éditions du Seuil, 1995). The 1998 estimate is from John Peterson and Elizabeth Bomberg, *Decision-Making in the European Union* (New York: St. Martin's Press, 1999), p. 38.

8. The new "subsidiarity" clause was vague and general. The consequence was significant intimidation of the Commission, which became exceedingly careful when it acted.

9. *Financial Times*, March 11–12, 1995.

10. There are two COREPERs. The second is where the ambassadors work on higher political matters; the first is where their deputies work out more technical issues.

11. Fiona Hayes-Renshew and Helene Wallace, *The Council of Ministers of the European Union* (London: Macmillan, 1997), p. 98.

12. There is also a Special Agriculture Committee that, an exception proving the rule, is not in the COREPER orbit.

13. Rotation was alphabetical by country when the EU was smaller. For some time, however, it has rotated in a more planned way.

14. On the Council presidency see Emil Kirchner, *Decision-Making in the European Community: The Council Presidency and European Integration* (New York: St. Martin's Press, 1992).

15. The Presidency Conclusions for the most recent European Councils are downloadable from http://europa.eu.int.

16. On the Parliament see Martin Westlake, *A Modern Guide to the European Parliament* (London: Pinter, 1994).

17. The treaty specified that the mode of election should be uniform across the Community, but uniformity has not quite been achieved. All EU countries except the United Kingdom, which sticks with its traditional first-past-the-post single-member-constituency system, use some form of proportional representation.

18. The other, much smaller, groups include, in order of strength, the Liberals, the Greens, the European Democratic Alliance, the European Right, Left Unity (Communists), and the Rainbow Group. There are also a few unaffiliated members.

19. This is the consensus of different studies of the 1994 polls. See Cees van der Eijk and Mark N. Franklin, eds., *Choosing Europe* (Ann Arbor: University of Michigan Press, 1996), and Juliet Lodge, ed., *The 1994 Elections to the European Parliament* (London: Pinter, 1996).

20. For a revealing ethnographic view of the Parliament see Marc Abelès, "Political Anthropology of a Transnational Institution: The European Parliament," in *French Politics and Society* 11, 1.

21. See Shirley Williams, "Sovereignty and Accountability in the European Community," in Robert Keohane and Stanley Hoffmann, *The New European Community* (Boulder: Westview, 1991).

22. The Parliament had an epiphany in 1999. During much of the Santer period there was parliamentary restlessness about the Commission's sloppy work habits, cronyism, and even corruption. Matters came to a head in later 1998 at a very hard-nosed parliamentary plenary session about the "discharge" (book closing) of the 1996 budget. A successful censure vote might then have occurred had the two major party groups agreed on what to do. Instead, the Socialist group, afraid of provoking an institutional crisis, backed off. In a gesture of reconciliation, and perhaps in relief at getting off the hook, the Commission agreed that an independent committee of experts should investigate the charges. The committee's report, issued on March 15, 1999, was a crushing indictment of the Commission. In general, as the report noted, "It is becoming difficult to find anyone [in the Commission] who has even the slightest sense of responsibility." With this report in hand, the Parliament looked set to pass a censure vote. Instead, the Commission resigned as a bloc.

23. Klaus-Dieter Borchardt, *The ABC of Community Law* (Luxembourg: European Commission, 2000), provides a solid introduction to the EU's legal order.

24. The original treaties dealt mainly with Europeans as "workers"—that is, marketized individuals. It was the European Court of Justice that progressively expanded this notion to incorporate broader dimensions of citizenship, laying the groundwork for the insertion of citizenship into the treaty.

25. Political cooperation occurred at four different levels: at European Council meetings; at meetings of foreign ministers wearing their EPC hats (as opposed to their Council of Ministers caps—a venue that often caused the very same people to change the name of the conversations they were carrying on); at regular meetings of the "political committee," which included the political directors of foreign ministers plus the Commission political director; and at various working group meetings. EPC is presided over by the Council presidency.

26. The Amsterdam Treaty, recognizing the deficiencies and vagueness of Maastricht's CFSP formulations, created high representatives for CFSP and the new policy tool of "common strategies" toward countries and/or regions. The Nice European Council in 2000 further established a Political Security Committee, a

European Union Military Committee (EUMC), and a European Union Military Staff (EUMS, composed of military experts seconded by member states and responsible to EUMC). These changes were followed in 2002 by the establishment of a European Institute for Security Studies in Paris and a European Union Satellite Center just outside Madrid. The second Iraq war demonstrated yet again, however, that when member states disagreed fundamentally on a major issue, Mr. CFSP had to be speechless.

27. Monica den Boer and William Wallace, "Justice and Home Affairs: Integration Through Incrementalism?" chap. 18, in Helen Wallace and William Wallace, *Policy-Making in the European Union* (Oxford: Oxford University Press, 2000).

C H A P T E R

4

The EU and Its Policies

Policymaking in the European Union is not easy to understand, particularly when compared with national processes, largely because the EU is not a state, but rather the core of a complex system of multilevel governance. The actions of EU institutions are difficult enough to follow, but they also are networked in innumerable linkages with member states and European civil society organizations. When the EU is involved in making policy, therefore, it does so together with other jurisdictions, whether transnational, national, regional, or local. Furthermore, as Chapter 2 shows, the relative power and resources of different European institutions change as policy develops. In what follows, we present policymaking narratives that will illustrate the EU's policymaking uniqueness in key issue areas.

The Single Market

Market integration has always been the core of the EU. After the Common Market faltered in the 1970s, the program to complete the single-market program revived, arguably even saved, European integration. Initiated by the Delors Commission in 1985, it demonstrated the space for policy creativity that the Commission had in the EU institutional triangle in the right circumstances. The program generated changes in the EU's treaties, particularly in providing for the widespread use of qualified majority voting (QMV), which, in turn, strengthened the Commission and the European Parliament.

The Commission's 1985 White Paper on Completing the Internal Market brought new economic objectives, new economic integration, and, ultimately, political integration on the EU agenda. Its logic emphasized deregulation and market building to give firms greater economic space to innovate, grow, and develop capacities to win on a global scale, while transforming national economic outlooks toward new European perspectives. The single market involved relocating some sovereignty to the market itself, away from the member states accustomed to deciding many market regulations in political ways. It also created openings for "reregulation" on a European level, because of the need for complementary legislation in competition, environmental, regional, commercial, research and development, and other policy areas. The 300-odd measures proposed in the White Paper had become 1,475 by 2002. Table 4.1 describes the major axes of the "1992" program.

EU legislative output during 1985–1992 was vast, easily comparable to that of any member state, although it slowed considerably thereafter. Planning was itself an immense job because measures had to be scheduled over eight years and year-by-year priorities coordinated with the Council and Parliament. Under the guidance of a commissioner for the internal market, the whole Commission and its administrations had to draft specific proposals, which simultaneously involved political strategizing and wide consultation with interests, committees, national-level administrations, the Committee of Permanent

Table 4.1   Synopsis of "1992" White Paper Provisions

Measures to Regulate	Markets for			
	Products	*Services*	*Persons/ Labor*	*Capital*
Market access	Abolition of internal border controls Approximation of technical regulations, value-added tax, and excise taxes	Mutual recognition, end licensing restrictions in banking and insurance, transport deregulation (air and road)	End of border controls on persons Relaxation of residence requirements for EU citizens Right of establishment for professionals	Abolition of exchange controls Securities issued in one country admitted in another Facilitation of industrial cooperation and migration of firms
Competition	Paper on state aids to industry Liberalize public procurement Merger control	New competition policy for air transport Approximation of fiscal and/or regulatory practices	European "vocational training" card	Proposals on takeovers and holdings Approximation of double taxation, security taxes, parent-subsidiary links
Market functioning	Proposals on research and development in telecoms and information technology, standards, trademarks, corporate law, and the like	Approximation of regulation in banking, consumer protection in insurance, EU permits for road haulage EU standard for bank cards	Approximation of income and training provisions for migrants Mutual recognition of diplomas	European economic interest grouping European company statute Harmonization of property laws Common bankruptcy provisions
Sectoral policy	CAP changes Reduce steel subsidies	Common crisis regime in road transport, air transport policies, rules on mass risks insurance	Silence on labor market	Strengthen European Monetary System

Source: Adapted from Table 4.2 in Helen Wallace and William Wallace, *Policymaking in the European Union*, 4th ed. (New York: Oxford University Press, 2000), pp. 95–96.

Representatives (COREPER), and other Council bodies. Prepared texts had to be negotiated with Council and Parliament until a result was achieved. Member states had then to transpose the new measures into national law, monitored and policed by the Commission through resort to the European Court of Justice if necessary.

One of the more daunting tasks was harmonizing technical standards and norms. Traditionally this had happened in lengthy multilateral negotiations between member states that usually bogged down and often failed. The 1985 White Paper proposed using the new technique of "mutual recognition," facilitated by the *Cassis de Dijon* ruling of the European Court of Justice (ECJ) allowing products legally marketed in any member state to circulate freely throughout the EU. There was also a "new approach" in which EU directives could set out minimal standards across a broad range of similar products and processes, to which member states adjusted their own practices. The White Paper also necessitated legislation to promote the compatibility of different utility and transport systems. Promoting voluntary creation of European norms and standards for products was contracted out to semipublic European standards organizations.

Deregulation and reregulation for food and agricultural products was a huge job that called for harmonizing public health standards and specifying additives and materials in contact with food processing, labeling, food hygiene, and the like. This proved particularly controversial, leading to constant accusations about the Brussels bureaucracy's determination to regulate ancient local tastes. The Danes were thus forbidden to use an additive to color imitation Greek feta cheese. The French went into a mild uproar about regulations on natural Camembert cheese. The British press had a field day when an administrative mistake about additives threatened to forbid the production of flavored potato chips. The Germans, who penalized beers not brewed to German standards, had to be taken to the ECJ. Controversies over the height of tractor seats and pollution standards for cars were fierce.

Limits on market liberation were needed to protect against "races to the bottom" by countries seeking competitive advantage through lower levels of regulation. Public services (utilities, certain transportation networks) also needed sheltering from market mechanisms, but the extent of such sheltering was a difficult issue. The "1992" program led to deregulation in insurance, telecommunications, international transport, and audiovisual transmission. Free

movement of people was a most difficult area, partly because of intergovernmental problems of police and judiciary cooperation. Even so, rights of EU citizens to work and live in member states other than their own were established, plus procedures for recognizing the equivalencies of professional certifications. Finally, the single market brought major advances in consumer protection.

The program was not completed on time, and the Commission continued producing directives after 1992. Opening up markets in the services was particularly troublesome, for example, necessitating a special "internal market strategy for services" in 2000. Movement on food, veterinary, and plant health standards, intellectual and industrial property, and corporate taxation was also slow. Opening public procurement still remains far away in some areas. Transport, energy, and telecommunications sectors were not in the "1992" program but were gradually phased in later, often through Commission efforts. Liberalization of air transport, done in three successive "packages," has virtually eliminated the ability of member states to protect national airlines from competition through subsidies and has contributed to lower airfares. National telecommunications markets were opened to competition in 1999, cutting back price gouging by national monopolies, prodding innovation, and promoting new growth. An important proposal on European company law to allow European-level incorporation remained in contention until the Nice Summit in 2000. Conflict over what constitutes "services of general public utility," which could still be run as national monopolies, persists.

Integrating financial services and markets has been very hard, despite measures taken to open markets in banking, insurance, and securities trading, the introduction of the euro, and new electronic technologies. Financial services and markets and their place in the broader economic life have always been strongly national in Europe—hence resistance to rapid change. The financial sector in general has been classically prone to market failures, with bad economic outcomes often occurring because of the informational advantages that financial professions have over ordinary consumers. There can be no question, therefore, of making the financial sector a "free" market through Europeanization. Instead European reregulation is needed, but deciding what it should be and overcoming large vested interests to make it happen have not been easy. Slow integration has nonetheless left EU Europe behind its competitors. European capital markets are much smaller than their U.S. counterparts, for example. In 1996, the three largest EU stock exchanges (London, Paris, Frankfurt) averaged 12.8 billion euros in trade per day, as compared with Nasdaq at $13 billion and the New York Stock Exchange at $16 billion.[1] The Commission produced an action plan to speed things up, to be completed in 2005. But if member states do not want to have a single market in financial services and markets, they will probably prevent one from coming.

The single market has not been the magic economic bullet to propel the EU to world economic leadership that its advocates claimed. Still, the EU is undoubtedly more efficient and entrepreneurial with the single market than it would have been without it. The Commission's Internal Market Directorate-General concludes that EU gross domestic product (GDP) in 2002 was 1.8 percent higher because of the single market, that 2.5 million jobs have been created that would not have existed otherwise, that there has been a cumulative added value of 877 billion euros, that the single market has allowed EU firms to compete more effectively in global markets, and that the changes have made Europe a more attractive destination for foreign direct investment (FDI). In general, the single market has benefited European consumers by producing better choices, cheaper prices, lower airfares, and more mobility.

The EU Budget

Analyzing budgets is an exercise that reveals fundamental political truths, as is shown by the EU budgetary trends presented in Tables 4.2 and 4.3.

A Small Budget with Big Impact

The most significant insight offered by these numbers is that the EU budget, even though it expanded rapidly from the 1980s through the 1990s, is still small compared with national budgets.[2] The EU is held to a total expenditure level of less than 1.27 percent of the total members' GNP, which it has never reached. In contrast, the average budgets of EU member states hover around 40 percent of their GDP. EU poli-

---

Table 4.2   Financial Perspective Through 2000 (billions of ecu's)

	1993	1994	1995	1996	1997	1998	1999
Agriculture	35.23	35.1	35.72	36.36	37.02	37.7	38.4
Structural funds	21.28	21.88	23.48	24.99	26.53	28.24	30.0
Internal policies	3.94	4.08	4.32	4.52	4.71	4.91	5.1
External action	3.95	4.0	4.28	4.56	4.83	5.18	5.6
Administration	3.28	3.38	3.58	3.69	3.8	3.85	3.9
Reserves	1.5	1.5	1.1	1.1	1.1	1.1	1.0
Total	69.77	69.94	72.48	75.22	77.99	80.98	84.09
% Gross domestic product	1.20	1.19	1.20	1.21	1.23	1.25	1.26

Source: *Official Journal of European Communities* (93/C 331/01).

Table 4.3 Financial Perspectives Through 2006, EU15 (billions of euros, 1999)

	2000	*2001*	*2002*	*2003*	*2004*	*2005*	*2006*
Agriculture	40.9	42.8	43.9	43.8	42.8	41.9	41.7
Structural operations	32.0	31.5	30.9	30.3	29.6	29.6	29.2
Internal policies	5.9	6.0	6.1	6.3	6.4	6.5	6.6
External action	4.6	4.6	4.6	4.6	4.6	4.6	4.6
Administration	4.6	4.6	4.7	4.8	4.9	5.0	5.1
Reserves	0.9	0.9	0.6	0.4	0.4	0.4	0.4
Pre-accession aid	3.1	3.1	3.1	3.1	3.1	3.1	3.1
Total	89.6	91.1	94.2	94.9	91.9	90.1	90.7
% Gross national product	1.13	1.12	1.18	1.19	1.15	1.13	1.13

Source: David Galloway, "Agenda 2000—Packaging the Deal," in Geoffrey Edwards and Georg Wiessala, eds., *The European Union, Annual Review 1998/1999* (Oxford: Blackwell, 1999), Table 1, p. 21.

cies may shape member state expenditure patterns without the EU spending a great deal, but the EU's financial clout is clearly smaller than those of its member states. In this respect, as in others, the EU is not really a state but not quite a nonstate.

Combined, the Common Agricultural Policy (CAP) and structural funds comprise around 80 percent of EU spending. Both are redistributive. The CAP takes revenues from taxpayers (and consumers) and redistributes them to farmers (often larger ones) and rural areas, to a degree across national boundaries. The structural funds promote development by transferring money from wealthier to poorer areas of the EU. Were one to remove these two items, the EU budget would be very small indeed. Funding in other areas, including the EU's spending inside and outside its boundaries, is only 20 percent of the total budget.

Tables 4.2 and 4.3 also show that EU budgets grew in the 1980s, then stabilized in the late 1990s. Thereafter, finding additional money for any purpose, new or old, became hard to do. On the other hand, it has also been difficult for the EU to reduce spending in its key budgetary items. On the CAP side, reform has involved

close to steady-state spending to placate EU15 agricultural interests, making the quest for additional funding to phase new members into EU agricultural policy norms practically a zero-sum game. A similar problem exists for the structural funds, where finding pre-accession funding for East European members demands reconfiguring general guidelines at the expense of some current EU members. The 1999 Berlin budget deal, which did allocate big sums for the countries of Central and Eastern Europe (CEECs), was also constrained to conclude that any general reconfiguration of the funds would only apply fully to the structural funds at the end of the next budgetary period, probably 2013. In the meantime, money is short, and there is intense bargaining.

Transferring national revenues to other nations in the broader interests of "Europe" is one of the more interesting modifications of national sovereignty flowing from European integration. Table 4.4 provides a rough index of these transfers in recent years. This redistribution has always been precarious, however. As noted in Chapter 2, the British were too eager to get in in the 1970s and they ended up paying disproportionately, leading to the "British Check" issue and Prime Minister Thatcher's strident "I want

Table 4.4   Member State Shares in EU Financing and EU15 GNP (1997 data)

Country	Share in EU GNP	Share in Financing EU Budget
Austria	2.6	2.8
Belgium	3.1	3.9
Denmark	1.9	2.0
Finland	1.4	1.4
France	17.2	17.5
Germany	26.0	28.2
Greece	1.5	1.6
Ireland	0.8	0.9
Italy	14.2	11.5
Luxembourg	0.2	0.2
Netherlands	4.5	6.4
Portugal	1.2	1.4
Spain	6.6	7.1
Sweden	2.7	3.1
United Kingdom	16.1	11.9

Source: Wallace and Wallace, *Policymaking in the European Union*, Table 8.3, p. 234.

my money back" and willingness to block EU progress on other issues. Subsequent British governments have protected the deal on their "check" through thick and thin, even though it is no longer justifiable.

The EU budget stabilized in the late 1990s because members insisted on clear limits to transfers of their taxpayers' contributions to other member states. And even if countries continue to accept redistribution, the issue of proportionality remains: What is a "fair" contribution, measured against those of others, and what criteria should be used to decide? The common policies that redistribute EU revenues affect member states in unexpected ways. The British have always felt unjustly treated because the CAP favors countries with large agricultural establishments (France's, for example), while

Britain's agricultural presence is small. Yet the shortfall in United Kingdom contributions shown in Table 4.4 explains growing impatience on the part of other EU members with the continuing "rebate" that Prime Minister Margaret Thatcher negotiated in 1984. The Spanish, despite their relative poverty, feel similar to the British.

The Budgetary Process

Since the mid-1980s, the budgetary process has had two steps. The first and most important one is an intergovernmental "grand rendezvous" every five years or so to agree on medium-term spending patterns. There have been three complete package times—in 1987, 1992, and 1998–1999—with dealings on a fourth beginning in 2004. Agreement reached, the "triangle" institutions then pledge budgetary discipline to keep within guidelines. These programs allow middle-range planning for EU activities and free EU institutions from annual financial squabbling. But "package" negotiations themselves have become a moment of truth when member state priorities are expressed in the hard currency of financial commitment.

The Commission drafts the "package," assessing what it thinks member states are willing to accept and finding a strategy for funding what it most wants to pursue. The Commission typically asks for more than it can expect in anticipation of eventual compromise, making tough dealing inevitable. The Commission's budget package papers—for example, *Making a Success of the Single Act: A New Frontier for Europe* (1987); *From the Single Act to Maastricht and Beyond: The Means to Match Our Ambitions* (1987); and *Agenda 2000* (1997)—are always built around the Union's large objectives, often themselves the result of treaty changes, and provide invaluable indicators about the Commission's goals.[3]

Leaders negotiate the final compromise at European Councils. In 1988, after the first Delors package had been turned down once before, member states pledged to double regional development funds over five years, signed on to controlled growth of CAP spending, and agreed to a new "fourth resource" tied to GNP and a new "own resource ceiling" so that, by 1992, the EU budget would not exceed 1.2 percent of member states' combined GDPs.[4] Despite the fact that the later 1980s were years of economic growth, the package passed only because the Germans were willing to pay for it.[5] At Edinburgh in 1992, the deal on a "financial perspective" covering 1993 to 1999 involved another near-doubling of regional policy funding, reflecting the power and resolution that the "cohesion" countries had come to have in EU financial struggles. But economic circumstances had changed. The Germans faced huge unification costs and were unwilling to repeat their generous gesture of 1988. This, combined with recession, desire on the part of some member states to slow down European integration, and public disenchantment, meant that the Commission did not do as well in 1992 as it had in 1988.[6] A similar situation existed for the *Agenda 2000* discussions at the end of the 1990s. Because of transfers associated with the coming enlargement, almost all of the EU15 were becoming "net contributors." Again the Germans were determined not to write new checks, and net contributors were in general determined to pay less. Yet the French refused to allow cuts to the CAP, and Spain, followed by other southern members of the EU15, adamantly opposed financing enlargement at the expense of their structural funds. Everyone except the Commission was against continued budget growth, and the result was a "stabilized" EU budget, despite imminent enlargement.

The second level of the budgetary process is annual discussion on expenditures. The European Parliament, with no control over revenues but power over expenditures, becomes an important participant. The exercise begins when the Commission drafts an annual budget, usually by late May, which goes to the Council and Parliament. The Council examines it (having had considerable input already), and the Parliament

officially adopts by the end of July. The draft budget has been divided between compulsory and noncompulsory expenditures, and the Council of Ministers has had final say over compulsory expenditures, defined as those items needed for the EU to meet its internal and external obligations—that is, treaty and legislative commitments like the CAP. The Parliament had the last word on noncompulsory expenditures. The balance between these two expenditure types shifted from 80-20 in the early 1980s to 50-50 by the mid-1990s, helping to make Parliament a prime target for lobbyists. The distinction between compulsory and noncompulsory expenditures will disappear after the 2004 Constitutional Treaty is ratified, making Council and Parliament equal participants.

The Parliament's first reading on the final annual budget draft occurs in early autumn of the preceding year, when it can ask for modifications up to a preestablished "maximum rate of increase." The revised draft then goes to the Council of Ministers for final decisions on compulsory expenditures in November. Parliament's second reading, in December, focuses on noncompulsory expenditures. Once it has reached its conclusions, the Parliament can accept the entire budget by a majority vote of its members and three-fifths of the votes actually cast. If it rejects the budget, a system of "provisional twelfths" comes on line, with monthly expenditures allowed only to the limit of one-twelfth of the previous year's total.

Parliament's involvement continues, however, in the "discharge procedure." When the budgetary year is over, the Commission must submit a financial statement that Parliament must "discharge," helped by a statement from the Council and a very important, and often critical, annual report from the EU's Court of Auditors.* The timing of the discharge procedure is complicated. During the first year after the end

*The Court of Auditors, in place since 1977 and based in Luxembourg, became a "European Institution" at Maastricht, giving it the power to bring cases to the ECJ.

of a particular budget, the Commission and the Court of Auditors prepare reports. It is not until the next year, or perhaps even two, that Council and Parliament actually review the auditors' report. The Council then must recommend to Parliament about voting, and Parliament itself debates and votes resolutions. In November of this second year, the Commission prepares a new report responding to Parliament's resolutions. Such a confusing timetable means that a five-year Parliament has to spend its first two years discharging two budgets that were implemented before it was elected. Moreover, in its entire term, a Parliament only considers two budgets in which it has been directly involved. The discharge procedure is important, despite its complexity. It was a discharge debate (on the 1996 budget at the end of 1998) that began the processes leading to the momentous resignation of the Santer Commission in 1999.

"Horizontal" Policies

The EU treaties have created "horizontal" common policies in which member states have conferred quasi-governmental power on the Commission, even though its initiatives are scrutinized and constrained by member states in varying ways. Competition policy, regional development, social policy, environmental policy, and fiscal policy are the most important.

Competition Policy

Articles 85 to 94 of the Rome Treaty established a policy to ensure that "competition in the internal market is not distorted." Article 90 applied less stringent rules to publicly owned undertakings. Article 89 granted the European Commission exclusive responsibility for enforcing these rules, such that its rulings are not submitted to Council votes and are subject only to judicial review by the ECJ. The object has been to provide instruments to knock down artificial walls protecting special producer interests and states inside the EU.

The Commission does most of Europe's larger antitrust enforcement on its own, a rare federal activity. Anticompetitive firm behavior—unfair market power, trusts, and monopolies—is outlawed, and the Commission reviews cases above a certain minimum size. It also reviews any state aid to firms (subsidies, grants, special tax advantages, etc.) that could create unfair market advantage. Its powers were enhanced after 1989 when, after seventeen years of hesitation, it acquired the right to oversee and control mergers.[7] The Commission can impose penalties for violations. To account for its actions in this area, the Commission must submit an annual report to the European Parliament.

The Commission's powers are both negative—prevention of illegal behaviors—and positive—regulatory and authorizing. The Commission's Competition DG is charged with most of the work. It has a two-hundred-strong A-level staff of lawyers and economists monitoring conditions, devouring the business press, and observing market developments, with special merger control units since 1989. The Competition DG can request information from firms and carry out investigations. Member state governments are required to notify the Commission of aids and subsidies. Each year the Competition DG looks into hundreds of cases, submits the most important to broader Commission consideration, and informs member states when their state aid practices are under investigation. Commission proceedings are often heated because competition matters are important to member state governments and firms. Commission credibility can be at stake, and there is give and take. The ECJ ultimately sets limits to the Commission's operations by way of litigation, and a specific Court of First Instance handles most competition cases.

Commission investigations of potential violations are quite often ended informally in negotiations that lead firms and member states to redefine their plans. When informal dealing fails, the Commission may levy quite substantial fines—French state-owned companies like Renault and Pechiney, the Belgian chemical giant Solvay, and the Swiss-Swedish packaging company Tetrapak were all fined in the early 1990s, for example. Major cartels have been ferreted out and dismantled in several areas, even if the play of national interests may have allowed other potential violations to escape sanctions. The most spectacular recent ruling has been against U.S. software giant Microsoft's "bundling" practices, still under litigation after a Microsoft appeal to the ECJ.

Merger control regulation, in effect since 1989, has provided the Community with a powerful new tool, first used in 1991 when the Commission voted to forbid the takeover by Alenia-Aerospatiale, a producer of commuter airliners, of DeHavilland Canada, a North American company. The procedure usually involves legal judgments about the nature of markets and the likely restraint of trade were the merger to be allowed. The number of merger cases considered has increased each year to reach the hundreds, in the process creating clearer procedures and jurisprudence. The Commission has struck down only a few large merger deals, but when it has, there have often been global implications, exemplified when it prevented U.S. giants General Electric and Honeywell from merging even though U.S. authorities had already approved. More often mergers are allowed after company plans are reformulated to meet the Competition DG's concerns.

The problem of state assistance to companies is difficult because jobs and votes may be at stake. Moreover, some member state governments—and not only the French—have traditions of state-centered industrial policy, notwithstanding the single market. Community competition law has nonetheless become active and effective when government-controlled companies engage in commercial activities and where governments have acted like private owners. In the airline industry, for example, heavily subsidized national carriers have run up against Commission efforts to deregulate the EU airline market. The treaty also grants the Commission certain powers to deregulate in telecommunications and energy (in Article 90). Promoting "third-party access" to national monopoly energy networks caused endless political disputes, with the introduction of energy liberalization stalled until after 1999. Telecommunications deregulation took a decade until it began in 1998 and stimulated frenetic mergers and acquisition action. The Commission and Community have also become much more active in regulating intellectual property.

Complicated jurisprudence separates EU competition policy competencies from those of national governments and courts. In smaller matters, the Commission observes a *de minimis* rule (e.g., a threshold below which the EU does not act). Moreover, the area is in constant evolution. For public services, opening markets without undercutting the equitable provision of public goods remains a legal and political frontier. The private sector has also been in persistent furor over threats to exclusive distribution arrangements—car dealerships constrained contractually by manufacturers, for example—and franchises. There has also been persistent debate about establishing an EU antitrust agency independent of the Commission, but this has never reached a point of decision, even if a measure of decentralization to member state levels on antitrust matters was decided in 2004.

Regional Development

Regional development funding—the "structural funds"—is the EU's second-largest budgetary item and an expression of solidarity between better-off and less developed regions. It was not always thus. There was slight bowing to regional development in the Rome Treaty, a payoff to the Italians for their underdeveloped southern regions. A European Regional Development Fund (ERDF) was then founded in the 1970s to complement development in agriculture, but the funds were small, uncoordinated, and often seen as supplements to member state national budgets.

Enlargement to poorer countries (Ireland in 1973, Greece in 1981, Spain and Portugal in 1986) led to more energetic efforts. The Single European Act (SEA) made "economic and social cohesion" a new common policy, and the reform of the structural funds in 1988 sought to target the combined effects of the three funds on regional development while doubling their financing over five years. The Delors II budgetary package in 1993 brought another doubling by 1999. The third budgetary package in 1999 was more complex because of commitment to pre-accession help for the countries of Eastern and Central Europe. The amounts have become quite large, upwards of 40 billion dollars by 1997.

Until 1999, general structural fund principles concentrated on priority objectives to promote partnership—close cooperation between the Commission and the "appropriate authorities" at "national, regional, and local levels." EU funds were allocated to complement, rather than replace, national funding, and to advance multiannual, multitask, and multiregional programs rather than uncoordinated individual national projects.[8] The Commission initially assumed a strong planning role. The priority objectives were as follows:

- Objective 1: Assisting underdeveloped regions
- Objective 2: Aid to deindustrialized regions
- Objective 3: Combating long-term (over twelve months) unemployment and integration of young people (under twenty-five) into the labor market
- Objective 4: Helping workers to adapt to technological change
- Objective 5: a. Structural reform of agriculture
  b. Aid to rural areas

After accession of Sweden and Finland in 1995, a sixth objective for Arctic regions was added.

For the period prior to *Agenda 2000*, all of Greece, Ireland, Portugal, Corsica, Sardinia, Sicily, southern Italy, all of Eastern Germany except Berlin, and most of Spain were Objective 1 areas and received roughly two-thirds of all

funding. The Maastricht Treaty added a "cohesion fund" to compensate "cohesion countries" for participation in the EU's environmental and transport policies. The amounts involved, modest in absolute terms, were significant in relationship to the investment needs of poorer EU15 countries. Throughout the 1990s, member states tried very hard to "renationalize" the financing process. Eastern Germany and southern Italy, for example, received more from the funds than comparable regions in other parts of Europe. This, plus scatter-plotting small projects funded from Brussels (indicating national patronage politics), demonstrate the working of factors other than those strictly related to regional development.[9]

After the Amsterdam Treaty, prospective enlargement began to change the picture. The Commission's *Agenda 2000* programmed steady-state structural fund spending (0.46 percent of Community GDP) through 2006 and set aside 20 percent of this for pre- and post-accession help to new EU members. This meant taking money from existing Western recipients, and the Commission redefined the objectives so that the percentage of the EU15 population getting some funding would drop from over 50 percent to 35–40 percent and cut the number of objectives to three. Objective 1, aiming at less developed regions, was retained with tougher eligibility criteria; Objective 2, aimed at declining areas, often in the EU15, was more precisely targeted; Objective 3 focused training and employment policies.

The EU15 "cohesion" areas whose living standards had risen above the cutoff point (75 percent of EU average GDP) tried to block the changes. Northern EU15 members then insisted on their pet projects for underdeveloped and declining areas. The Berlin 1999 results were not quite what the Commission had hoped for. Funding for prospective new members was protected, but the funding level was reduced, particularly in areas where the Commission had power. Key member states insisted on funding for "particular situations," structural fund principles and objectives notwithstanding. The Commission was weakened, and further renationalization occurred. The 2004 enlargement was bound to change existing arrangements even more.

The cumulative effects of the structural funds catch-up cannot yet be known. It is clear, however, that they have provided incentives to EU15 member states to avoid "races to the bottom" through strategies of low-wage and minimalist social policies. Regional levels of government in poorer areas have also developed stakes in European integration, a bonus. The structural funds have been good for many donor states because they have increased purchasing power in poorer areas to spend on goods and services from the rest of the EU. Structural funds have also been catalysts for administrative reforms in recipient states, with a considerable amount of money dedicated to this in the CEECs. Finally, EU regional development aid has helped consolidate democracy in the three southern countries that emerged from dictatorships in the 1970s, and it is likely that the same things will occur with the CEECs admitted in 2004.

Social Policy

Social policy, while a "horizontal" policy area, is also one where the EU has little formal power. The Treaty of Rome's social provisions were narrowly limited to labor market mobility, training, and equal opportunity for men and women (Article 119). The treaty also created a European Social Fund to make "the employment of workers easier, increasing their geographical and occupational mobility within the Community," but with vague indications about scope and implementation. The reasons for initial social policy modesty were not mysterious. The EU's founding coincided with the consolidation of modern European welfare states where social policy was the epicenter of national politics. The EU thus grew together with as wide a variety of social policy regimes as it had members.

Initial attempts to transcend EU weakness in social policy in the earlier 1970s failed. Progress in "equal opportunities" began only after the ECJ's 1976 *Defrenne v. Sabena* case (which made equal opportunity a matter of direct legal effect on individuals).[10] The 1985 White Paper made little mention of social policy either, excepting workplace health and safety.[11] The snail's pace of harmonization in health and safety prompted a "new approach" in the 1980s in which framework directives for products were limited to defining "essential safety requirements" or other "requirements of general interest" without detailed technical specifications. The new approach brought speedup in health and safety harmonization, but it took qualified majority in the SEA's Article 118A to accelerate the pace. Elsewhere in social policy areas decisions were governed by unanimity rules, even if the Commission was required to "take as a base a high level of protection" whenever measures concerned "health, safety, environmental protection and consumer protection." By the mid-1990s, a solid body of European-level health and safety regulation was on the books.

The Delors Commission's *Community Charter of Basic Social Rights for Workers* in 1989 was a "solemn commitment" to a set of "fundamental social rights" for employees, but it added nothing legally and instead sought to mobilize around any unfulfilled social promises that the Community's treaty base already contained. Any "teeth" the Social Charter had were contained in an Action Program proposing forty-seven different measures. Here, however, excepting health and safety, Council unanimity was required.

The SEA also included a new Article 118B stating that "the Commission shall endeavor to develop the dialogue between management and labor at European level, which could, if the two sides consider it desirable, lead to relations based on agreement." Commission efforts at getting the European-level "social partners" to bargain only began to work in the early 1990s under the pressure of the Maastricht negotiations, however. At

Maastricht, Commission proposals became a Social Protocol in which the Commission, when it
desired to propose social policy action, could first
ask the "social partners" to negotiate in the area.
If negotiations succeeded, the results could become EU legislation. If the "social partners" were
unable to negotiate, the Commission could
then go to legislation. With this in the treaty,
European-level employers, to that point opposed
to European-level bargaining, decided that accepting such a "negotiate or we'll legislate" clause
was preferable to legislation. British prime minister John Major refused to accept this proposal but
could not prevent the other eleven member states
from going ahead.

After the ratification of Maastricht in 1993,
the Commission proposed a directive for establishing European Works Councils (EWCs) in
multinational companies that had been blocked
several times since 1970. EWCs would encompass all of an undertaking's operations within
the EU, with competence limited to transnational, as opposed to national, matters concerning the group in question. The "social partners"
decided that they preferred legislation to bargaining, however, and a directive was passed in
the fall of 1994. "Negotiated legislation" worked
for the Commission's next proposal in 1995,
leading to an agreement on parental leave. Negotiations to regulate different dimensions of
atypical work (part-time and short-term contracts) were successful in the later 1990s.

By the time the British signed the Social Protocol at Amsterdam in 1997, the EU had lost its
enthusiasm for legislating in core social policy
areas. Employment and competitiveness had become much more important concerns, and paths
shifted toward the decentralized "soft" procedures of the open method of coordination
(OMC) discussed in Chapter 2. The EU's direct
influence in social policy remains limited, therefore. What exists is a patchwork, including
"equal protection," health and safety legislation,
together with Social Charter directives, the
slight opening of EU-level bargaining, and the
OMC. The core welfare state is not part of any
conceivable EU mandate, except in indirect,
long-term ways. Conventional welfare state
matters remain solidly ensconced behind borders of national sovereignty.

European social policy has always been constructed around a concept of subsidiarity that is
now embedded in EU treaties. From the outset,
leaders decided that national polities were the
appropriate places for confronting the social
problems their citizens faced. The EU, in contrast, was better placed to promote policies to
promote the step-by-step development of a European market. This market-building approach
could not help but have major *indirect* effects on
national social policy dispositions, however, particularly after the 1970s, when the relative self-
sufficiency of national development models
broke down. Since the 1980s, the single market
and the Economic and Monetary Union (EMU)
have both been powerful influences over national social policies. Among other things, the
single-market program has been an instrument
to promote greater flexibility in labor markets,
enjoin wage restraint, and pressure social protection programs whose relative costs might become important factors in determining national
competitiveness. EMU, institutionalized in ways
that made monetary policy completely independent of national and European political influence, consolidated a new macroeconomic regime
that prioritized price stability over employment
and growth, and the Stability and Growth Pact
placed constraints on national budgetary and financial practices that limited the resources governments had for social policy purposes. There
are many other factors working to change national social policy practices, such as changed demographics, rising medical costs, and changing
workplaces, but European-driven market liberalization and monetary policymaking clearly play
important roles. The correlates have been declining trade unions, changes in labor laws to favor
employers more than they had, and strong pressures to reform welfare states. Social policy thus
demonstrates that the EU can have great indirect
effects even when it has few legal prerogatives.

Environmental and Fiscal Policies

Many environmental problems cannot be remedied effectively by national governments and are better addressed transnationally. Moreover, different national environmental standards might easily become nontariff barriers to trade. EU environmental policy has become quite important, therefore. The EU and the Commission's DG have worked primarily on the basis of multiyear action programs, which the Council and Parliament approve. The EU treaties set out general principles of policy formation—primacy on preventive action, "the polluter should pay," and correction at the source of the problem. Recent environmental programs have promoted the codes of conduct, particularly through "green labels" on products. The treaty also advocates that firms use an "eco-audit." A range of legislation has been passed about water and air pollution, noise, waste disposal, and transporting dangerous substances. Environmental impact assessments are now compulsory for all projects above a certain size. In general, EU action has raised environmental standards far above any low common denominator. EU-level environmental policy has also become a favorite of public opinion, and the Commission has tried very hard to reinforce this through new projects. The annual rating of the quality of bathing beach water was one way it devised to fly the EU flag.

By the 1990s, however, certain member states, like the United Kingdom, had begun to resent EU "meddling" in environmental matters. Others, like Spain, which received the new cohesion fund at Maastricht partly in compensation, objected to the high costs of compliance. The Commission's most daring proposal, a tax on CO_2 emissions, has been bogged down for years, however, and environmental policy has become a favorite target for arguments about subsidiarity. Nonetheless, EU environmental policy is in many respects a genuinely federal approach to environmental problems. It has been effective in deciding ways to share the diminution of greenhouse gas emissions, for example. The EU also is

an important international agent in multilateral environmental negotiations. Here, as in social policy, one sees today a mix of different approaches, reflecting a more mature recognition of the meaning of subsidiarity—with multiple policy foci ranging across global programs, EU-wide programs, and efforts to coordinate national and local policies.[12]

The EU has limited power over taxation. This is not surprising, because practically everything member states do depends on raising necessary revenues. Certain types of taxation make good nontariff barriers, however, and this has necessitated a Community role in indirect taxation—value-added taxes (VATs, general consumption taxes assessed on value added to goods and services) and excise taxes (on particular consumer goods of social and cultural importance—tobacco and alcohol, for example—often heavily taxed for health reasons). For VAT taxes, the single market demanded cross-border rate harmonization and, with "fiscal borders" removed, a new collection system. VAT levels were thus harmonized around 20 percent, with member states having constrained possibilities for declaring certain goods and services of fundamental social and cultural importance—food, books, medical fees, and a few others—and being eligible for reduced rates. VAT harmonization was surprisingly easy, even though it obliged member states to make significant changes to revenue raising. The issue of collection was easily resolved. Consumers paid the VAT tax where goods were purchased with an EU-level clearing system to prevent revenue shifts between states. For excise taxes, the Union promoted harmonization of structures and levels.

EU intervention in the realm of direct taxation—mainly income and wealth levies on individuals and corporations—has been more or less taboo. Variations in certain direct tax levels, particularly those on individual savings, could nonetheless establish advantages for member states in the single market. Given free capital movement, for example, savers might shop for tax havens to shelter their money. Confronting this took years because of member state opposition. In 1999 the EU decided that countries had two choices: either a uniform 15 percent tax or official notification about deposits to tax authorities in the depositor's country of residence. Harmonizing corporate profit taxation also became an issue because of the incentives that transnational companies had to manipulate national differences in shifting taxable income to lower-tax countries within the Union. Two important but insufficient directives were thus passed in the early 1990s. EU regulation of direct taxation remains an important issue, however, because of the possibilities of national "tax dumping" and because EMU will intensify the need for tax convergence to achieve optimal economic "policy mixes."

Sectoral Policies

The Common Agricultural Policy

The CAP continues to be a source of negative legend about European integration. It was put into the Rome Treaty to create a Common Market in agricultural products and modernize a then-backward Western European agricultural sector (Article 37). CAP financial administration went to a European Agricultural Guarantee and Guidance Fund (EAGGF) run by the Commission. The CAP's double-price system involved price supports for agricultural products in ways that kept Community prices simultaneously above what might otherwise have been market-clearing levels in the EU and above those on the world market. The Commission set internal or indicative prices for each agricultural product market and established intervention levels to enable the EAGGF to buy up products for storage and export when prices fell below a certain point.

Modernization happened quickly, and by 1968 European agriculture had become an important exporter. Perverse consequences came quickly as well. The double-price system encouraged farmers to produce too much, leading to surpluses that were stored at great expense

and, when necessary, dumped on the international market at prices below their production costs, affecting global price levels. Other major producers, including the United States and Australia, were incensed, even if they were not averse themselves to following similar practices from time to time. The CAP also created incentives for farmers to overuse chemical fertilizers, creating pollution and affecting water tables. These developments were worrisome enough to prompt serious reflection about change by the later 1960s, but by then farmers had created very powerful groups to protect their interests. The CAP and its costly absurdities thus persisted, along with the repeated budgetary crises and diplomatic problems connected to it.

DG Agriculture became the largest single administrative unit in Brussels. Inside its buildings, technocrats measured carrots, administered milk quotas, rented storage barns, and sold surplus goods on the world market. Because fraud was tempting in such highly regulated markets, DG Agriculture also policed farmers to make sure that they actually produced what they claimed. The DG spent vast amounts of money, tried valiantly to account for it, and projected how much more would be needed in years to come. And when these brave civil servants annually prepared to propose specific prices and regulations, they were lobbied incessantly by agriculture ministers and hard-nosed farmers' organizations that were not averse to mobilizing their sheep and cows in the streets of Brussels to get their way. Each particular product area had its own management committee, and the entire system was carefully tracked by the COREPER committee on agriculture.

The CAP has been redistributive in several ways, not all felicitous. In simple terms, it shifts income from taxpayers and consumers to farmers. It also shifts money from country to country: some member states have gotten more than others from the EU budget. Several poorer countries (Greece, Ireland, and Spain) along with two much wealthier ones (Denmark and France) have been big CAP beneficiaries, with Danish farmers getting the biggest per capita payments. Germany has lost the most, followed by Italy and the United Kingdom. The price support system, when it has led to the international dumping of agricultural goods, involves transfers from Europeans to non-European others plus storage costs. EU export subsidies had by the 1990s become the CAP's single largest spending category.[13] There are additional transfers between urban and rural areas, both to more inefficient agricultural regions and to very efficient producers, like French wheat farmers, hiding politically behind laggard colleagues.

Acrimonious intergovernmental negotiations about the CAP started soon after the CAP began. Certain member states, Britain and the Netherlands in particular, rebelled against big transfers to phantom Italian tobacco growers, Bavarian hop growers with Mercedes cars, gigantic French beet-sugar conglomerates, and prosperous Danes. Small changes began in the 1980s with new quotas on milk production, stabilizers to reduce subsidies automatically if dangerously high levels of production were reached, and multiyear budget projections. More serious CAP reform began in the early 1990s, when the CAP's price support system and international surplus dumping became barriers to completing the General Agreement on Tariffs and Trade (GATT) Uruguay Round. EU member states and manufacturers had high stakes in freer international trade, diminishing the clout of the protectors of the CAP. The Commission could thus use threats from GATT partners to corner farmers and their allies. Commission reforms reduced guaranteed price levels and shifted CAP aid toward land set-asides along U.S. lines—"deficiency payments"—rather than price supports. The battle was noisy, and the French came close to blocking CAP changes and the Uruguay Round, but reform was accepted in 1992. Movement since has been away from price supports and toward direct income subsidies. Because paying farmers off was an important part of the politics of reform, the new approach has not saved money, however. Fitting the CAP to East-

ern European agriculture has been a more recent challenge. When member states stabilized the EU budget at Berlin in 1999, they set up a zero-sum game between applicant countries and EU15 beneficiaries. The Poles and others were given transition periods before full participation in the CAP as a result.

Integrating new CEEC EU members will eventually oblige more reform, if international trade negotiations do not get there first. The international community remains at war with the CAP. The new dispute mechanisms of the World Trade Organization (WTO), for example, were clogged immediately by U.S. complaints about the EU's banana regime, an odd spectacle in which the EU tried to protect special arrangements for "ACP countries" (colonies and ex-colonies of Africa, the Caribbean, and the Pacific) against U.S. accusations made on behalf of two large companies (Chiquita and Dole), neither of which grew bananas in the United States. There were also WTO disputes about U.S. exports of hormone-fed meat and genetically modified agricultural products, which the EU is reluctant to accept, raising complicated questions about health risks in agricultural trade, intensified by Europe's mad cow disease scare.

One of the achievements of Pascal Lamy, the 1999–2004 trade commissioner, has been to maneuver a reluctant world into the WTO Doha Round. Since the United States and other important agricultural exporters have not given up attacking the CAP, pressure for reform is bound to intensify despite EU trade openness in other areas and its recent "everything but arms" approach to developing countries. The prospect of renewed collision between broader international trade questions and the CAP cannot be excluded, therefore. In the meantime, the EU has been arguing that agricultural subsidies are justified for environmental reasons.

Industrial and Research Policies

EU industrial policy stretches back to the European Coal and Steel Community (ECSC), which had strong powers over producers and did not hesitate to use them. More than once, for example, the ECSC invoked a situation of "manifest crisis" to implement structural changes. The Community more broadly has also been involved in similar activities to reconfigure troubled industries—restructuring shipbuilding and textiles, for example. It has often provided financial aid, subsidized training programs, trade protection to promote cooperation among firms, and voluntary trade restriction agreements with foreign producers. Most such actions have been of the bailout type. But by the 1990s, the structural funds had partly taken over the job of aiding rustbelt areas, and EU focus had shifted elsewhere.

Today's issue is the vulnerability of European industry, including its most up-to-date sectors, to more intense global competition. In the early 1980s the EU, prodded by Commission activism, began funding research and development (R&D). The pioneering Esprit program, which provided funding to transnational research cooperation among companies in the electronics area, is now but one example among many of EU-sponsored research and development efforts organized in a long list of different titles. The Esprit experience, however, illustrates the problems and paradoxes of promoting a European-level industrial backbone in electronics. The Information Society DG, the agency that administers such programs, has been accused by liberals of French-style *dirigisme* (statist planning) and of being in the pockets of the big electronics companies.

Despite such criticism, EU research and development programs have proliferated. The SEA granted the EU broader responsibilities in research and development, resulting in multiyear "framework programs" for research funding, put together by the Commission. The Fifth Framework Program for research and development for the period 1998–2002 totaled slightly more than $15 billion. The effort has been hampered by difficulties and controversies, however. European R&D efforts, largely national in focus, have been fragmented, and EU-level research

funding, subject to huge national pressures, may simply add another layer of fragmentation. Moreover, the EU has insufficient money to make much difference. In addition, given globalization, ascertaining whether the sectors to be helped are actually European anymore has become difficult. Should the EU help European firms deeply enmeshed in strategic alliances all over the world? Another large issue is whether the EU should promote pure research, or help firms bring products closer to the market. Heavy-handed Commission efforts to use standard-setting prerogatives for high-definition television in the early 1990s at the behest of large consumer electronics firms were a political and technical fiasco, as were similar efforts to use EU money to entice big computer firms into greater collaboration.

Divergent member state perspectives about industrial policy are not easily resolved. Those who believe that market signals should be the ultimate guide to producers' decisions, like the British, are skeptical. Others, like the French, believe that there needs to be a consciously woven European economic and industrial fabric to allow Europe to compete successfully. The Maastricht Treaty included a new clause allowing industrial policy but restricted it by requiring unanimity. It also included a clause about the need for trans-European networks in transport, telecommunications, and energy. The reluctance of the European Council to come up with the money has been patent, however.

The most important recent steps occurred at the Lisbon European Council—referred to by some as the "dot-com" meeting—in spring 2000. There EU heads of state and government declared that they would make the EU "the most competitive and dynamic knowledge-based economy in the world" by 2010, in the process restoring full employment. The new approach proposed a stronger liberalizing program to promote the "information society," more labor flexibility, and new social policy objectives, in the process generalizing the new "open method of coordination" (OMC) pioneered in the European Employment Strategy. Lisbon also proposed the development of a "European Research Area" to stimulate greater transnational cooperation among think tanks, universities, and other sources of innovation, with particular focus on use of the Internet. Progress has been limited, however, in large part because of a new recession that fell over most of Europe beginning in 2001. We return to these matters in Chapter 5.

Trade Policy

EU trade policy is central to European economic success and foreign policy. Forging a consistent trade policy toward the outside world has been one of the central pillars of a common, then single, market. By the 1990s, the EU had become tremendously important in international trade, by far the largest and most open zone in the global system, comprising 38 percent of world trade. Administering trade policy is a Commission responsibility, carried out by the International Trade DG. The international trade commissioner has become an important world figure, comparable to the U.S. trade representative. He bargains internationally on the basis of member state mandates and is in regular give-and-take with the Council and Parliament. EU member states have had different approaches to trade policy. Northern industrial countries are free traders who are loath to interfere in trade flows, while the south, including France, leans more toward managed trade for shaping domestic economies. Over time, the areas covered by international multilateral trade negotiations have expanded—from industrial goods to agriculture, services, and intellectual property rights, for example, in the GATT Uruguay Round. This has created a situation in which some matters are EU Commission responsibilities, some are "mixed," and some remain in member state hands.[14]

The EU gives privileged trade positions to the "ACP countries," whose trading relationships with Europe are regulated separately (the ACP countries are exempt from EU customs). It is these arrangements that fell afoul of the United States over bananas in disputes before the WTO. The Commission also negotiates for the EU in important multilateral trade venues such as GATT and WTO and deals with specific countries as well, largely through the EU's trade and diplomatic delegations in world capitals. The Uruguay Round, which lasted several years, saw conflicts between the EU and the United States over agriculture and ended in the substantial lowering of European trade subsidies of key agricultural products. Subsequent trade discussions over services and intellectual property ended with European-American agreement to disagree over trade in audiovisual materials, with Europe (behind which lay the French) insisting upon the cultural importance of protecting film and television.

The GATT Uruguay Round stimulated conflict inside the EU in ways that laid bare the hidden importance of external trade dealing to EU life, as we have discussed with reference to the CAP. The WTO, which emerged from the Uruguay Round, established a binding dispute resolution system with sanctions tougher than earlier GATT rulings. The first years of the WTO's life saw disputes between the United States and Europe about bananas, beef hormones, mufflers for airplanes, genetically modified organisms, and U.S. tax havens for exporters (the Foreign Sales Corporation). Managing endemic conflict has been a constant challenge. As the WTO's scope expands beyond manufacturing, international trade has become ever more important to the EU, and, in response, the EU is ever more preoccupied with international trade issues. In the first years of the new millennium, for example, the EU pushed to expand WTO dealings beyond manufactured and agricultural goods further into services, intellectual property, and trade-related investment. At the same time, the EU trade commissioner pushed to expand the areas in his EU negotiating mandate by incorporating new sectors where member states had earlier dealt on their own. Trade politics, in other words, has become ever more central to the EU internationally and an ever more significant matter in the EU's internal life.

Controversies about globalization and the centrality of international trade rules for developed and developing nations mean that trade issues will be central in years to come. As the dimensions of trade under the WTO's remit grow, for example, matters that used to remain outside trade talks, such as health, environmental, and labor standards, are on the table. Private diplomacy by large economic interests and the emergence of a lively international civil society composed of protest groups and nongovernmental organizations are now facts of life. The Seattle ministerial meetings of the WTO in 1999, with their street protests and ultimate breakdown, were harbingers of future conflicts. In all this, the EU has had new openings to act creatively. Despite protests, Pascal Lamy and his American counterpart, U.S. Trade Representative Robert Zoellick (a good friend of Lamy's) managed to engineer the beginnings of the Doha Round, the first WTO multilateral trade session.

Doha has revealed all the complexities of a rapidly changing economic world. Protests and pressure continue, but other problems lie even deeper. Bringing the poorest of developing societies into the trade game without exploiting them is very difficult, since their meager comparative advantages lie largely in agriculture, where northern and EU trade protection does not give away easily; in raw materials, where markets have been depressed by northern consumer nations; and in different environmental and labor standards. With new areas of the world, particularly the Far East (China) and Southeast Asia (India), in rapid, probably sustainable, development based in part on their lower costs, there are new threats to established northern interests. The collapse of the Doha Round ministerial talks in Cancún in 2003 demonstrated these processes at work. International trade will continue to be a bumpy road for the EU, and those responsible for moving forward on this road within the EU, particularly in the Commission, will have ever more important and difficult jobs to do.

Notes

1. European Commission, *The Internal Market: Ten Years Without Frontiers* (Luxembourg: European Commission, 2002), p. 36.

2. See Brigid Laffan, *The Finances of the European Union* (London: Macmillan, 1997).

3. *Making a Success of the Single Act* (Luxembourg: EC, 1987); *From the Single Act to Maastricht and Beyond: The Means to Match Our Ambitions* (Luxembourg: EC, 1992); and *Agenda 2000: Financing the European Union* (Luxembourg: EC, 1998).

4. Over time, agricultural levies and sugar duties, never large, have steadily declined; the VAT resource, which had reached 68 percent in 1988, has also declined, with the "fourth resource" climbing from 10.6 percent in 1988 to its present level.

5. See Brigid Laffan and Michael Shackleton, "The Budget, Who Gets What, When and How," Helen Wallace and William Wallace, *Policymaking in the European Union*, 4th ed. (New York: Oxford University Press, 2000).

6. Michael Shackleton, "The Delors II Budget Package," in Neill Nugent, ed., *The European Community 1992: Annual Review of Activities* (Oxford: Journal of Common Market Studies/Blackwell, 1993).

7. For general discussions see European Commission, *EEC Competition Policy in the Single Market* (Luxembourg: EC, 1989), and Stephen Weatherill and Paul Beaumont, *EC Law* (London: Penguin, 1993), chaps. 22–27.

8. Taken from Box 9.2 in David Allen, "Cohesion and the Structural Funds, Transfers and Trade Offs," chap. 9 in Wallace and Wallace, *Policymaking in the European Union*.

9. See Loukas Tsoukalis, *The New European Economy Revisited* (New York: Oxford University Press, 1997), chap. 9, for an excellent review of these issues.

10. A set of directives then led to a progressive widening of the meaning of equal treatment to include most elements of the labor contract, including hiring and firing, access to training, working conditions, social security programs, and discrimination against women around certain family issues (pregnancy and employment security, for example). By the mid-1980s, the Commission had set up an "equal protection unit" in its Employment and Social Affairs DG and begun to produce "medium-term action plans" establishing priorities.

11. In the SEA, the application of qualified majority decision making in the general area of "harmonization" (Article 100A) was excluded for two single-market areas central in the EU's very thin social policy legacy provisions "relating to the free movement of persons" and those "relating to the rights and interests of employed persons."

12. Alberta Sbriagia, "Environmental Policy: Economic Constraints and External Pressures," in Wallace and Wallace, *Policymaking in the European Union*, chap. 11.

13. Elmar Rieger, "The Common Agricultural Policy: Politics Against Markets," in Wallace and Wallace, *Policymaking in the European Union*, p. 192.

14. The most frequently used short-term trade tool in the EU's toolbox, under GATT and WTO rules, is the antidumping procedure. Antidumping measures, taken by the Commission after appeal from industries in the Community, have been used recently at a rate of twenty per year, a figure that some observers claim is too high. Article 19 of the GATT Treaty also allowed invocation of "safeguard clauses" in urgent situations.

5

Euro-Politics in Transition:
Three Challenges

European integration has succeeded beyond its founders' dreams. Today the European Union touches the lives of EU citizens in innumerable and irreversible ways. Moreover, everything in previous chapters points to the fact that integration is far from concluded. As the EU moves forward, it is bound to change, and these changes will demand constant reassessment of the EU's function, mission, and rationale. For five decades the EU's advocates asserted that integration was a good in itself, worth doing almost no matter what. This argument held sway while memories of terrible warfare on the Continent remained in people's minds. But for Europeans today, whether elites or ordinary citizens, the EU is much more a fact of life than a moral imperative. It has existed and exists in multiple ways that can and should be judged on their own terms. Moreover, this existing EU continually creates situations in which actors must decide whether and how it should grow and change. Europeans can no longer avoid addressing the really hard questions: What has the EU already done, and is it what we wanted? Where is the EU going? What is it for? Who is it for?[1] This final chapter will discuss three of the largest challenges presently confronting EU Europe in the light of these questions, and the challenges of peace and power in a post-9/11 world, prosperity, and democracy.

Peace and Power: Europe and the World After 9/11

What is the EU's place in the world? The end of the cold war and the repercussions of 9/11 have created a new geopolitical situation. Moving forward in economic realms was the EU's history. But what then? Jacques Delors repeatedly and rhetorically asked whether the EU would remain a "big Switzerland," an economic giant but a foreign policy dwarf. With the United States guiding the North Atlantic Treaty Organization (NATO) with a firm hand and with NATO's interests constraining the EU's ability to define its own interests in foreign policy and security matters, being a "big Switzerland" has had its advantages.[2] It has allowed the EU to act on the economic matters that it did best and left Europeans to focus on what they wanted most, being prosperous. It was also cheaper than any alternative. Finally, it allowed member states to maintain what remained of their sovereignty in the foreign political arena.

The Union's recent foreign and security policy story illustrates this "big Switzerland" dilemma. A powerhouse in the world economy and international trade, effective in the use of "softer" foreign policy techniques, the EU has seemed clueless in the uncertain new post-1989, post-Yugoslavia, post-9/11 world best symbolized by the second Iraq war. America's new willingness to leave behind its traditional strategic restraint in favor of more aggressive and less multilateral approaches has underlined Europe's problem. To a degree this was understandable. The cold war subordinated European defense efforts into NATO, which had one purpose: to deter and, if need be, stop any hostile Soviet moves in Europe. Once the long moment of the cold war ended, EU member states needed first to understand their new security environment, then to decide which new threats needed to be anticipated, to make plans to defend against them, and finally, to come up with the money to make such plans credible.

Doing all this would have been difficult, and circumstances made it even more so. The EU's "near neighborhood"—the ex-Yugoslavia—caught fire before central questions about security had been answered. The result was an impression of an absence of EU commitment and great confusion. At the same time, the United States, with long-standing ideas about hard power issues extending far beyond European territorial defense, a willingness to invest in such ideas, and a gigantic technological lead, played very shrewdly in Europe by tying existing European NATO members as closely as possible to a U.S.-led reconfiguration of NATO while at the same time expanding NATO to the countries of Central and Eastern Europe (CEECs) with greater energy than the EU could muster.[3] Economic conditions were terrible across most of the EU until the brief boom that began in 1998, and member states had to labor strenuously to meet the Economic and Monetary Union (EMU) convergence criteria, leaving few financial and political resources for large new security initiatives. Finally, key EU member states—France, Britain, Spain, Italy, and Germany—tended to have distinct and different positions on security issues concerning problems beyond Europe and insisted on pursuing these positions on their own, outside of any framework of EU coordination.

Some agreement had been reached nonetheless on a European rapid-reaction force backed by reluctant but real commitments of troops and money. Just when this—small—battle seemed won, however, 9/11 occurred. Europeans unanimously expressed massive support and sympathy for Americans after the attacks on New York and Washington. EU member states and the EU itself bent over backwards to assist U.S. intelligence services to track Al Qaeda activity and beef up European counterterrorism dispositions. They supported and aided the U.S.-led expedition to Afghanistan. However, the new global challenge of terrorism forced EU member states to look beyond the immediate European security environment. Here they had serious disagreements.

U.S. insistence on invading Iraq to dislodge Saddam Hussein exacerbated these disagreements. Europeans, for the most part, recognized that the Iraqi regime was extremely repressive, corrupt, and dangerous. Not everyone agreed that this justified "preemptive" military action, nor were they convinced by the U.S. argument that the Iraqis possessed hidden weapons of mass destruction (WMDs) in violation of United Nations resolutions. In addition, it seemed obvious to Europeans that the United States would invade Iraq with or without European support (this was made clear even to the British). This attitude deeply offended Europeans, who believed strongly in the virtues of multilateralism and in the importance of European influence in matters of war and peace. The outlines of a difficult situation became clearer when German chancellor Gerhard Schröder won reelection in autumn 2002 by opposing U.S. plans for war in Iraq. French president Jacques Chirac agreed with Schröder and insisted on further UN discussions. The British predictably supported U.S. plans and impatience from the beginning but nonetheless hoped for a new UN resolution to justify war.

As the invasion neared, Europeans were deeply divided over whether conflict should depend on the results of continuing UN weapons inspections. The United States was willing to wait only for a new UN resolution justifying invasion to go through the Security Council. The French vetoed the proposed resolution in no uncertain terms, vividly underlining the United States's new and strident unilateralism. Iraq was thus invaded by a "coalition of the willing" that included EU members Spain, Italy, several CEEC applicants to the EU, and the United Kingdom, in the face of strident opposition from the French, Germans, and others. European public opinion, across the board, was massively opposed to the U.S. war, including in the countries supporting the United States.

The saga continued when the United States generated a pair of letters from a host of European governments (the "Euro 8" followed by the "Vilnius 10"), including many CEEC accession candidates, in support of the war. U.S. Defense Secretary Donald Rumsfeld was then moved to praise the "new" Europe and denounce the "old." The inability of the coalition to find any WMDs, the repeated shifting of U.S. justification for the war, and the deterioration of the military situation on the ground after President Bush had brashly proclaimed "mission accomplished" fueled European opposition to the Bush administration and renewed anti-Americanism.

The Iraq story underlined the EU's profound foreign and security policy dilemmas. The Union is far from devoid of international clout, but its major tools are largely of the "soft power" variety. The Community—the Commission in the lead—has responsibility for trade and development cooperation, and the EU trade commissioner plays a very large role in international trade dealings, most recently in the WTO. The EU is a major player in the current international exchange rate regime, thanks to the euro, and in international environmental regulation. Moreover, the otherwise troubled 1990s produced enhanced and more effective EU approaches to humanitarian aid and conflict management. Finally, the accumulation of common foreign and security policy (CFSP) positions has not been negligible, even if it avoids major geostrategic matters.

Javier Solana, Mr. CFSP, commented in 2002 that the common foreign policy was not meant to be a single policy.[4] Solana was correct: EU foreign and security policy was not meant to replace completely what member states did. Hence the CFSP may increase the Union's international dilemmas as much as it resolves them. In addition to underlining differences, 9/11 and Iraq revealed huge issues about Europe's place in the post–cold war world. Divisions between the pro-NATO and pro-American "Atlanticists" and the "Gaullists," who sought greater international autonomy for Europe, have been present from the beginning. The 2004 enlargement brought widespread pro-Americanism and NATO engagement among new CEEC members and reinforced the Atlanticists. But the open-ended uncertainty of the new post-1989 world disorder has created new reasons for such old divisions. The overpowering reality is that what the United States, the only remaining "great power," does is of crucial importance to Europe. Moreover, the Madrid bombings of spring 2004 demonstrated that both Europe and the United States are confronted with similar threats from international terrorism.

What to do, or rather what will the EU do? Given Europe's unwillingness to invest the large sums of money and effort needed to build a larger global security capability, should the EU rely on the United States: its good intentions, its global interests and perspectives, and its greater willingness and capacity for using military force? At first glance, this makes sense, but it runs up against another dimension of the new reality revealed by the Iraq saga. Europe is much less significant strategically to the United States today than it was in the cold war. To be sure, the sequels of Yugoslavian dissolution illustrate the possibility of regional European trouble that might destabilize the broader global order. But what really counts for the United States, and will count even more in the future, lies elsewhere. A global superpower must focus on global terrorist problems, nuclear proliferation, instabilities in the Middle East and Central Asia, and a changing economic and geostrategic scene characterized by the rapid industrialization of giant countries like China and India.

In the post–cold war world, in other words, there is a growing asymmetry between U.S. and European global interests and capabilities. In consequence, the United States is bound to define problems differently than Europe does. Moreover, it is likely to act on these definitions whatever the Europeans think. This may be the deeper lesson of the Bush administration's crusading unilateralism in Iraq. Insisting on the pursuit of multilateralism, as the French, Germans, and others did on Iraq, demonstrates simultaneously Europe's different way of seeing things globally and its way of attempting to keep the United States "under control." There is a great deal to recommend cautious multilateralism in our perilous world, and this kind of resistance may be wise. On the other hand, it could boomerang and accentuate U.S. impatience both with the opacity and snail's pace of the UN system and with "old" Europe. More to the point, Europeans are unlikely to influence outcomes or bring America on board to a worldview that sees the use of force as truly a last resort—and only to be used as part of a genuine multilateral exercise.

Iraq revealed, in new circumstances, that the EU's foreign and security policy limitations were based primarily on persistent disagreement among its members. This disagreement undoubtedly fuels the desire of member states to retain significant independent foreign policy capacities, if only to make sure that their voices can be heard. Throughout the Iraq crisis, as in earlier crises, the pursuit of national diplomacy, whatever the EU did, remained an important resort for most EU members. The prospect of disunity tends to deepen disunity and lock the EU into the "big Switzerland" dilemma. In an era of globalization, the EU's economic and "soft power" dimensions are global, yet its geostrategic visions and "hard power" are narrowly regional. U.S. and EU definitions of their global interests will often be similar. Sometimes they will be different, however, as Iraq illustrates. Without "hard" global conceptions and capacities, the EU, in a situation of global crisis, will face a very difficult choice: It can either support the United States, even if the United States is pursuing a course with which large numbers of Europeans disagree, or it can oppose the United States and more often than not lose in the unequal battle of wills with a determined superpower. Will the EU be able to resolve this dilemma? Much will depend on future U.S. foreign policy and the ability of Europeans to persuade the United States to adhere to multilateral approaches. Given power asymmetries, however, the likelihood is that, on

occasion, this ability will not be enough. At the limit, however, the perspective of a world in which the United States and EU Europe have genuinely different global conceptions and capacities should comfort no one.

Prosperity

Western Europe has been transformed economically by European integration, and Europeans in general are vastly better off as a result, even if the EU's newer southern and eastern members are still lagging behind. European incomes are higher, life choices greater, and education more widespread. The purposes of European integration have primarily been economic. Creating a more open European market has been at its heart a liberalizing project, designed to free up markets and expand the role of market decision making in European societies. This project has been more or less compatible with the social model that Western Europeans consolidated after World War II, characterized by generous welfare states and labor markets regulated to provide security for working people.

The economies of EU15 countries grew at around 5 percent annually from 1961 to 1973, the height of the postwar boom, and their unemployment was on average a very low 2 percent. From 1973 on, the numbers have been very different, however. Between 1973 and 1982 growth dropped below 2 percent, and unemployment rose above 5 percent. Things did not get better thereafter—growth stuck at around ± 2 percent, and unemployment at nearly 10 percent from 1982 to the present. EU members did extremely well during the first period of integration, when the Common Market was handmaiden to strong national development strategies. They did badly, as one would anticipate, during the crisis period of the 1970s. But since then, despite new activism, they have also not done very well. It is misleading to claim that the single market, EMU, and other changes have failed. It is likely that without them EU members might have found themselves in an even worse position. That said, no one can deny that the U.S. economy has outperformed the European economies since the early 1980s. There are a variety of plausible arguments about why the EU has fallen behind. It is possible, for example, that the EU's transitions from Keynesianism to price stability macroeconomic policy approaches and from relative national market isolation to an open Euro-market—all spurred by globalization—simply need more time to achieve greater success. Perhaps Europe is merely suffering from temporary transitional economic shocks that European countries—for political reasons—have been slow to confront. Mass unemployment, to choose only one of the largest of these shocks, is much harder to address in societies committed to high levels of social protection and welfare, like those in most of continental Europe. The path to success may be deceptively simple: elites should hang tough, fine-tune the policies they have put in place, and persuade their constituents to wait and see the positive results just around the corner. However, after twenty-five years of relatively bad news, these constituents just might be skeptical.

Another common argument, usually from neoliberals, is that despite the considerable market opening that has occurred, European institutions remain insufficiently flexible to face the harsh winds of globalization. Harder-line versions of this argument, often advanced by Anglo-American critics, advocate "structural reform" in European labor markets and welfare states so that they come more to resemble the United States with its weak unions, thin labor law, greater inequality, and private, individualized social protection programs. Much of what the Europeans built after World War II to create gentler and less harsh social market economies should be dismantled, the argument goes. Softer versions of these arguments are advanced by European Central Bank (ECB) leaders, and traces of them are also built into the European Employment Strategy, which seeks consensual progress toward greater flexibility.

Others claim that the absence of an effective "E" in EMU (i.e., an economic policy dimension)

is the key problem. In practice, EMU amounts to little more than centralized monetary policy-making in a politically independent ECB, while budgets and broad economic strategies are left to the member states, who may scatter in different directions. The result, many economists will be quick to say, is a suboptimal "policy mix" for the Union as a whole—hence growth, employment, and other problems.[5]

This architecture leaves separate EMU governments as "takers" of policy from the ECB, with fragmented resources to respond. Are things changing for the better? The constitution of an institutionalized "Euro-Group" (composed of EMU members), the rapid development of Euro-level, but nonbinding, methods to produce annual "broad economic policy guidelines," and new language in the 2004 Constitutional Treaty signal efforts to rebalance price stability and employment in a way that tries to narrow the gap between Union and national policies. Despite these efforts, critics assert that none of the reforms in place or contemplated are likely to be adequate to the task. What is needed is Euro-level macroeconomic policy governance as a counterweight to the ECB, and no one expects to see that anytime soon.

EU leaders are as aware of these issues as their critics. The most significant response to this point has been the so-called "Lisbon strategy," set out at the Lisbon European Council in 2001, whose—perhaps overoptimistic—aims were to transform EU Europe into the world's most competitive knowledge base and to achieve full employment by 2010. The central objectives of the strategy were

- Preparing the transition to a knowledge-based economy and society by better policies for the information society and research and development (R&D), as well as by stepping up the process of structural reform for competitiveness and innovation and by completing the internal market

- Modernizing the European social model, investing in people and combating social exclusion

- Sustaining the healthy economic outlook and favorable growth prospects by applying an appropriate macroeconomic policy mix

The Lisbon strategy was a judicious and enthusiastic mix of the new and the old. It proposed first an "information society for all," around the dissemination of Internet access and e-commerce. It then suggested establishing "a European area of research and innovation" to encourage more and better coordinated R&D in growth areas such as biotechnology, innovations in environmental technologies, defense, and space. Here the program looked like the "industrial policy" of bygone days. Then came more familiar themes like providing a friendly environment for creating new businesses, especially small and medium-sized ones. The rest of the document urged achieving a "complete and fully operational internal market"—the unfinished business of the "1992" program, with particular stress on financial market integration and taxation changes.

The Lisbon European Council occurred at the peak of one of the EU's rare moments of rapid growth since the 1970s—hence its reference to "the healthy economic outlook" and its belief that annual growth of 3 percent was possible. Alas, this felicitous situation barely lasted out the Portuguese presidency, and the downturn that followed was difficult indeed. What was most disturbing about the new recession was that it showed that the German economy, once the legendary "Modell Deutschland," motor of European growth and backbone of EU successes, had won the uncoveted title of "sick man of Europe." Partly because of this, Europe's downturn was greater and its recovery slower and less robust than that of global competitors. To make things more difficult, the United States began promoting devaluation of the dollar, pushing the euro up by nearly 20 percent. If a low euro had earlier favored European exports, a low dollar favored the opposite. In this new situation, much of the enthusiasm for the Lisbon strategy dried up, along with resources needed for progress. By

2004 it was clear that many, if not most, of the Lisbon goals were unreachable.

The economic bad news included problems with EMU. The ECB's initial accommodating policies gave way to excessive toughness. The bank set its inflation target at 2 percent annually, a figure that financial officials and experts judged more restrictive than necessary. Because the target was so low, the threshold of ECB inflation-control credibility was constantly close. Since little was more important for the new Central Bank than building credibility, ECB policy was bound to be overly restrictive. Thus, when recession developed in 2000, the bank refused to loosen its policies, regularly announcing that key market actors were responsible, not the bank. In brief, the ECB was determined not to provide countercyclical monetary policy room to slumping EU members it regarded as economic miscreants.

There were more EMU problems to come, however. Recession, as always, reduced governments' revenue flows and increased their expenses, particularly for social policy. The Stability and Growth Pact (SGP) enjoined that annual deficits not exceed 3 percent, however. This meant that euro-zone governments could not engage in countercyclical actions to fight the slump. Instead they faced situations where they were relatively powerless against unemployment and their own budgetary problems. Governments wanted to be reelected, however. Thus the French and the Germans, who had insisted on the SGP in the first place, rebelled and exceeded the 3 percent limit. By 2004 they had become repeat offenders and had been joined by the Italians, the Dutch, the Portuguese, and the Greeks. The SGP had procedures to be followed when governments did this. The Commission, with Council oversight, declared the offenders to be in excessive deficit and to insist on changed national policies to meet the 3 percent target. In case of persistent noncooperation, major penalties could be assessed. Despite Commission president Prodi's public announcement that he found the SGP "stupid," the Commission diligently pursued the excessive deficit process only to discover that EU leaders Germany and France simply refused to cooperate, the Germans with regret and contrition, the French in defiance. This made it much easier for others to disregard the SGP. Thus by 2004 practically everyone agreed that the SGP needed to be changed to make 3 percent a target for the economic cycle as a whole and not an annual goal. The SGP was enshrined in the treaty, however, and few wanted to change the treaty because of the effects that this could have for the EMU and ECB credibility.

Serious flaws in EMU and the SGP had been laid bare, but fudging became the order of the day. Given ECB restrictiveness and the SGP corset, how could the costs of economic adjustment within euroland be distributed without widespread defiance and dangerous criticism of EMU? The EMU's "one size fits all" monetary policy might enhance broader welfare in the medium term, but it was also likely to privilege certain regions to the advantage of others. Would EMU stimulate member states to undertake the structural reforms to complete transition to the "new economy"? Would it be possible to steer a course between monetary gentleness that allowed too much laxity and harshness that might destroy the uniqueness of the humane "European model of society"? EMU could eventually promote (and require) greater harmonization of member state social policies or, at the very least, much greater coordination, but if this meant a "race to the bottom," the threats to social cohesion and political stability would almost certainly be great, along with national opposition.

Where will the new 2004 EU members fit in EMU? Most are not eligible for immediate membership, even though accession agreements contained timetables and programs for eventual membership, since EMU is part of the *acquis communautaire*. This will make EMU temporarily much more of a two-speed club, with CEECs joining Denmark, Sweden, and the United Kingdom as EMU outsiders. The implications of this for EMU are difficult to foresee, but the implica-

tions for the EU more broadly are clearer. A solid core of member states will become "insiders," with ongoing reasons to meet and coordinate economic matters separately from the non-EMU "outsiders" (in an expanded Euro-11, for example). The outsiders will then have to find ways to cope. This, as we will later see, is in line with stronger "flexibility" provisions into the EU treaties to facilitate such "two-speed" arrangements. An EU based on widespread "variable geometry" would be very different from the one that emerged after the Treaty of Rome.

The EU's continuing success may well depend on its future ability to produce economic benefits for its citizens and member states. But will it be able to deliver the goods? The answer to this question is trickier than many suspect. For a start, the contrasts between the EU and the United States since the early 1990s may not be as stark as critics think. Europe's productivity has grown almost as rapidly as the U.S. economy, since differences in GDP per capita are largely attributable to European choices to work fewer hours—arguably an option that produces greater social welfare—while virtually all of the general underperformance can be laid at Germany's door.[6] Germany's economic problems, which flow primarily from unification, could persist, however, with continuing negative consequences for the Union more broadly. Combined with the effects of globalization and EMU, the EU's demographic future is also dangerous. Very low birthrates plus public rejection of new immigration will mean greater healthcare costs, higher pension replacement rates, and difficult dilemmas for public finances. The EU's stubbornly high unemployment levels plus increasing poverty and inequality remain very large problems at member state levels and, in consequence, for the EU's public image and credibility. The record of half a century of European economic integration is thus mixed. Things would undoubtedly have been worse without it. But Europeans still remain to be fully convinced that they are better off with it. And it is what Europeans think that will ultimately determine the future.

Democracy and Effectiveness: EU Institutions

The Euro system was never designed as a system of governance, let alone a state, and it did not begin in a search for an ideal constitution. Many who participated in composing the initial treaties hoped that beautiful democratic institutional flowers would eventually bloom, but they had little idea what varieties would grow, if any. They also knew that because European peoples had not been prepared for great changes, the garden would have to grow plot by plot. "Europe" would have first to prove its usefulness. The new European experiment was purposively begun in economic matters. In time, the founders hoped, "Europe" would grow beyond them, through "spillover."

The EU's institutional configuration of an appointed Commission, an intergovernmental Council of Ministers, and a weak Parliament, plus institutions like the European Court of Justice (ECJ), was designed to allow the EU's six original members to work together for limited purposes. In the EU's brief history, the scope and prerogatives of these institutions have been expanded beyond anyone's anticipation. Accompanying expanding mandates and membership, European leaders have periodically updated the treaties on which the system is based, and since 1985 there have been few moments when the EU has not been holding an intergovernmental conference (IGC), digesting a recent one, or preparing a new one.

By the turn of the century, leaders were aware that the EU faced issues that went well beyond tinkering. In the words of Joschka Fischer, German foreign minister:

> In the past, European integration was based on the "Monnet method" with its communitarization approach in European institutions and policy. This gradual process of integration, with no blueprint for the final state, was conceived in the 1950s for the economic integration of a small group of countries. Successful as it was . . . this approach has proved to be of only limited use for the political integration and democratization of Europe.[7]

Fischer was opening a "great debate" on the future of Europe. Other leaders with differing views quickly joined in. British prime minister Tony Blair queried, for example:

> Europe, yes, but what sort of Europe?
> . . . The trouble with the debate about Europe's political future is that if we do not take care, we plunge into the thicket of institutional change without first asking the basic question of what direction Europe should take. . . .
> The most important challenge for Europe is to wake up to the new reality: Europe is widening and deepening simultaneously. There will be more of us in the future, trying to do more. . . . The issue is not whether we do this, but how we reform this new Europe so that it both delivers real benefits to the people of Europe, addressing the priorities they want addressed, and does so in a way that has their consent and support.[8]

The redesign of the EU's "house" was really the issue. EU institutions had worked to get the Union into a new century, but in balky, convoluted, and sometimes obscure ways. Institutions that were already creaking and groaning with fifteen members were likely to seize up for good in an EU of twenty-five and more. Beyond this, EU institutions were unprecedented experiments in transnational governance and thus unmapped territory for democratic responsibility. As Joschka Fischer underlined, the EU had grown, following the "Monnet method," by adding functions for existing institutions rather than reflecting on and redesigning these institutions.

Enlargement: The Institutional Challenge

The 2000 Intergovernmental Conference in Nice was mandated to confront the immediate issues posed by enlargement. In the words of three "wise men" charged to think about institutions and enlargement, "A significant increase in the number of participants automatically increases problems of decision making and management. Interests are more different, discussion is slower, decision more difficult, management more complex. Problems in the working of the European institutions are already apparent today. . . . They are bound to increase."[9] More qualified majority voting (QMV) was necessary lest national vetoes increase geometrically, along with prospects for paralysis. Enlargement also necessitated reweighting votes in the Council so that majorities would more accurately reflect the size and population of member states. Next, enlarging the Commission could destroy the Commission's capacity to function as a college, so other approaches were needed.[10] The IGC was also to devise better procedures for "reinforced cooperation" to allow more energetic and ambitious member states to forge ahead in particular dimensions of integration (as EU members already had done in EMU and the Schengen group). Finally, the IGC was charged to draw up a European Charter of Rights that might eventually be integrated into the treaties.[11]

These were the urgent problems and also the "easy" ones. The resulting Treaty of Nice (December 2000) did not bode well, however.[12] Tit-for-tat bargaining on extending QMV fell far short of the objective of removing unanimity in forty areas. There was some QMV progress on external trade matters (on services and intellectual property, with France insisting, however, on maintaining unanimity on culture, health, and education), but unanimity continued in both fiscal and social policy. Finally, where QMV was extended, there were often long transition periods. On immigration, QMV would not happen until 2004, with the Germans also insisting on maintaining a veto beyond this date on asylum policy. The Spanish allowed QMV on the structural funds, but not until 2007, giving Spain and its allies a veto lasting through negotiation of the EU's next new budgetary "package," itself likely to be for six years, lasting until 2012! Reweighting Council voting (which included establishing the number of Council votes that new members would receive) provoked a bitter struggle between larger and smaller members that the larger members won. If the four largest members of the EU15 voted together, they would constitute a blocking minority against all the smaller countries. The smaller countries were paid off on Commission size, however, because in 2005 the large countries would lose their second commissioner, but all members would get one. The only real advance was that designating the Commission president could be by QMV rather than unanimity. In other areas, inflexible bargaining led to institutional impasse.

A Great Debate?

Nice stumbled even on the easy questions. Its most important result was official commitment to hold another IGC in 2004 to confront the larger ones. In the meantime, the democratic deficit thrived. There was record low participation in the 1999 European elections, the Danes voted no on EMU in 2000, and the Irish refused to ratify Nice in a 2001 referendum, while unpleasant national populists like Jörg Haider in Austria and Jean-Marie Le Pen in France mobilized supporters—and shaped public opinion more broadly—by bashing the EU along with their usual anti-immigrant rants. The EU was rapidly closing in on a new enlargement that could cause huge confusion and deadlock unless serious reform efforts were undertaken. After an extremely trying and difficult post–cold war decade, the Union also found itself at a moment of low credibility and public support. What was to be done?

Amidst the high-level hand-wringing that followed, the Laeken European Council in fall 2000, prompted by the Belgian presidency, called a "convention" of "the main parties involved in the debate on the future of the Union."[13] The convention, to begin in early 2002 and to present a final report prior to the 2004 IGC, was given a very large mandate that included bringing citizens closer to European goals and institutions, resolving the outstanding institutional issues posed by enlargement, and proposing how to make the EU into a force for stability and a model in world affairs.[14] Included was the possibility of a total rewrite of the EU's dense, opaque, and inadequate treaties. There were few limits on what it might do, in fact, except that whatever it did had to be realistic enough to pass member state muster in 2004. This was no small matter, however. The big EU15 member states were divided on fundamental constitutional issues between strongly pro-European federalists (Germany); intergovernmentalists like the French, whose president had resurrected de Gaulle's rhetoric about a "Europe of nations"; and pragmatic minimalists like the British, who really wanted less Europe altogether. Nice had also revealed that smaller EU15 members were anxious about opening up institutional questions. Reasonably, they feared that negotiations about fundamental institutional change could increase the power of the bigger members and unbalance the delicate equilibrium that had earlier been struck. Finally, there were the applicant countries who would become members in 2004, with their own more pro-American outlooks and their preferences for market solutions over traditional European social protection, whose role in EU institutions was unpredictable, but who were bound to bring change.

The convention was meant to bypass the gridlock and the dwindling imagination caused by the intergovernmental haggling that had characterized the 1990s and the Nice Treaty. It also targeted the democratic deficit, soliciting suggestions, contributions, and commentaries from anyone in the Union who cared to participate, whether individual citizens, NGOs, "social partners," lawyers, or even politicians. The goal was a genuine EU-wide debate on institutional change and the future that could clear the air, enhance the place of EU Europe in the minds of Europeans, and reengage EU citizens in the project of European construction. In certain ways this goal was reached. Thousands of NGOs, interest groups, think tanks, and citizens submitted contributions that were lodged on the convention website for anyone to read (http://europa.eu.int/futurum).

The official "conventioneers" who were charged with summarizing what they heard, debating the issues, and producing proposals for EU constitutional change were a more restricted group composed of thirty delegates from national parliaments, sixteen from the European Parliament, fifteen representatives of national governments, and two representatives from the Commission. Leadership and organization would come from a Presidium composed of a president and two vice presidents, plus nine other convention members. The accession countries participated fully (each through two parliamentarians and one governmental representative) even though enjoined not to block any consensus arrived at by the EU15.

The convention's president, seventy-eight-year-old Valéry Giscard d'Estaing, was a former president of France and longtime participant in EU life, an aristocratic man who saw the task of constitution building as his last great appearance on the European stage. The two vice presidents, Jean-Luc Dehaene, federalist former prime minister of Belgium, and Giuliano Amato, twice former premier of Italy and a gifted intellectual, were also extremely good choices.

Philadelphia 1776?

The term *convention* in French had the connotation of a constituent assembly that might prepare a constitution, even though this was not its explicit mandate. Giscard clearly had this in mind in his persistent references to "Philadelphia 1776" and the U.S. constitutional experience. Giscard hoped to produce a framework for the future EU that would stand the test of decades. The convention had eighteen months to work these miracles. Giscard structured its processes, suggesting that it should first "listen" to what Europeans had to say about the EU, then, in light of what it heard, break into working groups to "study" the big issues and ideas about Europe that were on the table. Finally, in its last stage the convention would prepare recommendations for the 2004 IGC.[15] The president also insisted, wisely as it turned out, that the convention would work on principles of consensus, avoiding votes, and that it would produce a complete "no options" document that did not leave major open choices for governments to make.

Whatever the product, the project of taking distance to reflect and having the freedom to propose outside the daily routines of EU life was an extraordinary moment in the history of European integration. The processes involved serious reflection, debate, and struggle among the conventioneers, who often disagreed but who developed a real esprit de corps in their time together. Over the eighteen months there were 26 plenary sessions (52 days) open to the public and the media, during which there were some 1,800 speeches by the conventioneers and 23,000 official documents. In short, the convention in itself was a work of democracy even though, like all such, it also became a prize location for complicated strategies, plots, tough confrontations, and maneuvering. But the product was very important as well, and it had to be realistic to have any chance at all for getting through the IGC. The convention could not move too far away from what member states would approve.

Thus the convention proposed a "draft constitutional treaty" in June 2003 that began with a preamble and continued in several parts. The preamble, largely composed by Giscard, began with a citation in Greek from Thucydides—which the European Council later deleted—describing the sources of Europe, "a continent that has brought forth civilization," whose inhabitants "gradually developed the values underlying humanism: equality of persons, freedom, respect for reason," and continued in much the same general way to note that reunited Europe wanted good things like prosperity, culture, democracy, and peace and would be "united in its diversity" in a "special area of human hope." The major dispute over the preamble, which continued through the 2004 IGC, was about recognizing God and Europe's Christian roots. Giscard and the convention had studiously avoided this through general talk of humanism, rights, and the rule of law, but a broad alliance of

Christians, including the Vatican, the Poles, Bavarian Christian Democrats, and the Christian Right in Italy and Spain, pushed hard for God. They ultimately failed, but made a great deal of noise until then.

The complexity of the EU and the world around it frustrated Giscard's aspirations to have the convention produce something that would be accessible to any intelligent secondary schoolchild. The convention's mandate, to construct a single treaty that could serve as a constitutional base and at the same time consolidate and clarify what half a century of European integration had already created, enjoined a product that could not be too stark and simple. The product also fell short of what many participants and observers felt was needed to refound a more effective, dynamic, and democratic EU. In particular, it failed to agree on the creation of an "economic government" to work on the macroeconomic policy side as a counterweight to the overly restrictive and monetarist ECB to advance the prospect of a more growth- and employment-oriented policy mix. A British-led struggle to defend "redlines" over fiscal and social policies prevented important, and probably needed, QMV procedures in areas where the single market and EMU created potential instability. The convention proposals nonetheless made the EU much more intelligible than EU treaties had ever been before while also innovating in important ways. Because it is impossible to do full justice to a carefully composed legal document in a few brief paragraphs, Table 5.1 summarizes the most important innovations proposed by the convention.

The convention's draft Constitutional Treaty went directly onto the table of a new intergovernmental conference in July 2003, where it very nearly died. In the hands of an inept and ill-prepared Italian presidency, the European Council of December 13, 2003 could not reach agreement on a version of the convention's text. The issue around which failure occurred was a familiar one, the reweighting of national votes in QMV. The convention had inherited a situation from the

Table 5.1   Major Convention Proposals

Subject	*Convention Proposal*
PART I GENERAL AND INSTITUTIONAL PROVISIONS	
One vs. several treaties	Constitutional Treaty subsumes all earlier treaties, becomes unique legal basis for Union action.
Qualified majority extended	QMV becomes the rule, unanimity the exception. Codecision the rule. De facto end of Maastricht pillars. Extent of unanimity contested at 2004 Brussels European Council.
	QMV based on "double majority" (majority of states, representing 60 percent of population, required for passage). Precise weighting change from Nice Treaty contested at 2004 Brussels European Council. Codecision renamed the default "legislative procedure."
"Passarelle" (bridge) clause	Council of Ministers can decide, unanimously, to move particular areas from unanimity to QMV. Allows major changes without convening new IGCs.
Renaming and legal hierarchy of Union decisions	Regulation (applicable to all members as worded) becomes "European law." Directive (transposed into national legal language) becomes "European framework law."
Rotating Council presidency becomes President of European Council	President of European Council elected for two and one-half years, renewable once. Main function to organize, prepare, and oversee European Council work (cooperating with other institutions and without separate civil service).
EU foreign minister	EU foreign minister combines foreign relations commissioner (running EU's foreign service and diplomatic missions) and high representative of common foreign and security policy (conducts CFSP).
Number of commissioners	15 commissioners (13 plus president and vice president) rotating among member states after 2009. Contested at 2004 Brussels European Council.
European Parliament	Maximum size 750, minimum national representation 6, maximum 96.
EU as legal entity	Ends pillars, allows Union to negotiate and sign treaties as a legal party. Union as such can join international organizations.
Competences, subsidiarity	Union can only act in areas where power has been conferred (competences can be exclusive to Union or shared with member states). Union action in these areas is governed by subsidiarity.
	Protocol allows national parliaments to contest Union actions on grounds of subsidiarity (one-third of parliaments can ask for reconsideration) and/or take legal proceedings at ECJ. Treaty does not appreciably expand Union competences, however.
Common foreign and security policy	Unanimity preserved, constructive abstention allowed. Creation of a "European Defense Agency" to promote defense, industrial cooperation, research and development. Promotion of defense "vanguard."
Justice and home affairs	"Communitized" immigration, asylum policies—exceptions for passports, family law. Police cooperation.

Suspension of membership, exit from Union	Member states not following basic values of Union can have certain rights suspended and be sanctioned. Procedures for member state leaving the Union established.
Openness	Nothing about Union decision making is hidden, nothing inaccessible, a priori. Union legislators, including the Council of Ministers, sit in public. Access to documents is a right.
Reinforced cooperation	Possible in any area covered by treaty, must include at least one-third of member states, allowed by QMV in Council. Once allowed, "vanguard" makes its own decisions, pays its own bills (similar to Amsterdam and Nice).

PART II   CHARTER OF FUNDAMENTAL RIGHTS

| Union Charter of Fundamental Rights | Elaborated for Nice, incorporated as Part II of convention proposal. Only covers actions of Union, including those taken by member states in name of Union. Charter underlines that EU is not only a market, but also a community of citizen rights. |

PART III   UNION POLICIES

| | Detailed review of different Union policy areas. |

Nice Treaty in which qualified majority demanded 74 percent of the total votes and in which Poland and Spain had negotiated reweighted voting power that was only slightly less than that of the EU's largest states. Hence Poland, Spain, plus one additional small country could assert a "blocking minority." If allowed to stand, this arrangement would have paralyzed the enlarged Union and made it unmanageable. Nonetheless, Spain and Poland stood their ground. The EU thus enlarged on May 1, 2004, with no assurance that it would be able to function.

The story did not end there, thankfully. Instead negotiations were continued under the Irish presidency of the first half of 2004, with a final effort set for the June European Council. In the meantime key member states—France, Germany, and Britain in particular—looked themselves in the mirror and recognized that a coincidence of enlargement and petty quarreling that prevented the Union from adapting its institutions to a Union of twenty-five members was likely to produce a catastrophic turning point for European integration. Some good fortune also flowed from another catastrophe, the terrorist train bombings that occurred in Madrid

two days prior to the Spanish elections in March 2004. Aznar's center-right government, which had supported the United States in Iraq despite massive public opposition, looked almost certain to win reelection until the bombing. Unexpectedly, the center-right lost to the Socialists, in large part as a result of Aznar's clumsy effort to finesse the bombing disaster in cynical ways, insisting against emerging evidence that Basque terrorists were responsible. The change of government in Spain held huge implications for the EU. Not only was the new Zapatero government determined to withdraw Spanish troops from Iraq, but it was much more pro-European, and—most important of all—much more flexible on the key IGC issue of QMV. The virtual collapse of the Leszek Miller–led Polish government, whose popularity in the polls after a series of corruption scandals had dropped to 5 percent, also helped to advance the cause of effective constitution building. The British government remained steadfast in defense of its "redlines" against expanding QMV, part of Tony Blair's own domestic strategy to convince the British that the EU was not as much of a "superstate" as Britain's assertive and narrow-minded press and the Conservative Party claimed, but this was not enough to block a deal.

Constitutional Settlement—Or Confusion As Usual?

Pending ratification, the EU acquired a new constitutional treaty in June 2004 that incorporated almost all (90 percent, according to the experts) of the convention's proposals. The European Council would henceforth have a president and the EU its foreign minister, among the many other changes. The key was a compromise on QMV. The convention had proposed a dual majority system set at 50 percent of member states, representing 60 percent of the population. The final deal became 55-65. Since this implied that France, Germany, and the United Kingdom, were they to agree, would constitute a blocking minority (by virtue of their combined population), a new requirement was added that at least four countries had to agree to block. The Spanish and Polish gave up their Nice advantages in exchange for a procedure that granted a group of countries representing three-quarters of a blocking minority to delay a decision in the hope that a broader consensus might be achieved. The convention's proposal on the Commission was also changed by the IGC. The current composition of the Commission of one member per member state would continue until 2014, after which the size of the Commission would drop to a number equivalent to two-thirds of member states, chosen by a system of equal rotation. The United Kingdom maintained its redlines against QMV in taxation, social policy, and CFSP, while the introduction of QMV for the Union's budget packages was postponed.

The EU's sigh of relief in June 2004 was tempered. Elections to the European Parliament held just prior to the European Council, on June 10–13, 2004, were very bad. Turnout, at 44 percent, was the worst ever, six points lower than in 1999, when hand-wringing about public indifference to Europe had been widespread. Worse still, while EU15 turnout was 45.7 per-

cent, slightly higher than the general average, it was a mere 26.3 percent in the ten new member states. In addition, there was a strong correlation between very low participation rates and the success of Euro-skeptic party lists in Poland, Slovakia, the Czech Republic, Sweden, the Netherlands, the United Kingdom, and Austria. Finally, virtually everywhere, except in Spain and Greece, where there were new governments, the voters slammed governmental incumbents. The fact that the center-right European People's Party (EPP) won the most seats (276), followed by the Social Democrats (201), promising that the European parliamentary business was likely to go on as usual, was small consolation. National campaigns had been very confused, the media paid very little attention to them, and the EU was clearly unloved when ordinary voters even gave thought to it.

Feelings of exultation about the IGC deal were also bound to be temporary. The European elections meant that red lights were on all over Europe concerning the ratification of the new Constitutional Treaty. Several countries, including Ireland, Denmark, the United Kingdom, and the Netherlands, were committed to ratification by referendum, and a significant number more were likely to commit to referenda in the light of these election results. This raised the prospect of several countries voting against ratification, with Euro-political turmoil then following. The consequences could vary tremendously. Following past precedents, small "no" countries could be asked to vote again. Were the United Kingdom to vote "no" in the referendum proposed by Blair to occur after the next British general election, it might be asked, in contrast, to consider leaving the EU. The convention draft had suggested that in the event of ratification by only four-fifths of member states, the European Council would then have to reflect anew on ways to move forward. On top of this, the same European Council that reached agreement on the new Constitutional Treaty also decided to consider the Turkish candidacy for membership seriously, with the Council of Ministers deciding whether or not to go forward to negotiations on the basis of a Commission report due before the end of 2004.[16] National debates on ratification might take place, therefore, during a period of economic gloom, public disfavor with the EU, the very serious transition problems attending enlargement, and amidst passionate debates about Turkey's "Europeanness" (with the domestic ripple effects such consideration is all but certain to spark for Europe's Muslim communities). The June 2004 agreement over a draft constitution averted a debacle, but the storm clouds hovering over the EU could remain ominous.

The Dilemma of Democracy

Behind these tumultuous and complicated debates lay issues about the future of democracy in Europe. European integration has always presented delicate problems for democratic theory and practice. EU member states agreed to "pool" significant dimensions of sovereignty from the Rome Treaty onward, particularly in all-important economic areas. This pooling, through the "Monnet method," was initially meant to enhance economic success and the general welfare across the Union. In the process it spawned a Euro-level political system. The EU that resulted was largely "a market," but its political system came to pose serious problems for citizen scrutiny, control, and exercise of preferences over decisions.

The Rome European Economic Community Treaty promoted a hybrid political system with insufficient direct public responsibility and inadequate transparency. The European Commission, with its formal monopoly of proposal, was appointed. The Council of Ministers, the EU's original legislator, and the European Council, later enshrined as the EU's strategic guide, were intergovernmental (hence inevitably representing conflicting national interests rather than Union interests). As if that weren't sufficient cause for concern, the Council of Ministers and the European Council functioned behind the

thick screens of diplomatic secrecy. From the viewpoint of member state political systems, Europe was a matter of "foreign policy," and this allowed national elites to shroud their European activities behind executive prerogative. The European Parliament, despite its growing power, remained an odd body to which no government was responsible and without majority and opposition. These peculiarities made for foggy debates and opaque communication with European peoples. European law was juridically superior to national law, but its origin and nature have never been fully understood by citizens. Finally, all of these institutions worked in a baffling multiplicity of decision-making processes that only specialists could follow, even after the 2004 Constitutional Treaty.

Real democratic politics in the EU largely happens in national arenas. Here elections are fought around programs with reasonably clear issues, elected officials can be held responsible for their choices, and there is a government and an opposition that debate in parliament to clarify issues, to which ministers and civil servants are responsible. The relative clarity, consistency, and deeply ingrained logic of national democracies may in themselves be problems for democratic practices at European level. Except among elites, there exists as yet little European political culture. National parliamentary discussions rarely place European issues squarely before the public. Elections to the European Parliament remain tightly linked to national political debates. With notable exceptions—Denmark, for example, which constitutionally obliges its national parliament to debate European issues and submit key Euro-level legal matters to national referenda—most national parties and interest groups have barely begun to embrace European matters. One could fault member state leaders, analyze the reasons for their behaviors, and investigate the institutional and other incentives at national level that encourage such practices. But wherever the fault actually lies, the gap between the thickness of national democratic deliberative practices and the thinness of these practices at European level is clear, and the consequences are profound.

The euphoria about triumphant democracy that occurred at the end of the cold war assumed that "democracy was democracy." Once societies had confirmed their choice of constitutional political institutions committed to the rule of law and regular, free electoral consultations, the story had been told, full stop. In the strange, but at the time widely accepted, formula of Francis Fukuyama, the enormous post–cold war victory of democratic ways was "the end of history."[17] But even where basic definitional criteria for democracy have been fulfilled, democratic life remains subject to change. Economic shifts, changes in citizen preferences, the shape of social structures and social problems, relationships between sovereign nations, the scope of markets, and a host of other factors create variety in the nature of democratic life over history and between different democratic societies. In effect, *there may be more, less, or different democracy* in different places and times.

In Europe, as elsewhere, change has occurred rapidly. Sociologically, "workers" have declined, and those workers who remain are diversified in situation and outlook. The "middle classes" have become pivotal as consumers, producers, and voters. "Elites," earlier based primarily on the power of wealth, are now more bureaucratized and technocratic. Populations are aging in ways challenging established intergenerational patterns of distribution and placing great new strains on existing social protection systems. Over the past two decades, the rate of economic growth has dropped, bringing high unemployment, increased economic insecurity, greater inequality, new poverty, and social exclusion. The downturn in growth has weakened unions, key to postwar patterns of labor representation. Organized interests of all kinds have changed their strategic and tactical repertoires. In general, citizen expectations of government developed for an earlier era are now less realistic, with important consequences for public confidence in politics and politicians.

Patterns of political representation have changed in consequence. The effects of television, for example, raise deep questions about the role of media in political representation. Expensive television campaigning has obliged political parties to seek new sources of funds, often in the technically illegal ways that have filled recent decades with scandals. Modern scientific polling and connected political advertising, extremely useful for politicians in targeting constituencies and "median voters," help to short-circuit older patterns of aggregating preferences and to create new ones that are much more subtle and less transparent. The role and nature of political parties have changed. The mass-membership parties pioneered by European social democracy are being replaced by elite-run "electoral machines." Decentralized popular social movements, earlier obliged to seek effective political expression under the wings of these parties, now are heard on their own. Lobbies of all kinds are now central in public decision making.

Most important, the declining economic importance of national boundaries has diminished national state capacities. Europeanization and globalization have rendered national boundaries far more permeable to economic forces. These dual processes have also made effective government action to sustain national economic models and strategies far more difficult. Financial markets can now constrain and sanction national policy choices. Multinational corporations can play in a multilevel political arena while ordinary citizens remain confined to their national boundaries. Sovereignty has been lost or diluted, sometimes from national choice, but often unwillingly. Politicians now have considerable difficulty responding to the expressed needs and desires of citizens for levels of economic and social security that had earlier been assumed.

In general, "issue repertoires" in democracies have shifted. Older, statist approaches have been under siege for decades, and social democratic parties have shifted toward "third-way" and "supply-side" perspectives in which the state and the market coexist to the market's greater advantage. In a period of what many perceive to be one of relative deprivation, immigration has once again become a central issue in European politics, with new populist impulses bearing messages of intolerance with sufficient clout to affect policy in significant ways. In the future, Europe is likely to avoid new immigration to compensate for its demographic problems, for fear that it would make it even more difficult than it already is to sustain public services and social protection programs. Harsh, even punitive asylum policies are likely to deepen the "fortress Europe" mindset of many Europeans, and concerns about security—after 9/11 and the bombings in Madrid—seem certain to provoke ostracism and social exclusion of Arabs and Muslims within the EU.

If many of these changes exist in most northern democratic capitalist societies, in Europe, unlike elsewhere, they have been occurring in the context of European integration. The EU's "democratic deficit" has been less or more pressing to the degree to which decisions made at European level have been significant to EU citizens. Europe was not perceived as weighing greatly on what really mattered until the 1980s. This is no longer the case, however. European integration, for better or worse, is now decisive in the day-to-day lives of all EU citizens. Since 1985, substantial national state capacities and control have been transferred away from EU member states, as amply illustrated in the rest of this volume. In some areas, capacities have been relocated from familiar national democratic places to much less familiar transnational ones in ways that have shone new spotlights on the insufficiencies of Brussels institutions.

The story is even more complicated. Decisions producing this relocalization of state capacities have often been made by European-level methods whose relationships to democracy are murky. Europe has become a choice location for making decisions either by "foreign affairs" methods shielded from public scrutiny or by the "Monnet method" of engineered spillover (the Commission's preferred approach). Although

neither method undermines principles of constitutionalism or the rule of law, both have intensified the democratic deficit. These Euro-level decisions have often been based on a temporal logic that is quite different from those in national democratic lives. Euro-level deliberations are privileged locations for large choices of medium- and longer-term significance whose ultimate consequences ordinary Europeans have usually ignored at the moment when the choices were made. After all, something else—closer to home—always seemed more pressing. Ignorance about the longer-term effects of Euro-political matters has also been structurally reinforced by the shorter-term time horizons that govern domestic political arenas, where politicians must always have their eyes focused on impending elections. Euro-level decision makers have very often refrained from stressing the precise implications of their longer time horizons in public discussion, except perhaps to oversell policies whose consequences were usually unknowable. Euro-politics thus became a very useful way to circumvent the many blockages and veto-points of national politics.

The perverse dimensions of this are clear and broadly understood by European citizens. The European arena presents European political elites with a place where politically risky medium-term policies can be decided far more easily than at national levels. Elites have thus used Europe to reconfigure arrangements in member states to give themselves policy breathing spaces that they thought they needed but which they were far less likely to obtain through national politics alone. To make matters worse, European institutions have allowed these same elites to turn around, inoculate themselves against responsibility, and shift the blame for failure and disruption onto Europe. The consequences for democratic governance are very significant. Decisions made today at the EU level often foreclose proper deliberation on policies tomorrow at the national level. Hence decisions with significant long-term consequences take place behind the backs and above the heads of ordinary citizens and are never subjected to the rough-and-tumble of national political debate and the key mechanism of programmatic choice: the opportunity for voters to pay attention to alternatives and throw incumbents out.

The ways in which democratic representation and accountability work in EU member states vary, but by and large, national politics enjoys considerable legitimacy. Even after the 2004 Constitutional Treaty, the same cannot be said for the EU, which remains a confusing promiscuity of different types of representation and decision making, mostly behind closed doors, and subject to procedures and a body of regulation that almost nobody knows or understands. National political elites are represented in the workings of the Council of Ministers and the European Council, but, given the intergovernmental ways of these institutions, they can skirt accountability in many ways, diluting their risks in national elections. The Commission is not supposed to represent any particular Europeans, but to serve "Europe," an abstract notion at best and perhaps a dangerous one when pushing integration forward is taken to be a moral duty rather than a way of solving real problems. The Parliament neither engages the attention of those who elect it nor controls sufficiently those who propose and decide what happens in the EU. Members of the European Parliament (MEPs) are elected, for the most part, because of the national positions of their parties (or as a symbolic protest against national governments in an election that isn't thought to matter all that much on its own terms). MEPs are not elected because of voters' acquaintance with European matters. There is no clear choice between parties on Euro-policy lines, largely because there is no choice between Euro-platforms and governments. The European Parliament may do good work analyzing and scrutinizing proposals sent to it, but very few people know about this work, even fewer understand where it fits politically, and even fewer care enough to get very worked up about elections to the EP—or even to vote at all.

The Implications of Euro-Politics for Democracy in Europe

If there can be *different* democracy and also *more or less* democracy, then we must be very attentive to the effects of Euro-politics for democracy in Europe. The most obvious observation is that the ramshackle EU institutional complex makes democratic responsibility and accountability more difficult than it needs to be. Time and again, however, we have seen situations in which the confusing nature of the EU seemed to have been designed precisely to blur lines of democratic responsibility and accountability. But it is not at all obvious what to change and how to change it, as the brave and creative efforts of the European Convention have recently demonstrated. Designing transnational democratic politics is a dramatically new problem that must take place against the background of changing democratic politics more generally. Moreover, given the wide range of difference across the EU, basic constitutional change could rock the boat in ways that would be dangerous for European integration. Politicians and leaders are thus faced with a daunting and constant choice between confronting the EU's democratic dilemma at the potential cost of disrupting integration or moving forward with integration and hoping for the best.

Those who have built Europe are democrats and people who believe in the law, but European institutions as they presently exist do not facilitate democratic responsibility and accountability. Institutional muddiness, however innocently created over decades, is unlikely to foster politically innocent behavior. Postwar settlements in Europe created extremely dense national systems of political exchange, often fenced by difficult-to-change rules and powerful organizations. European integration, particularly over the past two decades, has been designed in part to undercut the dimensions of these settlements deemed by elites to be barriers to European economic success. Some actors, including business interests, have been able to adjust their strategies to influence these processes successfully. Other actors, particularly those with deeply rooted national resource bases, have been less flexible. It is no surprise, therefore, to learn that European integration has helped some groups more than it has helped others. The changes wrought by European integration justify questioning whether Europe in the twenty-first century will have different democracy or less democracy.

Like every lasting political entity on planet Earth, the new Europe's future will be full of problems, and the choices that it makes in confronting them are essential for everyone. The EU's past—integration is now more than fifty years old—shows clearly that Europeans are capable of making the right choices, however. The EU began as a unique political innovation to eliminate war on a continent that had made periodic bloodletting a habit. More than fifty years later, despite conflict in the Balkans around the disintegration of the former Yu-

goslavia, the promise has been redeemed. The chosen strategy for this great endeavor was market and economic integration. Fifty years later this has gone far beyond what anyone expected, and, despite numerous outstanding issues, it has brought prosperity and dynamism. Moreover, the original design foresaw economic integration spilling over to the more directly political arenas that are today's EU frontiers. Carrying this new political dimension further to fruition will be difficult and take time. Here again, the past brings comfort and confidence. Through its openness to enlargement, the EU has united the entire Continent for the first time in history. Finally, European integration has been central in consolidating democracy, first in Western Europe, next for southern Europe, and most recently in Central and Eastern Europe. Thus the Continent is not only united, it is also democratic. In a tormented world, these accomplishments bespeak unusual success. Just as surely, they promise success in the future.

Notes

1. Loukas Tsoukalis's *What Kind of Europe?* (Oxford: Oxford University Press, 2003) is the most thoughtful recent work that addresses these deep questions.

2. At Maastricht EU member states had clearly been loath to give up their remaining foreign and defense policy autonomy because, in most instances, it remained a real source of international leverage. The Gulf War helped set the stage for this reluctance, simultaneously dividing the Europeans and pushing them into line behind U.S. goals. The EU's disarray after Maastricht then facilitated a relatively rapid American strategic reevaluation, particularly with NATO. NATO thus moved to reconsider its missions and to expand in ways that guaranteed it a strong position in European security matters for the new era, even while the United States withdrew most of its troops and cut back on defense spending. On NATO changes, see David S. Yost, *NATO Transformed* (Washington, D.C.: United States Institute of Peace, 1998).

3. See Frank Schimmelfennig, *The EU, NATO, and the Integration of Europe* (Cambridge: Cambridge University Press, 2003).

4. Paraphrased in Peter Norman, *The Accidental Constitution: The Story of the European Convention* (Brussels: Eurocomment, 2003), p. 109.

5. For a strong statement of this point of view, see Stefan Collignon and Werner Weidenfeld, *The European Republic* (London: Kogan Page, 2004).

6. See *The Economist*, June 19, 2004, pp. 65–67.

7. Joschka Fischer, "From Confederacy to Federation: Thoughts on the Finality of European Integration," translation of advance text of speech at the Humboldt University in Berlin, May 12, 2000, p. 6.

8. 10 Downing Street, "Prime Minister's Speech to the Polish Stock Exchange," October 6, 2000; www.number-10.gov.uk.

9. Report to the Commission on "The Institutional Implications of Enlargement" by Richard von

Weizsäcker, Jean-Luc Dehaene, and David Simon (Brussels: European Commission, October 18, 1999), p. 5.

10. For a succinct summary of the issues, see the Report to the Commission on "The Institutional Implications of Enlargement" by three designated "wise men" (Richard von Weizsäcker, Jean-Luc Dehaene, and David Simon) (Brussels: European Commission, October 18, 1999).

11. For the draft Declaration on Fundamental Rights in the EU go to http://db.consilium.eu.int, the Council of the European Union website, and follow the links.

12. See *Traité de Nice, texte provisoire agréé par la Conférence intergouvernementale sur la réforme institutionnelle*, SN 533/00 (Brussels, December 12, 2000).

13. I have drawn on Peter Norman's superb book on the convention, *The Accidental Constitution*, for much of what follows. Should readers want to get a play-by-play flavor of the workings of today's EU, warts and all, Norman's book is the place to look. Olivier Duhamel, a French MEP, convention member, and constitutional lawyer, has written a similar excellent book, *Pour l'Europe* (Paris: Seuil, 2003).

The convention's vast collection of documents and debates is on the EU website, http://europa.eu.int.

14. Much of what follows has been culled from Norman and Duhamel.

15. At this point, when real choices were in the offing, a number of foreign ministers joined the convention to make sure that governmental desires were heard clearly.

16. It also decided to open negotiations with Croatia.

17. Francis Fukuyama, *The End of History and the Last Man* (New York: Avon Books, 1992).

Part II Bibliography

Borchardt, Klaus-Dieter. *The ABC of Community Law*. Luxembourg: European Commission, 2000. Succinct, coherent, sophisticated discussion of the EU as an organization of people of the law.

De Grauwe, Paul. *Economics of Monetary Union*, 4th ed. Oxford: Oxford University Press, 2000. The technical economics of the EU's farthest point of advance.

Delors, Jacques. *Mémoires*. Paris: Plon, 2004. Indispensable recollections by one of EU Europe's most important leaders.

Dinan, Desmond. *Ever Closer Union*, 2nd ed. Boulder: Lynne Rienner, 1999. A thorough, thoughtful textbook on the EU.

Getz, Klaus, and Simon Hix, eds. *Europeanised Politics: European Integration and National Political Systems*. London: Frank Cass, 2001. Good work addressing key question of "Europeanization" of national politics due to integration.

Hix, Simon. *The Political System of the European Union*. Basingstoke, England: Macmillan, 1999. Sharp political science analysis of Euro-politics.

Lamy, Pascal, and Jean Pisani-Ferry. *The Europe We Want*. London: Arch Press, 2002. Penetrating insights by Lamy, one of the EU's most successful practitioners, and Pisani-Ferry, a leading French economist, on Europe's future.

Martin, Andrew, and George Ross, eds. *Euros and Europeans: EMU and the European Model of Society*. Cambridge: Cambridge University Press, 2004. International research on the effects of EMU on European social policy.

Moravcsik, Andrew. *The Choice for Europe: Social Purpose and State Power from Messina to Maastricht*. Ithaca, N.Y.: Cornell University Press, 1998. Massive and impressive historical research in support of an international relations theory of European integration.

Neal, Larry, and Daniel Barbezat. *The Economics of the European Union and the Economies of Europe*. Oxford: Oxford University Press, 1998. Readable introduction to EU market integration and the national economies that are being integrated.

Rosamond, Ben. *Theories of European Integration*. Basingstoke, England: Palgrave, 2000. Good review of different social science theories of European integration.

Ross, George. *Jacques Delors and European Integration*. Cambridge, England: Polity, 1995.

Ethnographic exploration of the European Commission under Jacques Delors during the Maastricht years.

Scharpf, Fritz. *Governing in Europe: Effective and Democratic.* Oxford: Oxford University Press, 1999. Rigorous reflection on what EU Europe can and should do by one of Germany's leading political analysts.

Tsoukalis, Loukas. *What Kind of Europe?* Oxford: Oxford University Press, 2003. An unusually thoughtful essay on the real meanings of the EU.

Wallace, Helen, and William Wallace, *Policymaking in the European Union,* 4th ed. New York: Oxford University Press, 2000.

Weiler, J. H. H. *The Constitution of Europe.* Cambridge: Cambridge University Press, 1999. Essays on the EU and its constitutional problems by a leading legal scholar.

Journals

Among the many periodical publications that focus or help understand the EU are the following:

Agence Europe. Daily newsletter where the "Eurocrats" learn what is happening.

Economist. Weekly, highly intelligent, but beware British liberal bias.

European Union Politics

European Voice. Brussels weekly, "insiders" talk.

EUSA Newsletter

Financial Times. London daily, with Internet and U.S. editions.

Journal of Common Market Studies

Journal of European Integration

West European Politics

Websites

www. europa.int.eu: The official EU website is a treasure trove of documents, press releases, EU publications to download, statistics, and other important information. As befits the EU's complexity as a political system, this website takes work to navigate but is well worth puzzling through.

www.eurunion.org: Website of the European Commission's delegation in Washington, D.C. Useful for information on EU-U.S. relations, up-to-date reporting on latest EU news, help for researching and teaching. Links to EU centers available under "A to Z index of European Union Websites."

www.eustudies.org: Website of the European Union Studies Association (EUSA), the largest professional organization dedicated to EU studies. In addition to information about EUSA, provides much useful information about grants, scholarships, internships, plus links to different European Union centers in North America and Europe.

Think Tanks

There are now a number of distinguished think tanks that work on the EU, all with good websites. Among them:

Centre for European Policy Studies (Brussels): www.ceps.be

Centre for European Reform (London): www.cer.org.uk

Federal Trust (London): www.fedtrust.co.uk

Institut d'Études Européennes de l'Université Libre de Bruxelles (Brussels); includes many documents in English: www.ulb.ac.be/iee

Max Planck Institute for the Study of Societies (Germany): www.mpi-fg-koeln.mpg.de

Notre Europe (Paris); includes many documents in English: www.notre-europe.asso.fr

PART

Britain

Joel Krieger

CHAPTER

6

The Making of the Modern British State

British Politics in Action

On Saturday, January 24, 2004, Prime Minister Tony Blair, who was facing the most dangerous week of his political life, acknowledged that his job was on the line. On Tuesday, an extremely tough fight was anticipated over the Higher Education Bill to raise student fees in order to fund university education, a centerpiece of his legislative program. But Wednesday looked far more ominous, for that was the day when Blair would face the much-anticipated report of the Hutton inquiry on the suicide of David Kelly, the former UN weapons inspector and whistle-blower who challenged a key tenet of the government's justification for the war in Iraq.

The report would bring to a climax the miserable saga that began in May 2003, when the BBC reported that the most compelling evidence for the claim that Saddam Hussein posed an imminent threat—that Iraq could launch weapons of mass destruction on forty-five minutes' notice—was wrong. For an increasingly beleaguered Tony Blair, facing mounting criticism of the war in Iraq, the story could scarcely have been more damaging. Relying on an unnamed "senior official," the BBC asserted that Downing Street had ordered the government's claims against Saddam to be exaggerated or, as the BBC reporter unforgettably put it, "sexed up." After three weeks of merciless pounding in the media, Blair made a fateful decision: it was time to authorize a back-channel leak of the BBC's source, David Kelly. If Kelly were discredited, the BBC

would be put in its place, and the prime minister might reclaim the offensive.

His name revealed, Kelly was promptly placed before the harsh glare of television cameras on July 15 and grilled by the House of Commons Foreign Affairs Committee. Then, just two days later, he left his home in a village near Oxford for his usual afternoon walk, chatted with a neighbor, and never returned. There was little doubt that Kelly's death was suicide, but his tragedy put a human face on the misgivings many millions of Britons felt about the justifications for the Anglo-American invasion of Iraq. It unleashed a furious debate about what lengths Blair had gone to steamroll Parliament into backing his war aims and what pressure he was willing to exert to intimidate a well-meaning whistle-blower.

Blair was feeling the heat on all sides. Polls indicated that nearly 60 percent of the British people thought Blair should resign if Hutton found he had intentionally exaggerated the case for war. The prime minister came very close to accepting that view when he acknowledged that the issue was one of his integrity. Both allies and detractors knew that his future was on the line, and Blair agreed. In addition, the prime minister made it clear that a defeat on the Education Bill on Tuesday would be taken as a vote of no confidence in his leadership and bring with it the possibility of resignation. London was buzzing with political intrigue, with many insiders speculating that by Wednesday, even if Hutton's verdict about Blair's role in the Kelly tragedy

Britain

0   100 Miles

0   100 Kilometers

Shetland Islands

Orkney Islands

Outer Hebrides

Inner Hebrides

SCOTLAND

North Sea

★Edinburgh

•Glasgow

NORTHERN IRELAND

Belfast

Isle of Man

Irish Sea

REPUBLIC OF IRELAND

Dublin★

Isle of Anglesey

Manchester

Liverpool•

ENGLAND

WALES

•Birmingham

Thames

Cardiff★

•Bristol

London

Southampton•

Isle of Wight

ATLANTIC OCEAN

•Plymouth

English Channel

FRANCE

was relatively mild, Blair's premiership might be crumbling.

So how bad a week did Blair have? It was not nearly as bad as he—and most observers—expected. In fact, things got better as the week went on. On Tuesday (the very Tuesday New Hampshire Democrats gave John Kerry the victory that catapulted him to his party's nomination), Blair's party deserted him in droves. His 161-seat majority all but evaporated, and his reputation was badly bruised, but the Education Bill squeaked through by 5 votes. Overnight he seemed weakened and discredited: a push from Hutton, and he could be on the way to political ruin. Then on Wednesday the Hutton Report entirely vindicated his role in the Kelly affair, roundly blamed the BBC, and the Blair government was back in business.[1]

The week's events signaled a short-term victory for Blair, but hardly a reversal in political fortunes. Blair's decision to support the U.S.-led war in Iraq was very unpopular in Britain, increasingly so as weapons of mass destruction—the key justification for war—remained elusive. In January, Blair was damaged by the imbroglio over the Education Bill, and then saved by the Hutton Report. But, as the resistance to Anglo-American occupation intensified and evidence of severe American mistreatment of detainees surfaced (as well as allegations of lesser but still serious mistreatment by the British), it seemed more and more clear that Blair was hostage to events that he could not control. Once an enormously popular prime minister and a political leader with uncanny instincts, he seemed now to be lurching from crisis to crisis. How bad was it for Blair? Many pundits expected a Blair resignation by fall 2004 in favor of Gordon Brown, his chancellor and much-anticipated successor as leader of the Labour Party and prime minister. But by the end of May, it seemed that perhaps the worst had passed. Although poll results in the *Guardian* indicated that Blair's personal popularity had dipped further in the prior month, from minus 20 to minus 24, there was some good news for Blair as well. The prime minister

was still considered an asset to the Labour Party by a very healthy 76 percent of Labour voters. Nearly half (48 percent) wanted Blair to run for reelection and to serve a full third term. And best of all, given the buzz about Blair's quick exit in favor of Gordon Brown, only 17 percent of the Labour Party faithful wanted him to step down before the next election (expected in spring or summer 2005 and required before June 2006). Polls through the summer indicated that twice as many Britons were dissatisfied with Blair's performance than were satisfied with it, but the talk of an early departure in favor of Gordon Brown faded. In October 2004, when Blair announced his intention to win election a third time and to complete the full term in office, few voiced any doubts that he would do exactly that.

Geographic Setting

Britain is the largest of the British Isles, a group of islands off the northwest coast of Europe, and encompasses England, Scotland, and Wales. The second-largest island comprises Northern Ireland and the independent Republic of Ireland. The term *Great Britain* encompasses England, Wales, and Scotland, but not Northern Ireland. We use the term *Britain* as shorthand for the United Kingdom of Great Britain and Northern Ireland.

Covering an area of approximately 94,000 square miles, Britain is roughly two-thirds the size of Japan, or approximately half the size of France. In 1995, the population of the United Kingdom was 58.6 million people; the population is projected to peak at 61.2 million people in 2023.[2] To put the size of this once immensely powerful country in perspective, it is slightly smaller than Oregon.

Although forever altered by the Channel Tunnel, Britain's location as an offshore island adjacent to Europe is significant. Historically, Britain's island destiny made it less subject to invasion and conquest than its continental counterparts, affording the country a sense of security.

The geographic separation from mainland Europe has also created for many Britons a feeling that they are both apart from and a part of Europe, a factor that has complicated relations with Britain's EU partners to this day.

Critical Junctures

Our study begins with a look at the historic development of the modern British state. History shapes contemporary politics in very important ways. Once in place, institutions leave powerful legacies, and issues placed on the agenda in one period and left unresolved may present challenges for the future.

In many ways, Britain is the model of a united and stable country with an enviable record of continuity and resiliency. Nevertheless, the history of state formation reveals how complex and open-ended the process can be. Some issues that plague other countries, such as religious divisions, were settled long ago in Great Britain proper (although not in Northern Ireland). Yet others, such as multiple national identities, remain on the agenda.

British state formation involved the unification of kingdoms or crowns (hence the term United *Kingdom*). After Duke William of Normandy defeated the English in the Battle of Hastings in 1066, the Norman monarchy extended its authority throughout the British Isles. Although Welsh national sentiments remained strong, the prospects for unity with England were improved in 1485 by the accession to the English throne of Henry VII of the Welsh House of Tudor. With the Acts of Union of 1536 and 1542, England and Wales were legally, politically, and administratively united. The unification of the Scottish and English crowns occurred in 1603, when James VI of Scotland ascended to the English throne as James I. Thereafter, England, Scotland, and Wales were known as Great Britain. Scotland and England remained divided politically, however, until the Act of Union of 1707. Henceforth, a common Parliament of

Great Britain replaced the two separate parliaments of Scotland and of England and Wales.

At the same time, the making of the British state included a historic expression of constraints on monarchical rule. At first, the period of Norman rule after 1066 strengthened royal control, but the conduct of King John (1199–1216) fueled opposition from feudal barons. In 1215, they forced the king to consent to a series of concessions that protected feudal landowners from abuses of royal power. These restrictions on royal prerogatives were embodied in the Magna Carta, a historic statement of the rights of a political community against the monarchical state. Soon after, in 1236, the term *Parliament* was first used officially to refer to the gathering of feudal barons summoned by the

Critical Junctures in Britain's Political Development

1688	Glorious Revolution establishes power of Parliament
ca. 1750	Industrial Revolution begins in Britain
1832	Reform Act expands voting rights
1837–1901	Reign of Queen Victoria; height of British Empire
1914–1918	World War I
1929–1939	Great Depression
1939–1945	World War II
1945–1979	Establishment of British welfare state; dismantling of British Empire
1973	Britain joins the European Community
1979–1990	Prime Minister Margaret Thatcher promotes "enterprise culture"
1997	Tony Blair elected prime minister
2001	Under Blair's leadership, Britain "stands shoulder to shoulder" with America in war against terror

king whenever he required their consent to special taxes. By the fifteenth century, Parliament had gained the right to make laws.

The Seventeenth-Century Settlement

The making of the British state in the sixteenth and seventeenth centuries involved a complex interplay of religious conflicts, national rivalries, and struggles between rulers and the fledgling Parliament. These conflicts erupted in the civil wars of the 1640s and the forced abdication of James II in 1688. The bloodless political revolution of 1688, subsequently known as the Glorious Revolution, marked the "last successful political coup d'état or revolution in British history."[3] It also confirmed the power of Parliament over the monarchy. Parliament required the new monarchs, William and Mary, to meet with it annually and to agree to regular parliamentary elections. This contrasted dramatically with the arrangement enjoyed in France by Louis XIV (1643–1715), who gained power at the expense of the French nobility and operated without any constraint from commoners.

By the end of the seventeenth century, the framework of a constitutional (or limited) monarchy, which would still exercise flashes of power into the nineteenth century, was established in Britain. For more than three hundred years, Britain's monarchs have been answerable to Parliament, which has held the sole authority for taxation and the maintenance of a standing army.

The Glorious Revolution also resolved longstanding religious conflict. The replacement of the Roman Catholic James II by the Protestant William and Mary ensured the dominance of the Church of England (or Anglican Church). To this day, the Church of England remains the established (official) religion, and approximately two dozen of its bishops and archbishops sit as members of the House of Lords, the upper house of Parliament.

Thus, by the end of the seventeenth century, a basic form of parliamentary democracy had emerged, and the problem of religious divisions, which continue to plague many countries throughout the world, was settled. Equally important, these seventeenth-century developments became a defining moment for how the British perceive their history to this day. However divisive and disruptive the process of state building may have been originally, its telling and retelling have contributed significantly to a British political culture that celebrates democracy's continuity, gradualism, and tolerance.

As a result of settling its religious differences early, Britain has taken a more secular turn than most other countries in Western Europe. The majority of Britons do not consider religion a significant source of identity, and active church membership in Britain, at 15 percent, is very low in comparison with other Western European countries. In Britain, religious identification has less political significance in voting behavior or party loyalty than in many other countries. By contrast to France, where devout Catholics tend to vote right of center, there is relatively little association between religion and voting behavior in Britain (although Anglicans are a little more likely to vote Conservative). Unlike Germany or Italy, for example, politics in Britain is secular. No parties have religious affiliation, a factor that contributed to the success of the Conservative Party, one of the most successful right-of-center parties in Europe in the twentieth century.

As a consequence, except in Northern Ireland, where religious divisions continue, the party system in the United Kingdom has traditionally reflected class distinctions and remains free of the pattern of multiple parties (particularly right-of-center parties) that occurs in countries where party loyalties are divided by both class and religion.

The Industrial Revolution and the British Empire

Although the British state was consolidated by the seventeenth century, the timing of its industrial development and the way that process transformed Britain's role in the world radically shaped its form. The Industrial Revolution in the mid-eighteenth century involved rapid expansion of manufacturing production and technological innovation. It also led to monumental social and economic transformations and resulted in pressures for democratization. Externally, Britain used its competitive edge to transform and dominate the international order. Internally, the Industrial Revolution helped shape the development of the British state and changed forever the British people's way of life.

The Industrial Revolution. The consequences of the Industrial Revolution for the generations of people who experienced its upheavals can scarcely be exaggerated. The typical worker was turned "by degrees . . . from small peasant or craftsman into wage-labourer," as historian Eric Hobsbawm observes. Cash and market-based transactions replaced older traditions of barter and production for local need.[4]

Despite a gradual improvement in the standard of living in the English population at large, the effects of industrialization were often profound for agricultural laborers and particular types of artisans. With the commercialization of agriculture, many field laborers lost their security of employment, and cottagers (small landholders) were squeezed off the land in large numbers. The mechanization of manufacturing, which spread furthest in the cotton industry, upset the traditional status of the preindustrial skilled craft workers and permanently marginalized them.

The British Empire. Britain had assumed a significant role as a world power during the seventeenth century, building an overseas empire and engaging actively in international commerce. But it was the Industrial Revolution of the eighteenth century that established global production and exchange on a new and expanded scale, with particular consequences for the making of the British state. Cotton manufacture, the driving force behind Britain's growing industrial

dominance, not only pioneered the new techniques and changed labor organization of the Industrial Revolution but also represented the perfect imperial industry. It relied on imported raw materials and, by the turn of the nineteenth century, already depended on overseas markets for the vast majority of its sales of finished goods. Growth depended on foreign markets rather than on domestic consumption. This export orientation fueled an expansion far more rapid than an exclusively domestic orientation would have allowed.

With its leading industrial sector dependent on overseas trade, Britain's leaders worked aggressively to secure markets and expand the empire. Toward these ends, Britain defeated European rivals in a series of military engagements, culminating in the Napoleonic Wars (1803–1815), which confirmed Britain's commercial, military, and geopolitical preeminence. The Napoleonic Wars also secured a balance of power on the European continent favorable for largely unrestricted international commerce (free trade). Propelled by the formidable and active presence of the British navy, international trade helped England to take full advantage of its position as the first industrial power. Many scholars suggest that in the middle of the nineteenth century, Britain had the highest per capita income in the world (it was certainly among the two or three highest), and in 1870, at the height of its glory, its trade represented nearly one-quarter of the world total, and its industrial mastery ensured highly competitive productivity in comparison with trading partners (see Table 6.1).

During the reign of Queen Victoria (1837–1901), the British Empire was immensely powerful and encompassed fully 25 percent of the world's population. Britain presided over a vast formal and informal empire, with extensive direct colonial rule over some four dozen countries, including India and Nigeria. At the same time, Britain enjoyed the advantages of an extensive informal empire—a worldwide network of independent states, including China, Iran, and Brazil—whose economic fates were linked to it.

Table 6.1   World Trade and Relative Labor
Productivity

	Proportion of World Trade (%)	Relative Labor Productivity[a] (%)
1870	24.0	1.63
1890	18.5	1.45
1913	14.1	1.15
1938	14.0	0.92

[a]As compared with the average rate of productivity in other members of the world economy.
Source: Robert O. Keohane, *After Hegemony: Cooperation and Discord in the World Economy* (Princeton, N.J.: Princeton University Press, 1984), p. 36. Copyright © 1984 by Princeton University Press. Reprinted by permission of Princeton University Press.

Britain ruled as a hegemonic power, the state that could control the pattern of alliances and terms of the international economic order, and that often could shape domestic political developments in countries throughout the world. Overall, the making of the British state observed a neat symmetry. Its global power helped underwrite industrial growth at home. At the same time, the reliance of domestic industry on world markets, beginning with cotton manufacture in the eighteenth century, prompted the government to project British interests overseas as forcefully as possible.

Industrial Change and the Struggle for Voting Rights.   The Industrial Revolution shifted economic power from landowners to men of commerce and industry. As a result, the first critical juncture in the long process of democratization began in the late 1820s, when the "respectable opinion" of the propertied classes and increasing popular agitation pressed Parliament to expand the right to vote (franchise) beyond a thin band of men with substantial property, mainly landowners. With Parliament under considerable pressure, the Reform Act of 1832 extended the franchise to a section of the (male) middle class.

In a very limited way, the Reform Act confirmed the social and political transformations of the Industrial Revolution by granting new urban manufacturing centers, such as Manchester and Birmingham, more substantial representation. However, the massive urban working class created by the Industrial Revolution and populating the cities of Charles Dickens's England remained on the outside looking in. In fact, the reform was very narrow and defensive. Before 1832, less than 5 percent of the adult population was entitled to vote—and afterward, only about 7 percent.

In extending the franchise so narrowly, the reform underscored the strict property basis for political participation and inflamed class-based tensions in Britain. Following the Reform Act, a massive popular movement erupted in the late 1830s to secure the program of the People's Charter, which included demands for universal male suffrage and other radical reforms intended to make Britain a much more participatory democracy. The Chartist movement, as it was called, held huge and often tumultuous rallies, and organized a vast campaign to petition Parliament, but it failed to achieve any of its aims.

Expansion of the franchise proceeded very slowly. The Representation of the People Act of 1867 increased the electorate to just over 16 percent but left cities significantly underrepresented. The Franchise Act of 1884 nearly doubled the size of the electorate, but it was not until the Representation of the People Act of 1918 that suffrage included nearly all adult men and women over age thirty. How slow a process was it? The franchise for men with substantial incomes dated from the fifteenth century, but women between the ages of twenty-one and thirty were not enfranchised until 1928. The voting age for both women and men was lowered to eighteen in 1969. Except for some episodes during the days of the Chartist movement, the struggle for extension of the franchise took place without violence, but its time horizon must be measured in centuries. This is British gradualism—at its best and its worst (see Figure 6.1).

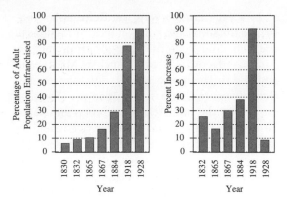

Figure 6.1   Expansion of Voting Rights

Expansion of the franchise in Britain was a gradual process. Despite reforms dating from the early nineteenth century, nearly universal adult suffrage was not achieved until 1928.

Source: From *The British Political Process, Concentrated Power Versus Accountability*, 1st Edition by Rasmussen. © 1993. Reprinted with permission of Wadsworth, a division of Thomson Learning: www.thomsonrights.com. Fax 800 730-2215.

World Wars, Industrial Strife, and the Depression (1914–1945)

With the matter of the franchise finally resolved, in one sense the making of the British state as a democracy was settled. In another important sense, however, the development of the state was just beginning in the twentieth century with the expansion of the state's direct responsibility for management of the economy and the provision of social welfare for citizens. The making of what is sometimes called the *interventionist state* was spurred by the experiences of two world wars.

The state's involvement in the economy increased significantly during World War I (1914–1918). The state took control of a number of industries, including railways, mining, and shipping. It set prices and restricted the flow of capital abroad and channeled the country's resources into production geared to the war effort. After World War I, it remained active in the management of industry in a rather different way. Amid a set of tremendous industrial disputes, the state wielded its power to fragment the trade union movement and resist demands for workers' control over production and to promote more extensive state ownership of industries. This considerable government manipulation of the economy openly contradicted the policy of laissez-faire (minimal government interference in the operation of economic markets). The tensions between free-market principles and interventionist practices deepened with the Great Depression beginning in 1929 and continuing through much of the 1930s and the experiences of World War II (1939–1945). The fear of depression and the burst of pent-up yearnings for a better life after the war helped transform the role of the state and ushered in a period of unusual political harmony.

Collectivist Consensus (1945–1979)

In the postwar context of shared victory and common misery (almost everyone suffered terrible hardships immediately after the war), reconstruction and dreams of new prosperity and security took priority over ideological conflict. In Britain today, a debate rages among political scientists over whether there was a postwar consensus. Critics of the concept contend that disagreements over specific policies concerning the economy, education, employment, and health, along with an electorate divided on partisan lines largely according to social class, indicated politics as usual.[5] It seems fair to say, however, that a broad culture of reconciliation and a determination to rebuild and improve the conditions of life for all Britons helped forge a postwar settlement based broadly on a collectivist consensus that endured until the mid-1970s.

Collectivism is the term coined to describe the consensus that drove politics in the harmonious postwar period when a significant majority of Britons and all major political parties agreed that the state should take expanded responsibility for economic governance and provide for the social welfare in the broadest terms. They accepted as a matter of faith that governments should work to narrow the gap between rich and poor through public education, national healthcare, and other policies of the welfare state, and they accepted state responsibility for economic growth and full employment. Collectivism brought class-based actors (representatives of labor and management) inside politics and forged a broad consensus about the expanded role of government.

Throughout this period, there was a remarkable unity among electoral combatants, as the Labour and Conservative mainstream endorsed the principle of state responsibility for the collective good in both economic and social terms. Although modest in comparative European terms, the commitment to state management of the economy and provision of social services marked a new era in British politics. In time, however, economic downturn and political stagnation caused the consensus to unravel.

Margaret Thatcher and the Enterprise Culture (1979–1990)

In the 1970s, economic stagnation and the declining competitiveness of key British industries in international markets fueled industrial strife and kept class-based tensions near the surface of politics. No government appeared equal to the tasks of economic management. Each party failed in turn. The Conservative government of Edward Heath (1970–1974) could not resolve the economic problems or the political tensions that resulted from the previously unheard-of combination of increased inflation and reduced growth (stagflation). The Labour government of Harold Wilson and James Callaghan (1974–1979) fared no better. As unions became increasingly disgruntled, the country was beset by a rash of strikes throughout the winter of 1978–1979, the "winter of discontent." Labour's inability to discipline its trade union allies hurt

the party in the election just a few months later, in May 1979. The traditional centrist Conservative and Labour alternatives within the collectivist mold seemed exhausted, and many Britons were ready for a new policy agenda.

Margaret Thatcher more than met the challenge. Winning the leadership of the Conservative Party in 1975, she wasted little time in launching a set of bold policy initiatives, which, with characteristic forthrightness, she began to implement after the Conservatives were returned to power in 1979. Reelected in 1983 and 1987, Thatcher served longer without interruption than any other British prime minister in the twentieth century and never lost a general election.

Thatcher transformed British political life by advancing an alternative vision of politics. She was convinced that collectivism had contributed to Britain's decline by sapping British industry and permitting powerful and self-serving unions to hold the country for ransom. To reverse Britain's relative economic slide, Thatcher sought to jump-start the economy by cutting taxes, reducing social services where possible, and using government policy to stimulate competitiveness and efficiency in the private sector.

The term *Thatcherism* embraces her distinctive leadership style, her economic and political strategies, as well as her traditional cultural values: individual responsibility, commitment to family, frugality, and an affirmation of the entrepreneurial spirit. These values combined nostalgia for the past and a rejection of permissiveness and disorder. Taken together and referred to as the *enterprise culture*, they stood as a reproach and an alternative to collectivism.

In many ways, the period of Margaret Thatcher's leadership as prime minister (1979–1990) marks a critical dividing line in postwar British politics. She set the tone and redefined the goals of British politics like few others before her. In November 1990, a leadership challenge within Thatcher's own Conservative Party, largely over her anti-EU stance and high-handed leadership style, caused her sudden

With characteristic aplomb, Prime Minister Margaret Thatcher greeted the annual Conservative Party Conference at the seaside resort of Bournemouth in October 1986.

Source: Stuart Franklin/Magnum Photos, Inc.

resignation and replacement by John Major. Major served as prime minister from 1990 to 1997, leading the Conservative Party to a victory in the 1992 general election before succumbing to Tony Blair's New Labour in 1997.

New Labour's Third Way

Some twenty electoral records were toppled as New Labour under the leadership of Tony Blair

(see the box on facing page) won 419 of the 659 seats in Parliament, the largest majority it has ever held. Blair was propelled into office as prime minister with a 10 percent swing from Conservative to Labour, a postwar record. More women (120) and members of ethnic minorities (9) were elected than ever before. In addition, the political undertow of this electoral tsunami was fierce. The Conservative Party, which had been in power since Margaret Thatcher's 1979 victory and was one of Europe's most successful parties in the twentieth century, was decimated. More cabinet ministers lost their seats than ever before. The Conservatives were nearly wiped off the map in London and other major cities and were shut out altogether in Scotland and Wales.

Blair's Agenda for Britain. After Tony Blair's election in 1997, there was an unmistakable sense in Britain that something extremely interesting and potentially significant was happening. New Labour aspired to recast British politics, offering what it referred to as a "third-way" alternative to the collectivism of traditional Labour and Thatcherism. Everything was at issue, from the way politics is organized to the country's underlying values, institutions, and policies. In electoral terms, New Labour rejected the notion of interest-based politics, in which unions and working people naturally look to Labour and businesspeople and the more prosperous look to the Conservatives. Labour won in 1997 by drawing support from across the socio-economic spectrum. It rejected the historic ties between Labour governments and the trade union movement, choosing instead to emphasize the virtues of a partnership with business.

In institutional and policy terms, New Labour's innovations were intended to reverse the tendency of previous Labour governments in Britain to provide centralized statist solutions to all economic and social problems. Blair promised new approaches to economic, welfare, and social policy; British leadership in Europe; and far-reaching constitutional changes to revitalize democratic participation and devolve (transfer)

Tony Blair

Born in 1953 to a mother from Donegal, Ireland (who moved to Glasgow after her father's death), and a father from the Clydeside shipyards, Tony Blair lacks the typical pedigree of Labour Party leaders. It is very common in the highest ranks of the Labour Party to find someone whose father or grandfather was a union official or a Labour MP. The politics in the Blair family, by contrast, were closely linked to Conservatism (as chairman of his local Conservative Party club, his father Leo had a good chance to become a Conservative MP). Often, like Tony Blair's two predecessors—Neil Kinnock from Wales and John Smith from the West of Scotland—leaders of the Labour Party also have distinctive regional ties. In contrast, Blair moved to Durham in the north of England when he was five but spent much of his youth in boarding schools, moved south when he was old enough to set out on his own, studied law at Oxford, specialized in employment and industrial law in London—and returned to the north only to enter the House of Commons from Sedgefield in 1983. Thus, Blair has neither the traditional political nor regional ties of a Labour Party leader.*

Coming of political age in opposition, Blair joined the shadow cabinet in 1988, serving in turn as shadow minister of energy, then of employment, and finally as shadow home secretary. An MP with no government experience, he easily won the contest for party leadership after his close friend and fellow modernizer John Smith died of a sudden heart attack in the summer of 1994. From the start, Blair boosted Labour Party morale and raised expectations that the party would soon regain power. As one observer put it, "The new Leader rapidly made a favorable impression on the electorate: his looks and affability of manner appealed to voters whilst his self-confidence, lucidity and clarity of mind rendered him a highly effective communicator and lent him an air of authority."† As prime minister, Blair combined firm leadership, eclectic beliefs, and bold political initiatives as he transformed the Labour Party to "New Labour." Blair will doubtless be viewed as a towering figure in British politics. Even before the war in Iraq, his lack of familiar roots and ideological convictions made Blair, for many, an enigmatic figure. His very personal decision to support the U.S.-led invasion of Iraq deepened the impression that Blair would follow his own inner voice above the preferences of party. It was also a decision that was very likely to define Blair's leadership and largely determine his legacy.

*See Andy McSmith, *Faces of Labour: The Inside Story* (London: Verso, 1997), pp. 7–96.
†Eric Shaw, *The Labour Party Since 1945* (Oxford: Blackwell, 1996), p. 195.

---

specified powers from the central government to Scotland, Wales, and Northern Ireland.

In the early months of his premiership, Blair displayed effective leadership in his stewardship of the nation during the period after Lady Diana's death and in his aggressive efforts to achieve a potentially historic peace agreement for Northern Ireland, with far-reaching constitutional implications. By the summer of 2000, however, a rash of embarrassing leaks from Blair's inner sanctum, including a document written by the prime minister that revealed him stewing over "a sense that the government—and this even applies to me—are somehow out of touch with gut British instincts," contributed to a growing sentiment that New Labour was spinning its wheels. Many observers, Labour supporters among them, suggested that Blair and his team were better at coming up with innovative-sounding ideas than at delivering the goods (better at spin than substance). Factionalism in the party and among the leadership was reemerging and skepticism growing that key promises—for example, in healthcare and education (to reduce waiting lists for hospital services and to reduce class sizes)—might not be met. In addition, a set of crises—from a set of fatal train crashes since 1997 to protests over the cost of petrol (gasoline) in September 2000 to an outbreak of mad cow disease in spring 2001—made Blair more politically vulnerable and made his grand promises seem a little shopworn. Nevertheless, until the war in Iraq, Blair remained a formidable leader, and a few months before the cataclysmic events of September 11, 2001, New Labour won what it most sought: an electoral mandate in June 2001 for a second successive term.

Britain in the Euro Era

In May 1998, eleven EU countries, led by Germany, France, Italy, and Spain—but not including Britain—signed on to the single European currency, the euro. One month later, the European Central Bank was established, operating with considerable institutional and political independence, and charged primarily with maintaining price stability and advancing the economic policies of the EU. At the beginning of 1999, exchange rates were locked in, the euro became legal tender, and euro-based foreign exchange operations began. Already, without Britain's participation in the single currency, much of the action on trading floors in the City (London's financial center) is conducted in euros. The introduction of euro bills and coins for everyday use within the euro zone commenced on New Year's Day 2002.

The introduction of the euro reflects the larger vision of creating a more fully integrated EU, or what many have called (some approvingly and some derisively) a "United States of Europe." More concretely, financial analysts point to increased trade, reduced transaction costs, and substantial savings on cross-border commerce. With a population larger than that of the United States

and with a bigger gross domestic product (even before its enlargement from 15 to 25 members in 2004), an integrated Europe poses a formidable competitive challenge to the United States. In addition, many observers expect that monetary union will accelerate and make irreversible a tendency toward greater European political and foreign policy cooperation. Britain's decision thus far not to join the Euro-club remains a significant nondecision in both economic and broader political terms, for it reflects the United Kingdom's ambivalent posture toward Europe.

Blair came to office determined to rescue Europe for Britain by redressing the problems caused by Thatcher's anti-Europe stance. He has been an enthusiast for the Common Foreign and Security Policy (CFSP), has helped galvanize the European role in Kosovo, and has worked with France and Germany to develop a more robust European military capability. But Britain remains stuck on the outside looking in when it comes to the euro and has made little or no progress in changing the mindset of Britons. In April 2004, under domestic political pressure, Blair further complicated the United Kingdom's relationship with the EU by announcing that he would put the ratification of the EU Constitution to a referendum. The implications of Britain's nonparticipation in the euro zone and challenges ahead in UK-EU relations are discussed further in Chapter 10.

After September 11. In the aftermath of the September 11, 2001, attacks on the World Trade Center and the Pentagon in the United States, Blair showed decisive leadership in assuming the role of a key ally to the United States in the war on terrorism. With Britain willing and able to lend moral, diplomatic, and military support, September 11 lent new credence to the "special relationship"—a bond of language and culture that creates an unusually close alliance—that has governed U.S.-UK relations and catapulted Blair to high visibility in world affairs. For a time, the war on terrorism seemed to bridge the gap between American and European foreign policy objectives. Before long, however, parliamentary opponents and editorial writers were mocking Blair's high-profile visits to trouble spots around the world (dubbed "designer diplomacy" by the Conservatives) and accusing him of neglecting pressing problems at home, from transportation to education and healthcare. From the British perspective, it was clear that Blair's willingness to run interference with allies and add intellectual ballast and nuance to President George W. Bush's post-9/11 plans was a big help to the United States, but it locked Britain into a set of policies over which it had little or no control, vastly complicated its relationships with France and Germany (which opposed the war), generated hostility toward the United Kingdom in much of the Arab and Muslim world, and imperiled both Blair's hold on office and the legacy of New Labour. We will return to the implications of the Blair-Bush special relationship and the consequences of the war in Iraq for Blair, New Labour, and Britain in Chapter 10.

Themes and Implications

The processes that came together in these historical junctures continue to influence developments today in powerful and complex ways. Our four core themes in this book, introduced in Part I, highlight some of the most important features of British politics.

Historical Junctures and Political Themes

The first theme suggests that a country's relative position in the world of states influences its ability to manage domestic and international challenges. A weaker international standing makes it difficult for a country to control international events, shape the policy of powerful international organizations, or insulate itself from external pressures. Britain's ability to control the terms of trade and master political alliances during the height of its imperial power in the nineteenth century confirms this maxim. In a quite different way, Britain's reduced standing

Playing Robin to President Bush's Batman turned Tony Blair into a foreign policy superhero in the aftermath of September 11. But once the "special relationship" led Britain into the war in Iraq, Blair's inability to control events precipitated a growing crisis in his leadership.

Source: © Dave Simonds.

and influence today also confirm the theme of the world of states today.

As the gradual process of decolonization defined Britain's changing relationship to the world of states, Britain fell to a second-tier status during the twentieth century. Its formal empire began to shrink in the interwar period (1919–1939) as the "white dominions" of Canada, Australia, and New Zealand gained independence. In Britain's Asian, Middle Eastern, and African colonies, the pressure for political reforms leading to independence deepened during World War II and in the immediate postwar period. Beginning with the formal independence of India and Pakistan in 1947, an enormous empire of dependent colonies more or less dissolved in less than twenty years (although the problem of white-dominated Rhodesia lingered until it achieved independence as Zimbabwe in 1980). Finally, in 1997, Britain returned the commercially vibrant crown colony of Hong Kong to China. The process of decolonization ended any realistic claim Britain could make to be a dominant player in world politics.

Is Britain a world power or just a middle-of-the-pack country in Western Europe? It appears to be both. On the one hand, as a legacy of its role in World War II, Britain sits as a permanent member of the United Nations Security Council, a position denied more powerful and populous countries such as Germany and Japan. On the other hand, Britain has remained an outsider in the EU, and it experiences declining influence in the Commonwealth (an association of some fifty states that were once part of the British Empire). Most significantly, Britain invariably plays second fiddle in its special relationship to the United States, a show of relative weakness that has exposed British foreign policy to extraordinary pressures since September 11. In particular, British governments face persistent challenges in their dealings with the EU. As Margaret Thatcher learned too late to save her premiership, Europe is a highly divisive issue. Can Britain afford to remain aloof from the fast-paced changes of economic integration symbol-

ized by the headlong rush toward a common currency, the euro, which has already been embraced by every other leading member state—as well as several of the newest members from East-Central Europe, who only gained admission in May 2004? It is clear that Britain does not have the power to control EU policy outcomes, and the schism over the war in Iraq has, for a time at least, weakened the United Kingdom's influence as an honest broker between the United States and Europe on a host of important issues, from European defense to global warming protocols and the future of both Iraq and the wider Middle East. Will British governments find the right formula for limiting the political fallout of EU politics, using the special relationship with the United States to extend British influence, and, at the same time, find the best approach to economic competitiveness?

A second theme examines the strategies employed in governing the economy and the political implications of economic performance and the choices government makes in the distribution of economic goods and public services. Since the dawn of Britain's Industrial Revolution, prosperity at home relied on superior competitiveness abroad, and this is even truer in today's environment of intensified international competition and global production.

When Tony Blair took office in 1997, he inherited a streak of prosperity in Britain dating from 1992—an enviable circumstance. The Blair government could thus work to modernize the economy and determine its budgetary priorities from economic strength. Will Britain's "less-is-more" laissez-faire approach to economic governance, invigorated by New Labour's business partnership, continue to compete effectively in a global context? Can Britain achieve a durable economic model with—or without—fuller integration into Europe? How can we assess the spending priorities and distributive implications of the third-way politics of the Blair government? Britain will never again assume the privileged position of hegemonic power, so a lot depends on how well it plays the cards it does have.

A third theme is the potent political influence of the democratic idea, the universal appeal of core values associated with parliamentary democracy as practiced first in the United Kingdom. Even in Britain, issues about democratic governance, citizen participation, and constitutional reform have been renewed with considerable force.

As the traditionally sacrosanct royal family has been rocked by scandal and improprieties, questions about the undemocratic underpinning of the British state are asked with greater urgency. Few reject the monarchy outright, but, especially after the perceived insensitivity of the royal family in the aftermath of Diana's death, the pressure to modernize the monarchy, scale it down, and reduce its drain on the budget gained new intensity. Nevertheless, the outpouring of affection during a four-day national holiday in June 2002 celebrating fifty years on the throne for Queen Elizabeth II could leave no doubt about the emotional and patriotic hold of the queen on the nation. Perhaps most significant, questions about the role of the monarchy helped place on the agenda broader issues about citizen control over government and constitutional reform. As a result, in November 1999, a bill was enacted to remove hereditary peers from Britain's upper unelected chamber of Parliament, the House of Lords, and although the final form of a reformed second chamber is not settled, the traditional House of Lords has been abolished.

Long-settled issues about the constitutional form and unity of the state have also reemerged with unexpected force. How can the interests of England, Wales, Scotland, and Northern Ireland be balanced within a single nation-state? Can the perpetual crisis in Northern Ireland be finally resolved? Tony Blair has placed squarely on the agenda a set of policies designed to reshape the institutions of government and reconfigure fundamental constitutional principles to address the "troubles" in Northern Ireland and modernize the architecture of the United Kingdom to recognize the realities of a state comprised of multiple nations. Key policy initiatives have included the formation of a Scottish Parliament and a Welsh Senedd (the Welsh Assembly), and the negotiations of a peace agreement for Northern Ireland that contains a comprehensive set of new political institutions and power-sharing arrangements— some involving the Republic of Ireland—with far-reaching constitutional ramifications, should the stalemate be resolved. Clearly, democracy is not a fixed result even in the United Kingdom, but a highly politicized and potentially disruptive process, as constitutional reform has taken a place front and center as perhaps the boldest item on Tony Blair's agenda.

Finally, we come to the fourth theme, collective identities, which considers how individuals define who they are politically in terms of group attachments, come together to pursue political goals, and face their status as political insiders or outsiders by virtue of these group attachments. In Britain, an important aspect of the politics of collective identities is connected to Britain's legacy of empire and its aftermath. Through the immigration of its former colonial subjects to the United Kingdom, decolonization helped create a multiracial society, to which Britain has adjusted poorly. As we shall see, issues of race, ethnicity, and cultural identity have challenged the long-standing British values of tolerance and consensus and now present important challenges for policy and the prospects of cohesion in Britain today. With the exception of Iraq, there is no more "hot-button" issue in Britain than nationality and immigration. Indeed, the concept of "Britishness"—what the country stands for and who comprises the political community— has come under intense scrutiny. For many, asylum policy, for example, is considered as much a statement about immigrants and an expression of a backlash against multiethnic Britain as it is a practical policy for policing borders and controlling the flow of refugees. At the same time, gender politics remains a significant theme, from voting patterns (where in recent years a gender gap first favored the Conservatives, then Labour, and now has dissolved) to questions of equality in the workplace and positions of political leadership. Moreover, the specific needs of women for equal employment opportunities and to balance the demands of work and family have assumed an important place in debates about social and employment policies.

Implications for Comparative Politics

Britain's privileged position in comparative politics textbooks (it almost always comes first among country studies in these books) seems to follow naturally from the important historical firsts it has enjoyed. Britain was the first nation to industrialize, and for much of the nineteenth century, the British Empire was the world's dominant economic, political, and military power, with a vast network of colonies throughout the world. Britain was also the first nation to develop an effective parliamentary democracy (a form of representative government in which the executive is drawn from and answerable to an elected national legislature). As a result of its vast empire, Britain had tremendous influence on the form of government introduced in countries around the globe. For these reasons, British politics is often studied as a model of representative government. Named after the building that houses the British legislature in London, the Westminster model emphasizes that democracy rests on the supreme authority of a legislature—in Britain's case, the Parliament. Finally, Britain has served as a model of gradual and peaceful evolution of democratic government in a world where transitions to democracy are often turbulent, interrupted, and uncertain.

Today, more than a century after the height of its international power, Britain's significance in comparative terms must be measured in somewhat different ways. Even in tough times, as today, the advantages bestowed on prime ministers by the formidable levers of power they control, and the relative strength of the British economy provide a platform for success. Particularly in the aftermath of September 11, with signs of intolerance rampant, all economies facing new challenges, and European center-left politics in disarray, the stakes are high. Britain's ability to succeed (or not) in sustaining economic competitiveness, resolving the euro dilemma, and revitalizing the center-left will send important signals to governments throughout the world. Is significant innovation possible in established democracies? Can a politics beyond left and right develop coherent policies and sustain public support? Can constitutional reforms help bind together a multiethnic, multinational state? What geopolitical sphere of maneuver does any state have in a global order dominated by the United States (where it is not easy to tell whether the "special relationship" is a blessing, a curse, or a one-way street with little benefit for the United Kingdom)? In fact, contemporary Britain may help define what the prospects are for middle-rank established democracies in a global age.

Notes

1. This vignette is based in part on a previous account. See David Coates and Joel Krieger, "Will Blair Walk the Walk?" www.globalpolicy.org/opinion/2004/0127blairwalk.htm.

2. Jenny Church, ed., *Social Trends* 27 (London: The Stationery Office, 1997), p. 28.

3. Jeremy Black, *The Politics of Britain, 1688–1800* (Manchester: Manchester University Press, 1993), p. 6.

4. E. J. Hobsbawm, *Industry and Empire* (Harmondsworth, England: Penguin/Pelican, 1983), pp. 29–31.

5. See Duncan Fraser, "The Postwar Consensus: A Debate Not Long Enough?" *Parliamentary Affairs* 53, no. 2 (April 2000): 347–362.

C H A P T E R

7

Political Economy and Development

The timing of industrialization and of a country's insertion into the world economy are important variables in explaining both how and how successfully the state intervenes in economic governance. Both the specific policies chosen and the relative success of the economic strategy have significant political repercussions. Economic developments often determine political winners and losers, influence broad changes in the distribution of resources and opportunities among groups in society, and affect a country's international standing.

In analyzing our "governing the economy" theme, some scholars have suggested that states that have institutionalized effective relationships with organized economic interests (such as France and Germany in Europe) have enjoyed more consistent growth and stronger economic competitiveness. It is true that Britain's annual growth rates were lower than those of Germany and France from the end of World War II through the 1970s. Rather than institutionalizing a dense network of relationships among government agencies, business, and labor, Britain has preserved arm's-length state relationships with key economic actors. With British political culture trumpeting the benefits of free-market individualism and with New Labour reinforcing Thatcherism's appeal to entrepreneurship, competition, and industriousness in the private sector, the British experience becomes a critical test case for analyzing the relative merits of alternative strategies for governing the economy.

In the first decade of the new century, it appears that the trend toward greater government management of the economy has reversed, breathing new life into the old economic doctrine of laissez-faire. In part this trend is due to the demonstration effects that have resulted from the relative success of the British and U.S. economies. In addition, the pressures of global competitiveness and the perceived advantages of a "one size fits all" style of minimalist government have encouraged the movement toward neoliberal politics (free markets, free trade, welfare retrenchment, and an attractive investment climate as the end game of every state's politics). Neoliberalism is a touchstone premise of Tony Blair's New Labour. Government policies aim to promote free competition among firms, to interfere with the prerogatives of entrepreneurs and managers as little as possible, and to create a business-friendly environment to help attract foreign investment and spur innovation.

We begin this chapter with a historical overview of Britain's economic development and its experience of the postwar settlement. We then consider, in turn, the principles of British economic management, the social consequences of economic developments, and the political repercussions of Britain's position in the international economic order.

The Postwar Settlement and Beyond

To understand the postwar settlement in Britain and come to terms with the contemporary debate about economic management, we must first step backward to analyze the historical trajectory of British economic performance. In addition to its claim as the first industrial nation, Britain is also the country with the longest experience of economic decline. In a way, it was a victim of its own success and approach to economic development. From the eighteenth century onward, Britain combined its naval mastery and the dominant position created by the Industrial Revolution to fuel expansion based on the foreign supply of raw materials and foreign markets. With plenty of profits available from this traditional overseas orientation, British entrepreneurs became complacent about keeping up with the newest industrial techniques and investing in machinery at home. Secure in the advantages of empire and the priority of international trade over domestic demand, the government stuck to its belief in free trade (low tariffs and removal of other barriers to open markets) in the international realm and a hands-off approach at home. With low investment in the modernization of industrial plants and little effort to boost efficiency by grouping small-scale firms into cartels and trusts as the United States and Germany were doing, Britain slipped behind its competitors in crucial areas: technological innovation, investment in domestic manufacturing, and scale of production facilities.

By the 1890s, Britain's key export, textiles, was slipping, and the international position of the machine-tool industry, which Britain also had dominated, was collapsing even more rapidly. Both Germany and the United States had overtaken Britain in steel production, the key indicator of competitiveness at the time, and the gap was widening. In 1901, the largest U.S. steel company alone was producing more steel than all of England![1] Thus, Britain has been concerned about relative economic decline for more than a century.

Thirty years ago, there was not much to admire in the British economy. Growth and domestic investment were low and unemployment high, and in 1976 the government received a Third World–style bailout from the International Monetary Fund to help stabilize the econ-omy. Britain was routinely called the "sick man of Europe." However, throughout the 1980s and 1990s, Britain's growth rate was right in the middle of the pack of the seven richest countries, or G7 (see Figure 7.1). During the same period, which spans the Conservative governments of Margaret Thatcher and John Major, as well as that of Labour's Tony Blair, living standards (whether measured by gross domestic product per capita or purchasing power parity) also placed Britain in the middle of the G7 and the group of twenty-nine Organisation for Economic Co-operation and Development (OECD) industrialized countries. Living standards were significantly below those of the United States and Japan, and roughly corresponded to others in Western Europe. As the *Economist* observed, "Britain is neither an economic paradise nor a wasteland."[2]

Perhaps because both praise and blame would have to be shared across party lines, debates about the health of the British economy are a mainstay of domestic politics. And, of course, a middling record leaves room for improvement. That said, the difference in the relative position of the British economy today from a generation ago has not gone unnoticed. For one thing, Britain has avoided the high unemployment and recession that have plagued many of the member nations of the European Union (EU). In May 2004, the UK unemployment rate was down to 4.7 percent, the lowest figure since records began in 1984,[3] while much of Europe remained mired in high unemployment, with key competitors Germany and France recording unemployment rates of 10.5 percent and 9.8 percent, respectively.[4] During the first quarter of 2004, the British economy grew by a healthy 0.6 percent compared with the previous three-month period, reflecting a healthy 3.0 percent growth in gross domestic product (GDP) since the first quarter of 2003.[5] The pattern of growth underlined the "two-track" character of the UK economy, with growth in the service sector offsetting a much weaker industrial sector performance,[6] but in general revealed continued overall

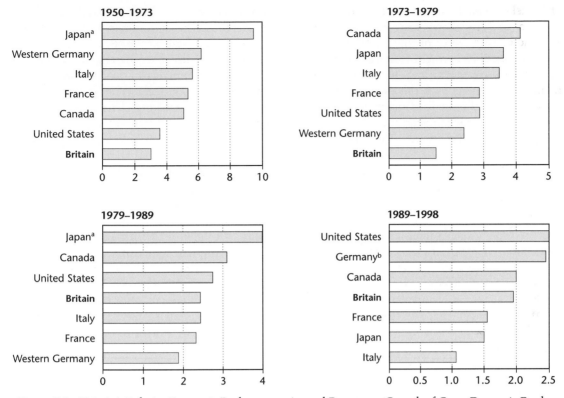

Figure 7.1   Britain's Relative Economic Performance: Annual Percentage Growth of Gross Domestic Product

A relatively bleak picture of early postwar economic performance left room for improvement in the 1980s and the 1990s as Britain began to catch up with and then overtake its European competitors.

---

[a]1952–1973.
[b]Western Germany before 1991.
Source: *Economist,* March 25, 2000. Copyright © 2000 The Economist Newspaper Group, Ltd.
Reprinted with permission. Further reproduction prohibited. www.economist.com.

strength (a judgment that was reinforced by OECD predictions of a slightly below 3.0 percent growth rate through 2005).

On the negative side, however, must be counted the continuing concern about a productivity gap between the United Kingdom and key competitors, persistent deficit in the UK balance of trade, as well as endemic concern about low rates of domestic investment and spending on research and development. In addition, the British model encompasses far greater inequality than its west European counterparts, and re-

lies on a system of production that tends to produce nonstandard and insecure jobs without the traditional social protections associated with the European social and economic model. Women and ethnic minorities are significantly overrepresented in this sector. As a result, within EU Europe (at least before the May 2004 enlargement eastward), Britain assumed a specialized profile as a producer of relatively low-technology, low-value-added products made by a comparatively low-paid, segmented, weakly organized, and easily dismissed labor force.[7]

Neoliberalism drives the economic policy orientation of Tony Blair's New Labour, and the economic performance of the UK economy today, in its sustained growth as well as its high inequality (discussed below in "Society and Economy"), reflects both the strengths and the weaknesses of the model. Government policies aim to promote free competition among firms, to interfere with the prerogatives of entrepreneurs and managers as little as possible, and to create a business-friendly environment to help attract foreign investment and spur innovation. At the same time, Britain's Labour government insists that its third way—as distinct from Conservative or conventional center-left projects—can blend the dynamism of market forces with the traditional center-left concern for social justice and commitment to the reduction of inequalities. How "new" is New Labour's approach to economic management? Are Britons across the spectrum enjoying the fruits of relative prosperity? How have the growing importance of the EU and the economic processes of globalization changed the political equation? In the next section, we analyze the politics of economic management in Britain and consider the implications of Britain's less-is-more, laissez-faire approach.

The State and the Economy

Whereas late industrializers, like Germany and Japan, relied on powerful government support during their industrial takeoff period, England's Industrial Revolution was based more on laissez-faire, or free-market, principles. When the state intervened in powerful ways, it did so primarily to secure free markets at home and open markets for British goods (free trade) in the international sphere.

With control of crucial industries during World War I and the active management of industry by the state in the interwar years, the state assumed a more interventionist role. After World War II, the sense of unity inspired by the shared suffering of war and the need to rebuild a war-ravaged country helped crystallize the collectivist consensus. In common with other Western European states, the British state both broadened and deepened its responsibilities for the overall performance of the economy and the well-being of its citizens. The leading political parties and policymaking elites agreed that the state should take an active role in governing the economy.

The state nationalized some key industries, assuming direct ownership of them. It also accepted the responsibility to secure low levels of unemployment (referred to as a policy of full employment), expand social services, maintain a steady rate of growth (increase the output or GDP), keep prices stable, and achieve desirable balance-of-payments and exchange rates. The approach is called Keynesian demand management, or *Keynesianism* (after the British economist John Maynard Keynes, 1883–1946). State budget deficits were used to expand demand in an effort to boost both consumption and investment when the economy was slowing. Cuts in government spending and a tightening of credit and finance were used to cool demand when high rates of growth brought fears of inflation or a deficit in balance of payments. Taken together, this new agenda of expanded economic management and welfare provision, sometimes referred to as the Keynesian welfare state, directed government policy throughout the era of the collectivist consensus.

Two central dimensions, economic management and social policy, capture the new role of the state. Analysis of these policy areas also reveals how limited this new state role was in comparative terms.

Economic Management

Like all other states, whatever their commitment to free markets, the British state intervenes in economic life, sometimes with considerable force. However, the British have not developed the institutions for state-sponsored economic planning or industrial policy that have been created by some countries with which they compete for global market share in key economic sectors. Instead, apart from its management of nationalized industries, the British state has limited its role mainly to broad policy instruments designed to influence the economy generally (macroeconomic policy) by adjusting state revenues and expenditures. The Treasury and the Bank of England dominate economic policy, which has often seemed reactive and sometimes skittish. As senior officials in these key finance institutions respond to fluctuations in the business cycle, the government reacts with short-term political calculations that abruptly shift policy agendas. As a result, state involvement in economic management has traditionally been relatively ineffectual.

Despite other differences, this generally reactive and minimalist orientation of economic management strategies in Britain bridges the first two eras of postwar politics in Britain: the consensus era (1945–1979) and the period of Thatcherite policy orientation (1979–1997). How has the orientation of economic policy developed and changed during the postwar period? How new is New Labour when it comes to economic policy?

The Consensus Era.   Before Thatcher became leader of the Conservative Party in 1975, Conservative leaders in Britain generally accepted the terms of the collectivist consensus. These Conservatives were also modernizers, prepared to manage the economy in a way consistent with the Keynesian approach and to maintain the welfare state and guarantee full employment.

Declining economic competitiveness made the situation for mainstream Conservatives and, indeed, for any other government, more complex and difficult. By the 1970s, public officials no longer saw the world as one they understood and could master; it had become a world without economic growth and with growing political discontent. Edward Heath, the Conservative centrist who governed from 1970 to 1974, was the first prime minister to suffer the full burden of recession and the force of political opposition

from both traditional business allies and resurgent trade union adversaries. Operating in an era marked by increased inflation and reduced growth (stagflation), Heath could never break out of the political constraints imposed on him by economic decline.

From 1974 to 1979, the Labour government of Harold Wilson and James Callaghan reinforced the impression that governments could no longer control the swirl of events. The beginning of the end came when trade unions became increasingly restive under the pinch of voluntary wage restraints pressed on them by the Labour government. Frustrated by wage increases well below inflation rates, the unions broke with the government in 1978. The number of unofficial work stoppages increased, and official strikes followed, all fueled by a seemingly endless series of leapfrogging pay demands that erupted throughout the winter of 1978–1979 (the "winter of discontent"). There is little doubt that the industrial unrest that dramatized Labour's inability to manage its own allies, the trade unions, contributed mightily to Thatcher's election just a few months later in May 1979. If a Labour government could not manage its trade union allies, whom could it govern? More significant, the winter of discontent helped write the conclusion to Britain's collectivist consensus and discredit the Keynesian welfare state.

Thatcherite Policy Orientation.   In policy terms, the economic orientations that Thatcher pioneered and that Major substantially maintained reflected a growing disillusionment with Keynesianism. In its place, monetarism emerged as the new economic doctrine. Keynesian demand management assumed that the level of unemployment could be set and the economy stabilized through decisions of government (monetary and fiscal or budgetary policy). By contrast, monetarism assumed that there is a "natural rate of unemployment" determined by the labor market itself. Monetary and fiscal policy should be passive and intervention limited (so far as this was possible) to a few steps that would help foster appropriate rates of growth in the money supply and keep inflation low.

By implication, the government ruled out spending to run up budgetary deficits as a useful instrument for stimulating the economy. On the contrary, governments could contribute to overall economic efficiency and growth by reducing social expenditure and downsizing the public sector, by reducing its workforce or privatizing nationalized industries. Monetarism reflected a radical change from the postwar consensus regarding economic management. Not only was active government intervention considered unnecessary; it was seen as undesirable and destabilizing.

New Labour's Economic Policy Approach. Can New Labour thinking on macroeconomic policy end the "short-termism" of economic policy and provide the cohesion previously lacking? In British commentaries on New Labour, much has been made of the influence of revitalized Keynesian ideas and reform proposals.[8] In some ways, government policy seems to pursue conventional market-reinforcing and pro-business policies (neoliberalism). In other ways, the New Labour program stands as an alternative to Thatcherite monetarism and traditional Keynesianism. Whether New Labour's approach to economic management constitutes a distinctive third way or a less coherent blend of disparate elements is a matter of political debate.

The first shot fired in the Blair revolution was the announcement within a week of the 1997 election by Gordon Brown, the chancellor of the exchequer (equivalent to the minister for finance or secretary of the treasury in other countries), that the Bank of England would be given "operational independence" in the setting of monetary policy, and charged with maintaining low inflation (which has been achieved). The decision transferred from the cabinet a critical, and highly political, prerogative of government. With Brown attuned to the pressures of international financial markets, and the control of inflation and stability the key goals of macroeconomic policy,

the transfer of authority over monetary policy confirmed the neoliberal market orientation of economic policy.

Central to the concerns of Brown and his Treasury team from 1997 were issues of macroeconomic stability. Brown (the "iron chancellor") insisted on establishing a "platform of stability" through explicit acceptance of the pre-existing (and Conservative specified) limits on public spending and gave a very high priority to policies designed to reduce the public debt. Only as he turned that debt into a surplus did the "iron chancellor" reinvent himself as a more conventionally Labour and social democratic chancellor. Starting in 1998, he released extra funds to the public at a projected annual real rate of increase of at least 2.75 percent for the three years to 2004.[9] Both Brown's success in achieving growth and economic stability and the credit he is given for a commitment to fund social policy position the chancellor well to make the most of any opportunity to assume leadership of the Labour Party.

Does the third way represent a genuine departure in economic policy? Although there is no ready agreement on how to best answer this question, the claim of a distinctive policy design is quite clear in the way Blair and Brown have articulated their priorities. What Tony Blair called "the principal elements of New Labour's economic thinking"[10] advanced four strategic policy areas: investment in industry, through tight and disciplined tax policies designed to "keeping inflation low and as stable as possible";[11] investment in infrastructure, through the expansion of public-private partnerships in education and training, defense, transportation, housing, and regional policy; investment in employment opportunities, through active labor market policies to move people from welfare to work; and through investment in people, with lifelong learning initiatives, better industrial training, and higher school standards. Brown was equally clear on the importance of investment in human capital as a key ingredient in economic competitiveness. He insisted that "access to skills, knowledge and access to the new technologies [were] a more critical determinant of [economic] success or failure than any other factor."[12] As Blair insisted, it was a cornerstone of New Labour policy that "the economic race now goes to the cleverest and the most innovative, not simply [to] the fastest and the cheapest."[13]

Above all, New Labour's economic policy approach emphasizes pragmatism in the face of global economic competition. Since capital is international, mobile, and not subject to control, industrial policy and planning that focus on the domestic economy alone are futile. Rather, government can improve the quality of labor through education and training, maintain the labor market flexibility inherited from the Thatcher regime, and help to attract investment to Britain. Strict control of inflation, low taxes, and tough limits on public expenditure help promote both employment and investment opportunities. At the same time, economic policy is directed at enhancing the competitive strength of key sectors and developing a partnership with business through research and development, training, technology, and modernization policies. New Labour is very focused on designing and implementing policies to create new jobs and get people, particularly young people, into the workforce.

It is hard to isolate the effects of particular policies within the overall development of the economy, and any claims of success are subject to partisan interpretation and debate. But there are some indications of success, in particular on the jobs front, where the government can reasonably take credit for strategic—and quite rapid—public sector job growth, particularly in education and healthcare. In 2003, the United Kingdom experienced the greatest public sector job growth in a decade (an increase of 162,000 jobs in the twelve months before June 2003, including 88,000 in education and 63,000 in healthcare).[14] Predictably, the Conservatives blasted New Labour for bloating the public sector, but government insisted that the growth represented an increase in much-needed front-line professionals, and independent economists were quick to note that the growth in public sector employment came at a very good time, since labor demand in much of the private sector was weak.[15] With New Labour having established its bona fides in terms of economic stability and budget tightening, and with record low unemployment, it was in a strong position to win the debate about public sector job growth and claim victory on the job creation front.

Because of both partisan debate and genuine ambiguity about the mix of neoliberalism, traditional Labourism, and genuinely new third-way initiatives that comprise New Labour's economic policy package, no consensus on the newness of New Labour is likely to emerge anytime soon. Blair, his economic policy team, and his supporters, however, can make a fairly convincing case that, despite problems in investment, productivity, trade imbalances, and persistent poverty and inequality, New Labour has sustained a stable and competitive economy. It further claims that its approach to governing the economy, with its emphasis on training and job creation, and its ambitions for steady growth spurred by the investment in people, should create an economy—and a society—in which all Britons have a personal stake (New Labour refers to its vision as "the stakeholder economy").

Political Implications of Economic Policy. Differences in economic doctrine are not what matter most in policy terms. In fact, British governments in the past have never consistently followed any economic theory, whether Keynesianism or monetarism. Today, the economic policy of New Labour is pragmatic and eclectic. The political consequences of economic orientations are more significant: each economic doctrine helps to justify a broad moral and cultural vision of society, to provide motives for state policy, and to advance alternative sets of values. Should the government intervene, work to reduce inequalities through the mildly redistributive provisions of the welfare state, and sustain the ethos of a caring society (collectivism/"Old

Labour")? Should it back off and allow the market to function competitively and thereby promote entrepreneurship, competitiveness, and individual autonomy (Thatcherism)? Or should it help secure an inclusive stakeholder economy in which business has the flexibility, security, and mobility to compete and workers have the skills and training to participate effectively in the global labor market (New Labour)? As these questions make clear, economic management strategies are closely linked to social or welfare policy.

Social Policy

Observers have noted that the social and political role of the welfare state depends as much on policy goals and instruments as on spending levels. Does the state provide services itself or offer cash benefits that can be used to purchase services from private providers? Are benefits limited to those who fall below an income threshold (means-tested) or universal? Are they designed to meet the temporary needs of individuals or to help reduce the gap between rich and poor?

The expanded role of government during World War II and the increased role of the Labour Party during the wartime coalition government led by Winston Churchill prepared the way for the development of the welfare state in Britain. The 1943 Beveridge Report provided a blueprint for an extensive but, in comparative European terms, fairly shallow set of provisions. The principal means-tested program is social security, a system of contributory and noncontributory benefits to provide financial assistance (not services directly) for the elderly, sick, disabled, unemployed, and others similarly in need of assistance.

In general, welfare state provisions interfere relatively little in the workings of the market, and policymakers do not see the reduction of group inequalities as the proper goal of the welfare state. The National Health Service (NHS) provides comprehensive and universal medical care and has long been championed as the jewel in the crown of the welfare state in Britain, but it remains an exception to the rule. Compared with other Western European countries, the welfare state in Britain offers relatively few comprehensive services, and the policies are not very generous. For the most part, Britons must rely on means-tested safety net programs that leave few of the recipients satisfied.

The Welfare State Under Thatcher and Major.
The record on social expenditure by Conservative governments from 1979 to 1997 was mixed. Given Britons' strong support for public education, pensions, and healthcare, Conservative governments attempted more limited reform than many at first anticipated. The Thatcher and Major governments encouraged private alongside public provision in education, healthcare (insurance), and pensions. They worked to increase efficiency in social services, reduced the value of some benefits by changing the formulas or reducing cost-of-living adjustments, and contracted out some services (purchased them from private contractors rather than providing them directly). In addition, in policy reforms reminiscent of U.S. "workfare" requirements, they tried to reduce dependency by denying benefits to youths who refused to participate in training programs. Despite these efforts, the commitment to reduced spending could not be sustained, partly because a recession triggered rises in income support and unemployment benefits.

To a degree, however, this general pattern masks specific and, in some cases, highly charged policy changes in both expenditures and the institutionalized pattern of provision. In housing, the changes in state policy and provision were the most extensive, with repercussions in electoral terms and in changing the way Britons think about the welfare state. By 1990, more than 1.25 million council houses (public housing maintained by local government) were sold, particularly the attractive single-family homes with gardens (quite unlike public housing in the United States). Two-thirds of the sales were to rental tenants. Thatcher's housing policy was extremely popular. By one calculation, between 1979 and 1983 there was a swing (change in the percentage of vote received by the two major parties) to the Conservative Party of 17 percent among those who had bought their council houses.[16]

Despite great Conservative success in the campaign to privatize housing, a strong majority of Britons remain stalwart supporters of the principle of collective provision for their basic needs. Thus, there were limits on the government's ability to reduce social spending or change institutional behavior. For example, in 1989, the Conservative government tried to introduce market practices into the NHS, with general practitioners managing funds and purchasing hospital care for their patients. Many voiced fears that the reforms would create a two-tier system of medical care for rich and poor.

More generally, a lack of confidence in the Conservatives on social protection hurt Major substantially in 1992, and it has continued to plague the party. Nothing propelled the Labour landslide in 1997 more than the concern for the "caring" issues. The traditional advantage Labour enjoys on these issues also helped secure victory for Blair in June 2001.

New Labour Social Policy. As with economic policy, social policy for New Labour presents an opportunity for government to balance pragmatism and innovation, while borrowing from traditional Labour as well as from Thatcherite options. Thus, the Blair government rejects both the attempted retrenchment of Conservative governments that seemed mean-spirited as well as the egalitarian traditions of Britain's collectivist era that emphasized entitlements. Instead, New Labour focuses its policy on training and broader social investment as a more positive third-way alternative. At the same time, New Labour draws political strength from the "Old Labour" legacy of commitment on the "caring" social policy issues.

For example, following Bill Clinton, Blair's New Democratic counterpart in the United States, the prime minister promised a modernized, leaner welfare state, in which people are actively encouraged to seek work. The reform of the welfare state emphasizes efficiencies and attempts to break welfare dependency. Efforts to spur entry into the labor market combine carrots and sticks. Positive inducements include training programs, especially targeted at youth, combined with incentives to private industry to hire new entrants to the labor market. The threats include eligibility restrictions and reductions in coverage. Referred to as the "New Deal" for the young unemployed, welfare reform in the United Kingdom has emphasized concerted efforts to create viable pathways out of dependence. Although beginning with a focus on moving youth from welfare to work, New Deal reform efforts expanded in several directions.

The New Deal was quickly extended to single parents and the long-term unemployed. In 1999, the government launched a "Bridging the Gap" initiative to provide a more comprehensive approach for assisting sixteen- to eighteen-year-olds not in education, employment, or training to achieve clear goals by age nineteen through a variety of "pathways" (academic, vocational, or occupational). "Better Government for Older People" was launched in 1998 and was followed quickly by "All Our Futures," a government report issued in the summer of 2000 with twenty-eight recommendations to improve the quality of life and the delivery of public services for senior citizens. A new initiative, "The IT New Deal," was launched in 2001 as a government-business partnership to address skill shortages in information technologies.

Although the jury is still out on the follow-through and effectiveness of New Labour social and welfare policy initiatives, the intent to create innovative policies and approach social policy in new and more comprehensive ways is clearly there. Late in 1997, the government inaugurated the Social Exclusion Unit, staffed by civil servants and external policy specialists. Initially located within the Cabinet Office and reporting directly to the prime minister, the Social Exclusion

Unit moved to the Office of the Deputy Prime Minister in May 2002. It was charged broadly with addressing "what can happen when people or areas suffer from such problems as unemployment, poor skills, low incomes, poor housing, high crime environments, bad health, and family breakdown." The Social Exclusion Unit has been actively involved in developing the New Deal initiative as well as in writing reports and recommending policies to take on problems such as truancy and school exclusion, homelessness, neighborhood renewal, and teenage pregnancy. This effort to identify comprehensive solutions to society's ills and reduce the tendency for government to let marginalized individuals fall by the wayside captures the third-way orientation of the Blair project.

Nevertheless, New Labour, like all other governments in Britain and many other countries, will be accountable above all for the failure or success of more traditional social policies, especially healthcare and education. The Department of Health acknowledged in a report issued in 2000 that the NHS suffered from chronic underfunding, overcentralization, and insufficient incentives to improve performance. In its annual Survey of the United Kingdom in the same year, the Organisation for Economic Co-operation and Development (OECD) gave the Blair government low marks on healthcare, noting that the ratio of doctors to population and level of spending are low for a developed country. It cautioned that healthcare results in the United Kingdom are in some ways mediocre, with cancer survival rates, for example, more typical of Eastern than Western European norms, and raised doubts about the effectiveness of NHS reforms. The 2001–2002 OECD Survey noted that some of the endemic problems in the NHS were being addressed with new budgetary allocations to add hospital beds, equip hospitals and doctors' offices with up-to-date information technology, and hire significant numbers of doctors and nurses, as well as specific targets to guarantee quicker appointments with primary care doctors and specialists.

By 2004, there was mounting evidence that record growth in the NHS budget had netted re-sults. Despite the report of a House of Commons select committee on the health dangers of obesity (particularly for children), there was widespread confidence that NHS quality and performance were improving, with waiting lists shorter and significant advances in the treatment of life-threatening diseases. And yet the government faced continued skepticism from the electorate. Consider the following observation from an influential journalist:

> Blair's third way has failed to change Britain into a progressive social democracy. Good is done by stealth while mimicking Tory critiques of the public service ethos. Why is Labour on the back foot over public services even when they are better than ever? Brilliant NHS results with plummeting death rates for cancer and heart disease and falling waiting times are not believed? Why? Because Blair's third way colludes with the Tories by telling the NHS it needs more radical reform, sending the message that it's not working.[17]

For a great many Britons, core policies and above all healthcare, much more than the battle against social exclusion, will determine the measure of success of New Labour's social policy.

Society and Economy

What were the *distributional effects*—the consequences for group patterns of wealth and poverty—of the economic and social policies of Thatcher and Major? To what extent have the policies of Tony Blair's Labour government continued—or reversed—these trends? How has government policy influenced the condition of minorities and women? It is impossible to ascertain when government policy creates a given distribution of resources and when poverty increases or decreases because of a general downturn or upswing in the economy. The evidence is clear, however, that economic inequality grew in Britain during the 1980s before it stabilized or narrowed slightly in the mid-1990s, and that ethnic minorities and women continue to experience significant disadvantages.

In general, policies initiated by the Conservative Party, particularly during the Thatcher years, tended to deepen inequalities. The economic upturn that began in 1992, combined with Major's moderating effects on the Thatcherite social policy agenda, served to narrow inequality by the mid-1990s. Since 1997, as one observer noted, Labour has "pursued redistribution by stealth, raising various indirect levies on the better-off to finance tax breaks for poorer workers."[18] As a result, Britain has witnessed a modest downward redistribution of income since 1997. Attention to social exclusion in its many forms, a 1999 pledge by the prime minister to eradicate child poverty (even though Britain at the time had the highest rates of child poverty in EU Europe), and strong rates of growth augur well for a further narrowing of the gap between rich and poor in Britain. Data from

March 2004 indicate that in 2002–2003, 17 percent of the population lived in low-income households (down from a peak of 21 percent in the early 1990s). In addition, there were clear indications that an ambitious agenda to reduce childhood poverty through a new set of inclusive tax credits for children, as well as other measures to transfer resources to poor families, showed significant signs of progress. After rising to a peak of 27 percent in the early 1990s, the percentage of children living in low-income households has held steady at 21 percent for each of the three years from 1999–2000 to 2002–2003.[19] Comparative analysis of poverty rates indicates that despite these efforts the United Kingdom has greater problems regarding income inequality than do most of its EU counterparts prior to the 2004 enlargement (see Figure 7.2).

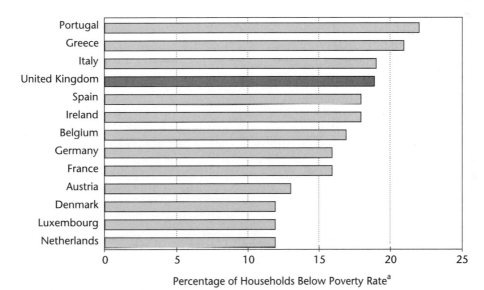

Percentage of Households Below Poverty Rate[a]

[a]Poverty rate is defined as income below 60 percent of the national median.

Figure 7.2   U.K. Poverty Rates in Comparative European Perspective

Britain has experienced more persistent problems with poverty and income inequality than most of EU Europe prior to the 2004 enlargement. New Labour's attention to social exclusion, its concern for childhood poverty, and a strong economy suggest that poverty may decrease in the years ahead, but improvements have been relatively modest.

Source: Adapted from the figure entitled "Poverty," *OECD Economic Surveys: United Kingdom 2001/2002,* OECD, 2002. Reprinted by permission.

Inequality and Ethnic Minorities

Poverty and diminished opportunity disproportionately characterize the situation of ethnic minorities (a term applied to peoples of non-European origin from the former British colonies in the Indian subcontinent, the Caribbean, and Africa). Official estimates place the ethnic minority population in Britain at 4.5 million in 2001–2002 (the most recent data available) or 7.6 percent of the total population of the United Kingdom. Indians comprise the largest ethnic minority, at 21.7 percent; Pakistanis represent 16.7 percent, Bangladeshis 6.1 percent, and Afro-Caribbeans and other blacks, 27.1 percent.[20] Because of past immigration and fertility patterns, the ethnic minority population in the United Kingdom is considerably younger than the white population. More than one-third of the ethnic minority population is younger than age sixteen, nearly half is under age twenty-five, and more than four-fifths is under age forty-five. Thus, despite the common and often disparaging reference to ethnic minority individuals as "immigrants," the experience of members of ethnic minority groups is increasingly that of a native-born population.[21]

Britain has adjusted slowly to the realities of a multicultural society. The postwar period has witnessed the gradual erosion of racial, religious, and ethnic tolerance in Britain and a chipping away at the right of settlement of postcolonial subjects in the United Kingdom. During the Thatcher era, discussion of immigration and citizenship rights was used for partisan political purposes and assumed a distinctly racial tone. Ethnic minority individuals, particularly young men, are subject to unequal treatment by the police and considerable physical harassment by citizens. They have experienced cultural isolation as well as marginalization in the educational system, job training, housing, and labor markets. There is considerable concern about the apparent rise in racially motivated crime in major metropolitan areas with significant ethnic diversity. Recognizing these problems, in 2000 the government brought to Parliament a bill to amend the Race Relations Act 1976 by outlawing direct and indirect discrimination in all public bodies and placing a "positive duty" on all public officials and authorities to promote racial equality. The Race Relations (Amendment) Act 2000 received final parliamentary approval in November 2000.

In general, poor rates of economic success reinforce the sense of isolation and distinct collective identities. Variations among ethnic minority communities are quite considerable, however, and there are some noteworthy success stories. For example, among men of African, Asian, Chinese, and Indian descent, the proportional representation in the managerial and professional ranks is actually higher than that for white men (although they are much less likely to be senior managers in large firms). Also, Britons of South Asian and, especially, Indian descent enjoy a high rate of entrepreneurship. Nevertheless, despite some variations, employment opportunities for women from all minority ethnic groups are limited.[22] In addition, a distinct gap remains between the job opportunities available to whites and those open to ethnic minorities in Britain. It is clear that people from ethnic minority communities are overrepresented among low-income households in the United Kingdom (see Figure 7.3). Almost 60 percent of Pakistani or Bangladeshi households are in low-income households (defined by income below 60 percent of the median). Just under half of black non-Caribbean households also live on low incomes after housing costs are deducted, as do nearly one-third of black Caribbeans. In contrast, only 16 percent of white people may be found in such low-income households before housing costs are deducted, and 21 percent after housing costs are deducted.[23]

Then there is the human side behind the statistics that reveals how difficult it remains in Britain for ethnic minorities to achieve top posts and how uneven the prospects of success are despite some pockets of modest success. It seems that the police have been more effective in recent

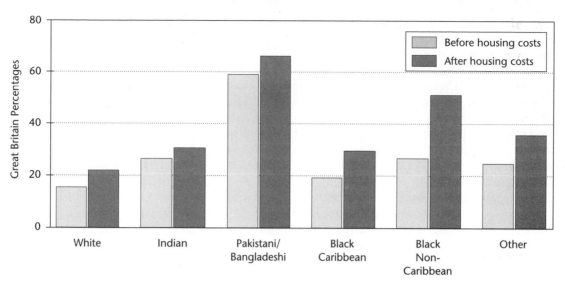

Households on low income: by ethnic group of head of household, 2001–02

Figure 7.3   Distribution of Low-Income Households by Ethnicity

People from Britain's ethnic minority communities are far more likely than white Britons to be in low-income households, although there are important differences among ethnic minority groups. Nearly 60 percent of Pakistani or Bangladeshi households are low-income households, while about one-third of black Caribbean households live on low incomes.

Source: National Statistics Online; www.statistics.gov.uk/CCI/nugget.asp?ID=269&Pos=1&ColRank=2&Rank−384.

years in recruiting and retaining ethnic minority police officers, and moving them up through the ranks, than have the further-education colleges (non-degree-giving institutions providing mainly vocational training for sixteen- to eighteen-year-olds not headed to university). "We don't have one black college principal in London in spite of having one of the most ethnically diverse student populations in the country," observed the mayor of London's senior policy director in May 2004. "There are many more young Afro-Caribbean men in prison than there are in university, and more black Met [London police] officers than there are teachers."[24] Ethnic minority police officers now make up 3 percent of the United Kingdom's 122,000-member police force, but only 2 percent of junior and middle managers in the more than four hundred colleges

in Britain, only five of which have ethnic minority principals. It speaks volumes to the level of ethnic minority inequality that a 3 percent representation of ethnic minority police officers is considered evidence that "the police have in recent years been undertaking a much-needed overhaul of equal opportunities."[25]

Inequality and Women

Women's participation in the labor market when compared to that of men also indicates marked patterns of inequality. In fact, most women in Britain work part-time, often in jobs with fewer than sixteen hours of work per week and often with fewer than eight hours (in contrast, fewer than one in every fifteen men is employed part-time). More than three-quarters of women working part-time report that they did not want a full-time job, yet more women than men (in raw numbers, not simply as a percentage) take on second jobs. Although employment conditions for women in Britain trail those of many of their EU counterparts, the gap in the differential between weekly earnings of men and women in the United Kingdom has narrowed in recent decades. Between 1970 and 1999, women's weekly earnings rose to 74 percent of the earnings of men, compared with 54 percent in 1970. Because even women who work full-time tend to work fewer hours per week than their male counterparts, the gender gap in hourly earnings is somewhat narrower. In 1999, women earned 82 percent of the hourly earnings of men.[26] In recent years, the gender pay gap in average hourly pay for full-time employees has narrowed further. In fact, in April 2003 the gender gap in pay dropped to 82 percent, its lowest value since records have been kept.[27]

The Blair government remains committed to gender equality in the workplace and affirmed its resolve to address women's concerns to balance work and family responsibilities. It has taken a number of steps to aid women at work and help reconcile the demands of family and employment. The government has implemented (or proposed) a set of "family-friendly" work-related policies, including unpaid parental leave of up to three months (the EU standard accepted by the United Kingdom under Blair as part of the Social Charter, an EU commitment to enhanced wage earner rights that was included in the 1991 Maastricht Treaty on European Union, to which previous UK governments had opted out). The unpaid leave supplements the statutory leave package (six weeks at 90 percent pay, plus twelve weeks at half-pay, plus an additional small supplement per week) and the right to refuse to work more than forty-eight hours per week. Other measures include a commitment in principle to filling half of all public appointments with women, a review of the pension system to ensure better coverage for women, draft legislation to provide for the shar-

ing of pensions after divorce, tax credits for working families as well as for child care, and a National Childcare Strategy. Nevertheless, the United Kingdom is likely to remain an EU outlier in the provision of day care, with responsibilities remaining primarily in private hands and the gap between childcare supply and demand far greater than elsewhere in Western Europe. Moreover, the government has continued the Conservative policy of promoting management flexibility, so it seems likely that the general pattern of female labor market participation and inequality in earnings will change relatively little in the years ahead. A recent report commissioned by the Cabinet Office's Women's Unit confirms a significant pattern of inequality in lifetime earnings of men and women with an equal complement of skills, defined by both a gender gap and a "mother gap."

The Generation Gap

There is another widely discussed and equally significant gap that helps shape British politics: the generation gap. In fact, its dimensions are most clear at the point where gender and generational differences come together, and they have done so acutely in elections. The issue of a gender gap in voting behavior has long been a mainstay of British electoral studies. From 1945 to 1992, women were more likely than men to vote Conservative. In addition, since 1964 a "gender-generation" gap has become well established and was very clear in the 1992 election. Among younger voters (under thirty years old), women preferred Labour, while men voted strongly for the Conservatives, producing a fourteen-point gender gap favoring Labour; among older voters (over sixty-five years old), women were far more inclined to vote Conservative than were their male counterparts, creating a gender gap of eighteen points favoring the Conservatives.

The modest all-generation gender gap that favored the Tories in 1992 (6 percent) was closed in 1997 as a greater percentage of women shifted away from the Conservatives (11 percent) than did men (8 percent). As a result, women and men recorded an identical 44 percent tally for Labour. The gender-generation gap continued, however, with younger women more pro-Labour than younger men and the pattern reversing in the older generation. Moreover, one of the most striking features of the 1997 election was the generational dimension: the largest swing to Labour was among those in the age group eighteen to twenty-nine years (more than 18 percent), and among first-time voters; there was no swing to Labour among those over age sixty-five.[28]

What are the implications of this overlay of gender and generational voting patterns? For one thing, it seems that a party's ability to recognize and satisfy the political agendas of women in Britain may offer big political dividends. Studies suggest, first, that issues at the top of the list of women's concerns (e.g., child care, the rights and pay of part-time workers, equal pay, support for family caregivers, domestic violence) do not feature strongly in the existing policy agendas of the political parties. Second, to the extent that women and men care about the same broadly defined issues, women often understand the issues differently than men do and express different priorities. For example, while men (and the three major parties) consider unemployment the central employment issue, women emphasize equal pay and pensions, access to child care, and the rights of part-time workers. Third, research indicates that distinct sets of issues concern different groups of women. For example, older women are most concerned about pensions and transportation. Because of the overrepresentation of women in lower-paid part-time jobs, working women express particular concern about the minimum wage and the treatment of part-time workers. Mothers find the level of child benefits more important than issues of tax cuts. Finally, younger women strongly support policies that would help them balance the responsibilities of work, family, and child care. This last point may be the most critical. Like the perennial focus on "work-

ing families" in U.S. presidential campaigns, political parties in Britain recognize that the successful political management of the gender-generation gap is becoming a critical electoral battleground. In particular, winning the support of working mothers or younger women who plan to become working mothers could pay huge political dividends.

On other aspects of the generation gap, there is far less clarity. The political apathy and self-interested materialism of the "youth of today" receive wide comment, but there is little evidence that can disentangle the attitudes of the millennium generation from the different stages and accompanying social and political attitudes each generation acquires during its life cycle.

After the 2001 election, analysis pointed to a generation gap in turnout. BBC exit polls revealed that young voters had the lowest turnout, most often saying the election "didn't matter." The new home secretary, David Blunkett, worried aloud that youth had "switched off politics." Polling data tend to confirm the impression that there is a generation gap in the connection between citizens and mainstream politics and that younger Britons are more divorced from politics. Three-quarters of young people aged fifteen to twenty-four have never met their local councillor, compared with just over half of those aged fifty-five or older. Also, older citizens are more than twice as likely to say that they know the name of their local councillor (46 percent compared with 20 percent of fifteen- to twenty-four-year-olds).[29] That said, the unprecedented participation of British youth in the massive antiwar protests in February and March 2003 tells a different story, one of young people with strong political views and an unexpected taste for political engagement. A BBC poll of schoolchildren in February 2003 reported 80 percent opposed to war, while Britain as a whole was more evenly divided. On March 5, thousands of teenagers across the country walked out of school and congregated in city centers, while some five hundred protested at the Houses of Parliament. "What's shocking isn't their opposition but the fact they're doing something about it," noted one electronic journalist on a youth-oriented website. "Considering that most 18–25 year olds couldn't even be bothered to put a cross in a box at the last general election this is a pretty big thing."[30] It was a big enough thing that New Labour strategists were left to ponder the consequences, knowing that the mobilization of support among young people, which was already a cause for concern, was likely to become more difficult in the aftermath of the war in Iraq.

The Dilemmas of European Integration

Since the beginning of the Industrial Revolution in the eighteenth century, Britain has been more dependent than most other countries on international commerce for the creation of wealth. Because Britain's economy is more interdependent with the global economy than most other leading industrial powers, it faces considerable external pressures on its economic policy. The dilemmas of European integration most vividly illustrate the interplay between economics and politics in an era of global interdependence.

Britain was humbled when its applications for membership in the European Community (EC) were blocked in 1963 and again in 1967 by France. Worse, since its admission in 1973, Britain's participation in the EC (in November 1993, it became the EU) has tended to underscore its reduced international power and ability to control regional and global developments. Many Britons remain skeptical about the advantages of Britain's political and economic integration with Europe and are uneasy about the loss of sovereignty that resulted from EU membership.

Economic Integration and Political Disintegration

During the Thatcher and Major years, the issue of economic integration bedeviled the prime minister's office and divided the Conservative Party.

The introduction of the European Monetary System (EMS) in 1979 set the stage for the political dramas that followed. The EMS fixed the exchange rates among member currencies (referred to as the Exchange Rate Mechanism, or ERM), and permitted only limited fluctuation above or below. Intended to stabilize European economies and promote trade among members, its success depended on the willingness of member states to pursue compatible economic strategies—and on their ability to maintain similar growth rates and levels of inflation. In retrospect, this plan seems highly unrealistic. How likely were Spain, Portugal, and Greece—or even Britain—to keep pace with Germany in the period of heady economic competitiveness before unification? But there was tremendous pressure to set up the ERM before political disagreements or recession could close the window of opportunity.

Thatcher opposed British participation in the ERM throughout the 1980s, insisting on British control of its economic policy. However, when her domestic economic policy failed to stem Britain's rampant inflation, Thatcher's anti-EC stance pitted her against senior ministers and leaders of Britain's EC partners, as well as against the bulk of the British business community. It seemed that everyone but Thatcher thought participation in European integration would ease inflation in Britain and enhance its competitiveness. In the end, Thatcher succumbed to the pressure to give up a measure of economic sovereignty, in effect, to Germany and its central bank (the Bundesbank), whose decisions would force Britain to follow in lockstep. She permitted Britain to join the ERM in October 1990. Ironically, just one month later, Thatcher was toppled from office in a coup led by those in her own party who most deeply resented her grudging attitude toward integration.

For the new government of Prime Minister John Major, participation in the ERM held enormous symbolic and political significance. As chancellor of the exchequer, he had quietly pressed Thatcher to join, and as prime minister, he staked his reputation on its success. He hoped that participation would stabilize European trade, reduce inflation, and pull Britain out of a stubborn recession.

Implications of Maastricht and the Common Currency

The Treaty on European Union (usually called the Maastricht Treaty for the small Dutch town where it was negotiated in 1991) represented a bold agenda for economic and monetary union and for deeper cooperation on foreign policy and security matters. Maastricht also established a plan to phase in a single EC currency and control of national monetary policy by a European central bank. In addition, Maastricht gave treaty status to the Community Charter of the Fundamental Social Rights of Workers, more commonly known as the Social Charter.

Unlike Thatcher, Major positioned himself as pro-Europe and was solicitous of his allies. But he stood his ground at Maastricht. Negotiating well, Major secured a crucial opt-out clause for Britain. The United Kingdom would not be bound by the Social Charter or by any single-currency plans. Unfortunately for Major and the Conservatives, almost before he could enjoy his Maastricht victories, Major's integration strategy faced a nearly fatal setback.

In September 1992, the EMS collapsed under the impact of downward pressures in the British economy and the strains of German unification. The prime minister's reputation was badly damaged, and the momentum for economic unity among EC countries was abruptly stalled. The Thatcherite anti-Maastricht hard core in the Conservative Party dug in against him on the key issues of economic and monetary union, thereby undermining his leadership and forcing him to squander his political capital on the lost cause of party unity on Europe. Major never recovered, and it took several years before plans for economic integration in the EU were put back on track. Remarkably, a single European policy (the ERM) led to Thatcher's downfall and politically haunted John Major throughout his premiership.

Developments in European integration present a formidable hurdle for Tony Blair or any successor government. On the one hand, few in Britain find it easy to countenance a common currency in place of the pound sterling (the British currency), a symbol of empire and national autonomy. Britons are also extremely reluctant to lose direct control over monetary policy to the European Central Bank (ECB), and the chancellor, Gordon Brown, has insisted on a cautious approach to British participation in the euro zone and has controlled the political terrain of the Labour Party position on participation. On the other hand, Blair's Britain wants to assume leadership in Europe, expand the foreign policy and military capabilities of the Union, and position itself on the cutting edge of globalization. Thus, Britain faces a significant dilemma over European integration, and the stakes have been raised significantly by the prime minister's surprise declaration in April 2004 that he would subject the UK ratification of the EU Constitution to a referendum. The continuing challenges to British government that are posed by European integration are discussed further in Chapter 10.

Britain in the Era of Globalization

The term *globalization* is often applied as a general catchphrase to identify the growing depth, extent, and diversity of cross-border connections that are a signal characteristic of the contemporary world. Some have argued that the radical mobility of factors of production, especially the capital of the "electronic herd" of investors and financiers who can shift vast sums of money around the globe at the speed of a mouse-click, has fatally weakened the capacities of nation-states. Students of comparative politics by and large argue, however, that claims of the demise of national policy controls and national economic models have been exaggerated. Each country study in this book illuminates the particular features of national economic models as they are shaped by the international political economy, all set against the critical backdrop of domestic policy legacies and political constituencies and programs.

Is Britain making the most of globalization? The answer to this critical question begins with the understanding that Britain plays a particular role within the European and international economy, one that has been reinforced by international competitive pressures in this global age. For a start, foreign direct investment (FDI) favors national systems, like those of Britain (and the United States), that rely more on private contractual and market-driven arrangements and less on state capacity and political or institutional arrangements. Because of such factors as low costs, political climate, government-sponsored financial incentives, reduced trade union power, and a large pool of potential nonunionized recruits, the United Kingdom is a highly regarded location in Europe for FDI.

From the mid-1980s onward, the single-market initiative of the EU has attracted foreign investment by according insider status to non-EU-based companies, so long as minimum local content requirements are met. Throughout this period, all British governments have, for both pragmatic and ideological reasons, promoted the United Kingdom as a magnet for foreign investment. For the Thatcher and Major governments, FDI was a congenial market-driven alternative to state intervention as a means to improve sectoral competitiveness, especially in the automobile industry. It had the added benefit of exposing UK producers to lean production techniques and to management cultures and strategies that reinforced government designs to weaken unions and enforce flexibility. New Labour has continued this approach, which helps advance its key third-way strategy orientation to accept globalization as a given and to seek ways to improve competitiveness through business-friendly partnerships.

FDI is only one part of a bigger picture. In very important ways, New Labour accepted the legacy of eighteen years of Conservative assaults on trade union powers and privileges. It has chosen to modernize, but not reshape, the system of production in which nonstandard and insecure jobs without traditional social protections proliferate, a growing sector in which women and ethnic minorities are significantly overrepresented. As a result, within EU Europe, Britain has assumed a specialized profile as a producer of low-technology, low-value-added products through the use of a comparatively low-paid, segmented, weakly organized, and easily dismissible workforce. Tony Blair's Britain preaches this model of "flexible labour markets" throughout EU Europe, and its success in boosting Britain's economic performance in comparison with the rest of Europe has won some reluctant admirers, even converts. Thus, Britain has been shaped by the international political economy in important ways and hopes to take full advantage of the economic prospects of globalization, even as it tries to reshape other European national models in its own image.

As our world-of-states theme suggests, a country's participation in today's global economic order diminishes autonomous national control, raising unsettling questions in even the most established democracies. Amid complicated pressures, both internal and external, can state institutions retain the capacity to administer policy effectively within distinctive national models? How much do the growth of powerful bureaucracies at home and complex dependencies on international organizations such as the EU limit the ability of citizens to control policy ends? We turn to these questions in Chapter 8.

Notes

1. See Paul M. Kennedy, *The Rise and Fall of British Naval Mastery* (Atlantic Highlands, N.J.: Ashfield Press, 1992), pp. 186–189.

2. "A British Miracle?" *Economist,* September 16–22, 2000, pp. 57–58.

3. National Statistics Online, "Labour Market: Unemployment Rate Falls Slightly to 4.7%," September 26, 2004; www.statistics.gov.uk/cci/nugget.asp?id=12.

4. "Economic and Financial Indicators," *The Economist,* May 15, 2004, p. 100.

5. National Statistics, "First Release: UK Output, Income and Expenditure, 1st Quarter 2004," May 26, 2004; http://www.statistics.gov.uk/StatBase/Product.asp?vlnk=1129&Pos=1&ColRank=1&Rank=272.

6. Mark Tran, "UK Economy Shows First-Quarter Growth," *Guardian,* May 26, 2004.

7. The discussion of the UK economy is drawn largely from previous work. See Joel Krieger, *British Politics in the Global Age: Can Social Democracy Survive?* (New York: Oxford University Press, 1999); Joel Krieger and David Coates, "New Labour's Model for UK Competitiveness: Adrift in the Global Economy?" paper presented to the Wake Forest Conference on the Convergence of Capitalist Economies, September 27–29, 2003 (unpublished, available from the authors); and Joel Krieger, *Globalization and State Power: Who Wins When America Rules?* (New York: Longman, 2005), chap. 3.

8. Will Hutton, *The State We're In* (London: Jonathan Cape, 1995).

9. This discussion of the tenets of the third way and the evaluation of its economic policy draws heavily on collaborative work with David Coates. See Joel Krieger and David Coates, "New Labour's Model for UK Competitiveness: Adrift in the Global Economy?"

10. Tony Blair, speech to the Keidanren, Tokyo, January 5, 1996, p. 4.

11. _____, The Mais Lecture at City University, May 22, 1995, p. 7.

12. Ibid, p. 6.

13. Ibid.

14. National Statistics Online, "News Release: Most New Public Sector Jobs in Education and Health Jobs in the Public Sector Mid-2003"; http://www.statistics.gov.uk/CCI/article.asp?ID=408&Pos=1&ColRank=1&Rank=224.

15. David Turner, "Britain's Public Sector Jobs Increase Is Fastest in Decade," *Financial Times,* May 27, 2004, p. 4.

16. Ivor Crewe, "Labor Force Changes, Working Class Decline, and the Labour Vote: Social and Electoral Trends in Postwar Britain," in Frances Fox Piven, ed., *Labor Parties in Postindustrial Societies* (New York: Oxford University Press, 1992), p. 34. See also David Marsh and R. A. W. Rhodes, "Implementing Thatcherism: Policy Change in the 1980s," *Parliamentary Affairs* 45, no. 1 (January 1992): 34–37.

17. Polly Toynbee, "The Janus Chancellor," *Guardian,* May 14, 2004; www.guardian.co.uk/comment/story/0,3604,1216417,00.html.

18. Steven Fielding, "A New Politics?" in Patrick Dunleavy et al., eds., *Developments in British Politics* 6 (New York: St. Martin's Press, 2000), p. 2.

19. National Statistics Online, "Low Income: Fewer Children in Poverty in Recent Years," March 31, 2004; www.statistics.gov.uk/cci/nugget_print.asp?ID=333. See also Adrian Sinfield, "UK Shows the Way on Child Poverty," *New Zealand Herald,* May 26, 2004; www.nzherald.co.nz/storydisplay.cfm?storyID=3568524&thesection=news&thesubsection=dialogue.

20. National Statistics Online, "Population Size: 7.9% from a Minority Ethnic Group," February 13, 2003; www.statistics.gov.uk/cci/nugget.asp?id=273.

21. Office of National Statistics Social Survey, *Living in Britain: Results from the 1995 General Household Survey* (London: The Stationery Office, 1997).

22. Gail Lewis, "Black Women's Employment and the British Economy," in Winston James and Clive Harris, eds., *Inside Babylon: The Caribbean Diaspora in Britain* (London: Verso, 1993), pp. 73–96.

23. National Statistics Online, "Low Income for 60% of Pakistanis/Bangladeshis," December 12, 2002; www.statistics.gov.uk/CCI/nugget.asp?ID=269&Pos=1&ColRank=2&Rank=384.

24. "All White at the Top," *Guardian*, May 25, 2004; http://education.guardian.co.uk/egweekly/story/0,5500,1223478,00.html.

25. Ibid.

26. Jill Matheson and Carol Summerfield, eds., *Social Trends* 30 (London: The Stationery Office, 2000), p. 88.

27. National Statistics Online, "Gender Pay Gap: April 2003 Difference Smallest on Record," October 16, 2003; www.statistics.gov.uk/cci/nugget.asp?id=167.

28. Pippa Norris, *Electoral Change in Britain Since 1945* (Oxford: Blackwell, 1997), pp. 133–135; ibid., "A Gender-Generation Gap?" in Pippa Norris and Geoffrey Norris, eds., *Critical Elections: British Parties and Voters in Long-Term Perspective* (London: Sage, 1999).

29. MORI, "Many Councillors 'Divorced' from the Electorate," April 30, 2002; www.mori.com/polls/2002/greenissues.shtml.

30. David Floyd, "British Youth Oppose 'Bomber Blair,' " *WireTap*, March 28, 2003; www.wiretapmag.org/story.html?StoryID=15505.

8

Governance and Policymaking

An understanding of British governance begins with consideration of Britain's constitution, which is notable for two significant features: its form and its antiquity. Britain lacks a formal written constitution in the usual sense; that is, there is no single unified and authoritative text that has special status above ordinary law and can be amended only by special procedures. Rather, the British constitution is a combination of statutory law (mainly acts of Parliament), common law, convention, and authoritative interpretations. Although it is often said that Britain has an unwritten constitution, this is not accurate. Authoritative legal treatises are written, of course, as are the much more significant acts of Parliament that define crucial elements of the British political system. These acts define the powers of Parliament and its relationship with the Crown, the rights governing the relationship between state and citizen, the relationship of constituent nations to the United Kingdom, the relationship of the United Kingdom to the EU, and many other rights and legal arrangements. Thus, it is probably best to say that "what distinguishes the British constitution from others is not that it is unwritten, but rather that it is part written and uncodified."[1]

More than its form, however, the British constitution's antiquity raises questions. It is hard to know where conventions and acts of Parliament with constitutional implications began, but they can certainly be found dating back to the seventeenth century, notably with the Bill of Rights of 1689, which helped define the relationship between the monarchy and Parliament. "Britain's

constitution presents a paradox," a British scholar of constitutional history has observed. "We live in a modern world but inhabit a premodern, indeed, ancient, constitution."[2] For example, several industrial democracies, including Spain, Belgium, and the Netherlands, are constitutional monarchies, in which policymaking is left to the elected government and the monarch fulfills largely ceremonial duties. In fact, Western Europe contains the largest concentration of constitutional monarchies in the world. However, Britain alone among Western democracies has permitted two unelected hereditary institutions, the Crown and the House of Lords, to participate in governing the country (in the case of the Lords, a process of reform was begun in 1999, which will be discussed further in Chapter 9).

More generally, constitutional authorities have accepted the structure and principles of many areas of government for so long that appeal to convention has enormous cultural force. Thus, widely agreed-on rules of conduct, rather than law or U.S.-style checks and balances, set the limits of governmental power. This reality underscores an important aspect of British government: absolute principles of government are few. At the same time, those that exist are fundamental to the organization of the state and central to governance, policymaking, and patterns of representation.

Organization of the State

The core constitutional principle of the British political system and cornerstone of the

Westminster model is parliamentary sovereignty: Parliament can make or overturn any law; the executive, the judiciary, and the throne do not have any authority to restrict or rescind parliamentary action. Only Parliament can nullify or overturn its own legislation. In a classic parliamentary democracy, the prime minister is answerable to the House of Commons (the elected element of Parliament) and may be dismissed by it. That said, by passing the European Communities Act in 1972 (Britain joined the European Economic Community in 1973), Parliament accepted significant limitations on its ability to act with power. It acknowledged that European law has force in the United Kingdom without requiring parliamentary assent and acquiesced to the authority of the European Court of Justice (ECJ) to resolve jurisdictional disputes. To complete the circle, the ECJ has confirmed its prerogative to suspend acts of Parliament.[3]

Second, Britain has long been a *unitary state.* By contrast to the United States, where powers not delegated to the national government are reserved for the states, no powers are reserved constitutionally for subcentral units of government in the United Kingdom. However, the Labour government of Tony Blair introduced a far-reaching program of constitutional reform that created, for the first time, a quasi-federal system in Britain. Specified powers have been delegated (the British prefer to say *devolved*) to legislative bodies in Scotland and Wales, and in Northern Ireland (although conflict there leaves the ultimate shape of the constitutional settlement still in doubt). "Boldly put, at least in terms of its governance the UK is not united," noted a pair of political scientists writing about multiple levels of governance in the United Kingdom. "Scotland, Wales and Northern Ireland in key domestic areas of decision-making can go their own way whether it is over university fees, beef on the bone or policies in relation to local government."[4] In addition, some powers have been redistributed from the Westminster Parliament to an authority governing London with a directly elected mayor, and additional powers may be devolved to regional assemblies as well.

Third, Britain operates within a system of fusion of powers at the national level: Parliament is the supreme legislative, executive, and judicial authority and includes the monarch as well as the House of Commons and the House of Lords. The fusion of legislature and executive is also expressed in the function and personnel of the cabinet. Whereas U.S. presidents can direct or ignore their cabinets, which have no constitutionally mandated function, the British cabinet bears enormous constitutional responsibility. Through its collective decision making, the cabinet, and not an independent prime minister, shapes, directs, and takes responsibility for government. Cabinet government stands in stark contrast to presidential government and is perhaps the most important feature, certainly the center, of Britain's system of government.

Finally, sovereignty rests with the Queen-in-Parliament (the formal term for Parliament). Britain is a constitutional monarchy. The position of head of state passes by hereditary succession, but the government or state officials must exercise nearly all powers of the Crown. Taken together, parliamentary sovereignty, parliamentary democracy, and cabinet government form the core elements of the British or Westminster model of government, which many consider a model democracy and the first effective parliamentary democracy.

It may seem curious that such a venerable constitutional framework is also vulnerable to uncertainty and criticism. Can a willful prime minister overstep the generally agreed limits of the collective responsibility of the cabinet and achieve an undue concentration of power? How well has the British model of government stood the test of time and radically changed circumstances? What are the constitutional implications of Blair's reform agenda? These questions underscore the problems that even the most stable democracies face. They also help identify important comparative themes, because the principles of the Westminster model were, with some modifications, adopted widely by former colonies ranging from Canada, Australia, and New Zealand to India, Jamaica, and Zimbabwe. British success (or failure) in preserving citizens' control of their government has implications reaching well beyond the British Isles.

The Executive

The term *cabinet government* is useful in emphasizing the key functions that the cabinet exercises: responsibility for policymaking, supreme control of government, and coordination of all government departments. However, the term does not capture the full range of executive institutions or the scale and complexity of operations. The executive reaches well beyond the cabinet. It extends from ministries (departments) and ministers to the civil service in one direction, and to Parliament (as we shall see in Chapter 9) in the other direction.

Cabinet Government

After a general election, the Crown invites the leader of the party that emerges from the election with control of a majority of seats in the House of Commons to form a government and serve as prime minister. The prime minister usually selects approximately two dozen ministers to constitute the cabinet. Among the most significant assignments are the Foreign Office (equivalent to the U.S. secretary of state), the Home Office (ministry of justice or attorney general), and the chancellor of the exchequer (a finance minister or a more powerful version of the U.S. treasury secretary).

The responsibilities of a cabinet minister are immense. "The Cabinet, as a collective body, is responsible for formulating the policy to be placed before Parliament and is also the supreme controlling and directing body of the entire executive branch," notes S. E. Finer. "Its decisions bind all Ministers and other officers in the conduct of their departmental business."[5] In con-

trast to the French Constitution, which prohibits a cabinet minister from serving in the legislature, British constitutional tradition *requires* overlapping membership between Parliament and cabinet. Unlike the informal status of the U.S. cabinet, its British counterpart enjoys considerable constitutional privilege and is a powerful institution with enormous responsibility for the political and administrative success of the government.

The cabinet system is a complex patchwork of conflicting obligations and potential divisions. Each cabinet member who is a departmental minister has responsibilities to the ministry that he or she must run, and unless the cabinet member is a member of the House of Lords, he or she is also linked to a constituency, or electoral district (as an elected member of Parliament, or MP), to the party (as a leader and, often, a member of its executive board), to the prime minister (as an appointee who shares in the duties of a plural executive), and to a political tendency within the party (as a leading proponent of a particular vision of government).

The cabinet room at 10 Downing Street (the prime minister's official residence) is a place of intrigue as well as deliberation. From the perspective of the prime minister, the cabinet may appear as loyal followers or as ideological combatants, potential challengers for party leadership, and parochial advocates for pet programs that run counter to the overall objectives of the government. Against this potential for division, the convention of collective responsibility normally ensures the continuity of government by unifying the cabinet. In principle, the prime minister must gain the support of a majority of the cabinet for a range of significant decisions, notably the budget and the legislative program.

The only other constitutionally mandated mechanism for checking the prime minister is a defeat on a vote of no confidence in the House of Commons (discussed in Chapter 9). Since this action is rare and politically dangerous, the cabinet's role in constraining the chief executive remains the only routine check on his or her power. Collective responsibility is therefore a crucial aspect of the Westminster model of democracy. Prime ministers, however, reserve the option to develop policies in cabinet committees, whose membership can be manipulated to ensure support, and then to present policy to the full cabinet with little chance for other ministers to challenge the results. In addition, the principle of collective responsibility requires that all ministers support any action taken in the name of the government, whether or not it was brought to cabinet. Does collective responsibility effectively constrain the power of prime ministers, or does it enable the prime minister to paint "presidential" decisions with the veneer of collectivity?

A politician with strong ideological convictions and a leadership style to match, Margaret Thatcher often attempted to galvanize loyalists in the cabinet and either marginalize or expel detractors. In the end, Thatcher's treatment of the cabinet helped inspire the movement to unseat her as party leader and stretched British constitutional conventions. John Major returned to a more consultative approach, in keeping with the classic model of cabinet government. "When John Major became Prime Minister it was as though he had read textbooks on British constitutional theory, had observed very closely the circumstances of Margaret Thatcher's downfall, and had come to the conclusion that he was going to do things differently—very differently."[6] After Thatcher's tight control, ministers were delighted with their new freedom, but in time the collegiality of Major's cabinet broke down.

Tony Blair, like Thatcher, has narrowed the scope of collective responsibility. Cabinet meetings are often dull and perfunctory, and debate is rare. The prime minister, a few key cabinet members, and a handful of advisers take decisions in smaller gatherings. In a striking example of this process early in the Blair premiership, right after the election when the full cabinet had not yet met, the government announced the decision to free the Bank of England to set interest rates. Blair has accentuated the tendency for shorter cabinet meetings (they are usually less

than an hour) that cannot seriously take up (much less resolve) policy differences.

More recently, the role of cabinet in the decision to go to war in Iraq underscores its weakened capacity to exercise constitutional checks and balances. The subject was often discussed in cabinet—and endlessly in bilateral meetings with key ministers and unelected policy advisers—but was never subjected to the full-scale debate and formal cabinet approval that is associated with the model of cabinet government and collective responsibility. "We have not had cabinet government in the textbook sense for a very long time," affirmed Bernard Crick in *The Guardian*. "To gain assent for the Iraq war the prime minister had summoned cabinet ministers individually."[7] In addition, when the cabinet did take up the issue of the war in Iraq, the conversation was more desultory than the strict exercise of cabinet responsibility would imply.

Consider this account by John Kampfner of the cabinet meeting on February 17, 2003, the morning after a very divisive debate on the war—and massive Labour defections—in the Commons:

> The . . . day's Cabinet was somber. They did not dwell on the vote. Blair moved the conversation quickly on to plans for the post-war reconstruction of Iraq. By the standards of this government, these meetings had become a little more open. On this occasion, John Prescott [deputy prime minister] was asked to wind up. "My assessment of the mood of the Cabinet is that we're backing the PM," he declared. "Anyone want to say anything to the contrary?" He slowly turned his head around the table twice, eyeballing each member of the Cabinet. There was silence. "I take it then that everyone's signed up for the policy," Prescott concluded. That is how decisions were endorsed. The Prime Minister's official spokesman announced that the Cabinet had been "rock solid." Technically he was not wrong. But underlying the public support for Blair by his Cabinet, the unease went well beyond the likes of Cook and Short [the most vocal critics within the Cabinet].[8]

Kampfner reports that at the cabinet meeting one week later, that support had weakened further: "Whereas the previous week the Cabinet had been described as 'rock solid'; this time Downing Street had to construct a phrase that support for Blair's position was 'broad.' "[9]

The point is not that Blair lacked a majority in cabinet, but that cabinet meetings had become largely beside the point. In addition, with eyes turned toward bruising debates in Parliament, where, as Blair acknowledged, defeat would compel him to resign, the prime minister took no steps to discipline ministers who spoke out against the war plan. In fact, Blair permitted both Robin Cook (former Foreign Secretary and the Leader of the House of Commons) and Clare Short (Secretary of State for International Development) each to resign in protest of the decision to go to war in a manner and at a time of their own choosing. In March 2003, Blair won the formal support of Parliament he sought. In so doing, perhaps he set a precedent that the presumed prerogative power of the prime minister or Crown to declare war had been handed over to Parliament.[10] Alternatively, many contend that the real decision to go to war in Iraq had been taken by the prime minister and President Bush long before, probably at President Bush's ranch in April 2002. Either way, there is no denying that the cabinet played a minor, almost incidental role.[11]

As the decision to go to war in Iraq underscores, both Blair and his close aides seem skeptical about the effectiveness and centrality of the cabinet as well as cabinet committees. The prime minister prefers to coordinate strategically important policy areas through highly politicized special units in the Cabinet Office such as the Social Exclusion Unit, the Women's Unit, and the UK Anti-Drugs Co-ordination Unit. In June 2001, the Prime Minister's Delivery Unit was introduced to take strategic control of the delivery of public services, a central commitment of Blair's second term of office and one with great political salience.

Finally, Blair has vastly expanded the role of one-on-one meetings with ministers or small informal chats with senior colleagues, often on the sofa in 10 Downing Street. In a lecture at the London School of Economics that caused quite a stir, a highly regarded historian and former writer for *The Economist*, Peter Hennessy, quoted a variety of Whitehall insiders (*Whitehall* is a street name referring to the London nerve center of the civil service) who lamented that Blair had killed off cabinet government. One of the luminaries was quoted as saying that "Blair makes Margaret Thatcher look like a natural consulter; to be a minister outside the inner loop is hell."[12]

On balance, cabinet government represents a durable and effective formula for governance, although the cabinet does not presently function in the role of supreme directing and controlling body it occupies in constitutional doctrine. It is important to remember that the cabinet operates within a broader cabinet system or core executive as it is sometimes called (see Figure 8.1) and that the prime minister holds or controls many of the levers of power in the core executive. Because the prime minister is the head of the cabinet, his or her office helps develop policy, coordinates operations, and functions as a liaison with the media, the party, interest groups, and Parliament. As Martin J. Smith puts it, "The culmination of a long-term process of centralization of power in the hands of the Prime Minister is seen in the declining role of Cabinet and the increased development of resources inside Number 10."[13]

Both cabinet committees (comprising ministers) and official committees (made up of civil servants) supplement the work of the cabinet. In addition, the Treasury plays an important coordinating role through its budgetary control, while the cabinet office supports day-to-day operations. Leaders in both the Commons and the Lords, the *whips*, help smooth the passage of legislation sponsored by the government, which is more or less guaranteed by a working majority.

The cabinet system, and the complex interplay of resources, interdependencies, and power within the core executive that tend to concentrate

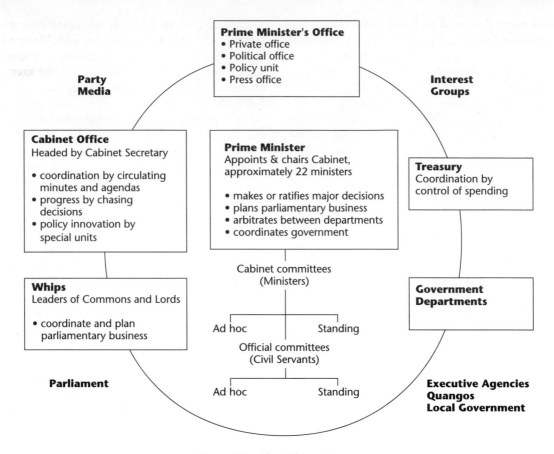

Figure 8.1   The Cabinet System

The cabinet is supported by a set of institutions that help formulate policy, coordinate operations, and facilitate the support for government policy. Acting within a context set by the fusion of legislature and executive, the prime minister enjoys a great opportunity for decisive leadership that is lacking in a system of checks and balances and separation of powers among the branches of government.

Source: Her Majesty's Treasury Budget Bulletin as found in *British Politics: Continuities and Change,* Third Edition, by Dennis Kavanagh, p. 251, Oxford University Press, 1996.

power at the top, ensure that there is no Washington-style gridlock (the inability of legislature and executive to agree on policy) in London. On the contrary, if there is a problem at the pinnacle of power in the United Kingdom, it is the potential for excessive concentration of power by a prime minister who is prepared to manipulate the cabinet and flout the conventions of collective responsibility.

Bureaucracy and Civil Service

Policymaking at 10 Downing Street may appear to be increasingly concentrated in the prime minister's hands. At the same time, when viewed from Whitehall, the executive may appear to be dominated by its vast administrative agencies. The range and complexity of state policymaking mean that in practice, the cabinet's authority must be shared with a vast set of un-elected officials.

How is the interaction between the civil service and the cabinet ministers (and their political assistants) coordinated? A very senior career civil servant, called a permanent secretary, has chief administrative responsibility for running a department. The permanent secretaries are assisted, in turn, by other senior civil servants, including deputy secretaries and undersecretaries. In addition, the minister reaches into his or her department to appoint a principal private secretary, an up-and-coming civil servant who assists the minister as gatekeeper and liaison with senior civil servants. According to the latest figures released by the Cabinet Office, in October 2003, there were 516,990 permanent civil servants (measured in full-time equivalents, FTEs), up from 482,690 in October 2001, but down from a height of 751,000 FTEs in 1976, a decline of nearly one-third. In terms of diversity, 52.4 percent of staff members were women (25.4 percent at the level of senior civil service), and 8.1 percent were from ethnic minority groups (3.2 percent at the level of senior civil service).[14]

Successful policy requires the effective translation of policy goals into policy instruments. Since nearly all legislation is introduced on behalf of the government and presented as the policy directive of a ministry, civil servants in Britain do much of the work of conceptualizing and refining legislation that is done by committee staffers in the U.S. Congress. Civil servants, more than ministers, assume operational duties, and, despite a certain natural level of mutual mistrust and incomprehension, the two must work closely together. To the impartial, permanent, and anonymous civil servants, ministers are too political, unpredictable, and temporary— *they* are tireless self-promoters who may neglect or misunderstand the needs of the ministry. To a conscientious minister, the permanent secretary may be protecting *his* or *her* department too strenuously from constitutionally proper oversight and direction. Whatever they may think, no sharp line separates the responsibilities

of ministers and civil servants, and they have no choice but to execute policy in tandem. Many of the activities traditionally undertaken by civil servants are now carried out in executive agencies established since a 1988 report on more effective government management. In addition, quite a range of administrative functions previously performed in-house are now provided through contracting out services to the private sector.

Like ministers, civil servants are servants of the Crown, but they are not part of the government (taken in the more political sense, like the term *the administration* in common American usage). The ministers, not the civil servants, have constitutional responsibility for policy and are answerable to Parliament and the electorate for the conduct of their departments. The significant influence of civil servants (and the size of even a streamlined bureaucracy) raises important questions about the proper role of unelected officials in a democratic polity. Indeed, the civil service has been assaulted from many directions. Since the early 1980s, the pace of change at Whitehall has been very fast, with governments looking to cut the size of the civil service, streamline its operations, replace permanent with casual (temporary) staff, and enhance its accountability to citizens. Beyond these pressures, the frustration of civil servants was deepened by Thatcher's evident impatience with the customs of impartiality and drawn-out procedures that slowed her aggressive policy agenda. In addition, the reinvigoration of parliamentary select committees has complicated the role of the civil service. Although tradition requires senior civil servants to testify on behalf of their ministers, the more aggressive stance of select committees in recent years has for the first time pressed them to testify, in effect, *against* their ministers if necessary to satisfy parliamentary concerns about misconduct or poor judgment. Some describe a situation of uncertainty and loss of morale.

As a result of the ongoing modernization of Whitehall (known as new public management, NPM), the civil service inherited by New Labour is very different from the civil service of thirty years ago. It has been downsized and given a new corporate structure (divided into over 120 separate executive agencies). Few at the top of these agencies (agency chief executives) are traditional career civil servants. More generally, a tradition of a career service, in which nearly all the most powerful posts were filled by those who entered the bureaucratic ranks in their twenties, is fading. Many top appointments are advertised widely and filled by "outsiders." The Blair government has continued the NPM trends toward accountability, efficiency, and greater transparency in the operations of the executive bureaucracy.

In recent years, many observers have expressed concern, however, that New Labour has done—and will continue to do—whatever it can to subject the Whitehall machine to effective political and ministerial direction and control.[15] A related concern, that the centrality and impartiality of civil servants is being eroded by the growing importance of special advisers (who are both political policy advisers and civil servants), came to a head as Blair made the case for war in Iraq. Key special advisers played critical roles in making the case in the famous "dodgy dossier" of September 2002 that the threat of weapons of mass destruction justified regime change in Iraq. "No. 10's handling of the dossier and its publicity gave impetus to longer-standing concerns that special advisers under the Blair government compromise the independence and integrity of the civil service," note Iain Byrne and Stuart Weir. "There is widespread agreement that special advisers can play a valuable role alongside ministers, but their presence raises concerns about their anomalous status . . . , their undefined functions and their accountability."[16] They are right to underscore the fact that the political neutrality of the civil service is a core element in British governance and policymaking and that the boundaries between ministers and civil servants as well as between special advisers and civil servants are not as clearly drawn as they should be. In September 2003, the prime minister rejected the recommendation of an April 2003 report of the Committee for Standards in Public Life (*Defining the Boundaries*) that the power of special advisers should be restricted as part of a larger effort to safeguard the civil service from politicization—and argued instead that special advisers should be given additional powers.[17]

Public and Semipublic Institutions

Like other countries, Britain has institutionalized a set of administrative functions that expand the role of the state well beyond the traditional core executive functions and agencies. The ebb and flow of alternative visions of government in the postwar period, from collectivist consensus to Thatcherism to New Labour, have resulted in substantial changes in emphasis. We turn now to a brief discussion of "semipublic" agencies—entities sanctioned by the state but without direct democratic oversight.

Nationalized Industries

The nationalization of basic industries was a central objective of the Labour government's program in the immediate period after World War II. Nationalization symbolized Labour's core socialist aspiration affirmed in the famous Clause IV of its party constitution ("to secure for the workers by hand or brain the full fruits of their industry . . . upon the basis of common ownership of the means of production, distribution and exchange"). Between 1946 and 1949, the Bank of England was nationalized, and coal, iron and steel, gas and electricity supply, and the bulk of the transport sector became public corporations. By 1960, nationalized industries accounted for about 18 percent of total fixed investment, produced about one-tenth of the national income, and employed some 8 percent of the UK workforce.[18]

During the eighteen years of Conservative government beginning in 1979, nearly 1 million workers transferred from public to private sector employment, and by 1995, the output of the nationalized sector was less than half the percentage of the gross domestic product (GDP) it had been in 1975. In his first speech as leader to the Labour Party conference in October 1994, Blair argued that a revision of Clause IV was necessary to make it clear that the Labour Party had broken with its past. Within months, a new Clause IV was in place that speaks to middle-class aspirations and rejects the notion that the capitalist market economy is immoral or inherently exploitative. For New Labour, a return to the program of public ownership of industry is unthinkable. Instead, when thinking of expanding state functions, we can look to a growing set of semipublic administrative organizations.

Nondepartmental Public Bodies

Since the 1970s, an increasing number of administrative functions have been transferred to bodies that are typically part of the government in terms of funding, function, and appointment of staff, but operate at arm's length from ministers. They are officially called nondepartmental public bodies (NDPBs) but are better known as quasi-nongovernmental organizations, or quangos. Quangos have increasing policy influence and enjoy considerable administrative and political advantages. They take responsibility for specific functions and can combine governmental and private sector expertise. At the same time, ministers can distance themselves from controversial areas of policy.

Despite Thatcher's attempts to reduce their number and scale back their operations, by the early 1990s a new generation of powerful, broadly defined, and well-funded quangos had replaced the smaller-scale quangos of the past. In 1990–1991, quangos were spending three times as much as they had in 1978–1979. The growth was particularly significant in locally appointed agencies, including bodies with responsibility for education, job training, health, and housing. By the late 1990s, there were some six thousand quangos, 90 percent operating at the local level.

They were responsible for one-third of all public spending and staffed by approximately fifty thousand people. Key areas of public policy previously under the authority of local governments are now controlled by quangos, which are nonelected bodies.

Some observers have expressed concern that the principle of democratic control is being compromised by the power of quangos, which are not accountable to the electorate. Some argue that the growth of local quangos has contributed to the centralization of power as agencies appointed by ministers take over many functions of local government. Although critical of the "quango state" while in opposition, New Labour took a more measured approach once in government, emphasizing reforms and more democratic scrutiny. Increasingly, the debate about NDPBs is less about the size of the public, semipublic, or private sector, and more about the effective delivery of services. For example, in May 2004 John Reid, the health secretary, announced detailed plans for a quango purge: the number of quangos sponsored by the department would be cut by one-half in order to reduce 20 percent of their spending (nearly 1 billion dollars) and streamline the staff by 25 percent.[19]

The elected authority in London, as well as the Welsh Assembly and Scottish Parliament, acquired extensive powers to review and reform many of the quangos under their responsibility. We will return later to consider local government in Britain, but we move now to a discussion of a set of formal institutions within and outside the executive.

Other State Institutions

Although British public administration extends well beyond its traditional focus on finance or foreign affairs or law and order, these policy areas remain critical. In this section, we examine the military and the police, the judiciary, and subnational government.

The Military and the Police

From the local bobby (a term for a local police officer derived from Sir Robert Peel, who set up London's metropolitan police force in 1829) to the most senior military officer, those involved in security and law enforcement have enjoyed a rare measure of popular support in Britain. Constitutional tradition and professionalism distance the British police and military officers from politics. Nevertheless, both institutions have been placed in more politically controversial and exposed positions in recent decades.

In the case of the military, British policy in the post–cold war period remains focused on a gradually redefined set of North Atlantic Treaty Organization (NATO) commitments. Still ranked among the top five military powers in the world, Britain retains a global presence, and the Thatcher and Major governments deployed forces in ways that strengthened their political positions and maximized Britain's global influence. In 1982, Britain soundly defeated Argentina in a war over the disputed Falkland/Malvinas Islands in the South Atlantic. In the Gulf War of 1991, Britain deployed a full armored division in the UN-sanctioned force arrayed against Iraq's Saddam Hussein. Under Blair's leadership, Britain was the sole participant alongside the United States in the aerial bombardment of Iraq in December 1998. In 1999, the United Kingdom strongly backed NATO's Kosovo campaign and pressed for ground troops. Indeed, the Kosovo campaign and Blair's "doctrine of international community," which the prime minister rolled out in a major speech in Chicago on the eve of NATO's fiftieth anniversary in 1999, assumed an important role in Blair's justification for the war in Iraq.[20] According to Blair, global interdependence rendered isolationism obsolete and inspired a commitment to a new ethical dimension in foreign policy. Throughout the war in Iraq and its bloody aftermath, Blair has persistently sought to characterize Iraq as an extension of Kosovo, an effort to liberate Muslims from brutal dicta-

torships, whether Serbia's Milosevic or Iraq's Saddam Hussein.

Until Blair's decision to support the American plan to shift the venue of the war on terror from Afghanistan to Iraq, the use of the military in international conflicts generated little opposition. Indeed, even in the case of the 2003 war in Iraq, the role of the military (as distinct from the decision to go to war) has generated little controversy. Although the International Committee of the Red Cross (ICRC) expressed grave concern about the treatment of some detainees—and the death of others—who were being held by UK forces, the allegations of mistreatment raised far fewer questions than those directed at the United States for its abuse of prisoners at Abu Ghraib. Hence the controversy over the ICRC findings focused more on questions about the conduct of ministers in failing to disclose the criticisms quickly enough and publicly enough, rather than on the conduct of the military. In addition, UK forces are widely credited with operations in and around Basra that have been as culturally sensitive and effective as could be expected under very difficult circumstances.

The role of the military in the dispute in Northern Ireland, however, has been more controversial. After a civil rights movement calling for Catholic political and economic equality helped provoke Protestant riots in the autumn of 1969, the British government sent troops to Northern Ireland. In a context set by paramilitary violence on all sides, the reputation of the army was tarnished by its use of techniques that were found to violate the European Convention on Human Rights (ECHR) as well as by accusations that it was used as a partisan political instrument to repress Irish nationalism.

As for the police, which traditionally operate as independent local forces throughout the country, the period since the 1980s has witnessed growth in government control, centralization, and level of political use. During the coal miners' strike of 1984–1985, the police operated to an unprecedented, and perhaps unlawful, degree as a national force coordinated through

Scotland Yard (London police headquarters). Police menaced strikers and hindered miners from participating in strike support activities. This partisan use of the police in an industrial dispute flew in the face of constitutional traditions and offended some police officers and officials. During the 1990s, concerns about police conduct focused on police-community relations, including race relations, corruption, and the interrogation and treatment of people held in custody. In particular, widespread criticism of the police for mishandling their investigation into the brutal 1993 racist killing of Stephen Lawrence in South London resulted in a scathing report by a commission of inquiry in 1999. The case raised basic questions about police attitudes toward ethnic minorities, as well as their conduct in racially sensitive cases, and focused renewed attention on necessary reforms. New Labour has advocated expanding police-community partnerships and improving relations with ethnic minority groups. At the same time, it considers tough action on crime as part of its broader approach to community that places considerable emphasis on the responsibilities of individuals and citizens (communitarianism).

The Judiciary

In Britain, the principle of parliamentary sovereignty has limited the role of the judiciary. Courts have no power to judge the constitutionality of legislative acts (judicial review). They can only determine whether policy directives or administrative acts violate common law or an act of Parliament. Hence, the British judiciary is generally less politicized and influential than its U.S. counterpart. In recent decades, however, governments have pulled the courts into political battles over the rights of local councils (municipal government), the activities of police in urban riots, and the role of police and trade unions in industrial disputes. For example, in the 1984–1985 coal miners' strike, the courts interpreted the new Employment Act of 1982 very broadly and froze the entire assets of the miners' union.

Jurists have also participated in the wider political debate outside court, as when they have headed royal commissions on the conduct of industrial relations, the struggle in Northern Ireland, and riots in Britain's inner cities. Some observers of British politics are concerned that governments have used judges in these ways to secure partisan ends, deflect criticism, and weaken the tradition of parliamentary scrutiny of government policy. Nevertheless, Sir Richard Scott's harsh report on his investigation into Britain's sales of military equipment to Iraq in the 1980s, for example, indicates that inquiries led by judges with a streak of independence can prove highly embarrassing to the government and raise important issues for public debate. The intensely watched inquiry conducted by Lord Hutton, a senior jurist, into the death of David Kelly confirmed this important public role of judges in the United Kingdom, although the question of Hutton's independence became very controversial in light of a "verdict" that exonerated the prime minister.

Beyond the politicization of jurists through their role on commissions and public inquiries, potentially dramatic institutional changes in law and the administration of justice are under consideration. In June 2003, Blair announced the government's intention to abolish the office of Lord Chancellor and move the law lords (who hold the ultimate authority of appeal in British law) from the House of Lords to a new "supreme court." The constitutional reform bill, introduced in 2004, faced strong opposition in the Lords (where Labour does not hold a majority). The prospects for ultimate passage remain clouded, straining relations between the Lords and the Commons, and generating considerable controversy over what is viewed by some "as a fundamental change in the relationship between law and politics."[21]

The European dimension has also significantly influenced law and the administration of justice. As a member of the EU, Britain is bound to abide by the European Court of Justice (ECJ), as it applies and develops law as an independent institution within the EU. For example, two decisions by the ECJ led to the enactment of the Sex Discrimination Act of 1986, since previous legislation did not provide the full guarantees of women's rights in employment mandated to all members by the EU's Equal Treatment Directive. Moreover, as a signatory to the ECHR with the passage of the Human Rights Act in 1998, Britain is required to comply with the rulings of the European Court of Justice on Human Rights (ECJHR). This has far-reaching potential for advancing a "pluralistic human rights culture" in Britain and providing new ground rules in law for protecting privacy, freedom of religion, and a wider respect for human rights.[22] Perhaps an indication of its broad influence to come, the adoption of the ECHR forced Britain to curtail discrimination against gays in the military. The Human Rights Act has also provided the judiciary with a legal framework (which Parliament cannot rescind) for addressing specific concerns such as asylum.[23] In addition, the UK Parliament's Joint Committee on Human Rights now reviews all bills for their compatibility with the Human Rights Act, thus imposing an important filter on controversial legislation as well as reporting on positive steps to secure human rights—for example, through a bill prohibiting the physical punishment of children.[24]

Subnational Government

Since the United Kingdom is a state comprising distinct nations (England, Scotland, Wales, and Northern Ireland), the distribution of powers involves two levels below the central government: national government and local (municipal) government. Because the British political framework has traditionally been unitary, not federal, no formal powers devolved either to the nations within the United Kingdom or to subnational (really subcentral or sub-UK) units as in the United States or Germany.

Although no powers have been constitutionally reserved to local governments, they historically had considerable autonomy in financial terms and discretion in implementing a host of social service and related policies. Before 1975, elected local governments set their own spending and taxation levels through the setting of rates (local property taxes). In the context of increased fiscal pressures that followed the 1973 oil crisis, the Labour government introduced the first check on the fiscal autonomy of local councils (elected local authorities) by introducing cash limits (ceilings on spending) beginning in fiscal year 1976–1977. In 1980, the newly elected Thatcher government introduced the Local Government, Planning and Land Act, further tightening the fiscal constraints on local government. Finally, in 1982, the central government set a ceiling on local rates (a rate cap). The outright abolition of London's progressive and multiculturally oriented city government (the Greater London Council, GLC) under the leadership of Ken Livingstone, and several other metropolitan councils in March 1986, completed the political onslaught on local autonomy. In 1989, the Thatcher government introduced a poll tax, an equal per capita levy for local finance, to replace the age-old system of rates. This radical break with tradition, which shifted the burden of local taxes from property owners and businesses to individuals, and taxed rich and poor alike, was monumentally unpopular. The poll tax proved a tremendous political liability, maintained the local edge to national politics, and helped lead to Thatcher's departure.

Although much of New Labour's agenda concerning subcentral government is focused primarily on the political role of nations within Britain, devolution within England is also part of the reform process. Regional Development Agencies (RDAs) were introduced throughout England in April 1999 as part of a decentralizing agenda, but perhaps even more to facilitate economic development at the regional level. Despite the fairly low-key profile of RDAs and their limited scope (they are unelected bodies with no statutory authority), they opened the door to popular mobilization in the long term for elected regional assemblies. Since 2002, the government's chief economic adviser has argued for a "new local-ism" to link local initiative and public policy co-ordinated through the No. 10 Delivery Unit.[25]

In addition, the Blair government placed changes in the governance of London on the fast track. The introduction of a directly elected mayor of London in May 2000 proved embar-rassing to Blair, as the government's efforts to keep Livingstone out of the contest backfired and he won handily. With characteristic panache, Livingstone began his victory speech with an obvious allusion to the abolition of the GLC: "As I was saying before I was so rudely interrupted 14 years ago . . . I want an all-embracing admin-istration that will speak with one voice on behalf of London."

Even before the debacle of the mayor's race in London, Blair and New Labour appeared gen-uinely ambivalent about decentralization with the loss of direction and control it entails. In the aftermath, it was even clearer that constitutional reform, once begun, can take on a life of its own. The movement for regional assemblies gained steam, with a series of referendums scheduled for late fall 2004 on introducing regional gov-ernment in the northeast, the northwest, Hum-ber, and Yorkshire. Once at least one region has voted for an elected assembly, the government plans to introduce enabling legislation to allow regional assemblies to be set up.

The European Dimension

In addition to devolution and constitutional re-form, British politics has been fundamentally re-structured by the delegation of more and more authority to the EU. As one observer neatly sum-marized this watershed development, "The result is a new kind of multi-level political system in which political power is shared between the EU, national and subnational levels, and decisions taken at one level shape outcomes at others."[26]

The European dimension has significantly in-fluenced law and the administration of justice. Parliament passed the European Communities Act in 1972 to seal Britain's entry into the European Community (EC), with the provision that existing EC law be binding on the United Kingdom. In any conflict between British law and EC (now EU) law, EU law prevails. The act specifies that British courts must adjudicate any disputes of interpreta-tion that arise from EU law. In addition, the Treaty of Rome (the treaty that formed the EC, to which the United Kingdom is bound by the terms of its membership) specifies that cases that reach the highest domestic appeals court—the House of Lords—be sent to the European Court of Justice (ECJ) in Luxembourg for final ruling.

As a member of the EU, Britain is bound to abide by the ECJ, as it applies and develops law as an independent institution within the EU. For example, two decisions by the ECJ led to the en-actment of the Sex Discrimination Act of 1986, since previous legislation did not provide the full guarantees of women's rights in employment mandated to all members by the EU's Equal Treatment Directive. The pace of supranational influences on Britain, in legal as in other policy areas, will doubtless increase as EU measures of economic and political integration proceed. Po-litically, the binding nature of EU laws and reg-ulations is likely to fuel the fear that Britain is losing sovereign control, whether to jurists in Luxembourg or bureaucrats in Brussels. More-over, the expanding scope of EU influences is likely to widen the role of the judiciary within British affairs. Since the EU's dispute resolution process relies to a much greater degree on legal instruments than has the domestic UK political system, the growing role of the ECJ as an agent of European integration promises to expand the role of the legal and judicial process in British political disputes.[27] In administrative and politi-cal terms, the consequences of the European di-mension are equally profound. Both ministers and senior civil servants spend a great deal of time in EU policy deliberations and are con-strained both directly and indirectly by the EU agenda and directives. Although still effectively in charge of many areas of domestic policy, more than 80 percent of the rules governing economic life in Britain are determined by the EU. Even when the United Kingdom has opted out, as in the case of the common currency, European influences are significant. Decisions by the Council of Finance Ministers and the European Central Bank shape British macroeconomic, monetary, and fiscal policies in significant ways. Nor are foreign and security policy, the classic exercises of national sovereignty, immune from EU influences, since multilevel governance has been extended to these spheres by the EU's Common Foreign and Security Policy.[28] Little is certain about the processes of European integration, except that they will continue to shape and bedevil British politics for many years to come.

The Policymaking Process

Parliamentary sovereignty is the core constitutional principle of the British political system. However, when it comes to policymaking and policy implementation, the focus is not on Westminster but rather on Whitehall. In many countries, such as Japan, India, and Nigeria, personal connections and informal networks play a large role in policymaking and implementation. How different is the British system?

Unlike the U.S. system, in which policymaking is concentrated in congressional committees and subcommittees, Parliament has little direct participation in policymaking. Policymaking emerges primarily from within the executive. There, decision making is strongly influenced by policy communities—informal networks with extensive knowledge, access, and personal connections to those responsible for policy. In this private hothouse environment, civil servants, ministers, and members of the policy communities work through informal ties. A cooperative style develops as the ministry becomes an advocate for key players in its policy community and as civil servants come perhaps to overidentify the public good with the advancement of policy within their area of responsibility. This cozy insider-only policy process has been challenged by the delegation of more and more authority to the EU.

As we will see in Chapter 9, not only the broad principles and practices of governance, but also the organization of interests and the broad dynamics of representation and political participation have been fundamentally reshaped in recent decades.

Notes

1. See Philip Norton, *The British Polity*, 3rd ed. (New York: Longman, 1994), p. 59, for a useful discussion of the sources of the British constitution.

2. Stephen Haseler, "Britain's Ancien Régime," *Parliamentary Affairs* 40, no. 4 (October 1990): 415.

3. See Philip Norton, "Parliament in Transition," in Robert Pyper and Lynton Robins, eds., *United Kingdom Governance* (New York: St. Martin's Press, 2000), pp. 82–106.

4. Jon Pierre and Gerry Stoker, "Towards Multi-Level Governance," in Patrick Dunleavy et al., eds., *Developments in British Politics*, vol. 6 (New York: St. Martin's Press, 2000), p. 31.

5. S. E. Finer, *Five Constitutions* (Atlantic Highlands, N.J.: Humanities Press, 1979), p. 52.

6. Anthony King, "Cabinet Co-ordination or Prime Ministerial Dominance? A Conflict of Three Principles of Cabinet Government," in Ian Budge and David McKay, eds., *The Developing British Political System: The 1990s*, 3rd ed. (London: Longman, 1993), p. 63.

7. Bernard Crick, "Blair Should Beware the Boiling Up of Little Irritations," September 29, 2003; www.guardian.co.uk/comment/story/0,3604,1051720,00.html.

8. John Kampfner, *Blair's Wars* (London: The Free Press, 2003), p. 278.

9. Ibid., p. 294.

10. Iain Byrne and Stuart Weir, "Democratic Audit: Executive Democracy in War and Peace," *Parliamentary Affairs* 57, no. 2 (April 2004): 455.

11. See Kampfner, *Blair's Wars*, p. 294.

12. Chris Brady, "Collective Responsibility of the Cabinet: An Ethical, Constitutional or Managerial Tool?" *Parliamentary Affairs* 52, no. 2 (April 1999): 214–229.

13. Martin J. Smith, "The Core Executive and the Modernization of Central Government," in Patrick Dunleavy et al., eds., *Developments in British Politics* 7 (New York: Palgrave/Macmillan, 2003), p. 60.

14. National Statistics Online, Cabinet Office News Release, "Latest Civil Service Numbers Published," April 22, 2004; www.statistics.gov.uk/.

15. See Kevin Theakston, "Ministers and Civil Servants," in Pyper and Robins, eds., *United Kingdom Governance*, pp. 39–60.

16. Byrne and Weir, "Democratic Audit: Executive Democracy in War and Peace," p. 458.

17. Ibid., p. 459. See also Committee on Standards in Public Life, *Defining the Boundaries Within the Executive: Ministers, Special Advisers and the Permanent Civil Service, Cm 5775, April 2003.*

18. Simon Mohun, "Continuity and Change in State Economic Intervention," in Allan Cochrane and James Anderson, eds., *Politics in Transition* (London: Sage, 1989), p. 73.

19. Nicholas Timmins, "Health Ministers Back Purge of Quangos," *Financial Times,* May 21, 2004.

20. Tony Blair, "Doctrine of the International Community," speech to the Economic Club of Chicago, Hilton Hotel, Chicago, April 22, 1999. For a detailed discussion of the speech and its implications for the war in Iraq, see David Coates and Joel Krieger, *Blair's War* (Malden, Mass.: Polity Press, 2004), chap. 6.

21. Sue Prince, "The Law and Politics: Upsetting the Judicial Apple-Cart," *Parliamentary* Affairs 57, no. 2 (2004): 288.

22. See Bhiku Parekh et al., *The Future of Multi-Ethnic Britain: The Parekh Report* (London: Profile Books, 2000), pp. 90–102.

23. See Andrew Gamble, "Remaking the Constitution," in Patrick Dunleavy et al., eds., *Developments in British Politics* 7 (New York: Palgrave/Macmillan, 2003), pp. 34–36.

24. Prince, "The Law and Politics: Upsetting the Judicial Apple-Cart," pp. 298–299.

25. Andrew Gray and Bill Jenkins, "Government and Administration: Too Much Checking, Not Enough Doing?" *Parliamentary Affairs* 57, no. 2 (2004): 274.

26. Simon Hix, "Britain, the EU and the Euro," in Dunleavy et al., *Developments in British Politics* 6, p. 48.

27. For a useful discussion of the repercussions of the EU on British governance, see ibid., pp. 47–68.

28. Ibid.

CHAPTER

9

Representation and Participation

As discussed in Chapter 8, parliamentary sovereignty is the core constitutional principle defining the role of the legislature and, in a sense, the whole system of British government. No act of Parliament can be set aside by the executive or judiciary, nor is any Parliament bound by the actions of any previous Parliament. Nevertheless, in practice, the control exerted by the House of Commons (or Commons) is not unlimited. In this chapter we investigate the powers and role of Parliament, both Commons and Lords, as well as the party system, elections, and contemporary currents in British political culture, citizenship, and identity. We close by offering an analysis of surprising new directions in political participation and social protest.

The Legislature

Is Parliament still as sovereign in practice as it remains in constitutional tradition? Clearly, it is not as powerful as it once was. From roughly the 1830s to the 1880s, it collaborated in the formulation of policy, and members amended or rejected legislation on the floor of the House of Commons. Today, the Commons does not so much legislate as assent to government legislation, since (with rare exceptions) the governing party has a majority of the seats and requires no cross-party voting to pass bills. In addition, the balance of effective oversight of policy has shifted from the legislature to executive agencies. In this section we discuss, in turn, the legislative process, the House of Commons, the House of Lords, and reforms and pressures for change.

Legislative Process

To become law, bills must be introduced in the House of Commons and the House of Lords, although approval by the latter is not required. The procedure for developing and adopting a public bill is quite complex. The ideas for prospective legislation may come from political parties, pressure groups, think tanks, the prime minister's policy unit, or government departments. Prospective legislation is then normally drafted by civil servants, circulated within Whitehall, approved by the cabinet, and then refined by one of some thirty lawyers in the Office of Parliamentary Counsel.

According to tradition, in the House of Commons the bill usually comes to the floor three times (referred to as readings). The bill is formally read upon introduction (the first reading), printed, distributed, debated in general terms, and after an interval (from a single day to several weeks), given a second reading, followed by a vote. The bill is then usually sent for detailed review to a standing committee of between sixteen and fifty members chosen to reflect the overall party balance in the Commons. It is then subjected to a report stage during which new amendments may be introduced. The third reading follows; normally, the bill is considered in final form (and voted on) without debate.

After the third reading, a bill passed in the House of Commons follows a parallel path in the House of Lords. There the bill is either accepted without change, amended, or rejected. According to custom, the House of Lords passes bills concerning taxation or budgetary matters without alteration and can add technical and editorial amendments to other bills (which must be approved by the House of Commons) to add clarity in wording and precision in administration. After a bill has passed through all these stages, it is sent to the Crown for royal assent (approval by the queen or king, which is only a formality), after which it becomes law and is referred to as an act of Parliament.

The House of Commons

In constitutional terms, the House of Commons, the lower house of Parliament (with 659 members since 1997), exercises the main legislative power in Britain. Along with the two unelected elements of Parliament, the Crown and the House of Lords, the Commons has three main functions: (1) to pass laws, (2) to provide finances for the state by authorizing taxation, and (3) to review and scrutinize public administration and government policy.

In practical terms, the Commons has a limited legislative function; nevertheless, it serves a very important democratic function. It provides a highly visible arena for policy debate and the partisan collision of political worldviews. The Commons comes alive when opposition members challenge the government, spark debates over legislation, and question the actions of cabinet members. During question time, a regular weekly feature of Commons debate, ministers give oral replies to questions submitted in advance by members of Parliament (MPs) and offer off-the-cuff responses to follow-up questions and sarcastic asides (often to the merriment of all in attendance). The exchanges create extraordinary theater and can make and unmake careers. The ability to handle parliamentary debate with style and panache is considered a prerequisite for party leadership.

The high stakes and the flash of rhetorical skills bring drama to the historic chambers, but one crucial element of drama is nearly always missing: the outcome is seldom in doubt. The likelihood that the Commons will invoke its ul-

timate authority, to defeat a government, is very small. MPs from the governing party who consider rebelling against their leader (the prime minister) are understandably reluctant in a close and critical vote to force a general election, which would place their jobs in grave jeopardy. Only once since the defeat of Ramsay MacDonald's government in 1924 has a government been brought down by a defeat in the Commons (in 1979). Contemporary constitutional conventions provide a good deal of wiggle room for the government. It was once taken for granted that defeat of any significant motion or bill would automatically result in cabinet resignation or a dissolution of Parliament. However, it is now likely that only defeat on a motion that explicitly refers to "confidence in Her Majesty's government" still mandates dissolution. Today, the balance of institutional power has shifted from Parliament to the governing party and the executive.

The House of Lords

The upper chamber of Parliament, the House of Lords (or Lords), is an unelected body that comprises hereditary peers (nobility of the rank of duke, marquis, earl, viscount, or baron), life peers (appointed by the Crown on the recommendation of the prime minister), and law lords (appointed to assist the Lords in its judicial duties and who become life peers). The Lords also includes the archbishops of Canterbury and York and two dozen senior bishops of the Church of England. There are roughly 1,200 members of the House of Lords, but there is no fixed number, and membership changes with the appointment of peers. Not surprisingly, the Conservatives have a considerable edge in the upper house, with just over one-half of peers; Labour runs a distant second at roughly one-sixth. About one-third are crossbenchers, or independents.

Traditionally, the House of Lords has also served as the final court of appeal for civil cases throughout Britain and for criminal cases in England, Wales, and Northern Ireland. This judicial role, performed by the law lords, drew international attention in 1998 and 1999 when a Spanish court attempted to extradite General Augusto Pinochet of Chile on charges of genocide, torture, and terrorism. As discussed in Chapter 8, if made into law, the constitutional reform bill, which was introduced in 2004, would transfer that function from the Lords to a new "supreme court."

In modern times, however, the Lords, which has the power to amend and delay legislation, has served mainly as a chamber of revision, providing expertise in redrafting legislation. Recently, for example, the House of Lords, which considered the Nationality, Immigration and Asylum Bill too harsh, battled the government for weeks and forced revisions before approving the legislation.

In 1999, the Blair government appointed a Royal Commission on the Reform of the House of Lords (the Wakeham commission) and in the same year introduced legislation to remove the right of hereditary lords to speak and vote. With the passage of House of Lords Act 1999, the number of hereditary peers was reduced to 92. In January 2000, the commission recommended a partly elected second chamber, enumerating alternative models. In February 2003, the Commons rejected seven options, ranging from a fully appointed chamber (Blair's preference) to an entirely elected one. The failure of a joint committee of MPs and peers to achieve consensus left reform plans in tatters. The government remains committed to the removal of hereditary peers and to an upper house that would be largely elected, but the fate of reform legislation is clouded by multiple divisions. It seems likely that Tony Blair has placed further reform of the Lords on hold until after the general election (expected in 2005, but not required until mid-2006).

Reforms in Behavior and Structure

How significant are contemporary changes in the House? How far will they go to stem the tide in Parliament's much-heralded decline?

Behavioral Changes: Backbench Dissent. Since the 1970s, backbenchers (MPs of the governing party who have no governmental office and rank-and-file opposition members) have been markedly less deferential than in the past. A backbench rebellion against the Major government's EU policy took a toll on the prestige of the prime minister and weakened him considerably. Until the war in Iraq was on the horizon, Blair seemed less likely to face significant rebellion from Labour MPs, although divisions did occur—relatively early in his premiership, for example, over social welfare policy and the treatment of trade unions. The Chapter 6 opening vignette described the extremely sizable and hard-fought rebellions Blair faced in January 2004 over the Education Bill. The defection of some one-third of Labour MPs on key votes in February and March 2003 authorizing the use of force in Iraq represents a far more historic rebellion. In May 2003, government whips managed to survive a rebellion over National Health Service (NHS) legislation by a narrow 17-vote margin (the bill polarized the divisions between "old" and "new" Labour concerning "foundation hospitals"—a new NHS entity that opened public hospital services to private sector corporations). Looking ahead, it is likely that any decision to join the euro would inspire significant backbench dissent once more. After Major's problems with backbenchers over the EU, many argued that weaker party discipline had become a permanent condition, and the rupture in the Labour Party over Iraq will fuel speculation that party discipline may no longer quell opposition on matters of great moment that inspire deep convictions.

Structural Changes: Parliamentary Committees. In addition to the standing committees that routinely review bills during legislative proceedings, in 1979 the Commons revived and extended the number and "remit" (i.e., responsibilities) of select committees. Select committees help Parliament exert control over the executive by examining specific policies or aspects of administration.

The most controversial select committees are watchdog committees that monitor the conduct of major departments and ministries. Select committees hold hearings, take written and oral testimony, and question senior civil servants and ministers. They then issue reports that often include strong policy recommendations at odds with government policy. As one side effect of the reform, the role of the civil service has been complicated. For the first time, civil servants have been required to testify in a manner that might damage their ministers, revealing culpability or flawed judgments. As discussed in Chapter 8, the powerful norms of civil service secrecy have been compromised and the relationship with ministers disturbed. On balance, the committees have been extremely energetic, but not very powerful.

In 1997, the Modernisation Committee was established, providing an avenue for the Commons to assess procedures and conventions critically. The committee's reforms have been generally regarded as productive but limited. Perhaps the most significant modernizing reform was the 1998 change in the system of scrutinizing EU affairs. These included the introduction of new committees and the strengthening of informal links with EU institutions. The prospects of parliamentary reform are limited by its very character and function within the broader political system. The dominance of party and executive constrains Parliament, not to mention "the fundamental fact that Parliament is a legislature in which the ambition of most of its members is to join the executive."[1] As a consequence, demands for significantly greater scrutiny over government are not likely to be made and are even less likely to be accepted.

Political Parties and the Party System

Like the term *parliamentary sovereignty*, which conceals the reduced role of Parliament in legislation and the unmaking of governments, the term *two-party system*, which is commonly used to describe the British party system, is somewhat deceiving. It is true that since 1945, only leaders of the Labour or Conservative parties have served as prime ministers. Also, from 1945 through 2001, the Conservative and Labour parties each won eight general elections. It is also true that throughout the postwar period, these two parties have routinely divided some 90 percent of the seats in the House of Commons. But a variety of other parties—centrist, environmental, nationalist, and even neofascist—have complicated the picture of party competition. (In addition, Britain has several national parties, such as the Scottish National Party [SNP] in Scotland or the Plaid Cymru in Wales, which are described below under "Trends in Electoral Behavior.")

The Labour Party

As one of the few European parties with origins outside electoral politics, the Labour Party was launched by trade union representatives and socialist societies in the last decade of the nineteenth century and formally took its name in 1906. From its inception in a Labour Representation Committee, supporters sought to advance working-class political representation and to further specific trade unionist demands. In the years preceding World War I, the party expanded its trade union affiliation but made only weak progress at the polls. Labour secured only 7.1 percent of the vote in 1910, but the radicalizing effects of the war and the expansion of the franchise in 1918 nearly tripled its base of support. In 1918, it received 22.2 percent, even with a shift of emphasis from the defense of trade union rights to explicitly socialist appeals. Its landslide 1945 victory promoted the party to major player status. At the same time, Labour began moderating its ideological appeal and broadening its electoral base.

Early in the postwar period, it was clear that Labour Party fundamentalism, which stressed state ownership of industry and workers' control of production, would take a backseat to a more moderate perspective that advocates the projects of the collectivist consensus (called revisionism or Labourism by contemporaries). In the 1950s and early 1960s, those not engaged in manual labor voted Conservative three times more commonly than they did Labour; more than two out of three manual workers, by contrast, voted Labour. During this period, Britain conformed to one classic pattern of a Western European party system: a two-class/two-party system.

The period since the mid-1970s has been marked by significant changes in the party system and a growing disaffection with even the moderate social democracy associated with the Keynesian welfare state and Labourism. The party suffered from divisions between its trade unionist and parliamentary elements, constitutional wrangling over the power of trade unions to determine party policy at annual conferences, and disputes over how the leader would be selected. In 1981, a centrist breakaway of leading Labour MPs further destabilized the party.

Divisions spilled over into foreign policy issues as well. Although Labour has been generally internationalist, persistent voices within the party challenged participation in the European Community (EC) on the grounds that EC policy would advance the interests of business over labor. However, the EC's adoption of the Social Charter to extend workers' rights and protections in 1989 helped turn Labour into a pro-EC party. On defense issues, there was a strong pacifist and an even stronger antinuclear sentiment within the party. Support for unilateral nuclear disarmament (the reduction and elimination of nuclear weapons systems with or without comparable developments on the Soviet side) was a decisive break with the national consensus on security policy and contributed to the party's losses in 1983 and 1987. Unilateralism was then scrapped.

The 1980s and 1990s witnessed a period of relative harmony within the party, with moderate trade union and parliamentary leadership agreeing on major policy issues. Tony Blair's immediate predecessors as party leaders—Neil Kinnock

(who served from 1983 until Labour's defeat in the March 1992 election) and John Smith (who replaced Kinnock and served as leader until his death in May 1994)—helped pave the way for New Labour by abandoning socialism and taking the party in a new pragmatic direction. Labour has become a moderate left-of-center party in which ideology takes a backseat to performance and electoral mobilization, although divisions over the war in Iraq have inspired some soul searching about what the party stands for. There is an increasing awareness that divisions run deep between traditional collectivist Labour and adherents of Blair's New Labour. Even more dramatic, the rupture over Iraq—which will not easily heal—exposed deep divisions within Labour Party foreign policy. In particular, it exposed the divide between two broadly defined camps, defined by support or opposition to the war in Iraq. Supporters want to anchor British foreign policy in the "special relationship" with the United States as a means of sustaining an imperial legacy of great power politics, and see the use of force as a necessary means for advancing British interests and values, even as in Kosovo and Iraq, without the authority of the Security Council. Those who opposed the war tend to look more critically at America's hegemonic project and to consider Europe the proper focus of British diplomatic and military policies. Like Robin Cook when he was foreign secretary, they want to advance an ethical dimension in foreign policy that emphasizes multilateralism, respect for international law, and a serious effort to narrow the development gap.[2]

The Conservative Party

The pragmatism, flexibility, and organizational capabilities of the Conservative Party, a party that dates back to the eighteenth century, have made it one of the most successful and, at times, innovative center-right parties in Europe. In contrast to some leading conservative parties in Italy and Germany, it has been a secular party wholly committed to democratic principles, free of the association with fascism during World

War II that tainted the others. Although it has fallen on hard times in recent years, it would be unwise to underestimate its potential as both an opposition and a governing party.

Although the association of the Conservative Party with the economic and social elite is unmistakable, it is also true that it was the Conservative government of Prime Minister Benjamin Disraeli (1874–1880) that served as midwife to the birth of the modern welfare state in Britain. The creation of a "long-lasting alliance between an upper-class leadership and a lower-class following" made the Conservative Party a formidable player in British politics.[3] Throughout the postwar period, it has also routinely (with some exceptions) provided the Tories, as Conservatives are colloquially called, with electoral support from about one-third or more of the manual working class. Even in Labour's recent landslide victories, the Tories continued to attract significant working-class support. In 1997, 28 percent of skilled manual workers and 24 percent of unskilled manual workers voted for the Conservatives, and in 2001 the corresponding figures were 31 percent and 25 percent.[4]

Contemporary analysis of the Conservative Party must emphasize the cost to the party of its internal divisions over Britain's role in the EU. The Tories have seldom, if ever, experienced divisions over an area of policy as serious as those over Europe in the 1990s. Wrangling among the Conservatives over Europe led to Thatcher's demise as leader and weakened Major throughout his years as prime minister. The bitter leadership contest that followed Major's resignation after the 1997 defeat only reinforced the impression of a party in turmoil. The new party leader, a centrist, William Hague, had his work cut out for him. The Conservatives were divided between the "Euro-skeptics," who rejected further European integration, and those who supported integration balanced by a firm regard for British sovereignty. In addition, despite party support for a unitary, not a federal, arrangement, the Conservatives under Hague had no choice but to find credible positions on the constitutional re-

forms that were already in the pipeline and some, like devolution, that had very considerable support, especially in Scotland. Finally, although economic and social policy divisions were eclipsed by the clash over Europe, Conservatives faced inner disagreements on social policy, industrial policy, and the running of the economy.

The pro-business and pro-market orientation of Blair's Labour Party and its perceived centrism limit the options for Conservatives in advancing economic and social policy that would mark out a distinctive alternative to Blair. In a clear effort to differentiate the Conservatives from Blair's third way, Hague launched a "British Way" initiative, appealing to "Middle England" and traditional values of entrepreneurship, individualism, and loyalty to local and national institutions.[5] In a related development, the party adopted hard-line positions on asylum seekers, gays, and ethnic minority rights that raised questions about tolerance and its much trumpeted compassion.

Whatever the divisions and policy challenges, the Conservatives faced the 2001 election with a confidence they had not experienced for several years, hoping for a good showing, although not expecting victory. But the election proved a stunning repudiation. A bid to lower taxes backfired with an electorate demanding better public services. Nor did the anti-euro stance gain support. Within hours of the result, Hague announced his resignation.

His successor as Conservative leader, Iain Duncan Smith, elected in September 2001, was viewed by many as a poor, even a suicidal, choice to revitalize the party. Since Hague was defeated fighting a "save the pound" campaign, what advantage would be gained by choosing a leader who was even more anti-euro and more right-wing on social issues? Starting from such low expectations, despite loyal support from party members who had elected him as leader, Smith suffered from opinion polls that consistently revealed that the public never embraced him as a potential prime minister. Persistent infighting and threats of rebellion, combined with his inability to capitalize on Blair's own political problems, led in October 2003 to Smith's ouster by Conservative MPs.

Many Conservatives feared a nasty and protracted leadership struggle, but in fact nothing of the kind occurred. Once the combative, experienced, and highly regarded Michael Howard—who had served in the cabinets of both Margaret Thatcher and John Major—threw his hat into the ring, no one else followed, and he was soon declared the party leader. His professed commitment to lead the party "from the center" offered the promise that he would make the battle for the electorate as broad based as possible, although his association with the introduction of the poll tax under Thatcher and his more recent sharp-edged criticism of the European Union clouded his prospects as the leader who could bring the Tories out of the electoral wilderness. Howard's assured performances from the front bench in Parliament seemed to revitalize the party, but, as one observer noted, "it remained to be seen whether Howard's competence, gravitas and apparent acceptance by his parliamentary colleagues would translate into popular support."[6] Although Howard pounded Blair on the failures of intelligence in the run-up to the war in Iraq and his handling of the David Kelly affair, Conservatives gave the prime minister far less trouble on Iraq than did members of the Labour Party itself. There was little evidence that the Tories were likely to capitalize politically on Blair's problems, whether domestic or international.

Liberal Democrats and Other Parties

Since the 1980s, a changing roster of centrist parties has posed a potentially significant threat to the two-party dominance of Conservative and Labour. Through the 1970s, the Liberal Party, a governing party in the pre–World War I period and thereafter the traditional centrist third party in Britain, was the only centrist challenger to the Labour and Conservative parties. In 1981, the Social Democratic Party (SDP) formed out of a split within the Labour Party. In the 1983 elec-

tion, the Alliance (an electoral arrangement of the Liberals and the SDP) gained a quarter of the vote. The strength of centrist parties in the mid-1980s led to expectations of a possible Alliance-led government (which did not occur), and observers of British politics began to talk about a party system with four major parties competing across much of the United Kingdom (Conservative, Labour, Liberal, and SDP). After the Conservative victory in 1987, the Liberal Party and most of the SDP merged to form the Social and Liberal Democratic Party (now called the Liberal Democrats, or the LD).

Under the leadership of Paddy Ashdown, the Liberal Democrats fought the 1992 election from the awkward stance of "equidistance" from the two major parties. After a disappointing result—17.8 percent of the vote and only twenty seats in the Commons—the party changed its position in 1994 and began working more closely with Labour. Most important, the two parties created the Joint Constitutional Committee, which developed a degree of unity on proposals for constitutional reform. Many credit the Liberal Democrats with inspiring Blair's constitutional agenda. Nevertheless, under Ashdown's effective leadership, the Liberal Democrats preserved their independence in the 1997 election. They targeted the seats where they had the greatest chance of victory, with impressive results. Although their share of the vote slipped slightly between 1992 and 1997 (from 17.8 to 16.8 percent), they won more than twice as many seats (forty-six).

Amid a growing debate about the relationship between Labour and the Liberal Democrats, early in 1999 Ashdown unexpectedly resigned as leader and was succeeded by Charles Kennedy, an MP from the Scottish Highlands. The success of the Liberal Democrats in the 2001 general election (discussed under "Trends in Electoral Behavior" below) positioned the party as a potentially powerful center-left critic of New Labour. The local government elections in May 2002 resulted in some significant gains (as well as some reversals) but did little to sustain the party's momentum. As the Blair government fought to emphasize its willingness to save public services (especially the NHS) at almost any cost, Kennedy's luster as leader and the optimism of the Liberal Democrats experienced at least a temporary decline. Although Kennedy won the political gamble in spring 2003 by opposing the war in Iraq, challenging the weapons of mass destruction (WMD) claim, and even attending the huge antiwar rally in February, he seemed reticent to take full political advantage of Blair's political weakness. Many remained puzzled at Kennedy's inability—or unwillingness—to galvanize either his party or the nation as opposition to the war in Iraq intensified in winter 2003.[7]

The appeal of smaller parties in Britain is constantly shifting. One party, the Greens (formed in 1973 by environmentalists and the oldest Green Party in Europe), surprised everyone (themselves included) by achieving a 15 percent third-place showing in the June 1989 elections to the European Parliament (but winning no seats). With public opinion surveys ranking "pollution and the environment" as the third most common concern, the major parties hustled to acquire a greenish hue. But the Green Party failed to capitalize on its 1989 showing. By the mid-1990s, party membership had declined, and environmental activists were focusing on a wide range of grassroots initiatives. In 1997, the Green Party ran only 95 candidates (down from 253 in 1992), with very little impact (it averaged only 1.4 percent in the constituencies it contested). A likely sign of the alienation of voters from the mainstream parties, in 2001 the Greens doubled their share of the vote in the constituencies they contested.[8]

The National Front (formed in 1967), a far-right, neofascist, anti-immigrant party, won seats on local councils and entered candidates (unsuccessfully) for Parliament. After the National Front faded in the late 1970s, the British National Party (BNP), formed in 1983, emerged as the most visible far-right party. Concentrating its electoral strategy on impoverished inner-city constituencies, in 1997 it ran fifty-seven candidates, who registered a meager 1.3 percent average share of the votes cast. The most dramatic and troubling result of the 2001 election was the performance of the far-right white racist BNP. Electioneering on the violent riots and racial tensions that enflamed Oldham, a town near Manchester, some ten days before the election, the BNP leader registered 16 percent of the vote in Oldham West and Royton, and party candidates won 11 percent in each of two neighboring constituencies. Although hardly rivaling Le Pen's National Front in France, the BNP results were a shock in the United Kingdom, representing the strongest showing of the far right in a general election in more than fifty years.

In addition to these center, environmental, far-right, and single-issue parties, Britain has several national parties, which are described below under "Trends in Electoral Behavior."

Elections

British elections are exclusively for legislative posts. The prime minister is not elected as prime minister but as an MP from a single constituency (electoral district), averaging about 65,000 registered voters. Parliament has a maximum life of five years, with no fixed term. General elections are held after Parliament has been dissolved by the Crown at the request of the prime minister. However, for strategic political reasons, the prime minister may ask the Crown to dissolve Parliament at any time. The ability to control the timing of elections is a tremendous political asset for the prime minister. This contrasts sharply with a presidential system, characteristic of the United States, with direct election of the chief executive and a fixed term of office.

The Electoral System

Election for representatives in the Commons (who are called members of Parliament, or MPs) is by a "first-past-the-post" (or winner-take-all) principle in each constituency. In this single-member plurality system, the candidate who receives the most votes is elected. There is no requirement of a majority and no element of proportional representation (a system in which each party is given a percentage of seats in a representative assembly roughly comparable to its percentage of the popular vote). Table 9.1 shows the results of the general elections from 1945 to 2001.

This winner-take-all electoral system tends to exaggerate the size of the victory of the largest party and to reduce the influence of regionally dispersed lesser parties. Thus, in 2001, with 40.7 percent of the popular vote, Labour won 413 seats. With 18.3 percent of the vote, the Liberal Democrats, despite targeting their most winnable constituencies, won only 52 seats. Thus, the Liberal Democrats achieved a share of the vote that was approximately 45 percent of that achieved by Labour, while winning fewer than 13 percent of the seats won by Labour. Such are the benefits to the victor of the system.

With a fairly stable two-and-a-half-party system (Conservative, Labour, and center), the British electoral system tends toward a stable single-party government. However, the electoral system raises questions about representation and fairness. The system reduces the competitiveness of smaller parties with diffuse pockets of support. In addition, the party and electoral systems have contributed to the creation of a Parliament that has been a bastion of white men. In 1992, 60 women were elected as MPs out of 650 seats (9.2 percent), an increase from 42 members in 1987 (6.3 percent). The 1997 election represented a breakthrough for women: the number of women MPs nearly doubled to a record 120 (18.2 percent). The 2001 election saw the number of women MPs decline to 118 (17.9 percent). In an effort to improve the prospects for female parliamentary representation, the Sex Discrimination (Election Candidates) Act, which received Royal Assent (the formal approval given by the queen after both parliamentary houses have approved an act) in February 2002, removes legal barriers to parties taking positive action to increase the number of women candidates—for example, through the use of women-only shortlists in the selection of candidates to run for Parliament (as Labour used from 1993 to 1996).

Also in 1992, 6 ethnic minority candidates were elected, up from 4 in 1987, the first time since before World War II that Parliament included minority members. The number of ethnic minority MPs rose in 1997 to 9 (1.4 percent) and to 12 in 2001 (1.8 percent). Although the numbers of successful candidates remain very low, recruitment has improved substantially: there were 57 ethnic minority candidates in 2001, compared with 5 in 1979. Another positive sign is that two of the ethnic minority MPs represent constituencies that do not have sizable ethnic minority populations. Despite the general trend of increased representation of women and minorities, they remain substantially underrepresented in Parliament.

Trends in Electoral Behavior

Recent general elections have deepened geographic and regional fragmentation on the political map. British political scientist Ivor Crewe has referred to the emergence of two two-party systems: (1) competition between the Conservative and Labour parties dominates contests in English urban and northern seats, and (2) Conservative-center party competition dominates England's rural and southern seats.[9] In addition, a third two-party competition may be observed in Scotland, where Labour–Scottish National Party competition dominates.

The national parties have challenged two-party dominance since the 1970s. The Scottish National Party (SNP) was founded in 1934 and its Welsh counterpart, the Plaid Cymru, in 1925. Coming in a distant second to Labour in Scotland in 1997, the SNP won 21.6 percent of the vote and six seats. In 2001, support for the SNP declined by 2 percent, and the party lost one of its seats. Both electoral and polling data indicate that Scottish voters are more inclined to support

Table 9.1 British General Elections, 1945–2001

| | Percentage of Popular Vote | | | | | | | Seats in House of Commons | | | | | |
	Turnout	Conservative	Labour	Liberal[a]	National Parties[b]	Other	Swing[c]	Conservative	Labour	Liberal[a]	National Parties[b]	Other	Government Majority
1945	72.7	39.8	48.3	9.1	0.2	2.5	−12.2	213	393	12	0	22	146
1950	84.0	43.5	46.1	9.1	0.1	1.2	+3.0	299	315	9	0	2	.5
1951	82.5	48.0	48.8	2.5	0.1	0.6	+0.9	321	295	6	0	3	17
1955	76.7	49.7	46.4	2.7	0.2	0.9	+2.1	345	277	6	0	2	60
1959	78.8	49.4	43.8	5.9	0.4	0.6	+1.2	365	258	6	0	1	100
1964	77.1	43.4	44.1	11.2	0.5	0.8	−3.2	304	317	9	0	0	4
1966	75.8	41.9	47.9	8.5	0.7	0.9	−2.7	253	363	12	0	2	95
1970	72.0	46.4	43.0	7.5	1.3	1.8	+4.7	330	288	6	1	5	30
Feb. 1974	78.7	37.8	37.1	19.3	2.6	3.2	−1.4	297	301	14	9	14	−34[d]
Oct. 1974	72.8	35.8	39.2	18.3	3.5	3.2	−2.1	277	319	13	14	12	3
1979	76.0	43.9	37.0	13.8	2.0	3.3	+5.2	339	269	11	4	12	43
1983	72.7	42.4	27.6	25.4	1.5	3.1	+4.0	397	209	23	4	17	144
1987	75.3	42.3	30.8	22.6	1.7	2.6	−1.7	376	229	22	6	17	102
1992	77.7	41.9	34.4	17.8	2.3	3.5	−2.0	336	271	20	7	17	21
1997	71.4	30.7	43.2	16.8	2.6	6.7	−10.0	165	419	46	10	19	179
2001	59.4	31.7	40.7	18.3	2.5	6.8	+1.8	166	413	52	9	19	167

[a]Liberal Party, 1945–1979; Liberal/Social Democrat Alliance, 1983–1987; Liberal Democratic Party, 1992–2001.

[b]Combined vote of Scottish National Party (SNP) and Welsh National Party (Plaid Cymru).

[c]"Swing" compares the results of each election with the results of the previous election. It is calculated as the average of the winning major party's percentage point increase in its share of the vote and the losing major party's decrease in its percentage point share of the vote. In the table, a positive sign denotes a swing to the Conservatives, a negative sign a swing to Labour.

[d]Following the February 1974 election, the Labour Party was thirty-four seats short of having an overall majority. It formed a minority government until it obtained a majority in the October 1974 election.

Source: Anthony King, ed., New Labour Triumphs: Britain at the Polls (Chatham, N.J.: Chatham House, 1998), p. 249. Copyright © 1998 by Chatham House. Reprinted by permission. For 2001 results, http://news.bbc.co.uk/hi/english/static/vote2001/results_constituencies/uk_breakdown/uk_full.stm.

the SNP for elections to the Scottish parliament than to Westminster and that devolution may have stemmed the rising tide of nationalism.[10] In both 1997 and 2001, the Plaid Cymru won four seats where Welsh is still spoken widely. In both Scotland and Wales, Labour is the dominant party, with the overwhelming majority of seats. Its experience is another illustration of the effects of the first-past-the-post system. With the Tories shut out in both Wales and Scotland in 1997 and with only one Scottish seat for the Conservatives in 2001, the prospects of a common two-party pattern of electoral competition throughout Britain are more remote than ever before.

For now, the winner-take-all electoral system has preserved two-party dominance in parliamentary representation. But the popular vote tells a different story. Except for 1979, the center and national parties combined have received more than one-fifth of the vote in every general election between February 1974 and 1992. They slipped slightly to 19.4 percent in 1997 and then, with the strong showing of the Liberal Democrats, rebounded to 20.8 percent in 2001. But the winner-take-all system preserves two-party dominance in parliamentary representation at roughly 90 percent. The British electoral system is more complicated than it seems at first glance.

In fact, one of the most significant features of the 2001 election was the further weakening of two-party dominance. With Charles Kennedy, the leader of the Liberal Democrats, running an effective, plainspoken campaign—arguing, for example, that improvement in public services would require tax increases—the party increased its vote tally by nearly one-fifth overall. It won fifty-two seats, the most since 1929, and knocked the Tories into fourth place in the popular vote in Scotland. As the Conservatives entered a period of introspection, the Liberal Democrats could credibly claim that they were, in effect, the leading opposition party, although translating that boast into an effective critique of New Labour, even at a moment when the government seems vulnerable on the war in Iraq

and unable to change the focus effectively to domestic policy, is easier said than done.

Local and European Elections: A Small Earthquake?

The papers dubbed the combined European and local elections held on June 10, 2004, "Super Thursday"—but the results were anything but super for both Labour and the Conservatives. Against the backdrop of Labour's uncharacteristic weakness in the wake of the war in Iraq and the grave problems posed by reconstruction and resistance to the Anglo-American occupation, Labour slipped into third place (with only 26 percent of the vote) in the local elections (compared with 38 percent for the Conservatives and 30 percent for the Liberal Democrats). Suffering the worst result ever for a governing party, Labour lost control of city government in strongholds like Leeds (which they had held for twenty-four years) and Newcastle (which they had held for thirty years).

Believe it or not, Blair's party fared even worse in the European elections, its share of the vote dropping to 22.6 percent, its lowest tally in any nationwide election since 1918. In fact, in the elections for the European Parliament (EP), with the Conservatives polling 26.7 percent and the Liberal Democrats 14.9 percent, none of the big-three parties in the United Kingdom could legitimately claim victory. That honor clearly went to the UK Independence Party (UKIP), which was founded in 1991 and contested the EP elections as a single-issue party dedicated to UK withdrawal from the European Union. Coming in third in the election with 16.1 percent of the vote (and twelve MEPs), UKIP's dramatic entry as a significant player in British politics left other parties struggling to adjust to the changed electoral landscape. Ironically, the Conservatives (who have the widest and deepest vein of anti-EU sentiment among the major parties) appeared to lose the most. Polls indicated that 40 percent of UKIP voters had voted Tory in the 2001 general election, compared with only

20 percent for Labour and 11 percent for the Liberal Democrats. Hence, the Tories faced the greatest risk of defection to UKIP.

Local and European elections in Britain are often seen as opportunities for disgruntled voters to make their feelings known to party leaders, and "Super Thursday" certainly achieved that result. UKIP supporters naturally hoped the EP election results revealed a fundamental shift in the landscape of British electoral politics. Conservatives argued that most Tory voters will not desert their party in a general election over Europe and that the next general election will be won or lost on Howard's ability to present the Conservatives as a credible alternative to Blair across the board. Meanwhile, despite the double debacle suffered by Labour, by fall 2004 the speculation about an early departure by Blair had died down from the fever pitch of gossip swirling around the capital in April and May. Despite all, Labour seemed to regard a victory in the next general election (anticipated in 2005) with a complacency that was not warranted by its terrible showing in both the local and European elections.

Political Culture, Citizenship, and Identity

In their classic study of the ideals and values that shape political behavior, political scientists Gabriel Almond and Sidney Verba wrote that the civic (or political) culture in Britain was characterized by trust, deference to authority and competence, pragmatism, and the balance between acceptance of the rules of the game and disagreement over specific issues.[11] Many have considered these characteristics the model for active, informed, and stable democratic citizenship. Viewed retrospectively, the 1970s appear as a crucial turning point in British political culture and group identities. It is too early to be certain, but the electoral earthquake of 1997 may represent another critical shift in British politics and culture.

During the 1970s, the long years of economic decline culminated in economic reversals in the standard of living for many Britons. Also for many, the historic bonds of occupational and social class grew weaker. Union membership declined with the continued transfer of jobs away from the traditional manufacturing sectors. More damaging, unions lost popular support as they appeared to bully society, act undemocratically, and neglect the needs of an increasingly female and minority workforce. At the same time, a growing number of conservative think tanks and the powerful voice of mass-circulation newspapers, which are overwhelmingly conservative, worked hard to erode the fundamental beliefs of the Keynesian welfare state. New social movements (NSMs), such as feminism, antinuclear activism, and environmentalism, challenged basic tenets of British political culture. Identities based on race and ethnicity, gender, and sexual orientation gained significance. Thus, a combination of economic strains, ideological assaults, and social dislocations helped foster political fragmentation and, at the same time, inspired a shift to the right in values and policy agendas.

Thatcher's ascent reflected these changes in political culture, identities, and values. It also put the full resources of the state and a bold and determined prime minister behind a sweeping agenda for change. As a leading British scholar put it, "Thatcher's objective was nothing less than a cultural revolution."[12] Although most observers agree that Thatcher fell considerably short of that aim, Thatcherism cut deep. It touched the cultural recesses of British society, recast political values, and redefined national identity.

To the extent that the Thatcherite worldview took hold (and the record is mixed), its new language and ethos helped transform the common sense of politics and redefined the political community. Monetarism (however modified) and the appeal to an enterprise culture of competitive market logic and entrepreneurial values fostered individualism and competition—winners and losers. It rejected collectivism, the redistribution of resources from rich to poor, and state responsibility for full employment. Thatcherism considered individual property rights more important than the social rights claimed by all citizens in the welfare state.

In addition to her positive appeals to the enterprise culture, Thatcher's reform agenda included negative appeals. A review of Thatcher's first general election reveals the repoliticization of race. She promised tougher nationality legislation to restrict immigration, expressed sympathy for those who harbored "fear that [Britain] might be swamped" by nonwhite Commonwealth immigrants, and associated minorities with lawlessness. In a similar vein, during the 1984–1985 miners' strike, she denounced the coal miners as the "enemy within," comparing them to the external Argentine enemy during the Falklands/Malvinas war of 1982. Thatcher symbolically expelled some groups—ethnic minority communities and the unrepentant miners—from the national community. In this way, Thatcherism involved an attempt to redefine national identity by implicit appeals to a more secure, provincial, and unified Britain. In addition, pressure for devolution and growing nationalist sentiment in Scotland and Wales fueled a center-versus-periphery division. Finally, working-class identity and politics were stigmatized as government sharply criticized the behavior of unions.

Social Class

One of the key changes in political culture in Britain in the last quarter-century has been the weakening of bonds grounded in the experience of labor. During the Thatcher era, the traditional values of "an honest day's work for an honest day's pay" and solidarity among coworkers in industrial disputes were characterized as "rigidities" that reduced productivity and competitiveness. Under the Conservative leadership of Thatcher and Major, governments held class-based interests at arm's length and worked to

curb their political and industrial power. A formidable combination of legislated constraints, trade union defeats in industrial disputes, and massive unemployment (particularly in the traditionally unionized manufacturing sectors) helped crystallize a pattern of decline in union membership, militancy, and power.

Although Blair's reasons are different—he emphasizes the realities of the new global economic competition—he has done little to create a more cooperative or productive relationship with the unions. In addition, New Labour has persisted in the negative characterization of social class as an impediment to competitiveness.

As many have noted, "tough on the unions" is a core premise of New Labour, and this has contributed to a fundamental erosion of the ability of working people in the United Kingdom to improve their lot through collective bargaining or to exert influence over public policy through the political muscle of the trade union movement. Class still matters in the United Kingdom, but not in the dominating way that it did in the nineteenth century or in the collectivist era.

The sources and relative strength of diverse group attachments have shifted in Britain in recent decades under the combined pressures of decolonization, which created a multiethnic Britain, and a fragmentation of the experiences of work, which challenge a simple unitary model of class interest. National identity has become especially complicated in the United Kingdom. At the same time, gender politics has emerged as a hot-button issue.

Citizenship and National Identity

As political scientist Benedict Anderson has observed, national identity involves the belief in an "imagined community" of belonging, shared fates, and affinities among millions of diverse and actually unconnected citizens.[13] Since the 1970s, the question of what constitutes "Britishness"—who is included and who excluded from the national political community—has become increasingly vexing. What constitutes "Britishness"? Of what may citizens be justifiably proud? How has the imagined nation stood the test of time? These questions are increasingly difficult to answer.

Questions about fragmented sovereignty within the context of the EU, the commingled histories of four nations (England, Scotland, Wales, and Ireland/Northern Ireland), and the interplay of race and nationality in postcolonial Britain have created doubts about British identity that run deep. As ethnicity, intra-UK territorial attachments, and the processes of Europeanization and globalization complicate national identity, it becomes increasingly difficult for UK residents automatically to imagine themselves Britons, constituting a resonant national community.

Thus, the imagined community of Britain fragmented into smaller communities of class, nation, region, and ethnicity that existed side by side but not necessarily in amiable proximity. Can New Labour recreate a more cohesive political culture and foster a more inclusive sense of British identity? Unlike Thatcher, Blair is a conciliator, and he has worked hard to revitalize a sense of community in Britain and extend his agenda to the socially excluded. The efforts of the Blair government to forge unity and build community and the obstacles that bedevil that agenda are discussed in Chapter 10.

Ethnicity

Britain is a country of tremendous ethnic diversity. As noted in Chapter 7, 4.5 million Britons (7.6 percent of the total population) are of African, African-Caribbean, or Asian descent. In Greater London, a little more than one-third of the population has community backgrounds outside Britain, and slightly more than one-fifth has backgrounds in Africa, Asia, or the Caribbean. The authors of a recent commission report on multiethnic Britain explained: "Many communities overlap; all affect and are affected by others. More and more people have multiple identities—they are Welsh Europeans, Pakistani Yorkshirewomen, Glaswegian Muslims, English Jews and black British. Many enjoy this complexity but also experience conflicting loyalties."[14]

In political terms, the past quarter-century has seen increased attention, both negative and positive, to the role of ethnic minorities in the United Kingdom. The politicization of immigration in the 1979 election marked an intensification of this process. It also underscored the resentment white Britons felt toward minority communities that maintained their own religious beliefs and cultures. Ethnic minority communities have experienced police insensitivity, problems in access to the best public housing, hate crimes, and accusations that they are not truly British if they do not root for Britain's cricket team. In a similar vein, the current controversy over immigration and asylum, coming as it does in the wake of intense scrutiny of the Muslim community post–September 11, contributes to the alienation of the ethnic minority community, particularly sections of the Muslim citizenry. The home secretary's talk about asylum seekers "swamping" public services, an almost eerie echo of Thatcher's remark a quarter-century ago, makes it look as if little has changed. And yet, in the aftermath of the attack on the World Trade Center and the Pentagon, public debate included a range of articulate, young, and confident Muslims from a variety of perspectives, and Faz Hakim, chief race relations adviser to the prime minister, played a visible public insider role. It is true that the experience of Islamic Britain has been framed by September 11 and by the riots in northern towns in the summer of 2001 (British Pakistanis in Bradford were responsible for the worst of the violent episodes). But it is equally true that Muslim university graduates are assuming leading roles in the professions, that there are more than 160 Muslim elected city councillors, and that the British society has become increasingly sensitive to Muslim concerns.[15]

Gender

Historically, the issues women care about most—child care, the treatment of part-time workers, domestic violence, equal pay, and support for family caregivers—have not topped the list of policy agendas of any political party in Britain. Has New Labour significantly changed the equation?

In 1997, Labour made a concerted effort to attract female voters and was handsomely rewarded. In addition to specific policy statements, the appointment of a series of shadow ministers for women, who worked hard to mobilize support through women's networks and organizations, contributed to Labour's success in closing the gender gap in 1997.[16] It is probably fair to say, on balance, that Labour does well among women voters less because of any specific policies and more because it has made the effort to listen to concerns that women voice. Labour stalwarts would insist that they have addressed key concerns that women (and men) share concerning healthcare, crime, and education. They would point with pride to the policy directions spurred by the Social Exclusion and Women's units.

In the absence of significant concrete policy achievements linked to women's experiences of work and family life, it is hard to place women decisively in Labour's column. Many women in Britain are quick to suggest that tax credits for working families and efforts to encourage businesses to adopt more family-friendly policies, however laudable, have not changed the basic equation. This puts in context the gender voting patterns in June 2001. Before the election, some New Labour enthusiasts called Labour "the natural party of women," but the votes did not turn out that way. Both men and women gave Labour about 46 percent of the vote, and both swung about 3 percent in the direction of the Conservatives, compared with 1997. New Labour has obliterated the old gender gap in which women favored the Conservatives but has not established a new pro-Labour women's vote.[17]

Interests, Social Movements, and Protests

Since the 1970s, movements based on ethnic and gender attachments (new social movements, or NSMs) have grown in significance. By contrast to the traditional interest-group-oriented social movements, the NSMs tend to be more fluidly organized and democratic, less oriented to immediate payoffs for their group, and more focused on fundamental questions about the values of society. For example, in the 1970s and 1980s, the women's peace movement protested Britain's participation in the North Atlantic Treaty Organization's nuclear defense and organized a string of mass demonstrations. In general, following the NSM approach, the women's movement in Britain has remained decentralized and activist. It has emphasized consciousness raising, self-help, and lifestyle transformations and spawned dozens of action groups, ranging from health clinics to battered women's and rape crisis shelters, to feminist collectives and black women's groups, to networks of women in media, law, and other professions. More recently, women have confronted government over inadequate child care and the difficulties posed by women's daily struggle to juggle the demands of work and family.

Simultaneously, the subcultures and countercultures of black Britain have been a vital source of NSM activity, often expressed in antiracist initiatives. "Rock Against Racism" concerts in the 1970s brought reggae and skinhead bands together in public resistance to the National Front; today, lower-profile efforts are made to sensitize local councils to the cultural and material needs of ethnic minorities and to publicize their potential political clout. Efforts to secure improved housing have been a persistent focus of ethnic minority political mobilization. Like the women's movement, such movements are decentralized and culturally engaged.

In recent years, partly in response to globalization, political protest has been on the rise in Britain. A radical strain of anticapitalist anarchism has gained strength. As protesters demand more accountability and transparency in the operations of powerful international trade and development agencies, a "Reclaim the Streets" march in London in June 1999 resulted in over eighty arrests and over $3 million in damage to the City of London (the equivalent of

Wall Street). In addition, London became the site of protests timed to correspond with the Seattle meeting of the World Trade Organization (WTO), which generated some 100,000 protesters in November 1999.

In addition, since the mid-1990s, the level and intensity of environmental activism have been unprecedented. The combined membership of Greenpeace and Friends of the Earth swelled substantially above 600,000 by 1993, but the level of environmental activism really took off with the growing attention to genetically modified (GM) crops in the late 1990s. A newly radicalized movement, worried that long-term consumption of GM food might be harmful and that once let loose, GM crops—referred to derisively as "Frankenstein food"—might cross-pollinate with "normal" plants, captured the popular imagination. A host of direct-action protests erupted in the summer of 1999, some including the destruction of crops. Opinion polls indicated that nearly 75 percent of the population did not want GM crops in the United Kingdom, and in November 1999, the government announced a ban on commercially grown GM crops in Britain.

In a movement that galvanized the country and raised critical questions about Blair's leadership, massive demonstrations that cut across constituencies and enjoyed huge popular support erupted in September 2000 to protest high fuel prices. A very successful and well-coordinated week-long protest stalled fuel delivery throughout the country, forced 90 percent of the petrol stations to run out of unleaded gasoline, and required the queen, on the advice of the prime minister, to declare a state of emergency. By the time the blockades came down, opinion polls for the first time in eight years showed the Conservatives for the moment surging past Labour.

A quite different kind of activism spread to the countryside among a population not usually known for political protest. Farmers who had been badly hurt by the BSE (bovine spongiform encephalopathy, more popularly known as "mad cow disease") crisis and other rural populations concerned about the perceived urban bias of the Labour government launched massive protests.[18] As the banning and licensing of fox hunting roiled Parliament, the Countryside Alliance, which represents country dwellers who see restrictions on fox hunting as emblematic of domineering urban interests, held mass demonstrations at party conferences and in London in an effort (thus far successful) to block restrictive legislation. Competing for attention with anti-hunt protesters, nearly a quarter of a million people who feared that hunts might soon be banned gathered on the day after Christmas 2002 for traditional Boxing Day hunts. With Blair still promising a vote in Parliament to ban fox hunting, supporters of the sport kept up the heat, mounting an angry protest at the Labour Party conference in September 2004.

On the far more significant matter of war in Iraq, a series of antiwar rallies were held in London. In September 2002, a huge protest rally was organized in London, led by the Stop the War Coalition and the Muslim Association of Britain. Organizers reported that 400,000 people joined in the Saturday march from the Embankment to a rally in Hyde Park, while police said that they counted more than 150,000 marchers. Whatever the exact number of protesters, it was one of Europe's biggest antiwar rallies. The mayor of London, Ken Livingstone, no stranger to social movement mobilizations, called it the largest march for peace that he had seen in thirty years. Another antiwar rally in mid-February 2003 challenged Blair's stand on Iraq with at least 750,000 demonstrators.

Both within the United Kingdom and among observers of British politics and society, many still endorse the Almond and Verba view of the political culture. Although pragmatism, trust, and deference may still be found in good measure, the persistence and mobilizing potential of a wide range of social movements suggest that quite powerful political subcurrents persist in Britain, posing significant challenges for British government.

Notes

1. Tony Wright et al., *The British Political Process* (London: Routledge, 2000), p. 232.

2. For a detailed discussion of the different historical currents and contemporary mindsets within Labour foreign policy, see David Coates and Joel Krieger, *Blair's War* (Malden, Mass., and Cambridge, England: Polity Press, 2004), chap. 6.

3. Samuel H. Beer, *The British Political System* (New York: Random House, 1973), p. 157.

4. John Bartle, "Why Labour Won—Again," in Anthony King, ed., *Britain at the Polls, 2001* (New York: Chatham House, 2002), p. 168.

5. For an excellent treatment of Hague's strategy, see Steven Felding, "A New Politics?" in Patrick Dunleavy et al., eds., *Developments in British Politics 6* (New York: St. Martin's Press, 2000), pp. 10–28.

6. Stephen Ingle, "Politics: The Year the War Was Spun," *Parliamentary Affairs* 57, no. 2 (2004): 247.

7. See John Kampfner, "He Says Blair Is a Disappointed Man and His Premiership One of Missed Opportunity. Has the Lib Dem Leader Also Missed the Boat?" *New Statesman* 19 (January 2004): 22–23.

8. Ivor Crewe, "A New Political Hegemony?" in Anthony King, ed., *Britain at the Polls, 2001* (New York: Chatham House, 2002), p. 228.

9. Ivor Crewe, "Great Britain," in I. Crewe and D. Denver, eds., *Electoral Change in Western Democracies* (London: Croom Helm, 1985), p. 107.

10. Bartle, "Why Labour Won—Again," p. 171.

11. See Gabriel A. Almond and Sidney Verba, *The Civic Culture: Political Attitudes and Democracy in Five Nations* (Princeton, N.J.: Princeton University Press, 1963); Almond and Verba, eds., *The Civic Culture Revisited* (Boston: Little, Brown, 1980); and Samuel H. Beer, *Britain Against Itself: The Political Contradictions of Collectivism* (New York: Norton, 1982), pp. 110–114.

12. Ivor Crewe, "The Thatcher Legacy," in King et al., eds., *Britain at the Polls 1992*, p. 18.

13. Benedict Anderson, *Imagined Communities*, rev. ed. (London and New York: Verso, 1991).

14. Bhiku Parekh et al., *The Future of Multi-Ethnic Britain: The Parekh Report* (London: Profile Books, 2000), p. 10.

15. For an excellent treatment of the complex experiences of British Muslims, see Philip Lewis, *Islamic Britain* (London and New York: I. B. Tauris, 2002).

16. For a detailed account of the efforts by Labour, as well as the Conservatives and Liberal Democrats, to attract women voters, see Joni Lovenduski, "Gender Politics: A Breakthrough for Women?" *Parliamentary Affairs* 50, no. 4 (1997): 708–719.

17. See Bartle, "Why Labour Won—Again," pp. 168–169.

18. For an excellent discussion of social movements and protest from which this account of anticapitalist and environmental mobilization was drawn, see Helen Margetts, "Political Participation and Protest," in Patrick Dunleavy et al., eds., *Developments in British Politics 6* (New York: St. Martin's Press, 2000), pp. 185–202.

CHAPTER

10

British Politics in Transition

In the fall of 1994, cease-fire declarations made by the Irish Republican Army (IRA) and the Protestant paramilitary organizations renewed hope for a peace settlement in Northern Ireland. Then, in a dramatic new development in early spring 1995, British prime minister John Major and Irish prime minister John Bruton jointly issued a framework agreement, inspiring mounting optimism about a political settlement. Although Major did what he could to secure public and parliamentary support, he lacked the necessary political capital to bring the historic initiative to fruition.

With his 1997 landslide victory, Tony Blair had political capital to spend, and he chose to invest a chunk of it on peace in Northern Ireland. Blair arranged to meet Gerry Adams, president of Sinn Fein, the party in Northern Ireland with close ties to the IRA—and shook his hand. He was the first prime minister to meet with a head of Sinn Fein since 1921. Blair later spoke of the "hand of history" on his shoulder.

Under deadline pressure imposed by Blair and the new Irish prime minister, Bertie Ahern, and thirty-three hours of around-the-clock talks, an agreement was reached on Good Friday 1998. It specified elections for a Northern Ireland assembly, in which Protestants and Catholics would share power, and the creation of a North-South Council to facilitate "all-Ireland" cooperation on matters such as economic development, agriculture, transportation, and the environment. Much was left unclear—for example, the details of how and when the IRA would give up its weapons (called "decommissioning"

in Northern Irish parlance) and questions about the release of prisoners affiliated with the paramilitary groups. It did not address the reform of the police force in Northern Ireland, which was overwhelmingly Protestant and partisan and did not enjoy the confidence of the Catholic community. Nevertheless, despite doubts about the fine print, both parts of Ireland voted yes in May 1998 in a referendum to approve the peace agreement. It appeared that a new era was dawning in Northern Ireland.

Handshake or not, devastating bombs have exploded from time to time in Northern Ireland since the agreement, and violent turf battles within and between each camp have created fear and repeated crises in the peace process. The Northern Ireland secretary felt compelled to suspend the devolved power-sharing government in February 2000, less than three months after it began, under Protestant Unionist pressure concerning the timetable for decommissioning of IRA weapons and amid allegations of bad faith on both sides. Through the winter of 2001, recurring crises over weapons—deadlines, procedures governing inspections by an international commission, what sort of interim meetings could take place—strained relations between the parties to the dispute and threatened to disrupt the Good Friday Agreement. Insisting that Sinn Fein cabinet ministers be barred from discussion until the IRA disarmed, hard-liners in the Protestant camp created a rash of challenges to David Trimble, the Ulster Unionist leader who remained committed to the success of the process. Sinn Fein, in turn, accused Trimble of sabotage and warned that the

IRA would not be able to control its own dissi-dents if the power-sharing arrangements were unilaterally dismantled.

In October 2001, the IRA began disarming under the sponsorship of third-party diplomats, and yet violence rose despite cease-fires by para-military groups: police reported eighteen killed in 2001 (mostly by the Protestant paramilitary groups) and more than three hundred "punish-ment beatings" inflicted equally by Protestant and Catholic gangs. The spring and summer of 2002 were rife with accusations and denials of the IRA training Colombian guerrillas in bomb-making techniques, fomenting street violence in Belfast, and stealing police antiterrorist intelli-gence in the United Kingdom. Was it a time of hope or a time of despair? In May 2002, a group of Palestinian and Israeli political leaders met in the English Midlands with figures who had ne-gotiated the Good Friday Agreement. They hoped to return to the Middle East with lessons about how a dangerous stalemate born of mis-trust and violence could be resolved through ne-gotiations. Yet, in October 2002, home rule government was suspended, and British direct rule was reimposed. Tony Blair and his Irish Re-public counterpart, Bertie Ahern, pledged to re-double efforts to get Northern Ireland's faltering peace process back on track, but progress has not been easy.

On the contrary, in November 2003, elections that were held for Northern Ireland's devolved assembly at Stormont made the hard-line Protestant Ulster Unionist Party the dominant political player and also strengthened Sinn Fein, the Catholic party with links to the IRA. By weakening the power of moderate groups and strengthening that of the classic sectarian adver-saries, the election results made it seem unlikely that the power-sharing framework envisioned in the Good Friday Agreement would be back in place anytime soon. Nevertheless, in September 2004, a full ten years after the cease-fire declara-tions, new hopes were raised that negotiations among rival Northern Ireland parties, Blair, and Ahern might break the deadlock. Although no

deal was struck at the initial talks at Leeds Cas-tle, participants and observers remained opti-mistic that an agreement might be within reach at long last.

The never-ending crises in Northern Ireland confirm the important proposition that unre-solved tensions in state formation shape political agendas for generations. Northern Ireland, how-ever, is but one of a host of challenges facing Britain on Tony Blair's watch.

Political Challenges and Changing Agendas

As our democratic idea theme suggests, no democracy, however secure it may be, is a fin-ished project. Even in Britain, with its centuries-old constitutional settlement and secure institutional framework, issues about demo-cratic governance and citizens' participation re-main unresolved.

Constitutional Reform

Questions about the role of the monarchy and the House of Lords have long been simmering on Britain's political agenda. Since the tradition-ally admired royal family was battered by scan-dal and misconduct in the 1990s, these concerns about the undemocratic foundations of the British state have gained credibility. "Why is the House of Commons not sovereign?" wondered one observer somewhat caustically. "Why does it have to share sovereignty with other, un-elected institutions?"[1] The balance of power among constitutionally critical institutions re-mains a major issue of contemporary political debate. Parliament is hamstrung by strong, cen-trally controlled parties and is easily overpow-ered by an executive whose strength in relation to that of the legislature may be greater than in any other Western democracy. Add to these con-cerns the reform of the unelected House of Lords and the absence of an "entrenched" bill of rights (one that Parliament cannot override), and it seems appropriate to raise questions about the accountability of the British government to its citizens.

In fact, in the heady days after Blair's 1997 election victory, amidst talk of an expanding array of constitutional reforms, it was commonplace to suggest that constitutional reform might become New Labour's most enduring legacy. The reform agenda, which has been very significant, has also been sidetracked or subjected to powerful political crosscurrents—or administrative complexities— that have slowed or stalled agreement on key elements. For example, the Freedom of Information Act was passed in 2002 but was not scheduled to achieve full implementation until January 2005. It was also weakened by the extensive range of information it permitted ministers to withhold and by its limited provision for independent review of such ministerial decisions.[2] The Blair government has begun to implement far-reaching reforms of Parliament, including the removal of the right of hereditary peers to speak and vote in the House of Lords and the redesign of the historic upper chamber, but as discussed in Chapter 8, the form of the new upper chamber has yet to take shape. In addition, the European Convention on Human Rights has been incorporated into UK law, and, more controversially, plans have been announced for the creation of a "supreme court," but strenuous opposition in both chambers has clouded the prospects for passage. New systems of proportional representation have been introduced for Welsh and Scottish elections, as well as for the European Parliament, and the possible use of proportional representation in UK general elections has been placed at least tentatively on the reform agenda (although reform in this area seems unlikely for now). In addition, New Labour's inability to control the outcome of London's historic mayoral contest in May 2000 illustrates the difficulties that may accompany far-reaching measures to devolve and decentralize power, a process that is now being expanded to local government in other parts of England.

Finally, the power-sharing initiatives in Northern Ireland (if the political deadlocks are ever broken) and arrangements between Westminster, the Welsh Assembly, and, most importantly, the Scottish parliament represent basic modifications of UK constitutional principles. Devolution implies both an element of federalism and some compromise in the historic parliamentary sovereignty at the heart of the Westminster model. But the potentially unsettling consequences feared by some have not come to pass. The Scottish parliament has asserted itself on occasion—for example, on care for the elderly and tuition fees—but this is a far cry from calls for independence. Devolution has begun to inspire a distinctive Welsh politics as well, but one that does not rock the boat very much, since it tends to be consensual. It is probably fair to say that devolution is less a fixed constitutional settlement and more a dynamic process, but not as unsettling a process for the United Kingdom as earlier anticipated.[3]

The range and depth of New Labour's constitutional reform agenda represent a breathtaking illustration of a core premise of our democratic idea theme: that even long-standing democracies face pressures to narrow the gap between government and citizens. If the British feel themselves removed from day-to-day control over the affairs of government, they are hardly alone. And despite the questions Britons raise about the rigidities of their ancient institutional architecture, others throughout the world see the Westminster model as an enduring exemplar of representative democracy, stability, tolerance, and the virtues of a constitutional tradition that balances a competitive party system with effective central government.

Identities in Flux

Although the relatively small scale of the ethnic minority community limits the political impact of the most divisive issues concerning collective identities, it is probably in this area that rigidities in the British political system challenge tenets of democracy and tolerance most severely. Given Britain's single-member, simple-plurality electoral system and no proportional representation, minority representation in Parliament is very low, and there are deep-seated social attitudes that no government can easily transform.

The issues of immigration, refugees, and asylum still inspire among white Britons a fear of multiculturalism and conjure up very negative and probably prejudiced reactions. In fall 2000, the report of the Commission on the Future of Multi-Ethnic Britain raised profound questions about tolerance, justice, and inclusion in contemporary UK society. In a powerful and controversial analysis, the report concluded that "the word 'British' will never do on its own. . . . Britishness as much as Englishness, has systematic, largely unspoken, racial connotations."[4]

Against the backdrop of intensified finger pointing directed at the Muslim community, the post–September 11 period has witnessed a hardening of government policy on asylum, refuge, and immigration. This controversial process culminated in the formal announcement in November 2003 that the Asylum Bill would force a heart-wrenching choice on failed asylum seekers: they must either "voluntarily" accept a paid-for return flight to the country from which they fled or see their children taken into government care.[5] By spring 2004, race, immigration, and asylum issues were even stealing headlines from the war in Iraq. Charges that there had been widespread fraud in the treatment of East European applications for immigration as well as efforts by the minister in charge of immigration and asylum, Beverly Hughes, to mislead Parliament led to her resignation. Official government data revealed the record levels of hate crimes in England and Wales. After an episode in which British-born Muslims set fire to the Union Jack in London, debate raged about the validity of "separateness" among ethnic communities, and the chairman of the Commission for Racial Equality, Trevor Phillips, called for a return to "core British values" and the abandonment of the government's commitment to building a multicultural society. As Britain experienced increased ethnic tension, polls indicated widespread unease with ethnic diversity.

How about other dimensions of collective identity? The situation is fluid. In political terms, the gender gap has closed for the time being, but concerns about women's employment, the disparate impact of social policy, the problems of balancing family and work responsibilities, and parliamentary representation remain. The electoral force of class identity has declined in Britain for the time being, and the Labour government's first term in office was free of pay disputes and strikes. New Labour's efforts to develop a partnership with business and to keep trade unions at arm's length appeared to weaken the labor movement, positioning it as an "internal opposition" with little ability to challenge the government on industrial relations and economic policy. By Labour's second term, however, the country faced an upsurge in industrial action. Public sector workers such as local government staff and firefighters have led the unrest. A new generation of militant leaders in two railway unions, the postal workers' union, and the government and health workers' union have created new challenges for the government. Against this backdrop, a dramatic series of work stoppages by firefighters in the autumn and winter of 2002–2003 were particularly noteworthy. The stoppages dramatized the return of industrial militancy in unforgettable images and raised difficult questions about Blair's ability to reform and improve public services, a pledge he takes very seriously and one the electorate will not soon forget. Many were asking whether the New Labour government could effectively resolve the upswing in industrial action and, at the same time, meet its commitment to modernize and upgrade public services.

The Challenges of European Integration

From 1989 to 1997, the seemingly endless backbiting over policy toward Europe in the Conservative Party sidetracked Thatcher and Major and cost them dearly in political terms. Britain's traumatic withdrawal from the Exchange Rate Mechanism in 1992 stands as a warning that deeper European integration can be economically disruptive and politically dangerous.

Against this backdrop, Tony Blair came to office determined to rescue Europe for Britain—to redress the problems caused by Thatcher's anti-Europe stance and reposition the United Kingdom both as a major player in Europe and as a powerful interlocutor (respected in both camps) to build bridges, when necessary, between the United States and EU Europe. To advance this agenda, Blair enthusiastically supported initiatives for a common foreign and security policy and helped bring Europe into the war in Kosovo in accordance with Blair's doctrine of international community, which insisted on military interventions when necessary to prevent or contain humanitarian catastrophes, such as ethnic cleansing. As one lesson of Kosovo, Europe tried to come to terms with its reliance on America's military muscle and unrivaled wartime technological capacities. Hence Blair worked with France and Germany to develop a more robust European military capability.

Yet the ambivalence of Britain toward Europe remains very strong. Britain remains on the outside looking in when it comes to the euro (it is one of but three of the fifteen members of the EU before enlargement on May 1, 2004, to remain outside the euro zone). By contrast, on the first working day after enlargement, the European Commission announced that Estonia and Lithuania would take the first formal steps toward joining the single currency by the end of the summer, with Slovenia and Cyprus to follow by the end of 2004 or early in 2005. To place British ambivalence in context, four new Eastern European countries needed less than a week to announce their clear intention to adopt the euro. Blair, in contrast, has made little or no progress on joining the euro club since he took office in 1997.

Chancellor of the Exchequer Gordon Brown has repeatedly declared that the decision on entry into the single currency will be based on how high the euro scores on a series of five key economic tests, and Blair has conceded the point. For his part, Blair has repeatedly hinted at his support for the "yes" vote to join the euro club, but instead of announcing a timetable for a British decision to apply for membership, which could be accomplished in Parliament, he has promised a referendum at an unspecified time—always, it seems, at a more propitious time after another general election. Because Blair hesitated to galvanize popular support for the EU in general and the euro in particular when he was riding high, little or no progress has been made in changing the mindset of ordinary Britons. A strong majority remain very skeptical about Europe and committed to the increasingly anachronistic glory of the British pound sterling as symbol of national pride and power.

With Blair's influence at low ebb, convincing a skeptical British electorate to vote yes on the euro poses a tremendous challenge, but that is not the only challenge that the EU poses for Blair and for Britain. In April 2004, under merciless sniping from the Conservatives, and worried that his own declining political fortunes made parliamentary passage of a bill on the EU Constitution increasingly contentious, Blair suddenly—and with virtually no consultation—announced that the EU Constitution would also be put to a referendum. With anti-EU sentiment running high and Blair's political capital depleted by the war in Iraq, the outlook appeared grim. In June, Ladbrokes, the famous British bookmaker that takes bets and sets odds for everything from sporting events to elections, placed the odds for British passage of the EU Constitution at 8:1 against!

By the time the leaders of the twenty-five EU members agreed on a constitution in June 2004, amidst open squabbles between Blair and Chirac, and a successful effort by France and Germany to scupper the candidacy of British candidate Chris Patten for European Commission president—in part because Britain was not a participant in the euro—there could be no mistaking how troubled UK-EU relations still were. And things were only likely to get worse. There was talk that any British referendum on the constitution would not be held until 2006 at the earliest. There was also speculation that the British were hoping that another country might reject the constitution before then, to minimize the wrath of EU stalwarts that would otherwise be directed at Britain if it were to delay or defeat the ratification of the constitution. (Assent by each of the twenty-five member states was required.) Clearly, Blair's high expectations that Britain could, under his leadership, assume a leading role in Europe, heal old wounds, and bridge the gap between Europe and the United States have not been realized.

British Politics, Terrorism, and Britain's Relationship to the United States

In the immediate aftermath of the terror attacks on the United States, Blair's decisive support for President Bush struck a resonant chord in both countries and (despite some grumbling) boosted Britain's influence in Europe. But by the spring and summer of 2002, Blair's stalwart alliance with Bush was looking more and more like a liability. The "axis of evil" motif of President Bush's State of the Union address in January 2002 worried many Britons (including Foreign Secretary Jack Straw), who considered it simplistic and potentially destabilizing. Would the special relationship—at the national level and between the two leaders—mean that Blair could moderate Bush's foreign policy and stall the plans for preemptive war against Iraq? Would it influence U.S. policy or at least calm the rhetoric about North Korea and Iran?

As Britons' instinctive post–September 11 support for America faded, many wondered whether Tony Blair had boxed himself into a corner by aligning himself too closely with George W. Bush, not knowing where the president's foreign policy initiatives might lead in the Middle East and Asia, and in a host of policy ar-

eas from trade policy to the conduct of the continuing campaign in Afghanistan, to global warming, to the International Criminal Court. Yet, throughout the diplomatic disputes in the run-up to war in spring 2003, Blair persevered in his staunch support for Bush's decision to go to war—this despite Blair's strong preference for explicit Security Council authorization for the use of force and his strong preference that significant progress in resolving the Israeli-Palestinian dispute be made before any military intervention to topple the Saddam Hussein regime.

Nonetheless, despite his inability to achieve either of these preferences, Blair refused all advice (including that from members of his cabinet as well as his chief of defense staff) to make support of the war conditional on achievement of these ends. Blair was convinced that the threats of weapons of mass destruction (WMDs), Al Qaeda terrorism, and rogue states justified the invasion of Iraq and that Britain should and must support the United States in its leadership of a global war against terrorism. Despite widespread opposition from Labour MPs; opinion polls indicating that only a quarter of the public supported Britain's participation in a war without a UN mandate; and the cabinet resignation of Robin Cook, leader of the House of Commons and former foreign minister, Blair persevered in his support of Bush. The prime minister insisted that the United Kingdom continue to stand "shoulder to shoulder" with the United States, and there they have remained throughout the revelations of horrific prisoner abuse by American forces (and the revelation of far less widespread abuse by British forces) and the devastation and chaos of occupation leading to the handover of power to the Iraqi interim authority on June 30, 2004.

Blair's unconditional commitment to support America's war in Iraq has cost Blair and New Labour dearly in political terms, especially as the initial justifications for war lost credibility. In the years ahead, the experience of the war in Iraq may contribute to a constructive reconsideration of the "special relationship" between the United States

One year after the start of the war in Iraq, Blair's political support had declined significantly, and his credibility was hurt as key justifications for war such as WMDs and Al Qaeda links to Iraq remained unproven. During an anniversary demonstration, and despite high winds, two Greenpeace protesters reached the clock face of Big Ben some 300 feet high and unveiled banners reading "Time for Truth."

Source: © Graeme Robertson/Getty Images

and the United Kingdom. It will certainly loom large in any assessment of Blair's contribution to British politics and the legacy of New Labour.

British Politics in Comparative Perspective

For many reasons, both historical and contemporary, the British case represents a critical one in comparative terms, even though Britain is no longer a leading power. How well have three centuries of constitutional government and a culture of laissez-faire capitalism prepared Britain for a political and economic world that it has fewer resources to control? Does Britain still offer a distinctive and appealing model of democracy? What are the lessons that may be drawn from Blair's New Labour, a modernizing politics that aspires to go beyond left and right?

Until the Asian financial crisis that began in 1997, it was an axiom of comparative politics that economic success required a style of economic governance that Britain lacks. Many argued that innovation and competitiveness in the new global economy required the strategic coordination of the economy by an interventionist state. Interestingly, however, the United Kingdom escaped the recession that plagued the rest of Europe for much of the 1990s. Britain is outperforming most major world economies and exhibits a good overall performance, declining unemployment, and relatively low inflation. Britain is not an economic paradise, but there is cause for continued optimism, notwithstanding persistent poverty, weak investment, problems with productivity, and trade imbalances.

The reasons for Britain's success and its economic prospects for the future continue to fuel debate inside the United Kingdom and attract considerable attention elsewhere. Perhaps Britain has already reaped the competitive benefits of ending restrictive labor practices and of attracting massive foreign investment looking for a European base with few restrictions, and it is time to introduce a more "European" high-skill, high-wage workforce and give it similar opportunities to participate in management. Or perhaps Britain's "less is more" approach to economic management, augmented by Tony Blair's business partnership and welfare reforms that encourage active participation in the labor force, provides an important and timely alternative to the more state-centered and interventionist strategies of Germany and France. In many countries throughout the world, politicians are looking for an economic model that can sustain economic competitiveness while improving the plight of the socially excluded. Tony Blair's third way—a political orientation that hopes to transcend left and right in favor of practical and effective policies—will be carefully watched and, if it is successful, widely emulated.

Beyond the impressive size of Blair's victory, nothing about the May 1997 election was clearer than the unprecedented volatility of the electorate. In previous elections, commitment to party (partisan identification) and interests linked to occupation (class location) had largely determined the results. In 1997, attachments to party and class had far less influence.

Beginning with the historically low turnout, the 2001 election underscored, as one journalist put it, that "instinctive party support" based on class and partisan traditions has been replaced by "pick and choose" politics. The tendency of voters to behave as electoral shoppers lends a perpetual air of uncertainty to elections. It seems that Blair's success in transforming Labour into New Labour blunted the social basis of party identification. At the same time, the modernization agenda of New Labour resolutely emphasized fiscal responsibility over distributive politics. As a result, it seems that specific issues and the needs of voters mattered more than deep-seated attachments. People voted as consumers of policies: they asked themselves who would make it easier for them to pay their mortgage, get the healthcare their family needs, best educate their children—and what role the government would play in underwriting or providing these goods.

The election in June 2001 was, paradoxically, a landslide and a powerful reminder that much of the electorate was waiting to be convinced that New Labour could deliver on its core promises of improved schools, hospitals, transport, and protection against crime. In winning

40.7 percent of the popular vote and a very commanding majority of 167 in the Commons, Labour achieved a historic result. For the first time, the party won two emphatic electoral victories in a row and was poised to lead the country for two full successive terms. Nevertheless, despite the overwhelming mandate, at 59.4 percent, the lowest turnout for a general election in Britain since 1918 indicated widespread apathy and skepticism (although, of course, a low turnout also reflected a sense that the outcome was never in doubt). Many wondered aloud whether in its second term, New Labour could dispel the notion that it was "more spin than substance." Even an exuberant Tony Blair noted that the mood in 2001 was more sober and less euphoric than it had been on election night four years earlier. Everyone seemed painfully aware of unfulfilled promises and the challenges that lay ahead.

Without the traditional constraints of partisan and class identities, citizens (whether as voters or as political activists) can shift allegiances with lightning speed. "What have you done for me lately?" becomes the litmus test for leaders and politicians. Taken together, the results of the June 2004 local and European elections in the United Kingdom suggest that foreign affairs may lend an additional dose of volatility to British politics. As the dictates of a post-9/11 war against terror, European integration, and globalization blur the distinction between governing the economy and the world of states, the scope of the "What have you done for me lately?" test may be expanding and the ways to fail growing.

These are tough times for national governments to maintain popular support and achieve desirable goals. Can a popular and resolute leader who is riding a wave of solid economic achievement in one of the most secure democracies govern effectively? Given Blair's past success, the competitiveness of the British economy, and the widespread influence of "third way" politics, the world will be watching to see whether Blair stumbles and falls. Or can he regain his momentum? If not, many will conclude that these tough times just got tougher.

Notes

1. Stephen Haseler, "Britain's Ancien Régime," *Parliamentary Affairs* 40, no. 4 (October 1990): 418.

2. Iain Byrne and Stuart Weir, "Democratic Audit: Executive Democracy in War and Peace," *Parliamentary Affairs* 57, no. 2 (2004): 453–468.

3. See James Mitchell and Jonathan Bradbury, "Devolution: Comparative Development and Policy Roles," *Parliamentary Affairs* 57, no. 2 (2004): 329–346.

4. Bhiku Parekh et al., *The Future of Multi-Ethnic Britain: The Parekh Report* (London: Profile Books, 2000), p. 38.

5. See Liza Schuster and John Solomos (and respondents), "Debate: Race, Immigration and Asylum," *Ethnicities* 4, no. 2 (June 2004): 267–300.

Part III Bibliography

Beer, Samuel H. *Britain Against Itself: The Political Contradictions of Collectivism.* New York: Norton, 1982.

Coates, David, and Joel Krieger. *Blair's War.* Cambridge, England, and Malden, Mass: Polity Press, 2004.

Coates, David, and Peter Lawler, eds. *New Labour in Power.* Manchester, England: Manchester University Press, 2000.

Cook, Robin. *The Point of Departure.* London: Simon & Schuster, 2003.

Dunleavy, Patrick, et al. *Developments in British Politics 7.* New York: Palgrave/Macmillan, 2003.

George, Bruce. *The British Labour Party and Defense.* New York: Praeger, 1991.

Giddens, Anthony. *The Third Way: The Renewal of Social Democracy.* Cambridge, England: Polity Press, 1998.

Gilroy, Paul. *"There Ain't No Black in the Union Jack": The Cultural Politics of Race and Nation.* Chicago: University of Chicago Press, 1991.

Hall, Stuart, and Martin Jacques, eds. *The Politics of Thatcherism.* London: Lawrence and Wishart, 1983.

Hobsbawm, E. J. *Industry and Empire.* Harmondsworth: Penguin/Pelican, 1983.

Kampfner, John. *Blair's Wars.* London: Free Press, 2003.

Kavenagh, Dennis, and Anthony Seldon. *The Powers Behind the Prime Minister: The Hidden Influence of Number Ten.* London: Harper-Collins, 1999.

King, Anthony, et al., eds. *Britain at the Polls, 2001.* New York and London: Chatham House, 2002.

Krieger, Joel. *British Politics in the Global Age. Can Social Democracy Survive?* New York: Oxford University Press, 1999.

Landes, David S. *The Unbound Prometheus: Technological Change and Industrial Development in Western Europe from 1750 to the Present.* Cambridge: Cambridge University Press, 1969.

Lewis, Philip. *Islamic Britain: Religion, Politics and Identity Among British Muslims.* London and New York: I. B. Taurus, 2002.

Marsh, David, et al. *Postwar British Politics in Perspective.* Cambridge, England: Polity Press, 1999.

Marshall, Geoffrey. *Ministerial Responsibility.* Oxford and New York: Oxford University Press, 1989.

Middlemas, Keith. *Politics in Industrial Society: The Experience of the British System Since 1911.* London: André Deutsch, 1979.

Norris, Pippa. *Electoral Change in Britain Since 1945.* Oxford, England: Blackwell Publishers, 1997.

Parekh, Bhiku, et al. *The Future of Multi-Ethnic Britain: The Parekh Report.* London: Profile Books, 2000.

Riddell, Peter. *The Thatcher Decade.* Oxford, England: Basil Blackwell, 1989.

Särlvik, Bo, and Ivor Crewe. *Decade of Dealignment: The Conservative Victory of 1979 and Electoral Trends in the 1970s.* Cambridge: Cambridge University Press, 1983.

Shaw, Eric. *The Labour Party Since 1945.* Oxford, England: Blackwell Publishers, 1996.

Thompson, E. P. *The Making of the English Working Class.* New York: Vintage, 1966.

Wright, Tony, ed. *The British Political Process.* London: Routledge, 2000.

Websites

The UK government official website for public services and general information: www.direct.gov.uk

The UK government website for on-line statistical data: www.statistics.gov.uk

The UK Parliament: www.parliament.uk

The Cabinet Office: www.cabinet-office.gov.uk

The Scottish Parliament: www.scottish.parliament.uk

The British Broadcasting Corporation (BBC): http://news.bbc.co.uk

MORI, Britain's leading political polling organization: www.mori.com

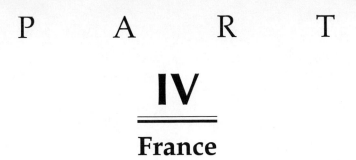

P A R T

IV

France

Mark Kesselman

11

The Making of the Modern French State

French Politics in Action

In late 2003, French president Jacques Chirac delivered a nationwide television address to announce a proposed public school reform. Did the proposal relate to the curriculum, educational standards, or school finance? Guess again. President Chirac declared that the government was planning to sponsor legislation prohibiting students from displaying "conspicuous signs of religious affiliation" in public schools. (The phrase is quoted from the law passed to implement Chirac's proposal.) The president explained that the rationale for the reform was to preserve the neutrality of schools, consistent with France's secular, republican tradition. Displaying religious symbols in a conspicuous manner violated France's secular tradition, and once the reform was implemented, students would be suspended from school if they did not conform.

What symbols were banned? Included on the list were large Catholic crosses and the Jewish yarmulke (skullcap). But it was clear that the main target of the reform—indeed, the reason it was proposed at all—was the *hidjab* (headscarf) worn by some Muslim girls.

How many French opposed a measure that might be interpreted as infringing on students' civil liberties and freedom of religion? The answer is very few: polls revealed that about 80 percent of the French supported the ban. The fact that only a few thousand among 1 million Muslim schoolgirls wear the headscarf to school mattered less to supporters of the ban than the fact that wearing the *hidjab* was interpreted as challenging dominant secular, republican values.

This was not the first time that controversy swirled around the issue of banning the wearing of headscarves in schools. An identical conflict erupted in 1989 after a school principal expelled four girls for wearing a headscarf. But after extensive debate, the conflict was resolved in a more pragmatic fashion. In 2003, President Chirac appointed a commission to study and make recommendations on how to reduce ethnic tensions. Although the commission report contained twenty-six recommendations, many involving positive measures to integrate Muslims into the French republic, Chirac accepted only one: a proposal to ban the conspicuous display of religious symbols in public places.

In early 2004, the French parliament passed the ban on displaying conspicuous religious symbols by an overwhelming majority. However, implementing the law produced some knotty problems. Ministry of Education administrators, school principals, and administrative courts had to decide whether—or under what circumstances—nontraditional garb like bandanas and kerchiefs were being worn not to make a fashion statement but to evade the ban. How can one distinguish between wearing a religious symbol in a discreet as opposed to a conspicuous manner? By late 2004, five Muslim girls had been expelled from schools for defying the ban and seventy-two other Muslim girls were suspended. In addition, three Sikh boys—whose turbans are both quite conspicuous and worn in compliance with Sikh religious dictates—were also suspended from school.

What does the headscarf controversy teach about French politics in action? First, the background to the dispute is ongoing tension between Muslims and other French citizens. President Chirac claimed that he was defending France's secular educational tradition. The ban on headscarves was also defended as a way to challenge Muslim fundamentalism as well as to protect Muslim girls from being intimidated by their families to wear the headscarf to symbolize their subordinate status.

That Chirac's proposal commanded such widespread support is also significant. In part, this suggests a large reservoir of anti-Muslim sentiment in France. But many French who are not religious bigots, and who identify themselves as being on the left, supported the measure to defend France's centuries-old secular, republican tradition against religious fundamentalism, the forced subordination of women, and a multiculturalist approach imported from the United States.

The headscarf incident also highlights that, despite important decentralization reforms in France in recent decades, the country remains highly centralized. Americans might be surprised that a dress code for public schools would be regulated by legislation and that a French president would make the measure a political priority. They might also be surprised that the dress code applies to all public schools throughout the country.

A final point is that the headscarf issue illustrates how countries that share durable democratic traditions may have quite different understandings of what is politically appropriate. The controversy encourages us to analyze the character of French political culture, the political institutions that communicate and reproduce that culture, and the relationship between France's political culture and the country's economy, institutions, and politics.

Geographic Setting

France is among the world's favored countries, thanks to its temperate climate, large and fertile land area, relatively low population density (about half that of Britain, Germany, and Italy), and high standard of living. France is by far the most popular tourist destination in the world, universally known for its natural beauty and superb architecture, culture, and cuisine. (With that said, the site in France most visited by tourists is Disneyland-Paris—which in 2003 drew twice as many visitors as the Eiffel Tower, the next most popular destination!)[1]

The French have a reputation for fine living (*joie de vivre* is the French term), ranging from a love of art, culture, and romance to fine food and wine. On a more mundane level, the country is poorly endowed in natural energy and mineral resources. For example, most petroleum must be imported, a reason why ever since the 1950s the government has sponsored an intensive nuclear power program. France must also import most minerals, a result of an initial scarcity of reserves and years of extensive exploitation. Thus, in order to compete internationally, France must concentrate on producing high-value-added products.

With a population of 61.1 million, France is one of the most populous countries in Western Europe, but its large size—221,000 square miles—means that its population density is low. An unusual feature of French national boundaries is that five overseas territories—the Mediterranean island of Corsica, the Caribbean islands of Guadeloupe and Martinique, French Guyana in South America, and the island of Réunion in the Indian Ocean—are considered an integral part of the country. They have a fundamentally different status than colonies. Their inhabitants are French cit-

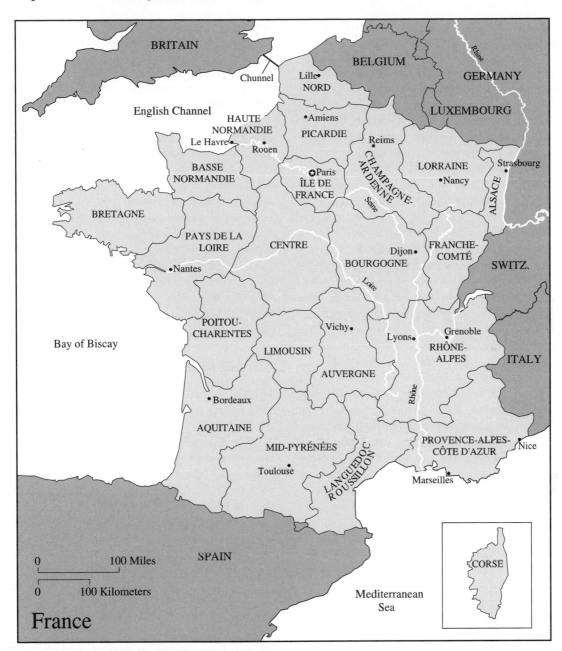

France

izens who enjoy the same civil rights and liberties as "mainland" French citizens; for example, they elect representatives to the French legislature. (Their situation is identical to that of citizens of Alaska and Hawaii in the United States political system.)

France's gross national product (GNP) of over $1.5 trillion and per capita income of more than

$25,000 make the country among the most affluent in the world. Nine families in ten own a color television, two-thirds own a VCR, 97 percent have a telephone, 62 percent a cell phone, and four-fifths an automobile.[2] Over half own their own home. France ranked sixteenth among the 177 countries of the world in the 2004 United Nations Development Programme's Human Development Index, a widely respected measure of the overall quality of life.

France occupies a key position in Europe, bordering the Mediterranean Sea in the south and sharing borders with Belgium, Switzerland, and Germany on the north and east, Spain in the southwest, and Italy in the southeast. France is Britain's closest continental neighbor. The two are separated by a mere twenty-five-mile stretch of the English Channel, a distance that shrank even more in 1994 with the opening of the "Chunnel," the railroad tunnel under the English Channel linking the two countries. France has quite secure natural borders of mountains and seas on all sides, save for the open plains of the northeast. The flat, open terrain separating France from Germany enabled German forces to invade France three times in the nineteenth and twentieth centuries.

France has a modern economy, and most people work in the industrial and service sectors. However, agriculture continues to occupy a significant place in the economy and—because until quite recently most French lived in villages and small towns—an even stronger place in the country's collective memory. (Though compared with the British and Germans, a significantly higher proportion of the French still live in rural areas and small towns.) No other French city rivals Paris, the capital, in size and influence, and Lille, Lyons, and Marseilles are the only other large cities in France.

Critical Junctures

A central feature of French history—from premodern times to the present—has been the prominent role played by the state. France was created by monarchs who for centuries laboriously knit together the diverse regions and provinces of what is present-day France—actions that in turn provoked periodic resistance. The French have often displayed toward the state both enormous respect for its achievements and intense resentment because of its characteristically high-handed intrusion into local life. The pattern of vigorous state activity and popular backlash persists to the present day. However, France's participation in the globalized economy and the EU, along with economic reforms and decentralization measures dating from the 1980s, has jostled the French state's preeminence. Until recently, political attention and energies were exclusively focused on Paris—the national capital and seat of the admired and feared ministries that governed French life. Nowadays, Paris must vie with regional and local governments throughout France—as well as Brussels, headquarters of the EU; Frankfurt, where the European Central Bank is located; and Strasbourg, home of the European Parliament.

Creating Modern France

For five centuries at the beginning of the modern era, the area that is now France was part of the Roman Empire. It was called Gaul by the Romans (the source of the term *Gallic*, sometimes used to describe the French). It took its current name from the Franks, a Germanic tribe that conquered the area in the fifth century A.D., with the breakup of the Roman Empire. The Merovingian dynasty ruled France for several centuries, during which time most of the population became Christian. It was succeeded by the Carolingian dynasty, whose most noteworthy ruler, Charlemagne, briefly brought much of western Europe under his control during the Holy Roman Empire in the ninth century.

Following Charlemagne's death in 814, the empire disintegrated. Norsemen from Scandinavia established a duchy in Normandy, in northwest France; their ruler, William the Conqueror, led a force that invaded England and defeated English troops at the Battle of Hastings in 1066. (The Bayeux Tapestry, woven soon after the invasion and now displayed in the Bayeux Museum in Normandy, describes the battle in rich detail.)

During the next two centuries, a succession of powerful French monarchs patiently and tenaciously sought to subdue powerful provincial rulers and groups in Burgundy, Brittany, and other regions to unify France. The country was invaded and nearly conquered by the English during the Hundred Years' War (1337–1453). Joan of Arc, a peasant who considered herself invested with a divine mission, finally led French forces to victory over the invading English army. Along with Charlemagne and a handful of other historic figures, she remains a symbol of intense national pride.

France flourished during the next several centuries, especially after Henri IV (who ruled from 1589 to 1610) ended religious conflict between Catholics and Huguenots (Protestants) by issuing the Edict of Nantes in 1598. The edict granted Protestants limited religious toleration. In the sixteenth century, France and England competed to gain control of North America. The rivalry between the two eventually ended with France's defeat, symbolized by the signing of the Treaty of Paris in 1763, when France accepted British domination in North America and India. (At a later period, France engaged in further colonial conquests in Africa, Asia, and the Caribbean.)

The seventeenth and early eighteenth centuries were the high point of French economic, military, and cultural influence throughout the world. France was the most affluent and powerful country in Europe, as evidenced by the exquisite châteaux throughout France, many still standing, built by monarchs and aristocrats. France was also the artistic and scientific capital of Europe, home of the Enlightenment in the eighteenth century, the philosophical movement that emphasized the importance of using scientific reason to understand and change the world.

The Ancien Régime

French monarchs continually sought to undermine local loyalties and foster uniform rules throughout the country. A turning point came when the powerful king Louis XIV (r. 1643–1715) sponsored the creation of a rela-

Table 11.1 Major French Constitutional Regimes

Ancien régime (Bourbon monarchy)	until 1789
Revolutionary regimes	1789–1799
Constituent Assembly, 1789–1791	
(Declaration of the Rights of Man, August 26, 1789)	
Legislative, 1791	
Convention, 1792–1795: Monarchy abolished and First Republic established, 1792	
Directory, 1795–1799	
Consulat and First Empire (Napoleon Bonaparte)	1800–1814
Restoration	1814–1830
July Monarchy	1830–1848
Second Republic	1848–1851
Second Empire (Louis Napoleon)	1852–1870
Paris Commune	1871
Third Republic	1871–1940
Vichy regime	1940–1944
Fourth Republic	1946–1958
Fifth Republic	1958–present

tively efficient state bureaucracy, separate from the Crown's personal domain. France began to be administered according to a legal-rational code in which standardized regulations were applied throughout the country. France was a pioneer in developing the absolutist state, which has shaped French development ever since.

But the modernizing, absolutist state created by Louis XIV and his successors coexisted with an intricate and burdensome system of feudal privileges that peasants, urban workers, and a rising middle class increasingly resented. Another target of popular discontent was the Catholic Church, a large landowner, tax collector, and ally of the feudal authorities. This complex patchwork of institutions was later described as the *ancien régime*, or old regime (see Table 11.1).

Pressure on the regime increased as Louis XIV and his successor, Louis XV, accumulated massive state debts resulting from military adventures in Europe and colonial conquests overseas. For most of the period from the mid-seventeenth to the mid-eighteenth century, France was at war with its neighbors. As historian Simon Schama notes, "No other European power attempted to support both a major continental army and a transcontinental navy at the same time."[3] France was the most powerful nation in Europe in the seventeenth century. But in the eighteenth century, Britain began to challenge France's preeminence, thanks to the economic advantages that Britain reaped from the Agricultural and Industrial Revolutions. France's stagnant economy could not generate the resources to compete with an increasingly productive England. As a result, the French monarchy had to borrow from the French to raise the necessary funds. By 1788, French state debt was so large that interest on past loans consumed over one-half of current state expenditures.[4] When Louis XVI tried to raise taxes, the bulk of which fell on the common people, the move provoked a violent reaction that sealed the fate of the French monarchy.

The Two Faces of the French Revolution, 1789–1815

An angry crowd burst through the gates of Paris's Bastille prison on July 14, 1789, and freed the prisoners, launching the French Revolution. This was soon followed by the toppling of the French monarchy and the entire *ancien régime* of nobility and feudal privileges. A succession of revolutionary regimes quickly followed, including the Constituent Assembly (which in 1789 issued the world-famous Declaration of the Rights of Man and the Citizen), the Legislative Assembly, the Convention, and the Directory. The most important changes involved the abolition of the French monarchy (as well as the monarch—Louis XVI was guillotined in 1793 for opposing the Revolution), the elimination of the entire

ancien régime of nobility and feudal privileges, and the proclamation of the First Republic in 1792. France was the first modern European nation to establish a republic based on the belief that all citizens, regardless of social background, were equal before the law.

It is difficult to overestimate the impact of the Revolution on French and European history. Historian Lynn Hunt observes, "The chief accomplishment of the French Revolution was the institution of a dramatically new political culture. . . . The French Revolution may be said to represent the transition to political and social modernity, the first occasion when the people entered upon the historical stage to remake the political community."[5]

The Revolution of 1789 was at the same time a *national* revolution, which affirmed the people's right to choose their own political regime; an *international* revolution, which inspired national uprisings elsewhere in Europe and sought to expand French revolutionary values internationally (often through military means); a *liberal* revolution, which championed the value of individual liberty in the political and economic spheres and proclaimed the importance of secularism and religious freedom, as opposed to state-mandated Catholic Church dominance in religious affairs; and a *democratic* revolution, which proclaimed that a nation's identity and the legitimacy of its government depend on all citizens' having the right to participate in making key political decisions. Thus, the Revolution was in part a social revolution, but perhaps even more importantly it was a revolution in thought, bringing forth new conceptions of people's relation to each other and their place in the world. The Revolution's provocative ideas have spread far beyond France's borders and have become part of our universal heritage.

The Revolution was not without flaws. At the same time that the revolutionary regime was proclaiming the values of liberty, equality, and fraternity, it acted with brutality and intolerance toward opponents. (At the extreme, during the Reign of Terror, the Jacobin state—so named for the revolutionary faction that triumphed over moderates within the revolutionary camp—guillotined those found guilty by revolutionary tribunals.) Historian Joan Landes has described how, despite some reforms in women's interests (for example, short-lived divorce legislation), the revolutionary ferment was quite hostile to women: "The [First] Republic was constructed against women, not just without them, and nineteenth-century Republicans did not actively counteract this masculinist heritage of republicanism."[6]

In other ways, too, the Revolution left a complex legacy. Alexis de Tocqueville, a brilliant French aristocrat and writer in the nineteenth century, identified two quite opposite faces of the French Revolution: at the same time that it produced a rupture with the *ancien régime,* it shared the goal long pursued by French monarchs of strengthening state institutions. In particular, many of the centralizing institutions created by the revolutionary regime and by Napoleon Bonaparte, the popular general who seized power and proclaimed himself emperor in 1802, remain to this day. Napoleon established the system by which state-appointed officials called *prefects* administer localities, and he created the Conseil d'État (State Council), an elite agency that supervises the central administration. He also developed the Napoleonic Code of Law, a detailed legal framework, whose two hundredth anniversary was celebrated with great pomp in 2004.

Since Napoleon's defeat and exile in 1815, French politics has often revolved around the question of how to reconcile state autonomy—the state's independence from pressure coming from groups within society—with democratic participation and decision making. Compared with some other successful democracies, notably Britain, France has been less able to combine the two within a stable political regime because of an overbearing state, which regulates important as well as many less important areas of social life. For example, the Ministry of Education issues a standardized curriculum used in all public schools, and until quite recently, local governments needed the approval of the Ministry of the Interior when naming city streets. While citizens often sought state help, they resented its heavy hand and periodically took to the streets to protest state policies and demand benefits.

Many Regimes, Slow Industrialization: 1815–1940

France spent much of the nineteenth and twentieth centuries digesting and debating the legacy of the Revolution. The succession of regimes and revolutions for more than a century after 1815 can be interpreted as varied attempts to combine state autonomy and direction with democratic participation and decision making. After Napoleon's final defeat in 1815, there were frequent uprisings, revolutions, and regime changes. The monarchy was restored to power in 1815 (hence the name, the Restoration, to refer to the change), but it was overthrown in a popular uprising in July 1830, which installed the king's distant royal cousin, Louis Philippe, as king. (This regime is known as the July Monarchy.) In 1848, another revolution produced yet another regime: the short-lived Second Republic. Louis Napoleon, the nephew of Napoleon Bonaparte, overthrew the republic after three years and proclaimed himself emperor. When France lost the Franco-Prussian War of 1870–1871, the Second Empire was swept away by a revolutionary upheaval that produced the Paris Commune in 1871, a brief experiment in worker-governed democracy. The Commune was violently crushed after a few months, to be succeeded by the Third Republic, created nearly by accident in the years following France's military defeat and civil war in 1871.

Although prior to the Third Republic, regimes alternated among monarchies, republics, and empires, since 1871 France has been a republic (save for a brief period during World War II). The Third Republic never commanded widespread support. It was described, in a famous phrase by conservative politician Adolphe Thiers, as the regime "that divides us [French] least." Yet it turned out to be France's most durable modern regime, lasting until 1940. (The second most durable regime is the current one, the Fifth Republic, which was created in 1958.)

The Third Republic was a parliamentary regime with two powerful legislative bodies, the Chamber of Deputies and the Senate. Its institutions were designed to prevent decisive leadership, given the legacy of Napoleon's illegal seizure of power and the ideologically and fragmented state of French society. Yet the republic survived the terrible ordeal of World War I and held firm against extremist forces on the right during the 1920s and 1930s, when republics were crumbling in Germany, Italy, and Spain. However, when France was defeated by Germany in World War II, following the Third Republic's failure to check the Nazi invasion, the republic was abolished.

The succession of regime changes in the nineteenth and twentieth centuries highlights the existence of sharp cleavages and the absence of political institutions capable of regulating conflict. However, in sharp contrast with the dizzying pace at which regimes came and went, the rate of economic change in France during this period was quite gradual. Compared with Germany, its dynamic neighbor to the northeast, France chose economic stability over modernization.

There have been endless attempts to explain why France did not become an industrial leader in the nineteenth century. Although it began the century as the world's second most important economic power, fairly close to Britain in terms of economic output, by 1900 France trailed the United States, Great Britain, and Germany in industrial development. A large peasantry acted as a brake on industrialization, as did the fact that France was poorly endowed with coal, iron, and petroleum. Historians have also pointed to the relatively underdeveloped entrepreneurial spirit in France. Within the ranks of the middle class, professionals, administrators, and shopkeepers outnumbered industrial entrepreneurs. In general, French manufacturers excelled in sectors that did not fuel industrial expansion, notably agricultural produce for local markets and custom-made luxury goods (silk weaving and porcelain), which did not lend themselves to mechanized production and for which mass markets did not exist.

Another factor inhibiting industrial development was the slow growth of the French population. In the middle of the nineteenth century, France was the second most populous nation in Europe (after Russia). However, although the British population more than tripled in the nineteenth century and the number of Germans more than doubled, France's population increased by less than one-half.[7] Whereas 15 percent of Europe's population in 1800 was French, only 8 percent was French in 1950.[8] Slow population growth meant smaller demand and less incentive for businesses to invest and increase productivity.

More important than technical or demographic factors was the role of the state. In Britain, the government removed restrictions on the free operation of market forces, and in Prussia (later Germany), the powerful chancellor Otto von Bismarck imposed industrialization from above. By contrast, the French state aimed to "maintain an equilibrium among industry, commerce, and agriculture and attempt[ed] to insulate France from the distress and upheaval that had struck other nations bent upon rapid economic advance."[9] France retained some of the highest tariff barriers in western Europe in the nineteenth and early twentieth centuries. The purpose of this protectionist policy was to shield small producers—farmers, manufacturers, and artisans—from foreign competition. Economic historian Richard Kuisel observes that "rarely, if ever, did [the French state] act to promote economic expansion, plan development, or advance economic democracy."[10]

Yet the state did not simply prevent economic modernization. In a tradition dating back to Colbert, the finance minister of Louis XIV who directed the creation of the French merchant marine, the state sponsored a number of large-scale economic projects. For example, in the

1860s under Louis Napoleon, the state consolidated several small railroad companies and organized an integrated national rail network; encouraged the formation of the Crédit Mobilier, an investment bank to finance railroad development; and guaranteed interest rates on bonds sold to underwrite railroad construction.

On balance, however, through much of the nineteenth century and well into the twentieth, the state sought to preserve political stability rather than promote economic modernization. Slow economic growth did not prevent political conflict. But it did contribute to France's humiliating defeat by Germany in 1940.

Vichy France (1940–1944) and the Fourth Republic (1946–1958)

World War II was one of the bleakest periods in French history. When France was overrun by Germany in 1940, Marshal Pétain, an aged French military hero, helped destroy the Third Republic by signing an armistice that divided France in two. The north was under direct German occupation; in the south, Pétain presided over a puppet regime, whose capital was at Vichy. The Vichy government took its revenge on progressive elements in the Third Republic by preaching authoritarian values. It collaborated with the Nazi occupation by providing workers and supplies for the German war machine and has the dubious distinction of being the only political regime in Western Europe that delivered Jews to the Nazis from areas not directly under German occupation. About 76,000 Jews, including 12,000 children, were sent to Nazi death camps. Vichy not only failed to resist Nazi genocidal policies and failed to protect foreign Jews who fled Nazi-occupied territories seeking asylum in France but on its own initiative rounded up French and foreign Jews and sent them to Nazi concentration camps.

Although the vast majority of French citizens did not challenge the Vichy government's authority, a small resistance movement developed among Communists, Socialists, and progressive Catholic forces. Charles de Gaulle, a prominent general and junior cabinet minister in the Third Republic, denounced the Vichy regime's collaboration with the Nazis and advocated armed resistance. He assumed leadership over the diverse anti-Vichy forces and consolidated them into what became known as the Resistance. At great personal risk, its members engaged in sabotage, such as blowing up bridges and assassinating Vichy and Nazi officials. However, Resistance efforts were more than offset by the valuable assistance offered by the Vichy regime to the Nazi war machine, including sending French workers to factories in Germany, shipping French manufactured goods and food to Germany, and participating in the Nazi propaganda campaign. Attempting to salvage French honor, de Gaulle sought to create the myth that most French supported the Resistance. His skillful actions enabled France to gain acceptance as a member of the victorious Allied coalition and to obtain one of the five permanent seats on the United Nations Security Council following the war.

After World War II, the French were reluctant to admit the country's dismal war record; a widely shared (although inaccurate) view held that the Vichy regime had been isolated and unrepresentative. It took fully half a century after the war for a French president to publicly acknowledge the state's responsibility for the crimes committed by the Vichy regime. In 1995, President Jacques Chirac declared, "Those dark hours will forever tarnish our history and are a disgrace to our past and to our tradition. We all know that the criminal madness of the [Nazi] occupying forces was assisted by the French, that is, the French state."

In 1945, following the Nazi defeat, de Gaulle sought to sponsor a regime that would avoid the errors that in his view had weakened France and contributed to its moral decline and defeat by Germany. He believed that the institutional design of the Third Republic, in which the executive was dependent on parliament, blurred responsibility for governing and prevented forceful leadership. He proposed creating a regime in which the government was independent and powerful.

Having just overthrown the authoritarian Vichy regime, French citizens opposed creating a new republic with a strong executive. When the attempt failed, de Gaulle abruptly resigned as leader of the provisional regime drafting a constitution and mounted an unsuccessful campaign against the new republic. The constitution of the newly created Fourth Republic was in fact very similar to that of the Third Republic.

The Fourth Republic, which survived for a dozen years (1946–1958), embodied an extreme form of parliamentary rule and weak executive. The constitution gave parliament a near-monopoly of power, which it exercised in a quite destructive fashion: governments were voted out of office an average of once every six months! This situation partly resulted from the fact that many parties were represented in parliament because the National Assembly, the powerful lower house, was selected by proportional representation. As in the Third Republic, rapid shifts in party alliances, as well as a lack of discipline within parties, meant that governments lacked the cohesion and authority to make tough decisions and develop long-range policies. Although the Fourth Republic was often regarded as highly unstable, the situation might better be described as one of political stalemate.

Neither the Vichy regime nor the Fourth Republic satisfactorily combined state direction and democratic participation. By their opposite excesses, they underlined the need for devising a new constitutional framework that would promote stable, democratic rule.

Despite some important achievements, notably setting France on the road to economic expansion and modernization, the Fourth Republic was unable to take decisive action in many important spheres. The regime was severely handicapped by the fact that the Communist Party and de Gaulle's political party had extensive popular support and large parliamentary delegations. They combined to topple one centrist government after another. However, the Fourth

Republic would doubtless have survived were it not for its failure to crush a rebellion by forces seeking independence in Algeria, France's largest colony.

The military stalemate during a long and brutal war enabled de Gaulle to regain power. When the French army stationed in Algeria threatened to invade mainland France to protest what it claimed was the republic's indecisive leadership, de Gaulle persuaded parliament to authorize him to propose a new constitutional framework to replace the Fourth Republic. The constitution of the Fifth Republic, drafted under his direction and approved in a nationwide referendum, broke with a nearly century-old tradition prevailing in the Third and Fourth Republics by creating a strong, independent executive and a weak parliament.

The Fifth Republic (1958 to the Present)

The contrast between the Fourth and Fifth Republics provides a textbook case of how institutions shape political life. The Fourth Republic could be described, cruelly but accurately, as all talk and no action: while parliament endlessly debated, and voted to make and unmake governments, elected political leaders did little to address the nation's pressing problems. On the other hand, the Fifth Republic created institutions enabling leaders to act decisively but, at least in the early years, avoid accountability to parliament or public opinion.

The history of the Fifth Republic is closely linked to the growth of the European Union (first known as the European Economic Community), which was created in 1957, a year before the birth of the Fifth Republic. The European Union (EU), as it is now known, helped to knit together historic rivals France and Germany, foster economic growth, and increase Europe's economic and political role internationally. The growing economic and political integration of Europe, in part a result of vigorous French efforts, represents a fundamental change after centuries of intense conflicts within Europe. The Fifth Republic has reaped handsome benefits from the growth of the EU, although participation has also created economic and political burdens.

Despite the fact that de Gaulle became first president of the Fifth Republic under quite unsavory circumstances, he commanded wide popular support because of his historic position. Resistance hero, commanding presence, and one of the political giants of the twentieth century, de Gaulle was able to persuade the French to support a regime in which democratic participation was strictly limited. He defended the new constitution on the grounds that a parliamentary regime along the lines of the Fourth Republic or the British Westminster model was not appropriate for a country as divided as France. Although the new constitution was approved by a large majority in a popular referendum, de Gaulle's high-handed governing style and the centralized institutions of the Fifth Republic eventually provoked widespread opposition.

The most dramatic example was in May 1968, when students and workers engaged in the largest general strike in Western European history. At the height of the May uprising, half of France's workers and even more students participated. For weeks, workers and students occupied factories, offices, and universities, and the regime's survival hung in the balance. Although de Gaulle temporarily regained control of the situation, he was discredited and resigned from office the following year.

The Fifth Republic was again severely tested in 1981. For twenty-three years, the same broad political coalition, representing the conservative forces that took power in 1958, won every single national election. In 1981, economic stagnation and divisions among conservative forces enabled Socialist Party candidate François Mitterrand to be elected president. In the parliamentary elections that followed, Mitterrand's supporters swamped conservative forces. Despite fears that the Fifth Republic would not be able to survive a Socialist government, the institutions of the Fifth Republic proved highly successful at accommodating political alternation.

"What!?? The president's a Socialist and the Eiffel Tower is still standing!??" "Incredible!"

Source: Courtesy Plantu, Cartoonists & Writers Syndicate, from *Le Monde*.

President Mitterrand's Socialist government sponsored one of the most ambitious reform agendas in modern French history, including strengthening the autonomy of the judiciary, the media, and local governments. The centerpiece was a substantial increase in the number of industrial firms and financial institutions in the public sector. However, by seeking to extend the sphere of public control of the economy, France was swimming against the international economic and political tide. During the 1980s, the predominant tendency elsewhere in the industrialized world was to strengthen private market forces rather than extend public control. (Margaret Thatcher in Britain and Ronald Reagan in the United States were elected to leadership positions at nearly the same time that Mitterrand captured the French presidency.) When the Socialist experiment began to provoke an economic and financial crisis in 1983–1984, the government reluctantly decided to reverse course. Since then, governments of left and right alike have pursued market-friendly policies. As a result, the ideological war of left and right in France, which raged for centuries, has declined. Since the 1980s, frequent changes in the governing coalition have occurred, but there has been extensive continuity in broad economic orientation.

Does the convergence between the major center-left and center-right parties mean the end of major political conflict in France? Not at all, as the 2002 presidential elections described below demonstrate.

France in the Euro Era: Decline or Renewal?

Although no single event can be identified as a critical juncture in the first years of the new millennium, France's increasingly close involvement in the EU, highlighted by the adoption of the euro, deserves special mention. In the 1970s, political scientist Stanley Hoffmann identified France's dilemma as "decline or renewal?" The same question can be used to identify the dilemma that the euro was designed to address.[11] The euro symbolizes the powerful way that France's fate is now intensely intertwined with that of the EU. Few national symbols are as important as a country's currency. A turning point was reached in 1991, with the creation of the Economic and Monetary Union (EMU) as a key element of the Maastricht Treaty, which deepened the process of European integration. With the exception of Britain, Denmark, and Sweden, Ireland, and all member states of the EU committed themselves to replacing their own national monetary units with the euro. In 2002, the euro entered into circulation in euroland (as it was informally called). The euro is now the only currency used throughout most of the EU, and the European Central Bank, headquartered in Frankfurt, regulates interest rates and exchange rates for member states.

Although European integration has been occurring ever since the creation of the European Coal and Steel Community in 1950, the adop-

tion of the euro qualifies as a critical juncture because it enmeshes France so deeply in the institutions and policies of the EU. Along with Germany and several other European countries, France helped form the EU to promote economic growth and political stability. France played a key role in accelerating the pace of European integration in the 1980s. Has EU membership in fact enabled France to achieve economic growth and political stability? On the one hand, as Chapter 12 analyzes, although the French economy has been flourishing, disquieting problems persist. Our major focus in this book is on political developments. And on that score, the news seems even less promising.

One reason is a rapid-fire series of electoral shifts that have occurred. Since 1981, France has had six parliamentary elections. In every single one, control shifted from the ruling coalition to the opposition. Voters thus are quick to demonstrate their displeasure with the "ins"—although it does not take them long to register their displeasure with the new ruling coalition!

A good illustration of voter volatility was provided in 2002–2004. In 2002, Jacques Chirac was reelected president, and a conservative majority was elected to parliament. A mere two years later, candidates from Chirac's center-right party were trounced by center-left candidates in elections to France's regional councils. As a result of this swift pendulum swing, Chirac's center-right coalition was substantially weakened.

A second reason is countless political scandals involving leading politicians, including party leaders, cabinet ministers, and the two most recent presidents (Mitterrand, president from 1981 to 1995, and Chirac, elected in 1995 and reelected in 2002). Third, a growing number of French citizens have turned against the major governing parties of both left and right, preferring to abstain or support fringe parties. Fourth, many scholars assert that underlying these changes is the fact that the French political system is unable to deal effectively with pressing social and economic challenges, stubbornly high levels of unemployment, French participation in the EU, and the meaning of French national identity in an era of globalization.

The persistent malaise in French politics was highlighted by the 2002 presidential elections. When the presidential election campaign began, it was universally assumed that the two candidates who would face off in the decisive runoff election would be two major workhorses in the mainstream of French politics: Lionel Jospin, Socialist prime minister, and Jacques Chirac, incumbent president and candidate of the center-right. (Two rounds of elections are usually required to select a French president. If no candidate at the first round gains an absolute majority, the typical case, a runoff election is held between the two front-runners.) Jospin and Chirac were perennial opponents: they had competed in the runoff in the previous presidential election, held in 1995, that resulted in Chirac's election as president. Virtually everyone assumed that the first ballot in 2002, when a record sixteen candidates competed, was a mere prelude to the decisive runoff between Chirac and Jospin. A best-selling book published in early 2002, *The Duel*, whose cover featured a photo of Jospin and Chirac in classic dueling position, said it all.

Given that the real action would not occur until the second ballot, it was understandable why the first-ballot campaign was lackluster. A day before the election, a *New York Times* reporter explained why voters were so bored: "Part of the problem, experts say, is that there is little suspense."[12]

The preelection analysis proved accurate about voters being apathetic—or confused by the large number of candidates. Turnout was a record low in French presidential elections. But predictions about the outcome of the first ballot were decidedly inaccurate: soon after the polls closed on April 21, apathy turned to stupefaction at the greatest electoral surprise in the nearly fifty-year history of the French Fifth Republic. Although Chirac came in first, according to script, incumbent prime minister Jospin was nudged out of second place by Jean-Marie Le Pen, candidate of the Front National (FN), a far-

right demagogue whose targets include Muslim immigrants, Jews, and mainstream politicians. The fact that Le Pen outpolled Jospin by less than 1 percent (17.0 percent to 16.1 percent) was less important than that the runoff would pit Le Pen against Chirac. Commentators routinely used terms like *bombshell* and *earthquake* to describe the first-ballot results. It was literally unthinkable that a politician regarded by a large majority of the French (and citizens from around the world) as a barely disguised racist would be one of the two candidates competing in the runoff election.

Le Monde, France's most influential newspaper, spoke for most French when it began its front-page editorial the day after the election: "France is wounded."[13] A cartoon in *Le Monde* graphically depicted Le Pen's success as France's equivalent of the September 11, 2001, attack against the United States.

Immediately after the first-ballot results were announced, massive anti–Le Pen marches and demonstrations were organized throughout France in preparation for the runoff election. The high point occurred on May 1, a holiday traditionally commemorating workers' struggles, when about 1.5 million people participated in demonstrations in Paris and other cities. *Le Monde* observed that "May 1, 2002, will go down in history as one of the largest popular demonstrations that the capital has ever experienced."[14] A poll reported that one young French person in two participated in a demonstration between the two ballots.[15]

At the runoff ballot on May 5, Chirac outpolled Le Pen by 82 to 18 percent, the most lopsided vote in the history of the Fifth Republic. Nevertheless, many questioned whether Chirac's overwhelming second-round victory offset the damage from Le Pen's first-ballot performance.

The memory of Le Pen's exploit in the 2002 presidential elections remains vivid in contemporary French politics, and the FN remains a significant presence in contemporary French politics. In the 2004 elections to the European Parliament, FN slates received 10 percent of the

Le Monde's cartoonist compares Le Pen's attack on Chirac and Jospin to the bombing of the twin towers of the World Trade Center.

———————

Source: Plantu, *Le Monde*, April 23, 2002, p. 1.

vote, fourth highest of France's many parties. A far larger proportion of French citizens support Le Pen's authoritarian views about Muslims, immigration, and law and order. The Le Pen phenomenon is disturbing evidence of a malaise in French political, economic, and social life.

France after September 11

France is home to the largest Muslim population in Western Europe, and, following the terrorist attacks on the United States of September 11, 2001, the country has been closely connected to the post-9/11 conflicts of global politics. On the one hand, France is itself a site in which terrorists have operated. In late 2001, Richard Reid, a British citizen, attempted to ignite explosives during a flight from Paris to Miami. In 2003, he was convicted and sentenced to life imprisonment. Zacarias Moussaoui, a French citizen, was tried in the United States in 2002 on charges that he helped plan the September 11 attack. In 2003, French antiterrorist police detained eighteen Algerians and Pakistanis in the Paris area on charges that they were accomplices of Reid and members of a network of Islamic militants

linked to Al Qaeda. In 2002, fourteen French technicians working in Pakistan were murdered. In a separate incident that year, a French oil tanker near Yemen was damaged by an explosive charge.

On the other hand, France has been actively involved in seeking to destroy terrorist networks while at the same time being highly critical of U.S. policies on some important issues. France supported the U.S. military action against Al Qaeda and the Taliban regime in Afghanistan in 2001. It voted for the U.S.-sponsored resolution in the United Nations authorizing military operations, and French troops served in Afghanistan during the war. However, France challenged the United States over the wisdom of invading Iraq in 2003 and helped organize an international coalition that opposed military action to remove Saddam Hussein's regime. France claimed that, prior to launching military operations, UN weapons inspectors should have more time to search for weapons of mass destruction.

The conflict between France and the United States over Iraq was intense. It had its comic aspects, as with the renaming of French fries to Freedom fries in the dining room of the House of Representatives! But the predominant tone was far from humorous. For example, influential *New York Times* columnist Thomas L. Friedman angrily described what he called "Our War with France." Friedman alleged that France had become an enemy of the United States.[16]

France's anti-American sentiment was intensified by criticism of President George W. Bush: a public opinion poll in the *New York Times* of May 9, 2004, reported that 85 percent of the French had a negative opinion of Bush. After photographs of the torture of Iraqi prisoners at the Abu Ghraib prison by American soldiers became public in 2004, a *Le Monde* editorial claimed that "the largest wave of anti-Americanism in history is sweeping the world."[17] It suggested that, while most people were in full solidarity with the United States after September 11, most opposed the U.S. attack on Iraq and were outraged by the Abu Ghraib revelations. In 2003, when a public opinion poll asked French citizens to name the greatest threats to world peace, the United States ranked among the top three countries in the world.

The roots of anti-Americanism go deeper than French opposition to George W. Bush or American actions in Iraq. Many studies have documented how the French have long viewed the United States as a political, cultural, and economic threat. Years before the Iraqi war, the French feared that the demise of the Soviet Union left American power unchecked in global politics. They coined the term *hyperpower* (a notch higher in the scale than *superpower*) to describe what they regarded as the threatening position of the United States. Although French society is highly divided these days on domestic political issues, public opinion is close to united in opposing what it regards as the arrogant, imperial stance of the United States.

Themes and Implications

Our analysis of the evolution of French development has identified some key turning points in French history. We can gain greater clarity on French politics by highlighting the distinctive ways that France has addressed the four key themes that provide a framework for analyzing European politics in transition.

Historical Junctures and Political Themes

Analyzing the four themes that frame *European Politics in Transition* suggests the extent of the current transition in French politics. The situation in France has changed quite dramatically within the past decade with respect to every one of the four.

France in a World of States. France's relationship to the rest of Europe and other regions of the world, particularly Asia and Africa, has heavily shaped state formation. For over a century following Napoleon's defeat in 1815, the country displayed an inward-oriented, isolationist orientation. For example, France erected high tariff barriers throughout the nineteenth century and the first half of the twentieth century to minimize international trade. Nevertheless, at the end of the nineteenth century, it aggressively extended the boundaries of its empire beyond North Africa to Southeast Asia, North and sub-Saharan Africa, and the Pacific. For close to a century, France exploited the mineral and other resources of its colonies with little regard for their own development. But the arrangement also damaged the French economy in the long run. By enabling France to avoid competing in the global economy, it contributed to the country's relatively slow pace of technological and industrial development.

France's tortured relationship with Germany— the two fought three devastating wars in less than a century—has weighed heavily on state development. The fact that the two countries developed cordial relations after World War II, in part thanks to the mutually beneficial expansion of the European and world economy, has provided France with vastly increased security. The alliance between the two countries has been vital in promoting closer European economic and political integration within the EU. They developed a joint military force that served in Afghanistan—a project that would have been unthinkable for the century of mutual hostility between the two countries. And they cooperated in opposing the U.S. and British military intervention in Iraq in 2003. The two countries continue to compete, but the competition is now confined to economic rivalry between French and German business firms rather than military confrontation.

Although France ranks far below the United States in military and geopolitical power, it remains an important player on the world stage. For example, it has developed nuclear weapons and sophisticated military technology, and France ranks among the world's leading arms exporters. France has been a major participant in the Western alliance led by the United States. But, in contrast to Britain and Germany, for example, France has often been a gadfly to the United States.

The French state has been a powerful, capable instrument helping the country adapt to the challenges posed by global economic competition. In recent decades, the state skillfully promoted internationally acclaimed high-tech industrial projects, including high-speed rail travel (the TGV, for *train à grande vitesse*); leadership in the European consortium that developed an efficient wide-bodied airplane (the Airbus); an electronic telephone directory and data bank (the Minitel); and relatively safe and cheap nuclear power plants. The fact that the French state has played such a key role in nation building and in economic and cultural development is why, as one observer notes, "No other nation in the world has as dense and passionate a relationship with the State as does France."[18] Yet France's statist tradition is under siege as a result of increased international economic integration and competition, highlighted by French participation in the EU, as well as ideological shifts and citizens' demands for more autonomy.

Governing the Economy. Our discussion of France's statist tradition sheds light on French economic governance. In the period following World War II, the French pioneered in developing methods to steer and strengthen the economy. As a result of planning, state loans and subsidies to private business, and crash programs to develop key industries, the French economy soared. However, the postwar style of state direction, useful in an era when France was relatively underdeveloped, has created problems in the current period, when rapidly changing technology and economic globalization put a premium on flexibility. The French state can be compared to a stately ocean liner that can move powerfully in one direction but has great difficulty changing course.

The Democratic Idea. France has had a complex relationship to the democratic idea. On the one hand, the statist tradition regards democratic participation and decision making as impairing rational direction by qualified leaders. On the other hand, France has been passionately attached to two divergent democratic currents. The first dates back to eighteenth-century philosopher Jean-Jacques Rousseau. The theory of direct democracy that Rousseau inspired claims that citizens should participate directly in political decisions rather than merely choose leaders who monopolize political power.

A second powerful democratic current in French political culture, identified with republican values, champions representative or parliamentary government on the grounds that direct democracy lends itself to demagogic leadership. The precedent often cited in this regard was Louis Napoleon's use of the referendum in 1851 to destroy the Second Republic and enshrine himself as emperor. Many opponents of de Gaulle regarded him as trampling on representative democracy and furthering *le pouvoir personnel* (personal power).

France's democratic theory and institutions face important challenges. One problem stems from French participation in the EU, which exhibits what has been dubbed a "democratic deficit"—that is, too much administrative direction and too little democratic participation and representation. Another strain derives from the continuing difficulty of reconciling state autonomy and democratic participation within France. For example, as we analyze in Chapter 13, the French executive centralizes enormous powers and exhibits a relative lack of accountability. The kind of democratic deficit that many assert is a weakness of the EU may also be said to characterize France's own political system.

Politics of Collective Identity. French national identity has always been closely linked to state formation. The Revolution championed the idea that anyone who accepted republican values could become French. The French approach to citizenship and national identity encourages immigrants to become French citizens on condition that they accept dominant cultural and political values. Such an approach stresses that what binds people are shared political values rather than racial or ethnic (i.e., inherited) characteristics.

At the same time, the French were deeply divided by social, economic, and cultural cleavages. In the postwar period, there was sharp opposition between a working-class subculture, closely linked to the powerful French Communist Party (Parti communiste français—PCF), and a Catholic subculture, in which the Church played a key role. In recent decades, these subcultures have declined in importance. Occupational shifts, notably a drastic decline in blue-collar jobs and the rapid expansion of a white-collar service sector, have blurred class boundaries. During this period, the PCF went from being one of France's most powerful parties to a minor party. There has also been a dramatic decline in religious observance. As a result, the Catholic Church is no longer a powerful source of collective identity.

If old cleavages have declined, new challenges have developed. French national identity has been destabilized recently by issues involving ethnic differences and globalization. After World War II, French economic reconstruction and in-dustrialization were fueled by a large wave of immigrants from North Africa. Although immigration was severely restricted following the economic slowdown in the 1970s, the issue of immigrants and their status in French society erupted into the political arena in the 1980s and continues to the present. Jean-Marie Le Pen gained widespread support by blaming many of France's problems, especially unemployment, urban decay, and crime, on immigrants and their children. At the same time, many children whose parents were immigrants consider themselves fully French yet refuse to conform to dominant cultural norms. They have affirmed their pride in being Algerian and Muslim, demanding cultural autonomy and the right to be different in their dress, food, and religious practice.

French national identity is also jostled by French participation in the EU and, more broadly, by an opening of France's geographic and cultural horizons as a result of globalization. Decisions affecting French citizens are increasingly made outside France—by officials in Brussels, headquarters of the EU, and by corporate executives and bankers in Frankfurt, London, New York, and Tokyo. The French can no longer believe what was always to some extent a myth: that they lived in a self-contained world they refer to (because of France's geographic boundaries) as the hexagon.

At the same time, France participates vigorously in shaping decisions made outside its borders. Along with Britain and Germany, France is one of the "big three" of the EU and a world-class economic competitor. A key issue is how effectively France will confront the challenge of closer integration in the European and world political economy.

Implications for Comparative Politics

The study of French politics offers rich lessons for the study of comparative politics. But before engaging in systematic comparison of France with other countries, we must answer a prior question: given the many distinctive features of

French history, politics, and culture, is comparison legitimate? Scholars have used the term *French exceptionalism* to highlight that French politics is unusual, possibly even unique. They claim that French politics has historically been characterized by an unusual extent of ideological conflict, which in turn has fueled political instability reflected in frequent regime change.

Does the exceptional character of French politics rule out comparison? Quite the contrary! Instead, it further suggests the utility of comparison. For without comparison, we cannot identify and explain what is exceptional about France.

Because France has continually tried to reshape its destiny by conscious political direction, it provides a natural laboratory in which to test the importance of variations in institutional design. To illustrate, comparativists debate the impact of diverse electoral procedures. Since French electoral procedures (along with many other features of political institutions) have often changed in a brief period, comparativists can make fine-grained comparison of the impact of institutional variation. The most recent example of devising electoral procedures to affect political outcomes is a 1999 constitutional amendment to ensure gender parity in political recruitment. Introducing the parity law had an enormous impact: from one election to the next, female representation doubled on municipal and regional councils; and virtually all municipal and regional councils now have nearly equal numbers of men and women.

At a more general level, the French have often looked to the state to achieve important economic and political goals. In countries without a statist tradition (for example, the United States and Britain), private groups are forced to rely on their own efforts. What can we learn from comparing the two approaches? What are the strengths and weaknesses of statism?

France also provides a fascinating case of a country that seeks to combine a strong state and a strong democracy. Combining the two is no easy matter. How successful is the French attempt? What can it teach us about this issue?

As a leading participant in the EU, France provides students of comparative politics with an excellent case of a country seeking to forge close economic and political ties with its neighbors while retaining an important measure of autonomy. The EU is an extraordinary experiment in regional cooperation. But participation involves costs as well as benefits. What kinds of strains have been produced within France as a result of its membership in the EU? How effectively has France been able to shape EU institutions?

A place to begin our analysis of current French politics is with France's political economy, for the way that a country organizes economic governance deeply influences the functioning of its political system.

Notes

1. INSEE, *Tableaux de l'Économie Française, 2003–2004* (Paris: INSEE, 2003), p. 47.

2. Ibid., p. 45.

3. Simon Schama, *Citizens: A Chronicle of the French Revolution* (New York: Knopf, 1989), p. 62.

4. Perry Anderson, *Lineages of the Absolutist State* (London: New Left Books, 1974), p. 111. We also draw here on Theda Skocpol, *States and Social Revolutions: A Comparative Analysis of France, Russia, and China* (New York: Cambridge University Press, 1979).

5. Lynn Hunt, *Politics, Culture, and Class in the French Revolution* (Berkeley and Los Angeles: University of California Press, 1984), pp. 15, 56.

6. Joan B. Landes, *Women and the Public Sphere in the Age of the French Revolution* (Ithaca, N.Y.: Cornell University Press, 1988), pp. 171–172.

7. William H. Sewell Jr., *Work and Revolution in France: The Language of Labor from the Old Regime to 1848* (Cambridge: Cambridge University Press, 1980), p. 199.

8. Georges Dupeux, *La société française, 1789–1970* (Paris: Armand Colin, 1974), p. 10.

9. Richard F. Kuisel, *Capitalism and the State in Modern France* (Cambridge: Cambridge University Press, 1981), p. 15.

10. Ibid., p. 16.

11. Stanley Hoffmann, *Decline or Renewal? France Since the 1930s* (New York: Viking, 1974).

12. Suzanne Daley, "As French Campaign Ends, Many Focus on Next Round," *New York Times*, April 20, 2002.

13. *Le Monde*, April 23, 2002.

14. *Le Monde*, May 8, 2002.

15. *Le Monde*, May 10, 2002.

16. *New York Times*, September 18, 2003.

17. *Le Monde*, May 15, 2004.

18. Laurence Ménière, ed., *Bilan de la France, 1981–1993* (Paris: Hachette, 1993), p. 12.

C H A P T E R

12

Political Economy and Development

France's gross national product (GNP) makes it the world's sixth-largest economy. It has accomplished this feat by a fortunate combination of skill, state management, and favorable historical and geographic circumstances. (France is in the center of one of the world's most prosperous regions.) During the first decades of the postwar period, France relied on an inward-looking strategy to promote economic development. The key to understanding the country's postwar economic success was the vigorous role of the state. However, the state's relation to the economy has shrunk in the past two decades as a result of changing ideological orientations, EU commitments, and participation in the global economy. Accompanying these changes has been a highly successful shift from an inward-looking economic posture to an export orientation that has transformed France into a major global economic actor. France ranks second only to the United States in terms of the amount of capital invested abroad and third in the world as a location for foreign investment. Yet the record is not without important flaws: the benefits of economic success are unequally distributed; not all sectors of the population have benefited from the shift; and new and old fissures linked to economic changes have produced intense political challenges.

During the early period of industrialization in western Europe, from the late eighteenth century through the nineteenth century, the French state pursued a quite distinctive goal compared with the British and German states. Along with the United States, these nations were the world's

leading economic powers in the nineteenth century. In Britain, the world's first industrialized power, the state sought to remove restrictions on the free operation of market forces. In Germany, the state fostered industrialization from above. The French state, by contrast, aimed to "maintain an equilibrium among industry, commerce, and agriculture and attempt[ed] to insulate France from the distress and upheaval that had struck other nations bent upon rapid economic advance."[1] The slow pace of economic modernization did not allay intense class and ideological conflicts within the Third Republic, linked to issues stemming from France's revolutionary past and the country's inability to forge an adequate political regime.

Political conflicts could be contained only so long as the state was able to protect France's economy and the nation from external threat. However, the weaknesses of this typical French pattern of economic defensiveness and political conflict were cruelly highlighted by the Third Republic's failure to meet the Nazi challenge in 1940.

The Postwar Settlement and Beyond

When France was liberated and the Fourth Republic was created in 1946, influential groups active in the Resistance concluded that economic and social modernization were essential to reverse the downward spiral. They agreed that this project required a fundamental transformation in the state's relationship to the economy. "After the war," economic historian Richard Kuisel observes, "what was distinctive about France was the compelling sense of relative economic backwardness. This impulse was the principal stimulus for economic renovation and set France apart from other countries."[2] The modernizers were enormously successful. One study described the postwar shift as "a new French Revolution. Although peaceful, this has been just as profound as that of 1789 because it has totally overhauled the moral foundations and social equilibrium of French society."[3]

The term *postwar settlement* describes the pattern of compromise (settlement) among key social classes and social forces that worked together to promote economic modernization and growth. The postwar settlement was found in countries as diverse as Sweden, Britain, Germany, and France. It was especially noteworthy in France, however, because it involved a dramatic contrast with prewar economic and political patterns.

State and Economy

The new French Revolution ushered in sweeping changes in the economy, society, and values. As a result of its long statist tradition, France was potentially well equipped to develop the institutional capacity to steer the economy—once the state could be reoriented from economic protection to economic expansion. Kuisel describes the new approach as follows:

> France resembled other capitalist countries in developing an arsenal of institutions for managing the economy. . . . Yet France found its own way to perform these tasks. It lodged responsibility in new public institutions and staffed them with modernizers. It relied heavily on state intervention and planning. . . . The result was a Gallic style of economic management that blended state direction, corporatist bodies, and market forces.[1]

From guardian of the established order, the state became the sponsor of social and economic progress. It helped transform France from a relatively stagnant, rural society to a dynamic industrialized participant in the world economy.

French-Style Economic Management

The French developed a variety of techniques to foster economic modernization. The state was the nerve center of the enterprise.

Planning. Soon after World War II, the French developed what they called *indicative planning.* A national Planning Commission of civil servants appointed by the government established broad national economic and social priorities for the next four or five years. The Planning Commission was assisted by modernization commissions, comprising public and private officials, which established targets for specific economic and social sectors. Successive plans determined maximum feasible rates of economic growth, proposed crash programs for the development of specific industries and regions, and identified high-priority social goals such as educational targets. The state then shaped legislative and budgetary priorities to achieve planning goals. Perhaps more important than the specific goals that were pursued was that planning helped transform France's political culture. The process of planning highlighted that change was to be welcomed, a striking contrast to the century-old conservative pattern.[5]

De Gaulle's Leadership. Planning began in the Fourth Republic, but the first steps were halting and uncertain. Vigorous leadership to overcome conservative forces opposing change was provided after 1958, when Charles de Gaulle, the most influential politician in twentieth-century French history, regained power and created the Fifth Republic.

De Gaulle was a complex, controversial, and contradictory figure. On the one hand, he was a faithful representative of traditional France, deeply attached to the values of order and hierarchy, which earned him the enmity of the left. On the other hand, his personal leadership and the Fifth Republic that he helped create provided the energy to undermine traditional forces and restructure the French political economy.

Dirigisme. General de Gaulle's return to power in 1958 continued and deepened the style of state-led industrialization and growth originating in the Fourth Republic. The state bureaucracy expanded the scope of its activity and developed new instruments to promote economic modernization. The state steered cheap credit toward favored sectors and firms; in key industrial sectors it encouraged the creation of large firms, which were dubbed "national champions." The French described the new relationship between the state and economy as *dirigiste* (directorial), in order to highlight the state's importance in steering the economy. (The pattern is also called *dirigisme*.) Many key economic decisions were made in governmental ministries, especially the Ministries of Finance, Economy, and Industry, as well as the planning agency. The state's multifaceted leadership compensated for the relatively weak role played by private entrepreneurs. Among the tools that the state deployed were:

- Offering subsidies, loans, and tax write-offs to achieve industrial concentration, specialization in new fields, and technological innovation. Until the 1970s, the state provided the bulk of capital for new investment, limited the outflow of French capital, created a host of parapublic banking institutions, and controlled private bank loans. The state provided favored sectors with cheap credit—and starved low-priority sectors and inefficient firms to hasten their demise.

- Restructuring key sectors, including steel, machine tools, and paper products, by steering credit and pressuring medium-sized industrial firms to merge in order to create "national champions" able to compete in world markets.

- Creating and managing entire industries. Some state-created and state-managed firms were in the vanguard of technological progress throughout the world. A prime example was nuclear power. The state reduced its dependence on imported petroleum by developing safe and reliable nuclear energy. Three-quarters of France's electricity is produced by nuclear reactors, and France is a world leader in designing, building, operating, and exporting nuclear power installations.

In sum, in the French economic model, the state was a (indeed, *the*) chief economic player.

France's Economic Miracle. During the period a French economist called "the thirty glorious years" (1945–1975), the planners and their allies were remarkably successful. Although other countries in North America and Western Europe grew steadily during this period, as did Japan, France's rate of economic growth was among the highest—a striking contrast to the 1930s, when the French economy declined at the rate of over 1 percent annually. (See Table 12.1.)

Economic growth produced higher living standards. Average yearly income nearly tripled between 1946 and 1962, producing a wholesale transformation of consumer patterns. For example, between 1946 and 1962, the proportion of homes with indoor plumbing more than doubled. The number of automobiles registered in France increased from under 5 million in 1959 to 14 million in 1973. The number of housing units built annually increased from 290,000 to 500,000 during the same period. In sum, after a century of economic stagnation, France leapfrogged into the twentieth century.

Table 12.1   Average Growth Rates in Gross National Product, 1958–1973

Japan	10.4%
France	5.5
Italy	5.3
West Germany	5.0
Belgium	4.9
Netherlands	4.2
Norway	4.2
Sweden	4.1
United States	4.1
United Kingdom	3.2

Source: Bela Belassa, "The French Economy Under the Fifth Republic, 1958–1978," in William G. Andrews and Stanley Hoffmann, eds., *The Fifth Republic at Twenty* (Albany: State University of New York Press, 1981), p. 209.

May 1968 and Beyond: Economic Crisis and Political Conflict. And yet despite the dramatic economic growth of the 1950s and 1960s—or, more likely, because of the way that economic restructuring was carried out— economic change generated political conflict. Political scientist Peter A. Hall identified a central dilemma in the planning process: "The reorganization of production to attain great[er] efficiency tends to intensify the social conflict that planning is also supposed to prevent."[6] The Gaullist regime was superbly equipped to direct change. But it limited consultation and participation in planning change to the higher reaches of the executive and the corporate elite. Trade unions, a broad range of interest groups not based in strategic sectors of the economy, and rank-and-file citizens were kept at a distance.

The result was that, despite the appearance of great stability, the regime was fragile. The most dramatic evidence was a nationwide series of strikes and demonstrations in May 1968 that immobilized the country for several weeks. The opposition movement was triggered by a variety of causes: government-imposed wage restraint, the reduction of trade union representation on the governing boards of the social security (public health) system, and the rapid expansion of higher education. (New universities were hastily constructed to accommodate the postwar baby boom, and students received little guidance.) What united the various groups of participants in the May movement was opposition to a high-handed style of authority in the most diverse spheres, including universities, political institutions, and workplaces.

Students and workers unite in a mass demonstration on the Left Bank of Paris, May 27, 1968.

Source: AP/Wide World.

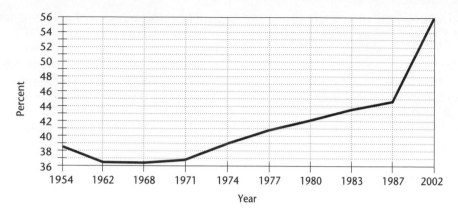

Figure 12.1   Women in the Labor Force

Source: INSEE, in Louis Dirn, *La Société française en tendances* (Paris: PUF, 1990), p. 108; 2002 data from INSEE, *Tableaux de l'Économie Française, 2003–2004* (Paris: INSEE, 2003), p. 77.

Although the May movement was overcome within several weeks, it ushered in a period of intense labor mobilization. Strikes in the early 1970s were frequent and often involved highly militant tactics, such as seizing factories, sequestering managers, and even organizing production directly. Striking workers challenged harsh authority in the workplace, speedups in the pace of work, and technological innovations that increased workplace hazards. A rapid increase in female employment beginning in the early 1970s (see Figure 12.1) also provoked some important strikes when women protested unequal treatment.

Economic Instability. Initially, discontent focused on the way that economic modernization was being orchestrated; this was compounded by a slowdown in economic growth beginning in the mid-1970s. First, the substantial shift of workers out of agriculture and from rural to urban areas began to reach its limit, which resulted in a slowdown in productivity growth. Second, France was badly damaged by international economic shocks in the 1970s, especially steep increases in petroleum prices. The restructuring of international capitalism in the 1970s further challenged French industry. On the one hand, developing nations, such as Taiwan, South Korea, and Brazil, began to outcompete France in such basic industries as textiles, steel, and shipbuilding. Hundreds of thousands of jobs were eliminated in these three industries alone. Entire regions were devastated.

On the other hand, other industrialized nations outstripped France in technological development. France was too small to be a world leader in high-tech growth industries like microelectronics, bioengineering, and robotics, and U.S. and Japanese producers rapidly captured markets in these fields. In brief, at the very time that the country needed to generate increased exports in order to finance petroleum price increases, French firms were losing export markets to some fast-growing Third World nations and importing advanced technology from Germany, Japan, and the United States.

These trends provoked a crisis in the French model of development. The postwar state-centered approach was highly successful in promoting crash programs for industrial reconstruction and modernization. But it was not equipped to adapt rapidly, decentralize economic decision making, and operate in the global econ-

"It's touching to see all these graduates." (ANPE—
Agence National pour l'Emploi—is the state
employment office.)

Source: Courtesy Plantu, Cartoonists & Writers Syndicate,
from *Le Monde.*

omy. The inadequacy of the postwar approach
was driven home by the failure of the Socialist
government in the early 1980s.

French Socialism in Practice—and Conservative Aftermath.   After conservative governments failed to meet the economic challenges of the 1970s, the left finally got the chance to try. A new era began in 1981 when, after twenty-three years in opposition, the left gained power. François Mitterrand defeated incumbent president Valéry Giscard d'Estaing in the 1981 presidential election. Immediately on gaining office, Mitterrand dissolved the conservative-dominated National Assembly (the more powerful of the two houses of parliament) and called for new elections. Capitalizing on Mitterrand's popularity, the Socialist Party and its allies gained control of the National Assembly, enabling the government to sponsor a range of economic measures to revive the ailing economy, create jobs, and recap-

ture domestic markets. The major Socialist reforms included:

- A hefty boost in social benefits, including increases in the minimum wage, family allowances, old-age pensions, rent subsidies, and state-mandated paid vacations.

- The creation of public sector employment.

- Higher priority given to environmental concerns. The Socialist government created a cabinet-level Ministry of the Environment and promised to reconsider France's heavy emphasis on nuclear energy. After declaring a moratorium on building new nuclear plants, it scaled back France's nuclear power program but did not end the construction of new plants.

- A vigorous industrial policy, including state assistance to develop cutting-edge industrial technologies (including biotech, telecommunications, and aerospace).

- The nationalization of many firms in the industrial and financial sectors.

On two previous occasions French governments had extended public control over the economy: in the Socialist government of Léon Blum during the Popular Front of 1936–1938 and, under de Gaulle's first period in power, in 1946, following the end of World War II. Between 1981 and 1983, the Socialist government went further. As a result of the nationalization measures, public sector firms accounted for 28 percent of France's gross domestic production (an increase of 7 percent), 23 percent of French exports (compared with the previous level of 11 percent), and 36 percent of investments (from 29 percent).[7] Thirteen of France's twenty largest industrial firms and virtually all banks were now in the public sector.

The Socialist approach was a radicalized version of the postwar *dirigiste* approach, supplemented by newly created mechanisms for increasing participation by rank-and-file workers and labor unions in economic decision making. Many French citizens reaped significant benefits from the Socialist program, and many of the newly nationalized firms, which were in financial difficulties when they were national-ized, were put on a firmer footing thanks to the infusion of government subsidies. But the pro-gram failed to revive economic growth, which was essential to fuel job creation and to generate revenue for the increased social spending. There were two reasons for the failure. First, business interests in France and abroad bitterly opposed the government's policy orientation on ideolog-ical grounds. Private investment by French and foreign firms declined sharply in the early 1980s. Second, an international economic reces-sion in the early 1980s reduced the demand for French exports at the same time that increased social spending enabled French consumers to buy foreign imports. In brief, foreign firms reaped a handsome share of the benefits from the Socialist reforms.

The Socialist reform agenda helped to mod-ernize the French economy, society, and state in the long run. However, in the short run, it drove France to the brink of bankruptcy. Budget deficits soared, international investors avoided France like the plague, and France's international currency reserves were rapidly exhausted. Something had to give—and fast.

The crisis cruelly demonstrated how limited was the margin of maneuver for a medium-rank power like France. Mitterrand's government was soon forced to choose between reversing its re-formist course or adopting strong protectionist measures to shield France from international competition. Adopting the latter course would have required France to withdraw from Euro-pean Union (EU) monetary arrangements and expose itself to retaliation from conservative governments abroad. After intense soul search-ing, Mitterrand ordered an about-face in economic policy in 1983. The government aban-doned its radical reformist course and set France on a conservative course from which it has not departed since.

France's failure to achieve autonomous state-sponsored development in the early 1980s has had profound ideological and policy conse-quences, both within France and elsewhere. It has often been cited as demonstrating the futil-ity of nationally based radical or democratic so-cialist reforms. Within France, it dealt a body blow to the traditional *dirigiste* pattern.

An indirect effect of the 1983 "right turn" was to propel European integration forward. Concluding that France could not exercise global power on its own, Mitterrand turned to the EU as the next best alternative. As one scholar ob-serves, "It was only in 1983, with the turn-around in the economic policy of the French government, that the French started . . . to be-come more pro-European, and started to see Eu-ropean integration as a way of compensating for the loss of policy autonomy."[8] After initially dis-playing a lukewarm attitude toward European integration, Mitterrand energetically began to promote European economic, monetary, and po-litical integration in the mid-1980s.

France's Neoliberal Modernization Strategy.
Although the state has continued to play an im-portant role in economic governance since 1983, it has scaled back its commanding role and defers to private decision makers on a host of key eco-nomic matters. Among the elements in this "neoliberal modernization strategy" are privati-zation, deregulation and liberalization, and other economic policies that conform to market-friendly EU directives.[9]

Privatization. A central element of the right turn in 1983 consisted of reversing the process of nationalization. After 1983, the Socialist govern-ment halted the process of nationalization. And when the conservative coalition led by Jacques Chirac won the 1986 parliamentary elections, it began the process of privatizing state-owned in-dustrial firms, banks, media, investment houses, and insurance companies. Since then, govern-ments of left and right alike have sponsored the third most extensive privatization program in Western Europe, after Margaret Thatcher's Britain and Germany (which sold off state-owned assets in East Germany following unifi-cation).[10] Although conservative governments were initially behind the initiative, Socialist governments in 1988–1993 and 1997–2002 energetically sold public firms to private investors.

The decision to support privatization was especially wrenching for the Socialists, who had passionately championed nationalization for generations and, as we have seen, sponsored an extensive increase in public sector firms when elected in 1981. However, privatization involved an about-face for conservatives as well. In the Gaullist view, public ownership was one of the tools in the state's arsenal that could be used to maximize French economic power.

The privatization reforms have produced a slimmer and more circumscribed state. This transformation of the state's relation to the economy is a key element in the "normalization" of French politics and the decline of French exceptionalism.

Although privatization may appear to represent a total shift from public to private control, this appearance is somewhat misleading. For example, there is considerable continuity in managerial ranks when firms are privatized. Many of France's largest private firms are directed by executives trained in state-run elite schools. They are steeped in a statist tradition and belong to cohesive elite networks, described in Chapter 13, that span the public-private divide. Another example: state-owned banks own large amounts of shares in private firms, which provide a lever for the state to influence managerial decisions. Indeed, one reason for France's successful performance in the global economy in the past two decades may be that an effective balance has been struck between public and private initiative in the economy.

Privatization has often generated intense opposition from employees of firms slated for privatization, who fear a reduction in wages and fringe benefits, job security, and rights to representation within the firm. Strikes in key sectors like transportation and power supply have caused considerable disruption. Employee concerns have proved quite justified. Indeed, a principal rationale for privatization was the calculation by political leaders that private firms would have a freer hand to sponsor cost-cutting measures.

Privatization has occurred throughout Western Europe (not to mention in formerly communist Eastern and Central Europe). However, within Western Europe, the move is especially noteworthy in France because it marks such a contrast with past practice.

Deregulation and Liberalization. Until the right turn in 1983, state officials defined technical standards for manufactured products, specified market share, set prices, interest rates, and terms of credit, and even determined the type and location of investment. Policymakers erected stiff tariffs to provide space to shield producers from foreign competition. The state regulated labor markets by restricting employers' freedom to schedule work time and lay off workers.

State regulations could provide important benefits. For example, the French public railway network has a superb record for safety and efficiency. State labor inspectors limited arbitrary employer actions. The French concept of public services involved the notion that the state should provide all citizens access to essential services, even if they could not be run at a profit. However, critics claimed that the French economy was being strangled by kilometers of red tape. Especially when economic growth was slow and the ideological pendulum swung against statism, the time was ripe for an assault on government regulation.

A key element in the Socialists' right turn, extended by governments of left and right since then, has been the deregulation of labor, financial, and commodity markets. For example, employers no longer need administrative authorization to lay off workers, and they have greater freedom to schedule work in a flexible manner. Price controls have been largely eliminated.

Deregulation has been especially sweeping in the financial sector. Market forces, not Ministry of Finance officials, now determine who should receive loans, how large they should be, and at what interest rates. Private firms are forced to fend for themselves, both for better—since they are forced to be more efficient—and for worse (since banks provide loans according to strictly economic criteria, which may ignore social needs).

Deregulation has meant that French firms can no longer rely on tariffs, technical standards, and government policies to prevent foreign competition. The result has been dramatic: France is now a world leader as both a destination for foreign investment and a source of investment abroad. In brief, the new policy stance relies heavily on market competition to achieve economic and technological modernization.

Impact of the European Union.   France's participation in the EU has further reduced the state's role in economic management. The adoption of the Single European Act in 1987, the Maastricht Treaty in 1991, and the Growth and Stability Pact in 1997 have tied France ever more tightly to its European neighbors. The Maastricht Treaty commits states to respecting *convergence criteria* that include limiting the state's budget deficit to 3 percent of the gross domestic product (GDP) and public debt to 60 percent of GDP. The EU can order stiff penalties for states that violate these commitments.

Important EU milestones include creation of the Economic and Monetary Union (EMU) in 1991 and the launching of the euro in 1999. The European Central Bank (ECB) was created in 1998 to manage the euro for the eleven member states who agreed to replace their currencies by the euro in 2002. The ECB is empowered to regulate interest rates, the euro's exchange rate, and the money supply of member states. Critics charge that the single-minded pursuit of price stability has come at the expense of other worthy goals, notably, economic growth and job creation. They claim that the tight-money policy pursued by the ECB is responsible for the EU's dismal record in these respects compared to that of the United States, where the Federal Reserve Bank has long maintained much lower interest rates.

Economic integration has also involved political costs. When states like France delegate EU officials the power to regulate the currency, interest rates, and the exchange rate, state officials and citizens lose control over core elements of sovereignty. The "democratic deficit" within the EU refers to the fact that unelected EU administrators make key decisions affecting citizens' lives.

Not surprisingly, the new policy initiatives have encountered stiff popular resistance. French voters came within a hair of rejecting the 1991 referendum on the Maastricht Treaty. Even more dramatic was the reaction in 1995 when the government announced a program of austerity measures designed to qualify France for the launching of the euro. In 1995, conservative prime minister Alain Juppé, at President Chirac's direction, announced cutbacks in state social programs, including retirement benefits for railway workers, civil servants' salaries, and reimbursement for medical costs. Massive strikes by public sector workers threatened the Juppé government's very existence. However, despite marginal differences among the economic policies of different governments since 1983, none has openly challenged the orientation chosen at that time.

The End of* Dirigisme *or* Dirigiste *Disengagement?   If the French have turned toward neoliberalism, they have done so in a distinctively French manner. Political scientist Vivien Schmidt observes that France has not

> abandoned its statist model. . . . The state . . . remains embedded in French culture and embodied in its institutions, with change able to come only through the state, not against it. . . . Governments have not stopped seeking to guide business, albeit in more indirect ways . . . and they as always play a primary role in deciding the direction of economic growth and the shape and organization of economic activity, even as they engineer the retreat of the state.[11]

Schmidt calls the shift in France's political economy "*dirigiste* disengagement." In recent years, the state has supervised the retrenchment of industries like steel and shipbuilding. It has steered the French economy toward integration within the EU and has shifted its efforts toward seeking to influence EU decision making. This is *dirigisme* of a different—and less overbearing—sort, but for better or worse, statism is alive and well in France. Moreover, elements of the old-style *dirigisme* remain. The state bailed out the Alstom engineering firm in 2003, and in 2004 it blocked the sale of a French pharmaceutical firm to a Swiss-based company. Instead, it brokered a merger of two French firms.

Social Policy

In part because of working-class pressure exercised in the streets and through political parties, the French have enacted among the most extensive package of welfare state programs in the world. Cradle-to-grave social services begin before birth, for pregnant women are entitled to free prenatal care, and extend through old age, with pensions and subsidies for home care. A key element of the social security system, as it is known in France, is health insurance, financed mostly by payroll taxes on employers and employees. In return for modest copayments, virtually all French are entitled to free medical care, hospitalization, and pharmaceuticals. French families also have access to low-cost public day care facilities staffed by highly qualified teachers. Families with more than one child receive a monthly subsidy.

Public education is excellent in France, and all students who pass a stiff high school graduation exam are entitled to virtually free university education. An extensive system of public housing and rent subsidies makes housing affordable for most citizens. Workers enjoy a minimum wage far higher than the level prevailing in the United States, six weeks of paid vacation every year, and the right to job training throughout their working lives. There is an extensive system of unemployment insurance and retraining programs for the jobless. The long-term unemployed are eligible to payments under a minimum income program.

The extensive system of social provision promotes solidarity and enables most French citizens to live in dignity. However, the price tag for the welfare state is high. France spent 29.7 percent of its gross domestic product for social welfare programs in 2000. As described below, the rising costs of social programs have generated intense political conflicts and ranked second only to Sweden among EU countries.[12]

The French are fiercely attached to their system of extensive social protection, which an American journalist described "as a global ideological rival" to the American model of social provision.[13] In the United States, social programs are designed to provide a bare minimum for the poorest members of the society, and the word *welfare* is often said with a sneer. The French system reflects the belief that the state should provide generous benefits on a universal basis—that is, to all citizens, not only to the very poor. Richard Kuisel suggests that the two societies have quite different social priorities: "Simply stated, for the French a good society offers equality and social protection and for Americans it provides opportunity and risk."[14] Yet, despite the fact that social programs in France channel significant resources toward those with low and moderate incomes, economic inequalities are severe and are increasing. In 1975, the wealthiest 10 percent of French households owned 40 percent of all assets; twenty years later, the wealthiest tenth owned 50 percent.[15] In the past decade, the figure further increased to 54 percent. For thirty years, French unemployment rates have ranked among the highest of advanced industrial countries. The present level of about 9 percent is lower than during the bleakest period (the 1990s) but it constitutes an unacceptably high level of social distress.

The Socialist government of Lionel Jospin (1995–2002) sought to reduce unemployment by work sharing. The goal was to encourage employers to take on more workers by reducing the number of hours employees worked each week.

Business interests bitterly opposed the reform, but in fact it provided employers with a significant benefit by authorizing them to flexibly schedule work in response to market demand for a firm's products and services. As a result, the reform has proved highly popular with both employers and employees. When a conservative government was elected in 2002, it sponsored minor changes in the arrangement but did not alter its basic outlines.

Despite France's prosperous economy and ample welfare state, many citizens are excluded from full participation in French society. The French have coined the term the social fracture to describe the existence of an excluded group of citizens—including those with temporary or part-time jobs, the long-term unemployed, the poor, and the homeless. The number of homeless in France has been estimated at between 200,000 and 500,000, and soup kitchens organized by nonprofit organizations serve 500,000 meals daily to the poor.[16] Nearly 2 million citizens receive grants under the minimum income program for the impoverished and long-term unemployed.

A key issue in French politics these days involves how to pay for the rising costs of the welfare state. On the one hand, the "Sécu" (shorthand for the social security system of health, unemployment, and retirement benefits) enjoys widespread popularity. Prior to 1995, not even conservative governments dared attack it frontally. However, tax revenues to finance social programs are being outstripped by rising costs resulting from soaring medical costs, high levels of unemployment, a slowdown in birthrates (which means fewer active workers to finance welfare benefits), and a demographic imbalance between retired and younger, employed workers. Nor will these structural problems ease with time. For example, the proportion of elderly within the total population is predicted to double by 2050. Currently, for every retired worker there are 3.0 French adults who work; in 2050, the ratio will drop to 1.5 employed workers for every retired worker. Since employed workers

mostly pay the taxes that finance pensions for the elderly, strains on social programs are bound to increase.

Although the specter of unemployment haunts large sectors of the society, certain groups—notably, youth, immigrants, and women—are far more likely to be jobless. For example, in 2002, unemployment among immigrants of North African background was more than triple the average for native-born French. The most unfortunate are those caught in a double bind. Young Algerians (under twenty-four years old) are the holders of this distressing record: a whopping 56 percent were unemployed in 2002.[17]

High levels of unemployment increase financial stress on the welfare state for two reasons. First, fewer employed workers mean less revenue from payroll taxes to support social programs. Second, more unemployed workers increase the size of unemployment insurance payments. Since the 1980s, France has experienced double-digit unemployment rates, among the highest of the industrialized nations. To illustrate the magnitude of the burden: when unemployment was low in 1973, unemployment expenditures amounted to less than 1 percent of French GDP. By contrast, the proportion of GDP devoted to unemployment expenditures is now four times higher.[18]

For years, voters have consistently ranked unemployment among the most pressing problems in France. The failure of successive governments to eliminate unemployment has contributed to the frequent electoral gyrations of the recent period. At the same time, there are severe pressures to contain the costs of social programs, stemming from the EU requirement to limit public deficits and debt, citizen opposition to tax increases, and the need to reduce production costs to meet international economic competition. As a result, there have been endless attempts to raise payroll taxes and trim benefits. Another impulse for reforms has been to reshape welfare from a tool for countering market dysfunctions and increasing social equity to a tool for using incentives and sanctions to promote the employment of the unemployed. These reforms have been highly unpopular. For example, in 1995, Prime Minister Alain Juppé's proposal to cut social spending provoked nationwide strikes and demonstrations that immobilized France and helped topple the conservative coalition in 1997. (The strikes are described in Chapter 15.)

A similar pattern occurred following Jacques Chirac's reelection in 2002. When Chirac's political ally Prime Minister Jean-Pierre Raffarin initiated an increase in the retirement age for public sector workers in 2003, over 1 million people turned out to protest, most air and rail travel services were cancelled, and many schools, hospitals, government offices, and the media were shut down. Although the reform was enacted, the rout of conservative parties in the 2004 regional elections was a vivid reminder of the intense opposition to trimming social benefits. Following the electoral defeat of the Union for a Popular Majority (UMP) in 2004, Chirac and Raffarin promised to heed public opinion in the future. Yet the government soon proposed further retrenchment, which in turn provoked new demonstrations.

Society and Economy

French economic performance has traditionally been hindered by stormy relations between management and labor. Typically, workers have gained benefits by protest at work and in the streets rather than by cooperating with their employers to seek mutually profitable solutions, the typical pattern in Germany. French labor unions have long had a beleaguered existence. For example, they obtained the legal right to organize plant-level locals only as a result of the May 1968 uprising. And employers were not required to bargain collectively with unions over wages and hours until reforms sponsored by the Socialist government in 1982. Because the labor movement has traditionally been quite weak, it has been especially vulnerable during the recent period of economic crisis and restructuring. The French labor movement has suffered severe declines in membership, and less than 10 percent of the wage-earning population currently belongs to a labor union.

Inequality and Ethnic Minorities

France long prided itself on its ability to integrate ethnic minorities. Yet France's vaunted openness was partially misleading, for there has also been a long tradition in France of suspicion (or worse) toward the foreign-born. (This issue is discussed in Chapter 14.) Immigrants face significantly greater hardships in the labor market. In 2002, a government study reported extensive racial discrimination and the existence of a glass ceiling that limits social mobility among immigrants and first-generation French citizens.[19]

Inequality and Women

The place of women in French society is fairly secure, but far from equal. On the one hand, France has been at the forefront of providing social services, such as day care facilities, that enable women to work outside the home. Mothers are entitled to six months' paid maternity leave, and in 2002 fathers became entitled to two weeks of paid paternity leave. French families have access to low-cost day care facilities staffed by highly qualified teachers. Families with more than one child receive a state subsidy, and the government headed by Jean-Pierre Raffarin sponsored legislation in 2003 to provide all mothers of young children with subsidies.

Policies that provide assistance to working mothers have facilitated an enormous increase in female employment rates in recent decades. The proportion of women aged twenty-five to forty-nine in the paid labor force soared from 49 percent in 1970 to 82 percent in 2003.[20]

However, women are far from achieving economic and social equality in France. Although laws mandate gender equality in the workplace and outlaw sexual harassment, France ranks at the bottom (along with Japan) among industrialized countries in terms of the proportion of female managers and administrators. The gender wage gap in France—that is, the gender wage disparity for comparable work—is 20 percent.[21]

The Generation Gap

An unanticipated result of France's extensive welfare state arrangements is to create a sharp generation gap. While social programs provide fairly generous assistance to the elderly, young people are treated far less well. Young workers are more than twice as likely to be unemployed as the national average. One reason is that the protections enjoyed by stably employed workers limit job creation. Thus, young people disproportionately absorb the costs of a generous welfare state.

Recent government measures to deregulate labor markets have proved a mixed blessing for the young. Although flexibility in scheduling work encourages new hiring and is especially helpful for those seeking their first job, two-thirds of newly hired workers in France are hired on a temporary or part-time basis, and these jobs enjoy significantly fewer benefits. Thus, there is a pronounced tendency in France toward a two-tier or dual labor market.[22]

The Dilemmas of European Integration

A government-commissioned study of France's long-term prospects observes, "[EU] legislation has assumed an increasingly important place in French economic and social life."[23] In such varied domains as the structure of business organizations, labor relations, the regulation of food and medicines, and even cultural life, the EU provides a regulatory framework. The attractive economic opportunities offered by EU membership have produced a change in France's economic orientation. Whereas the bulk of its international trade and investment in the post-war period were with its former colonies in Asia and Africa, over 60 percent of French imports and exports are currently with other member states of the EU.

Yet one should not consider the EU as simply external to France. After all, the Franco-German tandem has provided the leadership largely shaping the pace and character of European integration. Furthermore, the EU has provided France with immense benefits and opportunities. If the EU had not been created after World War II, Western Europe might have dissolved into violent strife, as occurred two decades after World War I. On the economic level, the EU has enabled Europe to aspire to the status of world-class economy. EU membership has contributed to French economic growth and has provided important financial assistance to particular sectors of the French economy. For example, since the creation of the EU, French farmers have received the largest EU agricultural subsidies of any single group in the EU. (However, reforms underway will severely reduce this benefit in coming years.)

France has also sought to transpose its *dirigiste* approach to the EU level. In 2004, France and Germany proposed that EU member states collaborate on producing European-wide industrial champions, modeled on the postwar national champions created by France that were described earlier in this chapter.

Yet the EU provides challenges and dilemmas as well as opportunities. The EU's emphasis on deregulation has harmed vulnerable economic groups and challenged the state-led pattern by which France achieved economic success and cultural distinctiveness. The style of economic governance in the EU is closer to that in Britain or Germany than France. EU regulations prohibit states from engaging in the kind of *dirigisme* that was the hallmark of the French state in the postwar period—although the French-German proposal to create European champions suggests that France hopes to resuscitate *dirigisme* on an EU level. As a result, France is forced to make greater adjustments in its style of economic management than is the case for other member countries of the EU.

The weight of the EU is evident in virtually every policy area imaginable. For example, following his reelection as president in 2002, Jacques Chirac announced plans to cut income taxes by 5 percent. The EU Commission promptly warned that doing so might violate the government's agreement to reduce budget deficits and balance the budget by 2004. After first blustering at the EU's warning, the government announced that it would respect its treaty obligations, although budget deficits in 2002 exceeded the convergence criteria, caused tense negotiations between French and EU officials, and provoked an EU reprimand in 2003. (Budget deficits and the public debt further increased, however, in 2003, when France again violated its treaty obligations.)

Another example: In late 2002, when French truckers mounted a strike for higher wages, they set up roadblocks throughout France. Since some of Europe's central transportation routes linking southern and northern Europe pass through France, the move threatened to bring commerce throughout Europe to a halt. The EU warned the French government that if this were to occur, it would violate EU treaty commitments not to impede the free flow of goods and France would be subject to stiff fines.

These examples demonstrate that, along with Paris, Brussels—the seat of the EU—can now be considered a site of decision making for French politics. The fates of France and the EU have become intertwined in ways that were inconceivable before the 1990s.

France in the Era of Globalization

France is highly integrated in the global economy. Imports and exports account for fully half of its GDP. Foreign investors, especially American pension funds, own nearly half of all shares traded on the French stock exchange. About one-third of all French workers are employed in firms that are at least in part foreign owned. France ranks among the top three countries of the world both as an exporter of capital and as a location for foreign investment. Some of the world's largest banks and transnational corporations are based in France. An example close to home is that Houghton Mifflin, publisher of *European Politics in Transition*, was owned for several years by the French media giant Vivendi Universal. (Vivendi sold Houghton Mifflin in 2002.) Contrary to the stereotype of France as a bucolic, rural economy, only about 5 percent of the population is employed in agriculture. France is a highly industrialized economy which can boast a large number of world-class industrial, banking, and high-tech firms. In *Forbes* magazine's 2003 list of the world's four hundred best-performing companies, the number of French companies was second only to the United States. French firms must be doing something right to be so successful in international competition.[24]

At the same time, French participation in the global economy, as well as the governance of the French economy more generally, has caused intense strains in domestic politics. The ways that economic factors are refracted in internal politics depends heavily on the shape of political institutions and partisan coalitions. We analyze these issues in the next two chapters.

Notes

1. Richard F. Kuisel, *Capitalism and the State in Modern France* (Cambridge: Cambridge University Press, 1981), p. 15.

2. Ibid., p. 277.

3. Henri Mendras with Alistair Cole, *Social Change in Modern France: Towards a Cultural Anthropology of the Fifth Republic* (Cambridge: Cambridge University Press, 1991), p. 1.

4. Kuisel, *Capitalism,* p. 248.

5. See Peter A. Hall, *Governing the Economy: The Politics of State Intervention in Britain and France* (New York: Oxford University Press, 1986).

6. Ibid., p. 163.

7. Laurent Ménière, *Bilan de la France, 1981–1993* (Paris: Hachette, 1993), p. 18.

8. Amy Verdun, *European Responses to Globalization and Financial Market Integration: Perceptions of Economic and Monetary Union in Britain, France and Germany* (New York: St. Martin's Press, 2000), p. 177.

9. Peter A. Hall described the economic policy followed by successive French governments since the mid-1980s as "neo-liberal modernization strategy." Hall, "From One Modernization Strategy to Another: The Character and Consequences of Recent Economic Policy in France" (paper presented to the Tenth International Conference of Europeanists, Chicago, March 15, 1996).

10. Jack Hayward and Vincent Wright, *Governing from the Centre: Core Executive Coordination in France* (New York: Oxford University Press, 2002), p. 196.

11. Vivien A. Schmidt, *From State to Market? The Transformation of French Business and Government* (Cambridge: Cambridge University Press, 1996), p. 442.

12. INSEE, *Tableaux de l'Économie Française, 2003–2004* (Paris: INSEE, 2003), p. 103. Also see Mark Kesselman, "The Triple Exceptionalism of the French Welfare State," in Gertrude Schaffner Goldberg and Marguerite Rosenthal, eds., *Diminishing Welfare: A Cross-National Study of Social Provision* (New York: Greenwood Press, 2001): 181–210.

13. Roger Cohen, "Paris and Washington Speak Softly," *International Herald Tribune,* October 20, 1997.

14. Richard Kuisel, "What Do the French Think of Us? The Deteriorating Image of the United States, 2000–2004," *French Politics, Culture, and Society* 22, no. 3 (Fall 2004).

15. Commissariat général du plan, *Rapport sur les perspectives de la France* (Paris: La Documentation Française, 2000), p. 30.

16. See *Le Monde,* October 22–23, 1995, and Assayers-CGT, *Rapport sur la situation économique et sociale, 1994–95* (Montreuil: VO Éditions, 1995), p. 9.

17. INSEE, *Tableaux de l'Économie Française, 2003–2004,* p. 87.

18. Ibid., p. 81.

19. *Le Monde,* June 4, 2002.

20. Commissariat général du plan, *Rapport sur les perspectives de la France,* p. 54. The age group for 2002 includes women aged 30–49 and is provided in INSEE, *Tableaux de l'Économie Française, 2003–2004,* p. 77.

21. *Rapport sur les perspectives de la France,* p. 17.

22. Ibid., p. 64.

23. Ibid., p. 45.

24. Sophie Meunier, "Free-Falling France or Free-Trading France?" *French Politics, Culture and Society* 22, no. 1 (Spring 2004): 98–107.

C H A P T E R

13

Governance and Policymaking

Despite frequent changes of regimes in the past two centuries, three guiding principles of the French state have remained nearly constant—until recently. That all three have changed in the recent period suggests a bedrock transformation in the character of the French state. First, for centuries, there was nearly universal agreement on the value of a unitary state. (Article 2 of the French constitution specifies, "France is a Republic, *indivisible*, secular, democratic and social.") Since the French Revolution, subnational governments have been regarded as an administrative arm of the state based in Paris; their primary purpose was to help implement national policy. Although there remains a strong consensus on preserving the unitary character of the state, a trend toward decentralizing power to subnational governments began in the 1980s, when the Socialist government transferred substantial powers to local, departmental, and regional governments. The conservative government of Jean-Pierre Raffarin went even further in 2003, when it sponsored additional transfers of power and a constitutional amendment that affirms the principle of decentralization.

Second, there has been a shift regarding the state's relation to French society. In the nineteenth century, observers as different as Alexis de Tocqueville and Karl Marx analyzed how the highly organized state force was an efficient, cohesive agency that was so overbearing that it discouraged French citizens from regulating their own affairs. This view contained a good deal of truth although it ignored countertendencies within the Jacobin state. But, as we saw in Chapter 12, the balance has shifted considerably: while the state continues to have an exceptionally central role, it now consults and persuades—and commands less than in the past.

The third change involves limits on state action from within the state itself. Until recently, the French accorded relatively little importance to the principle of constitutional supremacy. It may be surprising to learn that a nation that emphasizes the importance of formalized legal codes and that, along with the United States, boasts the modern world's first written constitution did not consider that the country's constitution should be scrupulously respected. The French conception of democracy held that the legislature, chosen by democratic elections, should have a free hand to govern and should not be hindered by constitutional or judicial restraint. Similarly, the executive rarely had to fear being restrained by the judiciary. Judges in France have traditionally enjoyed little autonomy and, indeed, have been considered part of the executive branch. This too has changed in the recent past. The constitution of the Fifth Republic is now regarded as the authoritative source for allocating power among political institutions; and the Constitutional Council has gained the vital power to strike down legislation and sanction executive actions that it judges to be in violation of the constitution.

In brief, along with important elements of continuity within the Fifth Republic, recent changes require us to analyze the political institutions of the regime with a fresh eye.

Organization of the State

The Fifth Republic is usually described as a semipresidential system, combining elements of presidential and parliamentary systems. In a presidential system, such as in the United States, the executive and the legislature are chosen separately and are not answerable to each other. The two branches have independent powers, and neither branch selects the other, is directly accountable to it, or controls its agenda. Moreover, both institutions have fixed terms in office, and neither one can force the other to resign and face new elections. The one exception to this generalization in a presidential system is that the legislature can impeach and force the president to resign when it deems that he or she has committed treason or other grave misdeeds. There is a similar impeachment procedure in the French Fifth Republic, although it has never been used: the requirement is that an absolute majority of both houses of parliament must vote articles of impeachment. The president's case is then judged by a High Court of Justice comprising twelve deputies and twelve senators elected from and by the two houses.

In a parliamentary system, as in Britain, the executive and legislature are fused. The government is accountable to parliament and must resign if parliament passes a motion of no confidence. At the same time, the government has substantial control over the parliamentary agenda and can dissolve parliament, thereby provoking new elections.

In the Fifth Republic, both the president and parliament are popularly elected. However, the French system differs from both presidential and parliamentary systems in that the French system provides for a dual executive: the president appoints a prime minister and government. As in parliamentary systems, the parliament can force the government (but, recall, not the president) to

resign by voting a motion of no confidence—what the French call a *motion of censure.*

Why is the Fifth Republic a semipresidential system? The *semi* refers to the fact that in two key respects—notably, the existence of a government responsible to parliament, and the government's ability to dissolve parliament and call new elections—the legislature and executive are not wholly separate, as they are in a pure presidential system. The system is called semipresidential, not semiparliamentary, because the executive dominates parliament, not the other way around. Whenever the Fifth Republic deviates from the purely parliamentary or the purely presidential model, the result is to strengthen the executive. The fusion of executive and legislative powers characteristic of parliamentary regimes strengthens the executive, for it enables the executive to control the parliamentary agenda and dissolve parliament. The executive is further strengthened by the fact that in contrast to parliamentary regimes, the French parliament cannot vote a motion of no confidence in the president. Although the National Assembly (the more powerful house of parliament) can vote a censure motion of the government, thus forcing it to resign, the president—the key office within the dual executive—is not answerable to parliament. On this fundamental matter, political institutions in the Fifth Republic reflect a separation of powers found in presidential systems. In brief, there is a particularly sharp imbalance between the French executive and legislature compared with the situation prevailing in both the classic parliamentary and presidential regimes.

Although there are many critics who judge that the executive is unduly powerful, the Fifth Republic is one of the most stable regimes in French history. For example, one poll found that 61 percent of the French judge that political institutions performed well in the Fifth Republic.[1] For the first time in modern French history, political conflicts are now played out within a widely accepted institutional framework. At the same time, there has been widespread criticism that, given the fact that the president enjoys extensive power, the seven-year presidential term did not ensure sufficient accountability. This was one reason for a constitutional amendment enacted in 2000 that shortened the president's term from seven to five years. Nonetheless, debate continues about the desirability of additional institutional reforms to democratize the regime.

Since the early 1980s, the Fifth Republic has survived two important political challenges: first, a shift in political control (alternation) between opposing political coalitions; second, the situation of divided institutional control, when the president leads one political coalition and parliament is controlled by a rival coalition—*cohabitation,* as it is called by the French, or power sharing. The first partisan alternation in the history of the Fifth Republic occurred in 1981, when the conservative coalition that ruled since the beginning of the Fifth Republic was defeated by the Socialists. Contrary to widespread predictions that the shock would destabilize the regime, the institutions of the Fifth Republic proved quite adequate to the challenge. Since then, alternation has become a normal feature of French political life.

For many years, the French judged that if opposing forces were to gain control of the executive and legislature—that is, if cohabitation were to occur—political stalemate (or worse) would result. The unthinkable finally did occur in 1986—nearly thirty years after the birth of the Fifth Republic. Following the honeymoon after François Mitterrand's election in 1981, voters became disaffected when economic difficulties developed in the mid-1980s. When parliamentary elections produced a conservative majority in the National Assembly in 1986, Mitterrand bowed to political realities and appointed Jacques Chirac, leader of the conservative coalition opposed to Mitterrand, to be prime minister. Despite many dire predictions, the event proved to be the mouse that roared. The two seasoned politicians quickly devised workable solutions to governing together, and despite a few tremors, the regime held firm.

The first period of cohabitation ended in 1988. When Mitterrand was reelected president

that year, he immediately dissolved the National Assembly and persuaded voters to elect a Socialist plurality. The second period of cohabitation began in 1993, when Mitterrand's second term had two years to run and conservatives won legislative elections. This time, however, there were no dire predictions: the informal rules of the game established the first time around were firmly in place.

Even less uncertainty occurred during the third period of cohabitation, 1997–2002. When the Socialists and their allies won the 1997 parliamentary elections, Jacques Chirac, who had been elected president in 1995, swallowed his disappointment and appointed Socialist leader Lionel Jospin as prime minister. By now, the leading political actors had fully memorized their lines, and the play proceeded quite smoothly through the five years of cohabitation, although the longer duration of cohabitation this time caused increasing discontent and provoked a constitutional change to reduce the possibility of a repeat performance. Cohabitation ended in 2002 when conservatives swept both the presidential and parliamentary elections. By shortening the presidential term to five years, the same length as that of the National Assembly, and holding elections for the two branches within a short time of each other, the chances of cohabitation recurring have been greatly reduced.

Three reasons might be suggested for why political institutions have been able to overcome the challenges of alternation and cohabitation. First, the ideological distance between the left and the right had declined *prior* to these challenges. The gap diminished even more after the Socialist government moderated its policies in the right turn of 1983. Second, the Constitutional Council (a court whose powers are described subsequently) has helped maintain a balance (equilibrium) among institutions. Finally, public opinion polls suggested that most French citizens want political institutions (and both alternation and cohabitation) to function without regime instability or change. These developments signify a profound change in French political culture, involving a diminution of ideological intensity and the development of a more pragmatic political style.

The Executive

France was the first major country to adopt a semipresidential system, although since then other countries have scrutinized the semipresidential system to evaluate its utility. After the fall of communism, Russia was inspired by the French example and adopted this constitutional design in the early 1990s.

In parliamentary regimes, the head of state—either a president or a monarch—exercises purely ceremonial duties, while the bulk of executive power is wielded by the prime minister and cabinet (they're known as the government). In France, the president is designated as the head of state but also often enjoys extensive policymaking and executive power.

How much policymaking power the president actually possesses depends in large measure on the political situation. When the president and prime minister are political allies and lead the same governing coalition, presidential preeminence is assured because the prime minister defers to the president's leadership. However, the situation changes dramatically when the National Assembly (the more powerful lower house of parliament) is controlled by a majority hostile to the president. Although at these times the president names the prime minister and other members of the government, the National Assembly can force the government to resign by voting a motion of no confidence. As a result, the president is forced to accept the harsh political reality that the National Assembly would overturn a government comprised of the president's political supporters. At these times, the president swallows hard and names the leader of the opposing coalition to head the government, and power is divided between the two. In this situation—cohabitation—the prime minister and government, not the president, control many major policy decisions. It thus makes a vital difference whether the president can count on the support of a parliamentary majority. As both Mitterrand's and Chirac's presidencies demonstrate, the outcome of legislative elections can make a decisive difference for the president's position. Mitterrand and Chirac shifted from exercising enormous power (when commanding a parliamentary majority, which enabled them to name a political ally as prime minister) to playing a quite subordinate role (when a parliamentary majority was elected hostile to the president, which resulted in the appointment of a prime minister who was a political opponent of the president).

During the third period of cohabitation (1997–2002), dissatisfaction with divided government was so great that a constitutional reform was adopted in 2000 that reduced the president's term from seven to five years. By making the term of the president and members of the National Assembly the same length, and holding elections for the two institutions at about the same time, the reform was designed to minimize the likelihood of cohabitation. In 2002, the first elections were held under the new system. Jacques Chirac was resoundingly reelected president, and his conservative supporters won a large majority in the National Assembly. Barring unforeseen developments, therefore, unified control of the executive and legislature will persist until at least 2007.

As is described below, an unusual situation, also described by commentators as cohabitation (but of a quite different kind), occurred as a result of the left's resounding victory in regional and European elections in 2004. Although conservative forces elected in 2002 remained firmly in control of the presidency and parliament, the right's defeat in regional elections significantly weakened President Chirac and his supporters.

To describe France as having a dual executive, as many do, obscures the power of the bureaucracy, a third key element of the executive. The bureaucracy is a large and sprawling organization that reaches far and wide to regulate French society. The three pillars of the executive provide the motor force of the French state.

The President

When both the executive and the legislature are controlled by the same party coalition—what we will term *united control*—the powers of the French president are immense. (We analyze below the very different situation during cohabitation—what we will term *divided control*.) At these times, the president combines the powers of the U.S. president—notably, command of the executive branch and independence from the legislature—with the powers that accrue to the government in a parliamentary regime—namely, control over parliament's agenda and the ability to dissolve parliament. The result is that the president's power exceeds that of the chief executive in virtually any other democratic nation.

The president occupies the office at the very top of the French state. The presidency has become such a powerful position because of (1) the towering personalities of Charles de Gaulle, the founder and first president of the Fifth Republic, and François Mitterrand, the Socialist president from 1981 to 1995; (2) the ample powers conferred on the office by the constitution; and (3) political practices of the Fifth Republic.

Presidential Personalities. Charles de Gaulle (1890–1970) was unquestionably the most influential politician in modern French history. He first achieved prominence in leading the Resistance forces in France during World War II. After he contributed to toppling the Fourth Republic in 1958, he designed the Fifth Republic to facilitate strong leadership. As first president in the Fifth Republic, de Gaulle established a precedent that presidents should be regarded as at the same time both above the partisan political fray and yet authorized to shape the state and nation's broad orientation.

The two presidents who succeeded de Gaulle, Georges Pompidou and Valéry Giscard d'Estaing (both were de Gaulle's political allies), were pale shadows of the Fifth Republic's founding president. The next president to expand presidential powers was François Mitterrand. Mitterrand was a youthful leader in the Resistance during World War II and an ally of de Gaulle, but personal ambition soon divided the two. When de Gaulle returned to power in 1958, Mitterrand joined many on the left in opposing the Fifth Republic as undemocratic and criticizing de Gaulle for creating a presidential office that would allow him to exercise power in an authoritarian manner. In the 1960s and 1970s, Mitterrand helped organize a coalition of leftist forces opposing de Gaulle, de Gaulle's policies, and the constitution of the Fifth Republic. During this period, Mitterrand twice ran for president, losing both times. However, he succeeded in remaking the Socialist Party into a major alternative to the Gaullist coalition and in 1981, on his third presidential bid, defeated the incumbent president, Giscard d'Estaing, who was running for reelection. Thus began Mitterrand's fourteen-year reign, the longest presidential term in the history of the Fifth Republic.

The supreme irony is that, as president, Mitterrand ruled in a manner strikingly similar to that of his archrival, de Gaulle. Many of the criticisms he had leveled at de Gaulle were applied to Mitterrand as well: he was solitary, capricious, and monarchical in his governing style. As he humorously remarked soon after taking office, "The institutions of the Fifth Republic weren't created with me in mind, but they suit me fine!" Under Mitterrand, the left became fully integrated within the institutions of the Fifth Republic. Mitterrand was largely responsible for the Socialist government's initial attempt to pursue a radical reform agenda, as well as for its right turn in 1983. He worked closely with German chancellor Helmut Kohl to promote European economic integration and monetary union. Political scientist Ronald Tiersky concludes that Mitterrand's most important contribution involved political institutions and legitimacy. "His legacy is to have restored an alternation of parties in power [and] to have made a success of partisan cohabitation. . . . In a word, his long presidency, for all its defects, created a widespread sense of legitimacy of French institutions."[2]

Mitterrand retired when his second term ended in 1995. The winning candidate in the presidential election that year was Jacques Chirac, who was reelected in 2002 and whose second term will expire in 2007. During much of his first term, Chirac was forced to share power with Socialist prime minister Lionel Jospin, who led the Socialist coalition that dominated the National Assembly. Although Chirac led the conservative coalition that won the 2002 legislative elections, and his coalition thus controls both the presidency and parliament, he has not thus far set his mark on the presidency by proposing important policy initiatives.

This review of presidential personalities suggests that the precedent for exercising powerful leadership exists, but that presidents must bring to the office their own personal vision. If they do so, and the political situation is favorable, they enjoy considerable constitutional powers to exercise strong leadership.

The Constitutional Presidency.

The constitution of the Fifth Republic endows the president with the ceremonial powers of head of state, the role occupied by the president in previous regimes. He resides in the resplendent Élysée Palace in a fashionable section of Paris, he is the symbolic embodiment of the majestic French state, and he represents France at international diplomatic gatherings.

The constitution also grants the president important powers that belonged to the prime minister in past republics, and adds new powers as well. Thus, the president both symbolizes the unity and majesty of the state and actively shapes broad policies.

A good place to start when reviewing the president's constitutional authority is with the method of selecting presidents. He (there has never yet been a female president in the Fifth Republic) is the only political official directly chosen by the entire French electorate. This provides an enormously important source of personal support. In order to be eligible to run, one must be a French citizen at least twenty-three

years old. Presidents are eligible for reelection without limit. The office of vice president does not exist in France; if a president dies in office, the president of the Senate (the upper house of parliament) acts as interim president, and a new election is held within a short time.

A two-ballot system of election is used for presidential elections. To win on the first ballot, a candidate must obtain an absolute majority, that is, over 50 percent of those voting. If no candidate receives a first-ballot majority, the case in every presidential election to date, a runoff election is held two weeks later between the two front-runners.

In order to be a candidate for president, five hundred local elected officials must sign a nominating petition. Because France has about forty thousand local elected officials, it is relatively simple to round up enough signatures; thus, many candidates typically compete in each presidential election. The record was 2002, when the field contained sixteen candidates! Although only candidates nominated by major political parties stand a realistic chance of winning, minor-party candidates can have an important influence on which candidates make it to the runoff ballot. The most dramatic example occurred in 2002, when Lionel Jospin, the major center-left candidate, failed to make the runoff because he came in third, behind Chirac and far-right candidate Jean-Marie Le Pen. A large number of leftist candidates that year drained enough support from Jospin to knock him out of the runoff.

During the first four decades of the Fifth Republic, the president was elected for a term of seven years. Given the enormous powers of the presidency, critics charged that it was undemocratic to elect someone to such a powerful office for seven years without adequate mechanisms of accountability. After many unsuccessful attempts to shorten the president's term, President Chirac and Prime Minister Jospin agreed in 2000 to sponsor a reform reducing the president's term to five years. The reform went into effect for the 2002 presidential elections.

Table 13.1   Presidents of the Fifth Republic

President	Term
Charles de Gaulle	1958–1969
Georges Pompidou	1969–1974
Valéry Giscard d'Estaing	1974–1981
François Mitterrand	1981–1995
Jacques Chirac	1995–present

The reform has promoted greater balance among France's political institutions. Furthermore, it considerably reduces the likelihood of cohabitation in future years, since henceforth both the president and members of the National Assembly will be elected for five years, generally within a few weeks of each other. (Table 13.1 lists the Fifth Republic's presidents and their terms of office.)

The constitution grants the president the following political powers:

- The president names the prime minister, approves the prime minister's choice of other cabinet officials, and names other high-ranking civil, military, and judicial officials.

- The president presides over meetings of the Council of Ministers (the government). Note that the constitution charges the president, not the prime minister, with this responsibility.

- The president conducts foreign affairs, through the power to negotiate and ratify treaties, as well as to name French ambassadors and accredit foreign ambassadors to France.

- The president directs the armed forces, bolstered by a 1964 decree that grants the president exclusive control over France's nuclear forces.

- The president may dissolve the National Assembly and call for new elections. If the president dissolves the National Assembly, he or she cannot do so again for a year.

- The president appoints three of the nine members of the Constitutional Council, including its president, and can refer bills passed by parliament to the council to determine if they conform to the constitution.

Four other constitutional grants of power strengthen the president's position. Article 16 authorizes the president to assume emergency powers when, in his or her judgment, the institutions of the republic, the independence of the nation, the integrity of its territory, or the execution of France's international (treaty) commitments are threatened. This power has been invoked only once, when President de Gaulle assumed emergency power to overcome an attempted military coup in 1961 that was provoked by his decision to grant Algeria independence. It is unthinkable that a future president would rely on Article 16 in any but the gravest of crises. Nonetheless, its existence provides the president with nearly unlimited potential power if such a grave situation were to occur.

Article 89 authorizes the president, with the approval of the prime minister, to propose constitutional amendments. Each chamber of parliament must approve the amendment, following which it must be ratified either by a national referendum or by a three-fifths vote of both houses of parliament meeting together as a congress.

The amendment procedure has been used with increasing frequency in recent years. Indeed, critics charge that adding so many amendments cheapens the constitution. Ten of the fifteen amendments to the constitution have been added since the 1990s. The most recent amendment was passed by both houses of parliament in 2004 (although it has not yet been ratified). It enshrines the principle of environmental protection, described in the Charter for the Environment, in the preamble of the constitution. It is thus equivalent in constitutional law to the 1789 Declaration of the Rights of Man and the Citizen, also an integral part of the constitution.

Article 11, amended in 1995, authorizes the president to organize a national referendum to approve important policy initiatives or reorganize political institutions, provided that the proposed change is first approved by the government. (This procedure is distinct from the process of amending the constitution—which, as we have seen, may also involve calling a referendum.)

Procedures like the direct election of the president, and the president's ability to call referenda, represent a sharp break with the traditions and practice of parliamentary dominance in the Third and Fourth Republics. The precedent of the two Napoleons led many to fear that popular leaders who had direct links to the people would be tempted to assume dictatorial powers. Consequently, the constitutions of the Third and Fourth Republics sharply limited presidential power, including the president's ability to mobilize popular majorities. One of de Gaulle's most important legacies was to create a presidential office endowed with strong powers and direct links to the people. While the president's ample powers have been used, as de Gaulle envisaged, to facilitate strong leadership, the fears of critics like Mitterrand in 1958 that this powerful office stifles political participation and representation have also proved justified.

The referendum was used several times in the early years of the Fifth Republic to bolster support for the republic. But use of the referendum is a high-risk strategy. When voters rejected a referendum that de Gaulle called in 1969 to approve his proposal to restructure the Senate and create regional governments, he resigned from office, on the grounds that he had lost popular confidence.

Because of the precedent de Gaulle set that a president whose referendum is defeated should resign, later presidents have used their power to call referenda quite sparingly. President Pompidou sponsored one referendum; President Giscard d'Estaing, none; President Mitterrand, two; and President Chirac, two. Although all five were approved, they received quite lukewarm support—for example, voting turnout in the referendum of 2000 to shorten the president's term was an embarrassingly low 31 percent. Thus, these "victories" didn't do the president much good.

Article 5 directs the president "to ensure, by his arbitration, the regular functioning of the governmental authorities, as well as the continuance of the State. He shall be the guarantor of national independence, of the integrity of the territory, and of respect for . . . agreements and treaties." The precise meaning of this grant of power is not clear. But because the president is the sole official delegated the awesome responsibilities of arbitrating among state institutions and guaranteeing national independence, this clause provides enormous legitimacy and power.

The Political President. The constitution creates a powerful office on paper. But to be effective, a president must translate formal powers into the actual exercise of influence. A president has important resources to pursue this goal, but success is far from certain.

The fact that the president is the only official elected by the entire nation sets the office apart. The democratic legitimacy conferred by electoral victory provides a powerful weapon that can be used in the president's combat with the opposition and is also useful in keeping the president's own allies in line.

Presidential leadership is given a powerful boost when the president commands a parliamentary majority—that is, the support of the dominant party coalition in the National Assembly. Prior to Mitterrand's election in 1981, the ties between the incumbent president and the dominant party were somewhat muted. De Gaulle professed to disdain parties, even the one formed to support him; Pompidou sought to remain distant from the Gaullist Party, which helped put him in office; and Valéry Giscard d'Estaing's power did not derive from his leadership of a party (he led a small party within the governing coalition, but it was overshadowed by the Gaullist Party). Mitterrand, however, reached the presidency in 1981 thanks largely to his effective use of the Socialist Party (Parti socialiste—PS).

Mitterrand's reliance on the PS did not mean that the party had much influence over government policy. Rather, as in the parliamentary regimes reviewed in this book, Mitterrand's control of the dominant party helped cement the executive's legislative leadership. Just as Mitterrand molded the PS to become the instrument of his personal and presidential ambitions, the same can be said about Chirac's leadership of the neo-Gaullist Union for a Popular Majority (UMP). Chirac or his handpicked assistants directed the party for decades.

The importance for presidential leadership of control over the majority parliamentary coalition can be gauged from how much weaker presidents are during the periods of cohabitation. When a party coalition hostile to the president dominates parliament, presidential power is considerably reduced.

During the periods of unified control, presidents have used their formal and informal powers to the hilt. In addition to the constitutional power to designate prime ministers, presidents have successfully claimed the ability to dismiss them (a power not granted in the constitution). The effect is to make the government responsible not only to the National Assembly, as specified in the constitution, but also to the president. Except during periods of cohabitation, prime ministers have accepted the fact—nowhere specified in the constitution—that they serve at the president's pleasure. Presidents have also assumed the power, assigned to the government by the constitution, to shape policy in virtually any domain that they choose. At the same time, the most powerful presidents do not direct the day-to-day operation of the far-flung executive. That responsibility falls to the prime minister and government.

The Prime Minister and Government

Anyone who referred only to the constitution would be surprised that presidents have made the key policy decisions during most of the Fifth Republic. The constitution designates the government, not the president, as the preeminent policymaking institution. Article 20 states that the government "shall determine and direct the policy of the nation. It shall have at its disposal the administration and the armed forces." And Article 21 authorizes the prime minister to "direct the action of the government. He [the prime minister] is responsible for national defense. He

assures the execution of the laws." Thus, when governments accept the president's leadership, as they invariably do during periods of unified control, it is because of *political dynamics* rather than *constitutional directive*.

The constitution directs the president to appoint the prime minister. Prime ministers are usually selected from leaders of the major party in the dominant parliamentary coalition. However, the president has ample discretion over the choice of prime minister in periods of unified control. President de Gaulle named Georges Pompidou as prime minister, a little-known banker and staff assistant to de Gaulle—and someone who had never held elected office. President Chirac appointed Jean-Pierre Raffarin, a senator from a small party in the president's coalition. Note that the fact that the president is directly elected by universal suffrage, whereas the prime minister is appointed by the president, gives the president an incomparable advantage.

The prime minister in turn nominates and the president appoints members of the cabinet or government, a collective body under the prime minister's direction. Most cabinet members, also known as ministers, are influential politicians from parties that control parliament. The constitution specifies that members of parliament who are named to the cabinet must resign their parliamentary seat. Positions in the cabinet are allotted to political parties in rough proportion to their strength in the majority parliamentary coalition. Care is also taken to ensure that there is some regional balance.

Cabinet ministers direct government departments and propose policy initiatives in their domain. If supported by the government and president, these proposals are included on the legislative and administrative agenda. One way for ambitious politicians to improve their standing is by dynamic performance as ministers.

The prime minister and other government ministers have extensive staff assistance to help them supervise the immense and far-flung bureaucracy. For example, the prime minister's office includes, in addition to his personal staff, the

General Secretariat of the Government, the general directorate for administrative and financial services, and the General Secretariat for National Defense. These powerful agencies are charged with coordinating policy and supervising its implementation by government ministries.

Although it is difficult to specify the respective responsibilities of presidents and prime ministers, an informal division of labor exists. During periods of unified control, presidents have uncontested responsibility for formulating the state's overall policy direction while prime ministers are responsible for translating these general policies into specific programs as well as for supervising the implementation of policy.

Even during cohabitation, presidents have predominant responsibility for overall defense and foreign policy. When control is unified, they are free to assume leadership in other policy areas as well. This has been made dramatically evident on occasions when presidents announced important policy initiatives without giving much advance notice even to the prime minister and government. Again, when control is unified, presidents are free to delve deeply and to propose innovations in any particular policy area of special interest to them. For example, President Mitterrand launched seven major projects that reshaped the architecture and character of Paris, including an opera house at the Bastille, a modernist glass pyramid that serves as the entrance to the Louvre Museum, and several book-shaped buildings that house the French national library. Finally, again especially during periods of united control, presidents seize control whenever a crisis strikes, whether a terrorist attack, an economic crisis, or a natural disaster. During periods of united control, the prime minister directs the executive establishment, but there is no confusion about which of the two leaders has the final word.

The situation is dramatically different under cohabitation. Forced to coexist with a hostile parliamentary majority, Presidents Mitterrand and Chirac retreated from center stage and cultivated the image of dignified statesmen presiding over France's longer-run destiny, while the prime minister assumed responsibility for shaping the government's policy orientation.

The prime minister occupies the second most powerful position in the Fifth Republic during periods of united control and, arguably, is the most important official during cohabitation. Most prime ministers have been prominent politicians, and serving as prime minister is regarded as a steppingstone to the presidency. Thus far, two prime ministers—Georges Pompidou and Jacques Chirac—have subsequently gone on to become president; several others, including Socialists Michel Rocard and Lionel Jospin and Gaullists Jacques Chaban-Delmas and Edouard Balladur, have actively sought the presidency. There has been one woman prime minister in the Fifth Republic, Edith Cresson, who directed a Socialist government in 1992–1993.

During periods of unified control, prime ministers provide the president with important assistance: leadership in shepherding government proposals through parliament, obtaining sympathetic media treatment, and supervising the bureaucracy. Again, when control is unified, the prime minister's most unpleasant function is to serve as a lightning rod to deflect criticism from the president. Prime ministers are expected to take responsibility for unpopular decisions and to give the president credit for popular actions. As a result, prime ministers typically become increasingly unpopular and are replaced after two or three years in office.

There is an inherent tension in the relationship between prime minister and president. This is most apparent during periods of cohabitation, when the two may express their disagreements in public—a major reason why cohabitation became so unpopular and why the president's term was reduced to five years. But even during periods of united control, open conflicts occasionally flare up. The most dramatic example occurred during the presidency of Valéry Giscard d'Estaing in 1976, when then–prime minister

Jacques Chirac resigned. In a letter to the president that Chirac made public, he claimed that Giscard had made his task as prime minister impossible by not providing him with sufficient autonomy. Chirac subsequently carried on a running skirmish with Giscard and ran against him in the next presidential elections, held in 1981. Although Giscard outpolled Chirac to qualify for the second-ballot runoff against François Mitterrand, one reason for Giscard's defeat in the runoff was that, although the two were both from the conservative side of the spectrum, Chirac provided only lukewarm support for Giscard.

Even at the best of times, prime ministers face difficult challenges. Political scientist Robert Elgie describes their thankless position: "When things go well, the President often receives the credit. When things go badly, the Prime Minister usually takes the blame. If things go very badly and the President starts to be criticized, then the Prime Minister is replaced. If things go very well and the Prime Minister starts to be praised, then the Prime Minister is also replaced."[3]

The prime minister is responsible for coordinating and supervising the work of the cabinet, which involves arbitrating conflicts among cabinet ministers over policy and budget priorities. This is no easy matter, for the cabinet typically comprises France's most prominent and ambitious politicians, who lead parties in the governing coalition with somewhat divergent interests and programs. Cabinet ministers thus have an autonomous power base, and many doubtless dream of using their cabinet positions as a springboard to become prime minister or president. For example, in the cabinet shuffle following the UMP's poor performance in the 2004 regional elections, Nicolas Sarkozy was switched from the Interior Ministry to Finance, and Dominique de Villepin was moved from the Foreign Ministry to Interior. It was widely believed that President Chirac was hesitating about which one to groom as his successor. Consequently, the two engaged in constant sniping, to the detriment of the rather weak prime minister, Jean-Pierre Raffarin.

Some prime ministers command enough political standing and personal respect to assure cohesion within the cabinet. Others, such as the affable but ineffectual Raffarin, lack the personal and political standing to restrain infighting among ministers.

Cabinet ministers direct the various government ministries. Cabinet positions differ widely in power. The minister of finance informally ranks second to the prime minister, because the ministry's responsibility for setting spending priorities gives it great influence over other government ministries. The Ministries of Defense, External Affairs, and Interior also rank high in importance. Presidents and prime ministers may configure ministries to highlight their particular priorities. Thus, for example, President Chirac ordered the creation of a Ministry of Social Cohesion in 2004 to coordinate government programs for social and urban problems.

Even more than is the case for cabinets in other political regimes, the French cabinet is not a forum for searching policy debate or collective decision making. Cabinet meetings are occasions where constitutional requirements are met—for example, authorizing appointment of key administrative officials—and where the president and prime minister announce decisions made earlier and elsewhere. The most important policy decisions are made at a higher level—at the Élysée or Matignon (official residence of the prime minister), or by interministerial committees—that is, informal working groups of ministers and high administrators from several ministries directed by the president, prime minister, or their staff.

Bureaucracy and Civil Service

The most prominent officials in the French state are found in the Élysée, the Matignon, and ornate government ministries scattered throughout Paris. The day-to-day work of the state, however, is performed by a veritable army of administrators. There are 2.3 million civil servants in the state administration, and another 2.7 million civil servants staff the public hospitals and subnational governmental bureaucracies. In brief, about one in twelve French citizens is a civil servant!

Given France's long-standing *dirigiste* tradition, the bureaucracy has long played a key role in shaping the country's social and economic life. The Fifth Republic further bolstered the bureaucracy's influence by limiting parliament's legislative power and extending the government's authority to issue binding regulations. French citizens may grumble about the bureaucracy, but they hold it in high regard and expect public services to be well run and accessible to all citizens. (In general, state-run activities—for example, the railroads, public hospitals, and electric utility—richly deserve their excellent reputation.) Securing a position in the bureaucracy provides lifetime employment, considerable prestige, and good pay and fringe benefits (significantly higher on average than in the private sector). Indeed, there is a strong cleavage between public and private sector workers in France, evident in such areas as union membership (unions are nearly nonexistent in the private sector and are powerfully organized in the public sector) and voting behavior: public sector workers are far more likely to vote for the Socialist Party; those employed in the private sector, for parties on the right.

The upper reaches of the bureaucracy, on which we focus here, offer among the most prestigious and powerful career possibilities in France. Recruitment is strictly on the basis of academic excellence. In order to be selected for a top post, one must be a graduate of one of the highly competitive educational institutions known as *grandes écoles*. While over 1 million students are enrolled in higher education at any given time (mostly public universities), only 3,000 students attend the few best *grandes écoles*.[4] The *grandes écoles* provide specialized education in diverse fields. More important, they convey certain shared beliefs that reflect and help reproduce French political culture, notably, the importance of academic excellence as a criterion for reaching high office (what has been called meritocracy), republican values of equality and secularism, and the desirability of state direction (*dirigisme*). At the same time, despite rhetoric about meritocracy, children from culturally and socioeconomically favored milieux have an immense advantage. The proportion of students from immigrant, nonwhite, and modest economic backgrounds is minuscule.

Students who graduate at the top of their class at a *grande école*, especially the two most prestigious ones, the École Nationale d'Administration and the École Polytechnique, are admitted into an even more select fraternity: one of the *grands corps*—small, cohesive networks with particular administrative specialties, such as the financial inspectorate or foreign service. Membership in a *grand corps* is for life and guarantees a relatively ample salary, high status, and considerable power. Members of the *grand corps* leapfrog to the very top of the bureaucracy at a remarkably young age. The *grands corps* have informally colonized government ministries. For example, members of the Finance Inspectorate monopolize top positions in the Ministry of Finance. Recently, members of the *grands corps* have also gained executive positions in public and private industrial firms and banks. Many run for parliament after compiling some administrative experience. Nor do their political ambitions stop there. Many have become cabinet ministers, over half of all prime ministers in the Fifth Republic were members of *grands corps*, and so were two of the last three presidents (Valéry Giscard d'Estaing and Jacques Chirac).

Among influential bureaucratic positions, particular mention should be made of what the French term a ministerial *cabinet*—that is, the personal staff advising a government minister. (In order to distinguish the *cabinet*, or personal staff, from the cabinet that refers to government ministers, we italicize *cabinet* when referring to the former agency.) Although most members of a *cabinet* are recruited from the ranks of the civil service (often from members of a *grand corps*), they are not considered part of the bureaucracy during the period they serve in a *cabinet*. The *cabinet*'s job is to provide information and advice to the minister, and to informally supervise the bureaucracy in the minister's name. The *cabinets* enable ministers to wield considerable power over the line bureaucracy. This situation contrasts with that in many parliamentary systems, such as the British, where ministers are dependent on line civil servants.

Given the French state's retreat to a more modest role since the 1980s, one might have expected that the *grandes écoles* would decline in importance. But the schools have adapted well to the increased importance of the private sector. After several years of obligatory service in the state bureaucracy, many graduates now obtain attractive positions in large banks and corporations. One study found that nearly half of all chief executives of France's two hundred largest firms are graduates of the two most selective *grandes écoles*.[5]

Although the French bureaucracy is organized in a pyramidal fashion that provides little voice to citizens, several organizational innovations provide some protection against executive domination. The office of mediator, created in 1973, handles citizen complaints against unfair treatment by bureaucratic agencies at all levels of government. The mediator is appointed by the president and serves for a six-year nonrenewable term. He or she is generally a distinguished elder politician with a reputation for impartiality. The mediator investigates citizens' grievances and can recommend solutions but has no judicial or administrative authority. The office has proved increasingly popular. When it was first created in 1973, it handled less than 2,000 cases. By 1999, that figure increased to over 50,000.[6]

Another organizational innovation that has become increasingly widespread and influential in the Fifth Republic is independent administrative authorities. These are agencies within the executive but not under the line authority of the government that are delegated responsibility for regulating particular sectors, such as the operations of the stock exchange, radio and television broadcasting, political campaign finance, and data protection. They have legal authority to issue binding rules within their area of competence—for example, providing political candidates with fair access to the airwaves during election campaigns. And they can levy financial or other penalties for noncompliance.

The state, and the bureaucracy that is the primary organizational instrument for implementing state policies, remain a formidable presence in French society. However, the heyday of *dirigisme* has passed. Since then, the increased power of the private sector, ideological changes, and the EU's role have diminished the scope of state activity and reduced the morale and prestige of the civil service.

Public and Semipublic Institutions

Since World War II, France has had an important array of public sector enterprises in basic industry, banking, transportation, energy, telecommunications, and services. Furthermore, the state controlled many investment decisions, both directly, through state-owned industrial firms, and indirectly, as a result of the credit policies of state-controlled banks and the Ministry of Finance. This sector has been downsized by the sale of state-owned enterprises beginning in the mid-1980s. Large and powerful semipublic agencies remain—for example, Electricity of France, a sprawling agency that monopolizes the distribution of electricity throughout France and that has been described as a state within the state. But like the civil service, semipublic agencies no longer enjoy the prestige and power of yesteryear. Many formerly state-owned bastions like France Télécom, Air France, and the Renault automobile company have been fully or partially privatized.

Other State Institutions

Given the far-flung reach of the French state, many state institutions would warrant close attention. We focus here on those that have the greatest power or that are described in the constitution.

The Military and the Police

In all countries, the military and police are key executive agencies that provide the coercive force to maintain law and order. In some countries, the armed forces play an important role in shaping policy and directing the state. In France, the army has traditionally played a minor role in politics. However, in a few instances, the army has intervened, as when it helped topple the Fourth Republic and return de Gaulle to power in 1958.

The French armed forces have traditionally been regarded as a pillar of the republic. As a result of universal male conscription, the army was seen as a device for socializing French youth from diverse social backgrounds. However, this pattern seemed quite old-fashioned and costly in an age when mass armies involving draftees with relatively little training have been replaced elsewhere by professional armies. In 1996, President Chirac ended conscription, downsized the army, and staffed it with professional recruits.

For many years, France deployed its armed forces in its former colonies in Africa and the Pacific to protect repressive regimes. In the process, France made a mockery of its proclaimed commitments to democracy and universal human rights. For example, international human rights organizations charged France with bolstering the Hutu-dominated regime in Rwanda that engaged in widespread genocide against the Tutsi population. Prime Minister Jospin announced an end to this policy in the 1990s, and the army is no longer available on call by dictators in France's former colonies.

Partly to compensate for its more modest unilateral role, France has become a major participant in United Nations–sponsored peacekeeping forces in postconflict situations, such as in Bosnia and Afghanistan, that are designed to promote peace, stability, and order in these areas. France has committed more troops to these efforts than any other country in the world.

The police forces in France operate with considerable freedom—far too much, according to critics. The "forces of order," as they are called in France, have a reputation for abusing power by illegal surveillance, arbitrary actions, and torture. Immigrants and French citizens from North Africa, black Africa, and the Caribbean are especially likely to be subject to identity checks, strip searches, and other indignities. The judiciary and high executive officials have rarely acted vigorously to restrain the police.

In the 2002 presidential campaign, Chirac and Le Pen repeatedly denounced the Jospin government for its alleged laxity in dealing with increased crime. Indeed, the issue of law and order dominated the campaign and heavily contributed to Jospin's first-round defeat. Immediately following Chirac's reelection, the Raffarin government sponsored legislation giving the police added powers to engage in surveillance (including wiretapping) and to detain suspects without formal charges.

The Judiciary

Traditionally the French judiciary had little autonomy and was considered an arm of the executive. In the past two decades, however, this condition has changed dramatically, with the growth in the powers of the Constitutional Council, as well as the increased power of independent administrative regulatory authorities in such varied sectors as broadcasting, stock market transactions, and commercial competition.

The Constitutional Council. The Constitutional Council might be considered the Cinderella of the Fifth Republic. One study of the council observes, "Originally an obscure institution conceived to play a marginal role in the

Fifth Republic, the Constitutional Council has gradually moved toward the center stage of French politics and acquired the status of a major actor in the policy-making system."[7]

The nine members of the council are named for staggered nine-year nonrenewable terms. The president of the republic and the presidents of the National Assembly and Senate each appoint three members. The president of the republic names the council's president. Those named to the Constitutional Council are generally distinguished jurists or elder statesmen. Ex-presidents are entitled to sit on the council. The first woman ever named to the council was appointed in 1992.

Three factors contributed to the substantial increase in the power of the Constitutional Council and the judiciary more generally:

- Broadening access to the Constitutional Council. At first, only the president of the republic and the presidents of the two houses of the legislature could bring cases to the council. A constitutional amendment passed in 1974 authorized sixty deputies or sixty senators to bring suit. As a result, the council is now asked to rule on most important legislation.

- Broadening the council's jurisdiction to include the power of judicial review—that is, the power to invalidate legislation that a majority of the council judges to be in violation of the constitution. The council exercises judicial review in a more limited way than does the U.S. Supreme Court, since it can only strike down recently enacted legislation. But that a judicial body can overrule the legislature is unprecedented in France, and the council now exercises this sweeping power in a bold and continuous fashion. If the primary innovation of the Fifth Republic in the first years of the republic was to consolidate the dominance of the executive over the legislature, the primary development since then has been to consolidate the primacy of the constitution, as interpreted by the Constitutional Council, over both the legislature and executive. The change has substantially expanded the powers of the council and provided greater balance among political institutions.

- Transferring the power to appoint judges from the executive to magistrates elected from among the rank of judges. This change required a constitutional amendment in 1993. The same amendment created a new Court of Justice of the Republic to try cases against government ministers accused of criminal acts committed while in office. The court comprises six deputies and six senators, elected by the two chambers of the legislature, and three senior judges. The change was designed to allay public criticism after government ministers in the 1980s were alleged to have authorized contaminated blood stocks to be distributed for transfusions, causing numerous patients to contract the HIV virus.

The Constitutional Council has periodically been the object of intense criticism after issuing controversial judgments. The council's composition is one reason that it may become the focal point of criticism. Owing to their nine-year terms, and particularly with the increasing frequency of political alternation, the majority of council members may have been appointed by political opponents of an incumbent government. The government sought to restrict the council's ability to overturn legislation by a constitutional amendment in 1995, which stipulates that a referendum can pass legislation that violates the constitution. The effect is to bypass the council's review procedure in such cases.

The French judicial system of Roman law, codified in the Napoleonic Code and other legal codes (for example, those governing industrial relations and local government), differs substantially from the pattern prevailing in Britain, the United States, and other nations inspired by the common law system. French courts accord little importance to judicial precedent; what counts is existing legislation and the codification of legislation in specific subfields. French judges also play an active role in questioning witnesses and recommending verdicts to juries. A judicial authority, the *juge d'instruction*, is delegated responsibility for preparing the prosecution's case. Criminal defendants enjoy fewer rights than in the U.S. or British system of criminal justice, although the Jospin government sponsored reforms that increased defendants' rights.

State Council. France has a system of administrative courts whose importance is linked to the great power of the bureaucracy and the wide scope of administrative regulations (many areas regulated by laws in other democratic systems are the subject of administrative regulation in France). There is a hierarchy of about thirty administrative courts. At the apex is the *Conseil d'État* (State Council), whose role as a watchdog on the executive is especially important in the French political system, where the executive has such great autonomy. (Members of the council belong to one of the most powerful and prestigious *grands corps*.) The council decides cases brought by individuals alleging that their rights have been violated by administrative regulations and actions, and it can order appropriate remedies. The State Council also provides advice to the government about the constitutionality, legality, and coherence of proposed laws. It can rule that administrative agencies have falsely applied the law, and can warn about damaging consequences that might result if proposed administrative regulations were implemented. One highly influential State Council ruling, later embodied in a constitutional amendment in 1992, declared that European Union treaty provisions and regulations have precedence over French legislation—that is, in the event of a conflict between the two, EU directives have primacy. Although the government can overrule the State Council, it rarely does so because the council's opinions command enormous respect.

The Economic and Social Council

The constitution designates the Economic and Social Council as a consultative body composed of representatives from business, agriculture, labor unions, social welfare organizations, and consumer groups, as well as leading citizens from cultural and scientific fields. The council has issued influential reports on important public issues, including job discrimination toward immigrants and reorganization of the minimum

wage system. However, it has no legislative power and occupies a modest role within the regime.

Subnational Government

Until the 1980s, responsibility for regulating local affairs was in the hands of nationally appointed field officers—for example, prefects, supervisors of civil engineering, and financial officers—who represented government ministries. Locally elected municipal governments were quite weak, and the local governmental structure extremely fragmented: there are 36,565 localities in France, more than in all other Western European countries combined!

The Socialist government sponsored a fundamental overhaul of local government in the 1980s. State supervision of local governments was reduced, regional governments were created, and localities were authorized to levy taxes and sponsor a wide range of economic, social, and cultural activities. Although local elected officials were able to prevent the government from consolidating localities into a smaller number of more viable units, incentives were provided for localities to form associations and sponsor joint public services. Similarly, at the time that regional governments were created, resistance by local politicians prevented the elimination of France's one hundred territorial departments (each with its own elected government). Consequently, France has three layers of subnational elected governments: municipal, departmental, and regional. Although this seems unusually cumbersome given the size of the population, citizens are deeply attached to local government: public opinion polls consistently demonstrate that local politicians command far greater respect than do national officeholders.

The Socialists also enlarged the space for political participation by limiting the *cumul des mandats*, a procedure that authorizes political leaders concurrently to occupy multiple elected positions like mayor, member, and possibly president of the departmental or regional council, deputy or senator, and/or member of the European Parliament. Most prominent politicians not only entered politics by first running for local office but also retain a local elected position(s) while serving in parliament or even in the government. For example, Jacques Chirac continued to serve as mayor of Paris (a post to which he was first elected in 1977) during the years he was prime minister (1986–1988). He resigned from his position as mayor when he ran for president in 1994. Socialist reforms restricted the *cumul des mandats* by prohibiting cabinet ministers or members of parliament from simultaneously serving as mayor or president of departmental or regional councils. (They are permitted to serve on the elected councils of local governments.)

The Raffarin government sponsored a constitutional amendment in 2003 extending the scope of decentralization. The amendment enshrines the principle of decentralization in the constitution and authorizes subnational governments to hold local referenda. Further, it requires the national government to provide local governments with adequate tax revenues when local governments are delegated responsibilities.

The decentralization reforms have had mixed effects. They have enabled regional, departmental, and city governments to gain significant control over education, transportation, social welfare, and other public sectors. Subnational governments used their newly acquired power to sponsor public transportation facilities linking cities in the provinces, thereby weakening the characteristic wheel-and-spokes pattern by which all French roads formerly led to Paris! They brought government closer to citizens. They enabled local governments to sponsor joint public-private economic development projects.

Yet critics of the reforms argue that decentralization has produced some new problems. For example, local officials in many localities have been convicted of taking kickbacks from contractors buying favorable treatment for construction projects, questionable land devel-

opment schemes, and municipal contracts. State reintervention often resulted from the mistakes made in the first flush of decentralization. (In a study of this pattern, political scientist Jonah Levy described it as the "statist two-step.")[8] The reforms have also increased economic and other inequalities among localities and regions. However, most people agree that the diffusion of power from Paris ministries to decentralized actors in local governments and civil society has produced far more gains than losses.

The European Dimension

Although we review state institutions in this chapter, political institutions in France, like those in other member states of the EU, no longer function in isolation from EU institutions. There is such tight integration between the two levels that French public officials spend considerable time participating in EU decisions and implementing EU decisions. The process begins at the top, since the president, prime minister, and cabinet are constantly involved in EU decisions. Most governments have included a junior minister responsible for European affairs. An agency within the prime minister's office is responsible for coordinating French governmental policies, legislation, and regulations relating to EU economic affairs. The process continues right down the bureaucratic hierarchy. Most ministries have a separate bureau specializing in EU affairs. Whether the topic is the quantity of fish that French commercial trawlers are permitted to harvest or standards for French pharmaceuticals, French legal and administrative regulations must conform to EU treaties and directives. To take another domain, French courts now routinely defer to EU directives and rulings by the European Court of Justice and the European Court of Justice on Human Rights when they decide cases brought within France. (This is no easy matter, since there are many thousand EU regulations governing French administrative activity.) When analyzing French political institutions, it is difficult to unravel where the "EU" begins and "France" leaves off.

The Policymaking Process

Prior to the first period of cohabitation in 1986, there was relatively great unity of purpose within the executive and a tight chain of command linking the president, government, bureaucracy, and parliament. The president, usually after consulting the prime minister, formulated major policy initiatives (although the more powerful presidents—notably de Gaulle and Mitterrand—sometimes announced major policy initiatives without prior notice to the government). Government ministers, assisted by civil servants, developed legislative proposals and administrative regulations. And the parliament generally approved the government's initiatives.

Even in the most extreme periods of heroic presidential leadership, the French state has never been a perfectly coordinated monolith. Even when a powerful president like de Gaulle or Mitterrand has been at the helm during periods of united control, tensions have erupted into more or less open turf conflicts at the very top—among different presidential advisers—as well as between presidents and their most loyal prime ministers, among different ministries, among agencies within a given ministry, and between the executive establishment and other public authorities. However, during periods of cohabitation, there has been agreement on deferring to the president as the ultimate decision maker. During periods of divided control, the prime minister has gained the dominant voice in policymaking, and the president has retreated to the political wings. At these times, uncertainty has increased about who has the last word in the event of policy disputes.

Moving outside the executive, there are fewer opportunities in France compared with most other democratic regimes for public and private actors outside government to influence policymaking. The constitution enshrines executive dominance at the expense of the legislature and popular participation. The bureaucracy is large, expert, and often domineering. The points of access for private interests are fewer than in most democratic regimes.

Yet the fact that a particular policy is adopted does not mean that it will be fully and smoothly implemented. One cannot predict the details of policy *outcomes* merely by knowing the content of policy *decisions*. The bureaucracy may be internally divided by competition among different ministries, and bureaucrats have expertise and power that can be used to protect their own and their agency's interests. Moreover, private interests have resources to resist legislative and bureaucratic directives, as evidenced by strikes, popular protest, and other forms of resistance analyzed in Chapter 14. As described above, the Constitutional Council has gained an important role in the policy process.

The position of the executive and the French state more generally have been affected in complex ways by France's participation in the global economy, especially French membership in the EU. First, EU commitments have limited the freedom of action of national states, although membership in the EU has been a way for France to leverage its modest power by gaining a leading voice in this influential multilateral organization. Second, EU membership has redistributed power among political institutions of the French state. For example, judicial authorities, notably the Constitutional Council and State Council, have gained increased power because of their authoritative role in applying EU treaty commitments and directives. Executive agencies have gained power relative to the French parliament, since members of the executive represent France in EU decision making, with parliament forced to accept the results. (A constitutional amendment of 1993 requires that parliament must be consulted prior to EU Council of Ministers meetings where important decisions are made; but parliament cannot amend or veto

France's official position.) At the same time, there is often confusion and conflict about which member of the executive branch speaks for France on EU-related issues: the president, prime minister, foreign minister, finance minister, or European affairs minister. Third, membership in the EU has increased the power of all political institutions relative to rank-and-file citizens.

As France has become more integrated within the EU and the wider global arena, the gulf has widened between political decision makers and ordinary citizens. There is widespread criticism of decisions made behind closed doors in Paris, Brussels, and elsewhere. This has further increased stress on the system of political representation, which was already shaken by conflicts involving political participation, identity, and inequality. As described in Chapter 14, representative institutions have not adapted effectively to these challenges.

Notes

1. Jean Charlot, *La Politique en France* (Paris: Livre de Poche, 1994), p. 27.

2. Ronald Tiersky, *François Mitterrand: The Last French President* (New York: St. Martin's Press, 2000), p. 242.

3. Robert Elgie, *The Role of the Prime Minister in France, 1981–91* (New York: St. Martin's Press, 1993), p. 1.

4. Ezra Suleiman, "Les élites de l'administration et de la politique dans la France de la Ve République: Homogénéité, puissance, permanence," in Ezra Suleiman and Henri Mendras, eds., *Le recrutement des élites en Europe* (Paris: La Découverte, 1995), p. 33.

5. Michel Bauer and Bénédicte Bertin-Mourot, "La tyrannie du diplôme initial et la circulation des élites: La stabilité du modèle français," in Suleiman and Mendras, eds., *Le recrutement des élites en Europe*, p. 51.

6. Robert Elgie, *Political Institutions in Contemporary France* (New York: Oxford University Press, 2003), p. 87.

7. John T. S. Keeler and Alec Stone, "Judicial-Political Confrontation in Mitterrand's France: The Emergence of the Constitutional Council as a Major Actor in the Policy-making Process," in Stanley Hoffmann, George Ross, and Sylvia Malzacher, eds., *The Mitterrand Experiment: Continuity and Change in Mitterrand's France* (New York: Oxford University Press, 1987), p. 176.

8. Jonah D. Levy, *Tocqueville's Revenge: State, Society, and Economy in Contemporary France* (Cambridge: Harvard University Press, 1999).

CHAPTER

14

Representation and Participation

Charles de Gaulle passionately believed that political parties and parliament had overstepped their proper role in the Third and Fourth Republics by capriciously making and unmaking governments through shifting parliamentary maneuvers. The result was to prevent vigorous, effective executive leadership and leave France unstable and weak. The constitution of the Fifth Republic was designed to free the executive from political parties, organized interests, and parliament so it could exploit the full potential of French power.

Although de Gaulle did succeed in limiting parliament's influence, he failed completely to curb political parties. Ironically, however, the development of strong, well-organized, centralized parties early in the Fifth Republic—squarely contrary to de Gaulle's intentions—has proved a principal buttress of decisive leadership and political stability, the general's highest priorities.

De Gaulle's decision to provide for popular election of the presidency has been the major reason for the development of strong parties. In order to compete effectively in the all-important presidential contest, parties had to become centralized, powerful organizations. The result has been to facilitate strong executive leadership, since parties have been able to mobilize popular majorities to support the president and government. But parties have also limited popular participation and representation. The result of their not providing a mechanism for popular expression is that France's centuries-old tradition of popular protest against state authority persists.

The Legislature

In the Fifth Republic, the operative assumption seems to be that parliament should be neither seen nor heard. What a distance parliament has fallen since its glory days in the Fourth Republic, when parliament majestically made and unmade governments an average of every six months. Parliaments everywhere have been described as ceding power to the executive. But the French parliament began higher (in the Third and Fourth Republics) and has sunk lower (in the Fifth).

In France's semipresidential system, parliament lacks the independence that legislatures enjoy in presidential systems, yet it cannot hold the executive fully accountable, as legislatures in parliamentary systems can, since the president is not responsible to parliament. In the Fifth Republic, parliament has rarely provided a forum for important national debates (one commentator notes that "it is no longer in the National Assembly that important debates occur but on television"), fails to represent conflicting interests adequately, and is a feeble mechanism for checking abuses of executive power.[1] In brief, parliament in the Fifth Republic has lost power to the president, government, bureaucracy, judiciary, television, subnational governments, and the EU!

The French parliament is bicameral and consists of the more powerful National Assembly and the upper house, the Senate. In the Third and Fourth Republics, parliament was regarded as the sole voice of the sovereign people. Under the Fifth Republic, parliament is no longer the seat of sovereignty and has been stripped of many powers. At the same time, the executive is granted extensive powers independent of parliament, as well as numerous weapons to control parliamentary activity.

Article 34 of the constitution, which defines the scope of parliament's legislative jurisdiction, represented a revolution in French constitutional law. Rather than authorizing parliament to legislate in all areas except those explicitly designated as off-limits—true to the tradition of parliamentary sovereignty prevailing most of the time since the French Revolution—the constitution enumerates those areas in which parliament *is* authorized to legislate and prohibits legislation on other matters. Outside the constitutionally specified areas, the executive can issue legally binding regulations and decrees without need for parliamentary approval. Even within the domain of parliamentary competence, Article 38 authorizes parliament to empower the government to issue ordinances with the force of law. This may happen, for example, if the government wishes to save time, avoid extensive parliamentary debate, or limit unwelcome amendments. The referendum procedure described in Chapter 13 and below provides yet another means for the executive to bypass parliament. Parliament's more modest role in the Fifth Republic can be gauged by the fact that it passes about 70 laws a year compared with the more than 200 laws that parliament passed annually in the Fourth Republic.

Within the limited area of lawmaking, the constitution grants the government extensive powers to control legislative activity. The government is mostly responsible for establishing the parliamentary agenda. As in other parliamentary regimes, the government, not backbenchers or the opposition, initiates most bills passed into law. (Over 90 percent of the laws voted by the legislature are government initiated.)

The executive can choose to dissolve the National Assembly before its normal five-year term ends. The decision to dissolve is delegated to the president, but the prime minister and government are closely involved in the process. (The executive cannot dissolve the Senate, but this matters little, since the Senate lacks two vital powers enjoyed by the National Assembly: the right to refuse to pass legislation and the power to force the government to resign by voting censure.) If the executive dissolves the National Assembly, it cannot do so again for a year.

The government's control over parliament's legislative and other activity is bolstered by some additional measures. Under Article 44, the government can call for a single vote—known as the *vote bloqué* ("blocked vote," or package vote)—on all or a portion of a bill. The government can select which amendments will be included with the text. Governments have used—or, according to the opposition, abused—the package vote procedure to restrict debate on many key legislative texts.

The government can curb parliament further by calling for a confidence vote on either its overall policies or a specific piece of legislation (Article 49). This provision applies only to the National Assembly. When the government declares a confidence vote, its text is considered approved unless the National Assembly passes a censure motion within twenty-four hours.

The constitution imposes an especially severe restriction for a censure motion to pass: it must be supported by an absolute majority of all deputies in the National Assembly. Thus, deputies who are absent or who abstain are counted as supporting the government. (Members of the National Assembly are known as deputies; members of the Senate are known as senators. Together the two groups are known as members of parliament.) The government uses these formidable weapons not only to check opponents but also to control deputies from its own coalition who might be tempted to oppose the government on a particular policy. When voting against the government may cause it to fall, which might lead it to dissolve the Assembly and call new elections, the government's supporters are inclined to silence!

Deputies can also submit motions to censure the government on their own initiative. Such a motion must be signed by one-tenth of all deputies in the National Assembly. The procedure for passing this kind of censure motion is the same as that called by the government, save that deputies who sign a censure motion of this kind cannot do so again during the life of the legislature. The result is to limit the number of parliament-initiated censure motions.

Given that the government normally commands majority support in the National Assembly, it need not worry about being forced to resign by a vote of censure. In fact, only one censure motion has ever passed in the Fifth Republic. In 1962, the majority of parliament was enraged when President de Gaulle convened a referendum to approve his initiative to elect the president by popular vote. Because the constitution prevents the National Assembly from holding the president accountable to parliament, deputies vented their spleen by censuring de Gaulle's prime minister, Georges Pompidou. However, parliament emerged weaker from the combat. Immediately after the censure vote, de Gaulle dissolved parliament and called new elections. When the Gaullist coalition won a legislative majority, de Gaulle sealed his victory by reappointing Pompidou prime minister.

Articles 38, 44, and 49 give the government powerful weapons with which to limit parliament, exceeding those possessed by the government in virtually any other democratic regime. When a government relies on these powers to overcome parliamentary resistance, which occurs frequently and on important legislation, the opposition cries foul. However, it has been impossible to abolish these devices because governments of both the left and right have found them highly useful. The result, however, has been to reduce parliament to a rubber stamp, limit the opportunity for useful national debate of vital political issues, prevent opposition parties from airing grievances, and force discontented groups to take to the streets rather than channel their demands through parliament.

Political scientist John Huber has analyzed how the package vote and censure procedures serve an important and little-noticed purpose.[2] Whereas most observers stress that the government can use these measures against the opposition, Huber suggests that the government can use them to promote binding agreements among the parties represented in the majority coalition. It is important to recall that the partners in a coalition are also rivals. The package vote and censure motion enable the prime minister to keep restless members of his own coalition in line.

Voting in the National Assembly is generally along party lines, and there is strong party discipline—that is, deputies from each party vote as a bloc. This means that the government can generally count on obtaining majority support for proposed legislation. Nonetheless, ministers may need to engage in behind-the-scenes negotiations with parliamentary supporters to assure their support, and there may be a revolt in the ranks, especially if the prime minister is vulnerable. For example, following the defeat of the Union for a Popular Majority (UMP) in the 2004 regional elections, for which Prime Minister Raffarin was widely held responsible, significant numbers of UMP deputies abstained in several votes on proposed government-sponsored legislation.

Parliament has especially limited control over the budgetary process. Members of parliament are prohibited from introducing budget amendments that will raise expenditures or lower revenues. Furthermore, parliament must approve the budget within seventy days after it has been submitted by the government or the government can enact it by decree (although this has never occurred in the Fifth Republic).

In some parliamentary systems, parliamentary committees—the French term them commissions—play a vital role. But not in the Fifth Republic. There are six permanent commissions: Foreign Policy; Finances and Economy; Defense; Constitutional Changes, Legislation, and General Administration; Cultural, Family, and Social Affairs; and Production and Exchange. (Special commissions may be appointed to examine especially important bills—for example, the Socialist government's nationalization reform in 1981.) Commissions are responsible for reviewing proposed legislation. Although they may propose amendments, the government can reject those it dislikes. The constitution also authorizes parliament to create commissions of inquiry to control the executive, but the few that have been created have proved ineffective.

In recent years, parliament has modestly increased its role. For example, whereas in the early years of the Fifth Republic, only one period a week was reserved for members of parliament to pose oral questions to the government, a constitutional amendment in 1995 added two more periods a week.

Since the government largely controls the parliamentary agenda, most bills that are given serious scrutiny and are eventually passed are sponsored by the government. However, a 1990 reform modestly increased the possibility for parliament to consider bills sponsored by members of parliament. Important antiracist legislation introduced by Communist deputies was passed in 1990. Members of parliament have exerted influence by skillfully using parliamentary procedures. One method has been to propose amendments to government-sponsored bills. Another has been the use of parliamentary commissions of inquiry, for example, an investigation of party finance in 1991 and Mafia influence in France in 1992. However, critics charge that the imbalance between executive and legislature remains a fundamental design flaw of the Fifth Republic.

The National Assembly is by far the more powerful chamber of parliament. It alone can censure the government, and it has the decisive role in passing legislation. The Senate has equal power in one key area. Since its approval is required for constitutional amendments to pass, it is coequal in this domain with the National Assembly and therefore possesses a veto power over constitutional changes.

How a Bill Becomes a Law

We provide here a somewhat simplified version of the complicated story of how legislation is enacted. A key feature is that the National Assembly has the last word in the event of a sustained conflict between the two chambers. Following a bill's introduction in one of the two houses of parliament (usually the National Assembly), the bill is reviewed and possibly amended by one of the six standing commissions in that chamber. Once the commission issues a report on the bill to the full house, the bill is submitted to the full chamber for debate, further amendment, and vote. If the text is approved, it is sent for consideration to the second chamber, where the same procedure is followed.

If a bill is passed in identical form by the two houses, it becomes law (unless struck down by the Constitutional Council). If the houses vote different versions of a bill, it is sent back for reconsideration by both. If the chambers cannot reach agreement on an identical text after two readings (that is, votes) or the Senate twice rejects a text approved by the National Assembly, a joint commission from the two houses seeks to negotiate a compromise version. This text is again voted upon by both chambers. If approved by both, it becomes law. If rejected by the National Assembly, the bill dies. If it is rejected by the Senate, however, the government can request the National Assembly to vote a fourth time, and, if approved by the National Assembly, the bill passes. The government is authorized to expedite this process (called the *navette* in French) by which a bill shuttles back and forth between the two chambers. (As noted above, the Senate is coequal—and thus can exercise a veto—when it comes to passing constitutional amendments.)

The National Assembly has overruled the Senate on some key legislative texts. This situation has been especially likely to occur when the Socialists control the government, since the Senate has always been in the hands of conservative parties.

After a bill is passed, the constitution authorizes the president of the republic, president of either chamber of the legislature, or sixty deputies or senators to request the Constitutional Council to review the text. The council can strike down the entire text or those portions that it judges to be in violation of the constitution. The council must be asked to rule on a text within one month after it is passed. If not, it becomes law and can never be reviewed by the council.

Why would the National Assembly and Senate hold different positions on a policy issue? One reason is that the two houses are elected by different procedures and represent different interests. Deputies are chosen from single-member districts for five years (unless the government dissolves the chamber before the end of its normal term). There are currently 577 seats in the National Assembly; thus, there are 577 districts. Districts are a fairly accurate reflection of France's demographic situation.

Electing the Legislature

Elections are held according to a two-ballot election procedure, similar in most respects to the one for presidential elections. In order to be elected at the first ballot, a candidate must receive an absolute majority of the votes cast in the district. If no candidate obtains a majority—the situation in most districts (although some popular deputies are reelected at the first ballot)—a runoff election is held the following week. Unlike the presidential election, in which only the two front-runners may compete at the runoff, all candidates receiving at least 12.5 percent of the votes can compete at the second ballot. Typically, however, most runoffs are duels between two candidates, since alliances are forged on either side of the left-right divide. The agreement specifies that lesser-place candidates in the alliance will withdraw in favor of the candidates in the alliance who received the most votes. Thus, most second-ballot elections pit a candidate on the left against one on the right.

Parties entering into electoral pacts obviously have a much better chance of electing candidates. However, fringe parties—notably, far-left parties and the Front National (FN)—can be spoilers if their candidates remain in the runoff, thus producing a triangular (or, in rare instances, a four-way) contest. Fringe candidates drain votes that might otherwise be cast for the "neighboring" major party. Thus, the presence of an FN candidate reduces support for the UMP; a far-left candidate takes votes from the Socialist Party (PS).

Since party alliances typically reflect the left-right divide, the system used to elect the National Assembly contributes to polarization within French politics. Thus, the system of alliances encouraged by the two-ballot system maximizes the chances of a cohesive coalition gaining a majority in parliament, and it thereby bolsters political stability in the entire political system. This is why political scientist Jean Charlot claims that the two-ballot single-district system "has proved . . . one of the most solid underpinnings of the Fifth Republic. The electoral law . . . weakens or even neutralizes the natural tendency of the French and their parties toward division."[3]

The other side of the coin is that the two-ballot system is designed to penalize small, fringe parties that cannot form agreements with major parties. The most dramatic example is the FN. The most extreme case was the 1997 parliamentary election, where the FN obtained 15 percent of first-ballot votes yet failed to elect a single deputy.

The procedure used to select senators produces a chamber that is responsive to different interests. There are 322 members of the Senate. Most are elected for nine-year terms by mayors and town councillors from France's 100 *départements* (the administrative districts into which mainland and overseas France is divided) as well as from several overseas territories. Twelve senators are chosen by a council elected by nonresident French citizens. The method of selecting senators ensures that the Senate will be particularly conservative and zealous in defending the interests of small towns and villages, since rural residents enjoy nearly double the representation that their numbers warrant in the electoral college, composed of local elected officials, that chooses senators. A Senate commission responded to criticisms of this situation by proposing an increase in the urban representation of the senatorial electoral college. The reform will likely be enacted in the future.

Political Parties and the Party System

We have described how the existence of powerful political parties—the very factor that de Gaulle feared would nurture division, instability, and paralysis—has promoted political stability in the Fifth Republic. Parties have facilitated stable leadership and political alternation in office. In recent years, however, the decline in ideological distance between the center-left and center-right has left many French citizens feeling unrepresented by the major established parties. The result has been an erosion of support for the governing parties and increased support for fringe parties at the ideological margins. Candidates from splinter parties received more than half the first-ballot votes in the 2002 presidential elections.

Popular election of the president has produced polarization, "presidentialization," and "Americanization" of the party system. *Polarization* describes the tendency for the electorate to divide into two camps as a result of the procedures used to elect the president (as well as members of the National Assembly). *Presidentialization* means that parties give priority, in terms of their program, internal organization, alliance strategy, and leadership, to winning the next presidential election. As parties have moved in this direction, some observers have described French politics as becoming "Americanized," for the emphasis on winning the presidential elections, the focus on candidates' personalities, and ideological centrism (designed to appeal to the broadest numbers of voters) are major features of American politics.

Counterpressures, however, constantly challenge these trends. In particular, because the major parties neglect certain groups by appealing to the ideological center, opportunities have opened up for a variety of fringe parties. Support for these parties produces a countertendency toward fragmentation within the party system. The point was dramatically illustrated by the performance of Le Pen and other minor-party candidates in the 2002 presidential elections. Fringe parties obtained a significant share of the vote in more recent elections as well, including the 2004 regional and 2004 European elections.

As a general matter, splinter parties perform especially well in elections to the European Parliament and to municipal and regional councils, where the stakes are lower than in parliamentary and presidential elections, and where representatives are chosen by proportional representation (PR). (These have been dubbed second-order elections by political scientists.) Since PR allots seats according to the proportion of votes each party receives, a party not able to gain a plurality or majority can nonetheless win seats. Hence, there is less incentive than in elections held in single-member districts by the plurality method for parties to ally or for voters to support large parties. Consequently, small parties generally fare better in elections held by PR.

The Major Parties

Two major parties—the Union pour un mouvement populaire (UMP) and the Parti socialiste (PS)—currently vie for national dominance. For the past several decades, each has dominated a rival coalition; the two coalitions have alternated control of key political institutions in the Fifth Republic. But the two parties are continually challenged by a host of smaller parties on their ideological flanks.

Union pour un Mouvement Populaire (UMP). Until General de Gaulle reached power in 1958, parties on the right of the French political spectrum were numerous and fragmented. Under de Gaulle's leadership, a new party was created that—largely thanks to his popularity—was the keystone of the Fifth Republic in the early years. Although the party lost its commanding position in the mid-1970s, it has reestablished its dominance in the current period.

The Union for a Popular Majority, or UMP, as it is now known (its name and political orientation have gone through many changes since the party was first created in 1958), has never had a precise program. It was originally created to support de Gaulle's personal leadership and his goals of championing France's national independence, providing strong political leadership, and modernizing French society and economy while preserving the country's distinctive cultural heritage. But its specific positions have changed considerably over time.

Beginning in the mid-1970s, the UMP slipped from first place. Jacques Chirac, who became leader in 1974, lost presidential bids in 1981 and 1988. The UMP regained its premier role in the 1990s. First, it led the coalition that won a swollen majority in the 1993 parliamentary elections. Next, Chirac won the 1995 presidential elections and named Alain Juppé, a close ally, as prime minister. However, the victory celebration soon ended. When Juppé proposed cutbacks in social benefits in 1995 (which we analyze in Chapter 15), massive strikes and demonstrations shook the regime to its roots. Chirac tried to regain control by dissolving the National Assembly and calling new elections. But the attempt backfired, and the victory of the Socialist-led coalition in the 1997 parliamentary elections produced five years of cohabitation through the remainder of Chirac's first term. The UMP survived this setback when Chirac won reelection in 2002 and the UMP won a comfortable victory in the 2002 parliamentary elections. Once again, however, the victory party ended quite soon, as voters deserted the party in the 2004 regional elections and the 2004 European elections (it gained only 17 percent in the 2004 European elections). Although its electoral victories in 2002 enable the UMP to control the presidency

and National Assembly until 2007, its political standing has been considerably weakened by the party's poor performance in the 2004 elections.

Throughout the Fifth Republic, the UMP has competed with other center-right parties for control of this portion of the political spectrum. In 2002, Chirac persuaded most center-right parties to merge with the newly renamed UMP. The price of unification has been internal conflict in the UMP, since those with loyalty to formerly separate parties have created factions with opposing ideological orientations. Moreover, the UMP faces formidable challenges from those center-right parties that resisted the 2002 merger.

The social base of the UMP generally reflects its conservative orientation. It draws the bulk of its votes from business executives, shopkeepers, professionals, the elderly, the wealthy, and the highly educated.

Parti Socialiste (PS). The PS is one of the major success stories in contemporary France. From a party of aging local politicians and schoolteachers in the Fourth Republic and a perpetual and ineffective opposition party in the early years of the Fifth Republic, it became a vanguard of the newly modernized France in 1981, when it swept presidential and parliamentary elections. Since 1981, the PS has rivaled the UMP for dominance. It has profoundly shaped present-day France by embracing the institutions of the Fifth Republic (many on the left opposed the legitimacy of the Fifth Republic in the early years), championing a moderate reformist policy orientation, and sponsoring sweeping reforms during its years in office.

The PS reached power in 1981 by advocating substantial, even radical, changes, and, as described in Chapter 12, it sponsored a whirlwind of reforms in its first years in office. However, the party lost its ideological bearings after the right turn of 1983. The party was further damaged when Mitterrand's long presidency drew to an end: Mitterrand's own reputation was tarnished by scandals involving his close personal associates and by revelations that during his university student days, before becoming a Resistance leader during World War II, he had been active in a far-right organization. The PS was also damaged when several of its leaders were convicted of receiving kickbacks to finance the party and for personal use. (PS politicians were not the only ones implicated in financial scandals: so too were UMP leaders, as well as leaders from other parties.)

But the PS has demonstrated remarkable resilience. It survived a steep falloff in support following its right turn of the mid-1980s, regained control of government in 1986–1988 and 1997–2002, and performed well in the 2004 elections for regional councils and the European Parliament (it obtained an impressive 30 percent of the vote in the 2004 European elections). Although the party is deeply divided by ideological conflicts, as well as by its top leaders' presidential ambitions, it continues to be a major contender. What explains the party's durable success? For one thing, although its achievements have fallen short of its ambitious goals, its policies when in office have been quite effective. Since 1981, it has presided over a thorough overhaul of the French economy and has played a leading role in strengthening European integration. It has sponsored social programs—including a minimum income program, the thirty-five-hour workweek, and expanded medical coverage—that benefit less favored groups in the population. It has demonstrated a capacity for governing that was unusual among previous left parties in France. At the same time, the fact that the PS has been a pillar of the established order distances the party from France's revolutionary traditions.

The PS draws support from civil servants, low-income groups, and educated professionals. While its support is to some extent the mirror image of the UMP's vote base, both parties tend to represent the more secure strata of French society. The most vulnerable and excluded groups, including unskilled workers, the unemployed, and school dropouts, have been especially likely to support fringe parties.

Small Parties

As the programs of the two political parties that dominate the party system have converged, many voters have decided that neither major party is responsive to their concerns. Thus, at the same time that there has been a consolidation of the center-left under the PS and the center-right under the UMP, parties that flourished in the past have managed to survive, and new parties continually form to fill new niches in the political universe. The extreme case was the 2002 presidential election, when sixteen candidates competed at the first ballot, and Jospin and Chirac, the PS and UMP candidates, were chosen by only 36 percent of the voters. The existence of splinter or fringe parties means that the current French party system exhibits conflicting tendencies between consolidation and fragmentation.

We review here the four largest splinter parties—the Parti communiste français (PCF), the Front national (FN), Les Verts (Greens), and the Union des démocrates pour la France (UDF). Other small parties champion nationalist opposition to the EU, far-left radical opposition to French and global capitalism, and the defense of recreational hunting and fishing. Splinter parties contribute to the diversity, vitality—and confusion—of French political life.

Parti Communiste Français (PCF). From 1945 until 1981, the PCF was one of the largest political parties in France. It claimed to be the heir to the French revolutionary tradition and maintained close links to both the French working class, whose electoral support was a key source of the party's power, and the Soviet Union. For much of this period, the PCF's stated goal was to substitute public ownership and state control of the economy for France's capitalist system, which, it argued, was undemocratically organized and exploitative. This put the party on a collision course with nearly all other political parties and forces.

PCF support began to dwindle when the party failed to adapt its Marxist program and highly undemocratic structure to the political, social, and economic modernization that began to transform France from the 1960s. Wave after wave of dissidents failed to persuade party leaders to reject the Soviet ideological model, promote internal party democracy, and modernize the party's ideology and program. From commanding over 20 percent of the vote in elections in the postwar period, PCF electoral support fell to under 10 percent by the 1980s—it has fallen further since then, in some elections to under 5 percent. (It received 6 percent of the vote in the most recent elections, those to the European Parliament in 2004.)

The PCF suffered another blow when in the 1970s workers began to desert the Confédération générale du travail (CGT), France's largest trade union and a close ally of the PCF. Moreover, the Soviet Union's implosion beginning in 1989 further isolated and discredited the PCF.

Thanks to an alliance with the PS at election time, the PCF continues to enjoy modest parliamentary representation and to control the city halls of a significant number of towns. PCF ministers served in Socialist governments in the 1980s and 1990s. But the party has become a shadow of its once-mighty self. The kinds of voters who supported the PCF in the past, especially workers, youth, and the less educated, have drifted to far-left fringe parties or to the FN, whose coarse opposition to established parties is appealing to those on the margin of French society.

Front National (FN). The FN has existed for decades, but its rapid rise in the 1980s was fueled by high unemployment, European integration and globalization, fears triggered by increased crime, and ethnic tensions. The FN's relentless criticism of a handy scapegoat—Muslim immigrants—provided a simple answer to complicated questions.

The FN was among the first political parties in Western Europe in the contemporary period to defend racist themes. The party's slogan, "France for the French," does not answer the question, "Who (and what) is French?" However, the phrase suggests that immigrants, especially those who are not white, have no place in France.

The party has advocated giving French citizens priority over legal immigrants in the distribution of social benefits like public housing—"national preference" were the code words for the proposal. Party leader Jean-Marie Le Pen has cracked anti-Semitic jokes about Jewish politicians and characterized the Holocaust as "a historical detail." However, the FN's major target has been Muslims (most of whom are Arab) from Algeria, France's former North African colony. They are a clever choice because hostility toward Algerian immigrants lingers as a result of France's bitter colonial war in Algeria in the 1960s.

The FN advocates giving French (that is, white French) citizens preference over immigrants in employment, social benefits, public housing, and education. In the 1990s, the party broadened its program and attracted increased support by dramatizing France's rising crime rate, the corruption of mainstream French politicians, and the problems caused by European integration.

Le Pen, the FN's flamboyant leader, has powerfully contributed to the party's success. In the 1988 and 1995 presidential elections, Le Pen gained 15 percent of the first-ballot vote, just behind the major candidates. Although the party split in 1998, Le Pen survived the setback and achieved unprecedented success in 2002 by outpolling Jospin in the first round of the presidential elections.

Le Pen has added to his anti-immigrant and anti-Semitic platform an appeal to nationalism and right-wing libertarian populism. Recent FN proposals include eliminating the income tax, withdrawing France from the EU, and outlawing abortion. In Le Pen's 2002 election campaign, he appealed for the support of "miners, metalworkers, and workers from industries ruined by EU-style globalization, as well as farmers doomed to a miserable retirement and victims of insecurity [that is, crime]." The fact that so many voters heeded the call highlights weaknesses in French democracy.

However, there is intense competition to succeed the elderly Le Pen when he retires. (His personal choice is his daughter, Marine Le Pen, but the contest remains undecided.) Le Pen's authority was further challenged during the 2004 elections to the European Parliament when he was unable to prevent open jockeying among FN politicians to gain favorable places on FN electoral slates.

No matter what the outcome of the leadership succession struggle, however, the FN continues to retain a loyal electoral following (it scored 10 percent in the 2004 European elections), and its influence reaches far beyond the party's core electoral support. In a 1998 poll, 40 percent of French respondents—twice as many as Germans or British—reported holding racist beliefs. This is why political scientist James Shields claimed (years before the 2002 presidential elections) that "the rise of a powerful extreme-right party in France is arguably the most important political development of the past fourteen years."[4] Indeed, the growth of the FN suggests that a new cleavage has developed alongside the traditional left-right cleavage in France, one that pits both center-left and center-right parties against the extreme right. The cleavage involves support or opposition regarding a racist, xenophobic, and homophobic platform.

Les Verts (Greens). The relative indifference to environmental concerns of both the state and other political parties provided the potential for a Green movement in France. For example, Greens first reached public notice by sponsoring antinuclear protests, and they have been the only party to challenge France's nuclear power program, the largest in Western Europe.

The Greens were on the French political scene for years before achieving a major breakthrough in the 1989 European elections, when they gained 10.6 percent of the vote. The success was linked to the "new look" that the party adopted in the late 1980s, which appealed to young, well-educated voters, who provide the bulk of support for the Greens.

To an even greater extent than other parties, the Greens have been divided by the personal ambitions of their leaders. One held the position of minister of environment in the Jospin government from 1997 to 2002. However, the Greens' internal divisions weaken their potential electoral support. Their score in the 2004 European elections was 7 percent, considerably less than their breakthrough in 1989 but sufficient to enable them to retain representation in the European Parliament.

Union des Démocrates pour la France (UDF). Created in 1978, the UDF was an umbrella organization for several small center-right parties that opposed the forerunner of the UMP. The party's best-known leader was Valéry Giscard d'Estaing, president from 1974 until his defeat for reelection in 1981.

In the first years of the Fifth Republic, there were good reasons to have two major center-right parties, since the two differed sharply on many issues: The Gaullist Party strongly supported de Gaulle; the UDF opposed him. The UDF supported European integration; the forerunner of the UMP was divided on the issue. The UMP favored state direction of the economy; the UDF preferred free enterprise. But these divisions are long gone. In 2002, Chirac tried to merge the UMP and UDF. Many in the UDF threw in their lot with Chirac. But UDF leader François Bayrou opposed the merger and ran against Chirac in the 2002 presidential elections. Although he received a meager 7 percent of the popular votes, and UDF candidates did poorly in the 2002 legislative elections, by obtaining 12 percent of the vote in the 2004 European elections (only 5 percent less than the UMP), the UDF remains an important center-right gadfly opposing the UMP.

Table 14.1   Electoral Results, Elections to National Assembly, 1958–2002 (percentage of those voting)

	1958	1962	1967	1968	1973	1978	1981	1986	1988	1993	1997	2002
Far Left	2%	2%	2%	4%	3%	3%	1%	2%	0%	2%	2%	3%
PCF	19	22	23	20	21	21	16	10	11	9	10	5
Socialist Party/Left Radicals	23	21	19	17	22	25	38	32	38	21	26	25
Ecology	—	—	—	—	—	2	1	1	1	12	8	4
Center Parties	15	15	18	10	16	21*	19*		19*	19*	15*	
Center-Right	14	14	0	4	7			42*				5*
UNR-RPR-UMP[†]	18	32	38	44	24	23	21	—	19	20	17	34
Far Right	3	1	1	0	3	0	3	10	10	13	15	12
Abstentions	23	31	19	20	19	17	30	22	34	31	32	36

* Number represents the percentage of combined votes for Center and Center-Right parties.
UNR = Union pour la nouvelle République; RPR = Rassemblement pour la Répulique.
Note: Percentages of parties do not add to 100 because of minor-party candidates and rounding errors.
Sources: Françoise Dreyfus and François D'Arcy, *Les Institutions politiques et administratives de la France* (Paris: Economica, 1985), p. 54; *Le Monde,* March 18, 1986; Le Monde, *Les élections législatives* (Paris: Le Monde, 1988); Ministry of the Interior, 1993, 1997; *Le Monde,* June 11, 2002.

Elections

French voters go to the polls nearly every year to vote in a referendum or in elections for municipal, departmental, or regional councilor, deputy to the European Parliament or National Assembly, and president. The most important elections are the legislative and presidential elections (see Tables 14.1 and 14.2).

In the 1980s, scholars identified a trend toward the "normalization" of French politics, following the Socialist Party's right turn and the PCF's decline. For example, 57 percent of the electorate report that they saw little difference between the PS and the center-right.[5] Another element in the process of normalization was that, for the first time in the Fifth Republic, alternation occurred in the 1980s between parties of the center-left and center-right. However, the steady rise of the FN—especially Le Pen's performance in the 2002 presidential election— shattered the assumption that France is moving

toward a stable structuring of the party system around center-left and center-right poles. Indeed, scholars now speak of a crisis of political representation and the party system:

- Support for fringe parties not part of the select "cartel" of governmental parties has soared: it was well over a majority in the first round of the 2002 presidential elections.

- Voting patterns have been increasingly unstable. Political scientist Pascal Perrineau notes, "A new type of voter is emerging, less docile to social and territorial allegiances, less faithful to a party or political camp, and less involved in the act of voting. . . . Voters are likely to change their minds from one election to another, or even from one ballot to another in the same election."[6] In every one of the six legislative elections held between 1981 and 2002, the governing majority swung between the center-left and center-right parties. Such shifts were unthinkable in the first decades of the Fifth Republic. Laurent Fabius, a former prime minister, probably identified the most important reason for electoral instability when he observed after the 2002 elections, "For the past 20 years, the principal feature of our political life is the rejection of incumbents."[7]

- Voting turnout has steadily dwindled. In the 2002 elections, abstentions reached record levels: 28 percent in the first ballot of the presidential elections (along with an additional 3 percent who cast a spoiled or blank ballot), and 36 percent in the first ballot of the legislative elections.

- In an exhaustive study of French political participation, a research team found that political participation in France has not so much diminished—in fact, they claim, it has increased as a result of participation in voluntary associations.[8] The researchers found that citizens are less attached to their former fixed allegiances of class, region, and so on, and more volatile in their voting choices. The result is that the French are not so much depoliticized as disillusioned, for the political system—including established parties, the administration, and the government—cannot respond to their aspirations.

- Political leaders and parties have been implicated in countless financial scandals. In recent years, former cabinet ministers, the president of the Constitutional Council, and large-city mayors have been hauled into court. In response to the public outcry, four party finance laws were passed between 1988 and 1995. The legislation authorizes public funds for parties and candidates, limits private political gifts for parties and candidates, and establishes ceilings for campaign expenditures in elections at all levels. An independent election commission can disqualify candidates who violate campaign finance laws.

- Yet new revelations of political corruption continue to appear. President Chirac himself has been implicated in several major scandals. Compelling evidence suggests that, while mayor of Paris between 1977 and 1994, he received illicit political contributions and kickbacks from housing contractors for lavish vacations. (A popular satirical puppet show on television depicts Chirac as "super-liar!") Alain Juppé, head of the UMP, former prime minister, and Chirac's close associate, was convicted on corruption charges in 2004 involving schemes in which Chirac was also closely implicated. Chirac himself has thus far been spared humiliating trials only because courts have ruled that a sitting president cannot be prosecuted while in office.

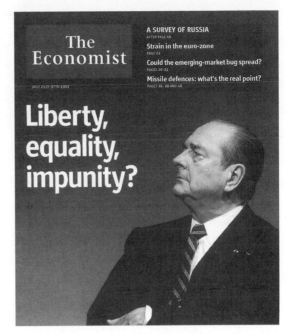

Allegations of corruption by President Chirac.

Source: Reuters.

Political Culture, Citizenship, and Identity

For close to a century, French political culture was structured in a quite stable fashion. Since the 1980s, however, traditional subcultures have eroded, and new forms of stable collective identity have not developed. This change helps explain the volatility in electoral behavior described above.

France's two most important traditional subcultures have disintegrated in recent decades. One was a predominantly working-class subculture structured by the strong grip of the PCF and the PCF's trade union ally, the CGT. The other subculture, attracting religiously observant, and politically and socially conservative French, was organized around the Catholic Church and its affiliated social organizations.

Both subcultures comprised a dense network of organizations in diverse spheres, including sports, culture, mutual aid, and professional

Table 14.2   Presidential Elections in the Fifth Republic (percentage of those voting)

	December 1965		June 1969		May 1974		April–May 1981	
	Candidate	Ballot Percentage	Candidate	Ballot Percentage	Candidate	Ballot Percentage	Candidate	Ballot Percentage
Extreme Right								
Center Right de Gaulle (Center-Right)	43.7	(54.5)	Pompidou (UNR)	44.0	(57.6)			Chirac (RPR)	18.0
Center Lecanuet (Opposition-Center)	15.8		Poher (Center)	23.4	(42.4)	Giscard	32.9 (50.7)	Giscard	28.3 (48.2)
Center Left Mitterrand (Socialist-Communist)	32.2	(45.5)	Defferre (PS)	5.1		Mitterrand (PS)	43.4 (49.3)	Mitterrand (PS)	25.8 (51.8)
Left			Duclos (PCF)	21.5				Marchais (PCF)	15.3
Abstentions	15.0	(15.5)		21.8	(30.9)		15.1 (12.1)		18.9 (14.1)

Note: Numbers in parentheses indicate percentage of vote received in second ballot. Percentages of votes for candidates do not add to 100 because of minor party candidates and rounding errors.

Sources: John R. Frears and Jean-Luc Parodi, *War Will Not Take Place: The French Parliamentary Elections of March 1978* (London: Hurst, 1976), p. 6; Le Monde, *L'Élection présidentielle: 26 avril–10 mai 1981* (Paris: Le Monde, 1981), pp. 98, 138; *Le Monde*, April 28 and May 12, 1988; *Journal Officiel*, May 14, 1995; *Le Monde*, May 5–6, 2002; *Le Monde*, May 7, 2002.

activities; they provided their members with distinctive (and opposed) political orientations, and social identities. The decline of the communist and Catholic subcultures has produced a vacuum. We analyze here changing forms of French political and social identity.

Social Class

For centuries, France was among the countries in which class cleavages periodically fueled intense political conflict. When Karl Marx sought an example of advanced economic development in the

April–May 1988		April–May 1995		April–May 2002	
Candidate	Ballot Percentage	Candidate	Ballot Percentage	Candidate	Ballot Percentage
Le Pen (FN)	14.4	Le Pen (FN)	15.0	Le Pen (FN)	17.0 (17.9)
Chirac (RPR)	19.9 (46.0)	Chirac (RPR)	20.8 (52.6)	Chirac (RPR)	19.9 (82.1)
Barre	16.5	Balladur (UDF)	18.9	Bayou (UDF)	6.8
				Saint-Josse (CNPT)	4.3
				Madelin (PR)	3.9
Mitterrand (PS)	34.1 (54.0)	Jospin (PS)	23.3 (47.4)	Jospin (PS)	16.1
				Chevènement	5.3
				Mamère (Greens)	5.3
Lajoinie (PCF)	6.8	Hue (PCF)	8.6	Hue (PCF)	3.4
				3 candidates (Extreme Left)	10.6
			20.6		27.9 (19.9)

nineteenth century, he studied Britain. When he looked for clues to how political and class conflict might develop, he studied the French revolutions of 1830 and 1848 and the Paris Commune. A watershed change in collective identities occurred during the 1970s and 1980s. Under the impact of economic change and ideological reorientation, declining numbers of French identified themselves as belonging to a social class (see Table 14.3).

The most extensive decline in class identification has occurred in the ranks of manual workers. There are many reasons for the declining

Table 14.3   Proportion of French Citizens
Identifying Themselves as Members of a Social Class

	1976	1983	1987
Total	68%	62%	56%
Occupation of respondents			
Higher executives, professionals	68	67	60
Middle executives, school teachers	57	66	63
Office workers	64	62	59
Manual workers	74	71	50

Source: *L'Expansion,* March 20–April 27, 1987, in
Louis Dirn, *La Société française en tendances* (Paris: PUF,
1990), p. 63.

importance of working-class identity—a tendency found throughout Europe. One reason is the massive economic restructuring that has occurred since the 1970s, with a shrinking of basic industries (including steel, shipbuilding, automobiles, and textiles), which has produced the closing of some of the largest plants and a general downsizing of the industrial workforce. Thus, the number of manual workers in France has shrunk by one-quarter in the past several decades.

Another reason why working-class identity is less salient is the decline and changing character of the trade union movement, a traditionally important source of working-class identity and activity. This development is described below.

Citizenship and National Identity

The French have traditionally taken pride in the fact that citizenship rights have been granted in a highly inclusive fashion. Sociologist Rogers Brubaker suggests that the traditional German understanding was based on blood or ethnicity; thus, only those born of German parents were entitled to become citizens. By contrast, the

French conception of citizenship is based on the principle of territory: anyone born on French soil, including the offspring of parents who are not citizens, automatically possesses citizenship rights.[9] These differing approaches also inform the ease with which immigrants can obtain citizenship: French naturalization rates have been several times higher than those in Germany. More generally, until recently France posed few barriers to immigration, with the result that large numbers of immigrants settled in France and eventually became citizens. Political sociologist Charles Tilly observes that France has "served as Europe's greatest melting pot."[10]

France has a two-sided approach to citizenship and national identity that dates back to the Revolution of 1789. On the one hand, the inclusionary aspect of the republican model specifies that any immigrant who accepts French political values and culture is entitled to citizenship; there are no ethnic, racial, or other ascriptive (inherited) restrictions on becoming a French citizen. On the other hand, there is an exclusionary side to this conception: the republican model insists that people's distinctive cultural identities and values should be considered purely private preferences and should play no role in the public sphere. The French believe that if ethnic identities were to be injected into the public sphere, the result would be to fragment the indivisible and culturally neutral French republic. According to the dominant French view, there should be no hyphenated identities—such as Algerian-French or Italian-French—of the sort common in the United States. Most French regard the American conception of multiculturalism as giving priority to ethnic or religious identity over common ties of citizenship. Yet France's dominant color-blind and ethnic-blind model has produced a virtual absence of minority representatives in key political institutions like the Constitutional Council, National Assembly, or government.

For generations, France has integrated millions of immigrants from many cultures and regions of the world. Moreover, the particular values that define the basis for inclusion in the political community—liberty, equality, fraternity, secularism, and rationalism—are admirable. However, France's characteristic approach is hostile to alternative conceptions of the public sphere and either rejects other values or relegates them to the private sphere.

The latent conflict between the secular, republican model and other conceptions of the political order has come to a head in the recent period, when the dominant model was challenged by some French Muslims. Since the 1980s, there have been important conflicts and debates involving demands by a minority of Muslims for substantial accommodation to their religious beliefs, for example, sex-segregated gym classes. The ban on Muslim girls wearing headscarves in public schools, which opened Chapter 11, is an important illustration of how divisions have hardened on this issue.

Ethnicity and Immigration

France has traditionally attracted large numbers of immigrants. Indeed, in 1930, the proportion of immigrants was higher in France than in the United States.[11] Today, one French person in four has at least one grandparent who is foreign-born. So what? Historian Gérard Noiriel suggests that the successive waves of immigration "allowed the country to preserve its rank on the international scene, whereas many observers in the late nineteenth century had predicted its irremediable decline."[12] Immigrants have made an invaluable contribution to France's economic performance. Moreover, immigrants have also contributed to France's scientific and cultural reputation. In the twentieth century, scientist Marie Curie, philosopher Henri Bergson, writers Paul Verlaine and Guillaume Apollinaire, painters Pablo Picasso and Marc Chagall, composer Igor Stravinsky—even the quintessentially French actor Yves Montand—were of immigrant background.

Contrary to a widespread belief that conflicts between native-born French and immigrants originated recently, historian David Bell observes, "The Belgians and Italians met as much hostility and prejudice in their time as Algerians and black Africans have done in contemporary France, and sometimes more."[13] Early in the twentieth century, tensions often ran high between immigrants arriving from Poland, Italy, and Portugal and native-born French.

The most recent wave of immigrants has mostly been Muslims (predominantly Arabs) from North Africa, especially Algeria, the former colony with which France fought a bitter war in the 1960s. There are about 5 million Muslims in France; about half are French citizens. During France's economic boom in the 1960s, the government actively recruited workers from North Africa to fill construction and factory jobs that native-born French rejected. When economic growth slowed in the 1970s, successive governments restricted immigration. Virtually all new immigration has been banned since 1993. Ironically, given France's aging population and dwindling birthrate, additional immigration would revitalize French society.

The relationship of Muslim immigrants to the secular republic has generated intense controversy. Many native-born white French resent the presence of immigrant families. Tensions run especially high in impoverished urban neighborhoods. One result of these tensions has been a challenge to the inclusive conception of citizenship described above. In the 1980s, the FN opposed automatically granting citizenship to immigrants' children born in France (second-generation immigrants from North Africa are known as Beurs—a term that some consider insulting). An FN slogan claimed: "To be French, you must deserve it." The conservative government of the time sought to capitalize on the popularity of this theme by modifying the procedure. Henceforth, immigrants' children must apply for citizenship. Further, in 2003 the criteria were tightened for gaining political asylum (that is, seeking to enter France to avoid abusive treatment in one's home country). Amnesty International, an internationally respected nongovernmental human rights organization, issued a report in 2004 criticizing the new asylum policy.[14]

There has thus been a sea change in French attitudes toward citizenship. Noiriel suggests that, since the 1980s, "the view that immigrants represented a threat to 'national identity,' originally launched by the far right, [came to be] held by large sectors of the public."[15] Public opinion polls document that racist attitudes are significantly more widespread in France than in most other EU member countries, although polls also suggest a slight decline from the high point of such views in the 1990s.

Gender

Women, the largest "minority"—in reality a 51 percent majority—have traditionally been highly underrepresented in the French political system. There has never been a female president of the republic and only one prime minister: Edith Cresson, who served briefly under President Mitterrand and was the object of considerable ridicule, in part because of her gender.

France was the home of modernist feminist thought. Philosopher and novelist Simone de Beauvoir's *The Second Sex*, published after World War II, is a landmark in this regard. In the 1960s and 1970s, French feminist theorists played a major role in reshaping literary studies around the world. However, these contributions have not been matched by comparable gains in the economic and political spheres: there is considerable gender inequality in France, and women's movements, like many other social movements, have been relatively weak in the face of a distant state.

Women's meager political representation means that state policy has often been unresponsive to women's concerns. Contraception, for example, was illegal in France until 1967. Abortion was banned until 1974. A law outlawing sexual harassment was not passed until 1992 (it was considerably strengthened in 2001). On the other hand, legislation bans publishing sexist material, and women's interests are served by extensive welfare state benefits, including paid parental leave, subsidized day care facilities, and public health programs.

Women have traditionally been highly underrepresented in politics. Although over half the electorate, women constitute less than 10 percent of the National Assembly, putting France toward the low end of women's legislative representation among EU countries.

This situation is in the process of changing. After years of mobilization, a constitutional amendment was passed in 1999 and legislation was adopted in 2000 that put France at the forefront of countries seeking to increase women's political representation. The 2000 parity law, as it is called, requires parties to nominate an equal number of male and female candidates in those elections where a list system is used, notably, municipal and regional elections and elections to the European Parliament. Parties may be disqualified if they violate the law. In elections held in single-member districts, parties that fail to nominate an equal number of men and women are given smaller public campaign subsidies.

The results to date of the parity law have been mixed. The 2001 municipal elections, the first held since the reform was adopted, produced a dramatic increase in women's representation. The number of women on municipal councils skyrocketed from 7,000 to 39,000. Similarly, in the 2004 regional elections, women nearly doubled their representation on regional councils; they now comprise 47.5 percent of all regional councillors. The proportion of women in the Senate increased from 11 to 17 percent following the 2004 elections.

Although the glass ceiling in French political institutions has been cracked, it is far from being shattered. The parity law mandates gender balance for representative institutions but is silent about the executives of these bodies, such as mayors or presidents of the regional councils.

Thus far, women have made few inroads at this level. Case in point: although women's representation on regional councils soared after the 2004 regional elections, only one of the twenty-two regional councils of mainland France elected a female president.

The second reason that the glass ceiling remains intact is the different treatment of elections held according to the single-member and list system. Parties incur a stiff penalty if they do not ensure gender equality in elections held by the list system, but the penalty for not achieving gender balance in nominations for single-member districts is relatively mild. Far from coincidentally, France's two most powerful political institutions, the National Assembly and presidency, are chosen from single-member districts! Regarding presidential elections, there is no mandate whatsoever for parties to nominate women. As for elections to the National Assembly, if a party does not nominate an equal number of male and female candidates, public campaign subsidies are reduced. But parties may calculate that this is a price worth paying. In the 2002 legislative elections, only one-fifth of the candidates nominated by the UMP, the major victor in the elections, were women. As a result, the number of women elected to the National Assembly in 2002 rose only slightly.

Thus far, the parity law provides a perfect illustration of the debate about whether the glass is half full or half empty. Although the reform has indisputably produced a major change in French political discourse and practice, women are not yet the political equals of men. Further, a key question—which it is too soon to answer—is whether women's increased political representation will result in legislative and policy changes that produce social and economic equality between men and women. The parity law thus provides a laboratory test of whether increasing political representation produces legislation that addresses gender inequality in the wider society.

Interests, Protest and Social Movements

The political party system represents one arena for citizen participation and representation. But, because parties have mostly confined their activities to electing a president and parliamentary majority, citizens have organized in other ways to pursue their interests.

Organized Interests

The overbearing French state has typically tended to limit possibilities for social movements and private interest groups. Although the Fifth Republic reinforced this tendency by strengthening the executive, organized interests do play varied roles. There is great variety in the relationship between administrative agencies and interest groups. At one extreme, the National Federation of Farmers' Unions (FNSEA) exercises immense power. Its representatives serve on the administrative commissions that determine agricultural prices and subsidies. It is sometimes difficult to distinguish where the Ministry of Agriculture ends and the FNSEA begins. Another powerful organization is the Movement of French Business Firms (Medef). Although they are not as powerful as the FNSEA or Medef, trade associations and labor unions play an important part in administering the public health system and state-financed vocational training programs. Representatives of interest groups also serve on the peak-level advisory body, the Economic and Social Council (described in Chapter 13).

At the other extreme, French labor unions are relatively weak (although they enjoy significant benefits from helping manage social insurance funds). French unions never organized as large a proportion of workers as did unions in other Western European countries. But they have steadily declined in strength from their postwar high: the proportion of the active labor force belonging to a union has plummeted from a high of over 30 percent to less than 10 percent—the lowest figure of any industrialized democracy. The bulk of union members are found among public sector workers.

The trade union movement is highly fragmented. There are five umbrella trade union confederations claiming to represent workers throughout the economy, as well as independent unions in specific sectors (such as teachers). Each confederation pursues its own course, often opposed to that of the others. Traditionally, divisions were heightened because each confederation was allied with a competing political party. The confederations' ties to political parties have weakened in recent years, but their mutual rivalry continues.

The low rate of unionization and divisions among unions are key factors in understanding unions' weak influence. Nonetheless, unions enjoy far wider support among workers and the general public than their small size would suggest, as evidenced by their ability to mobilize large numbers of nonmembers during strikes and the general public to turn out for demonstrations. For example, candidates sponsored by trade unions often run representative mechanisms like works councils. Union power is bolstered by the fact that collective bargaining agreements cover not only card-carrying union members but all workers in the sector. And, by a process known as extension, the Ministry of Labor often applies the terms of these agreements to nonunionized firms in an industry.

Yet because of their meager size and internal divisions, trade unions have little direct influence in shaping public policy. For years, the labor movement could not persuade the state to legislate even minimal protection for union officials in the face of arbitrary employer actions. Under these conditions, unions have often expressed their demands by direct protest rather than behind-the-scenes negotiations with private employers and state administrators. Their influence often is directed to blocking policies they oppose, such as the Juppé government's social reforms, rather than in persuading the government to adopt policies they favor.[16]

Social Movements and Protest

Although Fifth Republic institutions were designed to discourage citizens from acting autonomously, they have not overcome France's centuries-old tradition of direct protest. Throughout the nineteenth century, authoritarian regimes could not prevent mass opposition and revolution. More recently, the May 1968 uprising was "the nearest thing to a full-blown revolution ever experienced in an advanced industrial society" and a vivid reminder of how fragile political stability can be in France.[17] A repeat performance occurred in December 1995, when transportation workers brought Paris and other large cities grinding to a halt. (We describe the 1995 protests in Chapter 15.) And other important strikes and demonstrations occur periodically. Most recently, 2 million people turned out to protest changes in pension benefits in 2003. Among groups resorting to strikes and demonstrations in recent years were farmers, fishing interests, postal workers, teachers, high school students, truckers, railway workers, healthcare workers, the unemployed, immigrants and their offspring, research workers, and actors—to provide a partial list!

As should be clear, protest movements are not confined to manual workers. For example, French doctors waged a five-month slowdown in 2001–2002. A strike by actors and other cultural workers led to the cancellation of the Avignon summer theater festival in 2003. Several human rights advocacy organizations have existed in France for decades. In the recent period, movements have organized around additional issues, including AIDS, the homeless, the environment, women's rights, gay rights, racism, and undocumented immigrants. As described in Chapter 15, a vast antiglobalization movement has developed in France.

Another trend in recent decades is a sharp increase in the number of civic associations that are noncontestatory and focus on sports, leisure, and cultural activities. Whereas in 1975, about 20,000 new associations were created, 60,000 new associations have been created annually in the current period. Although these statistics reveal a sharp rise in civic membership, the French remain less likely to join such associations than citizens of neighboring countries. Although 39 percent of the French report belonging to one or more associations, the comparable figures are 53 percent in the United Kingdom, 58 percent in Belgium, 67 percent in Germany, and 84 percent in the Netherlands.[18]

To sum up the last two chapters, the Fifth Republic proved better at strengthening the state than in enabling citizens to organize their demands. Despite changes that have brought the state closer to citizens, an adequate balance has not yet been struck between the French state and civil society. This suggests an unsettling question: Does the French political system have the capacity to address current challenges?

Notes

1. Olivier Duhamel, *Le Pouvoir politique en France*, 5th ed. (Paris: Éditions du Seuil, 2003), p. 266.

2. John D. Huber, *Rationalizing Parliament: Legislative Institutions and Party Politics in France* (Cambridge: Cambridge University Press, 1996).

3. Jean Charlot, *La Politique en France* (Paris: Livre de Poche, 1994), p. 21.

4. James G. Shields, "Le Pen and the Progression of the Far-Right Vote in France," *French Politics and Society* 13, no. 2 (Spring 1995): 37.

5. Charlot, *La Politique en France*, p. 159.

6. Pascal Perrineau, "Election Cycles and Changing Patterns of Political Behavior in France," *French Politics and Society* 13, no. 1 (Winter 1995): 53.

7. *Libération*, July 4, 2002.

8. Pascal Perrineau, ed., *L'Engagement politique: Déclin ou mutation?* (Paris: Presses de la Fondation Nationale des Sciences Politiques, 1994).

9. Rogers Brubaker, *Citizenship and Nationhood in France and Germany* (Cambridge: Harvard University Press, 1992).

10. Charles Tilly, Foreword to Gérard Noiriel, *The French Melting Pot: Immigration, Citizenship, and National Identity* (Minneapolis: University of Minnesota Press, 1996), p. vii.

11. Patrick Weil, *La France et ses étrangers* (Paris: Gallimard, 1991), p. 28.

12. Noiriel, *The French Melting Pot*, p. 240.

13. David A. Bell, *The Cult of the Nation in France: Inventing Nationalism, 1680–1800* (Cambridge: Harvard University Press, 2001), p. 210.

14. *Le Monde*, May 28, 2004.

15. Tilly's paraphrase of Noiriel's position, in Noiriel, *The French Melting Pot*, p. xii.

16. See Anthony Daley, "The Hollowing Out of French Unions: Politics and Industrial Relations After 1981," in Andrew Martin and George Ross, eds., *The Brave New World of European Labor: European Trade Unions at the Millennium* (New York: Berghahn Books, 1999), and Herrick Chapman, Mark Kesselman, and Martin A. Schain, eds., *A Century of Organized Labor in France: A Union Movement for the Twenty-First Century?* (New York: St. Martin's Press, 1998).

17. Stephen Bornstein, "States and Unions: From Postwar Settlement to Contemporary Stalemate," in Stephen Bornstein, David Held, and Joel Krieger, eds., *The State in Capitalist Europe: A Casebook* (Winchester, Mass.: George Allen & Unwin, 1984), p. 64.

18. Commissariat général du plan, *Rapport sur les perspectives de la France* (Paris: La Documentation Française, 2000), p. 86.

CHAPTER

15

French Politics in Transition

The pace of change throughout the world has rapidly accelerated as space and time are compressed by the incredible technological advances of recent decades and national borders become more porous as a result of increased transnational economic, political, social, and cultural flows. To paraphrase the famous opening line of John Donne's poem, one might suggest that no country is an island; all are interconnected by globalization.

But just how does globalization influence a country's politics? After September 11, 2001, we have become painfully aware that globalization may involve not only increased knowledge, productivity, and efficiency, but also terrorism.

Thus, globalization is not a single process but a stream of processes, sometimes but not always interrelated. Similarly, countries vary in the ways that they participate in and are affected by globalization. A country's relationship to globalization is refracted through the prism of its political, economic, and cultural institutions. These remarks are a point of departure to analyze current political challenges and changing agendas in French politics.

Political Challenges and Changing Agendas

What a distance separates French politics in the first decade of the twenty-first century from an earlier period. Until the late 1980s, the major political parties were arrayed quite neatly along a left-right ideological continuum linked to social class divisions. In the 1970s, public attention was riveted on the opposition between an alliance of the Communist and Socialist parties, based on a radical reformist program, and the conservative center-right parties. In the early 1980s, the reform initiatives of the Socialist government dominated the news. When the center-right coalition gained a parliamentary majority in 1986, its first priority was to roll back many of the Socialist government's reforms.

Several years later, however, the governing parties on both sides of the ideological divide converged toward an acceptance of France's mixed economy, consisting of the coexistence of a reduced role for the state combined with heavy reliance on private market forces. These parties agreed that, for the sake of European integration, it was worth making unpopular economic policy choices to reduce government deficits and the public debt. By the mid-1990s, then, it appeared that substantial ideological controversy among the major political parties had ended. Might the result be the end of French exceptionalism?

In retrospect, the calm that prevailed was the prelude to the storm. We review here a series of political challenges since the mid-1990s that highlight continuities and changes in France's political agenda. They raise troubling questions about the adequacy of the existing system to confront that agenda.

The Strikes of December 1995: May 1968 Redux?

In late 1995, France was rocked by a series of strikes and demonstrations whose extent and intensity recalled those of May 1968. The strikes might be considered the first act of a drama involving the restructuring of the French welfare state that has yet to be concluded. Analyzing the strikes reveals elements of change that have recently occurred in France, elements of continuity, and some of the challenges that France is currently confronting.

The origins of the massive strikes in 1995 may be found in the conjunction of France's severe economic difficulties, expectations raised by Jacques Chirac's 1995 presidential election campaign advocating change, and intense disillusionment and anger when Chirac renounced his electoral pledges.

In Chapter 12, we reviewed how France has undergone extensive economic restructuring, involving both modernization for many industries and extensive dislocations for entire regions and sectors of the population. Since the Socialists' "right turn" in 1983, governments of left and right alike have promoted the intensive modernization of French industry by market-friendly means.

In the 1995 presidential election, Chirac attempted to differentiate himself from another conservative candidate, as well as from Socialist Party candidate Lionel Jospin, François Mitterrand's heir apparent. Chirac lamented what he called the "social fracture" that divided France into those enjoying economic prosperity and those excluded from its benefits. He promised that things would change if he were elected. A journalist commented that Chirac "was forced to adopt the strategy of an outsider, gambling that victory would go not to a candidate proposing continuity, but to the candidate who advocated change."[1] In a famous phrase during the campaign, Chirac declared, "Pay stubs [that is, decent wage levels] are not the enemy of employment." And it was no surprise that in his victory speech following the election, he proclaimed, "Our battle has a name: the struggle against unemployment."

Although Chirac's strategy was electorally successful, it soon proved politically costly. Only months after he had promised that things could be different, he abruptly announced an about-face in a television interview in late 1995. The need to comply with the strict fiscal requirements of the EU collided with electoral promises, and the promises lost.

Soon after Chirac's interview, Prime Minister Alain Juppé proposed some major reforms that amounted to a declaration of war on labor unions and large sectors of the French population. Proposed changes involved reducing civil servants' pension benefits and ending preferential retirement benefits for workers in key public sectors, raising payroll taxes, reducing social benefits, and increasing government control, while weakening union influence, over social spending. At the same time, Juppé announced cutbacks in higher education for hiring and construction of new facilities.

Reaction to the proposed reforms was swift and massive. Transportation workers soon struck, bringing France to a halt when service shut down on Air France flights, railroads, buses, and the Paris métro. The strikes quickly spread, and in short order the postal system ground to a halt, garbage accumulated on city streets, schools closed, and power slowdowns occurred. Demonstrations were mounted in support of the strikes. The high point was in early December, when 2 million people turned out to demonstrate their solidarity with the strikers. The strikes wound down when the government abandoned many of the proposed changes.

The 1995 strikes reveal the continuing vitality of the French tradition of popular protest. Other important strikes and demonstrations occurred in the trucking industry in 2002, in the healthcare sector in 2003 and 2004, in the cultural sector in 2003, around the issue of retirement in 2003, and in the electrical power industry in 2004. Yet another important strike may be making news while you read this book!

Oui *to Roquefort Cheese,* Non *to Genetically Engineered Products*

Several years after the 1995 strikes challenged social cutbacks, another movement developed to oppose what participants regard as the undemocratic process of globalization and Europeanization. The antiglobalization movement is quite diverse and includes environmentalists, far-leftists, intellectuals, and farmers. The movement's best-known leader is José Bové, a sheep farmer from southwestern France, where famed Roquefort cheese is produced. Small farmers like Bové oppose the standardized methods of farming that agribusiness corporations seek to impose (including the use of genetically modified seed), as well as farmers' loss of autonomy resulting from centralization of food distribution and processing by large corporations. Bové achieved worldwide prominence in early 1999 when he led a march that ransacked a McDonald's construction site in southwest France. For Bové and his millions of supporters, McDonald's symbolizes what is wrong about the EU and globalization: a U.S.-based multinational corporation purveying standardized fast food that might include genetically engineered products (genetically modified organisms, GMOs) and that produces meals that are an insult to traditional French cuisine.

Bové served six weeks in prison for the McDonald's attack and was sentenced to an additional prison term for an attack on genetically engineered crops in 1998. At the same time, he received support from across the political spectrum. President Chirac announced that he too dislikes McDonald's food and that he supports Bové's project of seeking to protect traditional French farming, cuisine, and lifestyles from the homogenizing forces of globalization.

When the World Trade Organization met in Seattle in 1999 to debate strengthening regulations requiring governments to guarantee free trade and investment, the French agriculture minister, who was a delegate, invited Bové to attend the conference and praised his efforts. (Bové managed to smuggle 100 pounds of Roquefort to Seattle and distributed it to the protesters.) After the EU banned American hormone-injected beef from European markets, the United States imposed punitive tariffs on EU food imports to the United States. Is it merely a coincidence that Roquefort cheese was included on the list?

Globalization. "And if Roquefort and Microsoft were to emerge?" Let's discuss it with José!"
This cartoon appeared when José Bové traveled to the Seattle meeting of the World Trade Organization in 1999.

Source: Plantu, Cartoonists & Writers Syndicate, from *Cassettes, Mensonges et Vidéo* (Paris: Le Seuil, 2000), p. 36.

France is a center of the antiglobalization movement. (Its members now refer to the movement as *altermondistes*—based on the movement's slogan: "Another world is possible." The name is intended to avoid the negative impression conveyed by the term *antiglobalization*.) In 1998, an organization named ATTAC was created, which quickly grew to over 25,000 members and nearly 200 local committees in France and other countries. ATTAC has sponsored forums and demonstrations to oppose free trade and capital movements and to support a plan, originally proposed by Nobel economics prize laureate James Tobin, to impose a tax on international financial speculation. (The name ATTAC stands for the Association in Support of the Tobin Tax.) ATTAC has been an organizer of the annual World Social Forums held annually in Brazil and India, where antiglobalization activists gather to strategize.

The Challenge of Le Pen and the FN

The antiglobalization movement is one response to France's changing position in a changing world. The growth of the Le Pen phenomenon and ethnic conflicts are others. The Front National (FN) has reaped a political harvest from the presence of Muslims in French society. Le Pen rose to political prominence in the 1980s by attacking what he alleged was the Socialist government's laxity toward Muslim immigrants. The FN's simplistic and racist response to rising unemployment, extensive layoffs in key industries, growing European integration, and budgetary austerity was to blame immigrants. Political scientist Pierre Birnbaum observes, "What the National Front proposes to the French people . . . is a magical solution to their distress, to their loss of confidence in grand political visions of the nation."[2]

At first Le Pen appealed mostly to groups on the far right of the political spectrum. However, he eventually attracted significant working-class support. In the 2002 presidential elections, the unemployed made up one-third of Le Pen's electorate.[3] Le Pen attracted a higher proportion of workers' votes than did any other candidate.

The FN's success may be due less to the substance of its ideas than to its position as critic of the established system. Polls show that a majority of FN supporters do not share the party's ideas but vote for Le Pen to protest against the established system of parties and politicians. Yet unfortunately one reason for the FN's popularity is that its xenophobic message has found a receptive audience. The proportion of French reporting that they agree with the party's program rose from 11 percent in 1999 to 28 percent in 2002.[4]

Muslim-Jewish Tensions

A recent addition to the list of challenges confronting the French political system is Muslim-Jewish tensions. Israel's occupation of the West Bank in early 2002 provoked hundreds of anti-Semitic attacks that included violent assaults on Jews and the defacing of synagogues, Jewish cemeteries, schools, kosher restaurants, and sports clubs. Of course, French Jews were not responsible for Israel's actions, but they provided a convenient target for Muslim youth—many of whom were the victims of unemployment and racial discrimination in France—who were outraged by Israel's actions. After synagogues were torched in Marseilles, Strasbourg, and Lyons over the 2002 Passover-Easter weekend, the government stationed police with submachine weapons outside synagogues throughout France. Parliament also passed hate-crime legislation providing for stiffer penalties for crimes committed because of a victim's ethnicity, race, or religion.

According to one specialist, these "incidents are linked to some very real social problems in France, where many Arabs who are having a hard time or are frustrated with what is going on in Palestine are taking it out on Jews."[5] Tensions are intensified because France has the largest number of both Muslims (5 million) and Jews (500,000) of any country in Europe.

From the Social Fracture to Law and Order

Problems involving law and order go beyond Muslim-Jewish tensions or immigration. The crime rate has risen steadily in France, especially in urban slums with high rates of poverty and unemployment. (To put the problem in perspective, however, U.S. homicide rates are four times those in France.) Public anxiety reached a fever pitch in early 2002 following a series of brutal murders, rapes, car burnings, and crime sprees that were luridly reported on television, and often given more prominent coverage than the presidential campaign that spring. Public opinion polls revealed that the issue that most concerned voters was a feeling of insecurity due to inadequate public safety. Le Pen and Chirac capitalized on and increased widespread fears by relentlessly criticizing the Jospin government's allegedly soft attitude toward crime. The barrage of criticism contributed to Jospin's failure to qualify for the runoff ballot.

Following his reelection and the victory of the Union pour un mouvement populaire (UMP) the following month in the legislative elections, Chirac quickly tried to preempt the issue by naming the dynamic Nicolas Sarkozy to be interior minister in Jean-Pierre Raffarin's cabinet. Sarkozy waged an energetic campaign to reduce crime. Although the Raffarin government was regarded as performing poorly in many policy areas, it was considered highly effective in improving law and order. As a result, the issue of personal safety faded from public prominence as quickly as it had developed.

At the same time, the underlying sources of violent crime persist—that is, poverty, unemployment, inequality, and discrimination. Following the UMP's disastrous showing in the 2004 regional elections, Chirac sought to deal with these structural problems by creating a superministry of employment, labor, and social cohesion headed by a rising young UMP politician. The ministry will be responsible for administering a "plan for promoting social cohesion" (it has informally been called a Marshall Plan) focusing on the 163 most dilapidated neighborhoods throughout France—those with the highest rates of crime, poverty, and social tensions. The plan earmarks substantial sums for housing construction and renovation in these neighborhoods. But the need to finance the plan collides with EU commitments to contain government spending—and the plan's future is uncertain.

Institutional Strains and New Issues and Sources of Partisan Conflict: Economy and Identity

In the past two decades, traditional ideological conflicts have waned, and major political parties have moved closer together. Debates involving the best way to organize the economy have been replaced by widespread acceptance of a mixed economy blending state regulation and market competition.

Significant institutional reforms, including the decentralization measures sponsored by the Socialists in the early 1980s and the Raffarin government in 2004, shortening the presidential term, and mandating gender parity in political representation, have produced a more balanced regime. Yet the important challenges described in this chapter have generated calls for additional institutional reforms. An extreme proposal—one unlikely to be adopted—involves transforming the Fifth Republic to a purely presidential system by abolishing the office of prime minister and prohibiting the president from dissolving parliament. More modest proposals include increasing parliament's role in preparing the budget, reforming the quite unrepresentative Senate, further restricting politicians' right to hold multiple elected offices (the *cumul des mandats*), and revising procedures for elections to the National Assembly and subnational governments to promote stable government by providing a bonus to large, mainstream parties and penalizing fringe parties. Debates about institutional reform will doubtless persist because France has not yet struck an adequate balance between vigorous political leadership and vibrant democratic participation.

Underlying the issue of institutional reform is a more general problem. The governing parties have been relatively unsuccessful in addressing two major issues: the economic challenge of ensuring jobs and decent living standards for all French citizens and the cultural challenge involving the redefinition of French identity.

"It's the Economy, Stupid."   Bill Clinton was elected president of the United States in 1992 over incumbent president George H. W. Bush because, during a painful recession, Clinton's major campaign promise was to "focus like a laser" on the economy. Bush's loss in 1992 is a reminder that politicians generally succeed when the economy flourishes and are punished when the economy stagnates. The uneven performance of the French economy in the past several decades helps explain the political gyrations that have occurred. (When French voters were asked what determined their vote in the 2004

European elections, the factor mentioned most often was unemployment.)[6] Although France has performed well in the global economy, high rates of unemployment and large numbers of marginalized citizens represent a heavy economic and social cost.

France faces a particular challenge in adapting its typical style of economic governance to current economic demands. As described in Chapter 12, after World War II the French excelled at state-directed promotion of large firms serving the protected home market and France's colonies. In the current economic race, however, victory often goes not to the large but to the flexible, and state direction may prove a handicap, not an advantage. Moreover, the cost of innovation in many new spheres now exceeds the capacity of a medium-sized power such as France. A further disquieting development is that France has reduced the proportion of its national income devoted to scientific research and development; it devotes significantly less than do Germany, Japan, and the United States.

Recall, too, our analysis in Chapter 12 of the challenge to finance the extensive social welfare sector in an era when unemployment is high, the proportion of the working population (which finances such programs) is declining, and EU treaty obligations impose severe fiscal constraints. The modest reforms achieved thus far have been highly unpopular and have failed to resolve the structural deficit resulting from rising costs outstripping revenue. Overall, public finances are fragile, and no solutions have yet been devised to bring the government's budget deficit and public debt below EU ceilings.

The Challenges of European and Global Integration

The EU and globalization pose particular challenges for French national identity and political, economic, and cultural autonomy. It is no coincidence that support for fringe parties of the left and the right—which are uniformly critical of France's participation in the EU—has increased

with the deepening of European integration in the past two decades.

Many have begun to oppose the EU because of what they believe is its failure to deliver adequate economic benefits, its undemocratic process of decision making, and its betrayal of French independence, sovereignty, and identity. The coalition is quite diverse, stretching from Le Pen's FN through the *altermondistes* to far-left parties. Its support derives from the fact that many people believe that mainstream parties and leaders on the center-left and center-right have failed to provide a convincing defense of the basic policy shift since the mid-1980s that involves the pooling of French sovereignty in the EU. Political scientist Pascal Perrineau has pointed out that there are no major political leaders nowadays like former presidents Mitterrand and Giscard d'Estaing who "describe Europe as a project, a dream, a utopia." Rather, Perrineau observes, "Europe is now widely regarded as a constraint."[7] French voters' lack of enthusiasm for the EU can be gleaned from the fact that 57 percent of voters did not bother going to the polls in the 2004 European elections, a record low in a national election—and a considerably lower level of turnout than the average turnout rate in EU member states. (Another reason for low turnout in France was that the two-ballot regional elections took place less than two months earlier.)

The relationship of France's Muslim minority to the wider political community is an economic and social challenge that French political culture is ill equipped to handle. Although France has stiff laws outlawing racial and religious discrimination, hate crimes, and incitement to racist violence, and welfare state programs distribute substantial benefits to individuals who qualify, political scientist Robert Lieberman notes that the French approach to exclusion "has not gone beyond the color-blind frame and the model of individual discrimination to embrace a more collective approach that attempts to compensate for inequalities between groups."[8] While there have been some recent attempts to provide affirmative-action kinds of programs designed to integrate Muslims within the French political community, much remains to be done.

In somewhat related fashion, the indivisible French republic has found it difficult to accommodate increasing demands for regional autonomy. Conflicts involving the status of the island of Corsica, an integral part of the French republic, have been especially intense. For years, movements demanded Corsican independence, and several sought to achieve this goal by violent means. For example, the prefect assigned to the island was assassinated in 1999. Recent decentralization reforms granted Corsica considerable autonomy, but it is too soon to say whether this will peacefully resolve the conflict. Equally likely is that the reform will prove too timid for Corsican nationalists but too extreme for French nationalists.

More generally, an important question is whether French national identity can be refashioned within the EU just when the French republican values of liberty, equality, and fraternity have become widely shared—and when regional and religious minorities within France have begun to challenge the dominant model of cultural assimilation in order to preserve their own distinctive identities.

The French have not been unaware of the challenges they face. Indeed, the country has been wracked by self-doubt in recent years. There has been a cottage industry of books published with titles like *France Falling* and *France's Disarray*. *France Falling*, a relentless critique of France's political and economic system that totally ignored anything positive, was on the bestseller list for months.[9] Alain Duhamel, a popular French commentator, observes in *France's Disarray*, "It is hard to deny that French society is sick, seriously and even profoundly sick."[10] One public opinion poll found that 63 percent of the French believe their country is in decline.

Indeed, political analyst Sophie Meunier chides the French for being unduly self-critical. She points out that at the very moment that countless books analyzing France's decline have been published, the country has excelled in international economic competition.[11] Yet this view overlooks the fact that, despite impressive economic achievements, France has not resolved major problems analyzed above, including economic inequality, social exclusion, fiscal crisis, and cultural strains.

The French have sought to address the challenges discussed here. Recently enacted reforms, including shortening the presidential term, the parity law, decentralization, and measures to reduce *dirigisme*, have promoted a welcome pluralism in politics and society. The state relies less on command and more on persuasion and dialogue. For example, the Jospin government sponsored the thirty-five-hour workweek in a manner that represented a significant contrast with the typical pattern of the state introduced changes in the past. The reform was implemented in stages, and the procedure provided ample opportunity for consultation, feedback, evaluation, and modification.[12]

France's formerly hierarchical pattern of state-society relations, in which most decisions originated in Parisian government ministries and were implemented by civil servants, has shifted toward a more pluralist pattern. Local governments have greater freedom to experiment. Citizens have greater freedom of choice in areas like television programming and telephone service. Private firms have more control over key aspects of their operations.

These gains are double-edged, however. Many French lament that economic modernization has jeopardized France's cherished way of life and may have contributed to the disturbing fragmentation of society. A key question is whether the positive features of the past can be preserved at the same time that past, present, and future problems can be addressed. No country (or person!) can have its cake and eat it, too—that is, sacrifices and compromises are inevitable. The dilemma, then, is how to achieve the optimum trade-off. What has to be sacrificed for the sake of what benefits? Political institutions and culture can help or hinder a political community in the attempt to frame this tough question and make hard choices. Will French political institutions and culture be able to meet this demanding challenge? A commission charged by the government to analyze France's capacity to confront the future rightly recognized the particular handicaps France faces. It asked, "Will the road toward democratic maturity, within the context of the globalization of values and a reduced role for national states, be more arduous in France than in other nations?"[13]

French Politics, Terrorism, and France's Relation to the United States

France's relationship to the issue of terrorism is quite different from that of the United States. Prior to September 11, 2001, the United States had been the target of only one terrorist attack organized from outside the country—the car bombing of the World Trade Center in New York in 1993. By contrast, for decades France was the target of numerous domestic and international terrorist attacks, although none comparable in scale to the destruction in New York and Washington, D.C., on September 11.

During the Algerian independence struggle in the 1960s, Algerian militants sought to weaken France's resolve to maintain colonial domination by unleashing attacks on French soil. At the same time, high-ranking officers in the French army and paramilitary forces also used violence in mainland France when de Gaulle announced his decision to grant Algeria independence. Although both threats were eventually crushed, in the 1990s Algerian radical Islamic militants again launched terrorist attacks to oppose France's support for Algeria's secular regime.

France remains a center of potential terrorist activity. The four million Muslims living in France are highly diverse: they hail from North Africa, sub-Saharan Africa, Turkey, the Caribbean, and South Asia. Nor do they share a common political orientation or practice their religious beliefs in the same way. But the number of Muslims drawn to a radical variant of Islam, who represent a prime source of potential recruits for terrorist activity, has grown, particularly among young, unemployed, second-generation Muslim men. In 2003, the government's central intelligence agency reported that there were 1,100 new converts that year to the most radical tendency within Islam.[14]

The government conducts an ongoing campaign against radical, repressive, and potentially violent forms of Islam. In 2004, a radical cleric was deported to his native Algeria for advocating wife beating, stoning adulterous women, and other reactionary views drawn from medieval Islamic texts. Also in 2004, three men were convicted and sentenced to prison for assisting Islamic terrorists elsewhere in Europe.

During the decades that France has been the target of terrorism, it has developed extensive intelligence and counterterrorist services based in the Defense and Interior Ministries. France has been quite successful in containing terrorism, at least thus far. There have been frequent police sweeps in which terrorist suspects have been arrested; many plots have reportedly been foiled (including an attack on the U.S. Embassy in Paris). At the same time that the threat of terrorism is disquieting, the government's antiterrorist activities have caused concerns. A shadow network of counterintelligence agencies, operating in secret with little accountability, has been accused of corruption, religious and ethnic discrimination, and abuses of human rights.

Following the September 11 attacks, France exhibited great solidarity with the United States. A lead editorial in *Le Monde* proclaimed, "We are all Americans now." (However, conspiracy theories were also rife, with one book, which sold 300,000 copies, claiming that the attack was organized by the U.S. government.) France joined the international military operation led by the United States to topple the Taliban regime and destroy Al Qaeda in Afghanistan in 2001. However, as described in

Chapter 11, this situation quickly changed. The government and the vast majority of French citizens passionately opposed the U.S. invasion of Iraq in 2003 and were highly critical of the U.S. occupation that followed. An illustration was provided by the sixtieth anniversary in 2004 of the U.S. landing in Normandy during World War II. A constant theme in the French media was the unfortunate contrast in the U.S. position in the world between 1944 and 2004. For example, the headline of an article by a respected French political analyst in London's *Financial Times* was "Bring back the America we loved and respected."[15]

French public opinion and politicians from virtually all parties have been relentlessly critical of the United States for not obtaining United Nations support for its actions before the war, for invading Iraq, and for its conduct of the Iraqi occupation. France was a leader of the international coalition opposing the U.S. action in Iraq, a reflection, for France, of the United States's more generally arrogant and unilateral posture. An illustration: Michael Moore's documentary film *Fahrenheit 9/11*, which is highly critical of President George W. Bush and his Iraqi policy, was awarded the *Palme d'or* (grand prize) at the Cannes film festival in 2004. For a country that is passionate about films, the award speaks volumes!

Summarizing French public opinion surveys, Richard Kuisel describes the French as "apprehensive about the United States acting as world leader, fearful of its hegemony, and mistrustful of its alleged ambitions and its motives. They, moreover, dislike many of America's social policies and are critical of our values."[16] French public opinion was critical of the United States prior to the presidency of George W. Bush and the Iraq war in 2003, but criticism reached a crescendo during the war and its aftermath. In a public opinion poll conducted during the 2004 American presidential campaign, 72 percent of the French supported the candidacy of John Kerry, 16 percent supported George W. Bush, and the remainder were undecided![17]

French Politics in Comparative Perspective

France has long provided a fascinating case for comparative analysis because of the endless attempts to analyze and explain French exceptionalism. An implicit question guiding our analysis has been whether French politics is becoming less exceptional. The case in favor partly rests on the claims that *dirigisme* and ideological conflict have declined in recent years. However, the jury is still out on both claims. We have described in Chapter 13 how, despite the fact that the scope of the state has shrunk, it continues to play an unusually vigorous role; we described in Chapter 14 how new forms of conflict have developed involving immigration, national identity, and social cohesion. Although "classic" left-right divisions have declined, one cannot conclude that ideological passions have waned in France. There is much to be learned, therefore, from including France in cross-national comparisons. One way to do so is by comparing France with other countries regarding the four core themes of this book: the world of states, governing the economy, the democratic idea, and the politics of collective identity.

The second kind of comparison to which France lends itself involves historical comparisons within France. For example, the Fourth and Fifth Republics provide fine case studies of the impact of institutions on political outcomes. The comparison of the two regimes can teach what to avoid and what to emulate. The Fourth Republic demonstrated the pitfalls of a fragmented multiparty system with undisciplined parties and a parliamentary regime with a weak executive. The Fifth Republic demonstrates the danger of an isolated and overly powerful executive. The Fifth Republic has adopted significant reforms designed to develop more balanced institutions, including a larger role for the Constitutional Council, stronger local governments, a shorter term for the president, and independent media. Although more is needed—for example, mechanisms to assure greater executive accountability—France's semipresidential system may prove attractive to countries seeking an institutional framework to achieve a balance between executive leadership and democratic representation. As was mentioned in Chapter 13, Russia has adopted the semipresidential system for this reason.

France also provides an exciting opportunity to analyze the efficacy of institutional changes to address inequalities in political representation. By adopting the gender parity reform in 2000, France became the first country in the world to mandate equal political representation for men and women. This bold experiment provides rich lessons for comparativists.

In addition, the Jospin government pioneered another attempt to promote social equality in 1999 with the creation of the civil solidarity pact (*pacte civil de solidarité*, or PACS), a civil union between unmarried couples of the same or opposite sex. The PACS provides many of the legal rights hitherto enjoyed only by married couples. The innovation reflects a liberalization of French cultural attitudes, as well as discontent about the institution of marriage. (Nearly half of all children are presently born out of wedlock.) On the one hand, the PACS has become highly popular. For every hundred new marriages performed nowadays, there are eight new PACS. On the other hand, it has been quite controversial. Defenders of conservative values oppose the procedure; other critics charge that it is an inadequate compromise and advocate the right of gay couples to marry.[18]

In 2004, a Green Party mayor of a small town near Bordeaux celebrated a gay marriage, the first ever in France, despite being warned not to do so by the state prosecutor and the justice minister. The justice and interior ministers quickly ordered the marriage nullified and the mayor

prosecuted for violating the law. It is uncertain whether the incident will remain isolated or will unleash further challenges to the traditional conception of marriage in France.

On the level of political culture more generally, France has prided itself on being among the first countries in the world to champion the values of liberty, equality, and fraternity. Every French school child is taught to revere the Declaration of the Rights of Man and the Citizen issued by the French revolutionary regime in 1789. But the very fact that these values have become part of the heritage of all people means that they are less distinctively French and therefore less able to serve as markers distinguishing France from other nations. Moreover, there is increasing conflict in France about their meaning, as the headscarf controversy that began Chapter 11 illustrates.

Another challenge to French political culture and national pride is that the French language—revered by the French for its beauty and precision, and for centuries the favored medium for international diplomatic communication—has largely been eclipsed by English. The contest is largely over outside France. But even within France, English has made enormous inroads in films, television programming, advertising, and popular music.

Comparativists can learn much from France's success—and failure—in seeking to achieve national cohesion while confronting extensive internal diversity and increasing integration in the international economic and political system. It is instructive to study how France adjusts to its more modest position in the world. France has linked its destiny to that of other European countries within the EU. But, as its opposition to the U.S. actions in Iraq demonstrates, France still aspires to play an influential role in world politics.

In brief, nearly forty years after youthful French protesters chanted in May 1968, "The struggle continues," the words have lost none of their relevance.

Notes

1. Patrick Jarreau, *La France de Chirac* (Paris: Flammarion, 1995), p. 9.

2. Pierre Birnbaum, *The Idea of France* (New York: Hill & Wang, 2001), pp. 278–279.

3. *Le Monde*, April 30, 2002.

4. Ibid., May 29, 2002.

5. *New York Times*, February 26, 2002.

6. *Le Monde*, June 15, 2004.

7. Pascal Perrineau, interview with Agence France Presse, reported at http://abonnes.lemonde .fr/web/dh/0,14-0@2-3224,39-23054751,0.html; accessed June 7, 2004.

8. Robert C. Lieberman, "Weak State, Strong Policy: Paradoxes of Race Policy in the United States, Great Britain, and France?" *Studies in American Political Development* 16 (Fall 2002): 139.

9. Nicolas Baverez, *La France qui tombe* (Paris: Perrin, 2003); Alain Duhamel, *Le Désarroi français* (Paris: Plon, 2003).

10. Duhamel, *Le Désarroi français*, p. 95.

11. Sophie Meunier, "Free-Falling France or Free-Trading France?" *French Politics, Culture, and Society* 22, no. 1 (Spring 2004): 98–107.

12. Gunnar Trumbull, "Policy Activism in a Globalized Economy: France's 35-hour Workweek," *French Politics, Culture, and Society* 20, no. 3 (Fall 2002): 1–21.

13. Bernard Cazes, Fabrice Hatem, and Paul Thibaud, "L'État et la société française en l'an 2000," *Esprit*, no. 165 (October 1990): 95.

14. *Le Monde*, June 4, 2004.

15. *Financial Times*, June 3, 2004.

16. Richard Kuisel, "What Do the French Think of Us? The Deteriorating Image of the United States, 2000–2004," *French Politics, Culture, and Society* 22, no. 3 (Fall 2004).

17. *Le Monde*, October 15, 2004.

18. INSEE, *Tableaux de l'Économie Française, 2003–2004* (Paris: INSEE, 2003), p. 26.

Part IV Bibliography

Bell, David A. *The Cult of the Nation in France: Inventing Nationalism, 1680–1800.* Cambridge: Harvard University Press, 2001.

Birnbaum, Pierre. *Jewish Destinies: Citizenship, State, and Community in Modern France.* New York: Hill & Wang, 2000.

———. *The Idea of France.* New York: Hill & Wang, 2001.

Brubaker, Rogers. *Citizenship and Nationhood in France and Germany.* Cambridge: Harvard University Press, 1992.

Célestin, Eliane DalMolin, and Isabelle de Courtivron, eds. *Beyond French Feminisms: Debates on Women, Politics, and Culture in France, 1981–2001.* New York: Palgrave Macmillan, 2003.

Chapman, Herrick, Mark Kesselman, and Martin A. Schain, eds. *A Century of Organized Labor in France: A Union Movement for the Twenty-First Century?* New York: St. Martin's Press, 1998.

Daley, Anthony, ed. *The Mitterrand Era: Policy Alternatives and Political Mobilization in France.* New York: New York University Press, 1996.

Daley, Anthony. *Steel, State, and Labor: Mobilization and Adjustment in France.* Pittsburgh: University of Pittsburgh Press, 1996.

Duyvendak, Jan Willem. *The Power of Politics: New Social Movements in France.* Boulder, Colo.: Westview, 1995.

Elgie, Robert. *Political Institutions in Contemporary France.* New York: Oxford University Press, 2003.

Gaffney, John, and Lorna Milne, eds. *French Presidentialism and the Election of 1995.* Brookfield, Vt.: Ashgate, 1997.

Gopnik, Adam. *Paris to the Moon.* New York: Random House, 2000.

Gordon, Philip H., and Sophie Meunier. *The French Challenge: Adapting to Globalization.* Washington, D.C.:, Brookings Institution, 2001.

Hall, Peter A. *Governing the Economy: The Politics of State Intervention in Britain and France.* New York: Oxford University Press, 1986.

Hall, Peter, Jack Hayward, and Howard Machin, eds. *Developments in French Politics*, vol. 2. New York: Macmillan, 1998.

Haus, Leah. *Unions, Immigration, and Internationalization: New Challenges and Changing Coalitions in the United States and France.* London: Palgrave, 2002.

Hayward, Jack, and Vincent Wright. *Governing from the Centre: Core Executive Coordination in France.* New York: Oxford University Press, 2002.

Howell, Chris. *Regulating Labor: The State and Industrial Relations Reform in Postwar France.* Princeton, N.J.: Princeton University Press, 1992.

Huber, John D. *Rationalizing Parliament: Legislative Institutions and Party Politics in France.* Cambridge: Cambridge University Press, 1996.

Ireland, Patrick. *The Policy Challenge of Ethnic Diversity: Immigrant Politics in France and Switzerland.* Cambridge: Harvard University Press, 1994.

Keeler, John T. S., and Martin A. Schain, eds. *Chirac's Challenge: Liberalization, Europeanization, and Malaise in France.* New York: St. Martin's Press, 1996.

Levy, Jonah. *Tocqueville's Revenge: State, Society, and Economy in Contemporary France.* Cambridge: Harvard University Press, 1999.

Lewis-Beck, Michael S., ed. *How France Votes.* New York: Chatham House, 2000.

———. *The French Voter: Before and After the 2002 Elections.* London: Palgrave and Macmillan, 2004.

Lieberman, Robert C. *Shaping Race Policy: The United States in Comparative Perspective.* Princeton N.J.: Princeton University Press, 2005.

Mazur, Amy G. *Gender Bias and the State: Symbolic Reform at Work in Fifth Republic France.* Pittsburgh: University of Pittsburgh Press, 1996.

Noiriel, Gérard. *The French Melting Pot: Immigration, Citizenship, and National Identity.* Minneapolis: University of Minnesota Press, 1996.

Pierce, Roy. *Choosing the Chief: Presidential Elections in France and the United States.* Ann Arbor: University of Michigan Press, 1995.

Sa'adah, Anne. *Contemporary France: A Democratic Education.* Lanham, Md.: Rowman & Littlefield, 2003.

Schmidt, Vivien A. *From State to Market? The Transformation of French Business and Government.* Cambridge: Cambridge University Press, 1996.

Smith, W. Rand. *The Left's Dirty Job: The Politics of Industrial Restructuring in France and Spain.* Pittsburgh: University of Pittsburgh Press, 1998.

Smith, Timothy B. *France in Crisis: Welfare, Inequality and Globalization since 1980.* Cambridge: Cambridge University Press, 2004.

Stone, Alec. *The Birth of Judicial Politics in France.* New York: Oxford University Press, 1992.

Tiersky, Ronald. *François Mitterrand: The Last French President.* New York: St. Martin's Press, 2000.

Tilly, Charles. *The Contentious French: Four Centuries of Popular Struggle.* Cambridge: Harvard University Press, Belknap Press, 1986.

Treacher, Adrian. *French Interventionism: Europe's Last Global Player?* Brookfield, Vt.: Ashgate, 2003.

Websites

The French Embassy site in Washington, D.C., in English: www.ambafrance-us.org.

The French president's site, in French: www.elysee.fr.

The prime minister's site, in English: www.premier-ministre.gouv.fr/en.

National Assembly site, in French: www.assemblee-nationale.fr.

French foreign ministry, in English: www.france.diplomatie.fr.

France's most respected newspaper, Le Monde, in French: www.lemonde.fr.

A center-left newspaper, Libération, in French: www.liberation.fr.

A conservative newspaper, Le Figaro, in French: www.lefigaro.fr.

P A R T

V

Germany

Christopher S. Allen

C H A P T E R

16

The Making of the Modern German State

German Politics in Action

Chancellor Gerhard Schröder sat with his head in his hands in a feature article of the prestigious British weekly *The Economist* during the early spring of 2004. This image seemed to crystallize all that had gone wrong with the once-redoubtable German model of economic policy. Unemployment remained stubbornly high, especially in eastern Germany; the country's income per person (for years among the highest in the European Union) had dropped below the EU average for the first time; the generous welfare state appeared to be creaking under a demo-graphic time bomb of too many retirees and too few employed; polls showed the ruling Social Democratic Party (Sozialdemokratische Partei Deutschlands, SPD) at 25 percent support two years before the next scheduled election; Schröder's economic structural reform package, Agenda 2010, seemed much less than needed; and the Germans, never a population with a particularly "sunny" disposition, appeared filled with much more *Angst* than usual. All seemed relentlessly bleak for the once-mighty postwar German juggernaut in mid-2004.

This criticism of the German model, however, was not new. Ever since the first post-WWII recession in the mid-1970s, critics of the German "variety of capitalism,"[1] with its "organized" corporatist structure, comprehensive regulatory framework, significant role for organized labor, and a generous welfare state, have predicted the demise of this set of economic policy options. These critics long argued that the German system of highly coordinated, regulated production stifled employers' ability to hire, fire, and set prices. Yet for decades the obvious reality of German economic growth and prosperity meant that these warnings fell on deaf ears. Yet for much of the subsequent thirty years, this "model" confounded a generation of largely free-market economists and politicians who kept predicting its demise. For much of the 1970s, 1980s, and even during much of the 1990s, German policymakers could brush off easily this criticism from its laissez-faire skeptics. However, beginning in the 1990s, the triple challenge of German unification, Europeanization via the growth of the EU, and relentless globalization

Schröder's *Angst*

© Graeme Robertson/Getty Images.

prompted a new critical look at the efficacy and structure of the German political economy. Despite the enviable strength of the institutions of the German political economy during the last half-century, the potential challenges facing the Federal Republic of Germany (FRG)* appear sharp and formidable.

These challenges are not merely economic ones. They have had profound effects on Germany's first left-wing government: the coalition of Social Democrats (SPD) and Greens, led by SPD chancellor Gerhard Schröder since the two parties won the 1998 federal election and were reelected in 2002. (A previous period of Social Democratic Party rule—1969–1982—included the centrist Free Democratic Party [FDP] as a coalition partner.) Unification has been a costly and still-incomplete attempt to integrate the five *Länder* (states) that comprised Communist East Germany from 1949 to 1990 into a larger Federal Republic of Germany. Europeanization—specifically, the growth of the EU to twenty-five countries in 2004—has been both a benefit and a liability. Some German firms have taken advantage of new market opportunities in the new EU states in Eastern and Central Europe. However, the more free-market-oriented pattern of growth in the entire EU—as opposed to the institutionally complex German style of postwar capitalism—has begun to undermine these dense networks of public and private sector actors that made the German model work so well. In other words, just as the EU opened up market opportunities, the process altered the rules of the game that formerly had so richly benefited the Federal Republic of Germany. Finally, globalization began to undermine the core of the most productive German industries by forcing these firms to lower their prices to compete against manufacturers from the developing world. The political impact of these pressures not only drove up unemployment but also threatened the

economic foundation of Germany's generous welfare state.

Given these formidable challenges, Chancellor Schröder's consternation about the appropriate policy options are quite understandable.

Geographic Setting

Germany is located in Central Europe and has been as much a Western European nation as it has an Eastern European one. A federal state, Germany is divided into sixteen states (or *Bundesländer* in German), many of which correspond to historic German kingdoms and principalities (e.g., Bavaria, Saxony, Hesse) or medieval trading cities (e.g., Hamburg, Bremen). It has a total area of 137,803 square miles (slightly smaller than the state of Montana) and a population of 82 million—the largest population of any wholly European country. (Table 16.1 presents a brief profile of Germany.) About 90 percent of present-day Germans have family roots within the borders of modern Germany; all of this group speak German as their primary language, and they are roughly evenly divided between Catholics and Protestants, approximately one-third each, with the remainder religiously unaffiliated or members of other religions. Until quite recently Germany has been relatively ethnically homogeneous; however, the presence of several million Turks in Germany, first drawn to the Federal Republic as "guest workers" (*Gastarbeiter*)—foreign workers who had no citizenship rights—in the 1960s, suggests that ethnic diversity will continue to grow. The new century saw a familiar echo of the importing of foreign workers in the 1960s. A shortage of information-age workers among the German population induced Chancellor Gerhard Schröder's government to permit the immigration of several thousand Indian computer professionals with Internet and programming skills. Furthermore, increased migration across borders by EU citizens has also decreased cultural homogeneity, since approximately 10 percent of the country's population traces its origins from outside the Federal Republic.

---

*The FRG was also the name of unified Germany in 1990, since the former East Germany officially reunified by joining the FRG as five separate, new federal states (*Länder*).

Germany

DENMARK

Baltic Sea

North Sea

SCHLESWIG-
HOLSTEIN

MECKLENBURG-
VORPOMMERN

HAMBURG
•Hamburg

BREMEN

POLAND

LOWER SAXONY

BERLIN
Berlin ★

NETHERLANDS

SAXONY-
ANHALT

BRANDENBURG

NORTH RHINE-
WESTPHALIA

Cologne •
Rhine
Bonn •

SAXONY

HESSE

THURINGIA

BELG.

Frankfurt
•

RHINELAND-
PALATINATE

LUX.

CZECH REPUBLIC

SAARLAND

•Nuremberg
BAVARIA

Danube

FRANCE

BADEN-
WÜRTTEMBERG

•Munich

AUSTRIA

0   100 Miles

SWITZERLAND

0   100 Kilometers

Table 16.1   Profile

Land and Population

Capital		Berlin
Total area (square miles)		137,803 (slightly smaller than Montana)
Population	2004	82.4 million

Economy

Gross national product (GNP) per capita	2003	$27,600
GDP growth rate	2004	1.1%
Women as percentage of total labor force	2003	46.7%
Income gap: GDP per capita (U.S.$) by percentage of population		
Richest 20 percent		36.9%
Poorest 20 percent		8.5%
Total foreign trade (exports plus imports) as percentage of GNP	2003	67.9%

Sources: German Information Office; German Statistical Office; OECD; CIA; Human Development Reports.

For a densely populated country, Germany has a surprisingly high 54 percent of its land in agricultural production. It comprises large plains in northern Germany, a series of smaller mountain ranges in the center of the country, and the towering Alps to the south at the Austrian and Swiss borders. It has a temperate climate with considerable cloud cover and precipitation throughout the year, a climatological feature that contributes to the famous German *Wanderlust,* as many often seek out warm-weather destinations for their annual six weeks of paid vacation. For Germany, the absence of natural borders in the west and east has been an impor-

tant geographic feature. For example, on the north Germany borders both the North and Baltic Seas and the country of Denmark, but to the west, south, and east, it has many neighbors: the Netherlands, Belgium, Luxembourg, France, Switzerland, Austria, the Czech Republic, and Poland. Conflicts and wars with its neighbors were a constant feature in Germany until the end of World War II.

Germany's lack of resources, aside from iron ore and coal deposits in the Ruhr and the Saarland, has shaped much of the country's history. Since the Industrial Revolution in the nineteenth century, many of Germany's external relationships, both commercial and military, have revolved around gaining access to resources not present within the national borders. The resource scarcity has helped produce an efficient use of technology since the industrial age, but in the past, the lack of resources also tempted German leaders to launch military aggression against neighboring countries to obtain scarce resources. This era appears to have ended, especially with the arrival of the EU.

Critical Junctures

Unification in 1990 represented a great triumph for democratic Germany, but this milestone also forces us to examine the specifics of *why* Germany was divided in the first place. By examining critical historical junctures from the eighteenth through the twentieth centuries, we can better understand Germany's dynamic evolution, including the havoc that earlier German regimes caused both the country's neighbors and its own citizens. This short review of the key periods that shaped modern Germany will take us through the volatile history of the country's nineteenth-century unification, the creation of an empire, a first world war, a short-lived parliamentary democracy, twelve years of Nazi terror and a second world war, military occupation after that war, forty years as a divided nation, and the uncertainties of European integration (see Table 16.2).

Table 16.2   Critical Junctures in Germany's Development

1806–1871	Nationalism and German unification
1871–1918	Second Reich
1919–1933	Weimar Republic
1933–1945	Third Reich
1945–1990	A divided Germany and the postwar settlement
1990–1998	The challenge of German unification
1998–2001	Germany in the euro era
2001–	Germany after September 11

Nationalism and German Unification (1806–1871)

There have been many attempts to unify a German nation in European history. The first was the Holy Roman Empire, founded by Charlemagne in A.D. 800 (sometimes referred to as the First Reich). But this wide-ranging, loose, and fragmented "empire" bore little resemblance to a modern nation-state. (In fact, someone once quipped that it was neither holy, Roman, nor an empire.) For more than one thousand years, the area now known as Germany was made up of sometimes as many as three hundred sovereign entities. Only in 1871 did the powerful Prussian military leader Otto von Bismarck unite the separate states into a united German nation-state.* Bismarck called it the Second Reich because the name suggested a German state that was both powerful and able to draw on centuries-old traditions.

There are three main points to make about state formation generally, and German state for-

*Prussia no longer exists as a state or province. It was an independent principality for hundreds of years until the end of World War II in what is now northeast and northwest Germany and part of Poland.

mation in particular.[2] First, state building requires an evolution of collective identity beyond the family, village, and local region to one encompassing a broader collection of peoples. Clear geographic boundaries may help define such an identity. Britain, an island, and France, a region surrounded by rivers and mountains, both developed as nation-states centuries ago. Germany, on the other hand, occupied central European plains with few natural lines of demarcation.

Moreover, religious, linguistic, or ethnic differences can hinder the development of a national identity. The Protestant Reformation, led by the German Martin Luther in 1517, not only split Christianity into two competing sects but also divided many European societies in ways that profoundly affected the evolution of nation-states. Bitter religious wars broke out among advocates of each side in many parts of Europe. Britain and France resolved these contests decisively in favor of Protestantism or Catholicism within their own borders, thereby getting rid of this decisive cleavage early on. In Germany, neither Catholics nor Protestants won, and the wars' extensive casualties deepened hostilities that lasted for centuries. Each side viewed the conflict as both a military and a spiritual war that needed forceful leadership. This clearly retarded the development of any liberal or democratic impulses in Germany. Although religious animosity subsided by the twentieth century, the north of Germany remains mostly Protestant and the south mostly Catholic.

Ethnic and linguistic divisions, sometimes involving widely different forms of spoken German, also delayed unification. Nevertheless, the similarities among Germans were great enough to produce a common cultural identity before the nation-state emerged. In the absence of clear geographic boundaries or shared religious and political experiences, "racial" or ethnic and cultural traits came to define Germans' national identity to a much greater extent than for other European peoples. For many nineteenth-century Germans, the lack of political unity stood in sharp contrast to the strong influence of German culture in such literary and religious figures as Goethe, Schiller, and Luther. For many German-speakers, romanticism thus remained a powerful organic counterpoint to secular French revolutionary values, which exercised a powerful influence on the fragmented German lands after the French Revolution of 1789.

A second point is that nation-states can promote economic growth more easily than fragmented political entities can. By the time Germany joined the global economy, it lagged behind Britain and France in industrializing and securing access to the natural resources of the developing world. Germany thus was forced to play catch-up with these other developed states.[3] Nineteenth-century leaders felt that Germany needed access to more raw materials than were contained within its own borders. Combined with the awakened German nationalism of the late nineteenth century, this pursuit of fast economic growth produced an aggressive, acquisitive state in which economic and political needs overlapped. Whereas Britain and France entered the nineteenth century as imperial powers, Germany's late unification and late industrialization prevented it from embarking on this quest for raw materials and empire until the late nineteenth century.

Third, military strength is a fundamental tool that many nation-states use in their formation and consolidation. Yet the rise of militarism and a corresponding authoritarian political culture were tendencies that were exaggerated in Germany for several reasons.[4] The map of Germany shows a country with many neighbors and few natural geographic barriers. This exposed position in the central plains of Europe encouraged an emphasis on military preparedness by nineteenth-century German state builders, since virtually any of Germany's neighbors could mount an attack with few constraints. And the lack of a solid democratic or liberal political culture in the various German-speaking lands before unification in 1871 allowed Prussian militarism an even greater influence over political and civic life.

German nationalism did not just appear out of the blue in the late nineteenth century. It had a long history and deep roots. Prussia had been a major military force in German-speaking lands since the seventeenth century, and it became Europe's greatest military power by the time of the Seven Years' War (1756–1763). Yet Prussia and most of the rest of Europe were overtaken by Napoleon in the early nineteenth century, as the French emperor swept eastward as far as Russia. During this conquest, Napoleon consolidated many of the smaller German-speaking principalities, particularly those from the northwest to the northeast of what is now Germany. But Napoleon's ambition exceeded his grasp, and he suffered defeat in 1814 by a coalition of European powers led by Britain. The Prussians, under the leadership of Friedrich Wilhelm III, conducted a "war of liberation" against French forces and further consolidated German-speaking states, but now under Prussian control.

The rise in Prussian influence in German-speaking areas continued through the first half of the nineteenth century as Prussian socioeconomic forces and political culture spread throughout what is now northern and central Germany. Prussian leaders were flush with military conquest and supremely confident that their authoritative—and authoritarian—leadership suited an awakening German-speaking population. Political and economic currents such as free-market capitalism and democracy did not find strong roots in the Prussian-dominated Germanic principalities. Rather, the dominant features of Prussian rule were a strong state deeply involved in economic affairs (an economic policy known as *mercantilism*), a reactionary group of feudal lords called *Junkers*, a patriotic military, and a political culture dominated by virtues such as honor, duty, and service to the state.

In 1848, German democrats and liberals (*liberal* in the original European sense of favoring free markets) tried to challenge Prussian dominance by attempting to emulate the democratic revolutionary movements in France and other European countries. The growth of free-market capitalism and the evolution of greater democracy in the United States and Britain served as catalysts in both France and Germany, and the center for this movement was in Frankfurt am Main, then as now an important trading city. However, German democratic forces were even weaker than in France because the Prussian state and authoritarian political culture were so strong. Thus, free-market and revolutionary democratic movements were violently suppressed. Yet Prussia—and eventually a united Germany—were to experience a different kind of revolution—a "revolution from above," political sociologist Barrington Moore has called it.[5]

After the democratic revolution failed in 1848, the most famous of the Prussian leaders, Otto von Bismarck, continued to forge unity among the remaining German-speaking independent principalities. Bismarck realized that the spread of German nationalism required firm economic foundations. Thus, Prussia, and a united Germany, would need to industrialize and modernize its economy to compete with Britain, France, and the United States. However, after the turmoil of the 1848 revolution, a democratic and free-market approach was not possible. Bismarck then put together the unlikely, and nondemocratic, coalition of the feudal *Junkers* in the northeast and the new industrial barons from the growing coal and iron ore industries in the northwestern Ruhr River valley. This alliance among grain-growing landowners and new-money industrialists under the guidance of a strong state was Bismarck's revolution from above. In other words, Bismarck's revolution relied on an alliance of elites rather than a mobilization of democratic or working-class support, a form common to the French and American revolutions.

Prior to 1871, the rise of nationalism and the formation of a united Germany out of the divided German states produced intense conflict. Militarism, not surprisingly, was a key component of Prussian nationalist political culture, and Bismarck used his armies to unite all German-speaking peoples under his influence. Such aggressive nationalism produced three bloody conflicts in the 1860s, as the Prussian armies defeated Denmark (1864), Austria-Hungary (1866), and France (1870) in short wars in which the modern German boundaries were established. The culmination of Bismarck's aggressive nationalism was the unification of Germany into a second "empire" or Reich in 1871, following the Franco-Prussian War.

Second Reich (1871–1918)

The Second Reich was an authoritarian regime that had some of the symbols of a democratic regime but very little of the substance. The failure of the democratic revolution in 1848 meant that nondemocratic forces (industrial and landed elites) in the newly united Germany mobilized and controlled both political and economic power. And these forces constructed political institutions to retain this power. Bismarck's regime was symbolically democratic in that the Iron Chancellor (Bismarck's nickname owing to his military successes and attacks on democratic forces) allowed for universal suffrage, but he retained real decision-making authority in nonelected bodies that he could control. The political dominance by nondemocratic forces took the form of a bicameral legislature consisting of a lower house (Reichstag) and upper house (Landtag). The Reichstag was popularly elected, but real power lay in the hands of the Landtag, the members of which were either directly or indirectly appointed by Bismarck. The Reichstag could pass legislation, but with little, if any, hope that it would become law.

Germany was led by Bismarck for the first twenty years of the regime (although the country was a monarchy, real power lay with the chancellor, or prime minister). The Second Reich saw as its primary goal rapid industrialization augmented by state power and a powerful banking system geared to foster large-scale industrial investment. Thus, it did not rely on British and American "trial-and-error" free markets. Germany became a leading industrial power by 1900, following the development of such key industries as coal, steel, railroads, dyes, chemicals, industrial electronics, and machine tools. The emphasis on the development of such heavy industries meant that the production of consumer goods was a lower priority. This pattern created an imbalance in which the industrialists reaped large profits while the majority of Germans did not directly benefit from the economic growth led by heavy industry. The resultant lack of a strong domestic consumer goods economy meant that a substantial portion of what Germany produced was directed toward world markets.

The rapid transformation of a largely feudal society in the 1850s to an industrial one by the turn of the twentieth century created widespread social dislocation and produced numerous forms of opposition. One was a general pressure to democratize the authoritarian system by providing basic rights for liberal (that is, free-market) and middle-class forces. A second was the growth of the working class and the corresponding rise of the militant Social Democratic Party. The SPD's primary goals were economic rights in the workplace and democratization of the political system. Greatly influenced by the writings and the active participation of Karl Marx and Friedrich Engels—who were, after all, Germans—the SPD grew as fast as the pace of German industrialization.

During much of his rule from 1871 to 1890, Bismarck alternately persecuted and grudgingly tolerated his democratic and socialist opposition. The combination of social and political pressures forced Bismarck, a conservative, to ban the SPD in 1878 but also caused him to create the world's first modern welfare state in the early 1880s to soften the rough edges of rapid economic growth. This combination of welfare and political repression (sometimes referred to as Bismarck's iron fist in a velvet glove) suggested that Bismarck was an astute politician who knew how far to push the opposition and when to give ground in the short term in order to maintain long-term political control.

Bismarck was also skillful in balancing the very different interests of the grain-growing feudal *Junkers* in East Prussia and the expanding industrialists in the north and west of Germany. In what has sometimes been called the marriage of iron and rye, these disparate social forces were united by mutual economic and political needs.[6] The *Junkers* needed a mechanism to get their agricultural output to market, and the industrialists needed a commodity (rye wheat) to ship on the expanding railroad system. Bismarck consummated the marriage with a tariff system that discriminated against foreign importers of steel and grain, giving German iron and rye greater breathing room. The marriage also helped the two reactionary forces remain united to stave off the clamoring democratic and socialist forces "below" them.

Bismarck used his skills to balance the divisive energy of nationalism with the need to maintain a coherent state policy. Invocation of nationalism enabled him to unite the diverse German-speaking peoples despite resentment by Bavarians and Rhinelanders (among others) toward the Prussian-dominated regime. But in time, nationalism proved difficult to contain. The spirit unleashed by a newly unified and rapidly industrializing Germany gave rise to a pan-Germanic feeling of nationalism among German-speaking Europeans in eastern Europe. This often took the form of militant anti-Semitism owing to the perception by some Germans that Jews had enjoyed a disproportionate share of wealth and influence in central Europe. In general, the pan-Germanic movement espoused themes that the Nazis later seized in justifying their claims of racial and cultural superiority.

Bismarck also powerfully influenced German political culture, with its state-centered emphasis that came to characterize the united Germany. The *Kulturkampf* (cultural struggle) was a prime example of Prussian, and Protestant, dominance. Led by Bismarck, it was essentially a movement against the Catholic Church, aimed at removing educational and cultural institutions from the church and conferring them on

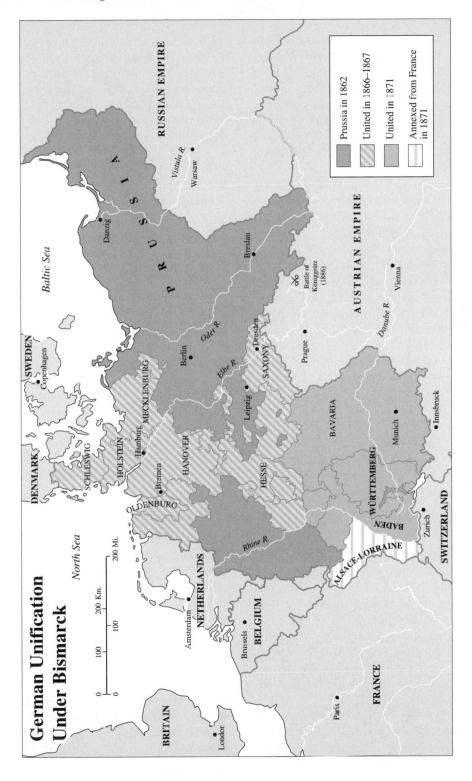

German Unification Under Bismarck

Legend:
- Prussia in 1862
- United in 1866–1867
- United in 1871
- Annexed from France in 1871

RUSSIAN EMPIRE

AUSTRIAN EMPIRE

P R U S S I A

Baltic Sea

North Sea

SWEDEN

DENMARK

SCHLESWIG

HOLSTEIN

MECKLENBURG

HANOVER

OLDENBURG

HESSE

SAXONY

BAVARIA

WÜRTTEMBERG

BADEN

ALSACE-LORRAINE

NETHERLANDS

BELGIUM

FRANCE

SWITZERLAND

BRITAIN

Vistula R.
Warsaw
Danzig
Breslau
Battle of Königgrätz (1866)
Vienna
Danube R.
Prague
Dresden
Berlin
Oder R.
Elbe R.
Leipzig
Hamburg
Bremen
Copenhagen
Innsbruck
Munich
Zurich
Rhine R.
Amsterdam
Brussels
Paris
London

200 Mi.
200 Km.
100
100
0
0

the state. This action polarized the church and many Catholic Germans and left a significant political legacy of both Catholic and Protestant influence in German politics to this day.

Clearly the unification of Germany in 1871 produced considerable economic strength in the late nineteenth and early twentieth centuries. However, as the tensions described above suggest, Germany remained politically fragile, unstable, and undemocratic.

As the German economy grew during the latter part of the nineteenth century, German business and political leaders faced an immediate problem: How could rapid economic growth continue if they could not be certain of obtaining needed raw materials or having access to world markets to sell their finished goods? Although Germany possessed considerable iron and coal deposits, it had little else in the way of natural resources. It had neither the colonial possessions of Britain and France, nor the geographic advantages of the United States, with its largely self-sufficient domestic market and plentiful natural resources. Having little influence in either North America or Asia, Germany participated in what historian Geoffrey Barraclough has called "the scramble for Africa."[7] However, Germany was a latecomer in this region and was able to obtain colonies only in what are now the countries of Namibia and Togo, whereas the British, French, and Belgians obtained colonies in regions of the continent with more easily exploitable resources.

From 1871 until World War I, the foreign policy of the German state was primarily concerned with extending its colonial and economic influence, only to be repeatedly checked by other colonial powers. This situation inflamed German nationalists, causing German leaders to invest in the rapid development of the shipbuilding industry to equip a commercial shipping fleet and a powerful navy that could secure German economic and geopolitical interests.

The combination of numerous factors—an undemocratic domestic political system, the lack of profitable colonies, an exposed geopolitical

position on the central European plains—joined with an increasingly aggressive nationalism to heighten Germany's aggression toward other nations. This volatile combination proved to be a blueprint for disaster and caused Germany to launch World War I.

Germany felt threatened by its inability to expand its economic and military resources and was allied with the Austro-Hungarian Empire. When the Austrian archduke Ferdinand was assassinated by a Serbian nationalist in 1914, the Austro-Hungarian Empire attacked Serbia (which was allied with Britain and France), and the war was on. Originally envisioned by German leaders as a brief war to solidify the country's geopolitical position and maintain socioeconomic power for dominant elites, it did neither. It turned out to be a protracted war that cost Germany its colonial possessions, hundreds of thousands of citizens who died in combat, and its imperial social order. The combination of weak leadership (Bismarck's successors were poor imitations of the original), lack of resources, and overconfidence in Germany's military prowess brought the Second Reich to an end at the conclusion of World War I. Germany's defeat and the collapse of the Second Reich left very weak foundations for the country's first attempt to establish a parliamentary democracy.

Weimar Republic (1918–1933)

Germany's military defeat in World War I had profound implications for questions of state formation and democracy. When the ceremonial head of state, Kaiser (King) Wilhelm II, abdicated the throne following the resignation of the last wartime government, Germany was without both a head of government (chancellor) and a head of state (*Kaiser*). The political vacuum was filled by the large but politically inexperienced SPD, as all other leading parties of the Second Reich had been discredited by Germany's defeat. In 1918, this new leadership proclaimed Germany's first democratic government, one that some would later call accidental, owing to the

SPD's unexpected assumption of power. The new government was born in defeat and lacked legitimacy in the eyes of many Germans. In other words it was a "republic without republicans."

This Weimar Republic, named after the city of Weimar, where the constitution was drafted, was a procedural democracy in the sense of holding regular elections and having multiple parties. The German Reichstag appeared to function like many other democratic parliaments at the time, such as those of Britain and France. It contained a broad spectrum of political parties, from the far left to the far right. Yet its eventually fatal weakness was that too many of the right-wing political parties and social forces, as well as the Communists on the left, did not accept the legitimacy of democratic government and actively tried to destabilize and undercut it.

The SPD leadership was on shaky ground from the beginning. The military leaders and industrialists who had so strongly encouraged Germany's aggressive nationalism were never held accountable for their actions. They faced neither criminal nor political sanctions for leading Germany into a destructive war. In fact, the republic's first government turned to the army to help restore order during late 1918, when the newly formed Communist Party (Kommunistische Partei Deutschlands, KPD) and various leftist groups challenged the government's authority. By asking the undemocratic army to "defend democracy," the SPD undermined its ability to make major changes in German society.

The outcome of the war intensified the nationalist impulses of many conservative and reactionary Germans. Many in the military believed that "cowardly" democratic politicians had betrayed Germany at the signing of the Treaty of Versailles following the German surrender to the Allies on November 11, 1918. Stung by the reparations payments assessed on Germany by the Allies, along with the demilitarization of the Rhineland, a region bordering on France, German nationalists branded the Weimar leaders as "Jews, democrats, and socialists" who had sold out Germany's honor. By controlling various right-wing newspapers and magazines, the nondemocratic right kept up a steady drumbeat of poisonous rhetoric that eventually crippled the regime.

A severe economic crisis in 1923, caused largely by Germany's payment of massive reparations to the Allies, as required by the Versailles Treaty, further played into the hands of the nationalists. Since the German economy was weakened by the mobilization during World War I, the added costs of the reparations payments made a bad economic situation much worse. The government's "solution" was to print more money. It used the shaky reasoning that a cheaper *Reichsmark* (the name of the currency then) would reduce the real costs of the reparations. This was no solution at all, because the government kept printing so much money that by 1923, inflation had reached astronomical proportions (e.g., one U.S. dollar was equal to approximately 12 million *Reichsmarks*). Individual Germans were powerfully affected in numerous ways. At the height of the inflationary wave, people had to receive their paychecks twice per *day*, once in the morning and once in the evening after work. The cost of basic foodstuffs was literally rising hourly, and people who waited to buy goods until after work (instead of shopping on their lunch break) would find the goods much more expensive. The simple act of depositing or withdrawing money at a bank also reached ludicrous proportions; some individuals used wheelbarrows brimming with nearly worthless *Reichsmarks* to go to and from the bank. To the nondemocratic right wing, the Weimar regime was a concrete demonstration that a democratic government was unable to create and supervise a stable economy.

In the early 1920s, Adolf Hitler, a little-known Austrian-born former corporal in the German army during World War I, founded the Nazi Party. *Nazi* is a German acronym derived from **Na**tionals**o**z**i**alistische Deutsche Arbeiterpartei, the National Socialist German Workers Party. Although it sounds like the name of a left-wing party, the use of the word *national* is important here. Hitler used nationalism as a weapon to attack both parties of the left, the SPD and KPD. He thereby undercut the socialist movement's German roots, which reached back to Marx and Engels. Taking advantage of a deepening economic crisis and a weakened democratic opposition, the Nazis mobilized large segments of the population by preaching hatred of the left, of "internationalism" (the key philosophical underpinning shared by both the SPD and the KPD), and of "inferior, non-Aryan" races. Hitler unleashed powerful racist social forces antagonistic to democracy, which ultimately undermined it and caused its destruction.

After the Great Depression began in 1929, Germany became even more unstable, with none of the major parties of Weimar able to win a majority or even form durable governing coalitions. The Communists, Social Democrats, Catholic Center Party, Democrats, Liberals, Bavarian People's Party, Nationalists, Conservatives, and Nazis all had fundamentally different views on how Germany should be governed, and many of them were not committed to the idea of democracy. In the wake of this political instability, the early 1930s saw numerous inconclusive elections. The last several months of the Weimar Republic (1932–1933) witnessed no fewer than six elections, all resulting in minority governments. At no time did the Nazis ever receive a majority. Their high point in free and fair elections was 230 seats out of 608 in the vote of July 1932, but the Nazis lost ground between then and the next Reichstag election four months later. The November 1932 election was considered the last one without violent Nazi intimidation of other political parties.

The Nazis relentlessly pressed for political power, while most Germans continued to underestimate Hitler's real intentions and to view his hate-filled speeches as merely political rhetoric. The Nazis were rewarded when Hitler induced Weimar's aging president Hindenburg, an eighty-four-year-old World War I general, to allow the Nazis to obtain cabinet positions in the last Weimar government in early 1933. Hitler immediately demanded the chancellorship from President Hindenburg, and received it on January 30, 1933. (Under the Weimar constitution, as in many other parliamentary systems, the head of state—the president—was assigned to choose the next head of government—the chancellor—if no one party or coalition received a majority of legislative seats.) Once in power, the Nazis began to ban political parties and arranged for a fire at the Reichstag that they tried to blame on the Communists. Hitler then demanded that President Hindenburg grant—by "emergency" executive order—broad, sweeping powers to the Nazi-dominated cabinet. This act made the Reichstag irrelevant as a representative political body.

Thus, the parliamentary democracy of the Weimar Republic was short-lived. From its shaky beginnings in 1918, the very stability of the state was mortgaged to forces that wished its destruction. Ironically, the constitutional structure of the Weimar regime was relatively well designed. The two significant exceptions were the "emergency" provisions allowing for greater executive power in crises and the lack of a mechanism to form and maintain stable governing coalitions among the various political parties. The more elementary problem with Weimar, however, was that not enough political parties and social forces were committed to democracy. The republic's critics included the military, many unemployed former soldiers, the Prussian aristocracy, elements of both the Catholic and Protestant churches, and large segments of big business. In addition, the KPD fundamentally criticized the Weimar Republic, but from the left. Unlike multiparty political systems in other countries, the Weimar Republic was plagued by a sharp and increasing polarization of political parties. Even parties expected to have at least some ideological affinities (the Communists and the Social Democrats, for example) were mortal enemies during Weimar. The KPD called the SPD "social fascists," and the SPD saw the KPD as a puppet of Moscow. The Weimar constitution was an elegant document, but without broad-based popular support, the regime itself was continually under attack.

Third Reich (1933–1945)

Once the Nazis controlled the chancellorship and the government, their next priority was establishing total control of the political system and society. The initial step was the systematic banning of political parties. The first party to be banned were the Communists, next were the Social Democrats and their trade union allies, and after that almost all of the democratic political parties. Even the organs of civic society such as clubs, neighborhood organizations, and the churches were subject to Nazi control, influence, or restrictions on independent action.

Ultimately the Nazis used propaganda, demagoguery, and the absence of a democratic opposition, which had been relentlessly hounded and then banned, to mobilize large segments of the German population. Through mesmerizing speeches and the relentless propaganda ministry led by his aide Joseph Goebbels, Hitler used his total control of political power and the media to reshape German politics to his party's vision. This was a vision that did not allow opposition, even within the party. For example, after establishing power, the Nazis even turned on their own "foot soldiers," the brown-shirted storm troopers (*Sturmabteilung*, SA). The SA was a large but ragtag group of street fighters whom the party used in the 1920s and early 1930s to attack Communists, Socialists, and trade unionists. The SA also was used to seize and burn opposition newspapers, as well as to loot and destroy businesses owned by Jews, foreigners, and other opponents of the Nazis. However, once the Nazis had established control and political opposition had been neutralized, the storm troopers became a major liability because their primary function—street brawling with left-wing groups—was no longer necessary. The SA and its leader, Ernst Röhm, believed that their valiant service should propel the SA to a stature equivalent or superior to that of the army. But to the ears of the Nazi

leadership and the generals who had now embraced Hitler, this notion was mutiny. The Nazis dispensed with the SA in 1934 by ordering the grisly murder of Röhm and the entire SA leadership in a predawn raid by Hitler's elite guard (*Schutzstaffeln*, SS) on a storm trooper barracks in Berlin, an event now known as the Night of the Long Knives, since most of the SA leadership were stabbed while they slept.

Domestic policy during the first few years of Nazi rule focused on two major areas: consolidating and institutionalizing centralized political power, and rebuilding an economy that had suffered through the monetary chaos of the 1920s and the Great Depression of the early 1930s.

The Nazis' new centralized political authority was different from past German political patterns. Until the Nazis came to power, German regional and local governments had enjoyed moderate political autonomy. Part of this autonomy was based on the independence that the German regions enjoyed while they were still sovereign states before the 1871 unification. Among the best-known semi-independent regions were Bavaria; the Rhineland, including the industrial Ruhr Valley; the Black Forest area in the southwest; and the city-states of Hamburg and Bremen. The Nazis chose to centralize all political authority in Berlin by making all regional and local authorities subject to tight, autocratic control. The main purpose of this top-down system was to ensure that Nazi policy on the repression of political opposition and of Jews and other racial minorities was carried out to the minutest detail. Such political centralization also enabled Goebbels's propaganda ministry to spread relentlessly the Nazi "virtues" of submission to authority, racial superiority, intolerance, and militarism. Nazi racist theories and practice were especially heinous, stressing Aryan racial purity and thus the persecution of Jews, Gypsies, and homosexuals as well as the sick and disabled.

The Nazis' economic program was also autocratic in design and execution. Since free trade unions had been banned, both private and state-run industries forced workers—and eventually slave laborers during World War II—to work long hours for little or no pay. The industries chosen for emphasis were primarily heavier industries (coal, steel, chemicals, machine tools, and industrial electronics), which required massive investment from the large cartels that formed in each industry, from the banking system, and from the state itself. Some segments of big business initially feared Hitler before he came to power. Yet with free trade unions suppressed, most of German industry endorsed Nazi economic policies. The Nazis also emphasized massive public works projects, such as creating the *Autobahn* highway system, upgrading the railroad system, and erecting grandiose public buildings that were supposed to represent Nazi greatness. These projects employed large numbers of workers under extremely repressive conditions. The emphasis on heavy industry and transportation clearly favored military production and expansion. Almost all of the industries that the Nazis favored had direct military application, and the *Autobahn,* similar to the modern U.S. interstate highway system, was built more to ease military transport than for pleasure driving.

During the Third Reich, Hitler fanned the flames of German nationalism by glorifying the warrior tradition in German folklore and exulting in imperial Germany's past smashing of rival armies in the mid-nineteenth century. In calling for a return to a mythically glorious and racially pure German past, he made scapegoats out of homosexuals; ethnic minorities such as Poles, Danes, and Alsatians; and especially Jews. In fact, the Germans' strident anti-Semitism helped give increased impetus to its growth in other European countries during the 1920s and 1930s. To nationalist leaders like Germany's Adolf Hitler, Italy's Benito Mussolini, Spain's Francisco Franco, and others elsewhere in Europe, anti-Semitism represented an important political force. It allowed these nationalist leaders to blame any political problems on this "external" international minority and target them

as an enemy of nationalism who should be relentlessly persecuted and suppressed.

On international issues, the Nazis refused to abide by the provisions of the Treaty of Versailles, signed by the Weimar government in 1918. One of these provisions called for severe restrictions on German military activity. After 1933, however, Nazi Germany began to produce armaments in large quantities using its heavy industry, remilitarized the Rhineland (the area of Germany closest to France), and sent aid to Franco's fascist army as it fought to overthrow the democratically elected Spanish republic from 1936 to 1939. The Nazis also rejected the territorial divisions of World War I, as Hitler claimed that a growing Germany needed increased space to live (*Lebensraum*) in eastern Europe. He ordered the forced union (*Anschluss*) with Austria in March 1938 and the occupation of the German-speaking Sudetenland section of Czechoslovakia in September 1938. The Third Reich's attack on Poland on September 1, 1939, finally precipitated World War II.

"Enemies of the Third Reich"

Hitler's grandiose visions of German world domination were dramatically heightened by the conquests of first Poland and then the rest of Europe. By the summer of 1941, he began to turn his attention to the only other continental power that stood in the way of his goal of total European domination, the Soviet Union. Hitler assumed that defeating the Soviet Union would be as easy as his other conquests. Therefore, in the summer of 1941, he violated the Nazi-Soviet nonaggression pact by embarking on a direct attack on the Soviet Union. The attack was the end of German military success and the beginning of the Third Reich's defeat, a process that would culminate almost four years later, in May 1945. Yet even as defeat loomed in 1945, Hitler preferred to see Germany totally destroyed rather than have its national honor "besmirched" by total surrender.

Germany saw tremendous physical and human destruction. Approximately 55 million people died in Europe during World War II, with approximately 8 million of those being German. In addition, Germany was occupied by the four victorious Allied powers (Britain, France, the United States, and the Soviet Union) and ceased to exist as a sovereign state from 1945 to 1949.

Clearly the most heinous aspect of the Nazi movement was the systematic execution of 6 million Jews and millions of other civilians in the concentration camps throughout Germany as well as occupied central and eastern Europe. Hitler explicitly stated in his book *Mein Kampf* (*My Struggle*) that the Germans were the "master race" and all other non-Aryan races, especially the Jews, were "inferior." But as with a lot of his other statements during his rise to power, many Germans chose to ignore the implications of this hatred or thought it was mere exaggeration. For example, a controversial book by political scientist Daniel Goldhagen makes a powerful case that many German citizens who were not directly connected to the Nazi extermination process nonetheless either ignored or turned away from clear evidence that systematic extermination of Jews took place.[8] Goldhagen

argues that many Germans voluntarily participated in brutal violence against Jews, not because they were forced to but because they were motivated by vicious anti-Semitism, the roots of which went back generations. Critics, however, argued that Germany was much less single-minded about Jews and that divisions among the left were a significant reason for Hitler's ascension to power.[9] The magnitude of Nazi plans for other races, religions, opposing political views, gays, and Gypsies, among others, became apparent after Hitler came to power, but by then any chance of domestic opposition had passed. Persecution of Jews and other racial and ethnic minorities grew steadily more atrocious until Germany's defeat in 1945. First, the Nazis placed sharp restrictions on the freedoms of Jews and other persecuted minorities, including Gypsies and Slavs. Then property was confiscated and destroyed, culminating in the *Kristallnacht* (Night of Broken Glass) of 1938, in which Jewish stores, synagogues, and homes were systematically ransacked. Last, the concentration and extermination camps were systematically constructed and filled with Jews and other minorities. The Nazis placed most of the extermination camps in occupied countries like Poland, but one of the most infamous was in Germany at Dachau, just northwest of Munich. These concentration camps existed for the systematic extermination by gassing of Jews and others the Nazis designated as opponents.

The Nazi period had a powerful impact on German state formation during the post–World War II years. It served as an "antimodel" of what any postwar democratic political system should avoid at all costs. Of course, the Nazi legacy has also served as a "model" for the various neo-Nazi groups that have sprung up in the Federal Republic of Germany (FRG), both in the mid-1960s and especially in the postunification years of the 1990s. Although there are constitutional prohibitions on neo-Nazi activities, numerous outlaw groups and their quasi-legal sympathizers still admire the horrors of the Third Reich. The number of active members of these groups is quite small, perhaps a few thousand at most, but some studies of public opinion show support for the goals, if not the tactics, of such groups at figures near 10 percent of the population. We examine these forces more closely in Chapter 18.

A Divided Germany (1945–1990)

From 1945 to 1949, a brief yet influential historical juncture, Germany was occupied by the four Allied powers. This was influential because the Western Allies seemed to impose democracy "from above" in a way that was quite effective. Yet as we will see, postwar democratic German leaders shaped this new democracy in a fashion quite different from British or U.S. democracy. Germany, as evidenced by both World Wars I and II, had proved to be one of the most unstable and threatening members of the international political system during the late nineteenth and early twentieth centuries. Through both the Sec-

ond and Third Reichs, Germany was viewed as an aggressive, acquisitive economic power and a political-military power that caused fear among its neighbors. This potent legacy of conquest and domination caused the victorious Allied powers (Britain, France, the United States, and the Soviet Union) to treat Germany differently from the other Axis powers, Japan and Italy. Unlike the latter two countries, Germany was occupied by the Allies, and its territory was divided into what soon became East and West Germany. At first, the reason for such a division and the physical dismemberment of the German state was that the country's history warranted such action. But the realities of the cold war soon offered a different and more powerful reason for Germany's division.

For the brief occupation period (1945–1949), Germany ceased to be a nation-state. It was only with the founding of the FRG in 1949 that a more stable, democratic form of government

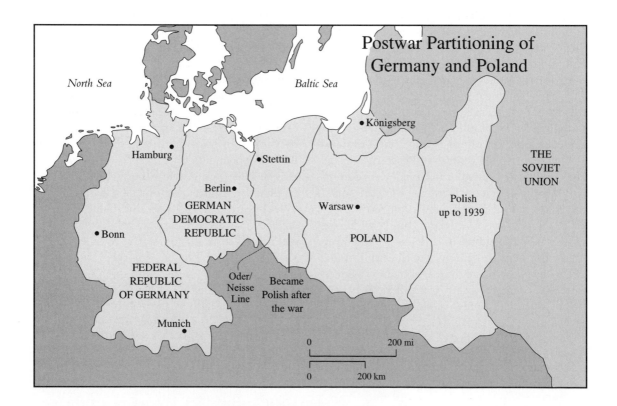

emerged and was known colloquially as West Germany. East Germany became a separate, Communist country (the German Democratic Republic, GDR) at that time. While nation-statehood returned nominally to the two Germanies in 1949, the lack of German sovereignty during the 1945–1949 period created an important legacy that lasted for much longer than the occupation period. From 1949 until 1990, both Germanies, for different sets of historical reasons, did not take on the kind of political responsibilities that "normal" nation-states did. The Federal Republic deferred to the United States in matters of international relations, as did the GDR to the Soviet Union. Both the United States and the Soviet Union felt it important to constrain independent and international German political activity, a legacy that dated from the occupation period. This constraint produced for the Federal Republic a so-called economic giant–political dwarf syndrome that began to change only in the 1990s.

In the years of the postwar occupation, both German and Allied officials imposed several important constraints that continued in the FRG. The first was the reduction of the powers of the central state in domestic politics, replaced in part by strong regional governments. The second was the limitation of the FRG's role as an international political power. The Allied occupation authorities prevented the German military from having a legal independent status until the mid-1950s, and even then it was closely monitored and controlled by the Western Allies and eventually the North Atlantic Treaty Organization (NATO). Third, German politicians reformed the party system, helping to create parties that were broader and less driven by narrow ideological considerations alone. Perhaps the most significant reform was the merger of Catholic and Protestant forces into Christian Democracy, comprising the Christian Democratic Union (CDU) and the Christian Social Union (CSU), the Bavarian branch of this movement. During Weimar, the Catholics and Protestants had their own parties, which were often uncooperative

with each other as well as with other parties. However, postwar Christian Democracy radically reshaped German political conservatism by embracing democracy, social welfare, antinationalism, and antimilitarism. Yet it also retained its conservative core in its emphasis on religious, family, cultural, and homeland (*Heimat*) values.

As the cold war intensified in the late 1940s and tensions grew between the Soviet Union and the other three powers, Germany became the dividing line between the two camps, and the two Germanies emerged. This division produced yet one more major historical juncture. Its most durable legacy was that it was a turning point in which an apparently stable democracy developed. That the country would remain divided for nearly half a century was not known in 1946. The cold war, however, changed many of the immediate postwar expectations of what Germany's future was to be. The transformation of the Soviet zone of occupation into the GDR and its inclusion in the Soviet-led Warsaw bloc, as well as the creation of the FRG and its inclusion in NATO, seemed to preempt any discussion of reunification indefinitely.

The Federal Republic became a parliamentary democracy, characterized by constitutional provisions for free elections, civil liberties, and individual rights, and an independent judiciary. However, it also banned both Communist and neo-Nazi parties during the 1950s and 1960s, and it initiated state-sponsored purges of the civil service in the early 1970s to root out presumed radicals who were believed to have obtained positions in the bureaucracy.

Forces on the democratic left such as the SPD, the Greens (the ecologically oriented political party that first won parliamentary seats in 1983 and joined the SPD in a left-leaning coalition government in 1998), and the trade unions grew into progressive movements that have strongly emphasized democratizing material resources. The clearest institutional examples are the legally mandated in-plant works councils (all firms with five or more employees are required to have independent organizations to represent worker interests) and firm-wide *codetermination* (that is, almost 50 percent of company boards of directors comprise trade union members). The 1952 codetermination law required firms with two thousand or more employees to let 33 percent of the board members be chosen by the trade unions. In 1976, the figure increased to 50 percent. However, management retained the tiebreaking vote. In addition, in 1972, the SPD-FDP coalition government also extended the provision of the *Betriebsverfassungsgesetz* (Works Constitution Act) to provide more rights for trade unions inside the works councils and thereby solidified unions' positions in the workplace. Most significant, this continued maintenance of an institutionalized presence for unions enabled them to participate in shaping the direction of the Federal Republic's economy on their own terms rather than forcing them reflexively to oppose any overtures by either management or a conservative government.[10] Beginning in the 1950s, this rank-and-file democratic participation, often called *democratic corporatism*, helped alleviate much of the social tension that had plagued Germany prior to 1945.[11] Under democratic corporatism, business, labor, and the government work together on economic and industrial relations issues and generally develop consensual policy solutions to national, regional, state, and local challenges.

The Germans have spoken of their "social" (not "free") market economy because of the deeply entrenched belief that business must share in the responsibility to provide a stable order, for both the economy and, indirectly, society. The development of this set of institutional and political structures—a mixed economy, democratic corporatism, and a generous welfare state—in Germany, as elsewhere in Western Europe, has been called the *postwar settlement*. Although this settlement proved generally beneficial for the political economy of the FRG, it was not a panacea. For example, the treatment of immigrant workers within German industry has at times seemed more exclusionary than inclusionary. Also, the illiberal right-wing extrem-

ists who have stigmatized and attacked racial and ethnic minorities have often met with less than thorough prosecution of these crimes by the German state.

The Federal Republic's democratic traditions since 1949 have their origins in the successful creation of a durable and flexible set of political institutions. The parliamentary system is bicameral, with a lower house (Bundestag) and an upper house (Bundesrat). The lower house is directly elected, and the upper house is made up of delegates selected by the sixteen federal states. The chancellor (head of government) is similar in power to the British prime minister and attains office by virtue of being the leader of the majority party or coalition in the Bundestag. The largely ceremonial president (head of state) is similar to constitutional monarchs like Britain's Queen Elizabeth. The multiparty system of five major parties covers a wide political spectrum and provides representation for diverse, democratic political opinions, and the independent judiciary respects the rule of law. Finally, the comprehensive state provides generous benefits to German citizens and works closely with private sector interests to maintain economic strength. However, the stresses placed on democratic institutions (both procedural and substantive) in the wake of German unification and European integration have caused many observers to reexamine German democracy in a more critical light.

The lack of democracy in the GDR—a "people's democracy," in Communist parlance—was a condition that remained throughout the GDR's history from 1949 to 1990. During the 1950s, many East Germans who wished to flee communism would travel to Berlin, which remained under the control of the four Allied powers (the United Kingdom, France, the United States, and the Soviet Union). Once in the free Western sectors of the city, they could travel without restriction to the FRG and receive immediate citizenship. Hundreds of thousands of East Germans migrated west, causing a labor shortage and a "brain drain" for the GDR. Finally, in August 1961, the GDR erected the Berlin Wall, making travel to the West impossible. The GDR called the wall an antifascist barrier, supposedly meant to keep the West Germans from "invading" East Germany, but all Germans, East and West, realized that its true purpose was to prevent East Germans from fleeing to the West. It thus solidified what many feared was a permanent division of Germany.

The GDR was a one-party state under the control of the Communist Party, which was known as the Socialist Unity Party (Sozialistische Einheitspartei, SED). Although the GDR provided full employment, housing, and various social benefits to its citizens, it was a rigid, bureaucratic, Stalinist regime that tightly controlled economic and political life under the leadership of party chairmen Walter Ulbricht, Willi Stoph, and Erich Honecker. The GDR assumed a universal consensus about the "correctness" of communism; all public democratic dissent was suppressed as being deviationist and undermining the "true path of socialism." East Germans trying to flee to the West were subject to execution on the spot. Numerous memorials to escapees who were shot stand along the site of the former Berlin Wall. Many observers have argued that recent antiforeigner attacks, which have been strongest in the former East Germany, can be attributed partly to the lack of a genuine democratic tradition of dialogue, tolerance, and public discourse there.

For more than forty years, Germany's role in the international arena was a limited one. Not only did Allied and NATO restrictions prevent unilateral German political action, but the *Grundgesetz* (Basic Law) prevented German troops from being used outside NATO (that is, largely Western European) areas. At the founding of the FRG and GDR, however, both West and East Germans believed that the country was likely to remain divided for the foreseeable future, which meant that the political role of the two German states was intentionally circumscribed by each of their alliance partners. Not

only was the GDR restrained by the Soviet Union; so too was the Federal Republic limited by the Western Allies, NATO, and the presence of a seemingly permanent garrison of foreign military forces. Even as the West German economy grew strong during the economic miracle years of the 1950s and became the leading Western European economy by the 1960s, the FRG's political role remained much more limited. The GDR experienced a similar pattern. It apparently became the strongest of the Eastern European Communist economies. However, since unification, the massive rebuilding required for the entire infrastructure in eastern Germany has suggested that the vaunted economic strength during the Communist period was largely a facade.

Germany's unification in 1990 took place rapidly and surprised West and East Germans alike. When the Berlin Wall came down in November 1989, the two German states envisioned a slow process of increased contact and cooperation while they maintained separate sovereign states for the short term. But when the trickle of East Germans moving west turned into a deluge, the Kohl government was forced to take action to stem the influx of East Germans into the West. One step was to provide a currency exchange whereby former East German currency could be exchanged for valuable West German deutsche marks. After hurried negotiations in late summer, the former GDR became part of the Federal Republic of Germany as five new FRG states.

Thus, through unification in 1990, the role of the German state in the international arena had remained muted. But the supposedly settled international political landscape that the cold war afforded, in which a divided Germany was taken for granted, was gone with the opening of the Berlin Wall and the coming apart of the Soviet Union in 1991. For better or for worse, Germany—as a single, powerful nation-state—had made a rapid reappearance on the international stage. This theme resonates throughout the chapters on Germany.

The Postwar Settlement

The postwar settlement in the FRG evolved in phases, or as Peter Katzenstein has called the first three of them, "republics."[12] These were not republics in the French sense, with separate constitutions; rather, Katzenstein associated them with the dominant political orientation of the respective FRG government in power at the time. In terms of governing coalitions, the period of the postwar settlement has swung from the moderate center-right (1949–1966), to the moderate center-left (1969–1982), to the moderate center-right (1982–1998), and now a democratic left government (1998–). Together these governments produced a set of basic policy options—with minor variations depending on which of the two major parties led the coalition—that have maintained continuity throughout this long period.

Important characteristics distinguished the postwar settlement in the FRG from the settlements in other Western European nations. Among the most significant were the highly organized nature of the business community (greater than in other European countries); a weak central state and strong regional governments; an active tradition of worker participation within a strong labor movement (i.e., corporatism); influential quasi-public institutions shaping and implementing public policy at all levels of society; and a continued commitment to the welfare state by both major parties.

The development of welfare services in the Federal Republic springs from several points of origin. First, it was the conservative Bismarck who created the initial welfare state in the 1880s to preempt the more radical demands of the left. Second, it owes much to the European Christian Social tradition, a major ideological tenet in the CDU-CSU coalition, and also an important influence on the small, more free-enterprise-oriented Free Democratic Party (FDP). Both Catholic and Protestant churches have, for more than a century, espoused a belief in public spending for services as a responsibility of the strong for the welfare of the weak. Third, the unions' and the SPD's demands for increased public spending ensured that the left was incorporated into the political order during the 1950s and early 1960s. Thus, the postwar settlement has produced a deeply rooted legacy of commitment to the public provision of welfare services.

We also want to elaborate a bit more on the concept of the German model, a theme used in much political science literature to describe how the FRG coheres in terms of its political and socioeconomic features.[13] Thus, the postwar period saw the development of the *Modell Deutschland* (German model), a term often used to describe the FRG's distinctive political and socioeconomic features: coordinated banking and industrial relations, export-oriented growth of high-quality manufactured goods, democratic participation by workers on the job, and extensive public sector benefits. Thus, German society is more "organized" than other countries in the sense that political institutions, social forces, and the patterns of life in civic society place more emphasis on collective action than does the individualism more characteristic of Anglo-Saxon countries.

"Find the money." German policymakers worrying about the costs of the welfare state.

Source: Atelier Rabenau/*Frankfurter Allgemeine Zeitung.*

Germans do have considerable individual freedoms; however, political expression, in both the state and civil society, revolves around group representation and articulation of a cooperative spirit in much of public action. Does it mean there is no conflict in Germany? Hardly! But it means that both private citizens and public authorities look to organized, collective responses rather than isolated individual action.

Helmut Kohl and the Challenge of German Unification (1990–1998)

Formal unification took place in the fall of 1990 as Chancellor Kohl, the "unification chancellor," won a strong reelection victory for his center-right Christian Democratic–Free Democratic coalition. The period of euphoria did not last, as the costs of unification placed increased stress on Germany's budget and democratic institutions. Unification has proved much more difficult than many observers first anticipated. Before unification, East Germany was considered the strongest of the Eastern European Communist economies. But the border opening and eventual unification soon showed that the East German economy was far more backward than most economists had thought. The Communist planned economy (sometimes called a *command economy*) was not sensitive to market signals since production of goods was determined more by rigid government dictates than by consumer needs. The East German level of technology was decades behind, especially when compared to the developed economies of the West. Simple telephone communication was usually an adventure, and the current unified German government has spent billions just to rebuild communication networks. Politically, East Germany was a state in which open political discourse and expression were discouraged, if not prohibited. Of course, people would meet and speak candidly among family or close friends, but a liberal democratic political culture did not exist.

Incorporating the disadvantaged East Germany had an adverse impact on a wide range of public policies, including unemployment expenses, structural rebuilding funds, and the large tax increases necessary to pay for it all. The large number of unemployed in eastern Germany— approximately 20 percent, more than double the figure in the prosperous West—helped fuel scattered ultra-right-wing political movements. They sought out foreigners (often Turks) as scapegoats, and there were several vicious attacks on minority groups in the 1990s.

The difficulties of unification were complicated by raised expectations by the Kohl governments throughout the 1990s. In order to win the support of eastern Germans, he sugarcoated the enormity of the unification process as well as its duration. In order to win the support of western Germans, he had to convince them that the 7.5 percent "unification tax" imposed on them in the early 1990s would be money well spent. Unfortunately for Kohl, the longer the unification process remained incomplete, the less willing the German electorate was to give him continued support. He was able to convince voters to continue to support the Christian Democratic–Free Democratic government in the 1994 election, in which the coalition was returned to power, albeit with a significantly reduced majority. The costs of unification were exported throughout Europe in the form of slow growth because of high interest rates needed to attract funds to finance the cost of rebuilding eastern Germany. Thus there was an economic recession throughout Europe in the early 1990s.

As the 1998 election approached, Kohl felt confident that he would win reelection. He believed that German unification, despite its remaining challenges, and the EU in which Germany would play a leading role would ensure victory. The voters did not agree, handing the Christian Democratic–Free Democratic coalition a resounding defeat in the September 27 election. Successfully convincing Germans that a change was necessary, newly elected SPD chancellor Gerhard Schröder, a generation younger than Kohl, entered into a coalition government with the Greens for the first time in the nation's history. Significant too was the continued high support for the former Communist Party in eastern Germany, renamed the Party of Democratic Socialism (PDS) (over 20 percent), which enabled it to gain more than 5 percent of the total German vote. With almost 54 percent of the electorate voting for parties of the left, clearly a new era had arrived in Germany.

The speed with which East Germany came apart after the fall of the Berlin Wall surprised everyone, not the least Helmut Kohl. Kohl can certainly be faulted for misjudging the economic and political costs of German unification. In fact, his overpromising of the pace of East German transformation in the early 1990s was a critical factor in his electoral loss in 1998. However, in acting quickly to integrate East Germany as five new *Länder*, when an independent, non-Communist East Germany proved unworkable in the spring and summer of 1990, Kohl helped alleviate what could have been a politically disastrous situation for both Germany and Europe.

Germany in the Euro Era (1998–2001)

Germany's leaders from Konrad Adenauer, the first postwar chancellor, through Schröder all have been strongly enthusiastic toward European integration. In its relations with other states after World War II, however, Germany has faced two different kinds of criticism. First was the fear of a too-powerful Germany, a country that had run roughshod over its European neighbors for most of the first half of the twentieth century. Second is the opposite problem, the so-called economic giant–political dwarf syndrome in which Germany was accused of benefiting from a strong world economy for much of the past fifty years while taking on none of the political responsibility. The fact that these are mutually contradictory points of view did not spare Germany from criticism.

Yet an integrated Europe promised the possibility of solving both problems simultaneously. Germany will likely remain the economic anchor of the EU, and its membership in the EU will enable it to do things and take on needed political responsibilities that it would be unable to do on its own. Former chancellor Kohl (1982–1998) realized this and was a firm advocate of all measures that would assist in a smooth, stable, and comprehensive EU. Germany, like all the other European nations that supported integration, has tended to see the glass as half full. From Germany's viewpoint, meeting both criticisms in the context of the EU was a positive-sum outcome.

However, the comprehensive integration process that began with the Maastricht Treaty of 1992 had an unusual mechanism of dealing with issues. European leaders, faced with fewer and more difficult tasks, made the choice to begin with the former and then address the latter. This meant that relatively easy steps—such as easing intra-European trade and travel and allowing for workers to cross borders for employment as long as they had the requisite linguistic and job skills—were taken first. The more complicated and difficult decisions—such as a single currency, monetary and fiscal policy, and democratic governance—were delayed. Optimistic European leaders, including the Germans, believed that a positive momentum, if not a "europhoria," would develop and thereby ease the transition toward continued integration.

The accelerating pace of European integration, however, with its movement toward a common monetary policy, a European Central Bank, and a single (virtual) currency in 1999, followed by the physical elimination of all national currencies in favor of the euro in 2002, placed additional pressures on the Federal Republic. Many Germans wondered whether the anchor of stability represented by the redoubtable deutsche mark (DM) and the inflation-fighting Deutsche Bundesbank would begin to drift in the uncertain sea of the EU. At the turn of the century, many Germans began to realize the costs associated with European integration that might threaten the economic and political stability they had so long prized during the first fifty years of the Federal Republic. The fall in value of the euro by some 25 percent in relation to the dollar in 1999 and 2000—and its subsequent rise to more than 30 percent greater than the dollar four years later—was worrisome to Germans long accustomed to a stable and predictable DM. More structurally, the lack of complete domestic control of Germany's monetary and fiscal policies (the latter due to the EU requirement that member states not run deficits greater than 3 percent of GDP) placed significant constraints—particularly with respect to social spending—on Chancellor Schröder.

With respect to open borders and seemingly free-flowing immigration, Germans also wondered whether Europeanization threatened to erode what it meant to be German. At the same time that immigration and political asylum increased in Germany during the 1990s, the birthrate, particularly in the former GDR, dropped precipitously. Far-right and even some moderate right-wing politicians used these demographic changes to whip up nationalist support for decreasing the flow of migrants to the FRG. Ironically, these demographic changes also coincided with the inability of the highly regarded secondary educational system to produce enough skilled workers for the information age. Germany's vocational educational system and integrated apprenticeship system have worked exceptionally well for traditionally strong German industries, but they have been less effective in producing highly qualified information sector workers. This "tech shortage" reached such a critical mass in 2000 that the Schröder government began to recruit software specialists from India who would be granted "green cards" (i.e., permanent residency status) upon their arrival! In other words, a new wave of *Gastarbeiter* was arriving precisely when some Germans were increasingly agitated about the immigration boom. In fact, some conservative politicians reacted to the arrival of the Indian software specialists with the phrase *Kinder statt Inder* (children instead of Indians), meaning that they would prefer that the government train German adolescents instead of inviting another wave of immigrants. The problem, however, was that the speed with which the German economy needed to embrace the information sector did not allow delays. The country needed both to increase Germany's presence in this complex sector and to enable its traditionally strong industries to adapt to new forms of international competition. The economic pressures did not allow the luxury of waiting the several years for the German secondary educational system to get up to speed.

Finally, the issue of democratic governance was an additional European challenge. Like most other forms of increased integration among nation-states throughout history, economic integration generally precedes political integration. The EU has been no exception. However, in the rush toward integration, questions of political accountability have been less well addressed. With fiscal and monetary policy essentially determined by either Brussels or the European Central Bank, where does democratic governance really lie?

Germany after September 11 (2001–)

The terrorist attacks in the United States had several significant effects on German domestic and international politics. Among the most significant were immigration/globalization, antiterrorist measures, and Germany's relationship with the United States.

The enlargement of the EU with the addition of ten Central and Eastern European countries in May 2004 highlighted the challenge that immigration poses for Germany. During the post-WWII *Gastarbeiter* period, immigration to Germany was comparatively straightforward. Workers came from southern Europe and Turkey, supposedly for limited periods, and would return home when economic conditions no longer required their services. Of course, several generations of Turkish Germans remain in the Federal Republic, illustrating the principle of unintended consequences. But in the first decade of the twenty-first century, migrants to a much more open Germany were coming not only for economic opportunities in a globalizing world but also for political asylum to a much more open EU.

The discovery that some of the 9/11 terrorists lived in Germany prior to the attacks only added to the tension. For a country that had prided itself in generously granting political asylum in the wake of the Nazi period, increased antiterrorist security requirements threatened to uproot decades of FRG postwar policy. Post-WWII Germany's sensitivity to the excesses of the Nazi regime was responsible for the liberal asylum laws because postwar German governments viewed with pride the country's openness to oppressed people facing repression. Yet the discovery of an Al Qaeda cell in Hamburg, where several of the terrorists lived before going to the United States, created uneasy discussion in Germany on the freedom-versus-security dimension. Clearly the Schröder government in the wake of 9/11 has increased domestic surveillance to locate additional terrorist cells, and has made a series of arrests and detentions. But such aggressive actions by police and security forces—while essential to identify potential threats to domestic and international security—rest uneasy with considerable segments of the German population. As a result, some officials in the Bush administration remain suspicious, if not openly critical, of the German commitment to antiterrorist measures.

Germany and the United States strongly disagreed about the war in Iraq. The FRG's post-WWII history had encouraged it to prefer multilateral negotiated approaches to international conflict, not preemptive attacks. Thus Germany's lack of support for the Iraq war drove a large wedge between the United States and the Federal Republic. The tension was exacerbated by the conduct of Gerhard Schröder during his 2002 reelection campaign. The less than robust German economy in the summer and early fall of 2002 did not give the chancellor a strong issue upon which to make the case for his reelection. His leading issue in the final weeks of the campaign—largely reflecting the preferences of the German public in avoiding an attack on Iraq—was direct opposition to the Bush administration's Iraq policy in the run-up to the start of the war in early 2003. While never degenerating to the level of American-French acrimony, the long-standing strong relationship between Germany and the United States took a significant hit because of this dispute. Further exacerbating these tensions were the acquittals of two Moroccan alleged terrorists in Germany in February 2004. Because the United States refused to release witnesses, held in detention in the United States, who could potentially exonerate the two Moroccan suspects in Germany, the judges in the two German courts were forced to release the two defendants because they could not present a proper defense. This conflict indicates a larger issue in the relationship between these two democracies. Democracy is grounded in the rule of law and self-determination, but when one country makes a different decision than its ally would prefer, the situation can call into question the very foundations of this bilateral relationship. As the American position in Iraq deteriorated in 2004, Germany and its continental European allies did not rush to embrace the idea of either EU or NATO action in an increasingly volatile and unstable Iraq, since the United States had favored such a unilateral position for the previous year.

Themes and Implications

We now step back and reexamine the historical junctures in light of the four political themes that comprise our analytical framework.

Historical Junctures and Political Themes

Germany's role in the world of states, the first theme, is contentious. For all states, military strength is a basic tool used to shape and consolidate. But in Germany, the rise of militarism and a corresponding authoritarian political culture were exaggerated for several reasons. Germany's exposed position in the central plains of Europe encouraged military preparedness because any of its many neighbors could mount an attack with few constraints. Since various German-speaking lands lacked a solid democratic or liberal political culture before unification in 1871, Prussian militarism exerted dominant influence over political and civic life. In other words, late unification accompanied by war created a state that caused tremendous fear among Germany's neighbors. The conduct of World War I and especially the Third Reich of the Nazis and World War II intensified this fear. Although more than fifty years have passed since the end of World War II and although Germany's independent political actions are constrained by the EU, many Europeans remain wary of Germany's international role.

The second theme, *governing the economy*, has been colored profoundly by Germany's late-nineteenth-century state building. Clearly, nation-states can promote economic growth more easily than can fragmented political entities. Delayed unification and industrialization prevented Germany from embarking on the race for empire and raw materials until the late nineteenth century. By the time it joined the global economy, it lagged behind Britain and France in industrializing and securing access to the natural resources of the developing world and was forced to play catch-up. This pursuit of fast economic growth combined with the awakened sense of German nationalism in the late nineteenth century produced an aggressive, acquisitive state in which economic and political needs overlapped. This fusion of state and economic power enabled Hitler to build the Third Reich. Consequently, post–World War II policymakers and political leaders sought to remove the state from actively governing the economy. The development of the German model was the preferred policy choice because it looked unlike the free-market traditions of countries like the United States and Great Britain and the more state-centered democracies like France and Japan. Rather, postwar Germany developed an organized capitalist model that placed primacy on coordination among private sector actors to promote efficiency and competitiveness. As a counterweight to concentrated economic power, the Federal Republic also developed a strong labor movement that used democratic corporatism to participate in fundamental decisions that were often left to management in other countries. This model served Germany exceptionally well until the late 1990s, but its future is uncertain in the new era of the EU. Will previously successful German economic institutions continue to function well in a unified EU? This remains an open question.

The *democratic idea*, our third theme, developed much later in Germany than in most other advanced industrialized countries. It was not until 1918 and the shaky Weimar Republic that Germany first attained democracy at all. And Germany's fragile democratic institutions were crushed by the Nazi takeover less than two decades later. Despite a formal democratic constitution, Weimar was a prisoner of forces bent on its destruction. Unlike stable multiparty political systems in other countries, the Weimar Republic was plagued by a sharp and increasing polarization of political parties. The constitution of the Federal Republic in 1949 was designed to overcome Weimar's shortcomings. A system of federalism, constitutional provisions to encourage the formation and maintenance of coalitions, and a streamlined political party system proved solid foundations for the new democracy. Electoral turnout of between 80 and 90 percent for almost all elections since 1949 suggests that Germans have embraced democracy, although skeptics argue that Germans were voting more out of duty than anything else.[14] However, four peaceful electoral alterations in the past fifty years in which both government and opposition functioned more smoothly than most other democratic regimes may finally put to rest doubts about German democracy. The remaining uncertainty is how well and how quickly the democratic culture will penetrate formerly Communist East Germany.

The fourth theme, the *politics of collective identities,* offers a unique look at the intersection of democracy and collectivity. More than in other democratic countries, German political institutions, social forces, and patterns of life emphasize collective action rather than the individualism characteristic of the United States. In other words, class is still important. Although it provides an important source of collective identity and is closely linked to party cleavages, it does not polarize and provoke stalemate. Religion, too, is an important collective identity, especially with the strong role that Christian Democracy plays in the political life of Germany. These collective identities should not imply that German citizens have less personal freedom compared with those in other developed democracies or that there is no conflict in Germany. It means that political expression, in both the state and civil society, revolves around group representation and cooperative spirit in public action. Certainly Germany's history from Prussian militarism through Nazism has led many observers to believe that collectivist impulses should be eradicated. However, to expect Germany to embrace a liberal, individualistic democracy as in the United States with no deep history of this is misguided. Germany's development of a collective identity since 1945 has relied on a redefinition of Germany in a European context. For example, one of the first provisions of the Social Democratic–Green coalition agreement was to alter Germany's restrictive immigration policies. The new law finally enabled long-established immigrants to gain German citizenship. Thus, German collective identity is changing.

Implications for Comparative Politics

Despite the surface similarities between Germany and the other Western European states covered in this book, there are substantial differences, and they give us a chance to develop and test more general theoretical claims in comparative politics. With respect to the organization of the state, the most significant difference between Germany, on the one hand, and England, France, and Italy, for example, on the other, is that Germany is a federal state, and the others are unitary. This German federalism has produced economic and political patterns quite different from those of its three major European neighbors.

Another important difference is that Germany's later industrialization produced a strong—though unbalanced—economic growth until after World War II. When this growth combined with nationalism and militarism in the late nineteenth and early twentieth centuries, Germany was feared by its neighbors, and with good reason. While late development can lead to catastrophic outcomes, it can also induce greater forms of cooperation and coordination among major actors, producing such institutions as corporatism.

A third difference arises from the fact that democracy was late in coming to Germany—it did not develop until after World War I with the creation of the Weimar Republic. Once it was destroyed by the Third Reich, parliamentary democracy did not return until the founding of the Federal Republic in 1949. Of course, the most significant difference between Germany and other Western European states is the Nazi period and the havoc the Third Reich caused. Many observers during the post–World War II period may have thought this difference had declined in significance. However, the current racist attacks on foreigners by neo-Nazis have forced many to rethink whether the evils of the Nazi period are confined entirely to the past. Also, the unification with the former Communist East Germany is an obvious important difference between Germany and its neighbors. The economic, political, cultural, and physical pressures of uniting two disparate societies have placed greater strains on the Federal Republic's politics and institutions than any other event since the state's founding in 1949. While postwar Germany has manifested most of the features of a stable capitalist democracy, these peculiarities and their legacies have created and maintained significant tensions within society.

Finally, Germany's role in the EU presents both opportunities and challenges to Germany and its neighbors. As the most populous and strongest European power, Germany has many economic and political advantages in an integrating Europe. However, it must deal with the suspicion its twentieth-century historical legacy produced in its neighbors, and it must also confront the question of whether its postwar political institutions, so well suited to it, will also suit Germany and other Europeans in the EU.

We suggest that the best way to answer these issues is to examine them historically, systematically, and rigorously through the prism of our four themes.

Comparative analysts seeking to understand Germany's history and future prospects have been guided by a number of assumptions that we explore more fully in the following four chapters. One is that relations among social groups—competing collective identities—have an important influence on a state's formation and development. In Germany's case, bitter religious, ideological, and regional social conflicts (among others) were partly responsible for delaying its unification and stable development. As a result, Germany lagged several centuries behind other Western powers in forming a modern nation-state.

Germany's late unification as a nation-state also gave it little time to develop strong civic and democratic institutions with which to address deep social divisions and fierce international competition. Democracies that evolve more gradually can usually meet such challenges more peacefully and effectively. In encouraging public discussion and compromise among competing social interests, such governments can diffuse potential conflicts and deliberate state options more fully. Germany's weak civic and governing institutions were unable to protect it and other nations from ruthless oppression by military elites who led the German people into

two disastrous wars. These tragic experiences were to have a profound influence on the postwar development of West Germany's democracy. This suggests that the clever design of political institutions can promote democracy; witness the success of the Basic Law in reconciling the need for effective government and democratic participation.

Another assumption we consider is that a state's relationship with private interests is established early and shapes its ability to develop effective economic policies over time. Such relationships formed to govern the economy help determine a state's wealth and ability to manage changes effectively. In Germany's case, delayed industrialization may have proved beneficial once democratic institutions became stronger and better able to reconcile economic growth with political accountability. Like Japan, Germany's government has played an active role in economic development from the start. In contrast, Britain and the United States industrialized early, with much less direct government intervention, and their economies rely much more on private market forces. Clearly, advanced industrialized democracies employ different economic policy models. In Chapter 17, we consider the implications of Germany's economic strategy for its postwar development.

A final assumption is that a state's position in the international system—measured in part by its resource base, level of economic development, and military power relative to other states—affects its ability to manage domestic and international pressures. By the time that Germany embraced industrialization in the late nineteenth century, it felt compelled to catch up with a world of more advanced industrial states such as Britain, France, and the United States, which had divided a large share of the world's primary resources and trade among themselves. Germany's intense effort to expand its industrial and military power through direct state involvement in the economy had important—and adverse—consequences for its development.

Notes

1. Peter A. Hall and David Soskice, *Varieties of Capitalism: The Institutional Foundations of Comparative Advantage* (New York: Oxford University Press, 2001).

2. Charles Tilly, ed., *The Formation of National States in Western Europe* (Princeton, N.J.: Princeton University Press, 1975).

3. Tom Kemp, *Industrialization in Nineteenth Century Europe,* 2nd ed. (London: Longman, 1985).

4. Gordon Craig, *The Politics of the Prussian Army* (Oxford: Oxford University Press, 1955).

5. Barrington Moore, *Social Origins of Dictatorship and Democracy* (Boston: Beacon Press, 1965).

6. Alexander Gerschenkron, *Bread and Democracy in Germany,* 2nd ed. (Ithaca, N.Y.: Cornell University Press, 1989).

7. Geoffrey Barraclough, *An Introduction to Contemporary History* (Baltimore: Penguin, 1967).

8. Daniel Goldhagen, *Hitler's Willing Executioners: Ordinary Germans and the Holocaust* (New York: Knopf, 1996).

9. Robert R. Shandley, ed., *Unwilling Germans? The Goldhagen Debate* (Minneapolis: University of Minnesota Press, 1998).

10. For a comprehensive treatment of the West German trade unions during the postwar period, see Andrei S. Markovits and Christopher S. Allen, "West Germany," in Peter Gourevitch et al., eds., *Unions and Economic Crisis: Britain, West Germany and Sweden* (London: Allen & Unwin, 1984).

11. Philippe Schmitter and Gerhard Lembruch, *Trends Toward Corporatist Intermediation* (Beverly Hills, Calif.: Sage, 1979).

12. The concept of the "three republics" of postwar West Germany has been drawn from Peter A. Katzenstein, ed., *The Politics of Industry in West Germany: Toward the Third Republic* (Ithaca, N.Y.: Cornell University Press, 1989).

13. William E. Paterson and Gordon Smith, *The West German Model: Perspectives on a Stable State* (London: Cass, 1981).

14. Ralf Dahrendorf, *Society and Democracy in Germany* (Garden City, N.Y.: Anchor, 1969).

C H A P T E R

17

Political Economy and Development

The Federal Republic of Germany (FRG) has taken a quite distinctive development path that emphasizes cooperative interaction with a dense interest group network of key social and economic actors. Post–World War II Germany has avoided both of the imbalances that plague many other nation-states: in one, powerful private interests (typically the leaders of a sector of the economy) may "capture," or dominate, state policy, which is often said to be an important feature of American politics; in the other, the state dominates or captures private interests, a pattern often described as characteristic of France. As we suggest in this chapter, by its unique forms of organized capitalism, combined with the social market economy, Germany has largely avoided the imbalance of state economic strategies that are subject to unpredictable changes and boom-and-bust cycles. This relative stability has been all the more remarkable given the triple challenges beginning in the 1990s: German unification, European integration, and globalization.

The Postwar Settlement and Beyond

The postwar settlement long seemed for many observers, both German and non-German, to be almost an immutable fact of nature. After emerging from its horrendous history during the first half of the twentieth century, the new FRG produced something quite different: a set of structures and institutions consisting of, first, an organized-capitalist, mixed-economy welfare state with a high degree of labor union involvement

and, second, a stable multiparty democracy. Yet like all other institutional arrangements, those in the FRG were neither immutable nor without tensions. A number of challenges to the postwar settlement arose beginning in the 1970s, at the end of the economic boom years, and have continued through unification and the era of European integration. This chapter characterizes the consolidation and maturing of the postwar settlement and contrasts it with the new political economy from the mid-1980s to the present. The new patterns are not simply a rejection of the old; there are important continuities between the two.

The transcending of the postwar settlement—the emergence of a Third Republic, in Peter Katzenstein's formulation—took place during this transitional period in the 1980s. In this process, the political economy of the Federal Republic emerged from a period of economic uncertainty—what some called Eurosclerosis[1]—to achieve its position as the leading nation in the process of European integration and accomplish its unification with the former German Democratic Republic (GDR). This Third Republic was again led by the Christian Democrats, this time in the person of Chancellor Helmut Kohl, who was consistently underestimated by his critics. It was the Kohl center-right coalition of the Christian Democratic Union (CDU) and the Christian Social Union (CSU) with the Free Democratic Party (FDP) that enthusiastically embraced the concept of the single European market and pragmatically moved to consolidate the former GDR into the Federal Republic. The opposition (the

Social Democratic Party, SPD; the Greens; and the former Communist Party of Democratic Socialism, PDS, in the five eastern states) was much slower to embrace either of these two momentous developments, to their political detriment.

The following example provides concrete evidence of a challenge to labor market policy, an area that had directly benefited from one of the long-standing institutional relationships of the postwar settlement. It also suggests that the institutional capacity to address such problems, although sharply challenged, has not fundamentally eroded.

The thirteen-year SPD-FDP center-left coalition government (1969–1982) led by Chancellors Willy Brandt and Helmut Schmidt collapsed largely because of a dispute over economic policy. The SPD's left-wing rank and file (but not Chancellor Schmidt) wanted increased stimulation of the economy, and the more moderate FDP did not. The FDP changed its coalition partnership and turned to the Christian Democrats. The new CDU/CSU-FDP coalition government, led by the new chancellor, Helmut Kohl, took office in October 1982 and faced the immediate problem of increased unemployment, owing largely to the residue of the twin oil shocks of the 1970s. One of the new government's immediate tasks was to shoulder the cost of sustaining the long-term unemployed through general welfare funds. However, a more serious structural problem lay beyond the immediate issue of cost: How could the Federal Republic's elaborate vocational education and apprenticeship system absorb all of the new entrants into the labor market? In a country that has prided itself on its skilled workforce, this issue represented a potential problem because it could have undermined one of the strong points of the German economy: the continued supply of skilled workers. This supply of highly skilled—and highly paid—workers has been one of the linchpins of the postwar settlement generally, and the German model specifically.

Despite these threats in the early and mid-1980s, the unemployment compensation system and the vocational education and apprenticeship system both weathered this period during the first years of the Kohl government. In a concentrated effort, the national and state (*Länder*) governments, employer associations, trade unions, and works councils, using a variety of formal and informal institutional mechanisms, found ways to reinvigorate one of the core foundations of the Federal Republic's labor market. They did so by a series of regionally specific industrial policies, targeted to such industrial needs as automobiles and machine tools in the Stuttgart area, industrial electronics in Munich, and the declining steel industry in the Ruhr Valley. They used such existing institutions as codetermination (*Mitbestimmung*), the works councils (*Betriebsräte*) present in almost all German firms, and the country's elaborate vocational education system, in which 40 percent of all Germans between fourteen and twenty-one attend vocational school. This system allows employers, unions, and governments to participate in shaping the curriculum to the needs of particular regions. Although some regions lagged, principally northern German regions such as the heavy-industry Ruhr Valley and the shipbuilding cities of Bremen and Bremerhaven, other regions prospered. Among the more successful regions was the southwestern state of Baden-Württemberg, where firms such as Daimler-Benz and Bosch have their headquarters outside the region's largest city, Stuttgart. The city of Munich and the *Land* of Bavaria (where the giant electronics firm Siemens is located) also prospered during the latter part of the 1980s to the mid-1990s.

The FRG has relied heavily on its skilled blue-collar workers throughout the postwar period. There has been much less erosion of this segment of the working class because of its importance in the flexible-system production processes of such industries as machine tools, automobiles, chemicals, and industrial electronics. Sometimes called "flex-spec," it relies on the continually reskilled manufacturing workforce and is greatly aided by such democratic corporatist institutions as the works councils. Although there has been some evidence of partial skilled worker erosion in weaker industries such as steel and shipbuilding, where there have been major job losses, blue-collar working-class decomposition has been far less pronounced than in either Britain or the United States.

Because of this reliance on high-skill and high-wage manufacturing, the FRG has seen only a small growth of service sector jobs. Unlike the United States, where a large proportion of the new jobs since the 1980s have been created in the service sector, Germany has resisted this option, largely owing to the belief that low wages would result. Some individuals on the right wing of the FDP in the mid-1980s at first argued that the country should emulate the United States by creating new jobs in services. The SPD and the trade unions countered with the assertion that most service sector jobs in the United States were low-paying jobs at fast-food restaurants with few benefits. They argued that the strains placed on society by this plan for employment growth, in the form of insufficient economic demand (owing to low wages) and increased social spending (owing to lack of fringe benefits), would represent a net loss for German society. The plan for high-productivity, high-wage unionized employment had sustained the economy for many years, and most labor market actors preferred to retain their dependence on that policy path. The U.S. "solution," they believed, was the wrong choice. From the mid-1980s until the first years of unification, German industry had not listened to the siren song of service sector jobs over manufacturing ones and had slowly reduced unemployment by relying on a traditional postwar pattern: manufacturing jobs in export-earning sectors helping to fuel economic growth and prosperity.[2] An additional institutional factor that prevented the erosion of the working class was the residual strength of organized labor.[3] (The role of unions is treated explicitly in subsequent chapters.) Their purposeful response to the economic downturn of the late 1970s and early 1980s pre-

vented the erosion of union strength that took place in other industrialized countries. For example, under the SPD-led governments, the unions were able to secure strong footholds in the political economy, which protected them during the more disadvantageous 1980s and 1990s. In 1976, under the SPD-FDP coalition government, the original codetermination law of 1952 was expanded to stop just short of the virtual full-parity codetermination that coal and steel workers had enjoyed since 1951.

The strains on the social market economy began in the early 1990s, after a false boom immediately after unification, which was fueled by a currency exchange that gave eastern Germans instant hard currency to spend. These policies exacerbated the huge costs of unification for rebuilding the eastern German infrastructure and finally seemed to transcend the postwar settlement as it pressed on the upper limits of Germany's capacity to pay for these costs. Larger budget cuts than ever previously proposed in the FRG became imperative by the early 1990s. The completion of the European Union's (EU) single market, supposedly the grand culmination of a post–cold war spirit of German and European unity, proved more difficult to realize than its planners first thought. The immediate impact in the early 1990s seemed only likely to strengthen the trends toward decentralization and deregulation already under way in Western Europe. Expanding markets is easier than building stable and durable political institutions, as the rapid expansion of the EU to twenty-five countries in 2004 has demonstrated.

More significant for the German regime, the market-based EU expansion threatened to disturb the organized capitalism of Germany's small and large businesses. Organized capitalism in Germany consists of an intricate, mutually reinforcing pattern of government and business self-regulation. Clearly, an Anglo-American push for deregulation would undermine these patterns because it relies more on fast-moving transactions, not the carefully constructed long-standing institutions characteristic of the German model. Plus, the rapid deregulation in European finance threatened Germany's distinctive finance-manufacturing links, which depend on long-term relationships between the two parties, not the short-term "deals" that quickly became fashionable in Europe. Thus, the trend toward Europeanization—in a way that challenged Germany's preeminent position—seemed to be incompatible with the highly consensus-oriented and coordinated nature of Germany's adjustment patterns.

In addition, tensions persist between former East and West Germans. The GDR economy was considered strong by Communist standards. It provided jobs for virtually all people, but many of these were not sustainable when Communist countries like the GDR collapsed. Industry in the GDR, as in most of the other former Communist countries, was inefficient by Western standards, and most firms were not able to survive the transition to the West German capitalist system. Among the most serious problems were bloated employment rolls and a tendency to churn out large quantities of shoddy goods that people refused to buy. Consequently, many East Germans lost their jobs. For the first few years after unification, they were generously supported by West German subsidies, but the recovery in the five new *Länder* lagged much more than the Kohl government originally thought it would. Easterners resented the slow pace of change and the high unemployment, and West Germans were bitter about losing jobs to easterners and paying increased taxes for unemployment benefits to eastern Germans as well as the cleanup of the ecological and infrastructural disaster inherited from the former East German regime.

On balance, the long years of the postwar settlement proved far more durable in Germany than in any of the other countries covered in this book. But the triple pressures embodied by German unification, European integration, and globalization that perplex Chancellor Schröder so greatly, combined with two new challenges to the political economy of the FRG in the twenty-first century in the form of the information economy and Germany's high tax status, will be explored in the remainder of this chapter.

State and Economy

Other country studies in this book make a sharp distinction between economic management and the welfare state. We do not do so with respect to Germany for a very good reason. The relationship between economic management and the provision of public goods (i.e., welfare) is interpenetrated among private, public, and what Peter Katzenstein calls "para-public" institutions.[4] In other words, it is not easy to demarcate these two policy areas in Germany as it is elsewhere.

The key general concept in understanding the FRG's political economy is that the relationship between state and market is neither free market nor state dominant. Rather, the state sets clear general ground rules, which the private sector acknowledges, but then allows market forces to work relatively unimpeded within the general framework of government supervision. Since the time of the first postwar chancellor, Christian Democrat Konrad Adenauer, the Germans have referred to the relationship between state and market as the *social market economy*. Basically, the concept refers to a system of capitalism in which fundamental social benefits are essential—not antagonistic—to the workings of the market. Among the social components of the German economy are generously provided healthcare, workers' rights, public transportation, and support for the arts, among many others. In some respects, these benefits are similar to those provided by the Japanese and French states. However, the provision of some public benefits by means of organized private interests—the quasi-public sickness funds that provide for health insurance, for example—makes the German social market economy a blend of public and private action to support and implement public policies.

Unlike Britain and the United States, Germany did not have the option of the kind of trial-

and-error capitalism that characterized much of the early nineteenth century. By the time it unified in 1871, Germany was forced to compete with a number of countries that had already developed industrialized capitalist economies. German business and political elites realized that a gradual, small-firm-oriented industrialization process would face ruinous competition from Britain, France, and the United States. Thus, the German state in the late nineteenth century became a significant and powerful—if antidemocratic—force in the German economy. It did so by building on the foundations established by the formerly independent states—Prussia, Bavaria, and the others—that became part of a united Germany in 1871.

Regional governments developed their autonomy before unification, resulting in a tradition of strong public sector involvement in economic growth and development. In the fragmented Germany of the late eighteenth and early nineteenth centuries, states had to develop governmental systems to provide for the material and social needs of their populations, and they had to do so without being able to rely on a centralized national state. These regional governmental actors worked both directly and indirectly with private economic interests, blurring distinctions between state and market.

The economic powers possessed by the modern states of the post–World War II Federal Republic are not products merely of the decentralized federalism that has characterized the political institutions of Germany. Rather, the *Land* governments have also built on a century-long pattern of regional government involvement in both economic growth and industrial adaptation. The most common metaphor for analyzing industrial growth in Germany during the nineteenth century has been that of Alexander Gerschenkron's late-industrialization thesis.[5] This argument maintains that Germany's transformation from a quasi-feudal society to a highly industrialized one during the latter two-thirds of the nineteenth century was characterized by a process of explicit coordination among govern-

ment, big business, and a powerful universal banking system. German banks are universal because, then and now, they are capable of handling all financial transactions and are not segmented into savings and commercial branches, for example. This nineteenth-century pattern has often been called rapid German industrialization, although a more accurate account would call it rapid Prussian industrialization, since it was Bismarck's vision and mobilization of Prussian interest groups that proved the dominant force.

Although Germany was not unified as a nation-state until 1871, the foundations for economic growth and the most spectacular early leaps of industrial modernization took place before 1871. The creation in 1834 of the customs union (*Zollverein*) that removed tariffs among eighteen independent states with a population of 23 million people was a crucial spur to industrial modernization as it greatly increased trade. This process was led by Prussia, and the dominant symbol for Prussia's hegemonic position was Bismarck's role in brokering the interests of grain-growing *Junkers* in the east with those of the coal and steel barons in the Ruhr. Bismarck used the development of the railroads as a catalyst for this marriage of iron and rye. He astutely realized that railroads were a primary consumer of coal and steel, yet they also provided an effective means of transportation to market for the *Junkers'* grain from the relatively isolated eastern part of Germany.[6] Although the Prussian-led image of rapid, state-enhanced industrial growth is important, the opening of trade among these independent principalities did not dislodge the distinct patterns of modernization that the less powerful states had developed on their own. Small-scale agricultural production remained in many parts of the southern states, particularly in Bavaria, and small-scale craft production continued in Württemberg, as well as in many other regions where feudal craft skills were adapted to the patterns of industrial modernization.

And because each of the states had different material needs and social circumstances, these regional governments perhaps did a more effective job of fulfilling needs than would a central state. Certainly Bismarck's welfare state measures brought economies of scale to those programs that needed to be implemented on a national basis. However, the strong role of the regional governments in the provision of certain specific needs continued, especially during the Second Reich of 1871–1918. Even as the Third Reich was overtaking the Weimar regime, the regional governments tried unsuccessfully to resist the Nazi state's goal of a massive centralization of policy.

Fundamental change was needed following the horrors of the Third Reich between 1933 and 1945, when the state worked hand in glove with German industry to suppress workers, employ slave labor, and produce military armaments. These events caused postwar policymakers to avoid such a strong state role in economic life under the Federal Republic. Unlike the French and Japanese states, which have been much more economically interventionist, the German state has evolved a rather unique relationship between the public and private sectors. Rather than seeing a relationship of state versus market, the German public and private sectors have evolved a densely interpenetrated association that avoids the kind of state planning characteristic of postwar Japan or France. It also has avoided the opposite pattern: the antigovernment free-market policies of Britain and the United States in the 1980s. Of course, the five *Länder* of the former GDR evolved no such balanced ground between state and market, as they were governed by a Communist regime in which the state ruled and markets did not. This past contributes to eastern Germany's continuing delayed integration into the economic and institutional fabric of the unified FRG.

The major principle behind the social market economy is that of a market system embedded within a comprehensive framework that encourages the interpenetration of private and public institutions. State policy is a conscious choice to provide a general regulatory boundary, without

involving itself in the minute details of policy implementation. The implementation of these framing policies produces a stable set of outcomes. It is organized and implemented by coordination among public and private sector actors that improves—rather than impedes—economic competitiveness. The politically independent Bundesbank (central bank) was just such an important actor until the introduction of the euro (further addressed in Chapter 18). Thus, the social market economy does not lie halfway between state and market but represents a qualitatively different approach. For example, German law in a particular area is often more general than specific, because it then expects that organized interests (business, labor, or other interest groups and social forces) will meet and negotiate the details within the law's general mandate. Moreover, strong, internally generated pressures from within each of these organized groups encourage their members to stay on-board and not depart from the negotiated collective outcomes. The combination of high wages, high social spending, and the necessity to keep German goods competitive globally for many years provided concrete reasons that such group-oriented outcomes were beneficial for the major social forces in the FRG. Not surprisingly, the five *Länder* of the former GDR fit uneasily into the dominant West German model. Not only are eastern German firms generally less competitive than those in the west, but the network of supporting institutions is either absent or is imposed by *Wessis,* a derogatory term akin to *carpetbagger* that is used to describe western Germans who try to exploit the less well-developed east.

Germany has long been an organized-capitalist country in which two sets of business groups, representing industry generally and employers specifically, are powerful and coordinated.[7] Rather than emphasizing the importance of either individual entrepreneurship and small business or large corporate firms as the defining characteristic of its economy, Germany has relied on an organized network of small and large businesses working together.[8] In addition, the banking system and financial community play a direct role in private investment and until recently have engaged in little of the financial speculation characteristic of Wall Street. Traditionally, they have seen their primary role as providing long-term investments for the health of the internationally competitive manufacturing industries, the foundation of the economy. This model generally holds for the regional and savings banks. However, a bifurcation has developed in the industry as the largest and best known of the German banks (Deutsche, Dresdner, and Commerzbank) have begun to move away from their traditional role and behave like large banks in New York, London, and Tokyo, unfettered by long-term relationships to domestic manufacturing firms.[9]

Government economic policy is indirect and supportive rather than heavy-handed and overly regulatory. It sets broad guidelines but often leaves the implementation of policies to coordinated negotiations among organized interests such as employers, banks, trade unions, and regional governments. This does not mean the government does not become involved in economic policymaking; it just does so more flexibly. The flexibility is produced in two ways. First, the German pattern of regulation addresses the general framework of competitiveness rather than the minute details more commonly addressed in other countries. In many cases, if the framework patterns are effectively drawn, microregulation is much less necessary. Second, among the major European economies such as Britain, France, and Italy, Germany has the smallest share of industry in government hands. This condition is accomplished by a cooperative federalism that delegates to the states the administrative powers of laws and regulations passed at the federal level. Both are integral parts of Germany's social market economy (*Soziale Marktwirtschaft*), discussed more fully later in this chapter.

Such policies are based on the German system of framework regulation and can best be explained in the words of one of the shapers of post–World War II economic policy, economist Wilhelm Röpke:

> [Our program] consists of measures and institutions which impart to competition the framework, rules, and machinery of impartial supervision which a competitive system needs as much as any game or match if it is not to degenerate into a vulgar brawl. A genuine, equitable, and smoothly functioning competitive system can not in fact survive without a judicious moral and legal framework and without regular supervision of the conditions under which competition can take place pursuant to real efficiency principles. This presupposes mature economic discernment on the part of all responsible bodies and individuals and a strong impartial state.[10]

By this method, German economic policy during the post–World War II period has avoided the sharp lurches between laissez-faire-led and state-led economic policy that have characterized Britain.

Germany is a prime case of a high-wage, high-welfare country that, despite slower growth since the turn of the century, has maintained its competitive world position far better than other advanced industrialized states for more than three decades since the oil crisis of 1973. Its success in combining strong competitiveness with high wages and social spending has surpassed even that of Japan. A high-skill emphasis in key export-oriented manufacturing industries has been the specific path that German economic policy has taken to maintain its competitive position. The foundation stones of this system are the elaborate system of vocational education combined with apprenticeship training. It is implemented through the works councils, which are elected by all employees in all German firms with five or more employees. This system of advanced skill training enabled Germany to resist the postindustrial, service sector orientation that countries such as the United States and Britain have tried. Relying extensively on this elaborate apprenticeship training program, Germany has maintained competitive positions in such "old" manufacturing industries as automobiles, chemicals, machine tools, and industrial electronics. The Federal Republic's strategy for international competitiveness was not to develop new high-tech industries, thereby deemphasizing the fulcrum sectors, but to employ high-technology *processes* in these comparatively old-fashioned industries. Economist Michael Piore and political sociologist Charles Sabel have called such process innovation "flexible-system manufacturing" because it emphasized the high skill levels and flexibility of the German workforce, thereby enabling these industries to find crucial niches in world markets.[11] To Americans, Mercedes, Audi, and BMW automobiles have been the most visible examples of the success of this strategy. By stressing the value that its highly skilled workforce adds to raw materials, Germany has defied predictions for more than thirty years that its industrial economy would erode, as have many other formerly manufacturing-oriented developed economies. Despite being poor in natural resources (like most of the rest of Europe), Germany maintains a surplus balance of trade and still has a large working-class population, which historically has *not* favored protectionism. With one in every three jobs devoted to exports (one in two in the sectors of automobiles, chemicals, machine tools, and industrial electronics), protectionism for German unions would be self-defeating. The skills of its workers help German industry overcome the costs of acquiring resources and paying high wages because German industry has emphasized high quality and high productivity as offsetting factors.

Enhancing this set of policies has been Germany's research and development strategy. It preferred not to push for specific new breakthroughs in exotic technologies or for inventing new products that might be years from market. Rather it chose to adapt existing technologies to its traditional, already competitive sectors. This has been the exact opposite of U.S. research and development strategy, for example. During the postwar years, this policy has enabled Germany to maintain a favorable balance of trade and a high degree of competitiveness. But how long will this model continue?

Early in the twenty-first century, however, the German political economy seems less rosy than in previous decades. European integration, German unification, and globalization have forced German industry and policymakers to examine whether this model remains appropriate or needs fundamental reexamination. Depending on others to make core discoveries and then quickly applying the technology to production is a delicate task that requires coordinated policies among all producer groups. Trying to institute the western German policy among former GDR workers who come from a different industrial culture has begun to prove difficult. In fact, the speed with which the information age and the Internet have penetrated into all facets of economic and public life has caught the German model somewhat unprepared. Are Germany's prevailing economic practices and policy styles still relevant for the new information industries, as well as existing industries transformed by the process? Can the vocational and apprenticeship system produce the kind of workers needed in the new century? The answer is uncertain, because despite unemployment at 9 percent in early 2004, German industry had to recruit programmers, web designers, and network specialists from India to meet gaping shortages in these fields in Germany. However, the deregulation of Deutsche Telekom, the formerly state-run telephone service, has begun to spur a belated development in Internet and information infrastructure technology. The question for observers of German political economy is whether the traditional German industrial pattern of integrating and applying innovations first developed elsewhere will apply to the information-age economy as well.

In general, however, Germany still seems well positioned among those developed countries to which the term *postwar settlement* applies in the sense of the embedding of a capitalist economic system within a parliamentary democratic polity. Given Germany's volatile history, these political and institutional arrangements were first imposed by the Allied powers as a way of preventing extreme economic and political outcomes. Once instituted, they were soon adapted and embraced by most of the major West German interest groups and political parties. The German state has played a guiding, though not imposing, role in developing and supporting the postwar settlement. Fearful of the excesses of centralized state control, manifested in extreme form by the Nazis of the Third Reich and the Communists of the GDR, German state policy has preferred to shape and frame outcomes rather than to control them directly. In general, social identities—the guest workers excepted—and political regulation remained relatively consistent from the founding of the Federal Republic until the 1990s. Here too, though, the postunification turmoil has created a much greater strain on the democratic political institutions of the Federal Republic.

Social Policy

With respect to state-society relations, we must stress the social market economy and its related concept of framework regulation, themes that will resonate throughout the three chapters that follow and that are unique contributions to democratic practice in German society. These institutional patterns characterize the relationship between private and public sectors and among major interest groups in German society. Rather than the state-centered polity of France and Japan or the market-centered polity of Britain and the United States, Germany has adopted a fluid, interpenetrated set of policies that govern state and market relationships. Democratic corporatism and the role of interest groups in shaping public policies (and not just through state policies) are two examples. In effect, these processes of "negotiated adjustment" allow the state to delegate certain public functions to private actors in return for these private actors' taking responsibility for implementing public policy.[12] Also, Germany enjoys a kind of overlapping federalism (in the sense of national and regional governments explicitly coordinating policies), which has produced strong institutional continuity. For example, federal law is ac-

tually implemented by regional and local governments, thus avoiding some of the duplication that plagues different levels of government in the United States. This German framework regulation has been maintained for much of the postwar period, though the tensions produced by unification have clearly placed strains on this system.

Such strains are particularly evident in the newer states that composed the former GDR. The complex network of institutions that evolved in western Germany for over forty years had to be created from scratch in the former GDR. Western German policymakers understandably attempted to transplant successful FRG models in a wide range of policy areas. Among these were labor market, educational, welfare, housing, and regulatory institutions, and virtually all of them were less successful in the five new *Länder* than in the other *Länder*. To scholars of institutional analysis, this lack of fit was no surprise. Wade Jacoby has written eloquently about just such "transplantation difficulty."[13] It is very difficult to impose institutional structures from outside. As Jacoby argues, successful adaptation of institutional change must be "pulled in" by indigenous actors in eastern Germany. That takes time. Furthermore, one usually organized segment of German society, business, also suffered from organizational fragmentation. Competitive pressures, principally in the east but also in the west, saw a weakening of the solidarity that had long characterized organized capitalism and began to complicate the usually smooth-running industrial relations system.[14]

Clearly the organized-capitalist model is not an unadulterated success in the minds of all Germans. Both the Greens and the small free-market-oriented sector feel that the organized, and perhaps closed, nature of producer groups privileges those who are inside the loop (such as industry organizations, employer groups, and the banking community) and excludes those outside. Moreover, the Greens are also critical of many business policies that they feel do not sufficiently guard against environmental consequences. The primary critique from the small-business sector is that the organized nature of large-firm dominance is not flexible enough in the creation of new products and industries. However, neither the Greens nor advocates of a more laissez-faire approach to economic policies have dislodged the dominant position of German organized capitalism in the shaping of economic policy. And the apparent limitations of the German model for eastern Germany have been largely responsible for the continued presence of the former Communist Party, renamed the Party of Democratic Socialism (PDS). This party has served as an important tribune for eastern Germans who would like greater resources from the federal government.

Beginning in the early 1990s, a sharp three-pronged challenge began to undermine the idea of a smoothly functioning German economic juggernaut. First, the Kohl government badly misjudged the costs of unification and the institutional resources necessary to integrate the five new *Länder*. By mid-1992, Kohl had finally acknowledged that the successful integration of the eastern economy into the western one would cost much more and take longer than originally predicted. Second, the structural challenges that the German political economy faced in the mid-1990s were far more extensive than any the Federal Republic had experienced since the 1950s. The amount budgeted in the early 1990s for reconstruction in Germany was approximately 20 percent of the entire FRG budget. In addition, funds from private firms and regional governments and other subsidies amounted to another 50 billion deutsche marks. Yet even these huge sums were not enough to make the assimilation process go more smoothly. There remains today a large gap in productivity levels between the two regions. Third, the West German integrated institutions (even when working well) became difficult to transfer as a model to eastern Germany.[15] For example, the Treuhand (the government reconstruction agency) privatized some 7,000 of the total of 11,000 firms that it had taken over in the former GDR as a result of the collapse of the old Communist economy. Some

1.2 million persons were officially unemployed, and another 2 million were enrolled in a government-subsidized short-time program (part-time work with full-time pay) combined with job training. Yet the latter program had its funds cut as part of an austerity budget. In short, the magnitude of the problems in eastern Germany has threatened to overwhelm the FRG's institutional capacity to handle them.

Some pessimistic observers finally began to suggest that these stresses had placed the German political economy in a precarious position by the turn of the century. Germany's economic prowess has resided in certain manufacturing industries whose goods are eminently exportable. But in these industries, many technologies must constantly be upgraded, and the cost of wages continues to rise. Throughout the 1990s and into the new century, the combination of unification, European integration, and the continued high-wage, high-tax, and high-welfare economy, followed by the pressures of the information economy on traditional "bricks-and-mortar" industry, led to the so-called *Wirtschaftsstandort* (literally, location for economic growth) debate. The essence of this turn-of-the-century criticism of the German economy was that the combination of domestic and international factors had made Germany a much less attractive place for investment by either international or German capital. In direct response to this challenge, the Schröder government passed a tax reform package in July 2000, followed by Schröder's Agenda 2010—a reform package that challenged many traditional labor market institutions to become more "flexible" along Anglo-American lines—which seemed to address directly the major criticism of the *Wirtschaftsstandort* by offering both personal and corporate tax cuts. These contentious issues were significant turning points for German social democracy and the social market economy. Although the reforms seemed to mollify the equities markets, they were not viewed with enthusiasm from the left-leaning rank and file of his Red-Green coalition (*red* is a colloquial term for all parties of the left, such as the SPD). For some of the rank and file within the coalition, Schröder's programs represented an abandonment of fundamental principles.

Thus, although the German model of economic growth has proved remarkably durable through almost all of the postwar period, the specific and demanding requirements of unification, European integration, and globalization have confronted this model with new pressures. The huge demands of unification are daunting enough. Complicating them is the need to align Germany's economic policies with those of its European neighbors and to respond to a competitive global economy.

Society and Economy

The social component of the social market economy also differs from those of other countries. Although the Federal Republic has always been generous with the provision of welfare benefits, they serve more than just distributive income-transfer purposes. For example, two of the most important provisions, government savings subsidies to individuals and a comprehensive vocational education system, have direct and positive benefits for the competitiveness of the German economy. They create both a stable pool of investment capital and a deep pool of human capital that enables Germany to produce high-quality goods.

During the boom years of the mid-twentieth century, German economic growth provided a sound foundation for social development. The social market economy of the Christian Democrats was augmented by the SPD-led governments from 1969 to 1982, under which the supportive social programs of the 1950s and 1960s were extended and elaborated. Such growth and corresponding social policies helped avoid the occupational and regional conflict common to many other countries. To be sure, there were—and are—divisions in Germany's society and economy. However, the strong role

of trade unions and the unwillingness of employers to attack their workers on wage and workplace issues (perhaps owing to trade union strength) minimized stratification of society and the workplace until the 1990s. Nevertheless, German unification, European integration, and new global competitive pressures on the German economy placed increasing strains on the social market economy by slightly increasing inequalities compared with the long preunification period of postwar prosperity. Such change increased German *Angst* about whether their social state could support citizens at levels they had come to expect.

Inequality and Ethnic Minorities

One indelible image of Germany in the postunification years is that of neo-Nazi skinheads setting fire to a hostel containing newly arrived immigrants in the early 1990s while chanting *"Ausländer raus"* (foreigners out) as local German residents look on without intervening. Although such heinous acts have been relatively rare in Germany—and have also occurred in other European countries—Germany's history during the Third Reich causes alarm bells to ring at the slightest hint of racial intolerance. Thus, among the concerns that affected the economy and society beginning in the 1980s was the role of ethnic minorities in Germany. The issue grew in prominence throughout the 1990s and has continued into the new century as unification and European integration intensify and immigration to Germany continues. The most contentious concepts are those of nationalism and ethnicity. Exacerbating the problem is the fact that the inhabitants of the former GDR were raised in a society that did not value toleration or dissent. Eastern Germans were also part of a society in which official unemployment did not exist. And the average GDR citizen rarely encountered, not to mention worked with, foreign nationals. West Germany, in contrast, has encouraged the migration of millions of guest workers from throughout southern Europe since the 1960s. At the same time, the FRG has provided generous provisions for those seeking political asylum, in large part to try to overcome the legacy of Nazi persecution of non-Germans from 1933 to 1945. East Germany, on the other hand, was a much more closed society, as were most other Communist regimes. Thus, when unification arrived—and was overlaid on the migration of different ethnic minorities into both the east and west—few former GDR citizens responded positively to the contact with foreign nationals.

Former GDR citizens were expected, first, to adopt completely Western democratic habits of debate and toleration of diversity without missing a beat. Second, they were expected to deal with a labor *market*, which sometimes did not supply an adequate number of jobs. In other words, gone was a world of lifetime employment, and in its place was one where structural unemployment claimed as much as 25 percent of the workforce in the five new *Länder*. Third, they were faced with a much more open and ethnically diverse society than they had ever known, and they often blamed the lack of employment on immigrants and asylum seekers. Consequently, many of those German citizens who were beginning to fall through the cracks of the German welfare state were also susceptible to racist pronouncements from demagogues who wished to blame ethnic minorities for all the major changes that had taken place in such a short time. The immigration of computer professionals from India in 2000 only added to the tensions.

Ethnic minorities—even long-term legal residents and new citizens of Germany—often face on-the-job discrimination, particularly in occupations unprotected by a trade union or a works council. Not surprisingly, ethnic minorities—in Germany as in most other developed countries—have found themselves often employed in workplaces where they are required to perform menial and often thankless work.

Inequality and Women

Women's role in the German workplace is a growing issue. First, the increase in female participation in the labor force (see Table 17.1) has created a departure from traditional German experience. Although still at lower rates than in the United States, the participation of increasing numbers of female employees has created new tensions in an area where men had dominated virtually all positions of authority in both management and unions. The unions have made far greater strides than has management in providing women with expanded opportunities with responsibility and authority.

Perhaps the most significant obstacle that German women have to overcome is not so much the substance of the benefits that they receive but the premise on which women's role in German society is defined.[16] By any measure, Germany's universal welfare state benefits are generous to all citizens, including women, but it is helpful to understand the context within which rights are granted. Benefits are generally cash based rather than service based (e.g., public day care), which means they are less women-friendly and do not encourage women to enter the paid labor force. This is in sharp contrast to a country like Sweden, which has publicly provided day care and a larger number of women in the workforce.

German welfare is a creation of conservatives and Christian Democrats and not that of the left. It was Bismarck who created the first modern welfare state in the late nineteenth century—not out of the goodness of his heart but to stave

Table 17.1 Labor Force Participation Rates, Ages Fifteen to Sixty-Five, 1993–2003 (in percentages)

	1993	1995	1997	1999	2001	2003
Male	81.3	81.0	80.3	80.2	80.1	80.3
Female	62.3	62.6	62.8	63.5	64.9	66.1

Source: Federal Statistical Office, Germany, 2004.

off Socialist revolution and preserve traditional German cultural values. Similarly, the postwar Christian Democratic creation of the social part of the social market economy was based on Christian values and envisioned a world of male breadwinners and women at home caring for—and having more—children. To be sure, the years of Social Democratic governance (1969–1982 and since 1998) have expanded benefits for women, but at its foundation women's benefits in German society have been tied more to their roles within the family than as individuals. This means that within the context of the labor market, individual German women face discriminatory aspects and assumptions about their career patterns that some American women have overcome. As increasing numbers of women enter the German workforce, it is harder for them to achieve positions of power and responsibility as individuals than it is for some of their American counterparts. Perhaps this is owing to the difference between a welfare state with paternalistic origins and a society that allows some women to achieve positions of authority. Of course, Sweden suggests that there can be a third option that provides positive, collective women-friendly measures.[17]

The Generation Gap

Modern generational issues first achieved political significance in the FRG with the emergence of the new social movements in the late 1960s. Several issues drove these movements, culminating in a wave of protests throughout West Germany in 1968, but here we concentrate on those that have affected the economy.

These social movements grew increasingly influential in the early 1980s. Elements of the citizen action groups became core supporters of the Green Party, formed in the late 1970s. In 1982, the presence of these groups—both the Greens and the young social movements outside the SPD—contributed to the final exhaustion of the SPD as a party of government. Willy Brandt, the first SPD chancellor, reflecting during the early 1980s

on these developments, termed these movements "the SPD's lost children," meaning, in retrospect, that the SPD ought to have listened to and incorporated their concerns into party policy.

Although increasingly important in the Federal Republic, these youth-led social movements were not usually associated with what French sociologist Serge Mallet has called the "new working-class" phenomenon (i.e., a change in the composition of the working class from older, male, blue-collar workers to a more diverse mix, including younger, female, and service sector workers) that had been identified in other countries. Political scientist Ronald Inglehart has named these social movements "postmaterialist," in the sense that their concerns were not those of traditional Marxist materialism.[18] In fact, in Germany they have not relied on class as a primary category to define themselves, as many tend to be university-educated children of the middle class. They have thus not been able to create an identity strong enough to challenge the highly skilled working class's dominance in the structure of the Federal Republic. If there is a new working class, it has arisen within the trade unions as members have increased their skills to engage in the flexible system of manufacturing. The still-dominant working-class culture of the Federal Republic has acted as a barrier to the postmaterialist social movement's attaining further influence. However, the movement has attained an important vehicle for systematic political representation in the Green Party.

The next aspect of the generation gap comes at the other end of the demographic scale: pensioners and older workers. The German birthrate fell markedly in the last decade of the twentieth century, particularly in the former GDR. Demographically this has placed great pressure on the German welfare state because the combination of the low birthrate and the increasing age of the baby boom generation means that fewer younger workers will be contributing to the welfare and retirement benefits of an increasing elderly population. This time bomb has not yet fully hit German politics, largely because the

Kohl government during the 1980s and 1990s essentially ignored it. In 2000, the Schröder government only began to address it in the context of the tax reform package. The Red-Green government has proposed augmenting the beleaguered public pension system with additional tax funds that will help Germans diversify their retirement options by developing tax-supported private pensions to accompany the public ones.

The Dilemmas of European Integration

The EU was embraced by most Germans and by the political and industrial establishment, especially in the first few years after unification. As Europe's leading power, Germany stands to benefit greatly from successful European integration, since its position of strength will likely be enhanced by wider market opportunities. Germany realizes that actions taken as a member of a twenty-five-nation European Union will be much more palatable to its neighbors than if Germany were using its size and economic power to dominate Europe.

From its international position in the early twenty-first century, Germany has confronted a number of difficult issues. One open question regarding the EU for Germany has been whether successful German-specific institutional arrangements—such as its institutionalized system of worker (and union) participation in management, its tightly organized capitalism, and its elaborate apprenticeship training—will prove adaptable or durable in a wider European context. What may work well inside Germany may be dependent on German-specific institutional, political, or cultural patterns that will not travel well outside the Federal Republic.

The challenge for Germany in the EU is a difficult one. Germany's particular form of organized capitalism during the postwar period clearly made its economy more successful than that of any other European country. One might then think that in looking for a European-wide model on which to base EU economic policy, Germany might serve as an attractive template. This has not

been the case, as EU economic policy seems modeled more on the British free-market policies reminiscent of Conservative 1980s prime minister Margaret Thatcher. What explains this anomaly? The short answer is that institutions take longer to build and establish than do laissez-faire markets. Moreover, German-style organized capitalism developed in a context specific to Germany and has been reinforced by thousands of overlapping and mutually reinforcing relationships built since the end of World War II. In short, German institutional practice is unlikely to extend beyond the borders of the FRG. The dilemma for the Germans is that to succeed in the EU economy will mean adopting the more free-market practices of the Anglo-U.S. model. The question for Germany is whether it will continue to flourish in Europe using the "German model," which is being pressed by more deregulatory patterns.

As for the question of the speed of European integration, countries that might see the value of emulating German institutions require not just strategies but also the means of implementing them. The lack of a cohesive European-wide institutional framework would severely hinder efforts to develop strategies appropriate to meeting the domestic and international challenges of European unification. Most other European nations know the goals to which they must aspire: a highly skilled workforce able to compete in international markets on some basis other than a combination of low labor costs and high-tech production strategies. But whether they can or want to emulate Germany's example remains to be seen, especially in the face of recent German economic difficulty. The preoccupation of Germans with their immediate domestic issues, plus the German-specific nature of the institutions of their political economy, has partially diminished the luster of German-style policies for the new Europe.

Germany in the Era of Globalization

The postunification years have altered Germany's political role on the world stage. As a mature democracy and the leading European power, more is now expected from it. Germany's economic and political power continued through the postwar period and saw its high point during the years between 1960 and 1990. Yet after the momentous events of German unification and European integration, many observers in Europe, Japan, and North America assumed that Germany would take on greater political responsibility based on its position of economic strength and newfound political unity. However, the international indecision and inaction of the Kohl government in the 1990s suggested that Germany was not yet willing or able to do so. Examples of this inaction can be seen in Germany's failure of leadership in such areas as the 1991 Gulf War, Somalia, and Bosnia, and—in the eyes of the G. W. Bush administration—its failure to support the 2003 Iraq war. Thus, some still believed that Germany would remain a "political dwarf," at least in a geopolitical sense.

Clearly Germany is being pressed to take greater political responsibility, both within the EU and as a sovereign nation-state, based on its economic resources and its political power as the leading European nation. Yet its first steps in the post–cold war arena of Eastern Europe when the former Yugoslavia came apart in waves of ethnic tension demonstrated its lack of diplomatic skill. Germany's initial inaction regarding Bosnia and how to support terrorized ethnic minorities from Serbian aggression paralyzed German (and European) foreign policy. Making a purposeful European response still more difficult was the Kohl government's impulsive recognition of the new states of Slovenia and Croatia rather than using more careful diplomatic negotiations. Germany's position was opposed by other Western powers, and it partially precipitated much of the violence when the former Yugoslavia came apart.

Europe as a united entity might find developing a regionwide geopolitical policy easier to accomplish if more skillful leadership came from Germany. But leadership requires working with one's allies and not simply taking an independent position diametrically opposed to one's allies' interests. Obviously future military issues are very much bound up with this question of leadership in the EU. Whether the United Nations, the North Atlantic Treaty Organization (NATO), or the EU itself are to take military responsibility for Europe remains uncertain, even more so in the wake of Iraq and the fissures it produced between the United States and the United Kingdom on the one hand and France and Germany on the other. This uncertainty has been prolonged by Germany's own ambivalence about its international political role. In their defense, the Germans have stressed the strains and huge costs of unification, as well as the difficulty of dealing with the political asylum issue. But Germany is experiencing nothing more than the obligations of political responsibility. Great nations have to find a way to do extremely difficult things at times when it is not convenient, but Germany is only beginning to develop these kinds of skills.

However, the arrival of Gerhard Schröder as chancellor seems to have moved Germany's foreign policy in a more decisive direction, much to the chagrin of the Bush administration. As the first chancellor with no direct memory of World War II (he was born in 1944), Schröder is less willing to defer to the United States and NATO on all international issues. In fact, the combination of moving the capital in the late 1990s from the sleepy Rhineland city of Bonn to Berlin—the seat of the capital from 1871 until the end of World War II—and Schröder's more independent foreign policy have already shown an increase in Germany's international political role. German participation in the United Nations peacekeeping mission in Bosnia is one example of this increased engagement, its agreeing to participate in opposition to Serbian aggression in Kosovo in 1998 another, and its sending forces to Afghanistan to attack Al Qaeda sites after the 9/11 attacks against the United States a third. In opposition, the SPD and Greens argue that because of the Third Reich's aggressive military expeditions to the east in World War II, it is impossible for the German military, under either UN or NATO auspices, to play a constructive role in Eastern Europe. Yet now in government, the SPD and Greens face increased international pressure for Germany to play a leading role in European foreign policy and not shirk the responsibility. While some European neighbors might express anxiety about increased German political power in Europe, the alternative is a political vacuum caused by an indecisive EU, hardly a stronger option. All of these involvements in Eastern and Central Europe are part of a larger vision of Germany and the EU expanding their eastward economic ties.

Other issues, such as trade, economic competition with Japan, the type of monetary policy to be favored by the EU, and the general pace of economic integration, remain areas of major concern. Although the passage of the General Agreement on Tariffs and Trade (GATT) in Uruguay in December 1993 promised smoother economic relations, events such as the contentious World Trade Organization conference in Seattle in 1999, as well as a more recent WTO meeting in Cancún, Mexico, suggest that these issues remain conflict laden. Serious U.S.-EU trade differences exist in such areas as genetically modified organisms (GMOs), agricultural subsidies, and steel tariffs, among many others. To its benefit, Germany, as a goods-exporting nation, has always favored an open trading system and has retained its role as the world's leading exporter in 2004. Both its management and its unions have realized that exports represent both profits and jobs, and that to seek refuge in protectionism would be self-defeating. The threat from Japan seemed to recede somewhat in the late 1990s as the Japanese experienced the recession that had earlier beset both Europe and North America. Germany had developed a different strategy to deal with the Japanese economic challenge than had other Western nations. Instead of believing, as Britain and the United States did, that older manufacturing industries should be given up in the face of the Japanese competitive onslaught, the Germans felt that these industries could remain competitive with a high-skill, high-value-added approach. In large measure, this approach has generally succeeded, but slow growth

and lingering stagnation in some regions and industries may question how quickly the German economy can bounce back. Simply showing stronger growth than Japan—with its decade-long recession—may not be such a great accomplishment after all.

Germany has enjoyed a greater degree of economic performance and institutional political stability since World War II than at any other time in its history, despite the large dose of *Angst* noted at the beginning of Chapter 16. Even the momentous European and German changes beginning in the late 1980s and continuing to the present do not seem to have fundamentally undermined the political structure. Part of the reason for this stability has been the ability of dominant economic and political leaders to retain a balance between the private and public sectors. Nineteenth-century history showed Germans the important role that the state played in the unification of the country and the development of an industrial economy. Yet twentieth-century German history—both the Nazi years and the GDR experience—showed Germans the dangers in placing too heavy a reliance on centralized state authority. Even the left has now realized that it must maintain a strong presence in both public and private sectors. The social welfare measures are important for their constituents, but so too are the institutions that workers have obtained within the workplace, and these institutions will be strongly tested as the five former GDR *Länder* struggle to attain the material benefits of the rest of Germany. Ultimately the lesson that the major actors in the Federal Republic's political economy seem to have learned from the confluence of Germany's pre–World War II undemocratic legacy, the GDR experience, and the FRG's post–World War II parliamentary practices is that a balance must be struck between the public and private sectors if the country is to be able to deal with the challenges of globalization. As this chapter suggests, Germany's response to economic challenges takes place by the public and private sectors working together. It is not likely that this pattern will substantially change.

Notes

1. Mancur Olson, *The Rise and Decline of Nations: Economic Growth, Stagflation, and Social Rigidities* (New Haven, Conn.: Yale University Press, 1982).

2. Steven Cohen and John Zysman, *Manufacturing Matters* (New York: Basic Books, 1987).

3. Andrei S. Markovits, *The Politics of the West German Trade Unions* (Cambridge: Cambridge University Press, 1986).

4. Peter J. Katzenstein, ed., *The Politics of Industry in West Germany: Toward the Third Republic* (Ithaca, N.Y.: Cornell University Press, 1989).

5. Alexander Gerschenkron, *Bread and Democracy in Germany*, 2nd ed. (Ithaca, N.Y.: Cornell University Press, 1989).

6. Colleen A. Dunlavy, "Political Structure, State Policy and Industrial Change: Early Railroad Policy in the United States and Prussia," in Sten Steinmo, Kathleen Thelen, and Frank Longstreth, eds., *Structuring Politics: Historical Institutionalism in Historical Perspective* (Cambridge: Cambridge University Press, 1992), pp. 114–154.

7. Rudolf Hilferding, *Finance Capital: A Study of the Latest Phase of Capitalist Development* (London: Routledge and Kegan Paul, 1981).

8. Gary Herrigel, *Industrial Constructions* (Cambridge: Cambridge University Press, 2000).

9. Richard Deeg, *Finance Capitalism Unveiled* (Ann Arbor: University of Michigan Press, 1999).

10. Wilhelm Röpke, "The Guiding Principles of the Liberal Programme," in Horst Friedrich Wünche, ed., *Standard Texts on the Social Market Economy* (Stuttgart: Gustav Fischer Verlag, 1982), p. 188.

11. Michael Piore and Charles Sabel, *The Second Industrial Divide* (New York: Basic Books, 1984).

12. Kathleen Thelen, *A Union of Parts* (Ithaca, N.Y.: Cornell University Press, 1992).

13. Wade Jacoby, *Imitation and Politics: Redesigning Germany* (Ithaca, N.Y.: Cornell University Press, 2000).

14. Steven J. Silvia, "German Unification and Emerging Divisions Within German Employers' Associations," *Comparative Politics* 29, no. 2 (January 1997): 194–199.

15. Jacoby, *Imitation and Politics*.

16. Joyce Mushaben, "Challenging the Maternalist Presumption: Gender and Welfare Reform in Germany and the United States," in Ulrike Liebert and Nancy Hirschman, eds., *Women and Welfare: Theory and Practice in the U.S. and Europe* (Rutgers, N.J.: Rutgers University Press, 2001).

17. Rianne Mahon, "Swedish Social Democracy: Death of a Model?" *Studies in Political Economy* 63 (Fall 2000): 27–60.

18. See Ronald Inglehart, *The Silent Revolution: Changing Values and Political Styles Among Western Publics* (Princeton, N.J.: Princeton University Press, 1977); Serge Mallet, *The New Working Class* (New York: Monthly Review Press, 1968).

CHAPTER

18

Governance and Policymaking

Political scientist Ralf Dahrendorf once stated that until the arrival of the Federal Republic, Germany had been a premodern country, having never developed a liberal democracy.[1] Between 1949 and unification in 1990, Germany had become much more like other Western industrialized countries, developing a stable parliamentary democracy. With the difficulty in integrating the two regimes after unification in 1990 and with the increasing uncertainty regarding the pace and scope of European integration, some of the more optimistic assumptions that Germany had purged its politics of antidemocratic elements came under greater scrutiny.

The governing principles of the Federal Republic of Germany (FRG) are a clear reaction to the catastrophic experiences that beset previous regimes in Germany. When the Federal Republic was established in 1949, the primary goals of the founders were to work toward eventual unification of the two Germanys and, more important, to avoid repeating the failure of Germany's only other experiment with democracy, the Weimar Republic.[2] Unable to accomplish immediate unification, the founders formulated the *Grundgesetz* (Basic Law) as their compromise. It symbolized the temporary nature of disunited Germany, since the founders preferred to wait until Germany could be reunited before using the term *constitution* (*Verfassung*).* However, their goal of ensuring a lasting democratic order

was a more complicated problem. Two fundamental institutional weaknesses had undermined the Weimar government.

One principal weakness was that provisions for emergency powers enabled leaders to centralize authority and to arbitrarily suspend democratic rights. The founders of the postwar system, heavily influenced by the Allied occupation authorities, sought to remedy the abuse of centralized power by establishing a federal system in which the states (*Länder*) were given considerable powers, particularly administrative powers. It is paradoxical that a constitution owing so much to the influence of foreign powers has proved so durable. Under the Basic Law of the Federal Republic, many functions that had formerly been centralized during the imperial, Weimar, and Nazi periods—the educational system, the police, and the radio and television networks—now became the responsibility of the states. Although the federal Bundestag (the lower house) became the chief lawmaking body, the implementation of many of these laws fell to the *Länder* governments. Moreover, the *Länder* governments sent representatives to the Bundesrat (the upper house), which was required to approve bills passed in the Bundestag.

There was little opposition from major actors within the Federal Republic to this shift from a centralized to a federal system. The Third Reich's catastrophic abuse of power with respect to Jews, political parties, trade unions, and human rights in general had created strong sentiment for curbing the state's repressive capacities. In addition, political leaders, influenced by the

*Since unification in 1990, the term *Basic Law* has been retained because most Germans rightly associate the "temporary" term with the country's longest and most successful experience of democracy.

presence in the Federal Republic of U.S. advisers, were inclined to support a federal system. Furthermore, the development of a federal system was not a departure but a return to form. Prior to the unification of Germany in 1871, the various regions of Germany had formed a decentralized political system. The regional states had developed such autonomous institutions as banks, universities, vocational schools, and state administrative systems.

The second weakness of the Weimar government was the fragmentation of the political party system that prevented stable majorities from forming in the Reichstag. This instability encouraged the use of emergency powers to break legislative deadlocks. By several methods, the new system overcame party fragmentation and the inability to form working majorities. The multiplicity of parties, characteristic of the Weimar Republic, was partially overcome by changes in electoral law. These procedures were designed to reduce the number of small parties and have resulted in a more manageable system. Only two large parties and four small ones have ever gained representation. The Bundestag in the FRG has succeeded in achieving working majorities, a situation in striking contrast to the chronic government instability in the Weimar Republic. Election laws require that the interval between elections be four years (except under unusual circumstances). This requirement gives an elected government the opportunity to implement its electoral goals and to take responsibility for success or failure. The electoral system, explained in the section on the Bundestag in Chapter 19, was also changed from proportional representation under the Weimar system, which proved unstable, to a combination of proportional representation and single-member electoral districts, which is now one of the most emulated in the world for democratizing countries. New constitutional provisions limited the possibility for the Bundestag to vote a government out of office. Under the Weimar constitution, negative majorities often garnered enough votes to unseat the chancellor but could not pro-

vide a mandate to install a replacement. The Basic Law of the FRG prevents this possibility by requiring that a chancellor cannot be voted out of office unless there is majority support for a successor. Another contrast with Weimar is that the Federal Republic's head of government, as the leader of the dominant party or coalition of parties, now has control over the composition of the cabinet. The federal president is merely the ceremonial head of state. Under the Weimar constitution, the president could wield emergency powers. Hitler used this rule to manipulate the system under aging president Paul Hindenburg in 1932–1933. In the Federal Republic, the president has been stripped of such broad power.

The principles of the Federal Republic's government contained in the Basic Law give the regime a solid foundation—an important reason why the FRG has proved able, at least thus far, to meet the challenge of assimilating the five *Länder* that comprised the former German Democratic Republic (GDR) when unification occurred in 1990. And with the Federal Republic having survived for more than forty years, it is clear that the most important goals of the Federal Republic's founders have been fulfilled. Nevertheless, neo-Nazi movements and racist violence in the 1990s surprised many observers who thought these sentiments had long since been purged from German politics.

Organization of the State

Germany is a parliamentary democracy with a chancellor as head of government and a ceremonial president as head of state (see Figure 18.1). Bonn was the capital beginning in 1949, but following unification, the capital was eventually fully transferred to Berlin, in 1999. In the early and mid-1990s, several ceremonial functions were held in the historic Reichstag in Berlin. But by 1999, after a massive renovation of the Reichstag and the building and rebuilding of numerous government ministries, almost all day-to-day activities were located in the new

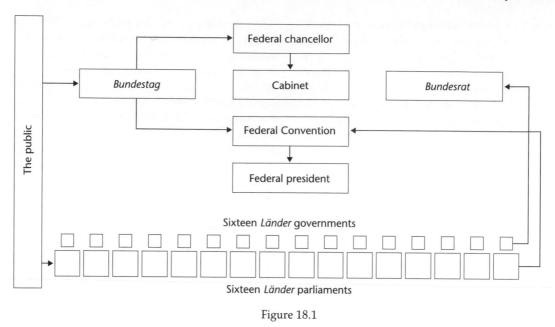

Figure 18.1

Constitutional Structure of Germany's Federal Government

capital, with only a few ministries remaining in Bonn.

The German state is organized as a federal system, with the sixteen *Länder* having considerable authority independent of the federal government. Most important are those powers that authorize *Länder* governments to raise revenue independently through the ability to own and operate firms, usually in partnership with private industry. Regional and local governments in Britain, Italy, and France have far fewer such powers. The functioning of the German federal government, however, is more like the parliamentary systems of its European neighbors. There is a fusion of powers in that the chancellor (the executive) is also the leader of the leading party (or coalition) in the Bundestag. This contrasts with the U.S. separation of powers, in which neither the president nor his cabinet officials can simultaneously serve in the Congress. Generally in the Federal Republic, the executive dominates the legislature, but this authority comes from the chancellor's role

as party leader coupled with a high level of party discipline. Most members of the governing parties support the chancellor at all times, as their own positions depend on a successful government. This circumstance has the significant result of avoiding the "lone ranger" syndrome, so common in the U.S. House of Representatives and Senate, where individual members of the House or the Senate act as independent political entrepreneurs.

The Executive

The division between the head of government (the chancellor) and the head of state (the president) was firmly established in the Federal Republic, with major political powers delegated to the chancellor. Responsibilities and obligations were clearly distinguished. For example, the chancellor could be criticized for the government's policies without the attack being perceived as a frontal assault against the state itself. In this sense, the division of the executive branch was crucial in gaining respect for the new West German state at a time when most of its neighbors remained suspicious of Germany's past. It was Chancellor Hitler, after all, who manipulated President Hindenburg in 1934 to increase the powers of the chancellor. When Hindenburg died shortly after, Hitler fused the offices of chancellor and president, producing the position of Führer (supreme leader).

The President

As head of state, the German president holds a much weaker position than that of the chancellor. Like constitutional monarchs in Britain, for example, German presidents stand above the political fray, which means that they take more of a ceremonial role than an active political one. Federal presidential powers are not autonomous but are constrained by the formal provisions of the Basic Law. The distinction between executive functions in the Federal Republic can be contrasted with the confluence of the roles of head of state and head of government in the United States. The president of the United States fills both of these roles, the implications of which have not always been positive for the country. Lyndon Johnson, Richard Nixon, and, some say, George W. Bush have hid behind the head-of-state mantle by suggesting that criticism of their government's policies was unpatriotic.

The German president has the following duties. As head of state, the president represents Germany in international affairs, concluding treaties with other countries and receiving the credentials of foreign ambassadors and envoys. He or she formally appoints and dismisses federal civil servants, federal judges, and officers of the Federal Armed Forces and may exercise the right of presidential clemency. He or she participates in the legislative process through the promulgation of laws, the dissolution of the Bundestag, and the formal proposal, appointment, and dismissal of the federal chancellor and the ministers. The political system of Germany assigns the president a nonpartisan role, often of

a ceremonial nature, with powers that rest largely on the moral authority of the office rather than on political power. An exception is the occurrence of a parliamentary crisis when no candidate can command the support of an absolute majority of Bundestag members. In this case, the president can decide whether the country is to be governed by a minority administration under a chancellor elected by a plurality of deputies or whether new elections are to be called (although the German president has never had to use the last provision).[3]

On July 1, 2004, Johannes Rau stepped down from the office after the completion of his five-year term, deciding not to seek a second term. His successor, Horst Köhler, an economist and former head of the International Monetary Fund (IMF), was elected president in May by a procedure specified in the Basic Law—that is, by the Federal Convention (Bundesversammlung), an assembly of all Bundestag members and an equal number of delegates elected by the state legislatures (the equivalent of an electoral college) according to the principle of proportional representation. Köhler, sponsored by the opposition Christian Democratic Union (CDU)–Christian Social Union (CSU) and Free Democratic Party (FDP), defeated Gesine Schwann, sponsored by the governing Social Democratic Party (SPD)–Green coalition in a narrow vote of 604 to 598. Schwann would have been the first female federal president. Herr Köhler took office on July 1, 2004.

The presidential term is five years, and a president may serve only two terms. The important point about the German presidency is that in the case of a political crisis affecting the chancellor, the president would remain as an overseer of the political process, providing continuity in a time of national crisis. However, such a situation has not arisen since the creation of the FRG in 1949.

The Chancellor

The chancellor is elected by a majority of the members of the Bundestag. In practice, this means that the chancellor's ability to be a strong party leader (or leader of a coalition of parties) is essential for the success of the government. A government is formed after a national election or, if the chancellor leaves office between elections, after a majority of the Bundestag has nominated a new chancellor, such as in the transition from Helmut Schmidt to Helmut Kohl in 1982. The new leader consults with other party and coalition officials to make up the cabinet. These party leaders have considerable influence in determining which individuals receive ministries. In the event of a coalition government— there has been only one noncoalition majority government, the CDU-CSU from 1957 to 1961—party leaders often earmark, even before the chancellor's election, members of their party who will receive certain ministries.[4] Negotiations on which policies a coalition will pursue can often become heated, so the choice of ministers is made on policy as well as personal grounds.

Once the cabinet is formed, however, the chancellor has considerable authority to govern, owing to the power of the Federal Chancellery (*Bundeskanzleramt*). This office is, in effect, the first among equals of all of the cabinet ministries, enabling the chancellor to oversee his or her entire government efficiently, as well as to mediate conflicts among the other ministries. It is a kind of superministry that has wide-ranging powers in many areas. The chancellor uses this office and its professional staff to supervise and coordinate policy among the other cabinet departments, such as the Ministries of Economics, Finance, Interior, and Labor, and the Foreign Office, as well as less influential departments. The chancellor draws the cabinet officials largely from the high ranks of the majority party or coalition partner. Germany's party system and its parliamentary legislative body place a premium on long service, which is expected before advancement is possible. Consequently, party officials often develop specific areas of expertise that the majority party or the chancellor's office can draw on when positions need to be filled. Rather than relying on outsiders from other professions for cabinet positions (as the U.S. executive often does), the chancellors draw their cabinet officials from a pool of individuals with long experience in both government and the party in power.

The Federal Republic has had a history of strong chancellors, although this has not always been the case. The first was Konrad Adenauer, who, as the leader of the CDU, served as the head of government from 1949 to 1963 and established the social market economy. A former mayor of Cologne in the Weimar years, he was known as *Der Alte* (the old man). His paternalism seemed reassuring to a majority of voters at a time when West Germany was rebuilding from the devastation caused by the war. His successor, Ludwig Erhard (CDU), had been economics minister under Adenauer and was widely credited with formulating the social market economy policies that produced the economic miracle during the 1950s and early 1960s. As chancellor from 1963 to 1966, Erhard was much less effective, however. Not only did he fail to respond to the slight recession that hit West Germany in 1965, but he lacked Adenauer's decisiveness. Still weaker was Kurt Kiesinger (CDU), the chancellor of the 1966–1969 Grand Coalition of the CDU and CSU with the Social Democratic Party (SPD). He was not a resolute leader, and his task was hindered by the increasing conflicts between the CDU-CSU and the SPD, and the strong foreign policy posture of Vice Chancellor Willy Brandt (SPD). It was also hindered by the growth of the Extraparliamentary Opposition (Ausserparliamentarische Opposition—APO) on the left and by the National Democratic Party of Germany (NPD), a reconstituted neo-Nazi party, on the right. Although the Grand Coalition had fused the two major parties in government, it also meant that there was no authentic opposition party. This period of "consensus" government proved short-lived.

Following the 1969 election, the SPD became the dominant coalition partner until 1982. Its thirteen-year tenure was largely due to the strong leadership of Chancellors Willy Brandt

(1969–1974) and Helmut Schmidt (1974–1982). Brandt was mayor of West Berlin during the 1960s, and during his years as chancellor, he emphasized *Ostpolitik* (encouraging relations with East Germany and the Soviet bloc countries). This policy proved highly popular and was continued even under the Christian Democratic leadership of Helmut Kohl after 1982. Brandt was forced to resign in 1974 when one of his personal assistants was discovered to be a spy for East Germany. However, Brandt remained party chairman through the mid-1980s and was a unifying figure for the party following the coming to power of the Christian Democrats in 1982. Helmut Schmidt replaced Brandt in 1974 and during his term was highly regarded for his skill in managing the economy. Schmidt steered the West German economy through the first oil crisis and through troubled economic straits during the late 1970s and early 1980s. Under his chancellorship, the German economy performed better than those of other European countries. His primary weakness was his inability to retain a close relationship with the rank and file of the Social Democrats. When the FDP, the SPD's junior partner in the governing coalition, broke with Schmidt in the early 1980s on economic policies, Schmidt lacked sufficient support among his own party to remain in power. As leaders of the SPD, both Brandt and Schmidt were adept at brokering conflicts between the left wing of the party and the centrist FDP coalition partner. Both also expanded and consolidated the welfare state.

Helmut Kohl took office in 1982. Many politicians and political observers underestimated his considerable political skills at their own peril. He expertly used the power of the chancellor's office: to hold the CDU/CSU-FDP coalition together; to fend off an attack from the right by the Republikaner (the Republican Party); and to keep the opposition SPD and Greens from making effective challenges to him in the elections of 1987, 1990, and 1994. By the time Kohl left office in 1998, he was the longest-serving and among the most influential chancellors in the history of the FRG.

"The scandal is . . . over?"

Source: © Andreas Karl Gschwind.

Following the urbane and worldly Helmut Schmidt was a difficult task for the career politician from the city of Ludwigshafen in the state of Rhineland-Palatinate. Unlike Brandt and Schmidt, Kohl did not speak English in public and often seemed ill at ease at ceremonial functions. He was a large and physically robust man who was said to typify to non-Germans avuncular and *gemütlich* (jovial) characteristics more appropriate for German travel posters than for a federal chancellor. Nevertheless, winning four consecutive national elections was no small accomplishment. Nor was shepherding Germany through the twin tasks of unification and European integration, his greatest accomplishments. Marring his postchancellorship legacy, however, was a campaign finance scandal in 1999 in which he refused to reveal the names of donors who had made illegal campaign contributions to the CDU, a clear violation of German law. Kohl claimed, in defense, that he was only honoring his pledge to these individuals not to reveal their names. Kohl's transgressions severely damaged the electoral fortunes of the Christian Democrats in *Land* elections in 1999 and 2000, at a time when his successor as chancellor, Social Democrat Gerhard Schröder, was struggling. Kohl's political ignominy reached its apex when, at the tenth anniversary of German unification in October 2000, he was not invited by his successor to the celebrations in Berlin.

Gerhard Schröder, elected chancellor in 1998, is the first German political leader truly of the postwar generation. Unlike Kohl, who was a teenager during World War II, Schröder was born at the end of the war in 1944, in the small Lower Saxony town of Rosenburg. He was nevertheless profoundly affected by the war in one sense: his father, a German soldier, was killed on the eastern front in Romania. As a young man, Gerhard Schröder had to work while he completed his education, serving a stint as a clerk in a hardware store before his university studies.

In his twenties, he became active in Social Democratic Party politics, belonging to the *Jungsozialisten* (Young Socialists), or *Jusos*, as they are known colloquially. Schröder embraced Marxism, as did most other *Jusos* at the time; this fact is not surprising given the Marxist roots of virtually all social democratic, socialist, and labor parties throughout the world. By the time Schröder received his law degree from Göttingen University in 1976, he had already become an influential young politician in the SPD. He became a member of the Bundestag in 1980 and in 1990 was elected *Minister-Präsident* (governor) of Lower Saxony. Even in his early years in public life, Schröder had high ambitions. One evening in Bonn in the 1980s, Schröder, who had taken perhaps an extra mug or two of German beer, was walking past the gate to the chancellor's office, then occupied by Helmut Kohl. Putting his hands on the gate, he exclaimed: "I want to be in there!" Schröder's personal life is not without controversy; he has been divorced three times, and is now married to his fourth wife. During the 1998 campaign, the youth wing of Helmut Kohl's CDU urged voters to reject Schröder and the SPD, proclaiming, "Three women can't be wrong."

During the 1998 election campaign, Germany's incoming chancellor was compared with British prime minister Tony Blair and U.S. president Bill Clinton. Observers stressed one apparent thread that tied the three young (all were in their forties or fifties) political leaders together. As heads of "left" parties on their countries' respective political spectrums, they seemed to share an affinity for moving their parties toward more centrist positions. In fact, the SPD slogan for the 1998 campaign was *"die neue Mitte"* (the new middle), suggesting just such a moderate tendency on Schröder's and the SPD's part.

Some more leftist members of the SPD acted as a brake on some of Schröder's more centrist-leaning tendencies, especially Oskar Lafontaine, the former chairman of the SPD and Schröder's first finance minister. Yet Schröder retained the upper hand when he forced Lafontaine from his cabinet position in the spring of 1999 in a power play to bring the governing coalition back toward *die neue Mitte*. The combination of Lafontaine's purging and Kohl's discrediting of the CDU gave Schröder needed breathing room as he consolidated his hold on the chancellorship in his first term.

The office of chancellor has played a pivotal role in the Federal Republic. The clearly defined role of the chancellor within the federal framework has resulted in a far more effective office than was the case in the Weimar period. And by requiring that the chancellor be the head of the majority party or coalition, the Federal Republic has avoided the disastrous scenario by which Hitler terminated the Weimar regime in 1933. One feature of this change is that the chancellor's more limited role within the context of a federal system has constrained the ability of the central government to take sweeping action. Many Germans have seen this limitation of centralized executive power as a welcome improvement.

As in all other parliamentary systems, in Germany the head of government is the dominant member of a governing team. Chancellors select a cabinet of ministers who can best support and strengthen the executive branch. The most significant cabinet ministries are those of finance, economics, justice, interior, and foreign policy (the Foreign Ministry). Chancellors generally select cabinet members from leaders of their own party or of coalition partners. Since many of the important deliberations and decisions occur prior to official cabinet meetings, those meetings have often a quite formal character. In many cases, chancellors rely on strong ministers in key posts, but some chancellors have often taken ministerial responsibility themselves in key areas such as economics and foreign policy. Helmut Schmidt and Willy Brandt, respectively, fit this pattern. The Economics and Finance Ministries always work closely with the Bundesbank, Germany's central bank.

Perhaps the most significant source of the chancellor's powers is the constitutional *constructive vote of no confidence*. To overcome the weakness of the cabinet governments of Weimar, the Federal Republic's founders added a twist to the practice, familiar in most other parliamentary systems, in which a prime minister is brought down on a vote of no confidence. In most systems, if prime ministers lose such a vote, they are obliged to step down or to call for new elections. In the Federal Republic, however, such a vote must be "constructive" in the sense that a chancellor cannot be removed unless the Bundestag *simultaneously* elects a new chancellor (usually from an opposition party). This constitutional provision strengthens the chancellor's power in at least two ways. First, it means that chancellors can more easily reconcile disputes among cabinet officials without threatening the chancellor's position. Second, it forces the opposition to come up with concrete and specific alternatives to the existing government and prevents them from being oppositional just for opposition's sake. As mentioned above, the only such occurrence was in 1982, with the transition from Helmut Schmidt to Helmut Kohl.

Nonetheless, chancellors face significant limits on their power, one of which involves the passage of legislation. As we discuss in Chapter 19, the Bundesrat must ratify all legislation passed in the Bundestag, unless overridden by a two-thirds vote in the lower house. In addition, the Bundesrat generally implements most legislation passed in the Bundestag, so it is important for chancellors to consider the position of the upper house on most issues.

Bureaucracy and Civil Service

Another crucial part of the executive is the national bureaucracy. The tradition of a strong civil service has deep roots that long predate the introduction of democracy. Particularly in a country like Germany, where the state stubbornly resisted democratic politics, the civil service was regarded as serving the state and not necessarily all citizens. Even in the democratic parliamentary Federal Republic, the perception remains strong among civil servants that their responsibility is first to the state and only secondly to the citizens. In Germany, positions in the bureaucracy are very powerful and are protected by long-standing civil service provisions. German civil servants (*Beamten*) had a reputation for being inflexible and rigid in the performance of their duties during the Second and Third Reichs. Even during the Federal Republic, when the bureaucracy has been under democratic supervision, there are certainly inefficiencies in the Federal Republic's public sector, as in all other public and private bureaucracies. Yet civil servants view the work that they perform as a profession—that is, more than just a job.

The most surprising fact about the German bureaucracy is that only approximately 10 percent of civil servants are employed by the federal government. The vast majority are employed by the various state and local governments. In the years before the founding of the Federal Republic, most of the civil servants were recruited from the families of the reactionary nobility, but selection of bureaucrats in the Federal Republic takes a more modern form. Most are either graduates of major German universities or from positions within the political parties. The federal bureaucrats are primarily policymakers and work closely with their ministries and the legislature. The bureaucrats at the state and local levels are the predominant agents of policy implementation, because the states bear most of the responsibility for carrying out policies determined at the national level. This overlapping of national, regional, and local bureaucracies is enhanced by the belief that certain crucial functions can be performed only by the public sector and that the civil servants' mandate is to perform these duties as well as possible. The ongoing institutionalized relationship among the various levels of the bureaucracy has produced more consistent and effective public policy than in some countries where federal and state governments are often at odds with one another. Social policy, particularly healthcare and education, is a good example. Policy is designed at the federal level but implemented at the *Land* level, but it occurs as part of an institutionalized process of formal and informal discussion.

Renowned for being officious, rigid, and unfriendly, the German bureaucracy has high—if grudging—political respect from the population. It is generally seen as efficient, although sometimes arcane. Selection of some bureaucrats is based on party affiliation. This derives from the traditional German pattern of *Proporz* (proportionality), in which all major political groups are represented in the bureaucracy. However, the 1970s witnessed attempts to purge the bureaucracy of suspected radicals, and the results—notably requiring civil servants to take loyalty oaths, arbitrarily dismissing many bureaucrats—tarnished the reputation of the bureaucracy for impartiality and fairness. Those who are chosen based on party politics—largely top federal officials—are in the minority. Selection to the status of civil servant is generally based on merit, with elaborate licensing and testing for those who advance to the highest professions. German bureaucrats are well known for a high degree of competence.

Public and Semipublic Institutions

Public and semipublic institutions in Germany are powerful, efficient, and responsible for much national policymaking. In countries that had a feudal guild system of representation, such as Germany, an inclusionary, often corporatist form of representation is common. Semipublic institutions combine aspects of both representation and implementation.[5] The corporatist interest groups are also very much intertwined with the Federal Republic's semipublic agencies, which we argue are institutions crucial for the functioning of the German political economy. Occupying a gray area encompassing both public and private responsibilities, the semipublic (or parastatal) institutions are an apparently seamless web that shapes, directs, implements, and diffuses German public policy.

In the late 1940s, the idea of a strong central state in Germany was discredited for two reasons: the excesses of Nazism and the American occupation authorities' strong affinity for the private sector. West German authorities faced a dilemma. How would they rebuild society if a strong public sector role were ruled out? The answer was to create modern, democratic versions of those nineteenth-century institutions that blurred the differences between the public and private sectors. These institutions have played a crucial, and long unrecognized, role in the German political economy.

Political scientist Peter Katzenstein has described these parapublic agencies as "detached institutions." He sees them as reducing the influence of the central state by acting as primarily mediating entities that operate from a principle of engaging all relevant actors in the policy community in continuous dialogue until appropriate policies are found.[6] Katzenstein finds that they have tended to work best in areas of social and economic policy, but less well in their interaction with the university system. Among the most important parapublic agencies are the Chambers of Industry; the Council of Economic Advisers (known colloquially as the Five Wise Men); the vocational education system, which encompasses the apprenticeship training system; and the institutions of worker participation (codetermination and the works councils). Even parts of the welfare system are parapublic, since the system of distribution for welfare benefits is often administered by organizations that are not officially part of the state bureaucracy. The most significant example is the *Krankenkassen* (sickness funds), which bring all major health interests together to allocate costs and benefits through an elaborate system of consultation and group participation.

Historically, the most important semipublic German institution for shaping economic policy, the politically independent Bundesbank, is not formally part of the government. Prior to the arrival of the euro in 1999, this institution was both the bankers' bank (in that it set interest rates) and the agency that determined the amount of money in circulation. This last point is the one that proved so contentious during the 1980s and 1990s. The Bundesbank's preference was for low inflation, both because this is a traditional demand of all central bankers and because of Germany's history of ruinous inflation during the Weimar Republic. The relevance for economic policy is that when the government wishes to expand the economy through increased spending or reduced taxes, the Bundesbank always preferred policies that favor monetary restrictions before fast economic growth. In other words, the government and the Bundesbank can be of opposite minds on economic policy, as has been the case in the years since unification.

However, the introduction of the euro has also been accompanied by the creation of the European Central Bank (ECB). Modeled after the Bundesbank, the ECB would seem to be poised to favor Germany. But because it serves all of Europe, the ECB has caused the Bundesbank to lose some of its former power and luster as a result of the new European-wide monetary regime. Exchange and interest rates are now set by the ECB. Some Germans are concerned not only about future monetary stability but also about whether European and German monetary interests will continue to be harmonious.

One of the policy areas already mentioned merits more extensive discussion: the parastatal

institutions involved in the implementation of policy concerned with industrial relations. This system of codetermination (*Mitbestimmung*) contrasts sharply with Anglo-American patterns. We cover this set of institutions here because the area of industrial relations in Germany is more than just a system of interest representation. It is also a shaper of public policy.

Providing for the institutionalized representation of workers—including, but not restricted to, union members—on the supervisory boards of directors of all medium-sized and large firms, codetermination gives unions an inside look at the workings of the most powerful firms in the Federal Republic. Based on laws passed in the early 1950s and expanded in the 1970s, codetermination gives workers and unions up to one-half of the members of these company boards. Labor representatives are chosen by democratic election among the workers of the companies where they are employed. Unions can thus understand, if not control, how and why major corporate decisions are made on such issues as investment and application of technology. What difference does codetermination make? A major benefit of representation is that it provides information about the operation of the company and forces management to defend its decisions. The problem for the unions in challenging management positions on contentious issues is that with the exception of the coal and steel industries, the laws always provide management with one more seat than workers have.

An additional institutional structure represents German workers and gives them access to the policy implementation process. In notable contrast to the trade unions' industrywide role of representation, all shop-floor and plant-level affairs such as social and personnel matters—but not collective bargaining, which is a union function—are the exclusive domain of the works councils (*Betriebsräte*), internal bodies of worker representation that exist in most German firms. These lines of demarcation were much clearer than they became in the late 1980s and early 1990s with the development of more flexible workplaces, in the sense of team work groups and multiple tasks within specific job categories. In fact, some of the structural economic reforms proposed by Schröder's Agenda 2010 threatened to modify or erode some of the powers of these unique labor market institutions under the goal of increased flexibility to deal with globalization.

The unions' legitimacy derives from a countrywide, multi-industry representation of a large number of diversified workers. The works councils, on the other hand, owe their primary allegiance to their local plants and firms. The two distinct and separate bodies definitely cause rivalries, periodic rifts, and different representations of interest. Despite the 85 percent overlap in personnel between unions and works councils and despite a structural entanglement between these two major pillars of labor representation in the Federal Republic, these divisions can produce tensions among organized labor. A period of general flux and plant-related, management-imposed flexibility in the mid- and late 1980s exacerbated these tensions. Specifically, micro (plant-level) concerns sometimes clashed with macro (industrywide) ones, partially threatening the broad labor solidarity that the unions desired. The unions have by and large successfully avoided the proliferation of any serious plant-level divisions among workers, although there have been some significant exceptions.

Other State Institutions

The chancellor, the president, the bureaucracy, and semipublic institutions are not Germany's only important state agencies for governance and policymaking. Among other state institutions that deserve attention are the military and police, the judiciary, and subnational governments.

The Military and Police

The German military was historically powerful and aggressive from the eighteenth century (when it was the Prussian military) through World War II. In this two-century period, it was responsible for many wars and major acts of aggression. However, all changed after World War II, and the German military today is completely under civilian control and tightly circumscribed by law and treaty. Germany has a universal service option requiring all citizens over the age of eighteen to perform one year in military or civilian service. In 1990, Germany had approximately 600,000 men and women in the military, but in 1994 the federal government set a cap at approximately 340,000. Germany spends 1.5 percent of its gross domestic product on the military, far less than other major European countries spend. Similar to the Japanese military, Germany's armed forces have been legally proscribed from acting independently beyond the borders of the FRG since the end of World War II, first by the Allied occupation and later by the Basic Law. The end of the cold war produced two other important changes in German military policy: the reduction in U.S. armed forces stationed in Germany and the payments made to Russia for removal of soldiers and materiel from the former East Germany.

Under the provisions of the Basic Law, the German military is to be used only for defensive purposes within Europe and in coordination with North Atlantic Treaty Organization (NATO) authorities. Only very limited military activity under tightly reined approval (e.g., via NATO, the United Nations, and perhaps eventually the EU) has altered the general prohibition. German participation in the UN peacekeeping mission in Bosnia in the mid-1990s was a very important, precedent-breaking step. Agreeing to participate in opposition to Serbian aggression in Kosovo in 1999 (a decision made by the SPD/Green government) was another, and sending troops to Afghanistan—even forming a joint Franco-German brigade—was a third.

Since World War II, two generations of Germans have been educated to deemphasize the military and militarism as solutions to political problems. The irony is that it is difficult politically—and until recently, constitutionally—for Germany to commit troops to regional conflicts, even under UN or other international auspices. Such issues are obviously related to Germany's aggressive historical role in the international political system. The dilemmas increase when the issue of Bosnia, Serbia, the former Yugoslavia, and now Afghanistan and Iraq is overlaid on this set of policy proscriptions. Humanitarian intervention and the peacekeeping role obviously seem diametrically opposite from aggression, although some within Germany reject this distinction. Part of the reason for German resistance to committing to military action other than strict defense of the Federal Republic's borders (the essence of NATO's cold war mission) is Germany's aggressive past actions in Eastern Europe. In fact, until their election in 1998, the SPD and Greens argued precisely that the Third Reich's aggressive military expeditions to the east in World War II make it impossible for the German military, under either UN or NATO auspices, to play a constructive role in Eastern Europe. Yet after coming to power, the Red-Green government chose to allow Germany to take on more geopolitical responsibility in the context of NATO and the EU. This has not been an easy issue, and it is made all the more difficult by the need for the Greens and left-leaning elements in the SPD to accommodate themselves to their power and responsibility.

Discussion of the German police needs to focus on two areas. The first is that of the postwar experience in the FRG, where police powers have been organized on a *Land* basis and—given the excesses of the Third Reich—have been constitutionally circumscribed to ensure that human and civil rights remain inviolate. To be sure, there have been episodes of abuse, as the German police will never be as well regarded as the British "bobby." For example, during the dragnets for the Red Army Faktion terrorists in the late 1970s, many forces in the SPD and among the *Bürgerinitiativen* (citizen action groups), the precursors to the Greens, argued that German police forces compromised civil liberties in their desire to capture the terrorists.

The second is that of the GDR's notorious secret police, the Stasi. The Ministry for State Security (Stasi's formal name) comprised some 91,000 official employees; moreover, in 1989, more than 180,000 East Germans and perhaps 4,000 West Germans worked as Stasi informants.[7] In proportion to the 16 million GDR citizens, the Stasi was more encompassing in the GDR than was the Gestapo during Nazi rule. Since unification, Stasi archives have been open to all, as the East Germans and later the FRG believed that full and open disclosure of Stasi excesses was essential in a democratic state. These disclosures generated huge scandals when it became known that some respected West German public figures had been spying for the Stasi.

The Judiciary

The judiciary has always played an important role in Germany because of the deep involvement of the state in political and economic matters. Late to unify and industrialize, the central state was a much larger actor in Germany than in most other countries, necessitating an extensive set of rules to define such wide-ranging powers. Thus, the German state has historically been supported by a strong legal system. The relationship between the state administration and the judiciary during the 1871–1945 period was an extremely close one, yet it engendered many abuses. During the Second Reich, the court was used to safeguard the privileged position of those in power—for example, by failing to rule against the Reichstag voting system, which allowed the small number of Prussian estate owners to have a majority of power. During the Weimar period, the court frustrated the further implementation of democracy when it ruled against the workers councils' demands for increased power within the workplace. Hitler abused the court system extensively during the Nazi regime, inducing it to make a wide range of antidemocratic, repressive, and even criminal decisions. Among them were banning non-Nazi parties, allowing the seizure of Jewish property, and sanctioning the death of millions.

The Federal Republic's founders were most concerned that the new judicial system avoid those earlier abuses. One of the first requirements was that the judiciary explicitly safeguard the democratic rights of individuals, groups, and political parties, stressing some of the individual freedoms that had long been associated with the U.S., British, and French legal systems. In fact, the Basic Law contains a more elaborate and explicit statement of individual rights than exists in either the U.S. Constitution or British common law.

Yet the Federal Republic's legal system differs from the Anglo-Saxon legal tradition. The Anglo-Saxon legal system is characterized by adversarial relationships between contending parties, in which the judge (or the court itself) merely provides a neutral arena for a legal struggle to take place. What emerges from these proceedings is an ad hoc system of case law based on precedent, as well as common law, which contrasts greatly with the continental system, including Germany, of codified law in which precedents have no weight.

This means that the judiciary in the Federal Republic is an active administrator of the law rather than just an arbiter. Specifically, judges have a different relationship with the state and with the adjudication of cases than they do in Anglo-Saxon systems. This judicial system relies on a belief in the "capacity of the state" (as political sociologist Theda Skocpol terms it) to identify and implement certain important societal goals.[8] And if the task of the state is to create the laws to attain these goals, then the judiciary should safeguard their implementation. In both defining the meaning of very complex laws and implementing their administration, German courts go considerably beyond those in the United States and Britain, which at least in theory avoid political decisions. The German courts' role in shaping policy has been most evident in its ruling in 1976 on whether to allow the unions to obtain increased codetermination rights. The court allowed the unions to obtain near parity on the boards of directors but stated that full union parity with the employers would compromise the rights of private property.

Autonomous and independent, the German judiciary generally makes its rulings consistent with accepted constitutional principles. It also remains outside the political fray on most issues, although a ruling in 1993 limiting access to abortion for many women—in direct opposition to the law on abortion in the former GDR—was a clear exception to the general pattern. It also was criticized in the 1990s for showing far too much leniency toward perpetrators of racist violence.

The Federal Republic has a three-pronged court system. One branch consists of the criminal-civil system, with the Bundesgerichtshof (Federal High Court) at its apex. It is a unified rather than a federal system, making it not subject to the *Länder* governments' control. In fact, it tries to apply a consistent set of criteria for legal issues in the sixteen *Länder*. As a court of appeals, the Bundesgerichtshof is the judicial body that addresses cases that have been appealed from the lower courts. It handles the range of criminal and civil issues common to most industrialized states, passes judgment on disputes among the *Länder,* and makes decisions that would be viewed in some other countries as political.

The Bundesverfassungsgericht (Federal Constitutional Court) deals with matters directly affecting the Basic Law. As a postwar creation, it was founded to safeguard the new democratic political order. Precisely because of the Nazis' abuses of the judiciary, the founders of the FRG added a layer to the judiciary, empowered for judicial review, to ensure that the basic democratic order would be maintained. The Federal Constitutional Court consists of federal judges and supporting staff.

Half of the court members are elected by the Bundestag and the other half by the Bundesrat. They may not be members of either house of parliament, the government, or any of the corresponding bodies of a state. Furthermore, the constitution and procedure of the Federal Constitutional Court are regulated by federal statute, which specifies in what cases its decisions have the force of law. The statute may require that all other legal remedies must have been exhausted before a complaint of unconstitutionality can be entered and may make provision for a special procedure as to admissibility.[9]

The most notable decisions of the Bundesverfassungsgericht in the 1950s were the banning of both the ultra-right Socialist Reich Party and the Communist Party as forces hostile to the Basic Law. During the early 1970s, a Radicals Decree was promulgated by Willy Brandt's SPD-led coalition. Targeting so-called 1960s radicals who had found work in the public sector, it caused some leftists their jobs as teachers, bureaucrats, or other public servants. The Constitutional Court ruled on the cases of several individuals who lost their jobs as "enemies of the constitution." During the brief terrorist wave of the late 1970s, in which several prominent individuals were kidnapped or killed by the ultraradical Red Army Faktion (RAF), this court was pressed into service to pass judgment on the violent actions of the terrorists. But it also sanctioned wide, indiscriminate investigation of all those who might be supporters of the RAF. In a state that claimed to be an adherent of Western-style liberalism and was ruled by an SPD-led government, such far-reaching action disturbed many who were concerned about individual freedoms and due process.

The Bundesverwaltungsgericht (Administrative Court) is the third branch of the court system. Consisting of the Labor Court, the Social Security Court, and the Finance Court, the Administrative Court has a much narrower jurisdiction than the other two. Whereas the Bundesrat, with its regional divisions, concerns itself with the implementation of the law within geographical boundaries, the Administrative Court system concerns itself with the implementation of the law within functional boundaries—that is, the specific topics such as tax disputes and welfare state programs that are regulated by these courts. Through administrative decisions, the state and its bureaucracy occupy a prominent position in the lives of German citizens. Thus,

this level of the court system acts as a corrective to the arbitrary power of the state bureaucracy. Compared with such countries as Britain and France, where much of public policy is determined by legislation, German public policy is much more often conducted by administrative action on the part of the bureaucracy. Through this court, citizens can challenge actions of the bureaucracy when, for example, they believe that authorities have improperly taken action with respect to labor, welfare, or tax policies.

Beginning in the 1990s, the courts have come under great pressure to deal with the intractable policy issues that unification and European integration have brought about. More and more, they are being drawn into the political thicket and coming under much more scrutiny regarding their decisions. Many critics wish that the courts would show the same diligence and zeal in addressing the crimes of neo-Nazis as they did in sanctioning those anti-left-wing-radical measures in the 1970s. However, the courts' response to the violence of the 1990s has not shown the same resolute action. The antiterrorist measures in the wake of 9/11 have placed additional pressures on the courts. For example, alleged Moroccan terrorists on trial in Germany for 9/11-related acts were released by the German court because the U.S. government would not allow the Moroccans to call witnesses on their behalf. These witnesses were being detained by the U.S. government as enemy combatants.

Subnational Governments

Unlike the weakly developed regional governments of Britain and France, for example, the sixteen *Länder* of the Federal Republic enjoy both considerable autonomy and significant independent powers. Each state has a regional assembly (*Landtag*), which functions much like the Bundestag at the federal level. The governor (*Minister-Präsident*) of each *Land* is the leader of the largest party (or coalition of parties) in the *Landtag* and forms a government in the *Landtag* in much the same way as does the chancellor in the Bundestag. Each of the sixteen state elections is held on independent staggered four-year cycles, which generally do not coincide with federal elections and only occasionally coincide with elections in other *Länder*. Like the semipublic or parastatal institutions, subnational governments in Germany are powerful, significant, and responsible for much of national policy implementation.

Particularly significant is Germany's overlapping federalism, in which policies developed in the Bundestag are often explicitly implemented by *Land* governments. Recall that only about 10 percent of all public employees work at the federal level, meaning the remainder work for state or local governments. A good way to show how Germany's functional federalism works is with an example: industrial policy.

Regional governments are much more active than the national government in planning and targeting economic policy, providing them with greater autonomy in administering industrial policy. Precisely because the *Länder* were constituent states, they were able to develop their own regional versions of industrial policy (*Ordnungspolitik*). They could take action regionally in ways that the federal government could not do nationally, since the national government was discouraged from centralizing economic power. The *Land* governments undertook this intervention in the economy—for industrial policies in Bavaria, North Rhine–Westphalia, and Baden-Württemberg—in the name of regional autonomy, not in the name of centralized economic planning.[10] Furthermore, because different regions had different economic needs and industrial foundations, these powers were perceived as legitimate and appropriate by most voters. The *Land* governments encouraged banks to direct investment and loans to stimulate industrial development in the respective *Länder*. They encouraged cooperation among regional firms—many in the same industry—to spur international competition. They also invested heavily in vocational education to provide the skills so necessary for high-quality manufacturing goods, the

core of the German economy. Organized business and organized labor too had a direct role in shaping curricula to improve worker skills through the vocational education system. The *Land* governments have enhanced industrial adaptation by qualitatively shaping the framework for adaptation rather than adopting a heavy-handed regulatory posture.

The general pattern of regionally autonomous economic policy in the *Länder* has an important common denominator: the legitimacy of regional state intervention. However, not all states pursue the same economic policies; there have been various models of specific government involvement in economic policy and industrial adjustment in these regions targeted to regional needs.

In the Federal Republic, state politics are organized on the same political party basis as the national parties. This parallel does not imply that national politics dominates local politics, but that voters are more often able to see the connection among local, regional, and national issues in ways that enhance both unity and diversity in the political system. Because the parties take positions and establish platforms for state and city elections, voters can discern the differences among parties and make choices based on issues as well as personalities. This does not mean that personalities play no role in German regional politics. In fact, the nature of the party system in the Federal Republic places a premium on national political figures' paying their dues through service at the levels of local and regional party and government. Because regional and local party actors are tied closely to the parties at the national level, there is an affinity among actions taken at different political levels.

Just as overlapping responsibilities (*Politikverflechtung*) make separating the institutions of federalism difficult from the national to the regional level, this phenomenon is at work between the regional and local levels too. In fact, the cities of Bremen and Hamburg, which were members of the Hanseatic League specializing in foreign trade from the thirteenth to the fifteenth centuries, remain city-states. Even today, they have overlapping municipal and *Land* governments. The unified Berlin city government now also fits into this city-state category. Echoing the powers that the regional governments held in the years before German unification in 1871, the FRG's local governments, growing out of such city-state traditions, have enjoyed far more power than their U.S. counterparts.

Local governments in the Federal Republic differ from those in Britain and France in their capacity to raise revenues by owning enterprises. For example, there is a wide degree of local government ownership of revenue-generating enterprises such as utilities and radio and TV networks. This is due in part to the historical patterns of public sector involvement in the economy, but it has also sprung from the belief that these levels of government are the stewards of a collective public good. Supporting art museums, theater companies, recreational facilities, and adequate housing complexes, and offering various direct and indirect subsidies for a city's inhabitants, are seen as crucial for maintaining the quality of life in modern society. Even during the recessions of the early 1980s and early 1990s, there were remarkably few cutbacks in ownership of public enterprises or these various types of social spending.

The European Dimension

The increased prominence of the EU offers both challenges and opportunities for FRG governance issues.[11] On the one hand, German policy formation at the European level is constrained because a much larger number of actors are involved in policies directly affecting the FRG. More significant, these actors generally operate in an environment quite different from the institutional continuity of German-style organized capitalism and democratic corporatism. Because pragmatic pluralist relationships are much easier to establish at the EU level than the deeply entrenched institutional continuities of the FRG, the shared understanding among German actors with long years of interpenetrated

relationships is much harder to establish at the EU level. Concretely, both the role of the Bundesbank and the cozy bank-firm relationships so long characteristic of the German model become decreasingly significant as the ECB usurps the role of the Bundesbank. In addition, the organized capitalist German mode—at least among the largest firms and banks—also gives way to a more Anglo-American deregulatory model. In that sense, what was unique about the German political economy in the postwar period became much less so the further European integration proceeded.

On the other hand, Germany possesses a significant institutional advantage over other European states as European integration continues. According to political scientist Vivien Schmidt, "To the extent that German institutional actors are now part of the larger, quasi-federal decision-making system that is the EU, this additional level of decision-making basically complements traditional German notions of democratic representation."[12] Unlike the unitary states of Britain, France, and Italy, for example, Germany has experienced fifty years of modern federalism. To the extent that the institutional structure of the EU is based on federalism, the organizational landscape for both German federal and regional actors is most definitely known territory. For example, one exceptionally important area within the EU is the complex of regional policies that enables Brussels sometimes to bypass national governments and implement directives within the regions of sovereign nation-states. While Britain and France have somewhat belatedly developed degrees of regional autonomy, the FRG has experienced regional political actors who can integrate themselves much more easily into the multilevel governance structures of the EU.

The Policymaking Process

The chancellor and the cabinet are the primary determinants of policymaking, but the executive does not wield arbitrary power in this area.

Despite the strong executive role, the policy process in Germany is largely consensus based, with contentious issues usually heavily and extensively debated within various public, parapublic, and private institutions. While the legislature also has a general role in policymaking, the primary driving force is the respective cabinet departments and the experts on whom these institutions call. Of course, the EU is now very much part of that policymaking process.

If policymaking is shaped primarily through the executive, then policy implementation is more diffuse. Along with the role of the corporatist interest groups and various parastatal organizations, the Bundesrat plays a significant role in policy implementation throughout the Federal Republic. This policy implementation takes place in a wide range of areas. Among the most significant are vocational education, welfare, healthcare, and worker participation. We can illustrate implementation most clearly by using the example of a specific form of economic policy.

In such an organized capitalist, corporatist political system, much of the policymaking takes place on an informal basis between and among overlapping institutions. A system of framework regulation sets only outer boundaries, within which all actors must function, and leaves detailed implementation to ongoing discussions among the major actors. For example, supervision of the banking system consists of a few general forms of regulation but very few specific ones. This structure gives considerable power to a parastatal institution (the Federal Bank Supervisory Office, FBSO) but also provides the private banks within the system both autonomy and responsibility (through self-regulation) for the implementation of policy affecting the important German banking industry. For example, the FBSO has stringent requirements to verify the competence and experience of banking executives, but these requirements also let the FBSO have great confidence that approved bankers will act responsibly and in the public interest.

There is considerable misunderstanding among many observers about exactly why and how institutions support the Federal Republic's economic policymaking process. At first glance, many observers of Germany see institutions such as regulatory agencies and parapublic interest groups that seem to inhibit economic freedoms. Yet closer examination reveals that German institutions regulate not the minute details but the general framework. Since all economic actors understand clearly the general parameters within which they must work, German regulatory policy is remarkably free of the nitpicking microregulations common to other countries. Moreover, many policies, particularly in the banking and manufacturing sectors, are reinforced by industry self-regulation that makes heavy-handed government intervention unnecessary.

What are the components of this economic policymaking process? First of all, it is a *system*, not just a collection of firms and discrete policies. It has followed a pattern in which business, labor, and the government work together from the outset of the process and develop consensual policy solutions to national, regional, state, and local problems. The Germans have spoken of their *social* (not *free*) market economy because of a deeply entrenched belief that business must share in the responsibility of providing a stable order, both for the economy and, indirectly, for society.

The foundation of this attitude lay in the fact that German business, labor, and government embraced a different conception of regulation from the one used elsewhere. Rather than seeing regulation as a stark choice between laissez-faire and heavy-handed regulation, Germany has used *Rahmenbedingungen* (framework regulation), which does not see a sharp market-state separation or a singly focused goal of regulating each government action toward the market. Rather, it contains the foundation of a looser, more encompassing framework for both the public and private sectors. This approach has produced a system that is often called externally rigid (in the sense of prohibiting easy entrance and exit with respect to firms and industry) but internally flexible (in the sense that large institutions and firms are often, to American observers, surprisingly flexible in adapting applied technologies to produce specialized goods). In short, this system regulates not the details but the encompassing rules of the game within which all actors must play.

Some would criticize such a system as being too cumbersome and inflexible. In fact, the relative slowness of the FRG in fully embracing the information economy would seem to confirm this stereotype. However, the Germans see a great advantage to this "all eggs in one basket" system in that it generally produces agreement on major policy direction without major social dislocation. Once agreement has been informally

worked out among all the major parties, moving forward with specific legislation is easier. This process is generally less conflict oriented than in Britain, since the German parliamentary system takes more explicit steps to include wider support among major interest groups.

This consensual system has been greatly challenged recently by the extraordinary nature of unification issues, which have put this informal style of policymaking under tremendous pressure. Among the issues that have proved most intractable are the noneconomic issues of political asylum, racist violence, and various scandals that have tarnished the reputations of major public figures, both political leaders and leaders of major interest groups.

Notes

1. Ralf Dahrendorf, *Society and Democracy in Germany* (Garden City, N.Y.: Anchor, 1969).

2. Gerhard Ritter, *The German Problem* (Columbus: Ohio State University Press, 1965).

3. http://eng.bundespraesident.de.

4. Michaela Richter, "Continuity or *Politikwechsel?* The First Federal Red-Green Coalition," *German Politics and Society* 20, no. 1 (Spring 2002): 1–48.

5. Parastatal institutions differ greatly from pluralist representation in countries such as the United States, where interest groups petition public authority for redress of grievances but themselves often stay at arm's length from the implementation process. See Robert Dahl, *Dilemmas of Pluralist Democracy: Autonomy vs. Control* (New Haven, Conn.: Yale University Press, 1982).

6. Peter Katzenstein, *Policy and Politics in West Germany: The Growth of a Semi-Sovereign State* (Philadelphia: Temple University Press, 1987).

7. John O. Koehler, *Stasi: The Untold Story of the East German Secret Police* (Boulder, Colo.: Westview Press, 1999).

8. Peter Evans, Dietrich Rueschemeyer, and Theda Skocpol, *Bringing the State Back In* (Cambridge: Cambridge University Press, 1985).

9. German Basic Law, Article 94, 1949.

10. Christopher S. Allen, "Regional Governments and Economic Policies in West Germany: The 'Meso' Politics of Industrial Adjustment," *Publius* 19, no. 4 (1989): 147–164.

11. Vivien A. Schmidt, "European 'Federalism' and Its Encroachment on National Institutions," *Publius* 29, no. 1 (Winter 1999): 19–44.

12. Ibid., p. 36.

19

Representation and Participation

The lack of a culture of democratic public dissent and dialogue was a long-standing, historic German problem. Only in the late 1960s did such normal civil society activities become widespread. As the Federal Republic of Germany (FRG) deepened and widened its democracy through the last several decades of the twentieth century, it found a synthesis of institutionalized parliamentary participation and public protest that was both inclusionary and genuinely democratic. However, in the new century of an expanded European Union, it still struggles with issues surrounding collective identities. Germany's history with its European neighbors combined with recent immigration has brought these concerns to the surface once again. Socializing disparate political cultures when respect for dissent and dialogue is not deeply ingrained is problematic for any society. In the wake of unification and European integration, the key issue for Germany in this regard is how to develop a system of democratic participation among newly arrived groups to Germany that encompasses both extrainstitutional protest and flexible and responsive democratic political institutions.

The Legislature

The legislature occupies a prominent place in the political system in Germany, with both the lower house (Bundestag) and the upper house (Bundesrat) having significant and wide-ranging powers. The Federal Republic's legislature is bicameral; the lower house—the 2002 Bundestag—has 603 members, and the upper house—the Bundesrat—has 69 members. Unlike the U.S. Senate and the British House of Lords, the Bundesrat is made up of elected and appointed officials from the sixteen *Länder*. In this sense, Germany's constitutional system allows more governmental institutional overlap than in many other countries that are either unitary (France, Italy, and Britain) or believe in sharp separation of powers within the federal government and a separation of powers between federal and state governments (the United States). The Bundestag members are elected in a basically proportional representation system (explained below), in which the leader of the major party, who is usually the leader of the largest party in a two- or three-party coalition, is the chancellor. As in most other parliamentary systems, the chancellor must maintain a majority for his or her government to survive.

The Federal Republic of Germany is similar to other parliamentary regimes having a fusion of power in which the executive is directly elected by the legislature and comes directly from the legislative branch. In other words, there is no sharply demarcated separation of powers between cabinet and legislature, on the one hand, and the balance of power between cabinet and legislature lies with the cabinet, on the other hand. However, as in other parliamentary regimes, such as the British, appearances can be deceptive, since the lines of influence do not simply flow from the legislature to the cabinet. Because the cabinet is composed of the senior leaders of the majority party or party coalition in parliament, the cabinet controls the legislature more than the legislature controls the cabinet.

The electoral procedures for choosing members of the two houses differ substantially, and their different orientations are a product of those different methods. For example, the citizens elect members of the Bundestag by direct ballot by a complex procedure described below. The Bundesrat's members, on the other hand, are officials who are elected or appointed to the governments of the states (*Länder*). Both branches of the legislature are broadly representative of major interests in German society, although some interests in the Bundestag, such as business and labor, are somewhat overrepresented and ecological and noneconomic interests are somewhat underrepresented. By design, the Bundesrat tends to represent principally regional interests.

The executive initiates important specific legislative proposals, since such issues as the federal budget and taxation are required by the Basic Law to come from the executive. That most bills are initiated in the cabinet does not diminish the influence of Bundestag or Bundesrat members, however, since party and coalition unity is important to ensure support for legislation. Also, many different groups, both inside and outside the legislature, can propose different policies. However, the chancellor and the cabinet are prominent. Since parties are generally ideologically coherent, there is usually strong consensus within parties and within coalitions about both the input and output of the legislative process. Parties and coalitions depend on party discipline to sustain majorities, which places high priority on agreement about major legislation.

When the chancellor and his cabinet propose a bill, it is sent to a relevant Bundestag committee. Most of the committee deliberations are behind closed doors, so the individual committee members have significant latitude to shape the details of legislation. The committees call on their own considerable expertise, but also solicit that of relevant government ministries as well as testimony from affected interest groups. This system appears to be a kind of insiders' club, and to some degree it is. However, the committees generally consult with a wide range of groups, both pro and con, that are affected by the proposed legislation. This inclusive form of deliberation—specifically consulting the democratic corporatist interest groups—helps produce a more consensus-oriented outcome. In contrast, in countries with a more pluralist (that is, less inclusive) form of lobbying, legislation is likely to be more contentious and less likely to produce general agreement. Under pluralism, it is relatively easy for groups to articulate issues. However, unlike democratic corporatist systems, pluralist systems tend not to ensure access in a systemic way and also often produce comparatively haphazard policy. Since no group has privileged access, it is more of a free-for-all. Under corporatism, there are fewer players and they play behind closed doors, so it's easier to reach consensus.

After emerging from committee, the bill undergoes final readings in the Bundestag. Although the major parameters of the bill have already been defined, this debate in the Bundestag often produces considerable criticism from the opposition and sharp defense by the governing coalition parties. The primary purpose of such debate is not some odd ceremonial feature; rather, its main function is to educate the public generally about the major issues being addressed. Following passage in the Bundestag, a bill must be approved by the upper house. Although usually accomplished easily, this approval also involves the Bundesrat's determining how a particular law will be implemented at the regional level. For example, if there are region-specific environmental, resource, or infrastructural issues, the Bundesrat can negotiate relevant specifics.

The social composition of the legislature has been largely male and of professional or middle-class orientation, a statement true even of the supposedly working-class Social Democratic Party (SPD), which in the 1950s had a much greater proportion of blue-collar workers elected to the Bundestag. From the 1950s to the 1970s, there were few women in the legislature, though this situation began to change dramatically in the 1980s and 1990s, particularly as the Greens—with their iconoclastic policies (and casual attire)—have seated a number of female Bundestag members (see Table 19.1).[1] By placing equal numbers of males and females on their party electoral list, the Greens forced other parties to include more women on their lists in response. The addition of newer parties, such as the worker-oriented ex-Communist Party of Democratic Socialism (PDS, the party of former East German Communists) and the continued presence of the Greens, has increased variety in the backgrounds of party members. If these parties maintain their representation to the legislature, it will continue to erode the Bundestag's middle-class, professional profile.

The Bundestag

The lower house of the legislature consists of 603 seats (see Figure 19.1), approximately half

Table 19.1   Percentage of Women Members of the Bundestag, 1949–2002

Year	Percentage	Year	Percentage
1949	6.8	1980	8.5
1953	8.8	1983	9.8
1957	9.2	1987	15.4
1961	8.3	1990	20.5
1965	6.9	1994	26.3
1969	6.6	1998	30.2
1972	5.8	2002	32.2
1976	7.3		

Source: Bundeszentrale für Politische Bildung, 2004 (http://www.bpb.de/suche/?all_search_action=search&all_search_text=%22Frauen%22+und+%22Bundestag%22); Women in National Parliaments, 2004 (http://www.ipu.org/wmn-e/classif.htm).

elected in single-member districts and half elected by proportional representation from lists compiled by the political parties. Citizens have two votes, one for an individual candidate in a local district, and one for their preferred political party.

The German parliamentary system represents a synthesis of the British and U.S. tradition of a single legislator representing one district and the proportional representation (PR) method more common in continental Europe, in which a group of party members represent a given region depending on the percentage of the party's vote in that region. This combination of two systems was unique when it was first devised. However, because its results have proved so successful in achieving a variety of views and producing a stable majority, it has become widely copied in newly democratizing regimes throughout the world. Single-member-district voting systems tend to produce a two-party system, and the PR system was melded with the single-member district of plurality voting because Germany wanted to ensure that all major parties, not just two, were represented. The German hybrid system, which is known as mixed-member (or personalized) proportional representation, requires citizens to cast two votes on each ballot: the first one for an individual member of a political party, almost always from the district, and the second one for a list of national and regional candidates grouped by party affiliation (see Figure 19.2). Thus, this system has the effect of personalizing list voting because voters have their "own" representative but also can choose among several parties. To ensure that only parties with significant support are represented, only those winning 5 percent of the vote or having three candidates who win individual seats directly gain representation in the Bundestag (or in any *Land* or municipal government). This provision exists because in the late Weimar period, sharp conflict among parties opened the door for the Nazi rise to power. Under the 5 percent rule from the founding of the

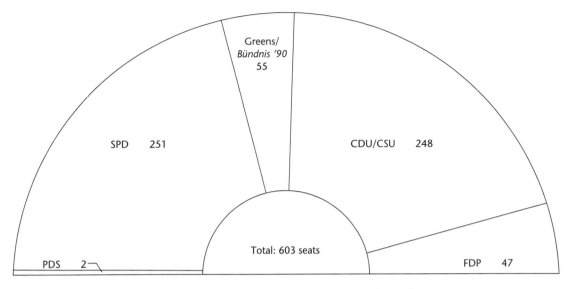

Figure 19.1   Distribution of Seats in the Fifteenth Bundestag (2002)

The Fifteenth German Bundestag was elected in September 2002. Currently,
603 deputies represent the Federal Republic of Germany's 61 million voters.

FRG until 1983, smaller parties tended to disappear, with most of their adherents gravitating toward the three major parties until the Green Party broke the 5 percent barrier and attained twenty-seven seats in the Bundestag in 1983. In the 1990 federal election, only the PDS and Bündnis '90 (an alternative, ecology-minded, former East German party, now merged with the West German Green Party) gained seats in the Bundestag as new parties. Both were successful in attaining representation in 1998, too, with the Greens joining the governing coalition for the first time. The extreme right-wing party, the Republikaner (Republicans), flirted with the 5 percent hurdle in several regional elections and threatened to exceed the threshold in the 1994 federal elections but ultimately received less than 2 percent of the popular vote.

Allocation of seats by party in the Bundestag, however, functions more like proportional representation. Specifically, the percentage of total seats won by each party corresponds to the party's percentage of the popular vote (providing the party receives the 5 percent minimum percentage to attain seats). For example, if a party's candidate wins a seat as an individual member, the candidate's party gains one fewer candidate from the list. In practice, most of the district seats are won by the two large parties, the Social Democrats and Christian Democrats (CDU), since the district vote is winner-take-all. The smaller parties' representatives, on the other hand, are almost always elected from the party lists. Thus, the list system creates stronger, more coherent parties. In countries with fragmented, individualistic parties, it is often harder to gain and hold effective majorities. In contrast, Willy Brandt's coalition governments from 1969 to 1974, formed from an alliance between the SPD and the Free Democratic Party (FDP), had

Stimmzettel

für die Wahl zum Deutschen Bundestag im Wahlkreis 136 Kreisfreie Stadt Wiesbaden am 2. Dezember 1990

Sie haben 2 Stimmen

hier 1 Stimme	hier 1 Stimme
für die Wahl	für die Wahl
eines/einer Wahlkreis-	einer Landesliste (Partei)
abgeordneten	- maßgebende Stimme für die Verteilung der Sitze insgesamt auf die einzelnen Parteien -
Erststimme	**Zweitstimme**

Figure 19.2   1990 Bundestag Election Ballot

With their "first vote," voters from the Bonn electoral district could choose a candidate by name from the left-hand column. The "second vote" in the right-hand column was to be cast for a party list at the federal level.

something harder to do when there are single-member districts.

We discuss the political parties below, but their general ideological coherence is essential to mention here, since Bundestag members belonging to the same parliamentary party almost always vote alike. This party unity contributes to consistency in the parties' positions over the course of a four-year legislative period and enables the electorate to identify each party's stance on a range of issues. Consequently, all parties and their representatives in the Bundestag can be held accountable by voters based on their support for their party's positions on the issues. This party discipline, in turn, helps produce more stable governments.

One direct result of party discipline is that the Federal Republic has high electoral participation (80–90 percent at the federal level). Some observers have argued that German citizens vote in such high numbers out of habit or duty.[2] Given the remarkable stability in the voting patterns of the three main postwar parties, with little deviation in each party's electoral outcome from election to election, it is more likely that high electoral participation is due to clear party ideology. And the newer parties, with similar kinds of ideological coherence, would seem to confirm this. For the FRG's fifty years, voting participation rates have matched or exceeded those of all other Western European countries.

The tradition of strong, unified parties in the Bundestag has had some drawbacks, however. The hierarchy within parties relegates newer members to a comparatively long period of apprenticeship as backbenchers. (Senior party members sit in the front benches of the Bundestag, as in other European legislatures, leaving the rear seats for newly elected members.) In fact, some of the Federal Republic's most prominent postwar politicians at the national level built up their visibility and political skill through long service in *Land* or local government service before using it as a springboard for national political power. For example, former

extremely narrow margins, and only strong party discipline enabled Brandt to remain in power. This mixed-member electoral system has become one of the most emulated in the world, particularly among democratizing countries because it combines local (geographical) representation with representation by ideology, class, gender, and/or religion. The list system enables party leaders to provide representation to diverse groups by placing individuals with different characteristics and attributes on the list,

SPD chancellor Willy Brandt was mayor of Berlin at the time of the construction of the Berlin Wall in 1961, former SPD chancellor Helmut Schmidt was mayor of Hamburg, and Helmut Kohl was for many years the dominant CDU regional official in his home *Land* of Rhineland-Palatinate.

Although this system does educate younger members in party ideology, it also frustrates particularly ambitious young legislators. They can become even more frustrated when their party is in power, because the dominance of the party elders increases at that time. The Federal Chancellery, as an administrative unit comprising the chancellor's top appointed officials, mentioned in Chapter 18, often controls the Bundestag by setting legislative agendas and making key policy decisions. Most bills originate with the chancellery and the ministries rather than with the Bundestag or Bundesrat. Thus, party discipline tends to channel committee discussion well within the broad position the party itself has taken, and the structure of the Bundestag discourages individual action by legislators.

The chancellor and the party leadership can lose touch with the backbench members of their party. For example, in the early 1980s Helmut Schmidt took positions—against stimulating the economy and for allowing the stationing of additional U.S. missiles on German soil—that the majority of his SPD strongly opposed. Thus, when the FDP attacked Schmidt on economic issues, his own party's rank and file also criticized him. Ultimately, any leadership of a governing party that fails to respond to its parliamentary membership or its voters, or both, will be forced to resign—as did Schmidt in 1982—or will lose in the next election.*

---

*The SPD/FDP coalition collapsed in October 1982 as the FDP chose to ally with the CDU/CSU. However, CDU leader Helmut Kohl believed that this unscheduled alternation of power needed ratification by German voters. So he called an early election in January 1983, and his newly formed coalition received a resounding victory.

The Bundesrat

As the upper house of the legislative ﹍ Bundesrat occupies a position quite ﹍ from those of the U.S. Senate and th﹍ House of Lords. The Bundesrat is the me﹍ by which the federal system of the coun﹍, ac-tually works. It is responsible for the distribution of powers between national and state levels and grants to the states the right to implement federal laws. It is literally the institutional intersection of the national and state governments, for it consists of members of the sixteen *Länder* governments. The total number of seats is sixty-nine, an increase from forty-five prior to unification, with each *Land* sending at least three representatives, depending on its population. States with more than 2 million residents have four votes, and states with more than 6 million have five votes. This system gives disproportionate representation to small *Länder* although nowhere near as disproportionately as the U.S. Senate gives to small American states. One might think that smaller states would be more conservative, but three of the small states are city-states (Berlin, Hamburg, Bremen) and usually vote for the left, so the political composition of the German *Länder* does not vary appreciably by size.

The political composition of the Bundesrat at any given time is determined by which parties are governing the *Länder*. Each of the sixteen *Länder* casts its votes in a bloc in the Bundesrat, depending on the views of the party or coalition in control of the state government at the time. Consequently, the party controlling the majority of *Länder* governments can have a significant effect on legislation passed in the Bundestag. And because *Länder* elections usually take place between Bundestag electoral periods, the Bundesrat majority can shift during the course of a Bundestag legislative period. For example, in the two years before the 1994 federal elections, the states governed by the SPD had a majority in the Bundesrat, which made it difficult for the Kohl government to implement all of its policies.

The Bundesrat must approve all amendments to the constitution, as well as all laws passed in the Bundestag that address the fundamental interests of the *Länder,* such as taxes, territorial integrity, and basic administrative functions. It also enjoys a *suspensive veto;* that is, if the Bundesrat should vote against a particular bill, the Bundestag needs only to pass the measure again by a simple majority to override the Bundesrat's veto. If a two-thirds majority of the Bundesrat votes against a bill, the Bundestag must pass it again by a two-thirds margin. In usual practice, however, the Bundesrat has not acted as a force of obstruction or gridlock. When the legislation is concurrent—that is, when the state and national governments jointly share administrative responsibilities for implementing the particular policy—there is almost always easy agreement between the two houses. Also, if a party or coalition has a stable majority in the Bundestag, then any possible obstruction by the Bundesrat can be overcome. For example, during most of his term as chancellor, Social Democrat Willy Brandt faced a Bundesrat that had a one-vote majority of Christian Democrats. However, since his SPD-FDP coalition also had a slim but firm majority in the Bundestag, he was able to overcome the Bundesrat's opposition on many issues and never lose a key vote.

The Bundesrat introduces comparatively little legislation. More bills are introduced in the Bundestag, though the majority of laws originate from the government itself through one of the ministries. However, the Bundesrat's administrative responsibilities are considerable. As *Länder* government officials, most of the members of the Bundesrat have significant experience in the implementation of particular laws. Their expertise is frequently called on in the committee hearings of the Bundestag, which are open to all Bundesrat members. This overlap (*Politikverflechtung*) is a unique feature of the Federal Republic. Many Americans make the mistake of equating German and U.S. federalism. Yet *Politikverflechtung* provides a qualita-

tively different relationship between national and state governments. The Federal Republic avoids the problems of administrative jurisdiction that sometimes plague other decentralized federal countries because many of the laws passed in the Bundestag are implemented at the *Land* level. This administrative arrangement enables the national government to use fewer employees than would be the case without *Politikverflechtung,* an extremely significant contribution of German federalism. Perhaps even more important, this arrangement avoids conflicts between the federal and state governments that often occur in the U.S. type of federal system of divided powers.

The Bundesrat's strong administrative role is a crucial component of the government. In different ways, this system avoids the shortcomings of both the fragmented legislative practices of the United States and the overly centralized policies of previous German regimes. Because the Bundesrat is concerned with shaping the framework of implementation, its role is more purposeful than that of the U.S. Congress, where laws that overlap or contradict previous legislation are frequently passed. For example, the Bundesrat coordinates the regional and national links between economic policies, vocational education systems, and the components of a major television network (ARD). The Bundesrat tends to be closer than the federal government to the concerns and needs of the entire country and provides a forum for understanding how national legislation will affect each *Land.* While the Bundesrat was originally envisioned to be more technocratic and less politically contentious than the popularly elected Bundestag, debates in the Bundesrat became strongly politicized in the 1970s and 1980s. The most common occurrence was increased conflict when regional elections caused a change in control of the Bundesrat, especially when this change gave more influence to the party, or group of parties, that was in opposition in the Bundestag.

With the increasing significance of the European Union (EU), the Bundesrat has a role to play here as well. It promotes representation for the *Länder* in EU institutions, most notably in the Council of Regions. It also successfully insisted on the German federal government's accepting that it could have a veto power over certain German positions on EU decisions.

The Party System and Elections

The following section details the functioning of the robust German political parties and identifies key patterns in FRG elections.

The Political Party System

Germany has a multiparty system that has proved remarkably stable for most of the post–World War II period.[3] Until the early 1980s, Germany had a "two-and-a-half" party system, made up of the moderate-left Social Democratic Party, the moderate-right Christian Democratic grouping (the CDU in most of the FRG and the Christian Social Union, CSU, in Bavaria), and the small, centrist Free Democratic Party (FDP). The ideological distance between these parties was not wide. Beginning in the late 1950s, the SPD broadened its base from its core working-class constituency to include more middle-class supporters. The CDU-CSU is a political grouping that includes both Catholics (mostly from the Bavarian-based CSU) and Protestants. The FDP is liberal in the European sense, meaning that it favors both free-market solutions to economic problems and extensive personal freedoms for individuals. Yet with only 5 to 10 percent of the electorate, it is a pragmatic party and almost always chooses to ally itself with one of the two large parties to form a government. During their time as the only parties on the political landscape (1953–1983), the SPD, CDU-CSU, and FDP presided over a stable, growing economy with a widely mixed public

and private sector agreement on economic and social policies.

During the 1980s and 1990s, three new parties arose to challenge the two-and-a-half major parties: the Greens–Bündnis '90, generally leftist and favoring ecology, environment, and peace; the PDS, the former Communist Party of East Germany; and the Republikaner, a sharply right-wing party, much more conservative than the CDU-CSU, that has emphasized nationalism and supported aggression toward immigrants and ethnic minorities. These additions have begun to complicate the comparatively tidy political landscape and promise to continue to do so. (See Table 19.2.)

The Greens–Bündnis '90 originated in 1979 and has been winning seats at national and regional levels; clearly it has become a permanent fixture. Because of the 5 percent rule, the Republikaner are not represented in the Bundestag, although the party has won seats in some local and regional bodies. The PDS is regionally concentrated in the five *Länder* of the former German Democratic Republic (GDR) and has received as much as 25 percent of the vote in the eastern German *Länder*, but it draws well under the 5 percent mark in the states of the former West Germany.

Because the parties are so important in shaping state policy, Germany has often been called a

Table 19.2 German Political Parties

Party of Democratic Socialism (PDS) (former Communist)
Greens–Bündnis '90 (environment)
Social Democratic Party (SPD) (left)
Free Democratic Party (FDP) (center)
Christian Democrats (right)
  Christian Democratic Union (CDU)
  Christian Social Union (CSU)
Republikaner (far right)

party democracy. However, criticism of the major parties surfaced in the late 1980s and throughout the 1990s owing to several financial and political scandals involving members of all three. For example, one major CDU state official was found dead under suspicious circumstances, former FDP officials have been subject to financial investigations, and former CDU chancellor Helmut Kohl's financial scandal has been the most recent. Such developments have provided increased opportunities for the new parties and could possibly disturb the relatively stable political party landscape.

Social Democratic Party. As the leading party of the left in Germany, the SPD has had a long history. Founded in the 1860s in response to rapid German (and Prussian) industrialization, the SPD survived Bismarck's attempts in the 1880s to outlaw it and grew to be the largest party in the Reichstag by 1912. The party was badly split by World War I, however, with the more "evolutionary" (or reformist) wing supporting the war and the imperial German government. The "revolutionary" wing saw the war as an opportunity to defeat capitalism in all countries; they viewed support of bourgeois governments' war efforts as representing a fundamental betrayal of the international working class.[4] Following World War I, the evolutionary socialists who controlled the SPD helped it become the leading party of the Weimar Republic during its early years. The revolutionary socialists joined either the Kommunistische Partei Deutschlands (KPD, the original Communist Party) or the short-lived Independent Social Democratic Party (Unabhängige Sozialdemokratische Partei Deutschlands—USPD), a party that lasted only until the early 1920s. Such splits among the left-wing parties proved fatal for the SPD in the Weimar period. The lack of a united left prevented a clear response to the growing economic and social turmoil and thereby indirectly helped the Nazis find a path to power.

When the SPD reemerged after 1945, it was initially in a strong position to play a dominant role in rebuilding Germany. Industrialists and the conservative Weimar parties had been discredited by their relationship with the Nazis, and the SPD retained its evolutionary commitment to both democracy and socialism. In the immediate postwar years, the SPD, under the leadership of Kurt Schumacher, led the call for the nationalization of industry under democratic control, the provision for a vast array of welfare state measures to rebuild the country, and a return to the participatory workplace structures (the workers councils) that had been curtailed by the early Weimar governments.

Despite its strong influence from 1945 to 1948, the SPD was able to obtain only about 30 percent of the popular vote from 1949 until the early 1960s, compared with the CDU-CSU's far larger 45 to 50 percent. Some of its critics observed that the party's inability to achieve wider influence resulted from its continued emphasis on its working-class origins and reliance on a Marxist-based ideology. More sympathetic observers believed that the cold war, the Communist GDR just to the east, and the economic miracle of the 1950s all played a major role in reducing the party's influence. In any event, the SPD was politically marginalized in the 1950s. The party formed municipal governments in a few of the major cities and regional governments in several traditionally strong northwestern *Länder*, but it exercised little national influence.

In an attempt to broaden its constituency, the SPD altered its party program at a 1959 party conference in Bad Godesberg. Abandoning its heavy reliance on Marxism, its new goal was to become what political scientist Otto Kirchheimer has called a "catchall party"[5]—a party seeking to "catch all" voters wherever they were located in the social structure or ideological spectrum. The SPD neither relinquished Marxism completely nor ceased to be a party representing the working class, but it began to seek and attract support from groups outside the traditional blue-collar working class. Among these were service sector workers, elements of the middle class, professional employees, and defectors from the Free Democrats or Christian Democrats. The Bad Godesberg conference transformed the SPD from a more rigidly Marxist party into a moderate center-left party more like other Western European social democratic parties.

The SPD finally won a place as the leading member of a majority coalition in 1969. It increased its share of the vote to 42.7 percent, compared with the CDU-CSU's 46.1 percent. However, it was able to propose a new coalition government with the FDP, which had received 5.8 percent of the vote. Although the two parties had less than 50 percent of the popular vote, their combined forces were larger than those of the CDU-CSU, and they attained a bare majority of the apportioned Bundestag seats after the smaller parties with fewer than 5 percent of the vote were discounted.

The center-left SPD-FDP coalition appeared shaky at first (it had a slim majority until its reelection in 1972), but it was able to stay in power for thirteen years.[6] The SPD brought to the coalition concern for increased welfare and social spending, arising partly from pressure by the Extraparliamentary Opposition (Ausserparliamentarische Opposition—APO), and the FDP brought its support for increased individual freedom of expression at a time when young people in all industrialized societies were raising this issue. However, the one factor that helped cement the interests of these two dissimilar parties for such a long time was the strong performance of the Federal Republic's economy. In fact, the coalition came apart in the early 1980s only after an economic recession prevented the increased social spending demanded by the SPD left. The recession also induced the FDP to define individualism less in terms of free expression and more in terms of an antistatist, free-market economic position.

Defeated in the 1983 Bundestag election, the SPD spent its many years out of power (until 1998) trying to formulate alternative policies to challenge the center-right CDU/CSU-FDP coalition. Unfortunately for the SPD, it did not take advantage of this opportunity. Under the leadership of Hans Jochen Vogel in the mid-1980s, Oskar Lafontaine in the late 1980s, Bjorn Engholm in the early 1990s, and Rudolf Scharping in the mid-1990s, it was unable to formulate clear alternative policies to make itself attractive to its members, supporters, and voters. Nor could it forge a durable coalition with the Greens to challenge the center-right coalition, develop positions on European integration that would induce supporters to turn in the party's direction, or take advantage of the opportunity to capture support in the former GDR during and after the unification process. After the 1994 Bundestag elections, the SPD remained uncertain about social and ideological identity. It continued to agonize over whether it should reemphasize its working-class roots and perhaps take support from the PDS in the east, or find some new synthesis of positions that could blunt the rising support going to the Greens. Its electoral support remained stuck in the upper 30 percent range. Options for the SPD seemed limited.

However, in 1998 the Kohl regime had exhausted its mandate, and voters punished Kohl for overpromising the speed of transformation in eastern Germany. An effective Gerhard Schröder campaign to search for a *neue Mitte* (a new center) enabled the SPD to step into the void created by the CDU's decline, increase the share of its vote by 5 percent over 1994, and emerge as Germany's leading party. Schröder's consolidation of power came at the cost of distancing himself from some of the left-leaning members of the party rank and file. The forcing out of Oskar Lafontaine, the party's left tribune, may have made Schröder's move to the middle easier in the short run. But alienating the party's hard core may prove costly in the long run, much as it did for Helmut Schmidt in the early 1980s. Schröder's prospects for reelection in 2002 seemed dim, given the slow economic growth that occurred in his first term. But his opposition to U.S. policy on Iraq proved to be the decisive factor in his reelection in the fall of that year.

Christian Democrats. The CDU is found in all *Länder* except Bavaria; the CSU is its affiliated Bavarian grouping.[7] Unlike the other older parties in the Federal Republic, the CDU-CSU did not originate until immediately following World War II, when most centrist and conservative parties wished to avoid the bickering and divisiveness of the Weimar period and establish a counterweight to the SPD.[8] The moderate leaders of the nonleftist parties feared that after the war the SPD would represent a mostly united left, while the forces of the right were both fragmented and discredited by the close ties some of their members had to the Nazi Party. Consequently, several of the moderate conservatives proposed the creation of a Christian party grouping, which not only would finally unite Catholics and Protestants in one confessional (Christian) party, but would also serve as a catchall party of the center-right, incorporating the various nonleftist elements (including "rehabilitated" ex-Nazis).

Programmatically, the CDU-CSU stressed the social market economy (*Soziale Marktwirtschaft*). The social market economy was neither a social democratic state (such as contemporary Sweden) nor a pure market economy (as expounded by the Reagan and both Bush administrations in the United States and by the Thatcher and Major governments in Britain). Rather, it blended elements of both forms to create a society that not only was procapitalist but also had a paternalistic sense of social responsibility. In fact, this synthesis joined the interests of a wide range of the party's supporters. The most active supporter of the market side of the equation was Adenauer's economics minister for most of the 1950s (and later the chancellor), Ludwig Erhard. Favoring the social side were the Christian trade unionists whose ideology derived from the Catholic tradition, which celebrated the value of human work, and from the Protestant work ethic.

After the SPD and the FDP established their center-left coalition in 1969, the CDU-CSU spent thirteen years as the opposition party.

During this period, the popularity of SPD policies and the unpopularity of the CDU-CSU leadership prevented the Christian Democrats from mounting a strong challenge to the SPD-FDP coalition. It was not until that coalition collapsed in 1982 over economic policies that the CDU-CSU returned to power in a coalition with the FDP. Political pundits called this *Die Wende* (the turnaround), but the Christian Democrats' return had more to do with the SPD's failure to manage the economy and the coalition with the FDP than with any new ideological tendency.

Despite the electoral rhetoric about change and a turnaround, the first CDU-led Kohl government (1983–1987) made no dramatic new programmatic overtures. In fact, many observers were predicting that the stolid and colorless Kohl would either lose the next election or be challenged within the party for the chancellorship. Kohl was not an ideologue in the mold of Britain's Margaret Thatcher and the United States's Ronald Reagan, and many criticized him for his plodding, pragmatic style. How, then, was he able to maintain his leadership of both the CDU-CSU and the center-right coalition for sixteen years, including four times that he led his coalition to electoral victory? It is important to stress that the nature of the German party system—in fact, of *any* parliamentary system—places a premium on the leader's ability to manage the party as an institution. In this task, Helmut Kohl was the consummate party leader. He reportedly knew the name of every Christian Democratic mayor (*Bürgermeister*) in the entire Federal Republic. With his mastery of such allegedly pedestrian skills, he maintained and reinforced his leadership of the Christian Democrats. There is, of course, nothing pedestrian about winning four consecutive federal elections—the most of any chancellor in the FRG!

During the mid-1980s, two additional factors played into Kohl's, and the CDU's, hands. One was the lack of a clear alternative position by the SPD opposition that could challenge the center-right coalition. The other was the strong CDU-CSU position in support of strengthening

European integration. The SPD, on the other hand, was more divided in its position on the EU. Taken together, these factors enabled the Christian Democrats and Helmut Kohl to find their stride as the dominant political forces in the Federal Republic through the early years after unification.

In the wake of the problems of the 1990s, some of the earlier criticisms of Kohl began to surface again, focusing on his apparent over-selling of unification and his lack of leadership in the face of the challenges of resurgent racism and Germany's geopolitical position after the cold war. With the end of the cold war and the tensions surrounding European integration and German unification, some party divisions surfaced. The first originated from the Bavarian CSU, led by Finance Minister Theo Waigel, and proposed a more conservative policy toward immigrants and minorities. The second was the more independent position—in favor of government intervention—of the regional CDU branches in eastern Germany. Concern also rose within the CDU/CSU-FDP governing coalition after the 1994 elections, because the FDP only barely achieved the 5 percent of the vote necessary for representation. The Christian Democrats reached political exhaustion with the 1998 federal election, in which they lost power for the first time since 1982. While the party can point to the truly significant accomplishments of German unification and European integration, it also had to face the daunting task of replacing both Helmut Kohl and his deputy Wolfgang Schäuble, both of whom were implicated in the disastrous fund-raising scandal of 1999 and 2000.

As it came to grips with its opposition role early in the new century, the Christian Democrats found themselves undercut by Gerhard Schröder's *neue Mitte* policies. Long accustomed to seeing themselves as the party that supported Germany's organized capitalist economy, they found that Schröder's government had "stolen" their primary base of support. As it searched for a new focus in opposition, the Christian Democrats have unfortunately seized on a mild form

of nationalism, stressing patriotism and German *Leitkultur* (guiding culture) as its new themes early in the new century. For most countries, such policies would be understandable—if not admirable—but the rules are different for Germany. At a time when new citizenship laws have been passed and German industry encourages increased immigration, particularly for information industry jobs, such calls for a stronger German culture are tinged with ugly memories of the Nazi period. Gerhard Schröder and even German business have criticized the Christian Democrats on this point, with the chancellor strongly stating, "The last time German conservatism gave into the seductions of nationalism, Social Democrats suffered and died fighting the fascists."[9]

The Greens. The Green Party is a heterodox party that first drew support from a number of different constituencies in the late 1970s and early 1980s: urban-based citizen action groups (*Bürgerinitiativen*), ecological activists, farmers, anti-nuclear-power activists, the remnants of the peace movement, and small bands of Marxist-Leninists. After making it over the 5 percent hurdle for the first time in the 1983 Bundestag elections, the party went on to win seats in most *Länder* in subsequent regional elections by stressing noneconomic, quality-of-life issues. The electoral successes of this "antiparty party" caused a new and serious internal division between its two ideological wings: the *Realos* (realists, or pragmatists) and the *Fundis* (fundamentalists, or hard-core environmentalists). In the mid-1980s, the realists, who thought it important to enter political institutions to gain access to power, won the upper hand over the fundamentalists, who unalterably opposed any collaboration with existing parties, regardless of whether some goals of the Greens could thereby be attained.

This choice was no guarantee of long-term success for the Greens, as all of the other parties began to include environmental and qualitative issues in their party programs. The position and direction of the Greens remained uncertain in the early and mid-1990s. To be sure, they continued to win seats in regional and local elections. But like the SPD, they were caught off guard by both the process of European integration and, especially, the rapid move toward German unification during 1990. Many Green Party members were opposed to both developments, and the party lost strength as the twin processes of unification proceeded.

Until the merger with Bündnis '90, the Greens' position looked bleak. The party's squabbling about *fundi* or *realo* positions undercut its credibility among potential new supporters. Its inability to grasp the seriousness of unification and develop relevant positions made it appear unwilling to deal with reality. The ability of other parties to address what had formerly been Green issues, such as the environment, made the Greens' specific appeal less distinctive. Finally, the Green Party's failure to motivate its own core constituency ultimately proved the party's undoing. Electoral turnout for general elections in the Federal Republic averaged between 84 and 90 percent for every election between 1953 and 1987. However, electoral turnout for the 1990 federal election reached only 78 percent; in 1994 it was up slightly, to 79 percent. Several postelection analyses found that a disproportionate share of the nonvoters were former Greens' supporters. Further embarrassing the party in 1990 was the success of Bündnis '90 in attaining seats by virtue of obtaining 6.0 percent of the vote in the former GDR territory. Before the general election, the Western Greens had spurned an offer from Bündnis '90 to run a joint ticket. Had the Greens done so, the resulting Green alliance would have won 5.1 percent of the total vote, enough for representation in the Bundestag. It was this embarrassment for the Greens that eventually led to merger with Bündnis '90.

The persistent ecological problems of the five *Länder* of the former GDR have presented the Greens with a tremendous opportunity to gain strength. With the Greens–Bündnis '90 merger

in 1993, a 5 percent electoral share and a position in parliament appeared certain for the foreseeable future. In the 1994 elections, however, the Greens attained a somewhat disappointing 6 percent of the vote after preelection polls had them closer to 10 percent. In 1998, the Greens raised their share of the vote to 6.7 percent and became the junior coalition partner of the SPD in the first democratic left government since the beginning of the Weimar Republic. Previous SPD-led governments in the FRG were coalitions with the centrist FDP. The Greens increased their strength to 8.6 percent in the 2002 elections, largely at the expense of the SPD. Joschka Fischer, the Greens' party leader, became the coalition's foreign minister, and the Greens obtained four of the fourteen cabinet ministries, the other three being the Interior, Health, and Environment Ministries. The party's base appeared to be a firm 6 percent, and it is likely to remain a permanent fixture in the German Bundestag, whether in coalition or on the opposition benches.

Free Democratic Party. The FDP's philosophy is Germany's closest equivalent to the individualistic impulses of the British liberal movement.[10] Here we emphasize again that *liberal* is used in the European context to mean an emphasis on the individual, as opposed to an activist state tradition.

The FDP's major influence is its role as a swing party, since it has allied with each of the two major parties at different periods since 1949. In fact, it has been included in the governing coalition for almost the entire history of the FRG. Clearly, the influence of the FDP has been disproportionate to its electoral strength of 5 to 10 percent of the voters. The primary reasons for the party's key position are the discrediting of the central state after the Nazi abuses, the role of the U.S. occupation forces and their preference for free-market economic arrangements, and the effects of the cold war. These factors increased the importance of nonleftist parties in the eyes of both the Allied powers and the citizens of the

Federal Republic, and the FDP was happy to play the nonleftist role.

The FDP's perspective is an expression of two ideologies, broadly characterized here as economic liberalism and social liberalism. During the postwar period, the FDP has relied on both philosophies to ally with the CDU-CSU and the SPD. Until 1998, the FDP was out of the cabinet only twice since 1949: during the CDU-CSU majority from 1957 to 1961 and during the Grand Coalition from 1966 to 1969. Moreover, the FDP has almost always had either the economics ministry or the foreign ministry, or both, in the various coalition governments.

The party has carefully nurtured its centrist position in the Federal Republic's politics by applying one or another of its political leanings to soften the ideological profile of the major party with which it is allied at the time. For example, in the early 1980s, during the latter years of the center-left Schmidt governments, the FDP acted as a strong counterweight to the leftist demands for more public spending made by many of the SPD rank and file. In fact, many of these SPD members described the FDP as the tail that wagged the SPD dog. On the other hand, after the center-right Kohl government took office in 1983, the FDP resisted the CDU-CSU's desire to increase the government's capacity for surveillance of individual citizens of the Federal Republic.

By adopting a strategy of allying with first one major party and then the other, the FDP has occasionally been accused of lacking strong political conviction. Critics view the FDP as a small collection of notables whose primary adherence to the party has been as a vehicle to gain important cabinet posts. Each time this accusation has been prominent, generally after a change of government, the FDP seems to have so disillusioned its voters as to fall below the 5 percent necessary for representation in the Bundestag. In fact, during the early and mid-1990s, the FDP failed to reach the 5 percent minimum in several *Land* elections. However, the Federal Republic's voters have generally been reluctant to give either of the two large parties an absolute majority. This occurred only from 1957 to 1961.

Throughout the history of the FRG, voters have always been induced to turn to the FDP as a buffer against the SPD and the CDU-CSU. But its flirting with the 5 percent electoral hurdle and falling below it in numerous *Länder* elections have been a constant worry for the party since unification. For years, many individuals have foretold the demise of the FDP, but the party has regularly frustrated these predictions. In fact, the party's stock rose considerably during the late 1980s and early 1990s, as it took leading and forceful positions—owing largely to the efforts of Foreign Minister Hans-Dietrich Genscher—on European integration and German unification. Yet just before the 1994 election, the FDP was again dropping badly in preelection polls. Under the leadership of Klaus Kinkel, the FDP survived the election with 6.9 percent of the vote, thus retaining its representation in the Bundestag.

The FDP's electoral drop from 1990 (when it received 11 percent) was very worrying for the party, especially when its electoral support dropped to 6.2 percent in the 1998 election (below the level of the Greens) and went into opposition for the first time since 1969. The party's fortunes looked especially bleak until the CDU financial scandal in 1999, when moderate German voters began searching for political alternatives. Under the leadership of Wolfgang Gerhardt, the party has rebounded in several *Land* elections since 1998 and once again seems to have avoided demise. Of course, what is different in the new century for the FDP is that it is no longer the balance wheel between the two large parties, serving as a constant coalition maker. Rather, the emergence of both the Greens and the PDS as contenders for non-SPD and non-CDU voters means that the political space for the FDP is threatened. Similarly, the emergence of other small-party alternatives means that the FDP will no longer have the luxury of serving as the political kingmaker in the FRG. However, the fact that the FPD increased its share of the vote in 2002 to

7.4 percent suggests that rumors of the party's demise were premature.

Party of Democratic Socialism. The PDS (known as the Sozialistische Einheitspartei Deutschlands [SED]—the Socialist Unity Party—in its GDR days) is concentrated in the five *Länder* of the former GDR. It has had a long and tortuous history. It sprang from the KPD's founding immediately after World War I, at the time of the Russian Revolution, when all socialist and labor parties split on the issue of evolutionary or revolutionary socialism. The KPD split from the SPD in 1919, following the success of the Russian Revolution, and continually attacked the SPD until both were outlawed and suppressed by the Nazis.

Following World War II, the KPD reappeared only briefly in West Germany and eventually disappeared in 1956, when it was banned by the Constitutional Court. Several factors were responsible for its demise. Prior to Hitler's rise to power in 1933, a major area of the KPD's support was in the northeastern part of Germany. After World War II, this area became the GDR. Within the newly defined West Germany, there remained a much smaller constituency for the KPD. In addition, the onset of the cold war in the late 1940s seriously eroded the KPD's support in West Germany, although the party did receive 5.7 percent of the vote in the Federal Republic's first election in 1949. However, the intensity of the postwar anti-Communist thrust was particularly damaging to the KPD in West Germany. West German leaders took advantage of these events to propagandize against communism, and the KPD's support diminished continually until the party was banned by the Constitutional Court.

In the GDR, on the other hand, the Communists had a very different history. This party dominated all aspects of life in the GDR under the successive leadership of Walter Ulbricht, Willi Stoph, and Erich Honecker, and was considered the most Stalinist and repressive of the Soviet client Communist parties. It was under this leadership that the dreaded Stasi secret police grew and ran roughshod on GDR citizens.

Thus, it is no wonder that the SED quickly changed its name to the PDS in 1990 as the process of unification gathered speed. Under the leadership of postunification party leader Gregor Gysi, the PDS showed considerable immediate strength in the five *Länder* of the former GDR, winning between 9 percent and 15 percent of the vote during the October 14, 1990, *Ländtag* elections and 11.1 percent of the vote in these *Länder* in the first all-German elections on December 2, 1990. The new PDS was plagued, however, by the legacy of corruption and wasteful extravagance under the Honecker regime and the secret transfer of millions of deutsche marks to the Soviet Union after unification had taken place in October 1990.

By the mid-1990s, the difficulties of unification had created renewed strength for the PDS. In regional and local elections in eastern Germany, it attained over 20 percent of the vote and won four directly elected seats in the 1994 federal election. The winning of four individual seats on the direct portion of the ballot gave the party representation in the Bundestag even though its overall vote percentage on the party portion of the ballot in the entire country fell just under the 5 percent threshold. In the 1998 election, the PDS not only won the same four individual seats but also crossed the 5 percent threshold to 5.1. It received only 4.0 percent in the 2002 elections, failing to get representation from the PR list voting. But it did win two directly elected seats in Berlin, so it had two members in the 2002 Bundestag. Thus, the PDS remains a significant force in German politics, especially in the east. It even formed a coalition government with the SPD in the *Land* of Saxony during 1994.

While the idea of the PDS's participating in governing coalitions in other *Länder* or at the federal level seems beyond the pale to many observers, this "permanent" political pariah status once was believed to prevent the Greens from participating in governing coalitions. Both the

Greens and the PDS quite likely have benefited from the democratizing influence of a multi-party parliamentary democracy that allows all significant parties to find their democratic voice. To some observers, the most interesting development regarding the PDS is that it is not really a Communist party anymore. Rather, it has become a regionally based party beseeching the national government for greater resources. In the new century, the PDS's primary challenge is not so much being seen as a legitimate party as much as its need to deal with its demographic problem. The average age of both PDS members and voters is between fifty and sixty. Until and unless the party is able to replenish itself with younger supporters, it might still have to worry about the 5 percent threshold, as the 2002 results suggest.

The Far Right.   There are three far-right political parties that have won seats in regional parliaments since the 1990s: the Republikaner, the Deutsche Volksunion (DVU), and the neo-Nazi Nationaldemokratische Partei Deutschland (NPD). None, however, have come close to winning seats in the Bundestag. The latter two parties have won regional seats in 2004, and will be discussed in Chapter 20.

The Republikaner were formed in the late 1980s when increasing numbers of non-Germans began arriving in Germany as European integration started.[11] There had been various splinter-group right-wing parties throughout the Federal Republic's history, but with the exception of the National Democratic Party of Germany (NPD), which received 4.3 percent of the vote in 1969, they had never seriously threatened to win seats in the Bundestag. The Republikaner's strength in local and regional elections in 1989 suggested that this right-wing party might finally break through the 5 percent threshold.

But the pace at which the Kohl government conducted the unification process in the early 1990s had a devastating impact on the far-right Republikaner and its leader, former Nazi SS soldier Franz Shönhuber. In effect, Kohl's speedy and comparatively pragmatic process of unification had stolen the very essence of the Republikaner appeal.

As the difficulties of European integration and German unification mounted in the mid-1990s, the Republikaner became a "safe" political outlet for the neo-Nazi sentiments that people did not publicly admit. In fact, in *Land* elections during 1992 and 1993, the Republikaner continually surpassed preelection predictions, because some of the party's voters did not tell pollsters how they would actually vote. In the mid-1990s, this far-right party apparently once again threatened to achieve the 5 percent threshold necessary for Bundestag representation. The continuing difficulties of unification should have been a major advantage for the Republikaner. One of the party's primary appeals had been to those in both the eastern and the western parts of the Federal Republic who wished to see the renewal of a resurgent German nationalism to counter the rising tide of internationalism that European integration represented. However, the 1994 elections were a disaster for the Republikaner, who fell to less than 1.7 percent of the vote. And in 1998, the Republikaner failed to approach 5 percent again. For a country that has had such a heinous history of right-wing extremism, modern German voters have been remarkable in failing to allow such parties into elected office.

Electoral Procedure and Results

The German electoral system has produced two significant outcomes. The first is coherence among the parties, since the system—and the constitution itself, for that matter—specifically supports the parties as essential organizations for political democracy. Second, the 5 percent hurdle ensures that only parties that command significant support attain seats in the Bundestag. This rule has helped Germany avoid the wild proliferation of parties in such democracies as Italy and Israel, which has made coalition formation difficult in those countries.

As Table 19.3 suggests, Germany has had no volatile electoral swings. There have been four major periods of party dominance since 1949: the CDU/CSU-FDP coalition from 1949 to 1966; the Grand Coalition "interregnum" (1966–1969); the SPD-led coalition (1969–1982); and the CDU-CSU-led coalition from 1982 to 1998. And with the election of the Red-Green government in 1998, Germany could be poised for a fifth period of stable rule. The major uncertainty will be how well the two new parties in the Bundestag since the mid-1980s and early 1990s (Greens and PDS, respectively) find their niche.

Political Culture, Citizenship, and Identity

Germany never had a strong individualistic ethos; rather it is a country dominated by organized collectivities, as shown by the organization of interests and social movements. This characteristic is visible not only among major economic producer groups but also among political parties (in which participatory membership is high) and a wide range of social groups. However, the FRG's strong collective identities have enhanced rather than diminished the country's relationship to democracy. Germany's political culture thus offers a strong contrast to the individualism characteristic of Anglo-American countries. German citizenship historically has been based primarily on the ethnicity of one's parents, making the granting of citizenship to those of non-German ethnicity problematic until relatively recently. For much of its history, including much of the post-WWII period, Germany has taken a comparatively restrictive—some even say racist—position. The opening of the EU could potentially change this landscape significantly.

Social Class and Cleavage Structures

In analyzing Germany's social forces since industrialization in the late nineteenth century,

class was and is a primary category. Germany's working class remains larger and more prosperous than those of Britain, France, or Italy, and it has thrived as postwar Germany's high-wage, high-skill, export-oriented industries have provided substantial material benefits to its mostly unionized workforce. While class remains a salient cleavage, other significant social divisions have been based on religion and region, with the former less significant than the latter. Although the population in the southeast, portions of the southwest, and along the Rhine as far north as Düsseldorf is predominantly Catholic, and although in the northwest, northeast, and portions of the southwest, one finds predominantly Lutheran Protestants, this cleavage is not particularly significant. Collective identities are also determined on regional divisions, which only rarely are based on religious cleavages. Many of the pre-1871 German states have retained considerable autonomy, which is often manifested in different traditions and customs. In many respects, the creation of a *Federal* (rather than unitary) Republic of Germany was due to these regional divisions. Of course, during the late nineteenth century, and particularly during the first half of the twentieth, ethnicity and race were major lines of social demarcation, with monstrous consequences.

Interest groups behave differently in the Federal Republic than they do in the Anglo-Saxon countries. In the Federal Republic, interest groups are seen as having a societal role and responsibility that transcends the immediate interests of their members. Germany's public law traditions, deriving from Roman and Napoleonic legal foundations, specifically allow private interests to perform public functions, albeit within a clear and specific general framework. The *Krankenkassen* (sickness funds), which provide national health insurance, are the best example. Thus, interest groups are seen as part of the fabric of society and are virtually permanent institutions. A social premium is placed on their adaptation and ability to respond to new issues. To speak of winners and losers in such an

Table 19.3   FRG Election Results, 1949–2002

Year	Party	Percentage of Vote	Government	Year	Party	Percentage of Vote	Government
1949	Voter turnout	78.5	CDU/CSU-FDP	1980	Voter turnout	88.6	SPD-FDP
	CDU/CSU	31.0			CDU/CSU	44.5	
	SPD	29.2			SPD	42.9	
	FDP	11.9			FDP	10.6	
	Others	27.8			Others	0.5	
1953	Voter turnout	86.0	CDU/CSU-FDP	1983	Voter turnout	89.1	CDU/CSU-FDP
	CDU/CSU	45.2			CDU/CSU	48.8	
	SPD	28.8			SPD	38.2	
	FDP	9.5			FDP	7.0	
	Others	16.7			Greens	5.6	
1957	Voter turnout	87.8	CDU/CSU		Others	0.5	
	CDU/CSU	50.2		1987	Voter turnout	84.3	CDU/CSU-FDP
	SPD	31.8			CDU/CSU	44.3	
	FDP	7.7			SPD	37.0	
	Others	10.3			FDP	9.1	
1961	Voter turnout	87.8	CDU/CSU-FDP		Greens	8.3	
	CDU/CSU	45.3			Others	1.3	
	SPD	36.2		1990	Voter turnout	78.0	CDU/CSU-FDP
	FDP	12.8			CDU/CSU	43.8	
	Others	5.7			SPD	33.5	
1965	Voter turnout	86.8	CDU/CSU-SPD		FDP	11.0	
	CDU/CSU	47.6	Grand		Greens	3.8	
	SPD	39.3	Coalition		PDS	2.4	
	FDP	9.5			Bündnis '90	1.2	
	Others	3.6			Others	3.5	
1969	Voter turnout	86.7	SPD-FDP	1994	Voter turnout	79.0	CDU/CSU-FDP
	CDU/CSU	46.1			CDU/CSU	41.5	
	SPD	42.7			SPD	36.4	
	FDP	5.8			FDP	6.9	
	Others	5.4			Greens	7.3	
1972	Voter turnout	86.0	SPD-FDP		PDS	4.4	
	CDU/CSU	44.9			Others	3.5	
	SPD	45.8		1998	Voter turnout	82.3	SPD-Greens
	FDP	9.5			SPD	40.9	
	Others	16.7			CDU/CSU	35.1	
1976	Voter turnout	90.7	SPD-FDP		Greens	6.7	
	CDU/CSU	48.2			FDP	6.2	
	SPD	42.6			PDS	5.1	
	FDP	7.9			Others	6.0	
	Others	0.9		2002	Voter turnout	79.1	SPD-Greens
					SPD	38.5	
					CDU/CSU	36.0	
					Greens	8.6	
					FDP	7.4	
					PDS	4.0	
					Others	3.0	

Source: American Institute for Contemporary German Studies, 2004 (http://www.aicgs.org/wahlen/index.shtml).

arrangement is to misunderstand the ability of existing interest groups to make incremental changes over time.

By being structurally integrated into the fabric of society, German interest groups have an institutional longevity surpassing that of interest groups in most other industrialized countries. But how does the German state mediate the relationship among interest groups? Peter Katzenstein observes that in the Federal Republic, "the state is not an actor but a series of relationships," and these relationships are solidified in what he has called "parapublic institutions."[12] As noted in Chapter 18, the parapublics encompass a wide variety of organizations; among the most important are the Bundesbank, the institutions of codetermination, the labor courts, the social insurance funds, and the employment office. Under prevailing German public law, rooted in pre-1871 feudal traditions, Katzenstein states they have been assigned the role of "independent governance by the representatives of social sectors at the behest of or under the general supervision of the state." In other words, organizations that are seen as mere interest groups in other countries are combined in Germany with certain quasi-governmental agencies so that together they have a much more parapublic role in the Federal Republic.

Employer associations and trade unions are the key interest groups within German society, but they are not alone.* Other, less influential groups include the Protestant and Catholic churches, the Farmers Association (Deutscher Bauernverband), the Association of Artisans (Handwerk Verein), the Federal Chamber of Physicians (Bundesaerztekammer), and the now nearly defunct League of Expelled Germans

(Bund der Vertriebenen Deutschen, BVD), which has represented the interests of emigrants from the GDR and Eastern Europe. Each of these groups has been tightly integrated into various parapublic institutions to perform a range of important social functions that in other countries might be performed by state agencies. These organizations are forced to assume a degree of social responsibility in their roles in policy implementation that goes beyond what political scientist Arnold Heidenheimer has called the "freewheeling competition of 'selfish' interest groups."[13]

For example, the churches, through the state, assess a church tax on all citizens who have been born into the Protestant or Catholic Church. This tax provides the churches with a steady stream of income and ensures institutional permanence, but it also compels the churches to play a major role in the provision of social welfare and in aiding the families of *Gastarbeiter* (guest workers). The Farmers Association has been a pillar of support for both the FDP and the CDU-CSU, and for decades has strongly influenced the agricultural ministry. It has also resisted attempts by the EU to lower the agricultural support provided to European farmers in the form of direct subsidies as part of the EU's common agricultural policy. The Association of Artisans is a major component of the German chamber of commerce (Der Deutsche Industrie- und Handelskammer—DIHK), to which all firms in Germany *must* belong, and the Chamber of Physicians has been intimately involved with both the legislation and implementation of social and medical insurance (social security and general welfare).

These interest groups, and the parapublic agencies within which they function, attempt to contain social conflict through multiple, small-scale corporatist institutions. The Federal Republic's corporatist variant in the 1980s was much more regionalized and industry-specific, and much less centralized, than earlier national-level conceptions of corporatism. Yet this system of interest groups and parapublics still must ex-

*German industry is represented by the BDI (Federal Association of German Industry), and employers are represented by the BDA (Federal Association of German Employers). The former addresses issues pertaining to industry as a whole; the latter focuses specifically on issues of concern to employers. German workers are represented by eight different unions, organized by industry, which belong to the DGB (German Trade Union Confederation).

press the concerns of member organizations, channel conflict, and recommend (and sometimes implement) public policy.

Citizenship and National Identity

Perhaps the most contentious issue of citizenship and identity has surrounded the political asylum question. Following World War II, Germany passed one of the world's most liberal political asylum laws, in part to help atone for the Nazis' political repression of millions. The German government granted immediate asylum status to all those who claimed persecution or fear of persecution based on violated political freedoms and allowed those asylum seekers to remain in Germany, with considerable monetary support, until each individual's case was heard. Often this process took years. With the end of the cold war and the opening of East European borders, the trickle of asylum seekers turned into a flood in the minds of some Germans. This sentiment caused the Kohl government to curtail drastically the right of political asylum, a step that called into question whether Germany's democracy was as mature and well developed as it claimed during the stable postwar period. Germany's commitment to democratic rights appeared to contain some new conditions, and many of them involved a definition of identity that looked remarkably insular in a Europe otherwise becoming more international.[14]

Examples of this restrictive aspect of naturalization are evident in the wake of the breakdown of the Eastern bloc. The immigration of ethnic Germans, the presence of *Gastarbeiter* who have been in Germany for two generations and are only now slowly obtaining citizenship, and the volatile political asylum question have all placed strains on the concept of citizenship in the post-unification years. Yet the expansion of the EU to twenty-five countries threatens to exacerbate questions of both citizenship and national identity. For many poor citizens in those ten new EU countries that are in Eastern Europe, Berlin looks like a very powerful magnet drawing these individuals in search for a better life. Until now, German post-WWII history has acted as a powerful brake on anti-ethnic, nativist sentiment. The FRG's generous asylum laws are a prime example of this commitment. However, the much more fluid world of the EU, in both citizenship and national identity terms, will likely prove a significant challenge for Germany.

Ethnicity

In the late 1980s and the 1990s, some of the optimistic views that Germany had become a "normal" parliamentary democracy were challenged by the nature of anti-ethnic and anti-immigrant violence. The attacks on foreign immigrants and even on *Gastarbeiter* families who had lived in Germany for more than thirty years raised questions among some observers regarding how tolerant the Germans really are. Owing to Germany's history of repression toward Jews and all non-Germans during the first half of the twentieth century, such concerns must be taken extremely seriously. More disturbing to many was the lack of leadership coming from the Kohl government at the time and the apathy—and, in some cases, enthusiasm—of some Germans toward the intolerant violence. To be sure, Germany was not alone among industrialized nations in racist violence, but Germany's history causes it to bear a special burden. The Schröder government has been more aggressive in using the bully pulpit of the chancellor's office as well as the German legal system to pursue racist attacks aggressively. On the tenth anniversary of German unification, a group of neo-Nazis attacked a synagogue in Düsseldorf, and the Schröder government issued a statement calling on German citizens to rise up against the "brown scum" in a "revolt of the righteous."

The full development of citizenship, democracy, and participation in Germany is not blemish-free, however. Germany has only recently altered an extremely restrictive position on immigration, as this was one of the first acts taken by the Schröder SPD-Greens government in 1999.

Immigrant workers have generally fared better in German society than those immigrants who are not members of trade unions or works councils and/or the democratic left political parties. Without the granting of German citizenship, such workers remain marginalized residents of the FRG. Unlike many other European nations, Germany until 1999 had made it difficult for immigrants to be naturalized, no matter how long they were in the country, and generally denied citizenship to offspring of noncitizens born on German soil. This prejudice was exacerbated by the end of the cold war and the demise of the Soviet Union. For example, "ethnic" Germans whose ancestors had not been in Germany for centuries were allowed to enter Germany legally and assume citizenship rights immediately. Yet the *Gastarbeiter* who had lived in Germany for decades—and at the express invitation of the German governments of the 1960s—were not given the same opportunities for instant citizenship.* The new law, which took effect on January 1, 2000, provided for German citizenship for all children born in Germany, provided their parents had resided lawfully in Germany for eight years or had an unlimited residence permit for three years. Naturalization now is possible after eight years of residence instead of the previous fifteen.

Gender

Gender did not appear to be a politically significant cleavage in Germany until the 1960s, as women remained politically marginalized for most of the first half of the Federal Republic's history. In other words, gender did not produce political divisions because many women appeared to accept their unequal position in postwar West German society. Taking to heart the Catholic admonition of *Kinder, Kirche, Küche* (children, church, and kitchen), many German women were socialized into believing that their

status as second-class citizens was appropriate. To be sure, there were pre-FRG exceptions to this pattern—such as the socialist activist and theorist Rosa Luxemburg and the artist Käthe Kollwitz from the 1910s—but until the social explosions of the 1960s, very few women held positions in society outside the home.

Even with the spread of feminism since the 1970s, German women have generally lagged behind their American counterparts by some five to ten years in terms of advancement in business and politics, at least on an individual level. However, as the data in Chapter 18 show, German women have quadrupled their representation in the Bundestag from approximately 8 percent in 1980, to over 32 percent in 2002. The differences between East and West Germany on social policy affecting women provoked great controversy after unification. Women in the former East Germany had far more presence and influence in public life and in the workplace than did their counterparts in West Germany.

In areas outside the formal workplace, the differences between the laws in the GDR and the preunification FRG created a firestorm of controversy. In the former East Germany, women had made far greater social and economic progress (relatively speaking) and enjoyed greater government provision for such services as child care and family leave. In fact, one of the hottest items of contention in Germany during the early 1990s was whether to reduce East German–style benefits to women (including abortion) in favor of the more conservative and restrictive ones of the Federal Republic. The more restrictive West German law prevailed after unification, to the consternation of many women, and many men.

Interests, Social Movements, and Protests

To be sure, Germans engage in significant strikes and demonstrations on a wide range of economic and noneconomic issues. But rather than being

---

*Turkish *Gastarbeiter* are disadvantaged because if they accept German citizenship, they generally surrender property rights in Turkey.

seen as a sign of instability or a failure of public institutions, these struggles should be seen as a success. Political institutions sometimes are mistakenly seen as fixed structures that are supposed to prevent or repress dissent or controversy. A more helpful way to analyze such conflicts is to take a "new institutionalist" approach. This theory argues that political organizations shape and adapt to social and political protest and channel such action in ways that are not detrimental to democratic participation but in fact represent its essence.[15]

This distinction has important implications for the role of interest groups and social movements in the Federal Republic. Rather than encouraging fractious competition, this system creates a bounded framework within which these groups struggle tenaciously yet usually come to an agreement on policy. Moreover, because they are encouraged to aggregate the interests of all members of their association, their policy total—the general interest of the group as a whole—will be greater than the sum of its parts—the aggregated concerns of individual members. These institutions are not omnipotent, however. If they fail and allow conflict to go unresolved, the failure challenges the effectiveness of the institutions and may allow elements of society to go unrepresented. A partial failure of certain interest groups and institutions led to the rise of a series of social movements during the 1960s and 1970s, particularly around university reform, wage negotiations, and foreign policy. The very existence of the Green Party is a prime example of a movement that arose out of the earlier inability of existing institutions to address, mediate, and solve contentious issues.

With respect to extrainstitutional participation and protest, a general system of inclusionary proportional representation has left few outside the political arena until recently. Those who are outside belong to political groups that fail to meet the 5 percent electoral threshold. The Republikaner, as well as other right-wing groups, might seem to fit into this category. Similarly, the substantial Turkish population, which accounts for over 5 percent of Germany's inhabitants, might be included here. First arriving as guest workers, many have now resided in Germany for decades. And compared to *Gastarbeiter* from EU countries such as Italy and Spain, Turkish residents have fewer rights in Germany. Finally, the once-active leftist community of revolutionary Marxists still retains a small presence, mostly in large cities and university towns. Some of these left-wing parties contest elections but never get more than 1 percent of the vote.

Still, during the years since the student mobilizations of the late 1960s, Germany has witnessed considerable protest and mobilization of social forces outside the established channels of political and social representation. Among the most significant forces in the postwar FRG have been the feminist, peace, and antinuclear movements. All three, in different ways, challenged fundamental assumptions about German politics and pointed to the inability of the institutional structure to respond to the needs and issues that these groups raised. From challenges to a restrictive abortion law in the 1970s, to demonstrations against stationing nuclear missiles on German soil in the 1980s, to regular protests against nuclear power plants since the 1970s, the spirit of direct action has animated German politics in ways that were not possible in the years before the late 1960s.

The 1990s, however, witnessed protest less from the left than from the right. Although the Republikaner are a legitimate party, illegal neo-Nazi groups have been responsible for numerous racist attacks, increasing since the summer of 2000, the most reprehensible one taking place at a Jewish synagogue on the tenth anniversary of German unification. Significantly, many of these attacks by the right-wing fringe have been met with spontaneous, peaceful marches, sometimes producing demonstrations of from 200,000 to 500,000 people in various cities. This reaction suggests that social protest, as part of an active democratic political discourse, has matured in the face of this new threat from the right. The challenge for

German politics is to maintain a system of democratic participation that encompasses both extrainstitutional groups and specific organized political institutions in a way that enhances democracy rather than destroying it. Germans would suggest that effective consensus is not something that is imposed from the top; it requires the engagement of contentious issues and the institutional capacity to successfully resolve them.

Notes

1. Frank Louis Rusciano, "Rethinking the Gender Gap: The Case of West German Elections," *Comparative Politics* 24, no. 3 (April 1992): 335–358.

2. Ralf Dahrendorf, *Society and Democracy in Germany* (Garden City, N.Y.: Anchor, 1969).

3. Christopher S. Allen, ed., *Transformation of the German Political Party System: Institutional Crisis or Democratic Renewal?* (New York: Berghahn, 1999).

4. Carl E. Schorske, *German Social Democracy, 1905–1917: The Development of the Great Schism* (Cambridge, Mass.: Harvard University Press, 1983).

5. Otto Kirschheimer, "The Transformation of the Western European Party System," in Roy C. Macridis, ed., *Comparative Politics: Notes and Readings,* 6th ed. (Chicago: Dorsey, 1986).

6. Gerard Braunthal, *The German Social Democrats Since 1969: A Party in Power and Opposition,* 2nd ed. (Boulder, Colo.: Westview Press, 1994).

7. Aline Kuntz, "The Bavarian CSU: A Case Study in Conservative Modernization" (Ph.D. diss., Cornell University, 1987).

8. Geoffrey Pridham, *Christian Democracy in Western Germany: The CDU/CSU in Government and Opposition, 1945–1976* (New York: St. Martin's Press, 1977).

9. Roger Cohen, "Is Germany on the Road to Diversity? The Parties Clash," *New York Times,* December 4, 2000, p. A13.

10. David Broughton and Emil Kirchner, "Germany: The FDP in Transition—Again?" *Parliamentary Affairs* 37 (Spring 1984): 183–184.

11. Hans-Georg Betz, *Radical Right-Wing Populism in Western Europe* (New York: St. Martin's Press, 1994).

12. Peter Katzenstein, *Policy and Politics in West Germany: The Growth of a Semi-Sovereign State* (Philadelphia: Temple University Press, 1987).

13. Arnold J. Heidenheimer, *Comparative Public Policy: The Politics of Social Choice in America, Europe, and Japan,* 3rd ed. (New York: St. Martin's Press, 1990).

14. Joyce Marie Mushaben, "A Search for Identity: The 'German Question' in Atlantic Alliance Relations," *World Politics* 40, no. 3 (April 1988): 395–418.

15. Sven Steinmo, Kathleen Thelen, and Frank Longstreth, eds., *Structuring Politics: Historical Institutionalism in Historical Perspective* (New York: Cambridge University Press, 1992).

C H A P T E R

20

German Politics in Transition

Is contemporary Germany best represented by a chancellor agonizing over a stagnant economy, declining poll ratings for his Social Democratic Party, and stalled political reforms? Has the German model finally reached its exhaustion point? Or is such concern by Gerhard Schröder more than understandable given the triple challenges facing the Federal Republic of Germany (FRG): the still-formidable uncompleted tasks associated with unification; the rapid expansion of the European Union (EU) and its free-market-style policy focus that is at odds with the institutionally based, organized-capitalist German economy; and the intense pace of globalization that threatens Germany's competitive edge and that has sent thousands of immigrants and asylum seekers to the FRG? That is, can the German political economy use its still-considerable institutional and political skills to respond as quickly to these challenges as it did in the wake of post-WWII devastation?

As we try to understand which image best represents Germany today, we should keep in mind that a balanced understanding of contemporary German politics requires giving due weight to both of these pictures. Both images are recognizable parts of modern Germany, and it remains a political challenge for all German citizens to see if the spirit of the latter image becomes more prevalent than that of the former.

Which path German politics takes will be determined by the resolution of the four themes around which this book is organized. The more pessimistic assumption could see a less than robust economy, an institutional sclerosis, and an erosion of confidence to address these economic challenges, resulting in a decreasingly influential Germany in the EU and attendant social tensions and conflict. Germany's political landscape now contains five political parties represented in the Bundestag, not just the three of the period from the late 1940s to the early 1980s. Can Germany's organized society (*Organisierte Gesellschaft*) and institutional political structure sustain the increased cooperation necessary to maintain a vibrant democracy? What of Germany's "economic giant–political dwarf" syndrome, discussed in Chapter 16? Can Germany assume the political responsibility that its economic stature would suggest it should? Do its European neighbors really want it to do so? And what of Germany's high-wage, high-welfare structure in the face of increased economic competition from lower-wage countries in Eastern Europe, Asia, and elsewhere? Negative outcomes to one or more of these questions could produce a much less satisfactory outcome for both Germany and its neighbors. This second path would be a dangerous one. It could see continued economic malaise producing rising social conflict; unstable domestic institutions; uncertain international relations, including a weakened EU; and difficulties in responding to global economic competition. Success or failure will most likely depend on how well Germany and the rest of Europe can rebuild economic growth, produce enough social equity, and create inclusionary and politically accountable forms of democratic representation.

The more optimistic assumption would see the institutional capacity of the German model to govern the economy respond to twenty-first-century challenges. This would entail overcoming the mutual suspicions between eastern and western Germans. The former resent the "elbow society" of the West, in which material goods seem to stand high in the hierarchy of societal goals, while the latter resent the huge costs—and increased taxation—required to rebuild the eastern *Länder*.[1] If a successful economic, political, and social integration occurs, it will take patience, a sound institutional foundation, and the ability of both *Ossis* and *Wessis* (Easterners and Westerners) to understand much more fully the context of each other's values. Once these domestic transitions are accomplished, Germany can devote more attention to the larger issue of European integration. This first path might see a rebuilding and/or reconfiguration of the German model to finally produce successes in the former East Germany so that its inhabitants can achieve the material prosperity and democratic political culture of their western counterparts. Such a development could help Germany to become the anchor in the expanding EU from a position of strength and not one of apparent weakness at mid-decade. Such developments might offer greater foundations for a more positive response to the challenges of globalization.

Political Challenges and Changing Agendas

For many years Germany was touted as a model for other industrialized societies to emulate. Yet in the years since unification, we have seen increases in racial intolerance, as well as the partial erosion of the country's formerly vaunted economic strength. What is the state of German democracy in the face of racist attacks and rising intolerance, and what is the state of the German economy in the face of contemporary structural challenges?

The continuity of democratic institutions has clearly balanced participation and dissent effectively, as the country's turbulent and often racist past has been offset by more than a half-century of well-established multiparty democracy. For example, Germany has evolved a stable system of alternation between a coalition of moderate left and moderate right parties in the more than fifty years of the FRG. And yet rather than the "stop-go" policies that characterized the alternation in power of British Labour and British Conservatives, Germany's alternation between a moderately conservative Christian Democratic Party and one of the most powerful and respected social democratic parties in the world has produced more continuity than sharp change. Despite the deregulatory and new information economy challenges, Germany has maintained its unique and successful industrialized democracy. The country is a bastion of advanced capitalism, yet it also possesses an extensive welfare state and government-mandated programs of worker, trade union, and works council participation in managerial decision making. Moreover, these economic and political successes have helped Germany participate more effectively in the wider world of other nation-states. Based on the post-WWII idea that neither a laissez-faire nor a state-centered economy was appropriate, the FRG developed its social market economy. And based on the idea that an organized and integrated labor movement could produce not only worker safeguards but also a high-productivity economy, Germany found a way to produce for over fifty years a "high-everything" (wages, skills, quality goods, competitiveness) political economy.

Let us briefly review the three major contemporary transitional challenges that the Federal Republic faces: unification; Germany's production profile and the welfare state; and immigration and the far right.

First, German unification has been both a tremendous accomplishment and a daunting challenge for all Germans. Few other countries could so quickly add 20 percent to their own population from an adjoining country with a completely different economic and social system. Such a challenge would likely have produced either a much less successful unification or far greater social chaos, or both, in most other countries. That official political unification took place within a year of the breaching of the Berlin Wall is an accomplishment of significant proportion. And the formal integration of the former German Democratic Republic (GDR) into the FRG as five new *Länder* is a tribute to organizational and political skills that combined both vision and pragmatism.

United Germany's democracy seems well established after more than fifty-five years of the Federal Republic and more than fifteen years of unification. It boasts high voter turnout, a stable and responsible multiparty political system, and a healthy civic culture.[2] Many observers now believe that Germany's broad-based political participation is part of the fabric of political life. However, several issues merit concern as Germany's political institutions are being extended to the five new *Länder*. How well have eastern Germans understood and internalized democratic practice after so many years of authoritarian Communist rule? For many eastern Germans, dissent was not political participation; it was treason. Similarly, can eastern Germans who have lost jobs and benefits in the transition to capitalism understand that ethnic minorities are not the cause of their plight? Can tolerance and understanding develop in all of Germany at a time when a right-wing fringe is preaching hatred and looking for scapegoats to blame for the costs of unification? Also, is the legacy completely gone of a bureaucratic state that as recently as the 1970s, under a social democratic–led government, purged individuals who appeared to have radical tendencies? In other words, if social and economic tensions continue to rise in the new century, how will the German state respond?

Beyond the immediate institutional features of this unification lie the more difficult issues of integration of economic and social systems and of the quite different political cultures of eastern and western Germany, which will take years to blend together. Furthermore, after the initial wave of construction and the economic mini-

boom in the first year after unification, a more sobering mood set in. As unemployment has remained much higher in the five new states than in the others in the early 2000s, Germans have realized that unification was far from a quick fix. The process of fully unifying the disparate parts of Germany will continue well into this century.

Second, Germany's famed social market economy, with its characteristic organized-capitalist features and strong emphasis on manufacturing over services, its privileged position for trade unions, and its generous social welfare provisions, has faced renewed pressures in the postunification years. Not only do German public and private officials continue to face criticism from countries that had more fully embraced postindustrial (service sector–driven) economic models; they also were criticized for maintaining the generous social welfare provisions that had been curtailed much further in countries such as the United Kingdom and the United States. Here, too, the pressures of unification added to the strains. Clearly these pressures were driving the push for the Schröder government in 2000 to pass the broad sweep of tax and pension reforms to help alleviate the problem of *Standort Deutschland* (Germany as an attractive location for investment). Likewise the Agenda 2010 economic structural reforms that were passed in Schröder's second term seemed to come from a position of weakness rather than strength. The continuing heavy costs of rebuilding the east have taken the form of infrastructural investments (in transportation, communications, housing, and new plants); large transfer payments to those in the east who could not find work or did not possess skills needed for the twenty-first-century capitalist economy; and now, more recently, the immigration of Indian computer programmers. Although Germans refuse to give up the generous welfare state benefits they have enjoyed since the 1950s, they have found that paying for these benefits in the new *Länder* does not come cheaply.

Germany's economy clearly faces transitional challenges in the new century. For many years it

A cynical western German view of money spent to rebuild eastern Germany.

———————

Source: Janusz Majewski/*Frankfurter Allgemeine Zeitung.*

has been characterized as "high everything," in that it has combined high-quality manufacturing with high wages, high fringe benefits, high worker participation, and high levels of vacation time (six weeks per year).[3] Since the first oil crisis in the 1970s, critical observers have kept insisting that such a system could not last in a competitive world economy.[4] Yet for most of the thirty-plus years since then, the German economy has remained among the world's leaders. More recently, however, the huge costs of unification, an expanding EU (discussed below), and continued pressures of globalization have caused many of the old criticisms of an extended and overburdened economy to surface again.

Pessimistic observers have begun to suggest that the stresses of the 1990s and the early years of the new century have placed the German po-

litical economy in a precarious position. This "anti–German model" consists of several related arguments.[5] The first is that Germany's economic prowess has resided in certain manufacturing industries, such as automobiles and machine tools, whose goods are exportable but whose technologies are decidedly low. Yet wage costs in these sectors have continued to rise. Second, the costs of the social market economy, as witnessed in the costs of unification, have pressed on the upper limits of Germany's capacity to pay for them. In addition, economic tensions remain at the heart of the conflict between former East and former West Germans. While eastern Germans have resented the slow pace of change and the high unemployment, western Germans are bitter about losing jobs to eastern Germans and paying increased taxes for the cleanup of the ecological and infrastructural disaster inherited from the former East German regime.

Third, racist movements and far-right parties, however marginal they were in the 1990s, still retain a presence in modern unified Germany in the 2000s. The far-right Republikaner Party threatened to break the 5 percent electoral threshold in the late 1980s and early 1990s, but by the 1998 federal elections it clearly had peaked as a political movement able to gain representation in parliament. However, in 2004 eastern German regional elections in Brandenburg, the extreme right-wing party, Deutsche Volksunion (DVU), received 6.1 percent of the vote and gained representation for the second consecutive *Land* election. Further to the right is the Nationaldemokratische Partei Deutschlands (NPD), which came close to gaining Bundestag representation in 1966 with 4.3 percent of the vote. But after years of relative dormancy, the NPD resurfaced in the 2004 regional election in Saxony, and obtained 9.2 percent of the vote and won seats in the regional parliament. It also has shown an increased extraparliamentary presence in demonstrations in large German cities, including several in eastern Germany. The attacks on foreigners, thought to have peaked in the early 1990s, returned again in the mid-1990s when a hostel for foreign refugees was fire-bombed and Jewish synagogues were attacked. While representing a tiny minority of the population, far-right racist movements nonetheless represent a significant concern for a democratic country with its catastrophic past. Whether these far-right regional electoral victories are just protest votes or harbingers of something more ominous bears watching.

In other words, in the area of collective identities, Germany faces numerous unresolved challenges. For example, the country's guest workers, a large number of whom are Turkish, remain essential to Germany's economy. But will the citizenship reforms of the 2000s prove sufficient to integrate them into the fabric of German political and social life? The opening of East Germany produced an influx of refugees and asylum seekers beginning in the late 1980s. This influx placed great strains on a country that paradoxically has had generous political asylum laws but significant restrictions on non-Germans' attaining citizenship. These factors have helped produce increased ethnic tensions as German nationalism, understandably suppressed since the end of World War II, has shown some signs of resurgence. In fact, the unification of Germany has partially contributed to this resurgence, as some younger Germans—two generations after the end of World War II—are asking what being *German* actually means. The dark side of such a development is manifested by the various extremist groups, which though still small in numbers, preach exaggerated nationalism and hatred of foreigners and minorities. Contributing to this climate is the reluctance of some German firms to settle reparation payments to aging workers who were slave laborers in World War II. Such tendencies are quite incompatible with a Germany that wishes to play a leading role in European integration.

The future of German politics depends greatly on how the country addresses these challenges, which relate clearly to the four primary themes that we have used to organize our analysis of the countries covered in this book: a world of states, governing the economy, the democratic idea, and the politics of collective identities. For much of the post–World War II period, Germany enjoyed a spiral of success, in that dealing well with one of these thematic issues enabled the country to confront others successfully. For example, problems of collective identities were handled in a much less exclusionary way as women, ethnic groups, and newer political parties and movements all began to contribute to a stable and healthy diversity in German politics that had been missing for most of the country's history.

However, in closely examining all four of these major themes, we find Germany at a crossroads. Can the country continue its successes in all four areas, or will tensions and difficulties undermine these successful patterns to produce a period of economic, political, and social instability?

There has been a significant change in the nature of German politics in the twenty-first century. Clearly the term *Modell Deutschland* (the German model), used in the 1970s and 1980s, is much less appropriate today. In the four preceding chapters, we reexamined the theme of democratic tolerance and respect for positions of other individuals and groups. The question remains, Can Germany evolve peacefully and democratically in a region where increased integration will become more likely? The expansion of the European Union in the 1990s—and once again with ten more countries in 2004—enabled more European citizens to live and work outside their home countries. What happens to German collective identity? Can the elaborate and, for fifty years, effective institutional structure that balances private and public interests be maintained and supported? Will the EU augment or challenge Germany's position in Europe? Will these challenges threaten Germany's enviable economic position in the face of increased competition from newly industrializing countries?

The Challenges of European Integration

The challenge that the EU presents offers both opportunities and dangers to the Federal Republic. Although the creation of a single market clearly can benefit the strongest European economy, Germany faces unique problems as it attempts to integrate its economy with that of other economies on the Continent. Clearly the weaker countries, such as Portugal and Greece, will look to strong countries such as Germany for assistance. Moreover, Germany's brand of organized capitalism is clearly out of step with the more free-market sentiments of other European countries. Defenders of the German model might rightfully say, why shouldn't the economy of all of Europe be modeled on Germany rather than on the free-market-oriented United Kingdom? However, transferring the deeply embedded structures of German capitalism to countries that do not understand how they work is much easier said than done, even assuming they would want to import the German model. Furthermore, the transition from the redoubtable deutsche mark to the uncertain euro has added further worries to the minds of German citizens. The volatility of the value of the euro—down some 25 percent after its introduction in 1999 until late 2000, and up 20 percent against the dollar in 2004—threatened to produce uncertainty regarding inflation fears in the former instance, and export worries in the latter.

The completion of the single market of the EU—now along with the enlargement of the EU in 2004 to twenty-five nations—has also complicated Germany's relationship with other states. The EU was supposedly the grand culmination of a post–cold war spirit of German and European unity. But unity has proved more difficult to establish than first anticipated. The outcome of recent reforms—the single market, the euro, a new EU constitution—has only strengthened the trends toward decentralization and deregulation already under way in Western Europe, rather than initiating EU political institution building. More significant for the German economy, such deregulatory tendencies, if spread throughout Europe, could potentially disturb the organized capitalism of Germany's small and large businesses. In addition, the wholesale deregulation in European finance—with the passage of a law in 2003 substantially lowering the capital gains tax and thus encouraging banks to sell their shares in industrial firms—has eroded Germany's distinctive finance-manufacturing links among the larger, internationally oriented banks (although the regional banks retain the old model).[6] In short, the specific direction that Europeanization is taking may be incompatible with the highly consensus-oriented and coordinated nature of Germany's adjustment patterns. Moreover, as Europe becomes more open to the rest of the world economy, how well will Germany's "high-everything" system be able to withstand increased economic competition from Asia and elsewhere? Politically, can Germany emerge from its political dwarf status and play a leadership role in integrating the East-Central European states into a wider EU?

For much of the post–World War II period, Germany's growing international economic prowess was not complemented by a similar level of international political responsibility. Yet in the 1990s and into the new century, Germany has confidently, and with the support of its neighbors and allies, taken a leading role in European integration. It is firmly anchored in Western Europe but uniquely positioned to assist in the transition of the formerly Communist East-Central European states toward economic and political modernization. Initial doubts concerning the capacity of Gerhard Schröder to continue Helmut Kohl's commitment to both a deeper and wider EU have been resolved, as Schröder seems to be speaking with an even greater sense of the projection of German responsibility in the EU than did his predecessor.

German Politics, Terrorism, and Germany's Relation to the U.S.

The good news for the Germans with respect to their relationship with the United States is that the Germans are not the French. The bad news is that the Bush administration considers Germany an unreliable ally, almost as "disloyal" as its neighbor to the west. Before the Iraq war, Germany strongly preferred to rely on the United Nations and to take a multilateral approach and keep nonmilitary options open as long as possible in dealing with Saddam Hussein. The Schröder government was unconvinced that unilaterally attacking Iraq would have any positive effect in challenging Al Qaeda. Thus the French and Germans prevented the United States from building a broad-based coalition to initiate the war. Only Britain as a major country supported the United States.

For anyone who understands German politics in the past fifty years, however, the German ambivalence about rushing pell-mell into Iraq alongside the United States and a relatively small contingent of British soldiers is completely understandable. Germany was explicitly discouraged by the United States from projecting a strong international political posture after WWII, and heavily constrained by the structure of the North Atlantic Treaty Organization (NATO), not to mention by the thousands of American troops stationed in Germany decades after the end of WWII—and even after the end of the cold war. For fifty years Germany was explicitly encouraged to concentrate on economic affairs and to leave geopolitics to the United States. To expect the Federal Republic, after educating two generations of its citizens about the folly of military adventure, to sign on to the Iraq invasion on a series of extremely dubious premises about "weapons of mass destruction," and against the wishes of the UN, represents a fundamental misunderstanding of German postwar politics.

For the Germans, the UN and NATO remain the primary international political vehicles for Germany to engage in international relations. And it's not that Germany is not willing to undertake responsibility in the fight against terrorism, as the deployment of forces in Afghanistan under a UN mandate has shown.

As for German domestic politics and terrorism, Germans are embarrassed that several of the 9/11 hijackers lived in Hamburg before moving to the United States. But Germany believes that the fight against terrorism can be better waged via domestic intelligence rather than by the approach that the Bush administration took in Iraq. A German court in 2004 reluctantly released Moroccan terrorist suspects because the United States would not allow detained "enemy combatants" in the United States—and at Guantánamo Bay, Cuba—to testify at the trials of the Moroccans in Germany, thus not permitting the alleged terrorists to receive a fair trial. In short, Germany believed that the fight against terrorism should not take place at the expense of the democratic rights of defendants to call witnesses to speak on their behalf. Germans found it ironic that these were rights that the United States encouraged Germany to develop in the wake of the Third Reich.

Finally, it is not as if Germany has not had experience in dealing with its own domestic terrorists of both the left and right. Clearly, some dubious measures were taken against the left-wing Red Army Faktion (RAF) terrorists and other political dissidents in the late 1970s, but successive German governments have engaged in less onerous forms of surveillance and counterterrorist measures. Many Germans would say that most of the provisions of the USA PATRIOT Act—such as holding suspects, both citizens and noncitizens alike, indefinitely, without formal charges, and without allowing them to consult a lawyer—would never have come close to passing in the Bundestag had a similar 9/11 event taken place in Germany.

Germany in Comparative Perspective

Germany offers important insights for comparative politics in several respects. Regime changes have occurred several times in Germany in the past century. By examining these upheavals, we can learn a great deal about the modalities of regime change, such as institutional capacities for change, breakdowns of economic performance, erosion and rebuilding of political culture, and respect for democracy so that political rivals are opponents and not enemies.

The first significant comparative issue is the role of organized capitalism. Germany has a model of combining state and market in a way that is unique in comparison to many advanced industrialized nations. Many models of political analysis choose to emphasize the distinctions between state and market. Debates about whether nationalized industries should be privatized and whether welfare should be reduced in favor of private charity, for example, are symptomatic of the conflict between state and market that animates the politics of most developed countries. Germany's organized capitalism, together with the social market economy, has effectively blurred the distinction between the public and private sectors. The FRG has refused to see public policy as a stark choice between these two alternatives, preferring to emphasize policies in which the state and market work together. Within the general framework of the model of governing the economy (outlined in Part I), the German state effectively pursues development plans that benefit from its cooperative interaction with a dense network of key social and economic actors. Despite Germany's prominence as a powerful advanced industrialized economy, this model remains surprisingly understudied. And despite the current economic difficulties,

largely brought about by unification and the strains of European integration and Anglo-American deregulatory policy styles, it is a model worthy of comparative analysis.

A second area of comparative interest is Germany's evolution of the principle of democratization and participation in a collectivist democracy. In many developed states, one thinks of democracy in the sense of individual rights, often taking the form of a series of individual choices, much as a consumer would choose to buy one product or another in a supermarket. Germany, on the other hand, has seen the evolution of a different model that, although it sometimes underplays a more individualistic democracy, does offer insights for participation and representation in a complex society. German democracy has emphasized participation within different groups. In other words, it has stressed the role of the individual not as a consumer in isolation from the rest of society, but as a citizen in a wider set of communities, organizations, and parties that must find ways of cooperating if the nation-state is to maintain its democracy. It is clearly within this complex of political actors that Germany is wrestling with its treatment of different groups within the Federal Republic.

Third, Germany offers insights concerning the question of tolerance and respect for civil rights for ethnic minorities. Can Germany's group-oriented democratic practices open up to allow those former *Gastarbeiter* who have now become German citizens to participate in and make a meaningful and significant contribution to German democracy? Can ethnic tensions be resolved in a way that enhances democracy rather than undermines it? Clearly, collective identities of Germans and non-Germans alike offer both powerful obstacles and large opportunities to address one of the most crucial noneconomic issues that Germany faces in the twenty-first century.

Fourth, can Germany really remake its political culture in the wake of the Nazi past? Many believed in the first half-century of the FRG that this was occurring, but several recent racist events and the recent revival of right-wing regional electoral support have raised questions about how fully German political culture has changed. To what extent have the educational system, the civil service, and the media addressed the Nazi past? To what extent do they bear some responsibility for the persistence of right-wing violence throughout Germany? Have the reforms in the educational system since the 1960s provided a spirit of critical discourse in the broad mainstream of society that can withstand the rise of right-wing intolerance? Can judges effectively sentence those who abuse the civil rights of ethnic minorities? Will the news media continue to express a wide range of opinion and contribute to a healthy civic discourse? Or will strident, tabloid-style journalism crowd out the more reasoned discourse that any democracy must have to survive and flourish?

Fifth, what is the role of a middle-rank power as a potential leader of a regional world bloc of some 454 million people after the 2004 EU expansion? To some extent, Japan also faces this issue, as it too struggles to take on political responsibilities commensurate with its economic successes. Into the new century Germany faces intense pressures not only from within its borders, such as conflict among ethnic groups, but also from a complex mix of external influences. Germany's role as both a Western European and an Eastern European power pull at the country in different ways. Should the country emphasize the Western-oriented EU and build a solid foundation with its traditional postwar allies? Or should it turn eastward to step into the vacuum created by the demise and fragmentation of the former Soviet Union? Can it do both? Can Germany's twentieth-century history allow either its western or eastern neighbors to let it begin to play the geopolitical role that its low-profile postwar political status has only postponed?[7] To some extent the "political cover" of the EU will allow Germany to do more as the leading country in a powerful international organization than it ever could as a sovereign nation-state with its unique twentieth-century political baggage.

Finally, Germany's historical importance on the world political stage during the past 150 years means that understanding its transition is essential for comparative purposes. It was late to achieve political unity and late to industrialize. These two factors eventually helped produce a catastrophic first half of the twentieth century for both Germany and the rest of the world. Yet the country's transition to a successful developed economy with an apparently solid democratic political system would seem to suggest that other countries, as they attempt to achieve economic growth and develop a political democracy, particularly in the Third World, may be able to learn from the successes and failures of countries such as Germany.

Notes

1. Robert Rohrschneider, *Learning Democracy: Democratic and Economic Values in Unified Germany* (New York: Oxford University Press, 1999).

2. Gabriel A. Almond and Sidney Verba, eds., *The Civic Culture Revisited* (Newbury Park, Calif.: Sage, 1989).

3. Lowell Turner, *Democracy at Work: Changing World Markets and the Future of Labor Unions* (Ithaca, N.Y.: Cornell University Press, 1991).

4. Bruce Nussbaum, *The World After Oil* (New York: Simon & Schuster, 1983); Michael Moran, "A State of Inaction: The State and Stock Exchange Reform in the Federal Republic of Germany," in Simon Bulmer, ed., *The Changing Agenda of West German Public Policy* (Brookfield, Vt.: Gower, 1989), pp. 110–127.

5. Peter Neckermann, "What Went Wrong in Germany After the Unification?" *East European Quarterly* 26, no. 4 (1992): 447–470.

6. Richard Deeg, *Finance Capitalism Unveiled* (Ann Arbor: University of Michigan Press, 1999).

7. Peter J. Katzenstein, ed., *Tamed Power: Germany in Europe* (Ithaca, N.Y.: Cornell University Press, 1997).

Part V Bibliography

Allen, Christopher S., ed. *Transformation of the German Political Party System: Institutional Crisis or Democratic Renewal?* New York: Berghahn, 1999.

Berger, Stefan. *The British Labour Party and the German Social Democrats: 1900–1931.* Oxford: Oxford University Press, 1994.

Braunthal, Gerard. *The Federation of German Industry in Politics.* Ithaca, N.Y.: Cornell University Press, 1965.

———. *The German Social Democrats Since 1969: A Party in Power and Opposition.* 2nd ed. Boulder, Colo.: Westview Press, 1994.

———. *Parties and Politics in Modern Germany.* Boulder, Colo.: Westview Press, 1996.

Craig, Gordon. *The Politics of the Prussian Army.* Oxford: Oxford University Press, 1955.

Dahrendorf, Ralf. *Society and Democracy in Germany.* Garden City, N.Y.: Anchor, 1969.

Deeg, Richard. *Finance Capitalism Unveiled.* Ann Arbor: University of Michigan Press, 1999.

Eley, Geoff. *Reshaping the German Right: Radical Nationalism and Political Change After Bismarck.* New Haven, Conn.: Yale University Press, 1980.

Evans, Peter B., Dietrich Rueschemeyer, and Theda Skocpol. *Bringing the State Back In.* Cambridge: Cambridge University Press, 1985.

Gerschenkron, Alexander. *Bread and Democracy in Germany.* 2nd ed. Ithaca, N.Y.: Cornell University Press, 1989.

Hager, Carol. "Environmentalism and Democracy in the Two Germanies." *German Politics* 1, no. 1 (April 1992): 95–118.

Hesse, Joachim Jens. "The Federal Republic of Germany: From Cooperative Federalism to Joint Policy-Making." *West European Politics* 10, no. 4 (October 1987): 70–87.

Hirschman, Albert O. *Exit, Voice, and Loyalty.* New Haven, Conn.: Yale University Press, 1970.

Inglehart, Ronald. *Culture Shift in Advanced Industrial Society.* Princeton, N.J.: Princeton University Press, 1990.

Jacoby, Wade. *Imitation and Politics: Redesigning Modern Germany.* Ithaca, N.Y.: Cornell University Press, 2000.

Katzenstein, Peter J. *Policy and Politics in West Germany: The Growth of a Semi-Sovereign State.* Philadelphia: Temple University Press, 1987.

———. *Tamed Power: Germany in Europe.* Ithaca, N.Y.: Cornell University Press, 1997.

Kemp, Tom. *Industrialization in Nineteenth Century Europe.* 2nd ed. London: Longman, 1985.

Markovits, Andrei S. "Political Parties in Germany: Agents of Stability in a Sea of Change." *Social Education* 57, no. 5 (September 1993): 239–243.

Moore, Barrington. *Social Origins of Dictatorship and Democracy.* Boston: Beacon Press, 1965.

Piore, Michael, and Charles Sabel. *The Second Industrial Divide.* New York: Basic Books, 1984.

Rein, Taagepera, and Matthew Soberg Shugart. *Seats and Votes: The Effects and Determinants of Electoral Systems.* New Haven, Conn.: Yale University Press, 1989.

Rueschemeyer, Dietrich, Evelyn Huber Stephens, and John D. Stephens. *Capitalist Development and Democracy.* Chicago: University of Chicago Press, 1992.

Rusciano, Frank Louis. "Rethinking the Gender Gap: The Case of West German Elections." *Comparative Politics* 243 (April 1992): 335–358.

Schmidt, Manfred G. "West Germany: The Politics of the Middle Way." *Journal of Public Policy* 7, no. 2 (1987): 135–177.

Schmitter, Philippe C., and Gerhard Lembruch, eds. *Trends Toward Corporatist Intermediation.* Beverly Hills, Calif.: Sage, 1979.

Shirer, William. *The Rise and Fall of the Third Reich.* New York: Simon & Schuster, 1960.

Thelen, Kathleen. *A Union of Parts.* Ithaca, N.Y.: Cornell University Press, 1992.

Tilly, Charles, ed. *The Formation of National States in Western Europe.* Princeton, N.J.: Princeton University Press, 1975.

Wever, Kirsten S. *Negotiating Competitiveness: Employment Relations and Industrial Adjustment in Germany and the United States.* Boston: Harvard Business School Press, 1995.

Websites

American Institute for Contemporary German Studies, Johns Hopkins University: www.aicgs.org.

German Embassy, German Information Center: www.germany-info.org/sf_index.html.

German News (in English), 1995–present: www.mathematik.uni-ulm.de/de-news.

German Studies Web, Western European Studies Section: www.dartmouth.edu/~wess.

Max-Planck Institute for the Study of Societies, Cologne: www.mpi-fg-koeln.mpg.de/inhalt/index_e.html.

WZB, Social Science Research Center, Berlin: www.wzberlin.de/default.en.asp.

PART

VI

Italy

Stephen Hellman

CHAPTER

21

Making the Modern Italian State

Italian Politics in Action

For nearly fifty years, the Italian political system was described as "blocked" or "frozen." The same parties had governed the country, uninterruptedly, from 1948. Other parties were permanently relegated to the opposition, with no hope of displacing the incumbents. Then, quite suddenly, the most immobile party system of any Western democracy simply imploded. In 1993, support for the governing parties dissolved, and by the time elections were held in 1994, a party that had not even existed five months earlier was the largest party in the country; its leader, Silvio Berlusconi, who had only entered politics when the party was created, became prime minister. His major coalition partners in a totally new center-right government included ex-Fascists on the one hand and former separatists on the other.

Barely a year after this political earthquake, the leader of the opposition, Massimo D'Alema, published a book in which he hoped Italy could complete its transformation into "a normal country." By this he meant not only that his own party—the Party of the Democratic Left, which used to be called Communist—would finally be able to govern the country, but that the act of replacing one government with another—a sine qua non of liberal democracy—would finally be accomplished in Italy.[1] In fact, within a year, a center-left government was in office. Two years later, this former Communist had become prime minister. His dream, not to mention his personal ambitions, seemed to have been realized. That the center-left lost the next election (in 2001), to

be replaced by the center-right, could even be considered proof of the completion of Italy's transition to normalcy.

Yet today, just a few years later, very few people outside the governing coalition would call the Italian political system "normal." As we will see, while many problems that plagued the old system have been left behind, an entirely new set has arisen. Most of these revolve around the personality and problems of a single individual: Silvio Berlusconi. If the old system was notable for a mass of gray politicos shuffling between positions of power as in a high-stakes game of musical chairs, the new system has a lightning rod who is anything but gray and anonymous.

Even people without much knowledge of Italy have heard of Berlusconi. He is the richest man in the country, but even more important is the *nature* of Berlusconi's wealth. In addition to extensive construction and financial interests, he owns three of Italy's four private television networks and Italy's largest advertising agency, along with a newspaper, an Internet company, and the largest publishing house. With politics increasingly conditioned (some would say dominated) by the mass media, this degree of control over a country's commercial means of communications raises all sorts of questions about whether it is even possible to speak in terms of a level political playing field.[2] Consider the implications for democracy during an election campaign: if Berlusconi's opponents want to put political ads on the much-watched private networks, they must pay his advertising agency for the privilege of appearing on his stations. The flip side of the coin is that the private networks provide notoriously lopsided coverage of Berlusconi, giving him many times more exposure than his opponents during campaigns, while avoiding his more embarrassing moments (for instance, when, in the European Parliament, he likened a German Eurodeputy to a concentration camp guard, this episode—covered extensively all over the world—was ignored on Italy's private networks).

Things become even more complicated when we consider that Italy also has a *public* broadcasting sector, consisting of three television networks. By convention, control over the two dominant national channels has gone to the party or coalition in power. The third, smaller and regionally differentiated network historically went to the opposition. Hence a Berlusconi-led government means that one man now has direct or indirect control over roughly 90 percent of all national programming in Italy.

Conflicts of interest, and the resulting problems raised for democratic governance, do not end with Berlusconi's businesses. He has also been plagued by numerous judicial proceedings, many of which allegedly relate to the highly questionable way he ran his companies, paid off political friends, bribed public officials, or evaded taxes, to name the most serious charges. His entry into politics was viewed as a move to defend his huge financial interests, and also to protect himself from what he considers a vendetta by politically motivated prosecutors and magistrates, whom he vilifies as "red robes."

Berlusconi's 1994 victory was followed by his exit from office after only seven months when his coalition collapsed. However, because the center-left failed to address the conflict-of-interest question, Berlusconi returned to office with no legislation on the books. In typically brash fashion, he promised to resolve the issue within a hundred days of taking office, which did not happen. When, after nearly a year, a law was drafted, it avoided the most important problems. It holds that "mere ownership" of a firm or of a significant financial interest does not represent a

conflict, which is deemed to exist only where the public interest can be shown to have been compromised.[3]

An assessment of Berlusconi's first two years back in power concluded that four of five major legislative initiatives were linked more to his legal problems than to anything else.[4] For instance, new laws were almost immediately passed that reclassified the falsification of corporate balance sheets, and the illegal export of capital, from serious criminal offenses to the Italian equivalent of a misdemeanor. This legislation was then applied retroactively—that is, to cases (including those involving Berlusconi and his collaborators) working their way through the courts at the time. The Italian government also drew attention to itself when it opposed EU initiatives for a European arrest warrant covering a range of crimes. Italy wanted to eliminate both financial crimes and racially motivated hate crimes from the list, while trying to make more restrictive the rules governing the admissibility of evidence gathered outside the country (widely seen as an effort to thwart an ongoing Spanish case against Berlusconi). In the case of the arrest warrant, unanimous pressure from the rest of the EU forced Italy to back down.

A final illustration of Berlusconi's potential for perverting the democratic rules of the game may be most telling of all. The Judiciary Committee of the Chamber of Deputies is chaired by Berlusconi's personal lawyer; another also sits on the committee. When they were not in Rome overseeing the rules governing judicial procedures, including trying to rewrite the powers of Italy's magistrates, these individuals were commuting to Milan to defend Berlusconi against charges of bribing a judge to win a favorable ruling for one of his companies.

Berlusconi is not running completely roughshod over Italian democracy, although many opponents do make this argument. Italian institutions, as well as movements in civil society, have shown that they still function. A law that granted immunity from prosecution to the top five officials of the Italian state as long as they occupied their positions was overturned by the Constitutional Court. The president of the republic vetoed as wishy-washy and self-serving an effort to regulate private television. And thousands of protesters turned out to circle and symbolically defend the Ministry of Justice against what were seen as attacks on the judiciary's autonomy.

As this discussion shows, if Italian democracy finally dealt with one anomaly in the early 1990s, it now finds itself confronting a new set of problems. Observers in the advanced democracies once tended not to take Italian politics too seriously because it seemed so chaotic; to this amusement has recently been added concern over Italy's continuing inability to address adequately some of the most basic issues confronting a modern democracy. Normalcy indeed appears to be a long way off.

Geographic Setting

Italy's boot may be the most immediately recognizable outline of any country in the world. Jutting into the Mediterranean, with 4,750 miles (7,600 kilometers) of coastline, it has been a strategic crossroads almost since humans began traveling, and conquering each other, for it dominates the central Mediterranean as well as the southern approaches into western and south-central Europe.[5] Phoenicians, Greeks, Normans, North Africans, Spaniards, and, more recently, Austrians, French, and Germans have all conquered or occupied parts of what became Italy.

Except for the flat, fertile Po Valley, Italy is mountainous. Half of all the Alps, Europe's largest range, are found in Italy. The rugged Apennines run down the rest of the boot, and smaller ranges cover most of the rest of the land. The Po is the only navigable river of any significance. Italy has been poorly endowed with the natural resources most central to the age of heavy industry, such as coal, iron, oil, and natural gas.

These physical characteristics have profoundly marked Italy's history and evolution.

Italy is the most marginally located of the large European countries. And this marginality was reinforced by a lack of resources that delayed industrialization. Italy was both a late industrializer and, in West European terms, a latecomer to the family of nation-states. Its weakness and strategic location made it easy prey for more powerful neighbors, so it remained carved up until 1870. Not surprisingly, the newly unified state was marked by extreme regional differences that reflected centuries of different political, social, and cultural legacies. Italy's rugged terrain also reinforced regional and local differences until well into the twentieth century, when a modern rail and highway system and, above all, radio and television finally unified the country culturally and linguistically.

With 58 million inhabitants, Italy has roughly the same population as the United Kingdom and France; its territory is somewhat larger than the United Kingdom and a bit smaller than Germany (France is nearly twice the size of Italy). All these countries have rapidly aging populations, and deaths are now outstripping births; Italy and Spain have recently been neck and neck for the lowest birthrate in the world. These trends lend a sense of urgency to the need to confront questions of pensions and welfare state restructuring, as well as immigration.

Italy's location gives it continuing strategic importance. Major U.S. Air Force bases are located in the northeast, and the U.S. Sixth Fleet has its home in Naples. Even in a post–cold war era, Italy remains a vital staging area for the United States and the North Atlantic Treaty Organization (NATO), as military operations in the Balkans in the late 1990s demonstrated. During NATO's campaign against Yugoslavia in 1999, air attacks were launched from bases in the northeast.

Critical Junctures

Its strategic location gave Italy a central role in the history of the West. The Romans established an advanced urban society and conquered most

Italy

of the known world two millennia ago. Their impact on the rest of Europe is evident in the Latin-based Romance languages, and also in the codified legal system, which they invented. Christianity spread rapidly into the Continent after becoming the religion of the emperor; it became the most powerful force shaping medieval Europe. Fiercely independent city-states in the north-center left important commercial and exploratory legacies, as well as establishing early democratic traditions.

But the rise of the nation-state found Italy lagging behind most of its neighbors. Because of its historical importance and strategic location, the country was carved up by successive waves of emerging powers. By the nationalist era of the nineteenth century, the glorious past served mainly as a unifying myth to patriots chafing under rulers who were either foreign or, as with the Papal States, considered backward and illegitimate by educated opinion. It is significant that the nationalists called their movement the Risorgimento (resurgence).

The Risorgimento and Liberal Italy (1848–1922)

In the mid-1800s, Italy expressed a nationalistic dream. The north was divided between the Kingdom of Sardinia under the Savoy monarchy (Piedmont and Liguria) and the Austrian-controlled northeast (Lombardy and Venetia). In the north-center, numerous small duchies and principalities led an uneasy existence. Across the entire middle of the boot, dominating most of central Italy, were the Papal States. Just south of Rome, embracing southern Italy and Sicily, was the Kingdom of the Two Sicilies, ruled by descendants of the Spanish Bourbons. This arch-conservative realm remained secure because, as a ruler once put it, it was surrounded "by salt water on three sides and holy water on the fourth."[6]

The Risorgimento finally triumphed in the second half of the 1800s. Victor Emmanuel II of Savoy and his skilled prime minister, Camillo Cavour, attracted middle- and upper-class moderate nationalists with their enlightened liberalism. Italy was thus created by extending Piedmontese hegemony over the entire boot.

Outside intervention determined the unification of the peninsula. Austria's defeat by France in 1859 forced the Habsburgs to cede part of the north to Victor Emmanuel II, who, in turn, gave Nice and Savoy to France. Eager to strike a deal, the French tolerated Piedmont's annexation of some of the Papal States, and limited their presence to a garrison in Rome. A parliament, elected by very limited suffrage, proclaimed the Kingdom of Italy in March 1861. Victor Emmanuel II of Savoy was its first monarch. No new consti-

tution was drawn up: Piedmont's 1848 *Statuto albertino* (named for King Charles Albert of Piedmont, Victor Emmanuel II's father) was extended over the whole country. This document differed from the more democratic republican constitutions of 1848, allowing extensive powers to remain in the king's hands.

The remainder of modern Italy's territory, save for Trento and Trieste, which were obtained at the end of World War I, was annexed thanks to Prussian military victories over Austria (1866) and France (1870), as the map of the unification of Italy shows. After the French withdrew from Rome, Italian troops seized Italy's historic capital, and difficult church-state relations followed, for the pope refused to recognize the new state.

Because of its narrow, and privileged, bases of support, the Risorgimento left basic social and political problems untouched. Italy's largest social group, the peasantry, was excluded from the independence movement and was then ignored by the new state. The new country's leaders were in no hurry to extend democratic participation in a society with 60 to 80 percent illiteracy rates. Northern elites guaranteed the loyalty of southern landlords by repressing restive peasants and introducing tariffs to protect inefficiently grown southern crops. But they otherwise pursued laissez-faire industrial policies, serving their own interests while devastating struggling new firms in the less developed parts of the country.

By the mid-1870s, Italy's free-market policies were proving inadequate for a country with so much ground to make up. Looking northward, the government noticed the impressive advances of another new state—Germany—and decided that interventionism was a far more appropriate model to emulate. In the course of the 1880s, a new economic policy evolved: taxes were lightened, tariff barriers were erected, and the state became more active in the economy.

Italy remained overwhelmingly agricultural well into the twentieth century. Not until the 1950s did industrial employees outnumber those in agriculture. This slow growth produced

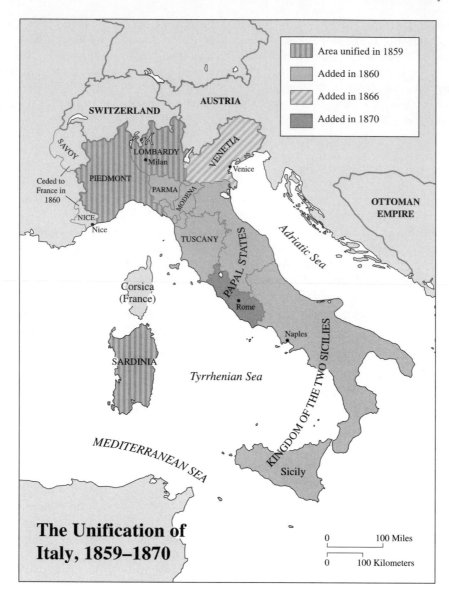

The Unification of Italy, 1859–1870

Map legend:
- Area unified in 1859
- Added in 1860
- Added in 1866
- Added in 1870

staggering emigration in the first half-century following unification. In peak years, over half a million people left Italy (nearly 900,000 emigrated in 1913), mostly for the United States and South America. The influx of so many Italians forever altered the culture, the class structure, and even the language of the United States and Argentina.

Emigration affected the entire country, but was greatest in the south. The outflow of so many young, able-bodied people distorted the population profile, but it did serve as a social safety valve, and was welcomed by both local and national leaders, who had good reason to fear the often-brutal class warfare that periodically erupted in the countryside.

Italy's location, late entry into the community of nations, and slow development made it a marginal European actor. Traditionally neutral,

Italy entered World War I following secret negotiations with the Allies. Although secondary by the standards of 1914–1918, the Italian front visited all the horrors of trench warfare on millions of (mostly peasant) conscripts, of whom approximately 600,000 died. The war extended Italy's border to the Brenner Pass in the north and to Trieste and Istria on the Adriatic, but when more ambitious demands were not met, the Italians abandoned the peace talks. This helped legitimize the extreme right. Wars expose the weaknesses of the countries that wage them and are especially hard on losers. It is indicative of Liberal Italy's rickety underpinnings that although the regime emerged from the slaughter of World War I on the winning side, its days were numbered. The Liberal regime collapsed because it lacked both the culture and the institutions that could attract mass support or regulate modern class conflict.

Liberal Italy's Political Contradictions and Collapse.

It is no easy task to deal with severe social inequality and class conflict, but the Liberal system barely recognized the demands of emerging social classes as legitimate. It tolerated corruption in the south, and practiced repression everywhere, to keep workers and peasants in their place. The ruling Liberal Party (Partito Liberale Italiano, PLI) relied on local power brokers instead of building modern parties or strengthening civil society. And it practiced *trasformismo* in Parliament—that is, constructing a majority by winning over enough deputies, irrespective of political affiliation, by whatever means prove most effective. What is ultimately "transformed" is the very meaning of the differences between parties, groups, and ideologies. If the opposition is absorbed into the government itself, so much the better.

Although the *Statuto albertino* made Roman Catholicism the official state religion, the Vatican rejected this effort at rapprochement. The church fiercely opposed liberalism for doctrinal reasons, since it could not countenance a philosophy that, at its core, questions established authority. But the Vatican also resented its loss of territory and population. In 1874, Pope Pius IX forbade Catholics from participating in the politics of the new state in his *non expedit* (noncooperation) decree. By the 1900s, political realism, and a less intransigent pope, gave Italy an openly Catholic Popular Party (Partito Popolare Italiano, PPI).

"Liberal" Italy was unworthy of the name. The polarized mass politics that followed World War I put the finishing touches on the old system of local power as the Socialists (Partito Socialista Italiano, PSI) and the PPI won more than half the votes in the 1919 elections. When the Socialists then swept local elections in industrial areas, the old parties' bases of support were drastically reduced.[7]

Then in 1920, workers occupied factories across the north, striking fear in the hearts of industrialists and the urban middle class. Frightened bourgeois looked to the extreme right when they felt the state could no longer keep peasants and workers in line. The classes that supported the original post-Risorgimento coalition had grown increasingly distant from what was supposed to be their own regime. Armed Fascist squads sowed terror in the countryside of Italy's central regions and openly attacked the unions and the PSI in the cities of the north, as the regime stood by and watched.

The Vatican's weak commitment to the Popular Party and democracy was revealed as soon as Mussolini, upon taking power, showed a willingness to compromise with the church and extend it financial aid. Pope Pius XI eventually abandoned the PPI in 1924 when a pro-Fascist group seceded and formed its own Catholic party.[8]

Fascism (1922–1945)

Liberal indifference to democracy and postwar fears of revolution (fanned by Socialist rhetoric) provided fertile terrain for the Fascist movement. Benito Mussolini, a charismatic ex-Socialist, built up a quasi-military party organization that preached and practiced violence. Within a few years, his denunciations of Italy's "betrayal" after World War I, his open contempt for democracy, and his willingness to attack the left won him support on the right and, more important, among masses of urban and rural property holders who had grown impatient with Liberal Italy's inability to adjust to the era of mass politics.

The Liberal system's fate was sealed following Mussolini's March on Rome in October 1922. This march was a successful act of intimidation. Tens of thousands of armed Fascist "Blackshirts" (the militia's uniform) paraded through the capital, and King Victor Emmanuel III asked Mussolini to form the next government. With only 32 of 530 seats in Parliament, the Fascist Party (Partito Nazionale Fascista, PNF) received support from the entire political spectrum (including the PPI), except the left.[9] Democratic freedoms were curtailed, and by 1926, following the murder of Socialist leader Giacomo Matteotti by Fascist thugs, a dictatorship was in place. Opposition parties were banned, the independent press was closed or brought to heel, and political opponents—mainly Socialists and Communists—were jailed or forced into exile.

Italian fascism's complexity and inconsistency help explain its broad appeal. Mussolini was openly contemptuous of the old political system; more important, he convinced people he would act decisively—especially to make sure that the left and the trade unions would be firmly put in their place. Denouncing the "decadence" of democracy, fascism claimed it would reclaim Italy's rightful place in the world as a great power, invoking the glory of the Romans. (Fasces, a Roman symbol of power and authority, are a bound bundle of rods symbolizing strength in unity.)

Mussolini had a particularly aggressive foreign policy. Before allying with Nazi Germany and Imperial Japan in World War II, Italy's 1936 conquest of Ethiopia led to condemnation by the League of Nations. When the military rose against the elected Spanish Republican government in 1936, Mussolini and Hitler joined the rebels in the Spanish Civil War, which lasted

three years and has been called the dress rehearsal for World War II. As Italy and Germany drew closer together, Mussolini passed anti-Semitic racial laws in 1938, stripping Jews of rights and property.

Political Trade-Offs. We must distinguish between the regime's claims and its accomplishments. Fascism's ambitions were openly totalitarian: Society was to be completely regimented. Mussolini, called il Duce (leader)—the living embodiment of all Fascist virtues—was at the very top of the pyramid. Citizens were to be made over in a new image, tough and uncorrupted by the materialistic softness represented by liberal democracy (or capitalism, for the really radical Fascists).

Coadiuvato

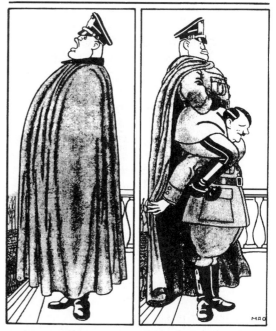

"Look at me, I'm a giant." Mussolini's reliance on Hitler is mocked in a 1939 cartoon.

Source: From Niccolò Zapponi, *Il fascismo nella caricatura* (Bari: Laterza, 1981).

Fascist legal and educational reforms indeed had totalitarian ambitions, but Mussolini was really more of a pragmatic maneuverer than a dedicated ideologue. Italy's entrenched problems continued under the dictatorship. For instance, Mussolini inherited a top-heavy state structure and centralized it even further. At the same time, local party officials often ran personal fiefs, which il Duce tolerated so long as leaders did not directly challenge his popularity.

Another trade-off was the Lateran Pacts, a series of agreements between church and state signed in 1929 that formalized the Catholic Church's privileged position in Italy. The most important was the Concordat, naming Roman Catholicism the official state religion, thus entitling the church to special privileges—above all, control over the compulsory weekly hour of religious teaching in Italy's public schools.* In return, the Fascist state obtained the recognition of the ecclesiastical authorities, which meant praise from thousands of pulpits every Sunday. The Vatican's approval of specific policies helped generate support for the regime and some of its more questionable adventures. When world opinion (except the Nazis) condemned Fascist aggression in Ethiopia, which not only was expressed in racist terms but also included the use of poison gas, Pope Pius XI applauded it. The pope also supported Mussolini's intervention on the side of Franco in the Spanish Civil War. And the Vatican was silent about the antisemitic racial laws of 1938.

In the economic sphere, fascism celebrated small producers in agriculture and industry but pursued policies that favored large firms. The Great Depression and League of Nations sanctions drove Mussolini to take protectionism to its logical conclusion: autarky, or economic self-sufficiency. He intended to continue his militaristic foreign policy, which required a heavy industrial sector. If others were going to try to

dictate policy to him, he would show that Italy could go it alone.

These decisions forced more state involvement in economic affairs, especially as the Great Depression took hold. The Institute for Industrial Reconstruction (Istituto per la Ricostruzione Industriale, IRI) was created in 1933 as a holding company for stocks that the state bought up as companies slid toward bankruptcy. Rome became increasingly involved in the ownership, and eventually the management and restructuring, of these distressed firms. In 1937, IRI became a permanent holding company geared to furthering rearmament and autarky. By 1940, about a fifth of all capital assets in all joint stock corporations in Italy were in IRI's hands, and important sectors of the economy, such as iron, steel, shipbuilding, and banking, were effectively monopolized by the state.

Fascism's End and the Republic's Birth (1945–1948)

By deposing Mussolini in 1943 and coming to terms with the Allies, Victor Emmanuel III and the army hoped to spare Italy further suffering and to salvage the monarchy in the bargain. But vacillating leadership allowed the Nazis to pour into Italy, set Mussolini up in a puppet regime in the north, and dig in along most of the length of the peninsula, guaranteeing a long, drawn-out war that only ended two weeks before Germany's final surrender. The 1943 declaration of war did legitimize the Resistance against the Nazis and their Fascist allies. In areas under Nazi and Fascist control, the Resistance became a brutal civil war. Its symbolic importance for the left cannot be stressed enough: it helped salvage national pride and honor, legitimizing the left, including Communists, as democratic and patriotic.

The war reinforced historic north-south divisions. The south was spared the worst of the conflict, as well as the brutal German occupation and the unifying liberation struggle. It was thus once more cut off from any direct role in some of Italy's most significant moments. This

---

*The others pacts recognized the Vatican as a sovereign city-state headed by the pope, and paid a large indemnity to the Vatican for property seized during the Risorgimento.

estrangement was apparent in the 1946 referendum to abolish the monarchy. The rest of the country could not forgive the king's role in supporting fascism and voted solidly for a republic, while the south opted for the monarchy, making the vote quite close (53 percent to 47 percent).

In 1946–1947, with the cold war brewing, a tense unity produced a constitution that reflected the few points of agreement and the many divisions of its writers (Chapter 23). At war's end, the Communists and Socialists were close allies. Combined, they accounted for 40 percent of the vote in the 1946 elections (see Table 21.1). Christian Democracy (Democrazia Cristiana, DC) was the largest party but garnered only 35 percent. Its favored status in the eyes of both the Catholic Church and the United States, and its social base in the small-holding peasantry and urban middle classes, ensured that the DC would not cooperate with the Communists and Socialists for long.

The 1946 vote, Italy's first exercise in truly universal suffrage, abolished the monarchy and elected a Constituent Assembly to serve as a temporary parliament and write a republican constitution within eighteen months. In 1947, as the constitutional exercise drew to a close, Christian Democrat prime minister Alcide De Gasperi ejected the Communists (Partito Comunista Italiano, PCI) and the pro-PCI Socialists from the government. The Socialist Party had split over how close its relation to the PCI should be, and De Gasperi and the DC would eventually be able to count on the breakaway Social Democrats (Partito Socialista Democratico Italiano, PSDI) as a reliable, if small, coalition partner. With cold war tensions at their peak, the DC won a crushing victory in 1948. This election saw lavish spending, and blatant intervention, by the United States on behalf of the DC. But many Italians needed little convincing to choose sides: in a totally polarized climate, they flocked to the DC as the surest defense against communism. For the only time in the history of the republic, a single party won an absolute majority of parliamentary seats (and over 48 percent of the popular vote).

Institutional Problems, Old and New. After il Duce, the consensus was that the legislature, not the executive, should be the supreme branch of government. From the beginning, a weak executive and fragmented party system produced unwieldy, unstable governing coalitions. Another sensitive issue was relations with the Catholic Church. As the cold war escalated, the Communists made a conciliatory gesture to the DC, and inserted the Lateran Pacts into Article 7 of the constitution. Notwithstanding this gesture, the PCI and PSI were soon in the opposition. Within a year, Pope Pius XII declared it a sin to uphold Marxist doctrine; by 1949 members of the PSI and PCI were excommunicated. The right and the church were now on the offensive. In fact, the Vatican went well beyond the considerable powers granted by Article 7 in the spheres of education and marriage to involve itself directly in Italian politics for a generation. Only in the 1980s, under a Polish pope and a Socialist prime minister, was the Concordat finally revised.

The DC-Dominated Postwar ("First") Republic (1948–1994)

Most Western European democracies saw postwar settlements between capital and labor, but in Italy and France, Communist leadership of the workers' movement produced a policy of *labor exclusion.* This was less a settlement than a lopsided truce: the left enjoyed political freedom and limited influence in the field of labor relations, with the tacit understanding that it was condemned to the role of permanent political opposition. It was clear by the late 1940s that the country would develop within the Western sphere of influence, with a more or less liberal-democratic institutional framework, but with precious little concern for the workers' principal representatives. Throughout the postwar period, the United States did not hesitate to intervene in domestic Italian politics to make sure that the Communists were kept in check. In the 1970s, the workers' movement made great gains, and

Table 21.1 Vote Obtained by Italian Parties in General Elections Under Proportional Representation During the "First Republic," 1946–1992 (percentage obtained by each party list in the 1946 Constituent Assembly and in the Chamber of Deputies thereafter)

Party	1946	1948	1953	1958	1963	1968	1972	1976	1979	1983	1987	1992
Far Left[a]	—	—	—	—	—	4.5%	2.8%	1.5%	2.2%	1.5%	1.7%	5.6%
PCI/PDS	18.9%	31%[b]	22.6%	22.7%	25.3%	27.0	27.2	34.4	30.4	29.9	26.6	16.1
PSI	20.7		12.7	14.3	13.9	14.5[c]	9.6	9.6	9.8	11.4	14.3	14.5
PR	—	—	—	—	—	—	—	1.1	3.5	2.2	2.6	1.2
Greens	—	—	—	—	—	—	—	—	—	—	2.5	3.0
PSDI	[d]	7.1	4.5	4.6	5.1	[d]	5.1	3.4	3.8	4.1	3.0	2.9
PRI	4.4	2.5	1.6	1.4	1.4	2.0	2.9	3.1	3.0	5.1	3.7	4.7
Leagues[e]	—	—	—	—	—	—	—	—	—	—	0.5	8.7
DC	35.2	48.5	40.1	42.4	33.3	39.1	38.7	38.7	38.3	32.9	34.3	29.7
PLI	6.8	3.8	3.0	3.6	7.0	5.8	3.9	1.3	1.9	2.9	2.1	3.0
Far Right[f]	8.1	4.8	12.8	9.6	6.9	5.8	8.7	6.1	5.9	6.8	5.9	5.4
Others	4.4	2.3	2.7	1.4	1.1	1.3	1.1	0.8	1.2	3.2	2.8	3.2
Total	100.0	100.0	100.0	100.0	100.0	100.0	100.0	100.0	100.0	100.0	100.0	100.0

[a] For 1964 and 1968, includes the PSIUP, which split from the PSI; from 1992, includes Rifondazione Comunista, which split from the PCI-DS.
[b] Result of united PCI-PSI list (Democratic Popular Front).
[c] Result of united PSI-PSDI list (United Socialist Party).
[d] Social Democrats were part of the PSI in 1946, split in 1947, then temporarily reunited with them during 1966–1969.
[e] Lombard League until 1992; Northern League thereafter.
[f] Uomo Qualunque and monarchists in 1946; neofascists and monarchists until 1972; MSI (neofascists) until 1992; AN thereafter.

Key: AN = National Alliance; DC = Christian Democracy; MSI = Italian Social Movement; PCI = Italian Communist Party; PDS = Democratic Party of the Left; PLI = Italian Liberal Party; PR = Radical Party (until 1992; Pannella list thereafter); PRI = Italian Republican Party; PSI = Italian Socialist Party; PSDI = Italian Social Democratic Party; PSIUP = Socialist Party of Proletarian Unity.

Source: For 1946 and 1948, Giuseppe Mammarella, *Italy After Fascism: A Political History 1943–1965* (Notre Dame, Ind.: University of Notre Dame Press, 1966), pp. 116, 194. Data since the 1953 elections compiled by author from newspapers.

the PCI contributed decisively to the stabilization of Italian democracy, but even when the Communists rose to over a third of the vote in the mid-1970s and their support was needed in Parliament, they were still denied a full share of political power. By the 1980s, union and PCI influence was again reduced as the tide turned in favor of business interests and the center of the political spectrum. Only the end of the cold war, massive scandals, and a total restructuring of the party system finally ended the DC-centered system of power in Italy and once more put the question of full governmental participation by a no-longer-Communist left on the agenda.

Christian Democratic Dominance. De Gasperi courageously resisted pressure from the Vatican and his own right wing to push Italy much further in the direction of a clerical, semi-authoritarian state. He thus looked to the center, not the extreme right, for his governing partners. Despite the notable achievement of presiding over the beginnings of Italy's "Economic Miracle," these centrist coalitions barely commanded a majority (see Table 21.1). Parliamentary arithmetic and hopes of increasing working-class support pointed to bringing the PSI—which grew increasingly distant from the Communists in the 1950s—into the government. This finally occurred in the early 1960s, against intense conservative resistance.

But the Socialists' alliance with the DC cost them votes and credibility on the left. Communist support grew steadily into the 1970s, and when the PCI reached its historic high of 34.4 percent in 1976, the DC was forced to make a number of concessions, including, for a time, accepting Communist votes in order to continue governing. The DC's sense of self-preservation, and the unacceptability of formal Communist participation in a Western government, thwarted PCI secretary Enrico Berlinguer's more optimistic ambitions of a historic compromise between the PCI and DC. By the end of the 1970s, a frustrated PCI was back in the opposition, where it languished and steadily lost votes.

PSI leader Bettino Craxi's aggressive strategy appeared to be paying off. When scandals weakened the DC, Craxi became prime minister in 1983, although his own party commanded barely 11 percent of the vote. His first government was the longest-lived of the entire postwar period, and he could boast important achievements, including a new Concordat in 1984. But his strategy was fatally flawed. His aggressive attacks on the PCI and the unions undermined Socialist credibility on the left. At the same time, the DC-PSI partnership degenerated into a shameless, increasingly corrupt struggle over political spoils.

And these spoils were abundant, for the DC leaders had found that they could use Italy's many public resources, inherited from fascism, to build a patronage structure that made the party less dependent on the Vatican, the United States, southern notables, and big industry. These spoils helped them build the party organization, while serving as a source of funds and favors for the party faithful—beginning with members of one's own faction. These measures gave the DC the glue that held its heterogeneous constituencies together.

The groundwork was laid for what one writer aptly called the DC's "occupation of power."[10] This colonization of state and parastate apparatuses accelerated throughout the 1960s and 1970s, contributing to Italy's huge public sector deficits while setting the stage for truly prodigious amounts of corruption.

Governing the Postwar Economy Through the 1970s. Chapter 22 addresses this topic in depth, but it is important to understand the social and political foundations of Italy's postwar development. *Labor exclusion,* in cold war conditions, meant that the unions were both weak and politically divided. Labor's major union, the General Confederation of Italian Labor (Confederazione Generale Italiana del Lavoro, CGIL), was dominated by the PCI and PSI; once the left was expelled from the government, its unity was doomed. Catholics left to found the Italian Con-

federation of Workers' Trade Unions (Confederazione Italiana Sindacati Lavoratori, CISL), which remained closely tied to the DC. A year later, Social Democrats and Republicans exited the CGIL to form the Union of Italian Labor (UIL), the smallest of the major confederations. These partisan divisions reinforced labor's weakness.

Following a brief season of promised reforms in the early 1960s, the workers' movement was finally able to take advantage of Italy's booming growth, which created conditions of near-full employment, giving the unions increased leverage in contract negotiations. Their growing strength also produced increasing cooperation among the previously divided union confederations. Political divisions suddenly mattered less than finally enjoying more of the benefits produced by the Economic Miracle. The result of the unions' new strength and unity was the militant period known as the Hot Autumn of 1969, which actually ran from 1968 into 1970. Divided and demoralized employers made concessions that drove up production costs. Weak governments granted most of the workers' demands, and then made costly commitments to the self-employed and other middle-class categories to guarantee their continuing support. The welfare state mushroomed. The price of this politically motivated generosity was evident in Italy's distressed public finances, a legacy that lingered into the 1990s, threatening Italy's membership in the emerging EU.

The Politics of Collective Identity. As social mobilization and gains for the left continued, democracy itself appeared threatened. Terrorists from both the extreme right and left arose on the fringes of mass movements, and tried to destabilize the political system and to provoke a coup (right) or a revolution (left). Although they failed miserably in their broader goals, these groups shook the country to its foundations throughout the 1970s and into the 1980s.

Terrorism was an extreme symptom of the profound changes that Italian society was undergoing and that its deadlocked political system was unable to resolve. Terrorism was also a distorted reaction by marginal groups to the widespread mass mobilizations that involved millions of Italians in the course of the 1960s and 1970s. Workers, students, and women erupted onto the political stage, sweeping aside entrenched but out-of-date values and practices. Nowhere is this more evident than in the 1974 referendum to repeal Italy's new divorce law. The referendum failed by a 40-to-60 margin, a gap that shocked everyone. (A 1981 referendum on abortion produced an even worse defeat for the church and DC.)

1992 to the Present: Toward a Second Republic?

Despite constant squabbling, the DC's and the PSI's hold on the reins of power appeared secure through the 1980s. Yet within a few years, the collapse of communism set in motion a chain of events that found the ruling parties fighting for their very survival—and losing. The DC, which had utterly dominated Italian politics for two generations, averaging almost 40 percent of the vote for most of that period, suddenly dropped under 30 percent in 1992; by 1994 the DC had renamed itself in a last-ditch effort to salvage some credibility. Its successor, however, barely obtained one vote in ten. The Socialists suffered an even greater collapse: from a more modest starting point, they had risen to almost 15 percent of the vote by 1992, and seemed to be on the verge of replacing the Communists as Italy's second largest party. Within two years, the PSI had effectively ceased to exist.

What accounts for this turnaround? Broadly speaking, the answer can be found in the four themes that inform the organization of this book. *The world of states* impinged directly on Italy at the end of the 1980s, most obviously in the collapse of communism. Within days of the fall of the Berlin Wall, the largest Communist party in the Western world announced that it would dissolve itself to become a new left-wing actor. This removed the DC's main rationale to be Italy's perennial governing party. And it also encouraged prosecutors to pursue corruption in governing circles with far more purpose, and courage, than they had in the past.

The other way Italy's international placement had a direct impact on the course of events overlaps with *governing the economy.* As the DC-PSI rivalry intensified, with an increase in lavish public spending, the global and European tide shifted decisively in the opposite direction. As the move toward European integration gained momentum, Italy simply could not continue business as usual. Changes in the *democratic idea* were most evident in the increasingly rapid erosion of support for the ruling parties, whose credibility plummeted under these combined pressures, particularly since they failed to grasp the changes taking place around them.

The rapid erosion of old *collective identities,* including the political loyalties that had shaped postwar history, was accompanied by the rise of entirely new identities. Various leagues sprang up in the north, doing best in historic DC strongholds in the Catholic northeast. Their origins were often separatist, but their major attraction was unquestionably an antiparty and anti-Rome rhetoric that appealed to the "little people," who saw greedy, corrupt politicians squandering their hard-earned money—especially on the south. By 1992 they had united into the Northern League (Lega Nord) and, with a quarter of the vote, were the largest party in Lombardy and the Veneto, two of the country's most dynamic regions.

Twice in the early 1990s, reformers tapped a tide of rising public disgust with the ruling parties, using abrogative referenda (Chapter 23) to force changes on the electoral system. In 1991, and again in 1993, referenda effectively forced Parliament to rewrite the electoral laws. On both occasions, the leaders of the DC and PSI openly opposed the proposed changes, and even counseled their followers not to vote. The public ignored these suggestions, and voted overwhelmingly to change the existing laws: 96 percent voted to abolish in 1991, while 83 percent did so in 1993.[11]

The outcome of the 1993 referendum was a predominantly first-past-the-post system for 75 percent of the seats and a more restricted proportional representation (PR) for the remaining quarter. A two-ballot electoral law for municipal elections was also instituted. Mayors are now directly elected, with a second, runoff ballot held if no candidate achieves a majority in the first round. This guarantees a clear mandate for individual candidates, thus limiting the leverage of the parties. Local elections held under this system in 1993 and 1994 were devastating for the DC and PSI. The once-mighty DC failed to make it to the second ballot in every important city, and the PSI was all but wiped out.

The old party system began to disintegrate in 1992, with evidence of a degree of corruption that shocked even hardened observers. As scores of politicians were arrested, the prestige of the ruling parties was obliterated, while investigators and prosecutors were turned into folk heroes. The scandal was dubbed *Tangentopoli* ("Bribesville"). Barely six months after the 1992 elections, five ministers had been forced to resign under a legal cloud. Within two years, roughly a fifth of the members of Parliament were in some form of legal trouble; the old style of politics was in terminal crisis. "Operation Clean Hands," as the entire anticorruption campaign was called, did not cause the ruling parties' downfall, but it certainly delivered the coup de grâce.

The End of the "First Republic."   Italy's economic woes compounded the political crisis. In 1992, the lira's weakness forced Italy's withdrawal from the European Monetary System (EMS), raising doubts as to whether the country could stabilize its currency and reduce its budget deficits sufficiently to meet the restrictive Maastricht convergence criteria for membership in the Economic and Monetary Union (EMU). Prime Minister Giuliano Amato, a Socialist appointed because of his clean reputation, responded with the most rigorous budget in living memory and is credited with starting Italy on the financial path to recovery.

It says everything about how seriously Italy took its economic plight to note that Amato was followed by Carlo Azeglio Ciampi, a former governor of the Bank of Italy. Ciampi's appointment was a clear signal to foreign markets that the economy remained in capable hands. Ciampi's was an explicitly nonpartisan technical government of specialists whose mandate was to address pressing economic problems and prepare the country for new elections.

The Emergence of a New Party System. As *Tangentopoli* ground on, the Northern League became the largest party in the north. The ex-Communist left began to rejuvenate, and swept local elections late in 1993. The most important of these took place in Rome and Naples, where the moribund DC failed to make the runoffs. The pariah of the First Republic, the neofascist Italian Social Movement (Movimento Sociale Italiano, MSI) appeared to be the only party able to fill the vacuum on the right. Running Mussolini's granddaughter in Naples and its own telegenic leader, Gianfranco Fini, in Rome, the MSI shattered its outcast status by making it into both runoffs. Silvio Berlusconi, a swashbuckling entrepreneur and media magnate closely tied to the former ruling parties, announced that if he lived in Rome, he would vote for Fini. In the runoffs, the MSI exceeded 40 percent, but the left won handily and appeared poised to do the same in what many were thinking of as the first general elections of the Second Republic.

Frightened by the left's successes, Berlusconi created his own party, called Forza Italia (FI), "Go Italy," which is the cheer for the national soccer team. He might owe his dominant media position to Italy's discredited former leaders (above all Craxi), but Berlusconi really did represent something new on the Italian political scene. Far more than a media phenomenon, Berlusconi was the center-right's political lifeboat. He was a respectable alternative to the Northern League and MSI, and veterans from the discredited parties flocked to FI, ready to

trade their much-needed experience for a chance to remain in power.

Berlusconi and his staff understood the logic of the new electoral system, and quickly set about finding attractive candidates to stand in Italy's new single-member districts in the 1994 general election. Undeterred by the fact that his major coalition partners could not stand each other, he engineered different alliances in the south and north: with the National Alliance (AN), as the MSI was rebaptized, and with the Northern League. Running a slick media campaign, the center-right won an absolute majority in the Chamber of Deputies, and a near majority in the Senate.

The March 1994 elections seemed to signal the definitive end of the First Republic. As anticipated, the new electoral law produced a rough bipolarity: the left-wing Progressive Alliance (Progressisti) and the two center-right groupings accounted for the vast majority of votes and seats alike. The PPI, which, as the DC, had dominated the republic's entire political history, tried to run as a centrist force. It managed 11 percent of the vote and was able to win precisely 4 of Italy's 475 single-member districts. Even allied with another ex-DC group, it obtained only 7 percent of the seats in the Chamber. The PSI fared even worse; it effectively disappeared. The largest vote-getter in the country, Forza Italia, had not even existed five months earlier.

Continuity and Change in the Political Sphere. When we recall the nature of the Italian party system for almost fifty years, the term *continuity* would seem to have no place in any discussion of the last decade. The old "frozen" party system has been swept away, replaced in the main by forces that either did not exist at all in the 1980s or have undergone radical changes since then. A political dynamic that permitted no alternation in power has seen, successively, a center-right coalition replaced by one of the center-left, which was then turned out of office by the center-right again. This might be a normal occurrence in most democratic systems, but in 2001, when the center-left lost to the center-right, there had not been a single occasion in the entire twentieth century when the opposition had replaced a sitting government.*

There were other novelties as well. In contrast to the old proportional system, with its parade of dividing the spoils behind the scenes, the new electoral system has—for better and for worse—personalized politics as never before. Nowhere is this more apparent than in the case of Silvio Berlusconi. And very few observers could have imagined, even as late as the 1980s, that a former Communist (Massimo D'Alema) would become prime minister, or that a neofascist leader (Gianfranco Fini) would be deputy prime minister.

Where, then, are signs of continuity? First and foremost in the dynamics of the party system: The individual parties have been transformed, but the party system remains highly fragmented, with all the problems this implies. Despite a new electoral system, there were actually more parties in Parliament after the 1994 vote than there had been previously. And while there may now be two large political blocs, neither can be called coherent or cohesive.

In fact, Berlusconi's first government lasted all of seven months before the Northern League withdrew its support. The year that preceded the 1996 elections saw the League join with the left to keep a caretaker government alive. In 1996, the ex-Communists learned from their mistake in 1994, and constructed a more broad-based coalition with an attractive leader. Romano Prodi was a prestigious economist, a Catholic who could appeal to middle-of-the-road voters. He led the center-left Olive Tree (Ulivo) coalition to victory, thanks above all to the fact that the Lega ran alone in the north, splitting the right-wing vote. Even so, the Ulivo had to rely on the votes of the far left to stay in power, and, after only two years, Prodi lost a confidence vote and was

*The previous occasion was 1876. When the center-left won in 1996, it did not replace the center-right, which resigned in 1995 and was replaced by a coalition of "technicians."

forced to step aside. When Massimo D'Alema replaced him, it was only thanks to the support of a small centrist party that bolted from the center-right. All this maneuvering, sabotaging of one's own side, and alliance switching recalled the First Republic, suggesting that Parliament was still very much at the mercy of the parties, even though most of them were new.

Berlusconi reconstituted the center-right in 2001, and his second government appeared to be the most solidly entrenched of the so-called Second Republic, with a clear majority in each chamber of Parliament. Importantly, this majority did not depend on the often-unpredictable League's support—although the coalition remained racked by internal rivalries and tensions. But in 2001, Forza Italia had become the largest party in the coalition, and the country, by far (see Table 21.2), enabling Berlusconi to ensure that his loyal followers occupied a much larger portion of strategic positions inside and outside the government.

Continuity and Change in the Policy Arena. In view of the First Republic's parliamentary immobilism, one of the strongest wishes of reformers was that a bipolar system would finally enable real alternatives to be proposed, and acted upon, if relatively coherent blocs or coalitions competed directly for power. None of the coalitions elected since 1994 has been a model of coherence, and much legislation passed since then reflects the sorts of compromises typical of heterogeneous governments. Some legislation has also managed to produce divisions within whichever majority was governing, and only passed because of help from within the ranks of the opposition.

Yet in some ways the hoped-for result has indeed been achieved, although this may turn out to be less of a blessing than reformers predicted. An electoral system that produces majorities out of a fragmented reality is electing representatives to a parliament in which the majoritarian principle is practically unfettered. Thus, during its five years in office, the Ulivo could boast of

Table 21.2   Election Results in the Chamber of Deputies, 1994–2001: Results since the Adoption of the New, Mixed, Electoral System

List or Bloc	1994 Single-Member Seats*	1994 PR List Seats	1994 Percentage of Vote**	1996 Single-Member Seats*	1996 PR List Seats	1996 Percentage of Vote**	2001 Single-Member Seats*	2001 PR List Seats	2001 Percentage of Vote**
Center-Right[a]	**301**			**169**			**282**		
Forza Italia	(69)	30	21.0	(85)	37	20.6	(127)	62	29.4
MSI/AN	1+(84)	23	13.4	(64)	28	15.7	(73)	24	12.0
Ex-DC	(29)	[b]		(18)	12	5.8	(41)	—	3.2
Minor Lay Parties	(8)	—	3.5	(2)	—	1.9	(11)	—	1.0
Lega Nord (part of Pole in 1994 and 2001)	(106)	11	8.4				(30)	—	3.9
Lega Nord (alone in 1996)				**39**	20	10.1			
Pact for Italy (1994)	**(4)**								
PPI (split in 1995)		29	11.1						
Segni Pact		13	4.6						
Progressives (1994)/ Olive Tree (1996, 2001)	**164**			**246**			**184**		
PDS/DS	(71)	38	20.4	(124)	26	21.1	(107)	31	16.5
Ex-PSI, Lay Parties	(14)	—	2.2	(24)	8	4.3	[d]	—	
Verdi	(11)	—	2.7	(14)	—	2.5	(18)	—	2.2
Other Leftist Groups	(30)	—	3.1	(19)	—	4.0	(9)	—	1.7
"For Prodi" (1996)	—	—	—	(63)	4	6.8			
Daisy List (2001)							(49)	27	14.5
Rifondazione Comunista	(28)	11	6.0	**15[c]**	20	8.6	[b]	11	5.0

Note: First used in 1994, the electoral system consists of 475 single-member constituencies (75% of all seats) and the remaining 155 seats distributed according to the proportion of votes obtained by party lists. Numbers may not add up to 100 percent or 630 seats because lists and blocs are selective.

*Boldfaced numbers indicate all single-member seats won outright by a bloc or list; numbers in parentheses refer to the distribution of single-member seats assigned to various parties within blocs.

**Percentage of vote is that obtained by individual lists on the separate proportional ballot.

[a] In 1994, ran as Freedom Pole (North) and Pole of Good Government (Center-South); in 2001 ran as Freedom's Home.

[b] Did not present a separate list in this election.

[c] In a stand-down agreement with the Olive Tree, but not officially part of the alliance.

[d] With Daisy List.

Source: Compiled by the author from various press and Web sources.

many important achievements. The health system was restructured. Administrative reforms began to streamline and simplify one of the West's most inefficient and unresponsive bureaucracies. Italy's entrenched (and, to many, tyrannical) criminal justice procedures were changed, amending the constitution to guarantee that the accused and the prosecution have equal status. The Ulivo also carried out important educational reforms, revamping the requirements, structure, and curriculum of the public school system and the universities. Another constitutional amendment changed the way the governments of the regions are elected and then devolved considerable powers to local governments, introducing a variant of federalism into the constitution.

This is an impressive record, and when the center-right won in 2001 it also undertook a number of highly ambitious reforms. One of the most notorious was a law that effectively forbade just about every form of assisted procreation, delighting orthodox Catholics inside the government (and the Vatican). There was also legislation one would expect from a more right-leaning government, such as a more restrictive immigration law, along with a tax simplification scheme. But the center-right also promptly set about to undo the Ulivo's educational and immigration reforms, as well as to propose its own much more extensive rewriting of the constitution in a federal direction. In short, alternation in power has indeed produced opposed proposals, but it has also thereby produced potential—and in the two cases just mentioned, real—dramatic swings in policy, whereby a new set of rules is hardly in place before it is abruptly replaced by another.

Italy in the Euro Era

The center-left's most striking achievements were economic and financial. Against many European leaders' confident predictions, and smug expectations, Italy met the Maastricht convergence criteria in mid-1998 and was thus present among the (eleven) founders when the euro was officially adopted in 1999. When the Ulivo took power in 1996, Italy was still a long way from meeting the criteria for inclusion in the establishment of the EMU. But starting with Amato's austerity measures in 1993, the country had embarked on a systematic effort that was eventually crowned with success during Prodi's premiership.

Prodi managed this feat thanks to considerable belt tightening, tax increases, and much cooperation from the unions.[12] His coalition depended on the external support of the far-left Communist Refoundation Party (Partito della Rifondazione Comunista, PRC), which made his tightrope-walking act even more precarious, for the PRC had threatened to bring down the government if it cut social programs. When Prodi's "EU Budget" was presented, not only did Rifondazione vote for it, but Forza Italia and the Lega abstained.

This outcome can be understood only in terms of Italy's obsession with being included in the euro zone and, more broadly, with being considered a serious country among its peers. Once this milestone was reached, Prodi and his successors would continue to impose far more restrictive budgets—in the name of maintaining Italy's commitments—than would have been imaginable a few years earlier. There is no doubt that Prodi's impressive achievements as prime minister paved the way for his selection by the governments of the EU as president of the European Commission once Rifondazione pushed him out of the prime minister's office in 1998.

As the domestic problems of Prodi, and his successor, D'Alema, show, Italian parliamentary bickering and maneuvering remain quite capable of paralyzing legislative initiatives and bringing down governments, suggesting disturbing continuities with the so-called First Republic. Yet, the "European imperative" had obviously introduced a series of constraints on almost the entire political class inside Parliament, as well as on significant actors, like the unions, outside the legislature.

We saw at the very start of this chapter that the new prime minister had his own personal reasons for bucking some European trends, particularly in the area of law enforcement. But by the time Berlusconi reentered Palazzo Chigi (the prime minister's residence), the bloom on the European rose also had faded. The goal of gaining entry to the euro zone had been achieved; the pain could now be blamed on the Ulivo. The economy was stagnant, and it had become fashionable to blame this and rising inflation on the euro. There were more profound factors at work as well. For one thing, as we discuss in Chapter 22, the new center-right government felt much less bound to sit down with the unions and work things out than had its predecessors. For another thing, there were members of the coalition who had become fiercely anti-European (the League) or at least euroskeptical (many members of Forza Italia, though not Berlusconi's closest collaborators). As a result, Berlusconi had to do some tightrope walking himself. In the first six months of the new government, there were so many discordant voices on the EU, and a distinct lack of firmness in bringing the critics to heel on Berlusconi's part, that his foreign minister was effectively forced to resign. It is a sign of the difficulties this subject created for him that Berlusconi had to take on the portfolio of foreign minister for nearly a year, until he finally named his own ultraloyal replacement from within Forza Italia without much consultation with the rest of his cabinet. He also took some foreign policy decisions (e.g., on collaboration in an Airbus initiative, on Russia, and on Iraq) that put him out of step with traditional allies in the EU.[13]

A final reason for tensions and difficulties between Berlusconi's government and the EU can be found in domestic political considerations. Romano Prodi not only is president of the European Commission but is also the consensus choice to lead the center-left into the next elections, scheduled for 2006; this makes him Berlusconi's current and future rival. Even with a less partisan and egotistical politician than

Berlusconi, tension would be inevitable in the Italian government's dealings with the Commission under these circumstances.

Italy After September 11, 2001. Italy has been no stranger to terrorism. Domestically, the Red Brigades and similar groups killed over four hundred individuals, including five-time prime minister Aldo Moro, because they were considered "class enemies"; although these attacks peaked in the 1970s, sporadic murders still take place. Between the Hot Autumn and the 1980s, fascist bombs struck more indiscriminately in train stations, banks, and other public places, killing several hundred Italians. International terrorism has also involved Italians, bringing the Middle East uncomfortably close to home. Separate massacres in 1973 and 1985 in Rome's airport killed over thirty people, while the hijacking of the cruise ship *Achille Lauro* made headlines in 1985 when the hijackers murdered a disabled Jewish passenger.

Among West European countries, it would be hard to find an ally more loyal to the United States than Italy in the postwar period, due to Italy's historical weaknesses (see below), and to the obvious benefits, ideological as well as material, it gained during the cold war. This loyalty—some critics call it subservience—continued even when the center-left was in power and a former Communist was prime minister, for Massimo D'Alema's government approved U.S.-imposed NATO air strikes directed at Serbia during the 1999 Yugoslav-Kosovo conflict, to the consternation of at least part of the left. But D'Alema was able to argue that the intervention was multilateral, and Italy was thus behaving very much within its traditional foreign policy framework. And Italy's participation in the overthrow of the Taliban in Afghanistan following September 11, involving the commitment of nearly 3,000 troops, fit very much within this mold.

Berlusconi's enthusiastic support for the much less multilateral invasion and occupation of Iraq put him at odds with France, Germany, and, latterly, Spain among the largest continental West European countries. He has in fact styled himself as George Bush's most loyal European ally, and—with the obvious exception of British prime minister Tony Blair—there is some truth in this assertion. There is also another parallel to Blair, in that Italian public opinion has consistently been among the most opposed to the invasion and subsequent occupation of Iraq among all EU members. Yet the Italian government has continued to express a preference for multilateral solutions to the Iraq question, and even the opposition (save for the far left and the Greens) is committed to a continued presence under international auspices. Italy's commitment to Iraq has been more than verbal: over 2,000 soldiers were sent there. This commitment has been costly. A suicide bombing late in 2003 killed 17 Italian soldiers, as well as 8 Iraqis, and the subsequent kidnapping of 4 Italian journalists, civilian contractors, and social workers (some of whom have been murdered) received worldwide attention as well as saturation coverage in Italy.

There have been domestic developments that might seem to be reactions to September 11, but it would be an exaggeration to give this terrible event too much weight in the Italian context. As we discuss in Chapter 22, the restrictive immigration law passed at the end of 2001 had been promised long before the summer of 2001.

Themes and Implications

Some of the four broad themes that inform this book are discussed more fully in subsequent chapters, but we can quickly review all four here.

Historical Junctures and Political Themes

The democratic idea has been no abstraction in Italian history. Each of Italy's critical junctures has been marked by deep differences over the very meaning of democracy and how much of it is desirable. The Risorgimento saw the victory of those with an extremely limited definition of democracy, but also the overt hostility of the Roman Catholic Church. The church's opposition to democracy continued throughout the Liberal regime, which tolerated blatant corruption and backroom deals (*trasformismo*) to avoid enfranchising the masses—and then to avoid responding to their demands. Fascism crushed the workers' movement, which attempted to broaden the meaning of democracy to include social issues, and it also crushed conservative democrats. Because of the painful past, the mass parties that built the postwar republic in the wake of war and Resistance defined democracy as, above all, a proportional principle of representation with a legislature that strictly limited executive powers. Cumbersome and prone to paralysis, this system survived cold war polarization, when the DC was able to pose itself as democracy's most reliable defender against communism.

The end of the cold war, changing economic realities, and the corruption that grew out of the DC's uninterrupted domination of Italy's postwar governments finally led to a break with the past. This was framed as allowing Italy to become a mature democracy in which government and opposition could alternate in power and in which voters would be able to translate their choices into effective political action. Conflicting visions of democracy—a participatory but fractious (and often paralyzed) conception of democracy versus more efficient and stable governments (with strong executives)—have been central to Italian political debate since the 1980s.

The world of states is a theme that Italy, from unification onward, has been unable to avoid. Powerful neighbors dictated the timing of unification and the country's eventual borders. National leaders consciously imitated Prussia's interventionist behavior as a more suitable model for a latecomer, and leaders tried, with less success, to imitate their neighbors' colonial triumphs. Exaggerated international ambitions

had the most profound effects on fascism's behavior, leading to international isolation, adven-
turism, and eventually complete disaster in World
War II. In the postwar world, Italy played a modest international role, often abjectly subservient
to the United States. But by placing itself squarely
in the Western camp, the country's political leadership ensured that the largest opposition party,
the PCI—identified with the other major camp—
would remain excluded from a governing role.
Because its party system, based on this division,
lasted so long, the collapse of the state socialist
systems of Eastern Europe had a dramatic domestic effect—not as great as in Germany, to be sure,
although the Italian party system certainly has
changed more than in any other country.

Governing the economy meant, from the
1870s until the triumph of free-market ideology
in the 1980s and 1990s, extensive state involvement in economic affairs. Italy came out of
World War II with the West's largest public sector. The "occupation" of this state by the DC
(and its allies) profoundly shaped the postwar
political economy. The system that evolved
eventually produced budget deficits and accumulated debt unrivaled among the major economic powers of the West. The profligate
practices of Italy's ruling parties made the country vulnerable in the changed international economic situation of the 1980s and played an
important role in creating the crisis of the political system in the 1990s.

The politics of collective identity has been an
elusive, problematic concept for Italy. At the
time of the Risorgimento, Italy was considered
more a geographical expression than a true
nation-state, and this generalization seemed
to hold true well into the late twentieth century.
In a pioneering study of political culture by
political scientists Gabriel Almond and Sidney
Verba, Italians stood out for their lack of
pride in the state or its institutions and instead
identified with Italy's artistic heritage and
natural beauty.[14] The term for localism—
campanilismo—expresses the sense that the

world that matters is within sound of the town
bell tower (*campanile*).

Stereotypes may reflect a partial reality, but
they also glide over uncomfortable facts. Mussolini's excesses were enthusiastically supported
by most Italians until Allied bombings and inva-
sions brought the war's brutal costs home.
Healthy second thoughts as well as outright embarrassment might account for the lack of nationalistic pride in the postwar period. It is also
true, as many have observed, that Italy's political institutions and elites have done little to win
citizens' allegiance.

Postwar politics were characterized by intensely held identities that underpinned cold war
polarization for nearly two generations. These
were explicitly *political* identities, built around
mutually antagonistic subcultures, Catholic
("white") and "red"—that is, identified with the
Socialist and Communist traditions, respectively.
Deeply rooted class divisions fed these subcultures, but neither had a very pure class base. The
DC, and even the PCI to a striking degree, were
able to win support across social groups on the basis of political allegiance. This explains the
longevity of their appeal: each was rooted in and
dominated specific areas of the country, guaranteeing a powerful political base. Only the dissolution of cold war polarization, compounded by a
rapidly modernizing society that weakened traditional political organizations and practices, finally
undermined these subcultures, though it has not
eliminated them altogether.

What has replaced the old identities? At times
nothing, or, more exactly, a politics based on
identifying not with tradition or ideological commitment, but with platforms and concrete policies. In other cases, as the success of the Northern
League indicates, new identities based on regionalism have filled the vacuum left by the collapse
of DC hegemony. The League initially targeted
southern Italians, reproducing one of Italy's oldest cleavages. But as the movement unified and
tried to expand, it increasingly focused on a new
"other": dark-skinned immigrants.

Implications for Comparative Politics

To study Italy is to take a continuing course in comparative politics. For many of its earlier historic junctures, interesting and fruitful comparisons could be drawn with Germany. Unified at about the same time, Italians consciously copied Prussia's interventionist model of development after laissez-faire policies (copied from Britain) failed to move the economy ahead at a satisfactory pace. Italy then was itself the pioneer; it invented fascism. Both countries had this grim legacy to overcome in their postwar democratic experiments, and both were dominated, though in different degrees, by Christian Democracy.

But despite these provocative parallels, comparisons with France in the postwar period are even more telling. Broad collaboration, followed by the isolation of the Communists, characterized both countries at war's end. But whereas new rules of the game under France's Fifth Republic laid the groundwork for reshaping the party system by the early 1960s, Italy kept the same rules and resembled the Fourth Republic's assembly-style democracy through the 1990s. In France, the Socialists became the dominant party on the left by joining the Communists, as the two-ballot electoral system required. In Italy, the Socialists tried to imitate Mitterrand's success by keeping the PCI at arm's length and were themselves crushed in the collapse of the old system.

In the area of policy, Italy, like other advanced capitalist democracies, faces daunting challenges in adjusting to the new international economy. It does so with a pair of distinct handicaps and one possible advantage. The first handicap is that in addition to considerable economic difficulties, Italy faces a full-fledged transitional crisis in the political sphere. The old party system has disintegrated, and a new one is struggling to be born. The process is fascinating, but it remains uncertain, and, as long as so much seems to depend on a single individual, it is also potentially destabilizing.

The second handicap aggravates the first. Italy's economic challenges are greater than those of other European countries. Its accumulated debt is enormous. And although it has moved, under unrelenting pressure from EU watchdogs, to divest the state of its considerable ownership of the economy, the very speed of this privatization guarantees that the process will be rather slapdash and not provide the country with the maximum benefits. Many other members of the EU face similar problems, but none is in worse shape along either of these dimensions.

Finally, Italy may have an advantage that grows, ironically, out of its historic shortcomings. Because the state has always been so weak and coherent direction of the economy so problematic, vast sectors of the Italian economy have flourished by taking advantage of local and international conditions. This remarkable resiliency has been much commented on, sometimes in exaggerated fashion, but there is no question that the demands of the new global economy reward these qualities.[15] The state and political sphere may stumble and stagger, but the economy seems, mercifully, to flourish despite its alleged political masters.

Notes

1. Massimo D'Alema, with Claudio Velardi and Gianni Cuperlo, *Un Paese normale: La sinistra e il futuro dell'Italia* (Milan: Mondadori, 1995).

2. David Hine, "Silvio Berlusconi, i media, e il conflitto d'interesse," in Paolo Bellucci and Martin Bull, eds., *Politica in Italia. Edizione 2002* (Bologna: Il Mulino, 2002), esp. pp. 293–294.

3. Ibid., p. 299; see also James L. Newell and Martin J. Bull, "Italian Politics After the 2001 General Election: *Plus ça change, plus c'est la même chose?*" *Parliamentary Affairs* 55 (2002): 640.

4. Felia Allum and James Newell, "Aspects of the Italian Transition: Introduction," *Journal of Modern Italian Studies* 8 (Summer 2003): 192.

5. Geographic details were obtained from the CIA's online factbook at http://www.cia.gov/cia/publications/factbook/geos/it.html#Geo.

6. Luigi Barzini, *The Italians* (New York: Atheneum, 1964), p. 241, quoted in Sidney G. Tarrow, *Peasant Communism in Southern Italy* (New Haven, Conn.: Yale University Press, 1967), p. 21.

7. The PSI won in over 2,000 of Italy's 8,000 municipalities. Frank M. Snowden, "From Sharecropper to Proletarian: The Background to Fascism in Rural Tuscany, 1880–1920," in John A. Davis, ed., *Gramsci and Italy's Passive Revolution* (New York: Barnes and Noble, 1979), p. 165.

8. Charles S. Maier, *Recasting Bourgeois Europe* (Princeton, N.J.: Princeton University Press, 1975), p. 548.

9. Paolo Farneti, "Social Conflict, Parliamentary Fragmentation, Institutional Shift, and the Rise of Fascism: Italy," in Juan J. Linz and Alfred Stepan, eds., *The Breakdown of Democratic Regimes: Europe* (Baltimore: Johns Hopkins University Press, 1978), pp. 23–26.

10. Ruggero Orfei, *L'Occupazione del potere: I democristiani '45–'75* (Milan: Longanesi, 1976).

11. Piergiorgio Corbetta and Arturo M. L. Parisi, "The Referendum on the Electoral Law for the Senate: Another Momentous April," in Carol Mershon and Gianfranco Pasquino, eds., *Italian Politics: Ending the First Republic* (Boulder, Colo.: Westview Press, 1995), pp. 75–92.

12. James I. Walsh, "L'incerto cammino verso l'Unione monetaria," in Luciano Bardi and Martin Rhodes, eds., *Politica in Italia, Edizione 98* (Bologna: Il Mulino, 1998), pp. 117ff.

13. Filippo Andreatta and Elisabetta Brighi, "La politica estera del governo Berlusconi: I primi 18 mesi," in Jean Blondel and Paolo Segatti, eds., *Politica in Italia: Edizione 2003* (Bologna: Il Mulino, 2003), pp. 263–265, 272–273.

14. Gabriel Almond and Sidney Verba, *The Civic Culture* (Boston: Little, Brown, 1959).

15. Richard M. Locke, *Remaking the Italian Economy* (Ithaca, N.Y.: Cornell University Press, 1995), esp. chap. 6.

CHAPTER

22

Political Economy and Development

Both a latecomer in the family of European nation-states and a late industrializer, Italy's development has been marked by considerable state intervention in the economy from the end of the nineteenth century. Even before the Fascists came to power, heavy industry had enjoyed a cozy relationship with the state. This favoritism was reinforced by Mussolini's militarism and his aggressively autarkic policies, which left huge portions of the economy in public hands by the end of World War II. The Christian Democrats (DC), who dominated the postwar republic for forty-five years, had few qualms about the large public sector they inherited, which they used for the common good but also, increasingly as time wore on, for narrowly political purposes. By the 1980s, problems common to all advanced societies were aggravated by two generations of an uninterrupted occupation of power. Joined by the Socialist Party (PSI) in the 1980s, the DC colonized great chunks of the state-owned parts of the economy. These parties increasingly used public enterprises to award contracts to their cronies, and to siphon off funds or collect kickbacks for the purpose of lining their parties' treasuries (and at times their own pockets).

The Postwar Settlement and Beyond

The postwar republic inherited from fascism very weak markets and a lopsided industrial structure that favored heavy industry. It also had the largest public sector among the Western economies. In some ways, this was an advantage:

the challenge of postwar reconstruction could never have been met by reliance on free-market forces alone.

State and Economy from Reconstruction to Crisis

Because the major parties that led the country in the immediate postwar period were either hostile to free-market principles (the Communists, or PCI, and the Socialists), or at least not opposed to interventionism (the DC), laissez-faire ideas were in a distinct minority. Long after the left's expulsion from government, the state continued to play an active role in Italy's economy. This interventionism helped set the stage for the impressive period known as Italy's Economic Miracle.

Yet for all its interventionism and high degree of public ownership of the economy, Italy never elaborated policies comparable to France's concerted *dirigisme,* or tradition of state-directed economic leadership. As a result, Italy's economic policies tended to be fragmented and uncoordinated, although they did produce impressive results starting in the 1950s.

Wartime devastation, the Resistance, and Italian capitalism's compromised position under fascism had initially favored the workers' movement. But cold war polarization meant that by 1947, the left had been expelled from the government. Italy's recovery was then built around low wages, a large surplus labor pool, and limited social spending. When the war ended, the United States put in place the European Recovery Plan (ERP, but also more commonly known as the Marshall Plan, after Secretary of State George C. Marshall) to get West European capitalism back on its feet. Administrators of the plan were soon openly criticizing Italy for, among other things, diverting hundreds of millions of dollars in aid earmarked for investments in order to bolster foreign reserves.[1]

The State and Private Sectors. Despite the prevalence of conservative policies, traditional economists did not completely carry the day even with the Communists and Socialists in the opposition. Some leaders, including Prime Minister Alcide De Gasperi, favored at least limited long-range planning and state intervention. Furthermore, the Marshall Plan required that recipient nations tell how their massive infusions of aid were being spent, and this aid was intended to stimulate the economy. (Italy eventually received $1.3 billion.[2]) Most important of all, the huge state holdings and banking and financial levers inherited from fascism were used in far-sighted fashion. Over the protests of both protected oligopolies and free marketers, huge sums were invested in key industries such as steel and chemicals. Successive governments gave free rein to public sector entrepreneurs, allowing them to reinvest dividends in state-held stocks with the result that Italy's industrial infrastructure was greatly strengthened. Before the DC seriously distorted the public sector of the economy for partisan (and private) ends, these policies paid handsome dividends. As Andrew Shonfield, a political economist who wrote an important study of postwar European economies, put it:

> It was another one of the characteristic Latin conspiracies in the public interest, of which France, in particular, has provided some outstanding examples. In Italy such things have to be done with greater stealth, because there is neither the instinctive French respect of the high public official, nor any of the confidence in his moral purpose.[3]

Public sector initiatives meshed well with the most dynamic parts of the private sector. By the late 1960s, Fiat had become Europe's largest auto manufacturer. Italian industry expanded enormously following Fiat's lead in mass-producing small cars, making the country a society of mass consumers. Aggressive export-oriented firms provided state-of-the-art products at low prices to increasingly affluent Europeans. By the mid-1950s, these companies were poised for maximum expansion. Earlier public sector intervention really paid off, as abundant steel, fuel, chemicals, and other goods enabled rapid expansion without many bottlenecks that inevitably would have occurred had free marketers won earlier debates about dismantling publicly owned firms. The groundwork for Italy's Economic Miracle was complete.

The Economic Miracle. In the early 1950s, a parliamentary committee of inquiry had described terrible living conditions. One family in eight lived in "utter destitution"; one house in ten had a bath; fewer than half of all Italians had an indoor toilet; and even fewer (38 percent) had indoor running water that was drinkable.[4] But then, throughout the 1950s and 1960s, Italy's economic growth ranked toward the very top of all West European countries.[5] Gross national product doubled between 1950 and 1962, finally reducing chronically high unemployment rates. Italy was forever altered in this period. By the 1970s, illiteracy was halved. Industrial workers surpassed the entire agricultural population in the 1960s, and the latter fell to a fifth of the total workforce by the 1971 census (see Table 22.1). New car registrations more than quadrupled in the 1960s. By other measures as well, such as televisions and telephones per capita, Italy was finally on a par with other large West European countries by 1971.[6]

But the miracle left important problems unresolved. Until northern factories expanded enough to absorb Italy's huge labor pool, only the steady emigration of (mainly southern) workers had avoided depression-era levels of unemployment. Between 1946 and 1955, net emigration totaled 1.6 million, and took a great deal of pressure off successive governments.[7]

Table 22.1   Occupation in Italy, by Sector of the Economy, 1951–2001

Economic Sector	1951 Employees	1961 Employees	1971 Employees	1981 Employees	1991 Employees	2001 Employees
Agriculture	43.9%	30.7%	20.1%	13.3%	8.4%	5.2%
All industries	29.5	34.9	39.5	37.2	32.0	31.8
All services, including government	26.6	34.4	40.4	49.5	59.6	63.0
Total	100.0	100.0	100.0	100.0	100.0	100.0
Number (000s)	(19,693)	(20,427)	(19,295)	(20,751)	(22,623)	(23,781)

Sources: For 1951, Kevin Allen and Andrew Stevenson, *An Introduction to the Italian Economy* (London: Martin Robertson and Co., 1975), p. 104. For 1961, CISL, *CISL 1984* (Rome: Edizioni Lavoro, 1984), p. 56. For 1971–1991, ISTAT (Italian Statistical Institute), *Italia in cifre*, 2000: "Lavoro," at www.istat.it, p. 2. For 2001, ISTAT, *Approfondimenti: 12_lavoro.pdf* at ibid., pp. 1, 2.

Much of the miracle was built on labor's weakness, which was only partially due to high levels of unemployment. After the left was expelled from government, the union movement split along partisan political lines, further weakening organized labor. The General Confederation of Italian Labor (CGIL), closely identified with the Communists and Socialists, was strongest among industrial workers. Nevertheless, because of its political affiliation, the CGIL steadily lost ground to the CISL, the predominantly Catholic Confederation of Italian Workers' Unions.[8] The much weaker UIL (Union of Italian Labor) consisted of more moderate non-Catholic unions, which tended to ally with the CISL.

The 1960s: The Tide Turns.   By the late 1960s, an improved employment picture and growing cooperation among the major confederations made unions increasingly aggressive as they tried to make up for their previous isolation and weakness. During the Hot Autumn of 1968 through 1969, they used extremely disruptive tactics to make impressive gains. The three major union confederations were not only cooperating but speaking of reunification. The Workers' Charter of 1970 guaranteed civil rights on the shop floor and entrenched the major con-

federations as bargaining agents. General strikes forced passage of a very generous pension scheme. Through the 1970s, Italy led the industrialized world in both the number and the intensity of strikes and other labor disputes. And even the statistics do not tell the whole story, for the workers adopted tactics that totally disrupted production at a minimum cost in terms of hours of pay lost. Colorfully named "checkerboard" or "hiccup" strikes, these work stoppages would spread across the entire factory floor in seemingly erratic fashion. Or they would suddenly flare up in one department, and then subside as another department was shut down; the process would be repeated until every department had downed tools once. At the end of the day, each worker might only have been docked for one hour's pay, but the cumulative damage to the company was immense.

Under these circumstances, contracts were so pro-labor that wages outstripped productivity (and inflation) through the 1970s, and overtime, layoffs, and even plant modernization became nearly impossible without negotiations with the unions. Wages were compressed, at the expense of more skilled workers, with a 1975 cost-of-living escalator (*scala mobile*) that kept wages in step with inflation. Because increases were based on the average worker's salary, they were equal for everyone, and hence bottom weighted: by design, the lowest salaries rose more than the highest. In an era of very high inflation like the late 1970s and early 1980s, the impact of the *scala mobile* was greatly magnified.

Crisis: The Late 1970s and Afterward

Italy's reliance on imported fuel made the oil shocks of 1973 and 1979 especially severe (see the inflation figures in Table 22.2). But by the mid-1970s, capitalist economies had a good deal more to worry about, and Italy was no exception. Growth slowed, unemployment rose, and militancy declined. The worst aspect of the crisis was—and remains—the fiscal problems of the Italian state. As Italy began to approximate a modern welfare state, expensive benefits won by workers were quickly granted by the DC to its own constituencies. The costs for these benefits were slapped onto an inefficient and irrational bureaucratic and fiscal structure that could neither deliver services effectively nor pay its own way.

The state managed to avoid alienating its major supporters by running up immense annual deficits, and hence the overall debt. Italy's soared over $100 billion in the 1980s, and the national debt rose well above 100 percent of gross domestic product (GDP). As successive governments had to face the consequences of their past actions, they began to raise taxes while making evasion more difficult. These measures aggravated the government's supporters, further undermining the ruling parties' legitimacy on the very eve of the *Tangentopoli* ("Bribesville") scandals.

The 1980s: The Tide Turns Again. Growing union weakness and the disappearance of hundreds of thousands of industrial jobs by the mid-1980s undercut militancy and emboldened management, which set out to reverse its defeats since the Hot Autumn. With the PSI and DC in government together again, tensions increased among the major confederations—and within

Table 22.2   Italian Economic Performance, 1971–2001 (odd-numbered years)

Year	Percentage Change of Real GDP over Previous Year	Percentage Rise in Consumer Prices over Previous Year	Percentage of Total Labor Force Unemployed
1971	1.6	4.8	5.4
1973	7.0	10.8	6.4
1975	3.6	17.0	5.9
1977	1.9	17.0	7.2
1979	4.9	14.8	7.7
1981	0.1	17.8	8.4
1983	1.2	15.0	9.8
1985	2.3	9.2	10.3
1987	3.0	4.7	12.0
1989	3.2	6.3	12.0
1991	1.2	6.2	10.9
1993	0.7	4.5	10.4
1995	3.0	5.2	11.6
1997	1.5	2.0	11.7
1999	2.1	1.7	11.4
2001	1.8	2.8	9.4

Sources: Real GDP and consumer prices through 1983: OECD and ISTAT figures cited in CISL, *CISL 1984* (Rome: Edizioni Lavoro, 1984), pp. 28, 32. Unemployment figures: ISTAT, *Annuario Statistico, 1983* (Rome: ISTAT, 1984), Table 292 for 1970–1982. For 1985, Ferruccio Marzano, "General Report on the Economic Situation of the Country in 1989," *Journal of Regional Policy* 10 (April–June 1990): 267–268. For 1986–1993: OECD, *OECD Economic Surveys: Italy* (Paris: OECD, 1995), pp. 144, 150. For 1994–2001, the 1999 ISTAT Yearbook: www.istat.it/Anumital/cifre.pdf, pp. 10, 20, and the 2002 *Rapporto Annuale*, Istat-2002.pdf downloaded from www.istat.it, p. 34.

the CGIL. By the time Socialist leader Bettino Craxi became prime minister in 1983, the stage was set for a showdown. Craxi ably played the CISL and UIL, as well as the Socialist minority in the CGIL, off against the Communists and their CGIL supporters. A head-on confrontation in the form of a referendum over limits imposed on the *scala mobile* led to a decisive political defeat in 1985, underscoring the PCI's isolation as well as the severity of the unions' crisis.

As Figure 22.1 shows, amidst a general decline in membership, the losses were worst for the CGIL starting in the late 1970s. This confederation's prominence has been due to its strength among industrial workers. Yet there is a reason that modern economies are called *post*industrial. By 1983, pensioners had replaced industrial workers as the largest single group in the CGIL. By the end of the 1990s, over half of all CGIL members were retired. The experience of the CISL was similar.[9] Table 22.1 shows that there were roughly equal numbers of service sector and industrial employees in the 1960s and into the 1970s, but by the 1990s, services outnumbered industry by two to one, which remains the current ratio. And even where industrial expansion has taken place, it has done so in small firms and in geographical regions (e.g., the Catholic northeast) where unions have historically had less organizing success.

Since the mid-1980s, the most intense contract disputes have involved white-collar and service sector workers, who often do not even belong to a major confederation. "Autonomous" unions, so called because of their independence of the CGIL-CISL-UIL, have become common in the public sector. They criticize the confederations as too tame, and undertake extensive job actions, often with considerable public disruption. Even more militant are the Committees of the Base (Comitati di Base, COBAS), which appeared in the mid-1980s in key state sectors such as railroads, air transportation, medicine, and education.[10] Finally, the PCI's transformation into the Democratic Party of the Left (Partito Democratico della Sinistra, PDS) led many hard-line Communists who refused to join the new party to form a more militant faction within the CGIL that is highly critical of the major confederations.

Organized labor was thus increasingly fragmented at the same time that its real weight in society was diminishing. Disruptive tactics fed

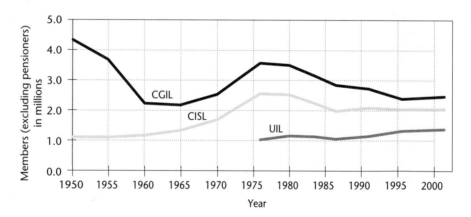

Figure 22.1   Total Union Membership, Excluding Pensioners, in the Major Confederations, Selected Years, 1950–2002 (in 000s)

Note: Reliable figures for the UIL are not available for 1950 through 1970.
Sources: For 1950–1970: Guido Romagnoli, ed., *La sindacalizzazione tra ideologia e pratica. Il caso italiano 1950–1977.* Vol. 2 (Rome: Edizioni Lavoro, 1978), Table 1.2. For 1976: Guido Romagnoli, "Sindacalizzazione e rappresentanza," in *Le Relazioni sindacali in Italia. Rapporto 1981,* ed. Guido Baglioni et al. (Rome: Edizioni Lavoro, 1982), Table 2. For 1980–1991: CESOS, *Le relazioni sindacali in Italia. Rapporto 1992–93* (Rome: Edizioni Lavoro, 1994), Table 3, p. 76. For 1986–1997: http://www.cisl.it/iscritti/isc86_97.htm. For more recent CISL data: http://www.cisl.it/iscritti/. For the UIL: http://www.uil.it/organizzazione/iscritti.htm For the CGIL, one must go to the home page at http://www.cgil.it/, and then follow the *Tesseramento* link, which provides access to membership figures between 1997 and 2003.

rising public impatience with, and resentment of, unions. These trends help explain why, in the early 1990s, the major confederations agreed to a reform of labor relations that institutionalized tripartite negotiations with management and the state. In terms of content, as we will see with regard to pension reforms, this framework of concertation guaranteed that the unions would be consulted and would be able to defend their interests in hard bargaining. In terms of formal structures, it gave them a solid representational base when their fortunes had waned.[11] And yet the unions, although weakened, remained relatively strong by international standards, still managing to organize roughly 40 percent of the labor force.

State and Economy

The very large state sector of the economy and the political uses to which it was put by the ruling parties ensured that Italy's embrace of laissez-faire, deregulation, and privatization would begin later (often against considerable resistance from within the ruling coalition) and be more limited than that of many other Western democracies.

Economic Management Since the 1980s

As we saw in the case of the unions, meaningful departures from earlier policies only began in the 1980s. The truly dramatic developments took place in the 1990s, as the ruling parties collapsed and the coming of the European Union required more forceful measures than in the past. When Craxi brought the Socialists back into the government in 1979, he demanded more leadership positions in the public sector, which led to intense battles between the PSI and DC over political spoils. But economic reality increasingly intruded into the infighting.

Privatization, Italian Style. If the governing parties did not rush to sell off Italy's immense public holdings in the 1980s, that is

because the stakes were enormous. State-owned enterprises employed 38 percent of the entire workforce in industry and services, and accounted for an even larger proportion (45 percent) of sales in those sectors.[12] But even though privatization at first proceeded at a fraction of the British or French rates, it did begin in the 1980s.[13]

Italian privatization has had a distinctive character, due to the (related) facts of the huge state sector, the weakness of Italian capital markets, and the domination of the private sector by a handful of large firms. The big companies have regularly colluded with Italy's largest private investment bank to dominate the stock market, making it very hard for small investors—and, above all, powerful competitors from outside Italy—to exert much influence.[14]

In the 1980s, changes in European Community (EC) rules explicitly excluded the sort of bailout operations the Italians had routinely practiced. Continued aid would only be given to governments that undertook serious restructuring of troubled companies—and "restructuring" increasingly came to mean the privatization of state-owned firms. When Italy began privatizing publicly owned companies in earnest in the 1990s, the state continued to keep a controlling share of these firms. Then, in an effort to circumvent EU policies, it adopted a "Golden Share" policy (using the English phrase). This amounts to veto power by the Italian Treasury when the sale of a company might compromise national security, as in defense-related industries, or where a private monopoly might result, as in utilities. These practices served domestic political functions, softening the rapid sell-off of so many firms, and reassuring more left-leaning members of the governing coalition. Such practices angered watchdogs in Brussels, who constantly threatened to take Italy to the European Court of Justice for violating EU rules.

But for all the foot dragging, the trend is clear and irreversible. The die was cast when the Ministry of State Holdings was eliminated in 1993. The most extensive sales took place under the center-left government of Romano Prodi between 1996 and 1998. By the end of the 1990s, once-sacrosanct areas of state intervention such as electric energy (nationalized under the first center-left government of the 1960s), steel, petroleum and natural gas, telecommunications, rail transport, autostradas, and innumerable industrial enterprises were sold off or were well on their way to being transferred out of state hands. When Italian Telecom was sold in 1997, it brought 26 trillion lire, or over $15 billion, into the Treasury and was the largest such sale in West European history, dubbed "the mother of all privatizations." Telecom had been one of the Institute for Industrial Reconstruction's (IRI) holdings, and its sale dropped IRI from the 35th-ranked corporation in the world to 157th.[15] By 2000 this symbol of Italian public enterprise had been totally liquidated. And in 2003 Berlusconi's second government announced that it was severely limiting the terms under which the Golden Share could be invoked.

The financial system was progressively deregulated starting in the 1980s; some of the most significant market-oriented changes occurred in the financial sector, mirroring trends everywhere in the advanced capitalist world. The Bank of Italy obtained its independence from the Treasury early in the decade. The bank had once been obliged to buy any government bonds not sold in the open market. Following this "divorce," higher interest rates were required to make the bonds more attractive.[16] In the mid-1980s, rules governing investment and borrowing abroad were liberalized. Toward the end of the decade, exchange regulations were loosened and banks were deregulated, greatly easing the flow of capital into and out of the country. By the end of the decade, experts called the financial sector "Anglo-Saxonized."[17] By the end of the 1990s, all financial markets had been privatized, and the tax system for investments was greatly simplified.[18]

Changing Industrial Relations. Relations between labor and capital have always been volatile in Italy. As the trends described above increasingly exposed Italy's economy to international competition, the strains increased. The most vulnerable firms were in the private sector, led by Confindustria (the Confederation of Italian Industries, the leading peak organization for private capital). They pressed, above all, for an end to the *scala mobile* and the introduction of much more flexibility into the labor market, which is another way of saying they wanted to see union power reduced dramatically. Although they won some political battles in this period, most notably on the *scala mobile,* their real advantage was that they had resurgent market forces on their side. By the mid-1980s, industrial jobs were disappearing in such large numbers that not even the vigorous small firms of the north, or the huge submerged economy, could absorb all the displaced workers. In the first four years of the 1990s, half a million manufacturing jobs disappeared.[19] These trends created enormous difficulties for capital, and their consequences were even more problematic for organized labor.

Given labor's vulnerability and Italy's history of fierce class conflict, why did the Italian unions not face the sort of onslaught that Margaret Thatcher unleashed on British unions? As we have already seen, in the early 1990s, the Italians adopted a policy of concertation, which involves cooperation among labor, management, and the state. Labor's weakness and fragmentation provided ample incentives for the unions to seek a more conciliatory stance, but why did the other major actors in this triad go along?

There could be no all-out conservative onslaught on labor because Italy lacked a genuine conservative party into the 1990s. The DC had never won the bourgeoisie's unqualified allegiance, and, with its strong peasant and middle-class base—not to mention a notable working-class component—it had numerous, and contradictory, interests to reconcile. It was not ideologically committed to laissez-faire policies, and its habit of lavishing public funds on pork-barrel projects never pleased business. But as long as it was the linchpin of the political system, the DC enjoyed the capitalists' support.

The rationales for this support had dissolved by the early 1990s. The Communist threat simply disappeared when the PCI (and the Soviet Union) ceased to exist. During the same period, globalizing trends and the move toward a more integrated EU drastically reduced the margins for maneuver that had permitted the old wasteful and corrupt practices. When the 1992 exchange rate crisis forced Italy's withdrawal from the European Monetary System (EMS), the political elite became convinced of the need for a stable framework of labor relations. *Tangentopoli* then made such an arrangement even more important in terms of Italy's international credibility.

Confindustria, its confidence growing with the unions' crisis, declared its effective political independence from the DC even before the final debacle of *Tangentopoli*.[20] But a number of changes on the entrepreneurial front and in the international economic situation soon persuaded many capitalists that concertation might be, if not the best, then the most prudent, path to follow. In the first place, Confindustria had grown much more diverse. Once dominated by large export-oriented firms, it had increasingly given voice to the small, extremely dynamic industries that have been the backbone of Italy's industrial dynamism in the past two decades. Although often not very hospitable to trade unions (except in the historic "red belt," the left's areas of greatest strength in the north-center of the country), these firms were far more interested in fighting for government deregulation and a lighter tax burden than they were in confronting the unions.

At the same time, galloping privatization was eliminating a historical division among the ranks of Italy's employers. Many of the largest, and most unionized, companies had been in public hands: the management of these companies had evolved far more cooperative relations with unions, going so far as to organize their own managers' association. With Italy's formal commitment to the elimination of state-owned industry in 1992–1993, the rationale for separate management representatives disappeared, and Confindustria basically absorbed these other organizations.[21] Concern over maintaining the unity of its very heterogeneous base thus made the employers' organization far more circumspect in its relations with the unions.

Finally, and significantly, employers and the government quickly learned, after the 1992 exchange rate crisis, that many old mechanisms no longer operated as they had in the past. For instance, under the pressures of increased competition and globalization, manufacturers found that they needed to worry about the quality of their products (and not just prices) and their skilled workers' job satisfaction, which are of course related. And these employers concluded that having a stable, predictable framework for negotiating with workers was preferable to confrontation—at least for the time being.

Labor Relations Reforms of the 1990s. Reforms enacted in the 1990s represented the most important departures in labor relations since the 1970s. Most were passed in 1993 when concertation was established.[22] The old *scala mobile* was abolished; wage increases now must be negotiated within projected inflation guidelines. Wages are now basically determined on a local level and are tied to rises in productivity rather than the cost of living, as was previously the case. The new agreement satisfied many of management's long-standing complaints and gave it more flexibility in hiring and layoffs. Furthermore, a larger share of benefit contributions now come from workers' paychecks rather than management's pockets, bringing Italian practices in line with the rest of Europe.

The 1993 reforms also reshaped workers' workplace representation. More inclusive shop floor institutions have been constructed. Two-thirds of the members of the new bodies are elected (by all workers), and the remaining third are appointed by any union taking part in contract negotiations. These changes are intended to increase the representativeness of shop floor organizations (ensuring a place for autonomous unions and COBAS, for instance), in the hope of revitalizing and relegitimizing the unions. There were signs that some of these hopes were being realized; the first elections held under the new system saw high turnout rates and striking victories for the confederations.[23]

The new framework served the unions well in negotiations with the government over pensions, starting with Lamberto Dini in 1995. The unions have made concessions, but—particularly when negotiating with center-left governments that needed their support—they were able to dilute many changes and draw out their implementation. These may seem like minor victories, but they are the sort of achievement that helped the unions regain a measure of legitimacy and support in the shop floor elections of the mid-1990s. They also explain why tensions have inevitably increased since Berlusconi returned to power in 2001 and almost immediately began to denounce the unions' "stalling" and "selfishness" on pension reforms. The center-right has much less need of organized labor's support, and (accurately) sees pensions as one of the most important, and vulnerable, items in the budget.

As a final illustration of a changed climate of labor relations, legislation in the spring of 2000 put more teeth into a 1990 law regulating strikes in "essential" public services. These services are primarily in transportation, where the autonomous unions' wildcat strikes have long bedeviled Italians, and tourists, since trains, ferries, and airports during peak travel periods are preferred targets. Several things stand out about the new rules. One is that public services are broadly defined—for instance, to include the self-employed in certain circumstances (truck drivers, for example). Another is that the major confederations agreed to these changes at the end of 1998, after Massimo D'Alema, the former Communist, replaced Prodi as prime minister. The legislation is a compromise, but it represents a breakthrough for Italy. Strikes are not forbidden, but they are restricted, including the introduction of mandatory cooling-off periods. If a strike does occur in an essential service, 50 per-

cent of services normally delivered must be guaranteed, as must the presence of 30 percent of regular personnel.[24]

These regulations were fiercely opposed by the most left-wing unionists. But most people in the major confederations welcomed the changes. These unions have always been sensitive to public opinion and generally try to avoid strikes that disrupt the lives of citizens and, especially, fellow workers. Those most affected by the new rules are the autonomous unions and COBAS, whose militancy has won them much support within the workplace but antipathy among the public. Already weakened by general trends in the economy, the major confederations assume that a more predictable and peaceful climate of labor relations will better serve their long-run interests.

Social Policy

Although Italy's social policies have a number of distinctive features, most of them in fact are typical of other countries as well.

Welfare all'Italiana. Maurizio Ferrera, perhaps the leading authority on the Italian welfare state, has shown that it conforms to the general pattern found along the Mediterranean rim of Europe.[25] These welfare states have fragmented social services and tend to provide cash transfers rather than services in kind. Abundant direct cash payments render such systems especially susceptible to clientelistic abuses and corruption. Most important, following the distinctions introduced by Richard Titmuss,[26] the underlying logic of these systems is particularistic; that is, benefits go to people as members of specified (and privileged) categories, in contrast to institutional welfare states, which provide (universal) benefits as a condition of citizenship. An example of a universal benefit would be a national health system or guaranteed free public education. Even as Italy developed a more modern welfare state, it has tended to be highly particularistic and highly inefficient.

Historically, the Italian state provided limited benefits, leaving most services in the hands of the workers' movement and, especially, the Catholic Church. Under fascism, as unions and democratic institutions were repressed, many benefits were rolled back. As the state got more engaged in the economy, it also assumed more responsibilities in the area of social security, reinforcing the fragmentation of an already haphazard structure. Given fascism's "corporate" ideology, benefits tended to be granted on an industrywide basis, with the result that some clerks and workers enjoyed reasonable treatment, while others were totally bereft of coverage. When fascism fell, there was nothing like a national system of benefits; those who lived off the land (the majority of Italians in 1945) had no entitlements at all.

Earlier patterns were reinforced and then expanded as the DC sought to consolidate its bases of support—for example, among the peasantry. Small farmers, small businesspeople, and professionals gradually were added to the rolls, and their benefits were increased in the 1970s and 1980s. In contrast to, say, Scandinavia, the Italian workers' movement did not press for universalistic benefits. Reflecting the Marxist orthodoxy of the period, they demanded that benefits be distributed to people as members of the working class, not as citizens. For this reason, the claims of many who were excluded from benefits—for instance, housewives or part-time employees—were not initially recognized by the unions. Furthermore, in the course of the postwar period, the DC's "occupation of the state" meant that many services became intimately interwoven with partisan political considerations and, finally, blatant corruption. For example, disability or veterans' pensions would be awarded not because a person qualified according to the rules, but because the local pension office was in the hands of a politician willing to hand benefits out in exchange for votes.

The expansion of the earlier fragmented system had long-lasting implications. First, because groups were included for partisan reasons, in piecemeal fashion, there was no sense that the system should be made to pay its own way. On the contrary: favored groups such as the self-employed could count on minimal contributions. In the 1960s, when benefits were limited, this was not so important, but as the welfare state expanded, it became critical. Second, the emphasis on privileged, already employed groups and cash transfer payments meant that historically underdeveloped areas remained perpetually underserved. To cite one telling example, Italy traditionally provided a tiny "subsistence" check for the chronically unemployed, paid out of public assistance funds, compared with a guaranteed 80 to 90 percent of the preceding wage, paid out of the main pension fund, for unemployed workers. Southerners, people with large families, and young people (especially women) have been least well served by the system's built-in biases.

The Italian welfare state expanded from the late 1960s onward, pushed by the first center-left governments and even more by the militancy of the Hot Autumn. Whenever the workers won concessions, the DC hastened to lavish similar benefits—with no concern as to how they would be funded—on its most important constituencies. By the 1980s, Italy resembled other Western countries in the proportion of gross GDP spent on social programs. But the Italian welfare state spends far more on pensions, and far less on all other benefits; Italy's nonpension welfare expenditures are less than half that of other EU members with a similarly high level of development.[27]

Deficit Reduction and Welfare State Reform.

High inflation and ballooning deficits in the 1980s forced some moderation on the pork-barreling DC and PSI. But fierce political competition between these parties ruled out dramatic changes that would hurt their key constituents. The dimensions of the phenomenon are quickly captured with a few figures: well over a tenth of the entire population—as many as one in three adults in some parts of the south—was receiving disability pensions; 180,000 new ones were being awarded every year.[28] Over 18 million pensions of all types are distributed in Italy, at a cost that amounts to 15 percent of GDP.[29]

The greatest fiscal threat comes from old-age and retirement pensions. Italy's pensions can be quite generous, particularly in the public administration. Public servants, including school teachers, used to be able to retire after fewer than twenty years on the job; Italians, using English, called these "baby pensions." Retirement benefits were historically funded out of general revenues, not contribution-based funds; payments were of the defined-benefit type and were protected from inflation by cost-of-living escalators.[30]

When Italian budget deficits climbed above 12 percent of GDP in the 1980s, they represented a record for Western Europe and a serious threat to continuing economic growth, let alone aspirations to adhere to EU standards. It took *Tangentopoli* and the collapse of the ruling parties, as well as the exchange rate crisis of 1992, for truly decisive action to be taken. The governments of Giuliano Amato and Carlo Ciampi, notable for the number of "technicians," or nonpolitical specialists, in their cabinets, pushed through extensive budgetary reforms and imposed numerous cuts and slowdowns in the growth of welfare programs.

These reforms were achieved after lengthy negotiations with the unions, leading many critics to complain that they did not go far enough. The critics have a point. For instance, those with eighteen years of contributions under the old seniority-based system were allowed to remain in the old system. The new contribution-based system will therefore not apply to everyone collecting a pension until 2036.[31] The minimum age at which someone can retire has moved upward at a glacial pace. Every government and almost every annual budget thus sees efforts to reopen pensions to further negotiations, and tensions between government and unions increase sharply when the center-right is in power.

By the 1990s, fraudulent pension and other welfare-related benefit claims came under increasingly intense scrutiny. By 1993, new disability pensions had fallen by over 100,000 per year,[32] and this obviously did not mean that Italians were suddenly healthier or more careful on the job.

Tax Evasion.   The *Economist*, certainly no enemy of private enterprise, noted twenty years ago that Italy is "a country where cheating on taxes by the self-employed is regarded as their entrepreneurial privilege."[33] The problem would be amusing were it not so serious. The total amount of income tax that goes unpaid each year has recently been estimated at a whopping 130 billion euros.[34] The inequities produced by rampant evasion are staggering; roughly half of national income is earned by dependent workers, and the other half goes to the self-employed— above all, shopkeepers and small businesspeople, professionals, and the like. But dependent workers, whose taxes are withheld at the source, pay 80 percent of all personal income tax.[35]

Tax evasion was winked at in the past, but even since the so-called First Republic ended, it has been dealt with erratically. Periodic amnesties are routinely employed to recover at least a portion of unpaid taxes without interminable administrative hearings and court battles. Individuals—and corporations—receive "discounts" on taxes owing if they pay up promptly. The equivalent of many billions of dollars per year have been recovered in this fashion. But the cause of civic responsibility is hardly helped by Prime Minister Berlusconi's tendency to state publicly his "understanding" of those who don't pay their taxes.

Deficit Reduction.   Serious austerity measures began to make an impact following the 1992 EMS crisis. Prodi had campaigned with the left's (and unions') support but was utterly committed to Italy's meeting the Maastricht convergence criteria. After winning the 1996 election, he created an economic "superministry," subsuming the budget portfolio under the Treasury and entrusting it to Carlo Ciampi. There can be no doubt that the rigor of successive governments played an important part in these achievements.

By the first years of the twenty-first century, the accumulated national debt had been steadily reduced, although it remained above 100 percent of GDP.[36] This gave Italy the largest debt relative to GDP of any country in the EU.

Society and Economy

Modern Italy has been marked by profound regional differences, none more serious than those between north and south, which were exacerbated from the Risorgimento on. Late industrialization and the powerful presence of the Roman Catholic Church meant that Italy encountered modernity later and in different ways than other advanced countries. Italy also suffered from seriously polarized class relations—fascism arose as a response to militancy in the factories and fields—which were then perpetuated and entrenched by cold war divisions.

A Legacy of Polarized Class and Political Relations

For much of the postwar period, Italy was among the world's leaders in strikes. From the left's expulsion from government in 1947 through the 1980s, Italian labor relations mainly revealed whether labor or capital had market conditions in its favor. When labor was weak, it was all but ignored; when it was strong, it played catch-up with a vengeance. When labor's fortunes flagged, capital tried to undo or ignore what had come before.

Successive governments, lacking strong ties to the labor movement and themselves internally divided, generally remained bystanders unable to produce a more institutionalized, less conflictual framework of labor relations. The welfare state, already fragmented and very uneven in the way it distributed resources, became even more so and was increasingly awash in a sea of red ink. Employed and organized workers, in both the public and private sectors, did relatively well but carried a crushing tax burden. The self-employed did even better, particularly

when authorities looked the other way at tax time. But historically unprotected groups remained so and often were able to achieve benefits only thanks to willful distortions of the system (e.g., disability pensions).

It took the end of the cold war, the collapse of the postwar party system, and a disastrous economic inheritance further constrained by external (EU) guidelines before a sustained attack on this legacy could be mounted. The unions' cooperation made meeting the Maastricht convergence criteria possible, but the center-right's more aggressive attitude, and above all its insistence on reopening the issue of pension reform, cast serious doubt on the likelihood of continued cooperation and relative labor peace.

A Legacy of Gender, Generational, and Regional Differences

Italy's social problems have deep and complex roots, but it is nevertheless clear that this legacy has had a clear impact in the three areas of gender, generational, and regional inequities.

Gender Inequities. A discussion of society and economy can only briefly address the legally sanctioned discrimination against women that lasted well into the postwar period. It is important to underscore the ingrained prejudice of a society where adultery was a crime that only a woman could commit, where women could not apply for passports without their husband's or father's permission, and where rape was defined as a crime against public morality. That such a society would not pay much attention to women's educational or employment opportunities is hardly surprising, nor, for that matter, would one expect much concern about providing day care or other facilities for working parents. In many societies of this type—and they are especially common in southern Europe—women are often actively dissuaded from working at all. Traditionally, the state expected them to produce children, not goods or services.

The state's slowness to offer many services can only be understood in terms of ingrained assumptions about the family's ability to provide these services. And, in this context, "family" is really a euphemism for "women." As noted above in the discussion of the welfare state, these attitudes were reinforced by the Catholic Church's "family values," but they were also prevalent for many years in the union movement as well. It took many years of struggle by the women's movement, including powerful pressure by feminists within the trade unions, before the major confederations embraced such ideas as gender-neutral unemployment lists, or demands for day care centers in the workplace.

Not surprisingly, the result has been a welfare state skimpy in its provision of services in kind, and hence in its modern infrastructure. The built-in biases of Italy's political economy are especially apparent in the extremely low female participation rate (37 percent) in the Italian economy (the proportion of women employed or those seeking employment as a proportion of all adults). This contrasts with a rate of 62 percent for men, which is also low. At over 12 percent, women's unemployment rates are nearly double the rate for men (7 percent).[37] And this despite the fact that women have for some time outnumbered men in university attendance and the completion of degrees.

This extremely low overall participation rate means that Italy has one of the weakest tax bases of all advanced capitalist nations. The entrenchment of gender-biased practices has also left Italy unable to address the challenges of persistently high unemployment, above all in economically weak regions. The female unemployment rate in the south, for example, is an extraordinarily high 29 percent.

Generational Inequities. Italian women are disadvantaged when compared with men, but this is hardly the only inequality built into the Italian labor market and welfare state. Young people as a whole—both men and women—are badly disadvantaged when compared with their elders, though women always suffer relatively more deprivation. The unemployment rate for youth, officially 27 percent (31 percent for women), was at the very top of all EU member states in 2002.

This does not mean that a quarter of all young men, or a third of all young women, have no job at all, for many do find part-time or "under-the-table" employment. But it does mean that they are much less well paid and have few, if any, of the guarantees that those with steady full-time employment enjoy. It also means that young people feel little attachment to trade unions, which defend many of the rigidities in the labor market, or sympathy for immigrants, who are portrayed as stealing jobs from Italians by accepting low wages and poor working conditions. Since the 1990s, the government has tried to encourage employers to hire young people for traineeships or at least part-time jobs, by paying a portion of their wages. These initiatives have met with limited success, as continuing high unemployment rates show. All too often, employers fail to extend the contract once the subsidies expire.

Regional Inequities. A north-south gap existed when Italy was unified, and persisted through the postwar period despite a massive infusion of resources. Not only does almost every important social and economic indicator show the south lagging behind, but the data often suggest that entirely different economic and social logics are at play in these two broadly defined parts of the country. Sidney Tarrow argued almost forty years ago that the south was not so much "backward" as systematically distorted by the way the DC had created a clientelistic network using the levers of a modern capitalist economy.[38] This distortion is still very much present.

Since the mid-1990s, for instance, the Italian economy has grown at a modest but sustained rate, while only recently making much of a dent in unemployment (see Table 22.2). But in the northernmost parts of the country, unemployment has steadily dropped, while it has actually increased in the south. Put another way, since the Economic Miracle, the north generally enjoyed an unemployment rate roughly half that of the nation as a whole, while the Mezzogiorno (the south) was roughly one and a half times the national average.[39] By the mid-1990s, regional differences had *increased*, with unemployment in the south rising to 21 to 22 percent, or roughly twice the national average, while unemployment in the north dropped to around 5 percent (central Italy was at 8 to 9 percent). Put another way, while the south had traditionally suffered three times the unemployment levels of the north, this was now better than four to one. And this regional difference compounds the gender and generational differences.

There are many other ways in which the south stands out from the rest of the country, ranging from birthrates and family size to migratory flows. In the south, births exceed deaths, and the population would in fact grow were it not for a net exodus of inhabitants. In the north, the dynamic is precisely the opposite: deaths exceed births, yet the population continues to increase, mainly because of immigration from outside Italy.[40] As with the employment data, the north and south are at the extremes, while the center tends to resemble the north more than the south.

The Politicization of Regional Identity.
Regional differences have been central to many aspects of postwar politics; the red zones of the north-center and the Catholic white zones of the northeast served, respectively, as the PCI's and DC's subcultural anchors (see Chapter 24). But except for a short-lived separatist movement in Sicily at the end of World War II,* local identities never served as the foundation of political movements or parties—that is, until the rise of the leagues. We will discuss this phenomenon at

length in Chapter 23, but it is necessary to mention it here, particularly since we address immigration immediately below.

As the DC lost political and moral credibility, the fortunes of the various leagues rose. Some earlier leagues made an unabashed ethnic appeal, first against southerners and then against foreigners. Others expressed more of the middle-class, populist tax revolt mentality that has recently appeared in many advanced capitalist nations. The terrible state of Italy's finances, and northerners' sense that the country's prosperity was based on their hard work while its problems were based on spendthrift central governments that channeled their hard-earned money into an insatiable—and lazy—south helped give these disgruntled citizens a strong sense of regional identity. The northeast, where the Northern League is strongest, finds the most polarized attitudes concerning demands for greater local autonomy and the most negative attitudes toward the welfare state and aid to the poorest regions of the country.[41]

Umberto Bossi created the Northern League (Lega Nord, LN) out of several regional leagues. For a time this was the largest party in the northeast, and occasionally the north as a whole, before Berlusconi's own party, Forza Italia, displaced it at the turn of the century. Bossi may be a mercurial and demagogic politician; however, he also embodies a political cleavage that may wax and wane but shows no signs of fading entirely from the scene.

From a Country of Emigrants to One of Immigrants: Ethnic Tensions

Bossi has helped keep immigration near the top of the political agenda in Italy, aided by other parties, including the post-Fascist National Alliance and, increasingly, Forza Italia. Italians were used to thinking of themselves as a country of emigrants and as therefore highly sensitive to the plight of strangers in a new land. But the rising tide of immigration, which began in

*There was also a separatist movement in the German-speaking Alto Adige in the 1960s, but this took the form of terrorist incidents rather than a mass movement.

the 1970s and which has accelerated since the end of the 1980s, has forced them to confront their own intolerance and lack of preparedness.

The dimensions of immigration, both legal and illegal, are small compared to those in France or Germany, but they are growing. In 2003, 1.5 million foreigners were legal residents in Italy; estimates for undocumented immigrants put the figure between 600,000 and 900,000.[42] The total is roughly 4 percent of the population, but there are much denser concentrations in various parts of the country—particularly the larger cities. Some sectors of society have reacted as if a flood of foreigners was invading the country, taking Italian jobs and boosting crime rates. At the same time, there have been undeniable connections between some immigrants and drug trafficking, forms of petty crime, and prostitution, and public opinion has shown growing sensitivity to immigration-related issues. Violent racist episodes have increased, and anti-Islamic sentiment was increasing even before the events of September 11, 2001, and their aftermath. Politicians, led by an increasingly strident and overtly racist Northern League, have not hesitated to politicize the issue. The Italian government passed four separate immigration laws between 1986 and 2001, tightening rules and increasing penalties on each occasion.

Italy at any rate would have had to address this issue because of its desire to be part of the EU's agreements on borders, which require standardized laws, controls, and restrictions on immigration among all participants. The most recent law was enacted under Berlusconi's second government, which tried to soften the law's more repressive aspects by promising an amnesty for undocumented workers who had already established themselves in Italy. Over half a million immigrants came forward to take advantage of the offer.[43] Like all such laws, many aspects of the current legislation are quite unrealistic, establishing arbitrary annual quotas and pretending that immigration can be made to conform neatly to the needs of the labor market. In recent years, the demand for labor in the north has been so great that the annual quotas have routinely been exceeded barely halfway through the year. Local employers, who have been among the League's staunchest supporters, then clamor—successfully—to have the quotas raised.

Public tolerance and bureaucratic incompetence will probably keep Italy from turning into a country that systematically tracks down and expels dark-skinned foreigners, although the growing willingness of politicians to exploit popular fears is not encouraging. Recent developments show that decision makers are only beginning to grasp the implications of economic trends and migration patterns that have become integral parts of a radically transformed, increasingly interdependent global economy.

The Dilemmas of European Integration

Italy has always occupied a peculiar place in what was originally the European Economic Community (EEC) and then became, in stages, the European Union (EU). Italian governments were among the most enthusiastic supporters of the project of European integration, as can be seen in constitutional provisions that recognize that sovereignty can be ceded to supranational bodies (Article 10), as well as the fact that the 1957 treaty that established the EEC was, after all, the Treaty of Rome. And Italians consistently ranked at the very top of public opinion polls in their enthusiasm for all things European, from positive general attitudes to their desire to see the EU expand more rapidly. Yet in spite of this general and official enthusiasm, Italy's reputation in the Community has always been rather spotty. The country's involvement in the actual shaping of European policies has historically been very sporadic, even when there were very real benefits to be had (e.g., the Common Agricultural Policy). Time and again, the other large members—France and Germany in particular—simply overshadowed the Italians, who, even as their economic weight increased, left the impression of being political and diplomatic light-weights. Nor was Italy's reputation helped by its erratic and indifferent application of European norms or, for that matter, its inability to collect and spend funds to which it was entitled.[44]

This terrible record is to some degree a reflection of the preoccupation of the political elite of the First Republic with its own backyard; the most important political benefits were to be had by controlling events in Rome, so for the longest time Italy tended to send more marginal figures to Brussels, with only a few exceptions. And the inability to collect and spend Community funds was yet another illustration of the degree to which the pathologies of the Italian state—in this case the notoriously inefficient bureaucracy—interfered with everything Italians tried to do.

As we have seen, however, by the 1980s Italy could no longer ignore international or European considerations in its political and economic activities. By the early 1990s, the same forces undermining the politics of the First Republic were also pushing economic policy in new directions. As the status quo collapsed, so did the attitude that had prevented numerous domestic reforms from being realized. The weight of international considerations in Italian economic policymaking is underscored by recalling that two of Italy's recent prime ministers (Lamberto Dini and Carlo Ciampi) were previously top officials of the Bank of Italy. A third (Romano Prodi) is an economist who built his reputation as a reforming president of IRI in the 1980s. Ciampi went on to be elected president of the republic, while Prodi became president of the European Commission. By the end of the decade, having made Italy's conformity to the Maastricht convergence parameters the central plank of their platform, successive center-left governments had enacted far-reaching changes in Italy's political economy, and the Italians appeared to be taking their European obligations much more seriously than they had in the recent past.

When Berlusconi returned to power in 2001, a more ambivalent attitude toward the EU came to the fore, reflecting the fierce Euroskepticism of some allies (most notably the LN) but also a deeply ambivalent attitude that runs through the center-right. Berlusconi had to assume the role of foreign minister himself for nearly a year after his first appointee felt compelled to resign over the constant anti-EU sniping from within the cabinet. Berlusconi also proved to be a less than enthusiastic supporter of several EU crime-fighting initiatives, most notably a Europe-wide search warrant and standardizing rules for the admissibility of evidence in criminal proceedings. As is often the case, the prime minister's objections seemed to reflect his own potential legal problems more than any coherent legal philosophy.

Italy's economic policies have not changed markedly since 2001, although as deficit projections for 2004–2005 threatened to exceed the 3 percent barrier, Berlusconi made clear that he did not consider the deficit ceiling to be sacrosanct. This could be a manifestation of the ambivalence mentioned above, but it should also be noted that both the Germans and the French have persistently exceeded deficit ceilings in recent years.

In some policy areas, such as privatization, events proceed apace, although at a slower rate than the EU's oversight authorities would like. And it can be argued than even where important changes can be documented, these have represented less a radical departure than the maturation of trends that began years earlier. Labor union strength had been declining for some time, and management had been moving toward more independence from the DC long before the ruling party imploded. Similarly, many policies that had long been paid lip service were now carried forward, or at least addressed, more decisively.

Significant external factors were simultaneously hastening the demise of old political and economic arrangements. Changes adopted in the early 1980s, above all Italy's membership in the European Monetary System, exposed the lira and monetary policy to greater international pressure. These pressures worked in a double sense. Most directly, from the mid-1980s on,

Italy, like all other EU members, had to meet guidelines concerning the exchange rate, inflation, and budgetary deficits and accumulated debt (all of them related). When Italy had to withdraw from the EMS in 1992, getting the financial house in order became an even more explicit priority.

But external factors have also worked indirectly. For example, Italian capitalists grew increasingly restive about very high, and therefore uncompetitive, payments for workers' benefits compared with those of their European counterparts. This was an old complaint, but with the approach of a single market, it could no longer be ignored. Similarly, Italy's grindingly slow bureaucracy and chronic governmental crises had always frustrated industrial and financial elites, but they now felt increasingly vulnerable without an efficient executive to defend their interests.[45] And observers of all stripes acknowledge that while Italian political institutions retain many of their more problematic characteristics, Prodi's adroit playing of the "European card" enabled him to gain concessions from the unions that few would have predicted.

Italy in the Era of Globalization

Much of what has just been said about Italy's engagement with Europe applies with equal force to Italy's place in the international political economy. Italy's postwar economy, like that of its neighbors, was built on an aggressive policy of exporting manufactured goods. Unlike its neighbors, however, Italy's investment in research and development was always relatively scanty, and its comparative advantage was largely a reflection of relatively lower labor costs in the mass production of durable consumer items. With the growth of international competition, particularly from East Asia, and the opening up of once-protected economies to increasing foreign penetration, many of these advantages started to slip away, as can be seen in a dramatic loss of markets for Italian household appliances,

office machines, and, especially, automobiles.[46] Fortunately for Italy, some older firms managed to adapt successfully to the new conditions, while many smaller firms responded very well to a more competitive international climate. Italian industrial and agricultural machinery, clothing, and specialized metallurgy have helped the country maintain a generally favorable balance of trade, despite its chronic reliance on imported energy, chemicals, and, increasingly, foodstuffs.

But Italy's economy, by general consensus, remains distorted in areas that are central to the new international economic order. One such area is research and development. Another is that Italian corporations remain, on the whole, family-run firms of rather limited dimensions. This perpetuates an undercapitalized stock market, and limits the country's attractiveness to foreign investment.

Recent efforts to remedy these historic shortcomings have met with mixed success. For one thing, opening Italy to the outside world has had unintended consequences. One has been to draw attention to many of the shortcomings of corporate practices that were previously hidden from general view. When the discovery of a massive 10 billion euro fraud forced multinational giant Parmalat to file for bankruptcy protection late in 2003, Italy's lax rules regarding corporate audits and the monitoring of market operations became painfully public. Aggrieved investors also quickly discovered how complicated it could be to file any sort of claim in Italy. In the past, these developments would be the source of head shaking and eye rolling among insiders, but those insiders would have been Italians. Now that investors come from all over the world, Italy can ill afford such publicity. Italian companies quickly began to feel the fallout, as international markets either shunned them entirely, or demanded higher interest rates if their books were not in perfect order.[47]

It is not easy to isolate domestic or international factors as the primary explanation for changes in policy. Even when we can say with certainty that one came first, it is the interaction between both that produces the final outcome. But given Italy's long history of political paralysis in the face of difficult decisions, and stalemated and polarized social relations, it is safe to say that the external pressure broke the deadlock, and internal political dynamics then determined just how far the reforms could go. It also appears safe to argue that—whether due to domestic or international pressures, or both—Italy's economic governance, and fortunes, were radically, and irreversibly, set on a new path in the 1990s.

Notes

1. Alan S. Milward, *The Reconstruction of Western Europe, 1945–1951* (Berkeley and Los Angeles: University of California Press, 1984), pp. 78–79, 98, 197–198.

2. Kevin Allen and Andrew Stevenson, *An Introduction to the Italian Economy* (New York: Harper & Row, 1975), p. 10.

3. Andrew Shonfield, *Modern Capitalism* (Oxford: Oxford University Press, 1969), pp. 186–187.

4. Allen and Stevenson, *Introduction to the Italian Economy*, pp. 11–12.

5. Gisele Podbielski, *Italy: Development and Crisis in the Postwar Economy* (Oxford: Clarendon Press, 1974), pp. 15, 100.

6. For example, 180 televisions per 1,000 population (versus 293 in the United Kingdom and 272 in the Federal Republic), or 174 telephones (versus 269 and 226, respectively). Allen and Stevenson, *Introduction to the Italian Economy*, p. 28.

7. George H. Hildebrand, *Growth and Structure in the Economy of Modern Italy* (Cambridge, Mass.: Harvard University Press, 1965), p. 117.

8. Guido Romagnoli, ed., *La sindacalizzazione tra ideologia e pratica: Il caso italiano, 1950–1977*, vol. 2 (Rome: Edizioni Lavoro, 1978), Table 2.2.

9. The CGIL's figures were: 5.4 million members, of whom 2.9 million were pensioners. The CISL, with 4.2 million, reported 2.1 million pensioners. The much smaller UIL reported a total of 1.8 million members, of whom 462,000 were retired. See Figure 22.1 for sources.

10. Lorenzo Bordogna, "'Arcipelago COBAS': Frammentazione della rappresentanza e conflitti di lavoro," in Piergiorgio Corbetta and Robert Leonardi, eds., *Politica in Italia: Edizione 88* (Bologna: Il Mulino, 1988), pp. 260–262.

11. Marino Regini and Ida Regalia, "Employers, Unions and the State: The Resurgence of Concertation in Italy?" in Martin Bull and Martin Rhodes, eds., *Crisis and Transition in Italian Politics* (London: Frank Cass, 1997), p. 226.

12. Anthony C. Masi, "Il complesso siderurgico di Bagnoli: La ristrutturazione e le relazioni industriali," in Raimondo Catanzaro and Raffaella Y. Nanetti, eds., *Politica in Italia: Edizione 89* (Bologna: Il Mulino, 1989), p. 213.

13. Patrizio Bianchi, Sabino Cassese, and Vincent Della Sala, "Privatisation in Italy: Aims and Constraints," *West European Politics* 11 (October 1988): 88.

14. Alan Friedman, "The Economic Elites and the Political System," in Stephen Gundle and Simon Parker, eds., *The New Italian Republic: From the Fall of the Berlin Wall to Berlusconi* (London: Macmillan, 1996), p. 269.

15. Guglielmo Raggozino, "Italia i miliardi delle privatizzazioni," *Il manifesto,* July 21, 1998.

16. Jeffry Frieden, "Making Commitments: France and Italy in the European Monetary System, 1979–1985," Working Paper 1.14, Political Economy of European Integration Research Group, 1993, pp. 22–23.

17. Gerald Epstein and Juliet Schor, "The Divorce of the Banca d'Italia and the Italian Treasury: A Case Study of Central Bank Independence," in Peter Lange and Marino Regini, eds., *State, Market and Social Regulation: New Perspectives on Italy* (New York: Cambridge University Press, 1989), p. 147.

18. Giacomo Vaciago, "Finance Between Markets and Politics," in David Hine and Salvatore Vassallo, eds., *Italian Politics: The Return of Politics* (Oxford: Berghahn Books, 2000), p. 198.

19. OECD Economic Surveys, "Italy" (Paris: OECD, 1995), Table H, p. 151.

20. Liborio Mattina, "Abete's Confindustria: From Alliance with the DC to Multiparty Appeal," in

Stephen Hellman and Gianfranco Pasquino, eds., *Italian Politics: A Review*, vol. 8, pp. 151–164.

21. Regini and Regalia, "Employers, Unions and the State," pp. 221–222.

22. Richard M. Locke, "The Abolition of the Scala Mobile," in Carol Mershon and Gianfranco Pasquino, eds., *Italian Politics: Ending the First Republic* (Boulder, Colo.: Westview Press, 1994), pp. 185–196.

23. Regini and Regalia, "Employers, Unions and the State," p. 219.

24. Riccardo De Gennaro, "Scioperi, da oggi si cambia," *La Repubblica*, April 19, 2000, p. 28.

25. Maurizio Ferrera, "The Uncertain Future of the Italian Welfare State," in Bull and Rhodes, *Crisis and Transition in Italian Politics*, pp. 231–249.

26. Richard Titmuss, *Social Policy: An Introduction* (London: Allen and Unwin, 1974).

27. Ferrera, "The Uncertain Future of the Italian Welfare State," pp. 232–233.

28. *L'Unità*, December 3, 1994, p. 9.

29. The data are from 2001. ISTAT, *Approfondimenti:* 12_lavoro.pdf, p. 4. Downloaded from www.istat.it.

30. Giuliano Cazzola, *Lo stato sociale tra crisi e riforme: Il caso Italia* (Bologna: Il Mulino, 1994), p. 66.

31. Marco Mira D'Ercole and Flavia Terribile, "Spese pensionistiche: Sviluppi nel 1996 e 1997," in Luciano Bardi and Martin Rhodes, eds., *Politica in Italia: Edizione 98* (Bologna: Il Mulino, 1998), p. 226.

32. *L'Unità*, December 3, 1994, p. 9.

33. "Will *la dolce vita* Turn Sour?" *Economist*, January 5, 1985, p. 58.

34. Maria Stella Conte, "Un paese con sempre più poveri," *La Repubblica*, February 1, 2003, p. 12.

35. Enzo Forcella, "Un paese senza ricchi," *La Repubblica*, January 4, 1990, p. 8.

36. ISTAT, "economia," in *L'Italia in cifre 2003* (Rome, ISTAT, 2003), p. 19. The economic document is downloadable at http://www.istat.it/Prodotti-e/ita2003/Economia.pdf; the entire report can be accessed, section by section, at http://www.istat.it/Prodotti-e/ita2003/index.html.

37. These figures refer to 2002. Ibid., p. 24.

38. Sidney G. Tarrow, *Peasant Communism in Southern Italy* (New Haven, Conn.: Yale University Press, 1967).

39. All figures obtained from ISTAT, *Serie storiche:* TAVrev9_17.doc (Rome: ISTAT, 2000), Table 17, available at www.istat.it.

40. ISTAT, *L'Italia in cifre 2003*, p. 2.

41. Ferrera, "The Uncertain Future of the Italian Welfare State," pp. 245–247.

42. Official figures: ISTAT, ibid., p. 1; estimates: Cinzia Gubbini, "Un'Italia più larga, 'sanata' malamente," *Il manifesto*, March 11, 2003, p. 11, and Giancarlo Mola, "Immigrati, 800mila in più nel 2002 è boom di 'regolarizzazioni,' " *La Repubblica*, May 14, 2003, p. 23.

43. For a discussion of various regularization efforts over the years, see Ferruccio Pastore, "A Community Out of Balance: Nationality Law and Migration Politics in the History of Post-Unification Italy," *Journal of Modern Italian Studies* 9 (Spring 2004): p. 44, n. 31.

44. A very good synthetic treatment of Italy's involvement in the EEC-EU can be found in Paul Ginsborg, *Italy and Its Discontents* (London: Penguin, 2001), pp. 232–242.

45. Vincent Della Sala, "Capital Blight? The Regulation of Financial Institutions in Canada and Italy," *Governance*, July 7, 1994, pp. 251–252.

46. Paolo Guerrieri, "La collocazione internazionale dell'economia italiana," in Paul Ginsborg, ed., *Stato dell'Italia* (Milan: Il Saggiatore, 1994), pp. 379–387.

47. David Reilly, "Italian Companies Hit by Fallout in Wake of Parmalat's Collapse," *The Globe & Mail* (Toronto), April 8, 2004, p. B9.

C H A P T E R

23

Governance
and Policymaking

Italy was saddled with chronic problems of governance and policymaking long before the writing of the postwar constitution—for instance, with a highly centralized state structure and far too much discretionary power in the hands of the executive branch of government. The *Statuto albertino* allowed the king to appoint Mussolini as prime minister, and it also allowed Mussolini to use emergency decrees to install a dictatorship. So it was understandable that the writers of the republican constitution would try to ensure that such abuses could never happen again. As time went on, it appeared that the framers had succeeded all too well: they produced an institutional framework that gave so much power to the legislature that it hampered the executive's ability to frame coherent policies, and to carry out such policies as it was able to articulate.

It would, however, be a serious error to blame all of Italy's governing problems on faulty constitutional design. Italian prime ministers do have less formal power than their counterparts in other parliamentary systems (e.g., Britain or Germany), although those powers have been strengthened over the years. But if fragmented and incoherent policy has been the hallmark of Italian governments for half a century, this has reflected the fragmented and often fractious nature of Italian cabinets. Governing majorities have often been numerically solid, but internally divided, and it is hard to produce coherent policies when many different parties—or factions of the same party (the Christian Democrats, DC)—are in fundamental disagreement with one another, or are trying to outmaneuver each other.

Another chronic obstacle to coherent governance and policy implementation has been Italy's notoriously inefficient bureaucracy, which the republic inherited, and which was then rendered even more inefficient by the way the ruling parties (again, above all the DC) occupied the state machinery for partisan ends. Here, too, institutional design certainly contributed to the country's problems—for instance, in concentrating so much power in the hands of a central administration. But the most serious pathologies are less the product of formal institutional arrangements than they are the result of the way these arrangements were used, and abused, by the people who ran the political system.

Understanding that Italy's problems result from the interplay of these several factors helps us see why it is no easy task to effect significant reforms. Recall that it took the end of communism, the near-bankruptcy of the state, and the *Tangentopoli* scandals to weaken the old parties, whose system of power was the glue that kept the First Republic together. Before 1994, even a growing sense of crisis had been unable to produce sustained, far-reaching changes. And even after that date, when it seemed that serious reform was finally on the political agenda, an initial effort to rewrite the constitution met with failure. Starting with the center-left government of 1996–2001 and then accelerating with the arrival of Berlusconi's second government, with its solid majorities in both chambers of Parliament, more ambitious reforms have begun to be implemented, involving both executive power and making Italy into a more federal state. It is, however, simply too early to tell how many of these efforts will be implemented, let alone what their eventual impact may be. Our examination of the major components of the Italian state will therefore discuss both their formal design and the actual practices that have shaped them over time, including the most significant efforts that have been made to change them.

The Organization of the State

Although it has become commonplace to speak of a First Republic when referring to the period 1946–1993, and of a Second Republic since 1994, this terminology is political shorthand. Formally, there is only one Italian Republic, in existence since 1946. It is a parliamentary republic with a bicameral legislature. Both chambers of Parliament are elected at the same time and have the same powers; the Chamber of Deputies has 630 members, while the Senate has 315 (see Chapter 24). Like other parliamentary republics, it has a dual executive, with an indirectly elected head of state, the president of the republic. The presidency is a largely ceremonial office, but its incumbents exerted considerable influence in the formation, and even the composition, of Italian governments during the tumultuous 1990s. The far more important executive office is that of the head of government, whose formal title is President of the Council of Ministers (as the cabinet is called), but who is generally referred to as the prime minister. As noted above, and as we will see at greater length below, the chronic instability of Italian cabinets has been the cause of many of Italy's governing dilemmas and the target of numerous reform efforts, most of which have not been successful.

The republic inherited the Liberal state's unitary and highly centralized administrative structure, which was consciously modeled on that of France, and includes prefects in the roughly one hundred provinces who are agents of the Ministry of the Interior in Rome. The republican constitution of 1948 decentralized some powers to the twenty regions of the country; over time the regions became the most important subnational level of government and acquired more power. But it took the rise of the Northern League to put serious decentralization, and federalism, on the political agenda. At the beginning of the twenty-first century, a rather weak form of federalism was instituted by the center-left; a few years later a more ambitious federalist rewriting of the constitution was being put in place by a center-right that included the League.

The judicial system has evolved dramatically under the republic, reflecting the interplay of conscious design and politics discussed at the start of this chapter. Judicial review was not part of the continental legal tradition, based in Roman law, but it was inserted into the 1946 constitution because of the Fascist past and U.S. influence. In another reaction against the past, the Italian judiciary, which, again following the continental tradition, includes prosecutorial as well as judicial powers, was granted far more institutional autonomy than its counterparts in France or Germany, but it acquired that autonomy very slowly. Eventually, it helped bring down the old party system thanks to its relentless—and, to some, reckless—prosecution of corruption during *Tangentopoli*.

As this brief summary suggests, it is not just Italian political processes, but the entire institutional framework, that has been very much in flux, and the rate of change has accelerated greatly since the 1990s.

The Executive

Throughout the First Republic, there were few exceptions to the general rule of an executive generally at the mercy of the parties—including the prime minister's own party. When the old party system collapsed, hopes were high that the old patterns would be left behind. It did not work out quite so neatly, and many aspects of the old system persist.

Cabinet Government all'Italiana: Chronic Problems of Governance

There is nothing unusual about the way Italians create their governments, which must command a majority in each of Parliament's two chambers. Following an election, the president of the republic consults party leaders and designates the most likely prime minister. The designee constructs a cabinet by consulting the leaders of the various parties that support the proposed government. In an (unsuccessful) effort to guarantee the collective responsibility of the government, the framers stipulated that the entire cabinet, and not just the prime minister, must then win the confidence of both the Chamber of Deputies and the Senate.

Governments are sworn in and remain in office until they no longer command Parliament's confidence or, much more common, the support of the governing coalition. In fact, on only one occasion since 1946 (Romano Prodi in 1998) has a government been brought down by a no-confidence motion. All other cabinet crises have been the result of internal divisions in the governing majority. When the prime minister no longer commands a majority, he (so far, there has never been a female prime minister) notifies the president, who can choose the incumbent or someone else to form a new government. If no coalition then obtains a majority or if Parliament's five-year term draws to a close, the president, after further consultation, dissolves the legislature and calls general elections, which must be held within a maximum of ten weeks of dissolution (Article 61).

During the First Republic, even though the outcome of the election was almost never in doubt, it could sometimes take months to find a prime minister and distribute ministerial portfolios in a manner that satisfied every party in the winning coalition. Since 1994, the new, mainly majoritarian electoral system now sends three-quarters of all deputies to the lower chamber (see Chapter 24). This change has forced the parties to construct their alliances before the elections, for this is the only way to agree on one candidate per single-member district—if the vote is split among two or more candidates from the same erstwhile coalition, it all but guarantees the loss of that seat. These alliances must also preselect the prime ministerial candidate around whom they will rally. Since 1994, it is therefore a foregone conclusion that the leader of the winning coalition will be the new prime minister, although it can still take a long time to dole out ministerial posts to all members of a coalition.

Since World War II, Italy has had sixty governments and twenty-three different prime ministers. Until the old party system collapsed in the early 1990s, this very high cabinet turnover actually masked the remarkable underlying stability of the party system. The same parties, and indeed many of the same people, occupied the key ministries of every government for forty years. This reflected postwar Italy's political arithmetic: in a fragmented Parliament, 35 to 40 percent of the seats regularly went to parties (Communists and neofascists) that had no chance of joining the government. Governing coalitions therefore had to be built from among the remaining 60 percent, which was extremely heterogeneous, though always dominated by the DC.

The utter predictability of the outcome of elections meant that there was never the chance that the opposition would win, and hence that the sitting government might truly be called to account for its policies. The most intense political competition often took place within the ruling coalitions, as governing parties jockeyed for marginal positional advantages in relation to their coalition partners and with respect to rivals within the same party. Serious reforms were rendered even less likely by the fact that the resistance of just a few key figures within the coalition could bring the government's support below 50 percent or precipitate crises and cabinet reshuffles that consumed weeks or even months.

The end of the old party system, and the disappearance of the rationale for the stable instability of the First Republic (the pariah status of the Communists and neofascists), has, so far, not produced the breakthrough that many hoped for. There has, to be sure, finally been true alternation in office between government and opposition. And by mid-2004, Berlusconi's second government had broken the record for the longest-lived cabinet in the republic's history by lasting three years. It is, however, a bit early to announce the dawn of a new era of stability in Italian politics. For one thing, Berlusconi's record-breaking cabinet consisted of four different parties, at least one of which was a coalition of several former political groupings. And the center-left, whose own government had witnessed four different cabinets in five years, and whose internal divisions then contributed to its defeat by Berlusconi in 2001, was fragmented into at least half a dozen different organizations. Electoral reform and the personalization of prime ministerial candidates had helped overcome one recurrent shortcoming, but only one government has so far proven able to survive the problem of a fragmented coalition—and it certainly has not solved that problem.

The Prime Minister's Powers. In formal terms, the Italian prime minister is one of the weaker heads of government in Western Europe, in part by design but especially due to the nature of Italian coalitions. When the dominant party is united, or when the governing coalition has an uncontested leader, the prime minister's power is enhanced. When coalitions prove to be less cohesive, as they did throughout most of the First Republic from the 1960s on, the prime minister's position will obviously be undermined. Socialist Bettino Craxi's leadership in the early 1980s showed that force of personality and pressing an agenda can make a difference, and his two governments at least gave the impression of decisiveness and action. But no amount

of dynamism can change the fact that under the existing rules, ministers owe their major debts to their own parties and factions, not to the head of government. Consider the case of Silvio Berlusconi, whose forceful personality surely did not change between 1994 and 2001. But while his first government lasted barely six months, his second—a coalition almost identical to the first—broke all previous records. It is true that his position within the coalition was stronger the second time around, but it is also true that he took much greater care in building and solidifying his second government.

In the waning days of the First Republic, the growing crisis of the parties finally permitted some strengthening of the prime minister's role vis-à-vis the cabinet, subjecting ministers to much more firm control. Then, at the end of the 1990s, far-reaching administrative reforms were implemented under Prodi and D'Alema. An economic "superministry" was created, combining the previously divided Budget and Treasury Ministries (Ciampi was the first incumbent), and budgetary procedures were restructured and modernized.[1] Other ministries were combined, and more coordination was established among ministries with overlapping interests. In the course of the 1990s, the powers of the prime minister in relation to his cabinet colleagues were further extended.

Because of the overriding need to divide positions between parties and factions, Italian cabinets not only have been politically cumbersome, but also have been physically ungainly. Every minister remains a member of the cabinet, and there were roughly thirty ministers in each cabinet through the early 1990s, when the number was briefly reduced to about twenty. Another old practice that was only briefly reformed in the mid-1990s was the naming of two junior ministers (undersecretaries) for each ministry. This guarantees the representation of diverse interests and the distribution of patronage and influence, but it obviously undermines coherent policymaking. Not surprisingly, as the solidity of the center-left coalition began to crumble, some old patterns resurfaced. D'Alema's cabinets and Amato's second government contained more ministries (twenty-four or twenty-five) and undersecretaries (more than fifty) than had their immediate predecessors, and there was no question that bloated cabinets were a price the leaders had to pay to keep fractious partners happy. Berlusconi's second government, which took a month to form, fit the same profile.[2]

The idea of giving more power to the prime minister, or the president, used to be dismissed out of hand with solemn reminders about Mussolini. Since the late 1990s, with the memory of Mussolini fading and the chronic problem of cabinet instability becoming all too apparent, new proposals to augment executive power have continually been put forward. Part of the left remains adamantly opposed to any such exercise, but most of the center-left now favors a strengthened role for the prime minister. The right is on record in support of a semipresidential system similar to that of France. More recently, however, Berlusconi has paid much less attention to the presidency and, instead, has revived the idea of directly electing the prime minister, a truly anomalous idea.* The underlying notion is both simple and time honored in democratic theory: If officials are chosen directly by the voters, they will be held more accountable for their actions—or, all too often in Italy, for their inaction. This idea informed the 1993 referendum that produced the mostly single-member system for parliamentary elections. It also contributed to the systems adopted for mayoral elections in towns with a population greater than 15,000 and for the regions, where voters cast a ballot (with a premium) for their preferred coalition candidate.† The success of both the municipal and regional electoral reforms is one of the reasons for the persistence of the idea of di-

rectly electing the prime minister. The notion of a direct popular mandate has special appeal for Berlusconi, a proven master of the mass media.

President of the Republic: A Sometimes Controversial Office

The president is the head of state and representative of national unity. Presidents are elected by secret ballot in a joint session of both chambers of Parliament, with an additional sixty representatives from the regions. On the first three ballots, a two-thirds majority is required; from the fourth, a simple majority suffices. The term of office is seven years, and although the constitution does not forbid reelection, no one has served more than one term.

The president's powers include designation of a prime minister and use of a suspensive veto, which can send a law back to Parliament unsigned with a note explaining the president's reservations. Vetoes can be overridden by a simple majority vote, in which case the president must then sign the bill. Presidents use this veto sparingly, but often to great effect. Since Italian governments are inevitably multiparty coalitions, the reservations of the head of state are usually enough to convince at least some members of the coalition to alter the bill. The president is also the chair of the Supreme Defense Council and the Supreme Council of the Judiciary (Consiglio Superiore della Magistratura, CSM). These are supposed to be honorific titles, but given the sometimes-stormy relations between politicians and the judiciary, this latter role can, at times, be politically charged: during the height of *Tangentopoli*, there were occasional clashes between President Francesco Cossiga and the CSM. The designation of a potential prime minister was once the president's most important power, for there were often several plausible contenders for the role. As the party system went into crisis in the 1990s, prime ministers were chosen from outside the parties in an even clearer assertion of presidential prerogative. For reasons

*Only Israel has ever tried such an experiment, and it was short-lived.
†See Chapter 24 for details on the national electoral system; details on the regional and municipal systems are examined later in this chapter.

outlined above, this discretion effectively disappeared as the new electoral system produced a more bipolar party system.

The office of the presidency became increasingly controversial in the 1970s. Some incumbents were clouded by scandal, and then the 1980s witnessed increasing outspokenness, usually involving denunciation of the slow rate at which Parliament was producing reforms. It became pronounced in the course of *Tangentopoli* and the collapse of the governing parties. This is hardly surprising: because almost all significant power rests in Parliament, and hence the parties, a crisis of authority inevitably resulted when their legitimacy crumbled. The resulting power vacuum created considerable freedom to maneuver in other branches of government. Into this vacuum stepped not only the president but the judiciary as well.[3]

The most dramatic developments occurred during the term of Oscar Luigi Scalfaro, a Christian Democrat who served from 1992 to 1999 and exercised unprecedented discretionary powers. In 1992, he informed Prime Minister Amato that politicians under a judicial cloud, no matter how strongly supported by their parties, would be unacceptable as members of cabinet. In 1993, he chose Italy's first nonpolitical prime minister (Carlo Azeglio Ciampi) to lead the country to general elections, and he then played an active role in choosing members of Ciampi's cabinet of specialists.[4] Finally, and most important, he resisted a furious campaign by the center-right in 1994 to call elections when Berlusconi's first government collapsed. A more cautious president might well have immediately dissolved Parliament, but Scalfaro feared that new elections might reproduce the paralysis that followed the 1994 vote, and further delegitimize Parliament.

Scalfaro was succeeded by Ciampi in 1999. His term in office has been less controversial than that of his predecessor, though he has criticized Berlusconi directly and indirectly, weighed in on governmental deliberations in various legislative areas, and vetoed a controversial telecommunications law. But with far more solid parliamentary majorities, the president has less opportunity to steer events than was the case in the 1990s.

The center-right was long on record in favor of strengthening the powers of the presidency, calling for something similar to the French Fifth Republic's semipresidentialism. This all changed under Berlusconi, who shifted his focus to the direct election of the prime minister. The center-right's proposed constitutional reforms now call for a weakened president and a strengthened prime minister. The left has historically been suspicious of anything that threatens Parliament's prerogatives. Yet in the face of Berlusconi's solid majorities and obvious ambition, it often found itself appealing to Ciampi to rein in the prime minister in the name of the integrity of the constitution.

The Bureaucracy and Civil Service

Few institutions enjoy much public respect in Italy, but the bureaucracy is especially reviled. Centralized and inflexible traditions, outmoded recruitment practices, low pay, ironclad job security, and practically every other shortcoming known to complex organizations are all combined in Italy's public administration. Italy's administrative system hardly ends with the formal ministerial bureaucracies and the career civil servants who staff them, however. Its most unique aspects are found in the state-owned firms, holding companies, autonomous agencies and enterprises, and special institutions that still saturate the country, despite the pace of reforms since the 1990s.

This sprawling structure is highly politicized *and* extraordinarily fragmented; it is also the key to understanding the paralysis built into the entire political system. It evolved and expanded at a time when the DC overwhelmingly dominated its coalition partners and therefore claimed most of the key ministries for itself while installing its own people in the top positions in the bureaucracy and state-controlled economic institutions. Its much smaller coalition partners received limited slivers of this pie. As its hegemony weakened, the DC was forced to provide its partners with larger shares. The system was fragmented from the very beginning, not only because of (limited) power sharing among coalition partners but especially because the DC itself was divided internally. This huge spoils system provided independent power bases within the ruling party. Forty-five uninterrupted years at the center of the system, at least thirty-five of which were spent carving it up, created a dynamic that did not end with the collapse of the DC and PSI.

The Regular Public Administration. With slightly more than 2 million people employed by central ministries and another 2 million scattered throughout all other levels of the public administration, the number of state employees in Italy may seem high at just under 20 percent of the total workforce, but it is not out of line with the rest of Western Europe.[5] The real problem lies in the way ministries—and to some extent the entire legal culture undergirding the Italian state—are organized: they seem designed to maximize inefficiency and demoralization through the ranks; they are overcentralized and rule bound; promotion disregards merit and rewards seniority and political connections; and the pay and working conditions are terrible. Especially at lower levels, absenteeism is widespread, second jobs are more the rule than the exception, and service is arrogantly delivered, appallingly slow, and susceptible to manipulation and corruption.

Like the judiciary, the bureaucracy's upper reaches in the first generation of the republic were staffed with Fascist appointees. A reform got much of the old guard to take early retirement in 1972, but it also sped the exit of highly professional upper-rank civil servants. The new top cadre, like the old, was highly sensitive to the political balance of power and the desires of the leaders of Italy's ruling parties. With politicians loath to delegate power and bureaucrats afraid of taking independent initiatives, the old system was perpetuated, and became increasingly rule-conscious as unionization spread through the lower ranks, giving workers a new awareness of their rights. Another reform in 1980 attempted to break down the rigid job classifications that contribute to the bureaucracy's inflexibility. But this reform, like so many others, met stiff internal resistance. One sensitive observer says these reforms were "ingested" and integrated into the system's old structures and processes.[6] Thanks to political favoritism and its own self-serving behavior, there is one way in which the Italian bureaucracy does stand out: its top grades are far more bloated than the upper levels of other Western democracies. Fully one of every eight Italian civil servants is found in the top ranks of the bureaucracy.[7]

The system is also perpetuated by its formalism: entrance examinations stress abstract concepts and knowledge of legal minutiae rather than technical skills. This, along with the low pay, helps account for the high proportion of southerners at all levels of the civil service. Tradition and the lack of other options in the Mezzogiorno, along with the high enrollment of southerners in legal and philosophical faculties in the universities, means that the civil service offers a chance to those who hope to earn a living without moving to the north or leaving the country.

Yet despite all the legal-rational trappings, the civil service, with a few exceptions, is highly fragmented and shot through with influence and patronage. Ministries set their own entry requirements and supervise their own examinations. A tradition of autonomous, centralized little empires was reinforced after World War II, as ministries were "colonized" by the ruling parties, often by one or two power groups within the DC. Especially for upper-level appointments, where long essays and oral exams are the allegedly objective basis on which candidates are judged, favored applicants easily get past the hurdles.

This colonization perpetuated fragmentation at the top of the system and penetrated down to the grassroots, making the bureaucracy an effective patronage machine but a much less satisfactory mechanism for the delivery of services. The results have been disastrous all along the line: division, incoherence, and infighting at the center, with indifferent service on the delivery end. A series of reforms beginning in the late 1990s began to streamline and decentralize the bureaucracy, and produced important innovations in center-periphery relations. Even more significant have been two recent revisions of the constitution, since 2001, the first by the center-left, and the second by the center-right, still in process as this chapter was being written in 2004. Each of these reforms was meant to introduce a degree of federalism into Italian institutional arrangements, decentralizing power down to the regional and subregional levels of government. As responsibilities for such vital functions as education, healthcare, and public safety, with their huge staffs and large budgets, are passed down to lower levels of the state, such decentralization has profound implications for the bureaucracy (see the discussion of local government below). It remains an open question whether the centralized bureaucracy's worst pathologies will be superseded by these measures, or whether they will simply be transferred down to the regions.

Public and Semipublic Institutions: State Enterprises and Autonomous Agencies

Italy's public agencies have counterparts nearly everywhere in the advanced capitalist world, although Italian agencies are astonishingly prolific. Their number ranges anywhere from forty thousand to over fifty thousand, depending on how one counts.[8] State monopolies in Italy may historically have covered a few unusual sectors (salt and bananas come to mind), and some public corporations may have slightly different structures elsewhere, but the state-run, nonstock corporation is a stranger to few modern capitalist societies. In Italy, key industries of this type, such as railroads and tele-

phone and telegraph services, date back to the turn of the twentieth century.

Health, pension, social security, and welfare agencies and institutions are also commonly nationalized services, although in most advanced societies many of these are under direct ministerial control. In Italy they evolved as autonomous agencies, parallel to Catholic and other charitable institutions. They are organized under the Ministry of Labor and Welfare, but the major institutions control the investment of their own funds, which amount to billions of euros. They operate under strict guidelines, but their potential leverage over the economy is immense. The largest agency is the Social Security Institute (Istituto Nazionale di Previdenza Sociale, INPS), and for at least twenty years there have been halting steps toward reorganizing and making the entire range of welfare agencies under INPS more efficient. This process has been resisted fiercely by thousands of local mini-agencies representing a variety of special interests.

All Western societies contain abundant examples of the political use of state services, but Italy is unique in the degree to which the control of state and parastate agencies, as well as the allocation of payments, became flagrant instruments of political patronage. Italy is also distinguished by the degree to which political parties have been the agents (and beneficiaries) of such practices.[9] A classic case is the political use of the disability pension. By the early 1980s, the total number of such pensions reached 7.2 million, accounting for 4.5 percent of GDP.

The extent and variety of public ownership of industry has made Italy unique among West European democracies. The Institute for Industrial Reconstruction (IRI) was not disbanded or its holdings privatized at war's end; its role in the economy steadily expanded, and other holding companies, most notably the National Hydrocarbons Agency, or ENI (Ente Nazionale Idrocarburi), an energy conglomerate, and EFIM (Ente Partecipazioni e Finanziamento Industriale Manifatturiera), covering state-owned industries in the south, were also created. The degeneration of the holding companies, along with unrelenting pressure from the European Union (EU), finally resulted in the formal dissolution of IRI in 2000, although much of its stock remains in the Treasury.

These extensive resources played an active role in Italy's reconstruction and in laying the groundwork for the Economic Miracle. From admirable beginnings, the picture increasingly became one of narrow partisanship and the indiscriminate distribution of positions to key power groups' numerous constituencies. Positions of immense influence were doled out in proportion to parties' (or factions') political leverage—a phenomenon the Italians call *lottizzazione*. The result was a system in which purely political, or extremely shortsighted, criteria governed decisions. Only with the collapse of the old party system and the establishment of more rigorous technical governments under Amato, Ciampi, and Dini in the 1990s was privatization undertaken in serious and sustained fashion. Even then, it was often ferociously opposed, and sometimes sabotaged, by entrenched interests inside the public firms as well as by powerful banking and industrial interests in the private sector that were in no rush to see the economy become too competitive.

Other State Institutions

With a centralized model copied in large measure from France, the Italian state reaches everywhere into society. We limit ourselves here to two areas of great importance for all democracies, and of particular importance in Italy's political history: the use of force, and the role of the judiciary.

The Military and the Police

The military has occasionally played an important role in modern Italian history. Under fascism, because the *Statuto albertino* remained in force, the military owed its primary allegiance to

the king, and not to Mussolini. This fact took on great significance when the king ordered the arrest of il Duce and turned power over to Marshal Pietro Badoglio, who then negotiated a truce and eventual alliance with the Allies. In the postwar republic, the armed forces primarily served to provide young men from the various regions of the country with a sense of national identity. A universal draft was in place for males over eighteen, and it was common to post southerners in the north, and vice versa. In the course of the 1980s and 1990s, the eighteen-month term of service was gradually reduced to a year, and exemptions became increasingly easy to obtain. Finally, in 2000, it was announced that, within seven years, the draft would be entirely abolished, by which date the armed forces would have been transformed into a fully volunteer service, much smaller in size, and characterized by the sort of professionalism required in a modern, high-tech army.

The line between the military and the police is not always a sharp one in countries like Italy, where centralized bureaucratic traditions run deep. In fact, in the Italian context, the term "forces of order" can refer to both the police and the military, and it is easy to understand why. The Carabinieri, for example, are a national police force trained and organized as a branch of the military, and historically staffed at the lower ranks with draftees. The regular police, in contrast, are responsible to the Ministry of the Interior. It is the latter whose functions are slated to be devolved to the regions in the center-right's federalist proposal, and some civil liberties activists worry about the impact this may have, for example, with regard to the treatment of immigrants.

Given the intensity and the nature of cold war polarization in Italy—above all the fact that the major union was affiliated with the largest Communist party in the Western world—as well as the extensive social movements that have marked Italian politics ever since the 1960s, the postwar period was marked by encounters that were often violent and frequently lethal. The

Italian military had several quick-response battalions of shock troops, called the Celere, stationed around the country, which were notorious for intervening in labor disputes. Well into the 1960s, encounters in which the police or military fired on demonstrating peasants or workers were not common, but they certainly were not unheard of. In the 1960s and 1970s, the use of deadly force decreased significantly, and was almost always limited to demonstrating students or youth; the most recent case was in antiglobalization protests in Genoa in 2001, where the forces of order shot one demonstrator to death, and physically assaulted dozens of others.

The Judiciary

No institution played a more controversial role in the transition to Italy's so-called Second Republic than the judiciary. Like the rest of the political system, it was plagued by blatant political manipulation from the earliest days of the republic. For a full generation, its top echelons were filled with people who rejected most of the constitution's innovations. Even under conditions of normalcy, the fight against organized crime and political corruption was often hampered when investigations got too close to centers of political power. Since 1992, corruption scandals showed how effective judicial investigators could be when not held back. The corruption scandals turned prosecutors into national heroes, but they sowed the seeds of bitter political resentment, reinforcing trends toward an increasingly politicized judiciary and raising troubling questions about the role of the courts in a modern democracy. Here, as elsewhere, Italy's institutional framework is far from consolidated.

Article 104 of the constitution affirms the judiciary's independence, and provides for a Superior Council of the Judiciary to guarantee that independence; another departure from continental tradition was the introduction of judicial review, with the stipulation that a Constitutional Court be the final arbiter of a law's constitutionality. These innovations were inspired by the

ease with which fascism had trampled Liberal Italy's legal structures. But it took many years for these (and other) provisions to be enacted, for the DC simply stalled their creation as long as it could.

The Constitutional Court has fifteen members, appointed on a rotating basis to nine-year nonrenewable terms. A third of its members are named by Parliament, a third by the president of the republic, and the remaining third by the highest courts in the country. Much like the U.S. Supreme Court, it can review cases only on appeal. It cannot, in other words, rule on the constitutionality of a law after it has been passed but before it is promulgated, as in France, nor can it be directly petitioned, as in Germany. But the

The major parties' perceived involvement in *Tangentopoli* (1993). The executioner is the period's leading prosecutor, Antonio Di Pietro, who eventually entered politics himself.

Source: Reproduced by permission of Giorgio Forattini from Giorgio Forattini, *Mascalzonate: Il Meglio di Forattini a Colori.*

appeals procedure has proven to be a very powerful tool, particularly in a country plagued by legislative paralysis. On a number of occasions, the Constitutional Court forced parliamentary action by striking down obsolete and regressive laws—for example, those regulating police powers and criminal procedures, or those governing family law and the role of women—that dated to the Fascist era. Faced with a legislative vacuum in the absence of the old laws, Parliament enacted far-reaching, modernizing reforms.

In the early postwar period, the highest-ranking appeals judges, mostly Fascist appointees, interpreted the constitution on extremely narrow grounds. These legal conservatives never accepted the principle of judicial review and often flouted the rulings of the Constitutional Court once it was established. They greatly delayed the evolution of the legal and judicial system until, by the end of the 1970s, they had largely faded from the scene. The reason the previous system of justice had remained intact through the late 1950s was nakedly political. During the height of the cold war, the government aimed to marginalize the left and weaken it in every possible way, and a Fascist penal code simplified that task. Because the 1931 code was intended to outlaw all political activity, it was easy to use the legal system to obstruct and harass the labor movement.

Pressures from above and below finally forced the system to change. The Constitutional Court's activism and relative independence—in spite of the fact that most of its members are political appointees—have made it one of the more respected political institutions in the country. This is much less true of the higher levels of the regular criminal courts: investigations take blatantly false and politically motivated paths for years, powerful judges shift the venues of investigations to sabotage them, decisions are rendered for extremely obscure motives, and so on.

Formally, the judicial branch is insulated from direct political interference by the Superior Council of the Judiciary, which was finally instituted in 1959. This is a twenty-four-member body, two-thirds of whom are directly elected by

members of the judiciary, thus further reinforcing its independence. The remaining third is chosen by Parliament from practicing lawyers and legal academics. It is presided over by the president of the republic, though its vice president, chosen from within the council's ranks, is the effective chief executive. In the course of a number of changes clearly meant to rein in the autonomy of the judiciary, the center-right weakened this body considerably in 2002, reducing its numbers (from thirty) and doing everything it could to diffuse and fragment the way the judges choose their own representatives.[10]

Changes in the judiciary were stimulated from below starting in the 1960s, when young recruits brought social ferment to the profession. The stranglehold of the conservative old guard was gradually broken, and the profession is now governed by civil service rules (e.g., tenure and de facto automatic promotion based on seniority) in a setting that can be highly politicized. Since the 1970s, judges have engaged in job actions and, more rarely, strikes. The Superior Council has been the site of highly politicized disputes that break along classic left-right lines, but also of more corporate struggles in which the judiciary as a body tries to assert its rights or prerogatives against outside interference.

The willingness of the judiciary to organize and promote itself aggressively, combined with numerous privileges granted it by law, has given this body immense power, raising serious questions about the judiciary's insulation from the political process.[11] The bureaucracy of the Ministry of Justice is, notoriously, the creature of the judges, who are legally entitled to its top positions. Judges lobby external agencies with little concern for what would be considered a conflict of interest in other countries. Judges are also entitled to stand for political office and participate in arbitration panels or other semipublic agencies. These privileges—or abuses—have generated efforts over the years to cut down their power, which then further politicizes their role.

Delayed Reform. All advanced capitalist democracies face serious problems in their systems of justice, but the Italian situation truly seems to be more acute. Texts written thirty years ago wondered how the system had survived into the 1970s, and matters have become much worse since.[12] Judges themselves evoke contradictory public responses. There is great public sympathy for prosecuting magistrates, who literally risk their lives when they exercise the duties of office. In the late 1970s and early 1980s, they were the targets of left-wing terrorists; since then, threats and murders have been carried out by the mafia. At the same time, the arbitrary workings of the regular courts are legendary. Wrongful prosecutions, endless delays, and damaging leaks to the press without the possibility of response by the accused have ruined many reputations.

In 1989, after a decade of delays and an additional four years of parliamentary debate, a new code of penal procedure was finally enacted in the wake of the referendum. It has been modified considerably since then by rulings of the Constitutional Court, continued tinkering on the part of Parliament, and even constitutional amendment. Although it mixes aspects of two different legal systems—not always coherently—it still is an improvement over the old (Fascist) code, in which, for instance, the accused was not informed of charges or evidence until a trial date was set. Pretrial investigations and trial deliberations are now far more open, but the new system takes even more time for evidence gathering and discovery than the old, and no revision in the statute of limitations adjusted for this. (Well-heeled defendants, and Berlusconi is a prime example, can simply drag a case out until it expires before being resolved in court.) The new code, after forty years, finally entrenched the constitutional principle of the equality of the accused and the prosecution. Preventive detention, which in the past could be drawn out for as long as ten years, has been reduced, although prosecutors used it to great effect during *Tangentopoli.*

But public prosecutors remain part of the judiciary in Italy and retain more police powers than similar figures in other Western constitutional democracies (where they are under the control of the executive branch). Aggressive prosecutorial techniques, combined with some magistrates' penchant for self-promotion and well-timed leaks to the press, created instant popular heroes in the 1990s, but also convinced some that the prosecutors had a political agenda. The worst abuses give pause to sober observers on all points of the political spectrum. Berlusconi's frequent railing against judicial abuses of power and conspiracies are obviously self-serving, but they resonate among people who are not necessarily his political allies. The best-informed experts agree that there is simply too much mutual suspicion to expect significant improvements in either the organization or the operation of the judicial system in the near future.[13]

This is a pity, for any improvement in the situation is long overdue. Cases are so backlogged, the machinery grinds so slowly, and the system is so inefficient that the intolerable becomes the norm. To cite but one example, when the new penal code was formally instituted in 1989, there was a backlog of 2.7 *million* criminal cases that would have to be tried using the old system in force when these arrests were made.[14] Those unfortunate enough to be jailed for minor offenses regularly serve the maximum sentence before coming to trial; an incredible 60 percent of Italy's prison population is awaiting trial, a situation that is regularly denounced by the European Court of Human Rights and the Council of Ministers. Lawyers regularly stall their clients' cases, knowing that amnesties are issued every few years to clear the docket. When sentences finally are handed down, they are often so lengthy and obscure that even experts have trouble deciphering them. In a country that produces a sarcastic remark for almost every occasion, few are as telling as, "Italy is the cradle of the law and the grave of justice."

Local Government

There are three main levels of subnational government in Italy: *comuni* (the Italian term for all municipalities, towns, and cities), provinces, and regions. As political entities, the *comuni* were by far the most important into the 1980s, and they remain the liveliest sites of local politics in the country, especially following important reforms in the 1990s. In terms of administrative importance, however, the province has historically been the major subdivision of the country, linked directly by the prefect, a member of the national bureaucracy, to the Ministry of the Interior in Rome and run at times like colonial offices. Because their boundaries are often arbitrary and the implementation of the regions seems to make them unnecessary, there is strong feeling that the provinces should be eliminated altogether. The regions, although steeped in history, had no formal status until the formation of the republic, and only the special regions had any significant powers until the 1970s. As federalism moved to the top of the political agenda, the regions recently came to occupy the most important place in subnational politics.

The Comuni

There are roughly eight thousand *comuni* in Italy. Their relatively large size means that towns are generally populous enough to reproduce most of the parties, and the partisan conflict, found at the national level. In 1993, a new law for towns with populations greater than fifteen thousand maintained list voting but introduced a separate, more important ballot for individual mayoral candidates.* Mayors are now directly elected, rather than being chosen by party leaders after the votes are counted. If no candidate

*For towns with fewer than fifteen thousand inhabitants, voters choose among lists. The list receiving the most votes, even a relative majority, receives two-thirds of the seats. The remaining third is divided proportionally among all other lists.

obtains an absolute majority on the first ballot, a runoff is held between the two candidates who got the most votes. The high voter turnout in general elections (80–85 percent) is nearly matched in local elections, which occur every five years. Mayors may only serve two full terms.

This new system, introduced as the old party system was imploding, has contributed to a rejuvenation of local-level politics in Italy. Since the mid-1990s, the mayors of larger cities have enjoyed very high visibility and legitimacy because they had a clear popular mandate. Some of them have used this leverage to vault onto the national political stage. Other prominent politicians have been "parachuted" into big cities to give themselves more visibility.

The left has been especially effective in building broad coalitions at the municipal level, finding high-quality candidates with wide public appeal. With the exception of Milan, where both Berlusconi and the Northern League have enjoyed exceptional success, the center-left has governed most of Italy's major cities since the new electoral system was introduced. At the same time, it has recently suffered humiliating defeats in some historic "red" strongholds when it got involved in internal power struggles and took public support too much for granted.

The Regions and Italy's Emerging Federal Structure

Two types of regions were spelled out in the constitution. Five special regions were granted significant autonomy almost immediately. These include Sardinia, Sicily, and three areas on the northern border of the country with strong French, Germanic, and Slavic cultural characteristics. Various powers were also supposed to be devolved to the fifteen ordinary regions, but Parliament did not pass the relevant enabling legislation until 1970.

The Communist Party's historic strength in the red zones, where it regularly obtained more than 40 percent of the vote, explains why the DC dragged its heels in devolving power to the regions, thus depriving the opposition of an important political lever. This was not the only instance of constitutional sabotage by the DC, but it was the most nakedly partisan in motivation.

Like the larger city governments, regional councils vary in size according to population. They are elected for five-year terms, and, as has happened at every level of Italian political life in the 1990s, a new electoral system, different from all the others, is now in place. Through 1990, regional councils were chosen by proportional list systems. A complicated dual ballot was introduced for the 1995 regional elections, and in 2000 it was further refined by a constitutional amendment that permits the direct election of regional presidents in a single ballot. (The direct election of mayors had a powerful influence on these changes.) Alliances are constructed by party lists around presidential candidates, with each list declaring its support of one or another candidate. Alliances are important, for only 80 percent of the seats are distributed proportionally to the lists. The remaining 20 percent serve as a premium to "top up" the winner's share, thus guaranteeing a working majority—generally a minimum of 55 to 60 percent of the seats. Winning majorities are "blocked" for two years—that is, alliances must be honored, or new elections are called. This avoids coalitions of convenience that would divide the victor's premium and then immediately dissolve, with each party keeping the additional seats for itself.

The erosion of Rome's centralizing tendencies has accelerated dramatically in recent years. Several laws passed in 1997 and 1998 extensively overhauled the central government's relations with local government. Even more significant developments have taken place since 2001. In that year, the center-left, almost as its last act in office, passed a far-reaching federalist reform that involved amending the constitution. The center-right, sensing that it was about to win the upcoming election, had fiercely opposed this reform, arguing that its own project of rewriting the constitution would introduce a far more thoroughgoing federalism. In October 2001, with Berlusconi back in power, the first ratifying referendum was called, and it upheld the changes by a 64-36 margin.* Berlusconi's new government, with Lega leader Umberto Bossi as minister of institutional reform, announced that it would proceed with its own constitutional revisions, and that process was still underway in 2004. Since the center-left's reform will have proven to be short-lived, and the center-right's reform was not definitively passed as this chapter was being written, all we can do here is sketch out the broad differences.

The center-left's is a rather "soft" interpretation of federalism, with a concern for maintaining national unity and not aggravating the already large gap between north and south.[15] But it does formally insert principles of federalism in the Italian constitution, including the explicit designation of some areas of legislation as exclusively the province of the regions, along with the principle of *subsidiarity*—that is, the idea that powers not explicitly reserved for the central state belong to its subnational units. The center-right, not surprisingly, has gone much further in its proposed reforms. Recognizing that everyone had appropriated the term *federalism*, Bossi made the English concept of *devolution* his own, though his final proposals—which respond to many reservations within the center-right—are a mix of both the Scottish and the Spanish experiences.[16] That is, the regions will be allowed to choose which services they wish to provide, and also whether to fund these services publicly or via some mix of public and private (the devolution pattern). At the same time, acknowledging that some regions will be ill equipped to assume extensive responsibilities in education, health services, and local public security matters—all of which are earmarked for devolution—subnational units of government may choose *not* to exercise powers in a given

---

*All previous referenda in Italy, save for the 1946 vote that abolished the monarchy, were of the abrogative variety (see Chapter 24). The turnout was only 34 percent but, in contrast with the abrogative referendum, a ratifying referendum does not require that half the voters turn out.

area, and may instead remain within a nationally structured framework.

Another significant innovation contained in the center-right's federalism package, missing from the center-left's reform, is the conversion of the Senate into a "Chamber of the Regions," much reduced in size from its current 315 members, and structured along the lines of the German Bundesrat (though chosen by direct election). Even if only partly put into practice, the center-right's reforms will represent the most far-reaching changes in Italy's institutional arrangements since the drafting of the republican constitution in 1947.

Evidence that the regions have become rooted in Italy is that they tend to reproduce the country's historical cleavages in their own operations. In a famous, and controversial, study, political scientist Robert Putnam argues that by almost all relevant measures—from how efficiently they deliver services to whether they even manage to spend the funds earmarked for their use— southern regions lag behind the rest of the country, while the red regions of the center and the industrialized areas of the north show the most initiative.[17] It is hard to argue with the evidence (though many critics take issue with Putnam's explanation for north-south differences, which he traces all the way back to the Middle Ages). Efforts to put the 1997–1998 reforms into practice once again saw the north and center in the lead, with the south well in arrears—making the "opt-in" clause of the proposed federal reform an absolute necessity in the eyes of many. Yet some recent developments suggest that the situation in the south might not be quite as irreversible as Putnam sometimes seems to suggest. For instance, the Campania region, and its capital city, Naples, have, by general agreement, made amazing progress since the mid-1990s.

The European Dimension

As is the case for every member nation of the EU, it is increasingly difficult to understand the functioning of many of Italy's political institutions in isolation from those of the EU. To cite just one example from the discussion of federalism immediately above: when the center-left revised the constitution, it made explicit reference to EU guidelines in rewriting Article 118. The new rules state that the central government has the right to determine whether regional legislation falls within EU legal guidelines; if it feels these are being violated, it can immediately refer the matter to the Constitutional Court.[18]

An even more revealing example concerns Italy's efforts through the 1990s to enter the Economic and Monetary Union (EMU), and then to remain a member in good standing. This required modification not only of the country's policymaking processes, but of many of its structures as well. To ensure compliance with EU directives, the Department for the Coordination of Community Policies was established and given ministerial status. The same pressures led to the deregulation of financial markets, the abolition of the Ministry of State Holdings early in the 1990s, and, perhaps more subtly, the creation of the Treasury and Budget superministry later in the same decade. These actions reflected the need to streamline and modernize economic decision making, but once EU standards had become imperative, such streamlining could not be avoided.

This is most evident with regard to privatization, although Italy is still under pressure to conform more fully to EU policies. Still, no serious observer of Italy's political economy could doubt that such a momentous step as the dissolution of IRI would ever have occurred without persistent pressure from the EU. European influence is even more unambiguously responsible for dramatic changes in Italian policymaking processes. Not only were budgetary structures changed, but budgetary decision making was profoundly altered, at the direct expense of the once all-powerful Parliament. With deficits and public spending under intense external scrutiny, and with the Bank of Italy free from government interference (see Chapter 22), governments had little, if any, maneuvering room of the kind that used to allow them to run up deficits, and spread largesse, with impunity.

The EU intrudes into Italy's institutional framework in more embarrassing ways. In 2001, in the wake of the September 11 attacks on the United States, the EU undertook to reinforce its own fight against terrorism by streamlining Europe-wide judicial investigations and procedures. One such measure was a European arrest warrant that covers a broad range of crimes, primarily terrorism and other violent activities, but also including fraud and corruption. Italy was the only government among the fifteen members to oppose these steps, arguing that the warrant should cover a much more limited number of abuses, and certainly not fraud or corruption. This appeared to be a nakedly self-serving move by Berlusconi to protect himself against pending charges originating in other countries (e.g., Spain). Under enormous pressure, Berlusconi's government backed down, but still dragged its feet over the next several years and only grudgingly implemented the measures needed to make warrants operational toward the end of 2004.

Policy Processes: Continuity and Transition

As this chapter, and indeed every chapter in this section, makes clear, all aspects of politics in the Italian Republic were indelibly marked by the intrusion of the country's parties into every nook and cranny of social, political, and economic life. This phenomenon was so pervasive that the Italian political system was described as a *partitocrazia*, or "party-ocracy." Its negative impact on the policymaking process is evident in everything from the sheer number of governments that Italy has had to endure to the tortured, fragmented, and conflict-riddled itinerary of so much of the legislation that successive governments have tried to shepherd through Parliament.

As we have just seen in our discussion of the European dimension of Italian governance and policymaking, some things have changed in

Italy, albeit only under incredible outside pressure. Nevertheless, even if they only did so under duress, Italy's governors proved that it is possible to streamline executive operations and executive-parliamentary relations, and to act decisively in areas of vital concern to the economy by producing budgets that many observers would have believed impossible a few years earlier.

These innovations were introduced thanks to several factors. One was a stronger and more assertive executive; it helped immensely that Prodi is an economist by training and also possessed an excellent understanding of governmental operations thanks to his previous experience at IRI. Another was the decision to combine previously fragmented ministries into an economic "super-ministry" and start its life under the leadership of a figure as prestigious as Carlo Ciampi, former governor of the Bank of Italy. The traditionally cautious and servile senior civil servants in the old economic departments were bypassed in the new decision-making process, which passed the initiative to technocrats from the Bank of Italy and the Treasury, as well as to academic economists from the Finance Ministry and various think tanks.[19] The enhanced control by the executive over financial policy, not to mention the coherence of that policy, was obviously noticed by Berlusconi, for he kept the same structures in place.

If the Italian system responds only to extraordinary pressure, the past dozen years show that not all extraordinary pressure to change has to be generated externally. It may have taken the political earthquake of *Tangentopoli* and the collapse of the old party system, but these triggered an effort to overhaul the country's entire political practice. Let us recall that much of the attention to institutional reform grows out of a desire to see Italy become a "normal country." The electoral reforms in the early 1990s, repeated schemes to strengthen the executive, and many other proposals reflect a widely shared desire to simplify the party system and to create a bipolar alternation in power between government and opposition. And at least some of these goals have been realized since the mid-1990s.

The second Berlusconi government seemed to some to mark the beginning of a new era in the annals of Italian governance. We will recall that while the center-left remained in office for the full five-year duration of the previous legislature, its tenure in office was marked by considerable internal division. With the very important exception of the budgets and related economic programs that brought Italy within the Maastricht convergence criteria, the center-left's travails did evoke the sort of infighting and paralysis that were so typical of the First Republic. Berlusconi's victory in 2001, in contrast, marked the first time the new electoral system had produced solid majorities in both chambers, and hence the conditions for the sort of majority rule that reformers had long hoped for. And, indeed, by mid-2004 the government had broken all previous longevity records. As the coalition stayed together, observers noted that Berlusconi's solid majorities allowed him to ram bills through Parliament in a fashion that was most unusual in Italy. Critics might disagree with the content of these laws (e.g., immigration, conflict of interest, telecommunications regulation, amnesties), but it did appear that something approaching true government by the majority—as opposed to the traditional mutual sabotage of the majority by its component parts—had finally arrived in Italy.

Although they do point to important departures from past practices, these assessments have turned out to be inaccurate. A careful analysis of the first two years of Berlusconi's second government, which compares its legislative output and efficiency with Prodi's cabinet, not only does not find the center-right to be more effective in getting its legislation through Parliament; indeed, along some important dimensions, the fractious center-left actually had a better record.[20] The fierceness of the debates over immigration, conflict of interest, and the like may have left the impression of a steamrolling majority, but systematic scrutiny of each coalition's overall output reveals far more similarities than differences.

It is also important to view the post-1994 governments as a whole. When we do so, we realize that, despite some significant departures, a good deal of continuity with the past remains. Berlusconi's first government was almost a caricature of the cabinet instability of the First Republic, lasting less than the nine months of its average predecessor. The center-left fared only slightly better, lasting a full five-year term, but with three different prime ministers. Thus only the second Berlusconi government suggested that the transition to a Second Republic might indeed finally be underway once more. But even this government was marked by constant threats from one or another of its components—most often the Northern League—and hardly projected an image of coherence or homogeneity. No matter how impressive its longevity might be, it will take more than one cabinet to constitute clear evidence of a new trend in Italian governance.

Notes

1. David Felsen, "Changes to the Italian Budgetary Regime: The Reforms of Law No. 94/1997," in David Hine and Salvatore Vassallo, eds., *Italian Politics: The Return of Politics* (Oxford: Berghahn Books, 2000), pp. 157–173.

2. D'Alema's short-lived second cabinet contained a record sixty-six undersecretaries by the time it was dissolved. Barbara Jerkov, "Il valzer dei 54 sottosegretari: dentro Minniti, Intini e Chiti," *La Repubblica*, April 28, 2000, p. 9. But Berlusconi's second government increased the number of ministers and also contained fifty-three undersecretaries. Silvio Buzzanca, "I ministeri sono aumentati e il centrosinistra insorge," *La Repubblica*, June 12, 2001, p. 4.

3. For details, see Enzo Balboni, "President of the Republic, Judges and the Superior Council of the

Judiciary," in Stephen Hellman and Gianfranco Pasquino, eds., *Italian Politics: A Review,* vol. 7 (London: Pinter, 1992), pp. 49–67.

4. Gianfranco Pasquino and Salvatore Vassallo, "The Government of Carlo Azeglio Ciampi," in Carol Mershon and Gianfranco Pasquino, eds., *Italian Politics: Ending the First Republic* (Boulder, Colo.: Westview Press, 1995), pp. 55–73.

5. David Hine, *Governing Italy: The Politics of Bargained Pluralism* (Oxford: Clarendon Press, 1993), esp. pp. 232, 237.

6. Paul Furlong, *Modern Italy: Representation and Reform* (London: Routledge, 1994), pp. 87–88.

7. Filippo Cavazzuti, "Finanza pubblica e pubblica amministrazione: Caratteristiche e limiti della nuova legge finanziaria," in Raimondo Catanzaro and Raffaella Y. Nanetti, eds., *Politica in Italia: Edizione 89* (Bologna: Il Mulino, 1989), pp. 104–105.

8. For the higher figure, see Furlong, *Modern Italy,* p. 88; for the lower number, see Hine, *Governing Italy,* p. 229.

9. Maurizio Ferrara, "Il mercato politico-assistenziale," in Ugo Ascoli and Raimondo Catanzaro, eds., *La società italiana degli anni ottanta* (Bari: Laterza, 1988), pp. 327–328.

10. David Nelken, "Berlusconi e i giudici: Legittimi sospetti?" in Jean Blondel and Paolo Segatti, eds., *Politica in Italia: Edizione 2003* (Bologna: Il Mulino, 2003), pp. 143–145.

11. Giuseppe Di Federico, "La crisi del sistema giudiziario e la questione della responsabilità civile dei magistrati," in Piergiorgio Corbetta and Robert Leonardi, eds., *Politica in Italia: Edizione 88* (Bologna: Il Mulino, 1988), esp. pp. 108–113.

12. P. A. Allum, *Italy: Republic Without Government?* (New York: Norton, 1973), p. 184; Raphael Zariski, *Italy: The Politics of Uneven Development* (Hinsdale, Ill.: Dryden Press, 1972), chap. 9, esp. p. 319.

13. Nelken, "Berlusconi e i giudici," p. 153.

14. Hine, *Governing Italy,* p. 255.

15. This discussion draws on Anna Cento Bull, "Verso uno stato federale? Proposte alternative per la revisione costituzionale," in Paolo Bellucci and Martin Bull, eds., *Politica in Italia: Edizione 2002* (Bologna: Il Mulino, 2002), pp. 205–223.

16. Ibid., pp. 213–215.

17. Robert Putnam, *Making Democracy Work* (Princeton, N.J.: Princeton University Press, 1993).

18. Cento Bull, "Verso uno stato federale?" p. 207.

19. Claudio M. Radaelli, "Networks of Expertise and Policy Change in Italy," *South European Politics and Society* 3 (Autumn 1998): esp. pp. 4–18.

20. Giliberto Capano and Marco Giuliani, "Il parlamento italiano tra logica di governo e logica istituzionale: Molto fumo per quale arrosto?" in Blondel and Segatti, *Politica in Italia: Edizione 2003,* pp. 174–182.

C H A P T E R

24

Representation and Participation

Memories of fascism put an unusual amount of power in Parliament's hands in relation to the executive. Then, for forty-five years, party-centered politics reinforced Parliament's centrality. As we saw in Chapter 23, the executive-legislative balance was changing before Berlusconi returned to office. In this chapter, in addition to describing long-established practices, we will discuss changes that have already occurred, as well as some reforms that have very recently been set in motion. We will also see that popular mobilization and protest have been in abundant supply for the past fifty years and show no sign of abating.

The Legislature

By design, but also because of the balance of power in postwar Italy, Parliament has remained the overwhelming locus of power in the Italian political system.

Parliament's Powers and Anomalies

As in other parliamentary systems, Italy's Parliament votes governments into and out of office and has wide latitude in passing laws. Additionally, in joint session, it elects (and may impeach) the president of the republic; it chooses a third of the members of the Constitutional Court and of the Superior Council of the Judiciary; and it may amend the constitution. There are two constitutional limits on parliamentary abuses of power. One is judicial review. The other is the abrogative referendum, which permits the nullification of all or part of some laws by popular vote.

Laws are made in the Italian Parliament in a fashion similar to other parliamentary systems, although numerous factors have undermined the executive's ability to control the legislative agenda. Laws can be proposed either by the government or by private members, and one of the ways Italy distinguishes itself is in not limiting the number of private-member initiatives. Government bills tend to originate in the ministries, but in contrast to a country like France, which has an activist state tradition (and highly competent top civil servants), in Italy this has historically meant that innovation-shy bureaucrats would pass along proposals put forward by the interest groups that incessantly lobby them. Only since the 1990s, with the innovations discussed at the end of Chapter 23, have cautious bureaucrats and lobbyists been displaced by a more expert and coherent corps of policymakers, at least in such areas as finance and the economy.

Proposals are then passed to the parliamentary committee that corresponds to the relevant ministry. Many proposals die in committee. A good number follow the "normal" legislative itinerary, familiar to any student of parliamentary politics—that is, after being picked apart and often amended, bills are reported out of committee and submitted to Parliament. But in Italy, for every bill brought before the entire Parliament, three are passed into law by committees: we discuss this anomaly below. Those bills that make it to the floor are debated in two stages. In the first, a general motion for approval is presented, and the broad principles of the law are discussed. In the second stage, specific articles are discussed in detail, and at this stage amendments can be presented. (A classic obstructionist tactic is to present hundreds of microscopically different amendments.) This process is identical in either chamber, and if the bill passes in one chamber, it must then be passed, in identical form, in the other.

As the above summary indicates, some of Parliament's rules seem designed to slow down operations, diffuse authority, and maximize potential mischief. Italy's legislature represents a case of pure bicameralism: the two chambers, with a combined total of roughly 950 members, have *identical* powers. Committees can pass laws without referral back to the floor. Government-sponsored bills enjoy no special status, such as limits to the number of amendments that can be proposed. Final votes on bills can be, and often are, conducted according to a secret ballot. And only in the past decade has the government gained control over the parliamentary agenda and legislative timetables. For nearly a generation, the balance of power in Parliament was so precarious that the agenda had to be agreed to by all parties, including the opposition. The most unusual of these provisions are worth a brief examination.

Pure Bicameralism

This clumsy arrangement was produced by Christian Democrat (DC)–left differences in the Constituent Assembly. Neither side got what it wanted and could only agree on something with no apparent virtues. Despite the two chambers' equality, no standing committee exists to reconcile different versions of the same law; each chamber must pass identical versions of a bill. The potential for stalling or sabotaging legislation is most evident when controversial legislation is at stake (e.g., abortion in the late 1970s, or conflict of interest in the late 1990s). Yet when the political will exists, party leaders can easily hammer out a deal. Most observers agree that pure bicameralism is an absurd impediment in a system that already has enough problems. The center-right's reform package (see Chapter 23) would put an end to this: the Senate would become a "Senate of

the Regions," akin to the German Bundesrat, but with its members elected, rather than appointed by the regional governments.

Committees That Legislate

As in some other legislatures, standing committees can take proposals and amend them beyond recognition or kill them by refusing to refer them to the floor of the Chamber or Senate. But committees can also pass a wide variety of proposals directly into law under conditions far less open to scrutiny than on the floor of Parliament. When a committee receives a bill under these conditions, it meets with deliberative powers (*in sede deliberante*). The cabinet, a fifth of the relevant committee's members, or a tenth of the members of the Chamber can demand that a bill be brought to the floor and voted up or down without debate. This option is exercised only with regard to controversial laws. As a result, Parliament's many standing committees often become miniature legislatures, which explains why Italy produces far more laws than any other European democracy. Over a thousand laws, most of them called *leggine* (little laws) because they deal with minor matters, are passed in a five-year legislature, and three-quarters of these are passed *in sede deliberante*. Yet even this high number represents a huge drop compared with the past.[1]

The Secret Ballot

A secret ballot was originally required for all votes in the Chamber of Deputies. Although not strictly required in the Senate, secret ballots are often used there as well, if requested by a small number of senators. The practice originated with the 1848 *Statuto albertino*, as a check on tyrannical party leaders, but its effect is to keep citizens from knowing how their representatives vote. Secret ballots have been a license to sabotage one's own party or coalition with impunity. Italians call this sniping, and it has seriously embarrassed many governments. Since the late

1980s, spending and revenue bills require an open vote, and only constitutional amendments, electoral regulations, and questions of personal morality and family law are now subject to secret balloting. Nonetheless, the secret vote can still disrupt Parliament and shield legislators from the consequences of their actions.

Representative Principles and the Electoral System

Adults over the age of eighteen are automatically registered to vote for the Chamber of Deputies. Suffrage for the Senate is restricted to those twenty-five or older. Both chambers are completely renewed in general elections. Parliament sits for a maximum of five years; the average life of a legislature has been just under four years. Senators must be at least forty years old, and deputies twenty-one. Through 1992, elections were held under a permissive form of proportional representation (PR), especially for the 630-seat Chamber, where 1.5 percent of the vote usually guaranteed seats to a party. Under PR, voters select a party list, and seats are then assigned in proportion to each party's vote.

The original goal of the 1993 referendum, discussed in Chapters 21 and 23, was to eliminate PR altogether. Reformers believed that a single-member, first-past-the-post system would reduce the number of parties and force elected representatives to be more responsive to their constituents. They also hoped that fewer parties contending in a winner-take-all system would produce a bipolar party system; it would be unrealistic to expect a party system as fragmented as Italy's to shake down to just a few parties, but it was felt that even two clear clusters or coalitions would represent a big improvement.

The New Electoral Systemp

The resulting reform produced a system similar to, but more complicated than, the one that elects the German Bundestag. Because the Parliament

that passed this law contained sixteen parties and was dominated by a DC committed to proportional principles, the resulting compromise was inevitable.[2] Since 1993, Italy has had a mixed single-member and proportional system. In the Chamber of Deputies, three-fourths of the 630 seats are assigned on a first-past-the-post basis; the remaining quarter are determined by PR lists. The new law is less permissive than the old: parties must get at least 4 percent of the vote to obtain any seats from the PR lists. Otherwise their PR votes go into a pool that is distributed only to lists that have exceeded the 4 percent floor. The major motivation for the reform was to reduce the number of parties and force the emergence of clear-cut coalitions that, it was hoped, would provide more stable governments and the possibility of an alternation in power between government and opposition.

In many ways, the new system has been a success. In 1994, it produced a complicated center-right alliance (which was really a northern and a southern coalition, both led by Silvio Berlusconi), as well as a left-wing Progressive Alliance. In 1996, voters faced a more simplified array, as (minus the Northern League) a single Freedom Pole (Il Polo della Libertà) represented the center-right throughout the entire country, and the Olive Tree coalition represented the center-left; the same two blocs faced each other again in 2001, with the center-right renamed the House of Freedoms (Casa delle Libertà). The new rules effectively compel rival blocs to unite behind a candidate for prime minister, giving a personal dimension to general elections. In the past, in contrast, backroom intrigues often determined both prime minister and cabinet only after the votes were counted. The new rules also force smaller parties to join one bloc or the other if they wish to obtain parliamentary seats—but this greatly increases the blackmail potential of the smaller parties, for if they run as "spoilers," they can cost an alliance closely contested seats.

Electoral systems are not magic bullets. The blocs that have been forced to form out of the existing parties are extremely heterogeneous. One need only think of the quick collapse of Berlusconi's alliance with Umberto Bossi's Northern League in 1995, or Romano Prodi's losing a confidence vote in 1998 when the far left abandoned him, or Massimo D'Alema's replacing Prodi only when a small centrist group deserted the Freedom Pole to support the center-left. Moreover, petty maneuvering that recalls the First Republic has returned. Battles regularly divide allies over the assignment of the safest seats or the highest positions on combined lists. Cynical deals between very different forces are a constant temptation, as can be seen in the courting of the League by both major blocs in 1996, before it decided to stand alone. In 2001, political reality brought these allies-become-enemies back together, even as Rifondazione Comunista's decision to run alone split the left-wing vote and contributed to the Ulivo's defeat.

The Referendum as a Direct Link to the People

Since 1970, two distinctive types of popular referendum have been possible. The first (see Chapter 23) may be called to ratify a constitutional revision. It has been used only once, in 2001, but it will probably be employed with growing frequency as efforts to alter the 1948 institutional framework proceed. The second is the abrogative referendum; as the name indicates, it is used to challenge all or part of an existing law. The first such effort was an unsuccessful attempt in 1974 to roll back the 1970 law that legalized divorce. Since then, this instrument has mainly been employed to raise issues that Parliament could or would not address.

Although referenda have occasionally had a profound and direct impact on the entire political system (most notably in 1991 and 1993, forcing changes in the electoral system that hastened the collapse of the old party system), they have been used so indiscriminately—fourteen times since 1974—that their future is now problematic.

A referendum's sponsors must specify the law, or parts of a law, to be eliminated. This requires half a million valid voters' signatures or identical motions passed by five regional councils. The Constitutional Court then rules on the validity of the challenge. If the referendum is declared admissible, a vote must be held within a prescribed period, with all the costs and disruptions that this implies. Should Parliament amend the targeted legislation before the vote, the referendum is nullified. If Parliament does not act in time, the vote is held, and if at least half the electorate turns out, the law is abrogated (a majority votes yes) or it stands.

Despite the positive role that some referenda have played, it is easy to understand why many people want to limit the topics that can be challenged, increase the number of signatures required, or both. After being used selectively on issues of great moment such as divorce, abortion, and the *scala mobile* (cost-of-living escalator), their abuse has produced understandable impatience. The turnout for referenda declined steadily through the 1980s, to the point where almost all recent efforts have failed to bring half the electorate to the polls, and hence have been nullified.

Political Parties and the Evolution of the Party System

The Italian political system was dominated for two generations by a handful of parties and a distinctive party system. All the formerly important parties either no longer exist or have undergone profound changes. In addition, new parties—some of them marginal—have arisen. A new party system is emerging and consolidating, but it remains relatively fluid. It is important to understand the current dynamic, its most important actors, and most likely scenarios. Yet ignoring the historical context of the present party system would render it incomprehensible.

The Party System Through the Late 1980s: Christian Democratic Centrality

Our starting point is the complete dominance of the First Republic by the Christian Democrats. Italy's postwar political experience demonstrates that there is no simple connection between social change and electoral behavior. For nearly thirty years, some of the most turbulent socioeconomic changes to occur anywhere in Western Europe barely rippled the surface of the Italian party system. The country as a whole showed stable electoral patterns, while the vote for the largest party, Christian Democracy (DC), wavered less than a single percentage point in five consecutive elections in the 1960s and 1970s (see Table 21.1). The "centrality" of the DC refers to two things: its occupation of the center of the political spectrum and the fact that it was the key player in every government of the First Republic. Its centrality reflected the unacceptability, to the majority of Italians, of the large left-wing and smaller right-wing opposition parties as participants in any government, for these parties were not considered loyal to the democratic rules of the game. The multiple divisions that resulted, faithfully mirrored by PR, created one of the most complex yet immobile party systems in the democratic world. Even as cold war tensions faded, the underlying dynamic determined the formation of every Italian government between 1947 and 1994.

For forty-five years, centrist or center-left coalitions governed Italy; the only mystery was which minor parties would be the DC's partner and share the booty. The center, totally dominated by the DC, held stable at around 40 percent through the 1970s. Three small lay (non-Catholic) parties were the DC's satellites. As the DC's share of the vote dropped well below 40 percent in the 1980s, its reliance on the Socialist Party (PSI) became absolute, a dependency the PSI was quick to exploit.

The left was divided between Communists and Socialists but was dominated by the PCI (Italian Communist Party) from 1948 on. Smaller parties—far left, ecological, and civil libertarian—occupied a limited space on this part of the spectrum. Even counting the PSI as part of the left (a problematic assumption by the 1980s), the left steadily rose to a high of more than 45 percent in the 1970s but slipped to closer to 40 percent thereafter.

The small extreme right was represented exclusively by the neofascist MSI (Italian Social Movement) from the 1970s on. The MSI was the real pariah of the party system, and not only because of its dubious history. Its commitment to democracy remained questionable into the 1980s, and in the 1960s and 1970s some party militants seemed uncomfortably close to antidemocratic and even terrorist groups.

The End of the Old Equilibrium (1989 and Beyond)

By the 1980s, the number of parties in Parliament and the proportion of the vote going to new parties was rising steadily. A dozen parties held seats at the beginning of the 1980s, and their number reached sixteen ten years later. More dramatic, the share of the vote going to lists that had not existed in the early 1980s went from a tenth in 1987, to a quarter in 1992, to nearly half in 1994. Before the tumultuous events between 1992 and 1994, the Northern League, which had barely a handful of seats even as late as 1987, appeared destined to reap the benefits of the DC's weakening grasp on its traditional constituencies.

The crumbling old system finally gave way under the combined onslaught of international and domestic events (the fall of communism, exploding deficits and accumulated debt, and the *Tangentopoli* scandal). Finally, the new electoral system, introduced in 1993, frustrated the crisis-riddled DC's ability to occupy the middle of the spectrum.

The old system collapsed with astonishing speed. By the 1994 elections, the PSI was all but wiped out. The once mighty DC lost its left wing, renamed itself the Popular Party, and then lost its right wing. It tried to run as a centrist alternative to the left and right in 1994, and plunged from 30 percent to a mere 11 percent of the vote. It split yet again in 1995. The neofascist MSI broadened its own appeal for 1994 and then undertook a more serious transformation after 1995. Berlusconi leaped to prominence at the head of Forza

Italia, which did not even exist five months earlier, and led a center-right bloc to victory.

Berlusconi's victory in 1994 appeared to confirm the emergence of a bipolar logic in the party system that made the construction of alliances absolutely essential. The left's defeat in 1994 convinced the PDS that the only hope of victory lay in a broad center-left alliance, which produced the Ulivo (Olive Tree) for the 1996 elections. Headed by Romano Prodi, a Catholic with impressive economic credentials, the Ulivo defeated a badly divided Freedom Pole. But serious divisions existed on the left and weakened the alliance from within and without.

Despite important changes, the new party system is more fragmented than the old. Even after the League abandoned him, deep differences in style and content separated Berlusconi from his post-Fascist partners. Adding the League to this mix renders it even more heterogeneous. The left is, if anything, just as divided. The far left, which has split several times, is ambivalent about formally supporting a center-left coalition. The center-left is divided over numerous issues, as well as by simple power struggles, and projects an image of constant bickering and maneuvering. Moreover, several old and new political groups, remnants of the former DC and some lay parties of the center, are unhappy with the system's bipolar logic. Uncomfortable in either bloc, they dream of controlling the balance of power from the center, which so recently seemed destined to irrelevancy.

We now turn to an examination of the specific political groups, or broad political families, as they have evolved and as they currently appear in Parliament.

Christian Democracy and Its Successors

The secret to the DC's success, ironically, was its lack of internal coherence: its catch-all multiclass, composite nature allowed it to be all things to all people. This may have denied Italy a true conservative party, not to mention consistency in economic or social policy, but it was an impressive recipe for raw political success. Its guaranteed governing role kept the DC united, despite often-bitter internal divisions.

The DC's support period rested on four pillars: religion, anticommunism, patronage, and the halo effect from being in power as Italy rapidly developed into a prosperous, advanced capitalist democracy. Over time, most of these factors were undermined, and anticommunism disappeared altogether. The decline of the other supporting pillars gave patronage increasing importance in holding together disparate constituencies. Its slipping strength compelled the DC to distribute more spoils to its coalition partners (above all, the PSI). The 1980s also finally saw limits imposed on state spending because of ballooning deficits and the growing national debt, policed by the European Community. The corruption scandals of the 1990s found the DC vulnerable enough to be attacked head-on. This was more a political than a judicial vulnerability, for the governing parties had weathered past scandals with impunity. With the alibi of anticommunism finally exhausted, it was open season on the old political elite.

The DC fell below 30 percent of the vote in 1992—*before* the most damaging revelations of *Tangentopoli*. Once the scandal broke, the DC went into free fall, and by 1994 it was down to 11 percent. It had long been losing ground to the League in its northern strongholds, and it was now being displaced by the MSI in the south. The 1994 name change to the Italian Popular Party (PPI) represented an effort to salvage some respectability for this once mighty machine (this was the party's original name when founded after World War I). But it was too late.[3]

The emerging bipolar logic of the new electoral system crushed the PPI between the Progressives and Berlusconi's Pole, and it lost support to both the left and the right. In 1994, it was most severely punished in the new single-member districts, where it won only four contests. Following this debacle, the conservative wing renamed itself the United Christian Democrats (CDU) and joined another ex-DC rump alongside Berlusconi. The PPI won the right to keep its name after a bitter and embarrassing court contest and joined the Ulivo. Within the center-right coalition, former Christian Democrats reunited in a single party, but failed to exceed the 4 percent floor in 2001.

Between Left and Right: Centrist Parties and Formations

The minor lay parties went into crisis in the 1980s, when Craxi moved the Socialists toward the center, crowding an already limited political space. Increasing bipolarity after 1994 effectively sealed these parties' fates, as people followed their ideological inclinations or political calculations. Most who allied with Berlusconi joined his party, Forza Italia. Others were among the founders of the Ulivo in 1995, or later joined other left-leaning centrists. Like most other centrists, including the remnants of the DC and PSI, however, they often preferred looser alliances that magnified their own pivotal role.

In 1996, and again in 2001, many left-leaning centrists felt vindicated. Under Prodi's leadership, they felt that the center, rather than the far left, would hold the decisive balance of power on the center-left. But the centrists' strategy was not a complete success. After the 1996 elections, Rifondazione Comunista's external support was essential for the survival of Prodi's coalition, at least in the Chamber of Deputies. When Rifondazione withdrew that support, Prodi fell. But the centrist parties had proven decisive in Prodi's electoral victory, and know they will play a decisive role if the center-left is to return to power.

But political grudges and maneuvering for position within the Ulivo have hurt the center-left's image. Prodi's followers, furious when he was pushed out of office, joined with others to form their own party, hoping to strengthen what they called the "centrist leg" of the coalition. This party then spent much of the next two years trying to undermine D'Alema, whom they blamed for allowing Prodi to be dumped. In

2001, Prodi's followers pulled together Catholics and lay centrists and gave concrete form to the "centrist leg," coming up with yet another botanical name—the Daisy (Margherita). In those elections, with 14.5 percent, this new group came close to equaling the DS's total vote in the election (see Table 21.2).

The Left

Italy is unique in the West in having a Communist Party or its successor dominate the left throughout the postwar period. Although the post-Communists have tried several times since 1989 to reinvent themselves and revitalize the left, they have not succeeded. In fact, the left hit a historic low following its defeat in 2001.[4]

The Communist Party (PCI)/Democratic Party of the Left (PDS)/Left Democrats (DS). A key reason for the cluttered, fragmented center is that the left continues to be dominated by the heir to the PCI. Despite its evolution before the end of communism and its total transformation since then, the "original sin" of the Left Democrats (Democratici di Sinistra, DS) is something neither opponents nor allies let it forget. Berlusconi misses no opportunity to drag up the past, while centrist coalition partners argue that moderate voters are leery of former Communist candidates for prime minister.

The PCI almost became a governing party in the 1970s, when it reached its historic high of 34.4 percent of the vote. In 1989, when the Berlin Wall fell, the PCI's fortunes had been declining for a decade. It embarked on a radical revision of its name, symbol, and structure. After two years of lacerating divisions and a schism, it formally became the PDS in 1991, adopting an oak tree as its new symbol, relegating the old hammer and sickle to the base of the tree. Completing its break with the past, the new party was accepted as a member of the Socialist International, the worldwide organization of socialist and social democratic parties that Communists used to denounce as insufficiently militant and radical.

In 1996, the PDS nosed out Forza Italia as the largest party in the country, though with a mere 21 percent of the vote. In 1998, seeking to expand its base and appeal, it changed its name, but aside from eliminating the hammer and sickle from its logo, the DS only succeeded in absorbing some minuscule leftist formations, leading observers to refer to an oak tree ringed by little "bushes." Later in the same year, its secretary, Massimo D'Alema, became prime minister—the first former Communist to lead a Western government. But a cabinet shuffle, not an election, put him in office. When the Ulivo chose a prime ministerial candidate for the 2001 elections, it named the centrist mayor of Rome; his main rival was the ex-Socialist prime minister Giuliano Amato. The DS did not put forward a candidate of its own.

An Electoral and Strategic Dilemma. The PCI was in crisis long before communism collapsed in the East. By the 1980s, it was steadily losing young people's support to newer parties, such as the Radicals, the Greens, and even the revitalized PSI. Changes begun in the late 1980s by Secretary-General Achille Occhetto, such as making ecology and feminism central planks in the party's platform, were an effort to make the PCI relevant to younger Italians while defining a new identity.

Nor did the loss of the most hard-line old-timers to Rifondazione Comunista in 1991 solve the identity crisis. Even those who supported the break with the past are divided. Most want the DS to become a modern social democratic party, whereas others are convinced that all old left-wing ideologies and identities are now obsolete. This group would like to see the DS merge with the center-left to form a single, even less ideological Democratic Party, like the one in the United States. For them, the Ulivo was not just a coalition but the precursor of a new political party (and some of them joined the Margherita when it was formed).

The PDS's beginnings were not very promising. It did poorly in the 1992 elections, gaining a mere 16 percent of the vote. It rose to just over 20 percent in 1994, but Berlusconi's victory drove home the point that if the left ceded the center of the spectrum to others, it would remain on the losing end of every election. Massimo D'Alema took over the party in 1994, and swiftly moved it even further toward the center. Under a new leader for the 2001 elections, the DS fell back to its historic low point and has been plagued with continuous internal squabbling, which further undermines its public image.

The Birth—and Death—of the Ulivo. Romano Prodi's emergence as its standard bearer finally gave the center-left a high-visibility leader to take on Berlusconi. Prodi reassured Italian capital, and particularly big business, that the Ulivo was committed to the sort of enlightened austerity programs that had marked Ciampi's government. His leadership was also intended as a bridge to Catholics and other centrists, who felt more comfortable voting for a coalition headed by a former left-wing Christian Democrat than for one headed by a former Communist.

The Ulivo won the 1996 elections, but that did not resolve the major dilemmas that the coalition or its largest partner faced. While D'Alema's government racked up impressive achievements, these were not reflected in the DS's fortunes. If anything, the shift of attention to the party's governing role disoriented its shrinking rank and file and further weakened an already atrophied organization. It remains rooted in the red zones of central Italy, but it had suffered defeats even in these strongholds by the end of the 1990s (most notably, losing the mayoralty of Bologna). By the time D'Alema resigned, the Ulivo had effectively ceased to exist, and the DS appeared to be floundering in search of a clear identity. Only several years in the opposition, and Prodi's impending return from Brussels at the end of 2004, seemed to partially revitalize the broader coalition, but new elections are not scheduled until 2006, and divisions within the coalition, as well as between it and other forces on the left, appear to be chronic.

Smaller Parties and Groups on the Left.
The rest of the left in Italy was always conditioned by the PCI's dominant role. The PCI's transformation into the PDS only changed the name of the major party; the dynamic remains the same.

The Ex-Socialists. No party was more devastated by *Tangentopoli* than the PSI. It barely managed 2 percent of the vote in 1994, after which it disintegrated into squabbling mini-groups. By then, Craxi was a fugitive from justice, and he died in exile in Tunisia in 2000. In 1994, a large group left the party to join the Progressive Alliance; a small ex-Socialist rump remains part of the center-left. When the reformist leadership of the PSI followed their comrades in a leftward direction, most of the *craxiani* became Berlusconi's partners; some joined Forza Italia while others formed their own tiny party.

The Far Left. From the 1960s on, the PCI's increasing moderation drove the most militant leftists outside the party. Even after the mass mobilizations of the Hot Autumn, this space remained restricted, although the small (2 percent) Proletarian Democracy (Democrazia Proletaria, DP) belied its name by becoming a vocal exponent of feminism, antinuclearism, and ecology as these themes gained support in Italy.

The 1991 creation of Partito della Rifondazione Comunista (PRC), or the Communist Refoundation Party, altered the nature of the far left. Its roots in the PCI gave the new party 150,000 members, close ties to militant trade unionists, and considerable mass appeal. But in addition to hard-line militants and radicals who left the old PCI, Rifondazione included the most closed and Stalinist remnants as well. When DP dissolved itself and joined Rifondazione en masse, the PRC became a grab-bag of everyone on the left who was unhappy with the PDS.

Rifondazione has polled between 5 and 9 percent of the vote in general elections, and over 10 percent in areas of historic Communist strength, giving it considerable leverage in Italy's fragmented politics. In 1994, the PRC joined the Progressive Alliance. In 1996, with the more moderate Ulivo contesting the elections, the PRC entered a "stand-down" (*desistenza*) agreement with the Ulivo in Italy's single-member districts. In exchange for a handful of safe seats, the PRC absented itself from all other single-member contests, instructing its supporters to vote for the Ulivo. This arrangement helped the Ulivo win, while Rifondazione earned an impressive 8.6 percent of the vote. After two years of supporting Prodi's government without joining the cabinet, the PRC decided that its identity outweighed its practical influence and it joined the no-confidence vote that forced Prodi to resign.

Rifondazione faces a delicate balancing act, as two internal splits attest: in 1995, and again in 1998, dissidents broke ranks to support the government in power. In the general elections of 2001, Rifondazione's support fell to about half of its historic high. If the center-left hopes to win the next election, some agreement with Rifondazione will be essential. The PRC is obviously aware of this and appeared to be seeking some accommodation with the Ulivo as the 2006 elections drew closer.

Other Small Formations. The Green phenomenon evolved slowly in Italy. Only in the late 1980s did Greens obtain parliamentary representation. The Green lists' late formation meant that many activists had previous political experiences and identities. A single group was formed in 1990 after years of mistrust. More moderate Greens remain suspicious of those with experience in DP or the Radical Party; there are also typical disputes over whether members should enthusiastically participate in existing political institutions or use them as a propaganda platform. Intensely committed to their own independence, the Greens initially refused to join the Ulivo but eventually supported Prodi and his successors, winning the environmental portfolio in three of four governments. Jealous of their autonomy, they have steadfastly refused to join a broader center-left coalition; in 2001, they presented a common list with leftist remnants of the old PSI and failed to exceed the 4 percent floor on the PR ballots.

Another group whose impact has been greater than its small size has appeared, since the late 1970s, as the Radical Party (PR) and under several other names. Its leader, Giacinto (Marco) Pannella, has been among Italy's most flamboyant political figures. He is given to hyperbolic statements and actions such as hunger strikes and was immodest enough to name the group after himself (the Pannella list) when he liquidated the PR in the early 1990s for egotistical reasons.[5]

The PR established its identity by embracing causes ignored by others: women's rights, civil rights (of a libertarian sort), conscientious objection, and ecology. Starting in the 1970s, it used the referendum more often than anyone else to embarrass the major parties.[6] It also emphasized developed countries' responsibilities to the Third World. The Radicals are hard to categorize using standard left-right criteria. For instance, Pannella supported Berlusconi in 1994 before growing uncomfortable with a departure from his usual gadfly role. The Radicals once represented an innovative form of protest politics. But they also have a limited repertoire of actions, as their multiple referendum proposals, and Pannella's attention-grabbing actions, suggest.

Centrist, "Third Pole" Ambitions. Some heirs of the DC and the lay parties continue to present lists independent of either of the two major blocs, almost always failing to exceed the 4 percent floor. This attests to the strength of the electoral system's bipolar logic. Smaller formations have little hope of obtaining parliamentary seats unless they ally—formally or informally—with a major bloc. But it hardly means that smaller parties cannot have a profound effect on any given election, as the Lega proved in 1996 when it cost the center-right the election. In 2001, three self-defined centrist lists won no seats but, combined, accounted for nearly 9 percent of the vote, indicating that while the bipolar trend may be clear, it is not yet fully consolidated.[7]

The Center-Right Freedom Pole/House of Freedoms

Divisions on the center-right are as great as those on the center-left, but the balance of power within the House of Freedoms gives it more stability than the Ulivo. Berlusconi's judicial and financial problems notwithstanding, he remains the only plausible candidate to lead this alliance. His party is more than twice the size of its next-largest ally, further reinforcing his leadership role. The volatile nature of some of his partners, and the natural tendency of minor parties in a coalition to demand more visibility, keeps Berlusconi busy—and convinces him of his indispensability. But all the squabbling should not obscure the fact that truly profound changes have taken place on this side of the political spectrum in Italy. Of the four major partners in the coalition, two were insignificant or nonexistent during the First Republic; the third had to undergo profound transformation to become a major player; the fourth is a rump of the party that totally dominated the political system for two generations.

The Ex-DC Centrists. These are the most moderate members of the coalition, many of whom accept the bipolar logic of the new electoral system through gritted teeth and probably would prefer to be part of a centrist "third pole." Some, such as the CDU, have already been on both sides of the divide. In 2001, the CDU joined the ex-Christian Democrats of the Christian Democratic Center (Centro Cristiano Democratico, CCD) in presenting an autonomous list affiliated with Berlusconi's alliance. Dubbed the "White Flower," they received a bit over 3 percent of the vote and thus no PR seats. Between 2002 and 2004, they were joined by a former DC trade unionist and his followers to form the Christian Democratic Centrist Union (Unione dei Democratici Cristiani e Democratici di Centro, UDC). Although they are both social and economic conservatives in Italian terms, these former Christian Democrats are also embarrassed by some of their coalition partners. In the 1990s, they had more reservations about the post-Fascists; more recently it has been the League's stridency (and often overt racism) that have strained relations within the coalition.

The Lega Nord. In 1991, several regional leagues, mainly in the northeast, combined to form the Northern League under the leadership of the strongest, the Lombard League, led by the mercurial Umberto Bossi. Leagues first appeared in DC strongholds, in areas historically hostile to the state and outside intervention. Ilvo Diamanti, an acute observer, notes that the various leagues departed from more traditional bases of identity and representation, such as religion versus secularism, or class, and took other long-standing cleavages (e.g., north-south, center-periphery, "common folks" versus big government) and expressed them in a new way, dramatically altering the political landscape.[8] In the words of another student of the phenomenon, the League turned the southern question into the northern question.[9] The small businesses and industries it represents have been dynamic contributors to Italy's resurgent economy. But for the League, they are also the repositories of traditional virtues in a rapidly changing world; they are the expression of family (as opposed to impersonal corporate) values and of deep roots in small communities.

The Lega began as an antitax, anti–big government movement. It presented itself as the defender of honest, hard-working "little people" of the north whose taxes were subsidizing a bloated Roman bureaucracy and its southern clients, portrayed in stereotyped terms as lazy parasites. In its earlier phase, the Lega was pro-EU, arguing that the virtuous north would be an integral part of a "Europe based on regions." Highly critical of Berlusconi and his post-Fascist ally, Bossi nevertheless led the Lega into the coalition that won the 1994 elections, effectively guaranteeing its victory in the north—and hence in Italy.

The alliance was short-lived. After barely six months, Bossi realized his grassroots support was slipping. The Lega pulled out of the coalition, bringing down Berlusconi's first government. From the opposition, Bossi sought to reinforce his party's identity by setting it on a more radical path. He resuscitated separatist ideas and became highly critical of the European Union, now viewed as the expression of American and international big business, economically and culturally antithetical to the interests and values of virtuous northerners. And while there was still no love lost for southern Italians, the truly menacing "outsiders"[10] were identified as immigrants, particularly those—overwhelmingly Muslim—who were seen as threatening Italy's Christian, European identity.

Bossi appeared to have committed political suicide by isolating his party and running alone in 1996, thus exposing it to the bipolar logic of the new electoral law. But thanks to its geographically concentrated strength, the Lega confounded predictions. It obtained more votes in the north than any other party and split the moderate vote, guaranteeing the Ulivo's victory.

This was the high point in Lega fortunes. By the end of the 1990s, its separatism and stridency made it easier for Forza Italia to attract the support of business. Moreover, Bossi's "go it alone" stance created tension within his own movement. Despite insistence that traditional left-right distinctions do not apply to the League, its activists felt far closer to the right and worried that isolation would guarantee the center-left perpetual victory—and deny the Lega access to governmental prerogatives.

Finally, pragmatism prevailed. Bossi spoke of devolution rather than separation. His criticism of the Vatican turned into an emphasis on traditional Christian values. The alliance between the Freedom Pole and the League was renewed in 2000 as the House of Freedoms, which permitted the center-right to present a single candidate in northern single-member constituencies, thus enabling it to win nearly three-quarters of all these seats in 2001.

The Lega's participation put Berlusconi back in power, bringing the Lega increased visibility.

From his position as minister of institutional reform, Bossi made sure that immigration reform
and, of course, devolution were put high on the
parliamentary agenda. Intemperate and sometimes racist outbursts against Islamic immigrants embarrassed many coalition partners, but
kept the Lega and its leader in the headlines.

But for all its posturing, the Lega entered the
second Berlusconi government in precarious
health (which helps explain its provocative behavior). Its support, on a downward trend after
1996, plummeted in the 2001 elections. And it lost
a larger share of the vote in its strongholds than
anywhere else. In 1996, aside from all the single-
member seats it won thanks to its geographical
concentration, the Lega attracted just over 10 percent of the national vote. In 2001, it failed (though
barely) to exceed the 4 percent floor in the PR
lists. Berlusconi could, if he wanted to, govern
without its votes in Parliament.

Forza Italia.   From the time Silvio Berlusconi
burst onto the political scene in late 1993, his
party was immediately dubbed the *partito-
azienda,* or "Company Party," since it was staffed
by lawyers, managers, and publicists from
Berlusconi's Fininvest business empire. Forza
Italia (FI) was more than a facade, however;
skilled advertising executives used their expertise to create a formidable electoral machine.
Berlusconi conducted a smooth American-style
campaign informed by focus group research and
extensive public opinion polling.[11] He avoided
face-to-face debates, fired off sound bites, proved
to be a masterful communicator, and won the
election. That someone with so many interests
would want to protect them is evident. That he
would vault into Palazzo Chigi (the prime minister's residence) as head of the largest party in
the country six months after entering politics is
extraordinary. And that in the course of this unprecedented personal triumph he would also
help radically reshape Italian politics, not least
by bringing the MSI into the democratic fold
and hastening its evolution, was yet another triumph for the man known as "Il Cavaliere" (for

his honorific title, Cavaliere del Lavoro, or
Knight of Labor). Grasping the implications of
the new electoral law before his competitors, he
devised a brilliant tactic: he formed separate
alliances with the Italian Social Movement–
National Alliance (MSI-AN) (in the south) and
the League (in the north), which cemented his
victory.

But Il Cavaliere proved a better campaigner
than prime minister, a better empire builder
than politician. He also claimed not to understand why people thought it problematic that he
owned three of Italy's four private networks and
directly or indirectly controlled all three public
networks. Berlusconi's obtuseness and insincer-
ity over conflicts of interest undermined his
credibility even among supporters.

Berlusconi did not simply sulk after being
driven back into the opposition in 1995. He realized that Forza Italia's lack of local roots had
compromised its effectiveness after the 1994 victory. Thus, while keeping a firm hand on the
helm, he dramatically reorganized the party, giving it more of a grassroots structure with incentives to ensure participation and a semblance of
internal democracy.[12] Externally, he lobbied incessantly for greater legitimacy and was rewarded in 1999 when FI was allowed to join the
European Popular Party (Christian Democrats)
in the European Parliament. By the time of the
2001 election, which swept him back into power,
his party was by far the largest in the country,
gaining over 29 percent. With two-thirds of the
center-right's votes, it dominated the coalition,
drawing votes from all members of the coalition,
though especially from the Lega.[13] Berlusconi
has made clear that he thinks Forza Italia needs
to be strengthened even further, for only then
will he be able to govern without constantly
having to placate his squabbling partners.

Since his return to office in 2001, Berlusconi's
behavior has continued to be self-serving, erratic, and often unstatesmanlike. His continued
legal problems (and a willingness to have Parliament pass made-to-measure laws to help him
and his cronies sidestep these problems), his in-

sensitivity to the very idea of a conflict of interest, his outbursts against the judiciary, and his "comprehension" with regard to tax evasion suggest an incomplete grasp of, and frequently an indifference to, the democratic rules of the game. Yet he remains the dominant figure on the center-right and the only one capable of uniting its disparate forces.

The (Former) Far Right. Since the postwar republic was explicitly antifascist and formally banned the reconstitution of the Fascist Party,[14] the MSI was the true pariah of the First Republic. It was the direct descendant of the Fascist Party in its ugliest, pro-Nazi phase. It flirted with antidemocratic elements and maintained an ambiguous attitude toward democracy well into the 1980s. As its leadership and original constituency aged, the MSI's appeal centered on anticommunism and a hard line on law and order. Evoking fascism's past, it called for a strong role for the state in the economy, rejecting free-market capitalism as antisocial. The MSI always championed family values, and despite strong anticlerical strains in the original Fascist movement, this party was pro-life and generally conservative on matters of church doctrine. But because it had been systematically excluded from sharing power during the postwar period, it could attack the degeneration of the party system. Its strong law-and-order stance also made it easy to root for the prosecutors who were filling Italy's jails with corrupt politicians.

The MSI was shaken by the end of communism. Its future appeared bleak as it became clear that proportional representation was on its way out. All the new electoral systems required alliances, and who would make common cause with Mussolini's heirs?

At this point, the DC's collapse rescued the MSI. Stepping into the vacuum, the party vaulted to national prominence in mayoral elections in Rome and Naples in December 1993. Silvio Berlusconi gave the neofascists a big boost by declaring that he would willingly vote for them against the left. It lost both runoffs, but the

MSI was now a force to be reckoned with. Its telegenic young leader, Gianfranco Fini, scrambled to reassure the public by adopting free-market rhetoric and creating a broad right-wing National Alliance (AN) with the help of a few refugees from the DC and PLI. But everyone knew that the AN was the creature of the MSI.

The postfascists became Italy's third-largest party in 1994, more than doubling their vote (to over 13 percent) and tripling their representation in the Chamber of Deputies. The AN became Berlusconi's most faithful ally, and its loyalty was richly rewarded in terms of cabinet seats, undersecretaries, and appointments to myriad patronage positions. After the government's forced resignation, the AN remained unswervingly loyal to Berlusconi.

The MSI's transition to full democratic respectability was incomplete, but Fini began to force the issue. Shortly after Berlusconi's resignation, the MSI was dissolved. The speed and relative painlessness of this transition led many to doubt the sincerity of this conversion.[15] Some veterans remained in the AN and grumbled, while a small hard-line faction refused to break with the past and created a party called MSI–Tricolor Flame (after the torch in the old MSI's logo). It became increasingly clear that Fini had set the party on a course from which there was no turning back—and he did so in a fashion that brooked no dissent.[16]

His methods were autocratic, but Fini's content was increasingly moderate. He embraced liberal democracy, denounced the racism and anti-Semitism that marked the Fascist regime from 1938, and even acknowledged the contribution of the Resistance to postwar Italian democracy. In 2003, now vice prime minister of Italy, Fini traveled to Israel and renounced fascism as "absolute evil" in a speech that drew even the left's admiration. This break with the past drove some nostalgic leaders (most famously, Alessandra Mussolini) out of the party and marked the AN's definitive move from the far end of the political spectrum. In the same period, Fini also surprised everyone—including Berlusconi—by suggesting that legal immigrants should be allowed to vote in local elections. He also drew closer to his ex–Christian Democrat coalition partners, expressing growing frustration at Bossi's headline grabbing, as well as Berlusconi's apparently limitless toleration for the Lega's antics.

These actions are meant to firmly establish the AN's legitimacy as a conservative, but moderate, member in good standing of the center-right—leaving the far end of the spectrum to the Lega (and the tiny MSI-FT). They are also meant to position Fini as Berlusconi's heir should Il Cavaliere be brought down by one of his legal problems. With 12 percent of the vote in 2001, the AN remained the second-largest party in the coalition, albeit less than half the size of FI. Yet no matter how statesmanlike or moderate he may appear, Fini and his party are condemned for the foreseeable future to bob along in Berlusconi's wake, and to follow the agenda set by Il Cavaliere.

Elections

Because of the changes that have swept Italy since 1992, both general electoral trends and the three landmark elections since 1994 have already been discussed here and in preceding chapters. Let us simply recall that the so-called First Republic, under proportional representation, provided almost monotonously predictable electoral results from the 1950s through the 1970s, and the results remained astonishingly stable until the 1980s (see Table 21.1). The largest three parties were exactly the same (DC-PCI-PSI) from 1948 to 1992, in the same exact order. And then, aided mightily by a new electoral system, the major governing parties were shattered, while new (or renovated) parties gave rise to a new party system. After no real change of governing formulas for forty-five years and no alternation in power at all, the elections of 1996 and 2001 saw alternation between two rival blocs.

Decades, and in some cases generations, of rooted political traditions do not disappear overnight. The "red" (Marxist) and "white" (Catholic) subcultures, although diminished, con-

tinue to be relevant. The PCI disappeared over a decade ago, but the red zones remain the areas where the left gets the highest vote and where all but a handful of single-member seats continue to go to this side of the spectrum. Similarly, the white zones of the northeast were both Catholic and conservative before and after the DC. These areas, along with other parts of the north, still choose between contending conservative forces: the League and Forza Italia. And religiosity remains a very strong, if imperfect, indicator of one's placement on the left-right spectrum. The south had been the most politically competitive area of the country after the collapse of the DC and PSI, but this changed in 2001, when Forza Italia improved its already strong standing while the DS lost nearly a third of its support in that area.[17] It is far too early to tell if this is a trend.

It is also important to recall that neither the Ulivo's 1996 victory, nor that of the House of Freedoms in 2001, was produced by massive shifts in public opinion despite the ever-evolving party system. The great swing to the Ulivo in 1996 was really the result of the League's running separately in that election. When it rejoined the center-right in 2001, it once again played an important role in Berlusconi's victory. As should be abundantly clear by now, the introduction of a predominantly single-member electoral system in 1993 made alliance formation the secret to electoral success.

A notable trend that began in the late 1970s and has continued in every election is a decline in voter turnout. Italy used to have one of the highest turnout rates in the world; it dropped below 90 percent in 1983 and has declined ever since, although in 2001 the decline was negligible. At 81 percent, turnout still remains high by comparative standards.

Political Culture, Class, Citizenship, and Identity

The intertwining of socioeconomic and territorial factors in Italian history makes it difficult to derive useful generalizations from any one of these phenomena considered in isolation from the other.

Social Class, Religion, and Regionalism

Class, religion, and regionalism have, historically, had a far more pronounced political dimension in Italy than is the case for any of the other countries examined in this text.

As noted above, the red and white subcultures linger, though in diluted fashion. Of course, these divisions were never equal in strength or geographical distribution. Catholicism has been a more powerful and diffused force in Italy than the various strands of Marxism. Furthermore, the strong subcultures were limited geographically to areas that sometimes surprise people unfamiliar with Italian history and politics. The red areas are not in the industrial heartland of the northwest but in the central regions of Emilia-Romagna, Tuscany, and Umbria. The white areas, where religion is most deeply rooted, are found mainly in the Veneto and eastern Lombardy. Political subcultures in Italy cut across classes more than is appreciated. This is less surprising for the white zones, for Catholic social thought rejects class conflict, but even the leftist subculture has a broad class base, owing to its agrarian, anticlerical origins. Italian Socialists and Communists were always less obsessed with the factory proletariat than were their counterparts elsewhere, such as France.

Far weaker, until recently, have been the variants of modern bourgeois subcultures, such as secular liberalism and conservatism, which never managed to acquire mass bases as they did in most of the rest of Western Europe and North America. These secular forces were stunted by *trasformismo*, repressed by fascism, and then delegated much of their role to the DC after 1945. Their historic political expressions survived and evolved in the form of the minor, so-called lay parties of the center, although secularization and the accompanying erosion of the major subcultures finally have produced a more "laical" political culture.

Class cleavages once ran deep in Italy, even though they were always mitigated, or crosscut, by religious and regional factors. Ironically, with the decline of the DC, class has become a more solid predictor of political preference than ever before. But some of the relationships between class, or closely related indicators such as formal education, and political preference depart from conventional expectations. It is not surprising that the party that draws the greatest share of independent businesspeople's vote is Forza Italia. But the most working-class party—in terms of the proportion of its supporters—is the Lega Nord. Even more striking, the center-right attracts a larger share of private sector wage earners than does the center-left. Wage earners in the public sector, in contrast, opt for parties of the left or center-left much more frequently. And more highly educated voters tend to prefer the center-left to the center-right.[18]

National, Ethnic, and Regional Identity

The Fascist experience appears to have inoculated Italians against nationalism. And the country's history since the Risorgimento has conspired to make Italians the most "European" of all West European publics. They are far more ready to delegate decision making to Brussels, which may be a reflection of the lack of pride they show in Italian institutions in general.[19]

Even under fascism, justifications for Italian nationalism often seemed contrived, as when Mussolini spoke of an "Italic" race, or later introduced legislation that defined Italians as "Aryan." With the exception of parts of the northeast that are adjacent to predominantly Slavic areas, ethnic identification was not a significant factor in Italian society or politics until the Northern League stimulated and politicized it. But the Lega was of course working with the raw material of history: regional identities have been extremely powerful in Italy, reflecting the extraordinary diversity of the various areas that were united in the nineteenth century. And northern disparagement of southerners took racist form long before the arrival of Umberto

Bossi: some of the more telling epithets for southerners include "Moroccan" and "African."

It is absurd to speak of the north-south cleavage in ethnographic terms; indeed, it is a gross oversimplification to speak of a southern culture or political style. It is the case, however, that the south's dependent development and resulting distorted class and social structures have had an undeniable effect on its political institutions, which do, in turn, shape public attitudes. The consequences of these distortions are most clear in the ways they have rendered southern politics especially vulnerable to patronage networks and clientelistic patterns of politics.

In related fashion, the League's emergence and consolidation show that in an era of rapid change, marked by the undermining of old certainties, local identities—which were always strong but not particularly political—may assume increasing importance, or even be invented out of whole cloth ("Padania" is the League's invented heartland). Such sentiments were far more diffuse, or obscured by other cleavages, in the past.

These new territorial identities have, as noted, occasionally been expressed in ethnic or racial terms. Most recently, the Lega has used September 11, 2001, to justify its anti-Islamic discourse, although it would hardly be fair to attribute all acts of intolerance against immigrants to the Northern League. Italians love to portray themselves as warm, tolerant people, as befits a country that has sent tens of millions of emigrants to other lands. But the fact is that Italian citizenship laws are among the most restrictive in the EU, and they were actually made more restrictive when the relevant legislation was rewritten in 1992.[20] Among other things, Italian law distinguishes between foreigners born in Europe and those born elsewhere, and sets far more restrictive citizenship requirements for non-Europeans.

Gender

As has already been noted in Chapter 22, discrimination against women in Italy is embedded in the ways that the welfare state is constructed, and in the structure of the labor market in both the north and, particularly, the south. Discrimination is not only a cultural or religiously rooted phenomenon, but one that was sanctioned by the law for a very long time, and in myriad ways. In the immediate postwar period, women needed their husband's permission to apply for passports, and adultery was a crime restricted to women. In parts of southern Italy, well into the 1960s, in order to preserve their family's honor, women were expected to marry the "suitors" who had kidnapped and raped them. It took a reform of family law in 1975 to establish parity between both partners in a marriage, or to permit a head of family to be of either sex. Divorce was illegal until 1970, abortion was illegal until 1978, and both these laws were challenged by referenda strongly backed by the Roman Catholic Church.

Many reforms were sped along by the existence of a strong and variegated women's movement, whose influence spread with extraordinary rapidity (see below). And it is a sign of just how much the country had changed that both referenda failed by overwhelming margins.

But the persistent gap between male and female employment rates, salaries, and opportunities for promotion remind us of how very far Italy has to go. And changes in public consciousness have hardly been accompanied by dramatic changes in many areas of society and politics. Only 5 (of 103) provincial prefects are female; 1 (of 20) regions is headed by a woman; the proportion of female deputies has actually declined since 1994, to just under 12 percent, putting Italy next to last in the EU.[21] The legislature found this last state of affairs embarrassing enough to pass a law mandating that in the 2004 elections to the European Parliament, at least a third of the candidates on the parties' lists had to be women. Of course, placing someone far down on a list (for these elections use PR) may meet the formal requirement and still produce a very low number of female Eurodeputies.

Interests, Social Movements, and Protest

Italy's political history, from unification through the cold war, is reflected in a civil society that has been far more volatile, and far more fragmented, than in most Western democracies.

Business Organizations

Because of the fragmentation of governing coalitions and the factional nature of the DC, interest groups in the First Republic had multiple, contending targets to lobby. Most groups in Italian society divided along left-right lines, but even the group that should have been largely immune to such division nonetheless found ample grounds for disunity along other dimensions.

The Confederation of Italian Industries (Confindustria) represents companies in the private sector. After the war, it continued to favor Italy's top-heavy, protected industry, as it always had. Other industrialists and managers, especially in technologically advanced firms and the large state sector of the economy (which had its own peak association), had ideas more in tune with changing times, and these divisions undermined Confindustria's unity and effectiveness through most of the postwar period.

The 1960s produced the greatest strains: the old oligopolies and the very numerous smaller firms (those with fewer than one hundred employees) were usually antilabor, while the dynamic large firms that produced consumer goods favored rapid agreements with the unions. They also supported broader social reforms—not only because they were more enlightened but also because theirs were more labor-intensive industries. They needed society to absorb the costs of improving the conditions under which working people lived; otherwise firms would have to foot the bill alone.

As labor weakened in the 1980s, the worst rifts in the capitalist front began to heal. Confindustria gave a greater voice to some of its historically silenced members; its presidents in the 1990s were chosen from the Association of Young Industrialists and then from the very dynamic small-firm sector. By the early 1990s, as state enterprises were sold off, Confindustria's ranks were expanded. In the course of the 1990s, Confindustria was instrumental in labor relations reforms, but it also became more politically assertive, demanding budgetary rigor, tax reform, and an overhaul of an inefficient bureaucracy and institutions. These demands were couched in terms of making Italy more responsive to European and international competitive pressures.[22] A sign of Confindustria's true independence is its support of Prodi and the Ulivo in 1996 out of the (accurate) conviction that the center-left, with union cooperation, would make entry into the single currency much more probable. In 2001, organized business sided much more openly with Berlusconi, lobbying for legislation that would make it easier to lay off workers in the name of "flexibility," although it continued to resist a confrontational relationship with organized labor.

Organized Labor

Organized labor has had an even more violent roller-coaster ride than has business. It suffered from two related weaknesses throughout the entire postwar period: it was politically divided, and, as a result of the exclusion of the Communists, no government was ever constructed in which labor's major representatives were all present. These limitations had a profound effect on every aspect of labor relations and reform legislation in Italy, but they did not always result in crushing defeats for the unions and the working class. Particularly when the unions were united, they often achieved more (in job security, guaranteed wage increases, and pensions) than counterparts in other countries did—even those who had the relative luxury of Socialist or Social Democratic governments to defend them. The flurry of legislation and contractual guarantees that followed the Hot Autumn of 1969–1970 are obvious examples.

The Hot Autumn brought the major confederations—the General Confederation of Italian Labor (CGIL), the Italian Confederation of Workers' Trade Unions (CISL), and the Union of Italian Labor (UIL)—close to reuniting. By the end of the 1970s, however, with the Communists' failure to enter the government and renewed tensions between the PCI and PSI, strains grew not only among the three confederations but also within the CGIL, where Communists and Socialists coexisted. By the 1980s and early 1990s, the major confederations were again divided and faced a shrinking class base, declining membership, and growing competition from autonomous unions and the Committees of the Base (COBAS).

Chapter 22 discussed the establishment of tripartite consultation among labor, management, and the government in the accords of 1993. Under Prodi, the trend continued and made a vital contribution to Italy's ability to meet the Maastricht convergence criteria. Under Berlusconi, the pendulum swung away from concertation, and back toward fairly obvious efforts to divide the confederations. Because the parliamentary opposition is so weak and divided, and because of such open antagonism toward the unions (above all on job security and pension-related issues), the CGIL took the initiative in resisting these attacks. It did this all through highly successful mass mobilizations and strikes.[23] These were so successful that they pushed the CISL and UIL into a more militant posture, although the tensions among the three confederations continue to be quite high.

The Church and the Catholic World

No discussion of Italian social and political forces since the war can ignore the immense role this unique institution has played. Provided with the opportunity to intervene decisively in postwar Italy, the church under Pope Pius XII did not hesitate to exercise its influence, often harshly. The church was supposed to stay out of politics, but it did not, most blatantly in its excommunication of Communist and Socialist party members at the height of the cold war. It regularly acted at all levels of politics to promote its own candidates and its own agenda. Fascist laws banning material offensive to the church, its moral standards (nudity or suggestiveness in magazines, films, or theater), or its dogma (e.g., information on contraception as well as the availability of contraceptives) were retained or expanded by the DC through the 1960s.

Blatant interference faded with the death in 1958 of Pius XII, whose anticommunism was matched only by his authoritarian methods and his beliefs that Italy should be made to adhere to church law. Under John Paul II, as one might expect of a non-Italian pope, direct involvement in Italy's internal affairs has lessened, although the pope's conservative doctrinal sympathies are well known and have influenced debates on abortion, procreation, family law, and related issues.

The church's position on contentious issues has varied according to the subject's doctrinal implications. A few cardinals have publicly expressed intolerant views, but the church as a whole has taken a compassionate approach to immigration, and this has softened the tones of public debate, and probably helped produce less harsh legislation on a potentially inflammatory topic. Relentless pressure on Catholics within various center-left governments resulted in a law far more favorable to religious schools than many secular members of the coalition would have liked. The center-right passed extremely restrictive legislation governing assisted procreation, again with the influence of the church very much in evidence.

Protest and Social Movements

Italy has a long history of both organized and spontaneous social movements. Extensive land occupations in the 1940s and 1950s, bloody rioting that closed the door to the right in 1960, and regional riots in Calabria in the 1970s have been the most dramatic episodes of the postwar period. Occupying a special place in the panoply of Italian social movements was the Hot Autumn of 1969–1970, which spilled out of the sphere of labor relations to engulf aspects of the entire political system. What all these phenomena have in common with the new social movements that have appeared since the late 1960s is that they arose outside, or quickly escaped the control of, established parties. They differ in that the new movements—and this justifies the adjective—have raised demands that do not easily fit the platforms and identities of the traditional parties.

New movements often became explosive because of Italy's slow, and sometimes paralyzed, political processes. Serious reforms are inevitably delayed or sabotaged, aggravating underlying problems. Furthermore, for most of the postwar period, the major parties blanketed the social sphere very effectively; their effort to absorb everything, capturing and channeling social activity in their own organizations, left limited room for the development of autonomous interest groups or citizens' movements. This controlling capacity began to break down in the late 1960s and had effectively vanished by the end of the 1980s. Most recently, the left's defeat and demoralization in 2001 appear to have provided a new occasion for extensive social mobilization as a sort of substitute for an effective opposition in Parliament.

In terms of size and impact on society, the most significant movement in recent times was the workers' activism that began in the 1960s and peaked during the Hot Autumn. Because of the explosive social and political context of the late 1960s, the boundaries between the labor movement and broader social movements were almost nonexistent. Spilling out of the factories, workers took up the banner of numerous social reforms, such as housing, transportation, healthcare, and other social services. The major cities also witnessed the growth of extensive urban protest movements that lasted well into the mid-1970s. Among other things, these movements helped to discredit Christian Democratic rule in the big cities and produced important reforms. The urban movements initially agitated against the se-

vere shortage of affordable housing, which led to spectacular, large-scale occupations of public housing projects. They also focused on services such as schools, health, parks, and day care.

Most recently, following the Ulivo's defeat in 2001, organized labor and a broader grouping of civil society groups have staged large, sometimes spectacular demonstrations against various policies of Berlusconi and the center-right—openly challenging the left to take more of the initiative itself. We have seen (Chapter 22) how the unions, led by the CGIL, took the lead in demonstrating against proposed pension reforms: some of these demonstrations became more generic antigovernment rallies and attracted millions of protesters. An even more original phenomenon has been the *girotondi*, or "ring around the rosy," phenomenon. Masses of demonstrators join hands around government buildings to protect them symbolically. The most notorious cases occurred outside the Ministry of Justice and the state-owned broadcast company against Berlusconi's attacks on the legal system and the independence of the judiciary, and his control of the media.

Student and Youth Movements. Student and youth movements have taken several different forms in Italy. In the late 1980s, they were sporadic, uncoordinated protests against barely functioning high schools and universities. But in the 1960s, they had a highly ideological leftist character. They often originated around protests against the Vietnam War, an event that was especially important in radicalizing young Catholics, putting them side by side politically for the first time with youths from different backgrounds. These movements peaked in 1967–1968, eventually furnishing activists for the far left that was emerging (or in some cases, had been revitalized) by the end of the 1960s. They provided critical contributions to factory and urban struggles and trained militants and future leaders for the traditional left. For example, nearly a quarter of all Communist militants, and over one-third of those who joined the party in the 1970s, had some experience in movements or groups (excluding the unions) prior to joining the PCI.

Autonomous Movements and Terrorism. A totally different movement appeared in the 1970s on the fringes of even the far left. Calling itself "autonomous" from all existing organizations, it was, broadly speaking, antipolitical with an extremist, nihilistic fringe, inclined to violence. Much smaller than the 1960s movement, it left a significant impression. It attacked all parties, as well as unions and the more privileged sectors of the working class. Even more deliberate, and lethal, violence occurred in the late 1970s, when left-wing terrorist groups such as the Red Brigades and Front Line reached their peak. These groups were never a mass movement, but they attracted diffuse sympathy among many disillusioned leftists, especially the young, at least until terrorism escalated from symbolic acts to kneecappings and then hundreds of murders. Former prime minister Aldo Moro was the best-known victim, but others included judges, police, journalists, politicians, and left-wing trade unionists.

Ultimately, the most interesting thing about Italian left-wing terrorism was how long it lasted. In part this reflects the clumsiness and brutality of the Italian forces of order. But as the breadth of support clearly indicates, it also reflects the deeper crisis of Italian institutions and society. Yet it is notable that Italy did not panic and enact a range of measures as repressive as those introduced by the West Germans when they faced a much less serious threat.[24]

The Women's Movement. As occurred elsewhere, the feminist movement of the 1960s and 1970s in Italy originated in the extraparliamentary left, which preached egalitarianism but relegated women to subordinate roles. The traditional left was also slow to appreciate the strength and depth of the feminist challenge. Feminists within the parties and unions kept up the pressure, however, and events, especially the momentous 1974 referendum on divorce, rapidly converted the unpersuaded. In fairness to the traditional left, the great referendum victories on divorce and abortion would never have been so lopsided without the left's full mobilization of its forces. Nor would the dramatic gains represented by the complete rewriting of family law have been possible without the left's active support in Parliament.

The ideas of the women's movement penetrated Italian society with striking speed, at least in the cities. Since the late 1970s, the women's movement in Italy, as elsewhere, has fragmented, although there remain umbrella organizations that occasionally mobilize women around specific issues, and certain strands of feminism are very influential in the universities.

Conclusions

The material examined in this chapter provides a deeper understanding of some of the worst pathologies of postwar Italian democracy, above all the *partitocrazia* that permeated civil society and politicized so many aspects of normal life. This in turn helps us understand the popularity of such different populistic appeals as that of Bossi and the League, on the one hand, and Berlusconi and Forza Italia, on the other. Each, in different ways, takes advantage of a cynicism toward politics and politicians that permeates broad strata of Italian society.

But the material examined in this chapter also provides a better understanding of the vibrancy of Italian democracy, despite its many flaws. In spite of an often cynical and self-serving political class—or perhaps because of the naked cynicism of established parties and politicians—Italy has seen extraordinary levels of social mobilization and various forms of popular pressure "from below," as well as aggressive prosecutors and reform-minded politicians acting within existing institutions. These activities, at times independently, on other occasions in more coordinated fashion, helped consolidate and reform

Italian democracy. Students of democracy know that it is not an end state that one achieves, once and for all, but rather a process that is continuous, with advances but also backsliding. One of the more intriguing questions about the current situation in Italy is whether the transition that began in the 1990s can still be considered to be limping along, or whether Berlusconi's return to office in 2001 is indeed finally laying the foundations of a Second Republic—even though what he seems to be putting in place is a long way from what most reformers imagined, and hoped for, when they launched their assault on the old system so many years ago.

Notes

1. In the early 1970s, the average was closer to 2,000 laws per full legislature. Paul Furlong, *Modern Italy: Representation and Reform* (London: Routledge, 1994), p. 129.

2. For details of the reform, see Richard S. Katz, "The New Electoral Law," in Carol Mershon and Gianfranco Pasquino, eds., *Italian Politics: Ending the First Republic* (Boulder, Colo.: Westview Press, 1995), pp. 93–112.

3. Douglas Wertman, "The Last Year of the Christian Democratic Party," in Mershon and Pasquino, *Italian Politics*, pp. 142–143.

4. Martin J. Bull, "Italy: The Crisis of the Left," *Parliamentary Affairs* 56 (2003): 58–59.

5. Mark Donovan, "I referendum del 1997: Il troppo stroppia?" in Luciano Bardi and Martin Rhodes, eds., *Politica in Italia: Edizione 98* (Bologna: Il Mulino, 1998), p. 201.

6. PierVincenzo Uleri, "I partiti e le consultazioni referendarie in tema di giustizia e nucleare," in Piergiorgio Corbetta and Robert Leonardi, eds., *Politica in Italia: Edizione 88* (Bologna: Il Mulino, 1988), pp. 203–204.

7. Stefano Bartolini and Roberto D'Alimonte, "La maggioranza ritrovata: La competizione nei collegi uninominali," in D'Alimonte and Bartolini, eds., *Maggioritario finalmente? La transizione elettorale 1994–2001* (Bologna: Il Mulino, 2002), pp. 222–229.

8. Ilvo Diamanti, "The Northern League: From Regional Party to Party of Government," in Stephen Gundle and Simon Parker, eds., *The New Italian Republic: From the Fall of the Berlin Wall to Berlusconi* (London: Routledge, 1996), p. 113.

9. Roberto Biorcio, "La Lega nord e la transizione italiana," *Rivista italiana di scienza politica* 29 (April 1999): 56.

10. See Paul M. Sniderman et al., *The Outsider: Prejudice and Politics in Italy* (Princeton, N.J.: Princeton University Press, 2000).

11. Renato Mannheimer, "Forza Italia," in Mannheimer, ed., *Milano a Roma: Guida all'Italia elettorale del 1994* (Rome: Donzelli, 1994), p. 40.

12. Emanuela Poli, *Forza Italia: Strutture, leadership e radicamento territoriale* (Bologna: Il Mulino, 2001), chaps. 3–5.

13. Roberto Biorcio, "*Forza Italia* and the Parties of the Centre Right," in James Newell, ed., *The Italian General Election of 2001: Berlusconi's Victory* (Manchester: Manchester University Press, 2002), pp. 96–97.

14. Item XII of "Final and Transitional Arrangements," of the Constitution. This was never enforced.

15. Piero Ignazi, *Postfascisti?* (Bologna: Il Mulino, 1994), esp. chap. 6.

16. Marco Tarchi, *Dal MSI ad AN: Organizzazione e strategie* (Bologna: Il Mulino, 1997), p. 146.

17. ITANES (Italian National Electoral Studies), *Perché ha vinto il centro-destra* (Bologna: Il Mulino, 2001), pp. 24–25.

18. Ibid., Chapter IV.

19. Liviana Tossutti, "Between Globalism and Localism, Italian Style," *West European Politics* 25 (July 2002): 52, 68f.

20. Ferruccio Pastore, "A Community Out of Balance: Nationality Law and Migration Politics in the History of Post-Unification Italy," *Journal of Modern Italian Studies* 9 (Spring 2004): 38.

21. For the prefects and regions: Giovanna Casadio, "Un 8 marzo in nome della parità cresce la sfida sulle 'quote rosa,'" *La Repubblica*, March 8, 2004, p. 3; data on deputies come from Luca Verzichelli, "Da un

ceto parlamentare all'altro: Il mutamento del personale legislativo italiano," in D'Alimonte and Bartolini, eds., *Maggioritario finalmente?* p. 341.

22. Liborio Mattina, "La Confindustria di Abete: Dall'alleanza con la DC all'appello multipartitico," in Stephen Hellman and Gianfranco Pasquino, eds., *Politica in Italia, Edizione 93* (Bologna: Il Mulino, 1993), pp. 269–272.

23. Aris Accornero and Eliana Como, "La (mancata) riforma dell'articolo 18," in Jean Blondel and Paolo Segatti, eds., *Politica in Italia: Edizione 2003* (Bologna: Il Mulino, 2003), pp. 252–253.

24. For an interesting comparison, see Donatella della Porta, *Social Movements, Political Violence, and the State* (New York: Cambridge University Press, 1995), chaps. 2–3.

C H A P T E R

25

Italian Politics in Transition

For all its shortcomings, postwar Italy became one of the world's richest societies, and its political system, for all its flaws, successfully evolved into a vibrant, open democracy against odds that once seemed formidable. These achievements provide a necessary context within which present difficulties must be viewed. Italy has clearly been undergoing a transition that represents much more than politics as usual, as terms like "First Republic" and "Second Republic" attest.

A full decade (and more) has passed since people started using the expression "Second Republic" to describe where Italy seemed to be going. Such terminology may make the Italian situation appear even more problematic than it is, for it obviously, and intentionally, invokes comparison with the French Fourth and Fifth Republics. Leaving aside the (happy) fact that, unlike France under the crisis of decolonization, Italy has at no time in the past decade seemed on the verge of civil war, the French transition was very much guided by a single individual who was able to impose a coherent vision on a traumatized nation. Although Silvio Berlusconi might like to think of himself as an Italian de Gaulle, the Italian transition has been so uncertain because it has been anything but a guided process: for better and for worse, it is the product of democratic give-and-take. As we have seen, the political forces struggling to redefine Italian politics have included those that were pure products of the old system, those that were entirely new, and those that had one foot in each.

Political Challenges and Changing Agendas

Italy has been fortunate in not having had to deal with the sorts of shocks and traumas that have confronted some of its neighbors since World War II (French decolonization and German unification come to mind). It does, however, have to face a number of separate, if related, challenges.

Transition—and Continuity— in the Party System

After more than forty years of immobility, the Italian political system became fluid and unpredictable in the mid-1990s. Optimism that the fall of the old political elite would swiftly be followed by a simplified party system and an improved, efficient government turned out to be premature. But if the period 1994–2001 failed to produce everything reformers hoped for, it did produce changes that were unimaginable just a few years earlier. Successive elections were won by alternating, opposed political blocs, and in 2001 a sitting government was ousted by the opposition for only the second time in Italy's history as a nation-state. The old elite has largely been swept away, and the parties that dominated Italian politics for nearly half a century have undergone profound changes, been reduced to bit players, or disappeared altogether. New electoral systems at all levels have helped speed the changes.

But despite these accomplishments, many of the worst aspects of the First Republic remain: Berlusconi's first government, along with those of both Prodi and D'Alema, were all forced to resign by divisions within their own majority, and by maneuvers between parliamentary blocs that recalled the *trasformismo* of old. And despite a serious electoral reform designed to simplify the party system, it became more fragmented after 1994. The First Republic was thought to have had too many parties, with somewhere between ten and twelve gaining parliamentary representation by the early 1990s. What, then, was one to make of the Ulivo coalition, which alone counted nine different political parties? Constant squabbling helped undermine the center-left's credibility and guarantee victory for Berlusconi and his allies in 2001.

The trend, however, is not simply toward greater fragmentation. It is the case that in 2001 fewer parties than ever before (five) made the 4 percent floor required to obtain seats from the PR lists, and many have seen this as a sign that the party system is finally becoming more simplified. Although there is truth in this observation, there is also a degree of wishful thinking. One of the success stories of the 2001 vote was the Daisy list on the center-left, which is made

VOTATECI, E' QUI CHE DOVETE PASSARE IL RESTO DELLA VITA.

"Vote for us, you have to spend the rest of your life here." Italy's governing parties are represented waist-deep in garbage for the 1985 local elections.

———————

Source: Reproduced by permission of Giorgio Forattini from Giorgio Forattini, *Forattini Classic, 1985–1990.*

up of at least three separate political organizations, each of which is quite jealous of its own identity. Moreover, three other lists—one consisted of two different parties—garnered between 3 and 4 percent; another three (with one composed of several small groups) obtained between 2 and 3 percent.[1] One can see the logic of the electoral system at work: there is an incentive for smaller parties to group together, and it is by no means guaranteed that they will win seats even if they do combine. But, to date, numerous smaller formations continue to exist, leaving the party system quite fragmented.

One explanation for the persistence of the smaller parties lies in the unintended, and perverse, effects of the logic of the new single-member districts (75 percent of all Chamber of Deputies seats). Even parties unable to attract 4 percent of the vote can guarantee themselves some seats by bargaining for a certain number of center-right or center-left nominations for single-member candidacies. With the margins of victory often very small in these head-to-head contests, even a tiny party's leverage—its blackmail potential—increases immensely. As time has passed, the doling out of seats to minor coalition partners in order to keep them happy has become so codified that observers refer to this practice as the proportionalization of the majoritarian system.[2]

Unresolved Political and Institutional Questions

It is obvious that Berlusconi's occupancy of the prime minister's office brings to the fore an issue that was submerged, and irresponsibly ignored, while he was in the opposition. But that is not the only open question Italy's democratic system currently faces.

Berlusconi's Personal Problems and Broader Implications for Italian Politics. Berlusconi has never shown much concern over his conflicts of interest, starting with his ignoring a Constitutional Court opinion in 1994 that three networks were too many for any single proprietor. His victory in several referenda in 1995 that would have limited his franchises or regulated commercials on the private networks reinforced his belief that he could sway public opinion when it really mattered. His insensitivity to this problem can be breathtaking; he has said that he "breaks out in hives" whenever the terms "conflict of interest" or "equal time" are mentioned. He has also insisted that his vast wealth should reassure the public, since it guarantees that he will not try to enrich himself at public expense—thus sidestepping the question of using legislative power to further enrich himself, or simply to pull his legal chestnuts out of the fire.

Since returning to power, Berlusconi has done little to reassure his critics, at least some of whom have taken to using the term *regime* to describe what they see as his own private vision of a Second Italian Republic.[3] For some observers, his control over, and self-serving use of, the media, his attacks on the judiciary, his efforts to write laws designed to benefit himself and his closest collaborators while doing everything possible to stall or derail his own trials—all the while claiming a special, direct link to the people who elected him—represent at least a potential despotism of the majority, and a genuine threat to liberal democratic institutions. In 2004, Freedom House downgraded Italy from a rating of "Free" to that of "Partly Free" and dropped it to seventy-fourth overall in its assessment of press freedom in the world, putting it in the company of Benin, Peru, and the Philippines. Reasons for the demotion are the conflicts of interest and continued manipulation of and interference in the exercise of press freedoms by the prime minister.[4]

In their efforts to portray Italy as on the road to normalcy, the major leaders of the opposition, although disturbed by Berlusconi's excesses and his seeming indifference to conflicts of interest, purposely avoid using terms like *regime*. Still, it remains one of the Ulivo's greatest failures that, in five years, it failed to deal with the conflict-of-interest issue. To obtain Berlusconi's cooperation, when a Bicameral Commission (Bicamerale) was established in Parliament to enact constitutional changes, the question of conflict of interest was consciously pushed to the sidelines. Massimo D'Alema, named by Prodi as the president of this commission, calculated that serious reforms would only be possible if undertaken in bipartisan fashion. Letting Berlusconi off the hook was considered a price worth paying for completing the transition to the Second Republic—including further changes to the electoral system, to the judiciary, and to the powers of the president and prime minister, as well as the introduction of some form of federalism. Berlusconi happily went along with the process until the end, when he announced that his allies would not accept the proposed reforms. D'Alema had been completely outmaneuvered by Berlusconi. While the Bicamerale dragged on, a conflict-of-interest proposal was tied up in the Senate; once it became clear that elections were imminent, there was no longer any hope of passing such controversial legislation, and it expired with the Ulivo's term in office. As we have seen, the legislation passed by Berlusconi's government sidesteps the issue instead of addressing it.

Constitution Revision: Suddenly Too Easy?

In 1947, the Italian political system appeared permanently fragmented; proportional representation guaranteed fair representation to all parties and also made it nearly impossible for one party to obtain an absolute majority of seats in both chambers of Parliament. Thus, the method for revising the constitution—absolute majorities in both chambers must pass identical versions of the proposed change on two occasions at least three months apart (Article 138)—was quite restrictive when written.

With a majoritarian electoral system, however, parliamentary majorities usually do not mirror popular sentiment. When the goal is to put together a government solid enough to last more than ten months, the trade-off is acceptable. But it is another matter altogether if an artificial (or extremely narrow) majority can then be used to alter the constitution. The elaborate amending formulas of most countries with majoritarian electoral systems reflect concern that constitutions not be able to be rewritten too casually. Even countries with proportional representation have established more restrictive conditions than Italy for altering their constitutions.*

Article 138 does stipulate that should the amending majority be less than two-thirds of each chamber, a popular referendum may be called within three months to vote to ratify the changes. And this vote—in contrast to that of an abrogative referendum—does not require that half of all eligible voters turn out. As we saw in Chapter 23, such a referendum was held in 2001 to ratify the Ulivo's semifederalist amending of the constitution. But as we also saw in Chapter 23, this did nothing to deter Umberto Bossi from proposing his own amendments to devolve far more powers to the regions than the Ulivo had. With solid majorities in both chambers, the center-right, despite misgivings among some members of the coalition, used those majorities to set far-reaching constitutional changes in motion in 2004. The opposition then announced that it would call a referendum to challenge any changes that threatened the unity of the country, and, above all, the principle of solidarity between north and south.

Whatever it does for solidarity, devolution has set a process in motion that will finally put an end to the redundancy of Italian bicameralism. In its original form, Bossi's proposal called for a reduction of the size of the Chamber of Deputies (it currently has 630 members), as well as a conversion of the Senate into a "chamber of the regions," directly elected but similar in other ways to the German Bundesrat, and much reduced from its present 315 members. Even many who are not convinced federalists agree that reshaping the Senate along these lines would represent a step forward.

*Sweden, for instance, has a provision similar to Italy's requiring two separate votes, but an election must intervene between these votes.

Although the opposition has loudly denounced the government's apparent intention to impose constitutional changes by simple majority, the center-left set the precedent for such behavior in the final months it was in power. After failing to get the center-right's agreement in the Bicameral Commission, the Ulivo rammed its reforms through Parliament by majority vote. Having seen how easily these changes were imposed, the center-right took a page from the same book. It remains to be seen whether there will be widespread use of this practice in the future. If there is, it will hardly serve to change Italians' already skeptical view of politics. It will also provide additional ammunition to those who think that Berlusconi wants to rewrite the democratic rules of the game to fit his own vision, and to serve his own interests.

The Executive.   Since the 1980s, Italians have discussed the need for a stronger executive. While the right has been the strongest proponent of this view, the left—with some exceptions— has also accepted that something needs to be done to resolve the perennial problem of governments being held hostage by the many parties (or factions) that compose them. In the ill-fated effort at bipartisan reform that floundered in the late 1990s, the opposing sides differed on many particulars, but both put forward proposals to strengthen the prime minister (the center-left) or for a semipresidential regime, such as France's Fifth Republic, with a directly elected president (the center-right).

Notwithstanding the brutal realities of coalition governments, in which leaders ultimately serve at the sufferance of their coalition partners, half-thought-out schemes are regularly put forward in the hope that they will solve the country's problems in one fell swoop, much as reformers used to believe that electoral reform could eliminate fifty years of party politics. One recurring proposal is for the direct election of the prime minister (a practice that briefly existed in Israel, and nowhere else). This would presumably give the head of government a popular mandate and make it easier to keep fractious coalition partners in line. But such a procedure would be far harder to implement than its supporters imagine, and could prove especially clumsy to apply at a national level. Another, borrowing from the recent change in the way the presidents of regions are elected, proposes awarding an electoral premium—that is, extra seats—to the winning candidate or coalition in an election. This would guarantee a working majority even when the mainly majoritarian electoral system fails to do so.

Berlusconi was once firmly committed to a semipresidential regime (in which he would be the first president under the new rules), but so was his strongest and most reliable ally, the post-fascist Alleanza Nazionale. Even the Northern League, having obtained its key demand in the form of devolution, went on record in favor of a strengthened executive. Giving much more power to an elected president of the republic while maintaining a fundamentally parliamentary regime, as is the case in France (and almost nowhere else), would pose particularly nettling problems for Italy, given the continuing fragmentation of the party system and the numerous powers that still reside in the legislature. Creating a semipresidential regime would therefore require a massive overhaul of the constitution, or it would result in a Frankenstein's monster of patched-together, and probably incompatible, institutional arrangements. The center-right, bowing to the complexities of an Italian version of semipresidentialism, as well as differences within the coalition, finally produced a constitutional reform proposal in 2004 that calls for a much-strengthened prime minister.

More Difficult Labor Relations

Almost from the day the second Berlusconi government took office, it expressed hostility toward the unions, declaring the 1993 concertation pact dead. While many industrialists have complained about union resistance to reforms of the labor market—that is, changes that would make layoffs and part-time contracts easier to achieve in the name of "flexibility"—many of those same industrialists were obviously uncomfortable with the government's aggressive posture toward the unions. Clearly signaling its discomfort with the government's tone as well as its policies, in 2004 Confindustria elected a leader who openly called for a rapprochement with organized labor.

Why, then, the more confrontational stance by Berlusconi's second government? Because if taxes are cut, and collected less assiduously, the only realistic way to keep deficits down is to reduce government expenditures—which would be expected from a more conservative government. And without question, the principal target for cost cutting is Italy's notoriously expensive pension regime. Current pension expenditures have leveled off at 15 percent of GDP,[5] but this is much higher than the EU average, and will rise dramatically as Italy's population continues to age, unless some fairly radical changes are imposed. This is a serious gamble by the government, for meaningful pension reform has thus far proven possible only via negotiations with the unions, which have shown themselves willing to call massive strikes to defend the existing system—and to show the government how costly it can be to try to steamroll them on this issue.

Italy's Changing Social Profile

Many people still think of Italy in terms that have little connection with reality. The image of a tradition-bound Catholic country was never true for the whole country, and even the most solidly Catholic areas have been dramatically transformed over the past generation. Ireland may have narrowly approved divorce in a 1995 referendum, but Italy did so massively in 1974, while almost 70 percent of Italians voted to uphold a liberal abortion law, funded through the national health system, in 1981. Another statistic demonstrates how much this country's problems have become those of a mature capitalist society, in which marriage is postponed and birthrates decline. By the end of the 1980s, Italy had the lowest fertility rate in the world; since 1993, deaths have outnumbered births.

This phenomenon is closely tied to another old stereotype: that Italy is a country of emigrants. This was true for the first century of its existence, but since the 1970s, Italy has seen more immigration than emigration. Many immigrants have been Italians, or their descendants, returning home, but since the 1980s, the country has faced a phenomenon typical of many other advanced economies: the massive influx of dark-skinned foreigners from developing countries. Were it not for them, the decline in population and the disproportionately high aged population would be even more marked.

Italy's New Immigrants

By the 1980s, the influx of *extracomunitari*, that is, people from outside the European Community, began to take on notable proportions. In that decade, foreign immigration tripled. It is impossible to obtain absolutely reliable figures with regard to this topic, but the best current estimates put the total immigrant population, legal and illegal, at roughly 2 million, or just below 4 percent of the entire population.

By the standards of the larger European countries, these numbers are low. But the fact remains that in just two decades, a country that had mainly experienced foreigners as middle-class tourists now encountered large numbers of black or brown field hands, street vendors, domestic laborers, and factory workers in its largest cities and in the smaller centers of the newly industrialized periphery of the north. The most highly visible minorities are North Africans and sub-Saharan Africans, whose presence has generated many reactions tinged with intolerance and racism. With the growth of immigration has also come the involvement of more marginal elements in drugs, prostitution, and other crimes. The underside of immigration inevitably gets extensive coverage in the sensationalist press, which plays into a growing public sense of insecurity related more to crime than to the threat of job loss.[6]

The Northern League has taken the lead in politicizing immigration, distinguishing itself for antiforeign pronouncements that often spill over into outright racism. The AN's recent proposal to give legal immigrants voting rights in local elections was probably motivated as much by the desire to distinguish itself from the Lega's intolerance as by any humanitarian impulse, enabling the postfascists to continue to espouse a hard line against illegal immigration, and in favor of law and order. (The restrictive new immigration law was, after all, coauthored by the leaders of the Lega and AN and is known as the Bossi-Fini Law.) Forza Italia has taken a somewhat more cautious approach, emphasizing law and order while delegating a more visible role to its coalition partners.

Former Christian Democrats within the center-right have been a consistent voice for tolerance—as has the Roman Catholic Church. Some on the right have expressed the usual fears and prejudices, including a defense of Christian values against groups identified as predominantly Muslim, but the church has remained a strong voice for moderation, although a few cardinals (but not the pope) have spoken out in decidedly intolerant tones.

The Challenges of European Integration: Changes in the Economy and Industrial Relations

It is generally acknowledged that the European sword of Damocles hanging over Italy in the 1990s forced the country to undertake measures it had previously avoided. To be sure, Italy's economy was in such bad shape by the end of the 1980s that even without the EU's impending arrival, serious corrective measures would have been required. It has been argued that the collapse of the party system would have occurred even without the end of communism, for the ruling parties had literally brought the country to the brink of bankruptcy.[7] But there can be no doubt that both the speed of Italy's recovery and the extent to which former sacred cows were sacrificed must be attributed to the willingness of successive governments to impose rigorous budgets, starting with Amato's first cabinet in 1992, and culminating in Romano Prodi's successful effort to bring Italy within the Maastricht convergence criteria by 1997. And there can equally be no doubt that this political decisiveness was the result of the pressure all these governments felt not to suffer the humiliation of being excluded from full partnership in Europe.

The seriousness with which this challenge was taken is nowhere more evident than in the choice of former Bank of Italy executives (Ciampi and later Dini) as prime ministers in crucial transitional periods. Prodi was chosen to lead the Ulivo for several reasons, but one of the most important was his reputation as a highly competent economist who had headed, and tried to reform, the Institute for Industrial Reconstruction (IRI) in the 1980s. Ciampi's election as president of Italy and Prodi's selection as president of the European Commission demonstrate the credibility these leaders earned while in office. When Berlusconi named Renato Ruggiero as his foreign minister in 2001, he appeared to be following a similar path, for Ruggiero had been director general of the World Trade Organization as well as a member of the European Commission.

Yet Ruggiero was basically forced to resign within six months by what he perceived to be the government's vacillating commitment to Europe. It would be an exaggeration to argue that Italy has embarked on a bold new course, but there are certainly signs to suggest that, under Berlusconi, attitudes toward Europe have become rather lukewarm for a country that has always been one of the most enthusiastic supporters of the Union. How can we account for this seeming turnabout?

Less "Euroenthusiasm"?

As we saw in Chapter 21, there are several reasons that explain this diminished enthusiasm, not the least of which is the fact that Berlusconi's prime ministership and Prodi's presidency of the EC have substantially overlapped, almost guaranteeing a more adversarial relationship between Italy and the EU. But there are also deeper reasons for the center-right's changed posture. When the Ulivo lost the 2001 elections, many supporters complained that it had not been very successful at communicating its achievements, starting with successfully meeting the Maastricht criteria. The center-left admittedly did not make running on the record of the previous five years easy, since its candidate for prime minister had played no role in any previous government (he was the mayor of Rome) and thus was hardly the ideal incumbent. But other observers have argued that the Ulivo may well have lost precisely because key social groups understood all too well what had been done over the previous five years, and, for that reason, they turned to Berlusconi and his allies. In a word, austerity meant that many who had previously been able to avoid a large share of their tax burden were no longer going to get a free ride—and they reacted accordingly.[8]

This line of argument is straightforward, if unflattering to Italy's huge independent stratum of shopkeepers, small-business persons, professionals, and proprietors of small industrial firms. These groups account for an astonishing 35 percent of the labor force, which puts Italy nearly 10 percent ahead of France, which has the next largest proportion among larger West European nations.[9] Simply put, these groups were once among the DC's major constituents, and the tacit understanding they had reached with the ruling party was, "We don't expect much from the state, but in turn we expect it to turn a blind eye to our tax evasion and other sidestepping of the rules." With the coming of austerity budgets from 1992, and especially 1996, they continued to get little from the state in the way of services. But they now saw not only a rise in their taxes—to be expected from left-leaning governments—but also a much firmer stance taken against tax evasion. Berlusconi's repeated campaign promises to reduce taxes and simplify the tax code were not simply a neoliberal reflex, but a conscious pitch to his most important constituency.

Once in office, statements to the effect that he understood the frustration of those who didn't pay their taxes, while his government provided generous amnesties to tax evaders and building code violators, were also hardly subtle signals.

These developments do not mark a dramatic turn toward Euroskepticism, for Italy is far too well integrated into the EU to afford such gestures, or the isolation from its neighbors that would ensue were it to pursue such a path. The more likely scenario that seems to be unfolding is a cooler attitude toward the EU, and an apparent drift back toward more toleration of tax evasion and other illicit activities that were so characteristic of the First Republic. In a country where respect for public political institutions was never high, this would be a clear indication of a return to a particularly ugly form of normalcy. It would also mean growing problems in the future with respect to the EU, since if taxes are both cut and evaded, how will Italy remain within the parameters of the Stability Pact?

Italian Politics, Terrorism, and Italy's Relation to the United States

Throughout the entire postwar period, Italian governments tended to keep a low and generally noncontroversial profile in foreign affairs, presenting their country as a reliable partner in the North Atlantic Treaty Organization (NATO) and an ardent proponent of European integration. With regard to NATO, critics and even sympathizers have noted that the Italians have shown a willingness to follow the lead of the United States to a degree that is sometimes slavish. Whether it reflected a realistic assessment of their own irrelevancy in foreign affairs or a tacit trade-off for unconditional support against the PCI, Italian pliability regularly served U.S. interests. When others balked over President Ronald Reagan's plan to deploy cruise missiles in the early 1980s, Italy agreed to accept them on its soil. When the Spaniards insisted that the Americans remove their F-16 fighters later in

the same decade, Italy promptly provided a base, which figured prominently in operations against the Bosnian Serbs in the mid-1990s. And when NATO controversially waged war against Yugoslavia over Kosovo, Italy again was in the forefront, actively supporting the effort. This support was all the more striking in that it came during the leadership of Massimo D'Alema, the former Communist.

This history casts Berlusconi's support for the invasion and occupation of Iraq, despite overwhelming public opposition, in slightly less dramatic light: he simply appears to be walking the well-worn path of Italian acquiescence to U.S. demands. At the same time, it is worth recalling that Italy has, over the years, been noted for its commitment to multilateralism and Europe; Berlusconi's position on Iraq does represent a clear departure from the former and, at the very least, puts him at odds with most of his neighbors. In addition, Iraq does not represent the only time Berlusconi has seemed to favor the United States over the EU. One of the reasons Foreign Minister Ruggiero resigned in 2001 was Italy's withdrawal from a consortium to produce a new Airbus jetliner and its pursuit of a collaborative deal on a jet fighter with Lockheed in the United States—without consulting Ruggiero.[10] Berlusconi also appalled Brussels when he traveled to Russia and endorsed President Putin's "antiterrorist" actions in Chechnya, despite the EU's official condemnation of human rights violations in that region. Observers tend to attribute these departures from tradition to Berlusconi's penchant to draw attention to himself and be taken seriously as a "player" on the international scene. These actions clearly do not seem to mark a new era in Italian foreign policy. But, as we saw above, it would be simplistic to see everything Berlusconi does in terms of character flaws. There are real (if venal) reasons for an increased dose of Euroskepticism, and there may well be quite realistic calculations that Italy's interests will also be better served by a closer relationship with the United States—particularly at a time when

American relations with France, Germany, and Spain are more strained.

Italy in Comparative Perspective

One way to conceptualize the Italian case is by undertaking specific country-by-country comparisons. No one would hold Italy up as a model to be emulated, but different aspects of Italian history and politics are by no means exceptional or unique. Indeed, extensive literature exists on many of these comparisons.

Many of the most interesting historical comparisons can be made with Germany, above all concerning late unification as nation-states and the subsequent reliance on an interventionist pattern of industrialization compared with Britain's laissez-faire model. Indeed, late in the nineteenth century, the Italians self-consciously shifted from a British to a Prussian pattern. Another quite stimulating, if unsettling, series of comparisons with Germany can be made surrounding the social and political alliances that dominated both countries through World War I, including their ultimate capitulation in the face of Fascist challenges to democracy. Christian Democracy was a widespread phenomenon in the immediate post–World War II period in Europe, but few countries were as dominated by Christian Democrats as Italy and Germany, even though the sister parties increasingly diverged as time wore on.

Japan provides the only comparison among advanced industrial democracies completely dominated by a freely elected single party for two generations.* For similar reasons, this comparison brings to light extraordinary levels of corruption, including collusion with organized crime, although the fact that Japan has a much stronger state tradition does represent a significant difference in a comparison with Italy.[11] Comparativists who prefer cultural explanations

for many political phenomena, including corruption, might want to pay special attention to this comparison and perhaps look to more straightforward political explanations such as the length of time a single party spends in power with no real opposition in sight.

France is the obvious point of comparison for Italy's most distinctive political feature, the postwar domination of the opposition by a Communist Party and a rebellious and divided labor movement. In the French case, this situation lasted until the end of the 1970s, when the French Socialist Party finally surpassed the French Communist Party. In Italy, because of its flexibility, the Communist Party's (PCI's) domination of the opposition lasted until the end of communism itself. The PCI's distinctiveness in turn conditioned the evolution of the rest of the left, above all, the Italian Socialist Party (PSI). Groping for its own space, Italian socialism decided that its fate lay in the center of the political spectrum, at the cost of its ultimate survival. Its path was not so different from that taken by Socialists and Social Democrats throughout southern Europe (e.g., Portugal, Spain, France, and Greece), and this phenomenon itself invites further analysis. But these other Socialist parties were far stronger than the PSI, which hovered between 10 and 15 percent of the vote from 1948 on, nor were they obliterated by corruption scandals, even though most of them have in fact been implicated in serious misbehavior. (The susceptibility of Socialist parties to corruption as they abandon their old identification and organizational structures is yet another interesting theme.)

On a broader level of comparison, Italian politics has been dominated for years by some of the classic questions of democratic theory: Which institutional arrangements provide the best guarantee of effective democratic government? What is the trade-off between stable government and the faithful representation of ideological and programmatic differences? Between stability and grassroots initiatives like the referendum? Can institutional engineering or

*Sweden, governed by the Socialists from 1932 to 1976, comes close.

manipulation produce desired results? Discussion of these issues has been the subject of national campaigns and is continuously aired in both the print and electronic media.

Italy's current situation may well be unique. This is not a transition from authoritarianism to democracy, which Italy underwent in 1945, and which so much of the less developed (including formerly Communist) world has undergone more recently. If the Italian transition is carried forward, it will be from a party-dominated, assembly-style democratic regime, with severe problems of political immobility, to another, ideally more efficient type of democratic regime. This may prove to be the rarest sort of transition of all, for despite the supposed flexibility of democratic institutions, democracies rarely undertake major institutional overhauls. And they simply *never* seem to do so unless massively disruptive and traumatic events such as war, revolution, or deep national division force their hand. It is worth recalling that the French transition from the Fourth to the Fifth Republic occurred as a response to the paralysis and trauma of decolonization and the Algerian War; *society* threatened to tear itself apart in a crisis that was far more than merely political. The Italian transition, in contrast, is exclusively political.

Italy has always lacked the French flair for political drama, although in its own crafty way it often manages to achieve more than its neighbor—like pension reform in the 1990s, but, even more tellingly, as a comparison of 1968 in France with Italy's Hot Autumn, reveals. Will it achieve the unprecedented—a transition to a Second Republic that is a radical new departure—without the trauma that such changes seem to require? Or will Italy continue to be the country of The Leopard,[12] where everything seems to change so nothing in fact really changes at all?

Notes

1. ITANES (Italian National Elections Studies), *Perché ha vinto il centro-destra?* (Bologna: Il Mulino, 2001), pp. 17–21.

2. Aldo Di Virgilio, "L'offerta elettorale: La politica delle alleanze si istituzionalizza," in Roberto D'Alimonte and Stefano Bartolini, eds., *Maggioritario finalmente? La transizione elettorale, 1994–2001* (Bologna: Il Mulino, 2002), pp. 79–129.

3. Paul Ginsborg, "The Patrimonial Ambitions of Silvio B," *New Left Review* (Second Series) 21 (May–June 2003): 21–64. See also Mark Donovan, "Berlusconi, Strong Government and the Italian State," *Journal of Modern Italian Studies* 8 (Summer 2003): 232–233.

4. For the general announcement, see the press release at www.freedomhouse.org/media/pressrel/042804.htm. The overall ranking can be downloaded at www.freedomhouse.org/research/pressurvey/allscore2004.pdf.

5. ISTAT, *L'Italia in cifre 2003* (Available at the ISTAT Web site www.istat.it), p. 25.

6. Carl Ipsen, "Immigration and Crime in Contemporary Italy," *Journal of Modern Italian Studies* 4 (Summer 1999): 275.

7. Stefano Guzzini, "The 'Long Night of the First Republic': Years of Clientelistic Implosion in Italy," *Review of International Political Economy* 2 (Winter 1995): 27–61.

8. Michele Capriati, "The economic context, 1996–2001," in James Newell, ed., *The Italian General Election of 2001: Berlusconi's Victory* (Manchester and N.Y.: Manchester University Press, 2002), p. 63, and Paul Ginsborg, *Italy and its Discontents, 1980–2001* (London: Penguin Books, 2001), pp. 176 and 252.

9. Ilvo Diamanti and Renato Mannheimer, "Le basi sociali del voto: La frattura che attraversa i ceti medi," in Mario Caciagli and Piergiorgio Corbetta, eds., *Le ragioni dell'elettore: Perché ha vinto il centro-destra nelle elezioni italiane del 2001* (Bologna: Il Mulino, 2002), p. 140.

10. Filippo Andreatta and Elisabetta Brighi, "La politica estera del governo Berlusconi: I primi 18 mesi," in Jean Blondel and Paolo Segatti, eds., *Politica in Italia: Edizione 2003* (Bologna: Il Mulino, 2003), pp. 270–271.

11. For a recent comparison of the two countries that starts in the nineteenth century and continues to the end of the twentieth, see Richard J. Samuels,

Machiavelli's Children: Leaders and Their Legacies in Italy and Japan (Ithaca, N.Y.: Cornell University Press, 2003).

12. The reference is to Giuseppe Tomasi di Lampedusa's classic novel of the Risorgimento, *Il Gattopardo* (*The Leopard*) (Milan: Feltrinelli, 1966), p. 24.

Part VI Bibliography

Blackmer, Donald L. M., and Sidney Tarrow, eds. *Communism in Italy and in France.* Princeton, N.J.: Princeton University Press, 1975.

Bufacchi, Vittorio, and Simon Burgess. *Italy Since 1989: Events and Interpretations.* New York: St. Martin's Press, 1998.

Bull, Anna Cento, and Mark Gilbert. *The Lega Nord and the Northern Question in Italian Politics.* Basingstoke, U.K.: Palgrave, 2001.

Bull, Martin, and Martin Rhodes, eds. *Crisis and Transition in Italian Politics.* London: Frank Cass, 1998.

Clark, Martin. *Modern Italy, 1871–1995.* 2nd ed. London: Longman, 1996.

Ferraresi, Franco. *Threats to Democracy: The Radical Right in Italy After the War.* Princeton, N.J.: Princeton University Press, 1996.

Furlong, Paul. *Modern Italy: Representation and Reform.* London: Routledge, 1994.

Gilbert, Mark. *The Italian Revolution: The End of Democracy, Italian Style?* Boulder, Colo.: Westview Press, 1995.

Ginsborg, Paul. *A History of Contemporary Italy. Society and Politics, 1943–1988.* London: Penguin, 1990.

———. *Italy and Its Discontents, 1980–2001.* London: Penguin, 2001.

Gundle, Stephen, and Simon Parker, eds. *The New Italian Republic: From the Fall of the Berlin Wall to Berlusconi.* London: Macmillan, 1996.

Hellman, Judith Adler. *Journeys Among Women: Feminism in Five Italian Cities.* New York: Oxford University Press, 1987.

Hellman, Stephen. *Italian Communism in Transition: The Rise and Fall of the Historic Compromise in Turin, 1975–1980.* New York: Oxford University Press, 1988.

Hine, David. *Governing Italy: The Politics of Bargained Pluralism.* Oxford: Clarendon Press, 1993.

Italian Politics: A Review. London: Frances Pinter, 1986–1993; Boulder, Colo.: Westview Press, 1993–1998; London: Berghahn Books, 1999–.

Lange, Peter, and Sidney Tarrow, eds. *Italy in Transition: Conflict and Consensus.* London: Frank Cass, 1980.

LaPalombara, Joseph. *Democracy, Italian Style.* New Haven, Conn.: Yale University Press, 1987.

Locke, Richard. *Remaking the Italian Economy.* Ithaca, N.Y.: Cornell University Press, 1995.

Lumley, Robert. *States of Emergency: Cultures of Revolt in Italy from 1968 to 1978.* London: Verso, 1990.

Lyttleton, Adrian. *The Seizure of Power: Fascism in Italy, 1919–1929.* London: Weidenfeld and Nicolson, 1973.

McCarthy, Patrick. *The Crisis of the Italian State: From the Origins of the Cold War to the Fall of Berlusconi.* New York: St. Martin's Press, 1995.

Procacci, Giuliano. *History of the Italian People.* Hammondsworth, England: Penguin Books, 1973.

Putnam, Robert. *Making Democracy Work: Civic Traditions in Modern Italy.* Princeton, N.J.: Princeton University Press, 1993.

Tarrow, Sidney. *Democracy and Disorder: Protest and Politics in Italy, 1965–1975.* Oxford: Clarendon Press, 1989.

Woolf, S. J., ed. *The Rebirth of Italy, 1943–1950.* New York: Humanities Press, 1972.

Websites

ISTAT, Italy's national Statistical Institute: www.istat.it/English/index.htm. Contains current, as well as historical, series of social and economic data.

Istituto Carlo Cattaneo: www.cattaneo.org/english/1index.html. Excellent archives of social and political data, often in historical series.

Italian Studies Web: www.lib.byu.edu/~rdh/wess/ital/polygov.html. Basic information, and links to websites of interest to students of politics and society.

P A R T

VII

East-Central Europe in Transition

David Ost

CHAPTER

26

The Making of Modern East-Central Europe

East-Central European Politics in Action

A few snapshots from the land that used to be called Czechoslovakia provide a perfect picture of the complex and astonishing events that have been shaping East-Central Europe in recent years.

Late 1989. Commentators around the world speak of the dawning of a new age of democracy, symbolized by the appointment of a non-Communist government in Poland, by the fall of the Berlin Wall in Germany, and then by the "Velvet Revolution" unfolding immediately afterward in Czechoslovakia. It is in Prague that the sense of promise and hope is most evident. Velvet is smooth, soft, and friendly, more an aesthetic concept than a political one. And that's what makes the term so appropriate. The strikes that bring down the government, in fact, are begun by actors who announce that they will use the stage to press for political freedom. Within days, first students and then the majority of workers join in. The protesters demand civic rights: freedom of the press and association, an end to the Communist Party's monopoly on power, a truly representative political system. Workers and intellectuals, urbanites and farmers, Czechs and Slovaks, liberals and conservatives—all come together behind the program of this democratic opposition. With a huge general strike showing the unity of the population, and the Soviet Union no longer ready to intervene, the government is powerless to resist. Every day

brings new concessions, until concessions are no longer enough and the government is forced to resign. By the end of December, veteran playwright and dissident Vaclav Havel, who has only recently been released from jail, is named the new president of Czechoslovakia. The country enters the new year and decade filled with hope, united behind a new leader promising tolerance for all and a velvet-smooth transition to a just, democratic, and prosperous new system.

Mid-1992. The Velvet Revolution is coming apart. The democratic movement has broken into pieces, and the new voices speak the language not of tolerance but of blame. Slovakia's leaders blame the Czechs for Slovak problems and say they want to secede. Leading Czech politicians say such a divorce is fine with them, while they in turn blame "Communists" for ongoing Czech problems even though the Communists are no longer in power. Those who remain loyal to the movement's original goals of freedom and tolerance warn against this new politics of witch hunt and resentment. But they are decisively beaten in the 1992 elections. Vaclav Havel resigns from the presidency as the country prepares to split apart. The revolution seems to have taken off its velvet gloves.

Early 1994. For all the tensions of the past year, the breakup of the country goes smoothly. It is a "velvet divorce," with the two lands agreeing amicably on dividing territory and property. Vaclav Havel is elected president of the new Czech Republic, a position he will hold for the next ten years. The country privatizes most companies, but also maintains the lowest unemployment rate of any country in the region. Optimism reigns as the new country's first parliamentary elections are held.

Mid-1999. As economic growth slows, corruption scandals explode, and unemployment rises (just when it's falling elsewhere in the region), the politics of blame reemerge. Fears of hard times drive some to vilify not Slovaks, not the corrupt elite, but Gypsies (Roma); in one depressed mining town, local officials erect a wall separating Roma from the rest of the population. The Czech Republic experiences international successes, but citizens are skeptical. It is chosen in 1998 as a future member of the European Union (EU), but is soon chastised by the EU for not doing what it takes to join. It enters the North Atlantic Treaty Organization (NATO) in 1999, but is largely critical of NATO's bombing of Serbia that same year. Is the Velvet Revolution coming unhinged?

May 2004. Along with nine other countries (including Slovakia), the Czech Republic becomes a new member of the EU. Yet the prior members have arranged the rules so that the newcomers are likely to see more costs than benefits, at least in the short term. Politically, too, the international arena has started to look unfriendly: the U.S. invasion of Iraq has split Europe, and the new members have to tread carefully to avoid alienating either the United States or Western Europe. The "transition" may be over, but a host of new problems emerge to which no one has answers.

These few snapshots show us the hopes and fears of the new Eastern Europe: the hopes that grand social transformation is possible, that border questions can be resolved amicably, that economic growth can embrace all; and the fears that national enmities will continue to arise, that no post-Communist economy can escape economic crisis, and that European integration creates as many problems as it solves.

While hope has mostly won out in the former Czechoslovakia, the fears have been borne out by the experience of the former Yugoslavia. In that country, the democratic aspirations of citizens came to fruition in 1990 with free elections in each of the six constituent republics. Unlike in Czechoslovakia, however, the language of blame pervaded the new system from the start. Citizens in each republic elected political leaders who claimed that local problems were the result of outside interference—meaning not foreign entities but the other republics making up the country. Within a year, Yugoslavia had not only divided into separate states but had exploded in wars that lasted nearly a decade. By the time the new century began, hundreds of thousands had lost their homes and often their lives, and foreign troops are still there keeping a tenuous peace. Many still wonder whether "freedom" was worth such a price.

The 1990s were a decade of enormous transformation in Eastern Europe, with each country having to create new political and economic systems at the same time. Many commentators say this is just a matter of doing what the West did in the past. In fact, it is something the West never even tried. Capitalism in the West began to develop in the sixteenth century, but political democracy had to wait a full four hundred years. Eastern Europe had to build capitalism and democracy at the same time. Economically, this meant abandoning the informal consensus of communism, by which workers were guaranteed jobs and a low but steadily increasing standard of living in return for their acceptance of Communist Party rule. In its place came a capitalist market economy, where people lost their economic security but gained political freedom. Western Europe has also moved away from guaranteeing economic security to citizens. But this substitution of the "new political economy" for the "old postwar consensus" has been much more painful in the East, where people began from a poorer position and where the underdeveloped economy left them with fewer possibilities.

By 2004, the worst part of the post-Communist transformation appeared to be over. Where the first years after 1989 saw economic declines greater than during the Great Depression in the West, since 1996 most countries in the region have been growing. All the countries have now had several multiparty elections, and basic freedoms are accepted everywhere. There is greater inequality than before, but also real political democracy. But not all the questions are resolved, and this is what makes the region still so fascinating to study. Having freed itself from dependence on the Soviet Union, how will it react to its new dependence on the EU? Can the many young people who lost job opportunities because of the economic crisis find their way, or will more of them turn to the kind of right-wing extremism that has emerged in recent years? After decades of legal equality but de facto discrimination, can women become full citizens? Democracy may prevail, but what kind of democracy will it be? These are the questions we will be exploring in the following chapters.

Geographic Setting

The borders of the countries in East-Central Europe have changed a great deal over the past century. Most of the countries discussed here did not even exist as independent entities when the twentieth century began, and all of them have seen their independence come and go over the course of the twentieth century. Even today, in parts of the former Yugoslavia, the process of state formation is not yet complete. What is East-Central Europe? Until 1989, the designation referred to the countries between West Germany and the Soviet Union that were ruled by Communist parties. (Thus the term had an ideological as well as a geographical referent. Vienna, for example, is located east of Prague, but was considered part of the West.) According to this definition, the region included East Germany, Poland, Czechoslovakia, Hungary, Yugoslavia, Romania, Bulgaria, and Albania. Since 1989, however, East Germany has disappeared. Czechoslovakia has split in two. Yugoslavia has split five ways, into Bosnia and Herzegovina, Croatia, Macedonia, Slovenia, and Serbia and Montenegro. (Kosovo remains formally part of Serbia, but is essentially run by the United Nations.) Six more countries then arose in the region west of Russia after the collapse of the

Soviet Union: the three Baltic republics of Estonia, Latvia, and Lithuania, plus Belarus, Ukraine, and Moldova. Except for the last three, all of these countries are today part of East-Central Europe.

The terrain in the region is quite diverse, getting steeper and more rugged the farther south you go. It ranges from the flat plains of Poland in the north to the rugged crazy quilt of hills, valleys, and mountains in the former Yugoslavia. Geography, of course, has its consequences, particularly in an area that has been the object of so much foreign intervention. The flat plains of Poland (*pole* means fields) have enabled strong armies to occupy the country with ease, while the sprawling mountains of the former Yugoslavia help explain why no single army (or even the former Yugoslav state) has ever been able to conquer it fully, leaving many different ethnic groups to coexist in the area. As you can see on the accompanying maps, all these countries are rather small. Poland is the largest in terms of population and territory, with a population of close to 40 million and a territory of over 186,000 square miles (about the size of New Mexico). Estonia is the smallest in population, with only 1.4 million inhabitants. Slovenia is the smallest in territory, with about 12,500 square miles (slightly smaller than New Jersey). See Table 26.1 for full population figures.

Although each country has its own unique history, the Communist and post-Communist experiences of all give them numerous features in common. In this book, we focus on three countries making up the political and geographical heart of this area: Poland, Hungary, and the Czech Republic. We also refer frequently to the Yugoslav experience, and the states that have emerged following its demise.

Critical Junctures

We can identify seven critical periods in the shaping of modern East-Central Europe: the long era of subordination to neighboring powers, the attainment of independence after World War I, the introduction of communism after World War II, the struggle for democracy from

Eastern and
Central Europe

Table 26.1   How Many Live Where?

Country	Population (est., 2003)
Albania	3.6 million
Bosnia and Herzegovina	4.0 million
Bulgaria	7.5 million
Croatia	4.4 million
Czech Republic	10.2 million
Estonia	1.4 million
Hungary	10.0 million
Latvia	2.3 million
Lithuania	3.6 million
Macedonia	2.0 million
Moldova	4.4 million
Poland	38.6 million
Romania	22.2 million
Serbia and Montenegro	10.7 million
Slovakia	5.4 million
Slovenia	1.9 million

Source: *CIA World Factbook;* www.cia.gov/cia/publications/factbook/docs/profileguide.html.

1956 to 1989, the collapse of communism in 1989, the process of European integration beginning in the mid-1990s, and the aftermath of September 11, 2001.

Underdevelopment and Subordination: From the Fifteenth Century to World War I

During the martial law period in Poland in 1982, the title of a popular protest song was "Let Poland Be Poland." Some Poles, however, thought such a notion was precisely the problem. "Let Poland be Sweden," they said, "Let Poland be England! Let us be anything but Poland!"

What the naysayers chiefly had in mind was Poland's location: between Russia and Germany, countries that have always dominated it. The theme of wanting to be some other country, however, is a recurring refrain in Eastern Europe. And it points to three central problems: domination by other states, a multiplicity of nationalities on the territory of one state, and a long history of economic backwardness.

The roots of Eastern European underdevelopment go back to the rise of capitalism in the West. Most of Eastern Europe began turning to the West for its manufactured goods as early as the fifteenth century, and this early dependency had serious consequences.[1] Up until the nineteenth century, no part of Eastern Europe except the Czech lands was able to make much progress in industrialization. Eastern Europe's economic woes soon led to political ones. Lacking the economic base on which to build viable states, the nations of Eastern Europe fell under the influence, and frequently the outright occupation, of stronger neighbors all around: Prussia in the west, Russia to the east, and the Habsburg and Ottoman empires in the south. The period of state formation in Western Europe therefore was a period of state erosion in Eastern Europe.

Poland stands as a classic example of this trend.[2] The largest country in Europe in the fifteenth century, Poland quickly began to decline as a state when the powerful gentry joined together to clip the powers of the monarchy. By the seventeenth century, the king was denied the right to raise taxes, create an army, dismiss officials, or enact any law without the explicit consent of the landowners. Poland's neighbors were creating strong absolutist states at the same time. In the inevitable ensuing conflicts with these absolutist neighbors, Poland rapidly unraveled. A series of wars decimated the country in the seventeenth century, destroying a large part of Poland's population and economy. Economic backwardness, political domination by the large landowners, and the expansionary tendencies of other states led to a grim finale. Beginning in 1772, Russia, Prussia, and Austria divided the country among themselves. By 1795, Poland had ceased to exist as a state. It did not regain its independence until 1918.

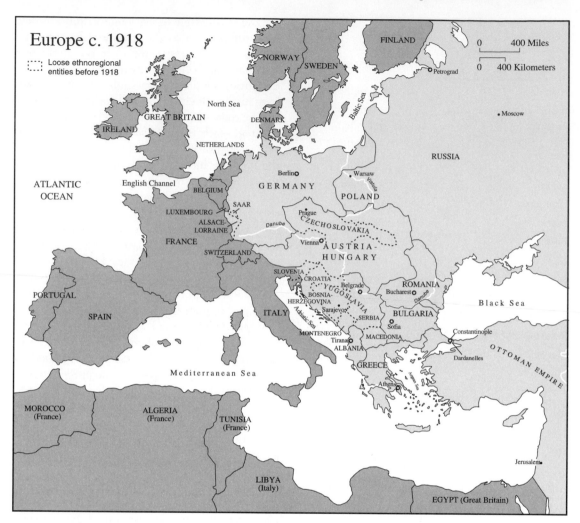

In 1918, the Czech Republic and Slovakia, former provinces of Austria-Hungary, united to form Czechoslovakia; and Serbia, Croatia, Bosnia-Herzegovina, Slovenia, Montenegro, and Macedonia united to form Yugoslavia. The dotted lines on the map show the borders of each former entity. Poland's border with Russia was in dispute during this period.

Although Poland's encounter with the world of strong states was perhaps most dramatic, the other Eastern European countries also suffered from being small countries in a region of large states. Hungary, for example, was conquered by the Turkish Ottoman Empire in 1526, and by Austria 150 years later, before carving out semi-independence in 1867. The Czechs came under the control of the Austrian empire in 1620, although, alone among conquered nations, they were able to turn this to their economic advantage, becoming a nation of prosperous bourgeois producers. They sought independence only when the Austrian Empire collapsed, and, together with the neighboring agrarian Slovaks, they formed their own state in 1918.

Yugoslavia followed the most complex path to statehood. Long dominated by the Ottoman Empire, large parts of it were later conquered by the Austrians. Serbia finally fought its way to independence in 1878, and then, after the breakup of the occupying powers in World War I, took the neighboring republics under its wing to form an independent Yugoslavia in 1918. Although linguistically quite similar, the new country was extremely diverse in matters of faith, with Catholicism, Orthodox Christianity, and Islam (represented most significantly by Croatia, Serbia, and Bosnia, respectively) all figuring prominently. While the northern and western (and Catholic) republics of Slovenia and Croatia were the most highly developed economically, the country was dominated politically and militarily by the lesser-developed Serbia. These political, economic, and religious differences laid the groundwork for conflicts that would emerge first in the 1920s, then in the 1940s, and most recently in the wars of the 1990s.

When the region's four annexing empires of Austria, Germany, Russia, and Turkey all crumbled as a result of World War I, the small nations of Eastern Europe were finally able to gain their independence. Maintaining that independence proved to be almost as hard as achieving it.

Independence (1918–1939)

As this brief historical account makes clear, a key problem for Eastern Europe after World War I, as again in much of the region today, was not so much the world of states on the outside, but the dilemma of how to build stable states given the multiplicity of nations on the inside. Several million Hungarians, for example, lived outside Hungary's borders. Millions of Germans lived far from Germany's borders. Poland had a large Ukrainian minority, and it also had the largest Eastern European Jewish minority. All other East-Central European states also had large Jewish minorities, as well as large Roma, or Gypsy, populations.

The Western powers responsible for the emergence of independent Eastern Europe states after World War I wished to create states that were ethnically homogeneous. With so many nationalities living in such close proximity, however, this goal was impossible to achieve. Moreover, the presence of many nationalities competing for land for their "own" nation-states led to the rise of *integralist* nationalism, which defines the national community in aggressive ethnic terms. This type of nationalism set in motion many of the ethnic antagonisms that have plagued the region even till today. It is East-Central Europe's plethora of nations, not its plethora of states, that has been one of the greatest obstacles to its democratic development.[3]

The interwar years were also a time of almost constant economic crisis, caused by the difficulties of developing after long years of foreign rule, and by the debilitating global economic depression. Altogether, continuing poverty, economic and social dislocation, and ethnic hatreds made it exceedingly difficult to consolidate democracy. The interwar years revealed the shakiness of liberal democratic institutions in Eastern Europe.

There is no space here even to begin to tell the story of World War II's impact on the people, economy, society, and psychology of Eastern Europe.[4] Millions of people were killed and tens of millions were terrorized. Nazi occupation and then the Soviet-led liberation left the economic infrastructure almost totally destroyed. By 1945, East-Central Europeans could be forgiven for considering the interwar years of independence after 1918 as one vast failure. The Communists, who had rejected the status quo before the war and represented the victorious power afterward, reaped the benefits of the growing desire for a total break with the past. They promised an end to what they called the capitalist legacy of poverty and dictatorship. And so it was not just the Red Army that brought socialism to East-Central Europe. After too many years of poverty, dictatorship, national rivalries, and war, many East-Central Europeans were ready for it themselves.

The Beginnings of Communism (1945–1949)

Many Eastern Europeans thought and hoped that the Red Army's expulsion of the Nazis meant that the region had finally become free of foreign domination. Instead, the outside world bore down on them again, this time in the form of the Soviet Union. Stalin's Red Army occupied East-Central Europe as it expelled the Nazis during its march to Berlin in 1944–1945. Hoping to make sure the region would never again become hostile territory, Stalin sought to create a buffer zone between the Soviet Union and the West by imposing a Soviet-style socialism on all of East-Central Europe.

The first years after the war saw some toleration of non-Communist parties and organizations. But by 1948, after the cold war had taken hold and the West had promoted the establishment of a new West German state, all pretense of tolerance disappeared. Stalin ordered the various Communist parties to eliminate all political rivals and to take power for themselves. From then on, East-Central Europe was governed just like the Soviet Union. Each country was ruled by the Politburo of the national Communist Party. Formally, each country had a single house of parliament, whose members were selected by Communist Party officials (though not all were party members) and then "elected" by the people, who were all but required to show up on election day to vote for the sole candidate on the ballot. The judiciary was dominated by the party, as was the civil service. The party exercised control through the *nomenklatura* principle, meaning that it chose the people not only for nominally elected offices but also for key positions in the national bureaucracy, local government, industry, trade unions, educational institutions, and most other public organizations.

Millions of people supported the Communist program in the 1940s. Young people were particularly attracted to the new system, for communism offered them something grandiose to believe in: the struggle to industrialize the country and build a great new world.[5] Communism also offered plenty of good new jobs. Indeed, for young people from peasant and working-class backgrounds, the Stalinist years were a time of unprecedented social mobility. In contrast to the unemployment lines of the past, the party had jobs to offer in industry, agriculture, the media, schools, the bureaucracy—anywhere one wanted. And the chief qualification for office was only that the applicant be committed to communism. Indeed, formal education often hindered chances for success, as it was considered a sign of a bourgeois background.

At the same time, the Stalinist years (approximately 1949–1955, though Stalin died in 1953) were an almost incomprehensibly brutal period. People were punished for their pasts, arrested for their private views, detained for telling jokes,[6] and even deported to Siberia without trial. Some defended these policies, saying that each country was engaged in a revolution and that enemies were lurking everywhere. But as the list of enemies kept getting longer and as police control embraced more and more of society, people turned increasingly against communism, seeing it as a betrayal of their hopes for a better world. Thus they entered on the long struggle for democracy.

The Rebirth of Democracy (1956–1989)

Prior to the mid-1950s, East Europeans seemed to treat independence and industrialization as more important than democracy. Yet by 1989, the very phrase "Eastern Europe" had become a synonym for democracy. Entire populations seemed to unite in the fight for democratic freedom, and the rest of the world looked on with awe and admiration.

In large part, it was the Communist experience itself that brought about the change. Communism had undeniably helped resolve the age-old problems of independence and economic backwardness. Despite Soviet influence, Eastern Europe was made up of independent entities with their own laws and armies. By the 1960s, no Eastern Europeans seriously expected their nations to disappear. Their economies may have been worse off than those in the West, but the debilitating poverty and monstrous inequalities of the past had been eliminated. Yet even after these accomplishments, communism continued to maintain a political repression that seemed increasingly inappropriate. People were ready to forgo democracy when the problems of independence and underdevelopment were central. As these old nineteenth-century problems dissipated, the struggle for democracy came to the fore.

Both concrete experience and conscious political activity contributed to this remarkable rebirth of democracy. Let us trace the evolution by looking at the events of 1956, 1968, 1970, and 1980.

Although no dissenting voices were tolerated during the peak Stalinist years beginning in 1949, that began to change soon after Stalin's death in March 1953. In June, pent-up anger broke out for the first time in East Berlin, sparking serious, if short-lived, working-class protests. Then, as new leaders in the Soviet Union began to abandon the policies of terror, a trickle of new voices began to be heard in Eastern Europe. These critics, known as revisionists, argued that socialism should be democratic and that Stalinism was an aberration of true socialism.

What began as a trickle turned into a torrent after the Twentieth Congress of the Soviet Communist Party in February 1956, when Soviet leader Nikita Khrushchev denounced Stalin as a tyrant and called for a return to "true Leninism." It is difficult to overestimate the impact of this congress on Eastern Europe. The region's rulers at the time all owed their positions directly to Stalin, who had picked them over rival Communist leaders during Soviet-sponsored purges of the late 1940s. The denunciation of Stalin constituted an endorsement of those who had been his victims and thus an invitation to Eastern Europe to make changes.

It did not take long for people to respond. Within months, protests inspired and led by the democratic socialist revisionists gripped both Poland and Hungary. Soon the intellectual critique gave way to protests from below, as workers challenged the harsh rules, low pay, and poor working conditions endemic to Stalinist socialism as contrary to the principles of "real" socialism. By fall 1956, both countries hovered on the brink of revolution. In Hungary, it turned into actual revolution, which the Soviet Union then crushed by sending in its army. Seeing the dire consequences for outright resistance, Poland opted for slower change under the continued leadership of the party.[7]

Nevertheless, 1956 had changed Eastern Europe forever: the era of "totalitarianism," or the absolute control of the state over society and the economy, had ended. Indeed, both Hungary and Poland soon embarked on innovative economic reform and gradually allowed critics of the party (including, in Poland, the Catholic Church) to take part in public life. The new Hungarian motto—"Whoever is not against us is with us"—constituted a stunning reversal of Stalinist ideology and seemed to acknowledge that the new democratic longings of society could not forever be repressed.

In Yugoslavia, meanwhile, democratic socialist ideology made even further progress, thanks to Stalin's decision to expel Yugoslavia summarily from the list of Communist nations. The only "crime" of the Yugoslav Communist Party and its dynamic leader, Josip Broz Tito, was to have remained independent of the Soviet Union. Although Tito saw himself as a Stalinist and tried to reproduce the Soviet model, Stalin never reciprocated. He hated Tito's independence and in 1948 denounced him as a fascist counterrevolutionary. As a result, Tito was forced to find his own road to socialism, ultimately choosing a nonstatist socialism based on regional autonomy and worker self-management. Although the party still retained control at the top and individual autonomy was allowed more in the workplace than in the political sphere at large, the Yugoslav reforms nevertheless constituted an important democratic innovation within socialism.

Then came 1968. The democratic fervor of 1989 cannot be understood apart from the legacy of 1968: the Prague Spring in Czechoslovakia and the student revolts in Poland and Yugoslavia. In the aftermath of these movements, a new generation rethought the whole strategy of revisionist opposition, developing an antistate orientation that would pave the way for the democratic revolutions of 1989.

The Prague Spring began as part of an effort for economic reform. The Stalinist economic program, developed as a crash industrialization strategy for a poor peasant country, had been particularly unsuitable for Czechoslovakia, with its strong industrial infrastructure and well-educated urban population. In 1962, Czechoslovakia became the first socialist country to record a decline in industrial output, sparking numerous calls for reform. Economists proposed a series of measures aimed at increasing managerial responsibility and promoting greater individual incentive. But inevitably in this country with strong democratic traditions, the call for greater economic freedom became a call for political freedom as well. Soon after Alexander Dubcek became head of the party in January 1968, party reformers promulgated a program of thoroughgoing democratic reform, declaring freedom of speech indispensable to a modern economy and arguing that authority should derive from knowledge and expertise rather than party affiliation.[8] By spring, Czechoslovakia had become a wide-open society, with censorship abolished and everyone speaking out on every possible issue.

The Soviets grew alarmed. Although set in motion by the Communist Party, the democratic changes seemed to make the party irrelevant, something the Soviets viewed as a threat to their security. And so in August 1968, the Soviets sent Warsaw Pact troops into Czechoslovakia to crush this democratic socialist experiment, thrusting the country into a long, gloomy period of political repression that would end only in 1989.

Poland's 1968 began over cultural issues, after officials closed a theatrical production of a nineteenth-century Polish play because of its allegedly anti-Soviet character. Students reacted with a wave of protests, attacking government repression and demanding freedom of speech. The government responded by arresting student leaders, organizing goon squads of workers to beat up demonstrators, and launching a vast anti-intellectual and anti-Semitic campaign. Why anti-Semitism? Not because of any "Jewish problem" in Poland, but to root out the entire liberal intelligentsia, to whom anti-Semitism was anathema. By the end of the year, hundreds of students and professors were expelled, government administration was purged of loyal civil servants, and the several thousand remaining Polish Jews were "invited" to leave the country for good.

The party's ugly campaign had more in common with native fascist traditions than with anything coming out of the socialist camp. Yet the party presented it as a "defense of socialism." Two years later, when shipyard workers in Gdansk and Szczecin took to the streets to protest price increases and demand independent trade unions, party authorities decided to "defend socialism" by shooting down dozens. For Eastern European oppositionists, the die had been cast. If official socialism could mean military invasion in Czechoslovakia and anti-Semitism and shooting down workers in Poland,

perhaps it was time to stop looking to the party to introduce "real socialism." Perhaps it was time to look inward for strength.

The new democratic oppositionists thus drew from 1968 the lesson that political change in Eastern Europe would not come from above. They now set out to force it from below through the promotion of a wide variety of independent social activity. The goal was to get people to do things—anything—just as long as they did it on their own, with no official mediation. Writing, printing, or reading an independent newsletter; organizing, publicizing, or attending an independent lecture series or discussion group: these were among the main forms of opposition activity. This was the time of the *samizdat* press (uncensored and self-published periodicals) and of "flying universities" (unofficial classes meeting in different homes each session). Such activity was considered the most important kind of political opposition possible. As conceptualized at this time, the aim of political opposition was not to take control of the state but to *democratize society.* If people felt and acted like free citizens, the opposition believed, then they would become free citizens. Eventually the state would have to follow along.

The East European opposition thus rediscovered the concept of *civil society:* the idea that politics meant not just government but the whole sphere of daily social interactions. People began fighting not so much for free elections and parliamentary democracy, which seemed far removed and perhaps beside the point, but for the right to have some social space free from the state. Writers wanted space to write about what they were interested in; students wanted space to study what and how they wanted to study; workers wanted space to form their own trade unions.

A number of brilliant writers and theoreticians emerged in East-Central Europe in the 1970s to give voice to these new aspirations; among them were Vaclav Havel in Czechoslovakia, Adam Michnik in Poland, and George Konrad in Hungary.[9] Organizations soon emerged, too, seeking to promote new civic activities and build an independent civil society. The most important and influential of these organizations was the Workers' Defense Committee, known by its Polish initials KOR. Formed by oppositionist intellectuals in Poland in 1977 to defend workers persecuted for going on strike the year before, KOR soon began sponsoring civic initiatives throughout the country, such as *samizdat* publications, lecture series, trade union organizing, and even some charitable work, often together with the Catholic Church. Combined with the independent workers' movement, KOR's activity helped bring about the remarkable Solidarity movement that spelled the beginning of the end of communism in East-Central Europe.

Polish workers had their own traditions, too. In 1970, shipyard workers had struck for the right to form independent trade unions. Ten years later, they went on strike again. In the new environment of civic activism, intellectuals from all over the country flocked to their aid, helping them print pamphlets and negotiate with the government. The strike ended with the signing of the Gdansk Accord on August 31, 1980, resulting in the formation of the "independent self-governing trade union Solidarity" headed by a thirty-seven-year-old electrician named Lech Walesa. It signified the beginning of the end of the state socialist system.[10]

Poland in the next sixteen months was the site of a unique democratic revolution. Without making any attempt to seize state power, workers in Poland acted as if they were already citizens of a free and democratic state. Solidarity was perhaps the most democratic trade union that ever existed. All leadership meetings were attended by journalists, who published detailed accounts in the union press, carefully documenting who had said what. Although the union did push for wage increases, its main goal was simply to exist—to make sure the state respected the rights of social groups to organize on their own. Long years of political repression had convinced workers that political freedom was the most important goal of all.

Solidarity was threatening to the Communist system not because it demanded political power—in fact, it did not—but just because it existed. Communism was based on central planning. The party made all public decisions and coordinated all public activities. Yet it could not do such things when millions of people gave their allegiance to an independent trade union that the party could not control. And so on December 13, 1981, the Polish authorities declared martial law and banned Solidarity. For the next seven years, the party tried to patch back together a system that had come apart at the seams. As it turned out, it could not be mended.

The Collapse of Communism (1989–1991)

In a breathtaking period of 1989, essentially from June 4 to December 20, Communist rule collapsed in one country after another in East-Central Europe. While everyone has heard of the fall of the Berlin Wall, which took place in November 1989, the real end to the Communist era happened not in Germany but in Poland, and it was a direct result of the decade-long struggle of Solidarity.

The turning point came in 1988, when workers went on strike in several key factories, protesting against the party's idea of economic reform, and demanding the relegalization of Solidarity. Having no other way to achieve economic reform, the Polish leadership, with the support of new Soviet leader Mikhail Gorbachev, agreed to meet with Solidarity's underground leaders. The strikes ended at once, and, in February 1989, Solidarity and the party entered into negotiations that ended two months later with Solidarity legal again and Poland preparing for its first real elections in the postwar period.

In those elections, Solidarity defeated the party so thoroughly that the latter could not even hang on to the formal state power it had been conceded. Although General Wojciech Jaruzelski, who had imposed martial law, became the new president, elected by parliament, Solidarity used its new power to force the selection of

Tadeusz Mazowiecki, a veteran oppositionist and Solidarity adviser, as prime minister. Mazowiecki took office in September 1989, and Poland became the first Eastern European country after World War II to have a non-Communist government. After Poland, Communist power fell swiftly elsewhere in the region.[11]

Democratization in Hungary came peacefully but decisively. Actually, reforms there had begun earlier—economic reforms after 1968, and political reforms in the 1980s. In 1984, in an effort to stave off a Polish-style crisis, Hungary became the first Communist country to experiment with multicandidate parliamentary elections. By 1987, opposition groups were forming political parties, and the government scarcely interfered. When the events of 1989 began in Poland, the Hungarian government was ready to talk with its opposition parties about managing a peaceful transition to democracy. In the end, change came more peacefully in Hungary than anywhere else in the region. With the elections of March 1990, a democratic political system was in place.

The changes in Hungary set off rebellion in East Germany (and then in Czechoslovakia, discussed at the beginning of the chapter). When Hungary opened up its borders on September 10, 1989, tens of thousands of East Germans, normally permitted to travel only within Eastern Europe, jammed the roads to Hungary, from there to cross over to the West. Ensuing mass demonstrations forced the ouster of party chief Erich Honecker in October, the fall of the Berlin Wall in November, and the hasty collapse not just of the party but of the entire state. In October 1990, East Germany merged into the Federal Republic of Germany to form a united Germany.

In the end, however, all these developments in East-Central Europe—including those not described here in countries such as Bulgaria, Romania, and Albania—were quite extraordinary. And they were topped off, in the summer of 1991, with the fall of communism in Russia itself. How do we explain all this? Perhaps the best explanation is the one put forward by Moshe Lewin in relation to the Soviet Union.[12] According to this view, East European societies simply outgrew the political systems in which they were encumbered. Communism was done in by modernization. At the start of the Communist period, most of the region was economically and socially underdeveloped, and many citizens wanted a strong government to take control. As economic and educational levels improved, however, people sought more responsibility for their own lives and no longer believed they needed the state to set all the rules. Soon even the party elite stopped believing that its rule was necessary for progress. Modernizing reformers started to chip away at party rule and eventually found no one holding them back. In the end, the old Communist political system was no longer appropriate to the socioeconomic world the Communists had built.

The Road to European Integration: 1998–2004

Having shed its Communist identity, Eastern Europe wanted nothing more than to "rejoin the West," in particular by entering the European Union. It took several years before that could be considered. The new governments had to reform their economic and political institutions, demonstrate that all major parties accepted the new "tilt" toward the EU, and then pass through their parliaments the panoply of EU laws known as the *acquis communautaire*, or the Community *acquis*: the body of common rights and obligations that bind all the member states together. These laws must be passed before a country can join the EU. While the first condition was satisfied in the first couple of years after 1989, the second had to wait till the mid-1990s, by which time the successor parties to the former Communist parties had won elections in Poland and Hungary and demonstrated their commitment to maintaining the new political direction. The Democratic Left Alliance won parliamentary elections in Poland in 1993, then the Socialist Party won in Hungary in 1994, but the crowning symbolic moment came in Poland in 1995, when former Communist Party official Aleksander Kwasniewski defeated legendary

Solidarity leader Lech Walesa in the presidential election.

Some people feared that these former Communists would try to undo some of the democratic and marketizing changes carried out since 1989. But as the end of the last section argued, most East European Communist parties (and particularly those in Poland and Hungary) had changed dramatically by this time. Their leaders no longer needed party dictatorships in order to advance their own interests, and many of them had changed with the times and become convinced democrats. In any case, once in power, these parties maintained pro-market policies and strict budgetary discipline, and pursued privatization with the same energy as their predecessors had. In other words, they were not much of a left at all, which had always opposed the market in the name of social equality. Or rather, they were very much like the contemporary social democratic left in Western Europe, which had long since made its peace with capitalism and sought only a slightly more socially concerned market economy. Despite their previous allegiances to Moscow, these former Communists also faithfully kept up the pro-Western orientations of the post-1989 governments, supporting entry into the EU and even NATO.

This demonstration of political continuity paved the way for European integration to begin in earnest. When everyone could trust the old Communists to be as liberal, democratic, and pro-European as those who had toppled their rule half a decade earlier, it was clear there was no going back, and that integration could therefore go forward. The stage was now set for expansion of the EU.

In the early 1990s, the EU put in place various association agreements with the countries of East-Central Europe and began numerous aid and education programs. Most EU countries allowed visa-free travel to citizens of East-Central Europe, thus facilitating increasing ties with the East. It was not until late in the decade, however, that the EU formally set in motion the accession process. The critical date here is March 1998, when the EU

selected ten countries as possible new members. Initially the EU divided the ten into two groups of five: those whose accession to the EU could be considered at once and those whose membership was conceivable but still a long way off. In the end, eight East European countries got into the fast track for accession: Poland, Hungary, the Czech Republic, Slovakia, Slovenia, and the three Baltic republics of Estonia, Latvia, and Lithuania. Bulgaria and Romania were in the second tier. Others were not even considered.

Even though no exact admission date was given at the time, the formal commitment to expansion dramatically changed East European politics. It meant that all the "anointed" countries had to reshape their policies and legislation to conform to EU requirements. This was no easy task. The EU has an eighty-thousand-page collection of laws and regulations (the so-called *acquis communautaire*) that all countries must meet in order to become members. In the first years of the new century, all prospective EU member countries began feverishly passing and rewriting their laws in order to meet *acquis* criteria. The countries of East-Central Europe were making internal political decisions based largely on how they would be perceived in the West.

Overall, however, the strategy worked. In 2003, the EU announced that the eight new countries would join the EU the following year, providing they maintained basic political and economic conditions. On May 1, 2004, the eight countries (along with Cyprus and Malta) became full members of the European Union. Provided they keep meeting their goals, Bulgaria and Romania can expect to enter in 2007.

This historic development has shaken the centuries-old divisions between East and West. Westerners are getting accustomed to the idea that Warsaw, Bratislava, and Talinn are proper European cities, while Easterners are on the verge of getting over their historical complex of being second-class European citizens. Although the process still has many tough times ahead, the historical magnitude of this process of European unification cannot be overestimated.

The EU is not the only sign of greater integration with the Western world. Besides the economic aspect of integration signified by the EU, there has been the security aspect represented by entry into NATO. The incorporation of the region into NATO began sooner than the EU accession process, and went much quicker. (As a U.S.-dominated military bloc rather than a complex economic and political union of independent states, NATO demands relatively little of its members besides the subordination of their armies.) The East European countries had lobbied for inclusion ever since the demise of the Warsaw Pact in 1990, seeing inclusion as a bulwark against future Russian pressure and as a clear sign of membership in "the West." Russia, undergoing its own democratization, called for the dissolution of NATO now that the cold war had ended. But neither the United States nor Western Europe wanted the United States to lose its influence in Europe. So NATO decided not to disband but to expand. Poland, Hungary, and the Czech Republic—East-Central Europe's new elite—became full members of NATO in March 1999. Exactly five years later, in March 2004, Bulgaria, Romania, Slovakia, Slovenia, and Estonia, Latvia, and Lithuania were admitted as well.

All this does not mean that East-Central Europe's problems are over. Less than two weeks after joining NATO, for example, Poland, Hungary, and the Czech Republic found themselves at war. This was the first time NATO ever fought a war, and it did so against another East European country, Yugoslavia (now called Serbia and Montenegro), on behalf of autonomy for the province of Kosovo. It was not the kind of welcome the new inductees had hoped for. The EU also has its costs. Unemployment is likely to rise at least in the short run, due both to cheap duty-free imports and to the inability of small East-Central European firms to follow all of the EU's regulations. Farmers in the "old" EU, moreover, continue to get levels of subsidies that farmers in the new countries are being denied. Full European integration will not be easy. Indeed, dis-

agreements over economic and political issues have made the promulgation of a new EU constitution very difficult. Nevertheless, joining both NATO and the EU is clearly a critical juncture in East-Central European history.

East-Central Europe After September 11

September 11, 2001, affected East-Central Europe profoundly. Nothing happened there that day, of course, but the ramifications of the planes smashing into the World Trade Center dramatically changed the world in which these countries live. The events of that day and, more important, the U.S. response to those events, simultaneously strengthened East-Central Europe's relations with the United States and hurt the region's ties to Western Europe. In 2005, this process continues to unfold in uncertain ways.

East Europeans reacted to the news of the day with the same horror, disbelief, and outpouring of sympathy for America as everyone else in Europe. Their support for U.S. military action in Afghanistan, against the fundamentalist Taliban movement which had been working closely with Al Qaeda, was also shared with the rest of Europe. Things changed, however, when the United States began preparing for an unprovoked invasion and occupation of Iraq, ostensibly aimed at finding weapons of mass destruction and toppling the regime of Saddam Hussein. France and Germany led the way in opposing American plans, calling for the continuation of sanctions instead. When the United States dug in its heels, the two countries persisted, using both NATO and the United Nations to vote against U.S. requests that an invasion be authorized. Suddenly East-Central Europe found itself caught between two rival powers, both of which the region had relied upon since 1989.

Things escalated dramatically in January 2003, when U.S. Defense Secretary Donald Rumsfeld derided his West European critics as representatives of an "old Europe," in contrast to a "new" Europe emerging in the East. The leaders of Poland, Hungary, and the Czech Republic promptly responded by joining those of Denmark, Italy, Portugal, Spain, and the United Kingdom in an open letter supporting the United States's Iraq policy. Not to be outdone, two weeks later ten other East European countries—Albania, Bulgaria, Croatia, Estonia, Macedonia, Latvia, Lithuania, Romania, Slovakia, and Slovenia—joined in, announcing that they, too, supported America.

There were ironies aplenty in all this. Here was a right-wing American administration treating its recent cold war opponent countries as its closest of friends, at a time when Poland, Hungary, and several other of these countries had governments run by former Communists! Why did East Europe take the position it did? It was a combination of choice and necessity. Poland, for example, has a long pro-American history, and has tried to stake out a role as the United States's most loyal Eastern ally, akin to the role played by Great Britain in the West. And many in the region, thinking of their own history, also sympathized intrinsically with the idea of getting rid of a dictator. Indeed, while citizens of the West European countries that were supporting the Iraq war staged massive protests against their own governments, citizens in East-Central Europe were far more restrained in their reactions.

But the governments of these countries also felt they had no choice. The United States was simply too powerful to alienate. All those countries hoping to get into NATO (only the three that signed the first letter were members at the time) felt that public support of the United States was obligatory, even at the risk of alienating the EU. And these actions did indeed alienate much of the EU. French president Jacques Chirac treated East Europe's open support for the United States, at a time when France and Germany were articulating a different position, as tantamount to betrayal. "These countries have been not very well behaved," he said, calling their statements "infantile" and "dangerous," and adding, "They missed a great opportunity to shut up." He even threatened that their entry into the EU might be delayed. (It was not.) Eastern Europe naturally reacted with outrage to the patronizing tone of the French, and in this way a new divide crept into Europe just at the moment when the various countries were finally coming together in the European Union.

Iraq remained a sore point of contention even after the U.S. invasion. Poland agreed to lead an occupation force of 9,500 troops in central Iraq, including 2,400 of their own and 1,600 from Ukraine, 1,300 from Spain, 500 from Bulgaria, with Hungary, Romania, Latvia, Slovakia, and Lithuania sending smaller contingents. Hungary also agreed to allow the Americans to use their territory to train a new Iraqi police force.

By 2004, things began to change. First the Poles began to waver. In March, President Kwasniewski complained about being "misled" by the United States about the reasons for the Iraqi invasion. Polish citizens also expressed disappointment that their country's strong support for the Bush administration has not resulted in any tangible benefits, such as visa-free travel to the United States for its citizens. By fall 2004, Poland announced that it would begin reducing its troop commitment starting in 2005. In November 2004, Hungary announced that it would withdraw its troops by March 2005. The Baltic countries also started backing out.

Another new development in the region after September 11 is the heightened fear of terrorism. When Spain became the target of a deadly terrorist attack on its railroads in March 2004, East European supporters of the Iraq occupation realized the threat was real. This has resulted in the same kind of challenges to civil liberties as has become common in the United States. When Poland hosted a global Economic Forum in April 2004, the Polish police treated antiglobalization protesters as potential terrorists. They prevented people from coming to the capital, blocked off much of the city, and, in the words of one press account, acted as if they were preparing for war.

The aftermath of September 11 thus poses a host of challenges, not just for the East but for all of Europe. Will East-Central Europe be able to maintain close ties with both the United States and Western Europe? Will all of Europe be able to get past the disagreements over Iraq and continue the process of deep integration? These are the questions and the challenges that lie ahead.

Themes and Implications

An old curse, attributed variously to Jews, Russians, or Chinese, goes like this: "May you live in interesting times!" Perhaps unfortunately for them, East Europeans have always lived in interesting times. The region has been in the center of all the great "isms" of the twentieth century: imperialism, nationalism, fascism, communism, and now global capitalism. Let us conclude this chapter by connecting this astonishing history with the main themes of this book.

Historical Junctures and Political Themes

Perhaps nowhere else in Europe is the link between this book's first two themes—the world of states and governing the economy—clearer than it is in the countries of the East. While the international environment and global competition affects every state's ability to govern its economy, this has been starkly evident at every stage of East-Central Europe's recent past. Since the region entered the post-Communist era with a large foreign debt, it needed support from the West to get its economies going. The International Monetary Fund (IMF) offered help for the region's stabilization plans in return for commitments to open up their economies to foreign investment and products. Since these countries hoped to get into the "world of states" that make up the EU, they were particularly open to goods and investment from EU countries—even though the latter did not reciprocate. When the process of entering the EU began accelerating in 1998, the supplicant countries had to open up not only their markets but their legal codes. By the early 2000s, most of the laws passed by most East European parliaments were about changing the legal environment to conform to the EU's *acquis communautaire*. Critics saw the EU as hijacking the democratic process. The link between international influence and domestic economic

governance has never been closer than in East-Central Europe's latest historical juncture.

The connection is also quite close, though in a very different way, in the former Yugoslavia. It was an IMF restructuring plan that pressed the country to impose painful economic measures in the late 1980s, creating the social unrest that would explode in war. When the conflict in Bosnia ended in the 1995 U.S.-brokered peace plan in Dayton, Serbia's economic options were limited by economic sanctions imposed by the United Nations. First Bosnia and then Kosovo came under direct UN control. How this region governed its economy could be explained only by its role in a particular world of states.

Just as this book's first two key themes are so closely related in East-Central Europe, so are its last two themes: the democratic idea and the politics of collective identity. One thing the ruling Communist parties were never able to do was to instill among the people a strong pro-Communist identity. They succeeded in making people dependent on the state but not in making them feel grateful to the state. On the contrary, since state control was so all-embracing, people commonly thought of the state as the enemy. Anyone with a complaint about anything could plausibly place blame on the state rather than on some other social group or on themselves. (In capitalist societies, of course, the reverse is true.)

In 1989, an antiparty collective identity became the dominant one. People saw themselves now as "citizens" fighting for "democracy" against an oppressive state. To be a democratic citizen meant to have a voice in public life. People did not organize in 1989 as workers or intellectuals, as urban or rural, as Czech or Slovak, as men or women, as gays or straights. They organized as citizens, united together and demanding democracy for all.

After 1989, this vision of democracy as entailing a grand sense of unity no longer made sense. Without a party and state to fight against, people had to develop new identities based on issues smaller (though not less important) than "us" versus "them." They still saw themselves as "democrats," but democracy for many people now meant the effort to build up the different social classes of a capitalist system. Democracy thus required that new collective identities come to the fore.

Class, paradoxically, is an identity that has not come easily. Communism discouraged class-based identities, since everyone was equal in relation to the state. The anti-Communist opposition also discouraged class identities, since everyone was supposed to be equal as citizens, fighting against dictatorship. In the day-to-day workings of a democracy, however, class identities play a very important role. Workers organize as workers to win higher wages and better working conditions, and in the process they come to feel they have a stake in the entire economic and political system. Organizing along class lines thus helps the consolidation of a liberal democratic system, as it allows large groups of people to win concrete benefits. The absence of class identities up until 1989, however, has meant a weakness of class identities since 1989. Workers find themselves angry over their economic situation, but not well organized to defend themselves. Only new elites began to organize themselves as a class, fighting to make sure public policy serves their interests. In this way, however, many workers have been alienated by the post-Communist system, and a system without the support of working people cannot be very strong or very stable.

East-Central Europe has not seen a great deal of identification along gender lines either. Women certainly faced a great many problems under communism, owing to poorer educational opportunities and a strong macho culture. (Because of endemic shortages, shopping and cooking were even more of a burden than in the West.) Nevertheless, women, like men, tended to see communism, and not gender relations, as the sole enemy. In fact, since communism claimed to have emancipated women, those struggling against communism often saw themselves as fighting *against* the emancipation of women. Even women sometimes argued that communism was a plot to take women out of the home

in order to promote the indoctrination of children in the schools![13]

Just as class differences have become more potent in the post-Communist era, so have gender differences. As enterprises began to cut back on their workforces, women were the first to be fired. Where good new jobs were to be had, women were increasingly hired on the basis of their looks, not their qualifications. Such experiences are leading to the emergence of a women's movement and new gender identities, but the legacy of the past makes this a slow process.

Far more than along class or gender lines, people in Eastern Europe identify themselves along national lines. That is, we see a clash today between nationalism and internationalism—or, as it is frequently characterized, between nationalism and "Europeanism." The Europeanist is one who feels part of a new, upwardly mobile, economically productive community, moving collectively into the twenty-first century. The most obvious candidates for this identity are the budding entrepreneurs, economic professionals, students studying business and foreign languages, and former dissident politicians who have moved into government.[14] But even many people who have lost out economically subscribe to this identity. They believe their sacrifices are short-term and feel pride in their country's path toward becoming "like the West."

The nationalist, on the other hand, is one who feels threatened by the new changes. To the nationalist, dependence on the East is being replaced by dependence on the West. Where communism once threatened traditional values, now liberalism, global capitalism, and secularism threaten those values. Those who embrace this new identity are usually those least able to prosper in the new environment, such as unskilled workers in dying industrial towns or the elderly living in rural areas. These people, who have reason to feel threatened by "the West" and all it implies, have been mobilized by right-wing parties to find solace in "the nation" instead. The "nation" is seen as a community of regular people—people just like them. Making policy in the interests of the nation means that state policy should benefit these "regular people," rather than the educated and the "cosmopolitans" who admire the West. We look more closely at the impact of these new identities in the chapters that follow.

Implications for Comparative Politics

Rarely can we see an entire region in such transition as in contemporary Eastern Europe, with so many exciting political, economic, and social experiments. Issues of democratization, globalization, privatization, and nationalism appear in this region in a way they appear nowhere else. While capitalism beckons, the old appeals of communism still tug. While the people are enticed by the opportunities to belong to a single global culture, their national pride and legacies of resistance keep them connected to local values too. With the eruptions of ethnic nationalism existing side by side with the desire to join the EU, we see the tensions that political scientist Benjamin Barber has described as "jihad vs. McWorld"—the former referring to people's desire to hold onto the local styles and traditions that "McWorld," or the push for global market uniformity, tends to sweep away.

The historic legacies of nationalism and communism have left East-Central Europeans feeling torn about their role in the world today. For the new elites, 1989 represented a chance to "join Europe," to become part of what they called the "normal world" of parliamentary democracies and a global economy dominated by large transnational corporations and international organizations. Many people in the area, however, still view the new global institutions skeptically. Echoing nationalist sentiments, they fear that in place of dependence on the Soviet Union will come dependence on the West. They feel that with their still-weak economies, they can "join Europe" only as paupers, not as real players. They like the EU's record of peace and prosperity, but then they see Western European farmers organizing to keep out cheap Eastern European products. They like the promises of massive aid that they hear from organizations like the IMF and the World Bank, but then find these organizations demanding internal changes that could greatly upset political stability. They want to like the outside world, but they keep seeing evidence that the outside world may not like them, and then they wonder if joining Europe might not hurt national interests more than help them. East Europeans still want to build their own strong states, but they fear that the international community is more interested in the region as a source of cheap labor than as a group of nations with interests of their own.

East-Central Europe thus continues to face an enormous number of pressing tasks in this era. It must consolidate democratic political systems at the same time as it builds a market economy. It must build the complex institutions of a market society, such as regulatory agencies and a new social welfare network, necessary to avoid the corruption scandals and poverty that can make people long for the past. It must try to avoid the dangers of fundamentalist nationalism by providing people with solid values to believe in now that the grand myths of communism no longer persuade. Can it manage all these tasks? Can it privatize the economy in a way that serves the interests of both the employees and the economy as a whole? Can it integrate even economic "losers" into a new democratic society and thus keep people away from the lure of demagogues and potential dictators? Can it make good on the grand democratic ideals that inspired people as citizens in 1989?

In looking at East-Central Europe, political scientists, sociologists, economists, and anthropologists have unprecedented opportunities for understanding the dynamics of social change. With the complex issues it faces and the transformations it is undergoing, it is surely one of the more fascinating areas of the globe today.

Notes

1. See Jacques Rupnik, *The Other Europe: The Rise and Fall of Communism in East-Central Europe* (New York: Pantheon Books, 1989), esp. chap. 1.

2. For an account of Eastern European states and nations in the premodern era, see Perry Anderson, *Lineages of the Absolutist State* (London: Verso, 1974).

3. See Raymond Pearson, *National Minorities in Eastern Europe, 1849–1945* (London: Macmillan, 1983).

4. For a brief but excellent account, see Joseph Rothschild, *Return to Diversity: A Political History of East Central Europe Since World War II* (New York: Oxford University Press, 1989), chap. 2.

5. For a wonderful account of why Czech and Slovak intellectuals chose to join the Communist Party, see Antonin Liehm, *The Politics of Culture* (New York: Grove Press, 1968). As to why workers joined, see Polish director Andrzej Wajda's 1996 film, *Man of Marble.*

6. See Milan Kundera's novel *The Joke* (New York: Harper and Row, 1982).

7. For an account of Eastern European protests up to 1980, see Chris Harman, *Class Struggles in Eastern Europe, 1945–1983* (London: Bookmarks, 1988).

8. For two inside accounts of the rise of reform communism, see Alexander Dubcek, *Hope Dies Fast* (New York: Kodansha International, 1993), and Zdenek Mlynár, *Nightfrost in Prague* (New York: Karz, 1980).

9. Vaclav Havel, *The Power of the Powerless* (Armonk, N.Y.: M. E. Sharpe, 1985); Adam Michnik, *Letters from Prison* (Berkeley and Los Angeles: University of California Press, 1986); George Konrad, *Antipolitics* (San Diego: Harcourt Brace Jovanovich, 1984).

10. On the Solidarity experience, from its early roots in the prewar period to the fall of the Communist government, see David Ost, *Solidarity and the Politics of Anti-Politics* (Philadelphia: Temple University Press, 1990).

11. See Timothy Garton Ash, *The Magic Lantern* (New York: Random House, 1990).

12. See Moshe Lewin, *The Gorbachev Phenomenon* (Berkeley and Los Angeles: University of California Press, 1994).

13. On gender issues in postcommunism, see Nanette Funk and Magda Mueller, eds., *Gender Politics and Post-Communism* (New York: Routledge, 1993); also Peggy Watson, "Civil Society and the Politics of Difference in Eastern Europe," in Joan Scott et al., eds., *Transitions, Environments, Translations: Feminism in International Politics* (New York: Routledge, 1997).

14. For a study of East-Central Europe's new elite and how they got there, see Gil Eyal, Ivan Szelenyi, and Eleanor Townsley, *Making Capitalism Without Capitalists: Class Formation and Elite Struggles in Post-Communist Central Europe* (London: Verso, 1998).

C H A P T E R

27

Political Economy and Development

From communism to capitalism, East-Central Europe has been through enormous changes in the course of a single generation. But what does this transformation mean for people's material lives? On the one hand, the era of shortages is over. On the other hand, many people now can't afford the goods in the stores. On the one hand, managers exercise tighter discipline and have made firms more efficient. On the other, managerial rule often tramples over labor rights, and zero unemployment has given way to high double-digit unemployment. From a planned economy to a market economy, East-Central Europe's economic transformation has been a bundle of paradoxes. Making sense of them is the aim of this chapter.

The Peculiar Settlement and Beyond

We hear a great deal now about communism having been an economic failure. Yet for most East Europeans in 1945, as noted in Chapter 26, it was capitalism that was synonymous with failure. The term evoked memories of mass unemployment, economic depression, vast social inequalities, uncontrollable greed, and war. The reason that communism was able to win support, or at least acceptance, from much of the population was that it promised something else: hope. Its proponents spoke of a planned economy with jobs for all, social mobility for society's poorest, stable prices, and general economic progress. It would carry out this program through a massive use of state power.

In the postwar period there was nothing so special about increasing the role of the state. In Western Europe this was a key component of the postwar settlement beginning to emerge. In the East, however, government sought not just to regulate the economy but to take it over completely so the state could plan everything in a "rational" way. The Communists had explicit totalistic aspirations: only by planning the economy totally did they feel they could eliminate the "anarchy" of capitalist production and build an economy that truly provided for people's needs. Total planning required complete ownership of factories, workshops, retail stores, and farms. It required ministries to determine how much of what products each firm should produce, as well as who should receive the finished products, and at what prices. Consumers were not compelled to buy the goods they found in the stores, but the absence of competition meant they had little choice but to do so. Constructing a planned economy—or, as it was often called, a *command economy*—therefore meant nationalizing all private property used for production and building a huge bureaucratic apparatus to administer all this property.

Clearly this approach was a very different kind of postwar settlement from the one that took hold in the western part of Europe. There, the government sought to mediate the relationship between capital and labor. Both groups retained their autonomy (and capital retained its property), but they were persuaded to moderate their antagonisms by a state that showed itself able to advance the interests of both groups. In Eastern Europe, the state abolished the relationship between capital and labor and essentially substituted itself for both groups. Property was taken over by the state; trade unions were turned into arms of the state. This was not quite a settlement between capital and labor, since capital as such ceased to exist, but it ended up achieving the same basic goals as the settlement in the West: a growing economy and major social welfare benefits to workers. It never led to the levels of prosperity of the West, but it did provide for social peace and steady growth.

The crucial difference was that the postwar settlement in the West was carried out on a democratic basis, whereas in Eastern Europe it entailed a suppression of democracy. Thus it was a *peculiar* settlement. No one was asked to accept it; instead, it was imposed by the ruling party. All other parties were banned. Newspapers, radio, and television had to follow the official line. There were elections, but only one candidate was on the ballot. The state tried to take workers' aspirations into account somehow, for it wanted to preserve social peace, but in the end it was answerable to no one. And with protests banned, strikes outlawed, and the media firmly under state control, there seemed to be no way for anyone to change the situation. Nevertheless, there is much evidence that people supported it. Just as in the West, people saw the postwar era as a time for economic growth and political peace. Many were tired of politics and welcomed an interventionist state, provided it could get the job done. Most surely wished such a process could occur while preserving political democracy, as in the West. But once it was clear that the Communists were not going to allow that, people were at least pleased that the social and economic arrangements of such a settlement would be put into place. (Indeed, the revival of the ex-Communists' popularity since 1993 shows that many people still want the social and economic commitments of a postwar settlement, although definitely not its political aspects.)

The Rise of the Peculiar Settlement

By 1949, the Stalinist transformation was largely accomplished: the state had effectively eliminated private property in the manufacturing and service sectors, with farming only slightly behind. From then on, the entire economy was to be managed by state-run institutions.

The state was able to accomplish several undeniably beneficial achievements. By concentrating resources, it was able to build up heavy industry quickly. It eliminated unemployment by bringing millions into the workforce, including peasants from the countryside and women, who now entered the labor market at rates only slightly lower than men. Having obtained a job, moreover, a person had it for as long as he or she wished, as a job was considered a right. The state kept prices on most essential goods at a low and affordable level, one of the reasons people often had to stand in long lines. And it facilitated vast social mobility. By taking over the entire economy, Communist governments suddenly had hundreds of thousands of good jobs that had to be filled. They filled them not so much with the old specialists, most of whom the new governments did not trust, but with loyal political activists, often regardless of their qualifications. In this way, hundreds of thousands of youths, unskilled workers, and illiterate peasants found that they suddenly had a future, if only they joined the party (see Table 27.1). In Hungary, 60,000 workers were made enterprise managers during the 1949–1953 period alone.[1]

On Soviet insistence, Eastern Europe carried out its new policies without help from the rest of the world. The West offered Marshall Plan aid, but the offer was rejected because it required recipients to open their economies to outside forces, and that would have prevented government planners from deciding just how the economy should be built. The West's response was to impose a boycott: no trade, no loans, and no exchange of technology. That symbolized relations between East and West until the détente of the late 1960s.

Forced to go it alone, the Eastern European states might have cooperated closely among themselves. However, for two key reasons that did not happen. First, each country wanted to build up its own heavy industry before working with anyone else; and second, Stalin opposed cooperation,

Table 27.1   Communism Brings Mobility in Eastern
Europe

	Agricultural Workforce (percentage)	
	1960	1980
Albania	71	62
Bulgaria	73	24
Czechoslovakia	38	13
East Germany	24	10
Hungary	49	24
Poland	56	26
Romania	74	30
Yugoslavia	70	33

Note: The way in which these data are collected
suggests that the shift from agriculture is slightly
underestimated by these statistics.

Source: Joni Lovenduski and Jean Woodall, *Politics and
Society in Eastern Europe* (Bloomington: Indiana
University Press, 1987), p. 130.

seeing it as a potential threat to Soviet domination. Stalin wanted Eastern European economies
to complement the *Soviet* economy, not each
other's. Each country therefore worked to create a
model Soviet economy at home, focusing on
large-scale industry, with giant, sprawling factories taking up hundreds of acres of land, employ-
ing thousands of workers, and producing iron and
steel goods used chiefly as intermediate products
in the production of ever more industrial goods.
Producing consumer goods was of secondary concern. Like the early Protestants and capitalists,
Communists too said that hard work today brings
gratification tomorrow.

The Stalinist economic strategy's main problem was that it did not take national particularities into account. Czechoslovakia, for example,
already possessed a solid infrastructure. The Stalinist program of building everything anew was
both unnecessary and counterproductive, as it
meant squandering a great deal of valuable experience. Hungary, on the other hand, was hurt by
the retreat from the global economy. With a small

population and poor energy resources, Hungary
had always relied heavily on foreign trade. The
Stalinist attempt at autarky, or complete self-
sufficiency, obstructed the country's natural way
forward. As for Poland, one of its chief problems,
ironically, was that it did not follow the Communist economic program fully enough. Its inefficient agricultural sector stemmed in large part
from the 1956 decision to allow private property
in land, while doing everything possible to discourage private agriculture from becoming profitable. Investment went to the more inefficient
state sector, and private farmers could not get the
mechanical equipment needed to expand and develop. For unindustrialized areas like Romania,
Bulgaria, and parts of Yugoslavia, the Stalinist
economic strategy played a very constructive role
by laying the basis of a modern industrial economy. Everywhere, however, the insensitivity to
specific national characteristics led to severe problems that these countries would have to address in
the future.

Failure and Demise

By the 1960s, the economies of East-Central Europe were in deep trouble, plagued by shortages,
budget deficits, and lack of imagination. Employment guarantees remained, but workers often had little to do. Opportunities for social
mobility had declined dramatically. Workers and
peasants, whose predecessors had been able to
move up rapidly in the initial postwar years, now
found career advancement blocked by those who
had advanced in the past and constituted a new
elite that tried to pass on privileges to their children. These children, meanwhile, sought better
and more creative jobs to match their levels of
education, but the system, stuck in its old ways,
could not generate such new opportunities.

The irony is that the economic problems of
the system were a sign not of communism's failure but of its success. Communist leaders had
wanted to build up big industrial economies.
Having done so, they just did not know what to
do next. Party authorities, in accord with the
plan, had built up an economy that was very

successful at producing large volumes of standardized goods, and very unsuccessful at producing specialized goods for particular markets.
Quantity, not quality, was key. The entire economic system came to resemble a giant enterprise, where decisions are made by a few at the
top and executed by the majority at the bottom.
The goods were produced, but initiative and
imagination were smothered—fatal flaws in the
high-tech global economy that was just emerging. As Daniel Chirot has noted, by the 1970s
this region had created

> the world's most advanced late nineteenth-
> century economy, the world's biggest and best,
> most inflexible rust belt. It is as if Andrew
> Carnegie had taken over the entire United States,
> forced it into becoming a giant copy of U.S. Steel,
> and the executives of the same U.S. Steel had
> continued to run the country into the 1970s and
> 1980s![2]

Eastern Europe needed reform, but how could
government take away the things people expected from the system without jeopardizing the
unwritten social contract on which it depended?
Could the government cut down on guaranteed
jobs, low prices on essentials, free education, and
cheap housing without giving way on one-party
rule as well? This would be the conundrum facing all of Eastern Europe in the last two decades
of Communist power. Beginning in 1968, the
various governments began their various experiments, the first tenuous shadows of an emerging new political economy.

Indeed, the Prague Spring itself should be understood as a first attempt to abandon the peculiar
Communist postwar settlement. The main proponents of reform were self-proclaimed economic
reformers who felt that the party needed to let
managers run businesses on a more market-
oriented basis, without constant instructions
from the bureaucratic center. But if the managers were going to try to make a profit, that
would mean eliminating some of a firm's social
welfare subsidies to its employees. Since that
would break the regime's end of the social contract, how could the workers' end (political obe-

dience) be maintained? The reformers proposed
precisely that it not be maintained. Thus, the
Prague Spring tolerated and even encouraged
political freedom as a kind of quid pro quo offered to society in return for giving up the social
contract. As it happened, the Soviets invaded the
country before the reforms could go very far.
Still, the word was now out: the peculiar settlement would have to be revised.

Hungary was the next to try to do so. In 1968,
it introduced the "new economic mechanism"
that reduced the role of the ministries and made
individual enterprises more responsible for their
own affairs. Unlike in Czechoslovakia, political reforms were not part of the bargain. That is one of
the reasons the reforms soon ran into trouble: different groups expressed their objections within
the party, and the leadership backed off its radical
plans so as not to promote political discontent.

In 1970, Poland was the next country that felt
it needed to moderate the peculiar settlement
and reduce the extensive subsidies leading to
chronic budget deficits. But instead of trying to
reduce waste and make management more efficient, as the Czechs and Hungarians had tried to
do, the Poles attempted to solve their problems
by challenging the workers head-on.[3] In May,
the party launched a propaganda campaign
against alleged worker laziness and then began
increasing work norms, cracking down on absenteeism, and cutting pay by reducing overtime. In
December, when Polish leader Wladyslaw Gomulka announced a dramatic rise in food prices,
shipyard workers in the port cities of Gdansk
and Szczecin responded with massive strikes.
Gomulka suppressed the strikes immediately,
leaving dozens dead. The price hikes were re-
scinded, but the economic problems remained,
and workers remained mobilized. The experience demonstrated that the peculiar settlement
could not be broken on one side only. Painful
economic reform might be tolerated only if political reform went along with it. Since neither
East-Central Europe's governments nor the Soviet Union seemed ready for political reform, the
crisis began to seem unresolvable.

Just as despair began to mount, a temporary solution was found. It was devised by Edward Gierek, who replaced Gomulka as party leader in Poland soon after the 1970 massacres. We can sum up the new strategy as "Let the West pay for it!" Eastern Europe would voluntarily reenter the global capitalist economy. The countries would turn to the West for the investment funds to help develop their stagnant economies and satisfy the appetites of their hungry consumers. Only Czechoslovakia, due to the recent Soviet invasion, refused to participate; all the other countries now got involved in the new global economy.

The West was willing to make loans to help finance its official enemy for three reasons. First, Eastern Europe was a good investment. Capitalist bankers paradoxically thought it safer to lend money to poor Communist countries than to poor capitalist countries, because in the former the political system was stable and labor was under firm control. Second, détente's temporary easing of the cold war, beginning in the late 1960s, made it politically possible to trade with Eastern Europe. Finally, the price hikes by the Organization of Petroleum Exporting Countries (OPEC) and the subsequent oil crisis made it economically possible to do so, as banks now held billions of so-called petrodollars (used to purchase oil at the new prices) that they needed to loan out. The West needed a market for capital just when the East needed a source.

So for a few years in the 1970s, Eastern Europeans lived rather well. Poland and Hungary, for example, imported not only machinery to make their industry more competitive, but also large volumes of Western consumer goods to placate the restive working class. But this "solution" in fact only sowed the seeds of a new crisis, for soon after all these goods were imported, the bills became due, and Eastern Europe had a hard time paying. Because the region was not part of the capitalist economy, it could not pay debts in its own currency. It needed hard currency, and for that it had to export goods to the West. Eastern Europe now learned that it was much easier to

borrow from the West than to sell goods there. There was an internal reason for the export difficulties and an external one. The internal reason was that Eastern Europe was still producing inferior goods. Although it had imported much new technology, it had difficulty integrating the equipment into the production process. Because managers were paid according to output and because changes tend to make things worse in the short run, managers often let new machinery sit idle instead of trying to bring it on line. (In 1981, Polish TV showed whole parking lots filled with Western machine tools that had been rusting in the rain for years.) The external reason was that the West, reeling from the oil crisis, was going through a serious recession and was not anxious to buy even well-made products, such as metal goods from Poland, electronic goods from Czechoslovakia, or buses from Hungary.

By the end of the decade, Eastern Europe was deep in debt, with spiraling interest payments making the future look bleak. Poland's $20 billion debt led the way, though Hungary, with a much smaller population, had the highest per capita debt. East-Central Europe's entry into the global economy had failed. It had fallen into a "debt trap" similar to the kind that had been crippling the Third World.[4] And the debt precipitated a general economic crisis and a new round of shortages. These shortages came about for two reasons. First, Eastern Europe had integrated just enough Western technology to make its economy dependent on Western inputs, and the debt now prevented it from obtaining those inputs. (A 1981 toothpaste shortage in Poland occurred because Poland's toothpaste producers had signed an exclusive contract with a West German firm to supply essential ingredients, and when Poland failed to pay its debts, the firm stopped shipping the ingredients.) Second, the debt burden forced Eastern Europe to export whatever would sell in the West, and the salable items tended to be items that the population needed itself, like ham from Poland or coal from Romania.

By 1980, it became clear that East Europe's attempt to borrow its way out of the crisis had failed. The crisis of the peculiar settlement now became even greater than before. Not only was the economy in even more serious trouble, but popular anger had been stirred up, both by the continuing lack of political freedom and, perhaps even more, by the sudden disappearance of the consumer goods that people were just getting used to.

In Poland, where the debt crisis had been worst, the attempt to raise prices sparked the general strike of 1980. Realizing that it could get the social support necessary for austerity measures only by easing the political monopoly of the past, the government legalized Solidarity in August 1980. Although it outlawed the union sixteen months later, it continued moving toward economic and political reform, culminating finally in the peaceful revolution of 1989.

While Poland was experimenting with political solutions to the crisis, Hungary experimented with economic solutions. Instead of giving workers political freedom, it gave them the chance to make money. For example, workers were allowed to band together in the factories where they worked, forming their own quasi-enterprises using state machinery, after hours, to fill orders that they had contracted for independently. Enterprises were given more autonomy than ever before, and the small private sector (called the *second economy*) expanded considerably. By the end of the decade, Hungary had some of the highest consumption rates in Eastern Europe, as well as some of the most profitable large firms, such as the Tungsram plant, which sold light bulbs on the Western market, and the Ikarus bus company, which produced for hard-currency customers as far away as Latin America. Hungary also had some of the most overworked workers; according to some estimates, it had a higher percentage of "moonlighters" (workers holding two or more jobs) than any other country in the world.

Romania chose yet another way of dealing with its debt crisis: paying off the debt as quickly as possible. The costs were horrific. Party leader Nicolae Ceausescu slashed domestic consumption

to prewar levels, exporting to the West essential items that the population itself needed in order to survive. Electricity was shut off for several hours each day, with heating nonexistent even in winter, while the government exported coal and oil to earn the money to pay back the debt.

By 1989, the peculiar settlement had collapsed completely. One by one, Eastern European countries turned to a democratic market economy, and Eastern Europe's peculiar postwar settlement gave way to a rapidly emerging new political economy.

State and Economy

The fall of communism can thus be traced in part to the woes that befell East-Central Europe when it sought reintegration into the global economy. Once a society seeks to play on capitalist turf, it is difficult to play only halfway. In the years since communism has fallen, East-Central Europe has moved decisively toward the creation of a full market economy and has eagerly sought integration into the global economy.

Economic Management

Since 1989, managing the economy has first and foremost meant marketizing it. In 1990, Poland embraced a series of marketization policies known collectively as *shock therapy*, or the rapid application of *neoliberalism* (which involves the ending of price controls, a free hand for business elites, and a reduced role for government in managing the economy). Although not all of these measures have been adopted elsewhere in the region, they do represent a model of economic reform that other governments measure themselves against. Let us look at some of this model's main features.

The main aim of post-Communist economic transition is to get the state out of the business of managing the economy and to allow the market to make most of the decisions that state planners used to make. This meant disbanding the planning ministries and granting firms full autonomy. Companies were no longer told what to produce, whom to produce for, or what prices to charge for their products. A firm that was not making a profit now had to make the necessary adjustments so it did make a profit or else go bankrupt. Firms were to do whatever it takes to survive, including firing their workers. The abolition of the old employment guarantee meant the end of the old social contract.

The aim of the state's withdrawal from the economy is to force enterprises to compete and become more efficient. But simple withdrawal is not enough. The old socialist economies frequently relied on one giant firm to produce everything the country needed; that is, they created monopolies. Freeing prices alone would mean that these monopolies would charge higher prices without having to become more competitive. Competition therefore needed to be brought from the outside. Thus, an essential part of Eastern European market reform was to reduce drastically or even eliminate tariffs on imported goods, particularly from the West. Until new firms arose to create internal competition, existing firms would have to compete against external competition.

Internal competition, meanwhile, was to be created by taking the state out of the business of management and creating a new class to do the job instead. In this sense, Eastern Europe's new economic policy is very much a "wager on the elite." Despite the fact that labor protest precipitated the overthrow of the Communist system, the new leaders sought to create a new monied, propertied elite that would lead the way into the promised new world. The aim was to create a new class of property owners who would have a personal interest in maintaining and developing the economy. The chief way they did this was through privatization of the previously state-owned economy.

There have been two kinds of privatization processes in East Europe, usually referred to as small and large. *Small privatization* was concerned with the retail sector, particularly small shops like groceries, bakeries, and repair shops.

This sector was privatized relatively quickly, sometimes by selling the shops to the highest bidder, more often by leasing them to those who worked there. This process was not very contentious, largely because there was not a great deal of money (or power) at stake. The real conflicts have come in the area of *large privatization*, concerned with the ownership transfer of the large state enterprises, with their large labor forces, enormous capital stock, and huge markets.

In Hungary, large privatization began even during the Communist era. Those who took the lead in privatizing the economy were not the new capitalists but the old Communist managers. The process is often referred to as *spontaneous privatization*, or *nomenklatura buyouts*, because it was carried out by the old managers themselves (members of the former *nomenklatura*, or party-appointed bureaucracy), without coordination by the state. The state supplied only the legal framework: laws allowing managers of state firms to create spin-off private firms with no starting capital, followed by laws permitting the transfer of assets from state firms to these new firms. The upshot was that managers simply got together to set up a new firm, transferred assets of the state firm to this new firm, and suddenly became new capitalist entrepreneurs. After 1990, the new government cracked down on this practice. Nevertheless, large privatization in Hungary remained very much an elite affair. Firms were sold to Western companies and domestic investors, and the population had little to do with it. In the end, foreigners appeared to be the main beneficiaries. Today, even such a crucial sector for development as banking is almost completely foreign owned.

One of the reasons Hungary could afford to leave the population out of this process was that economic reform providing benefits to workers had already come a long way before 1989. In Poland and Czechoslovakia, where previous opportunities for workers were more limited, governments made special efforts at least to appear to include more people in the privatization process.

In Czechoslovakia, aside from the sale of some major plants to Western buyers, the government decided to privatize industry through the use of a voucher system. In 1992, all citizens were allowed to purchase, at a nominal price, a booklet of stock shares, called points, that they could then invest in a company of their choice. By involving ordinary people in the privatization process, the government hoped to break the ethos of dependence on the state fostered by the old regime and to teach citizens the concepts of risk, profit, and ownership. By making people co-owners, the government hoped individuals would feel they had a stake in the entire process of marketization.

There were two problems with the Czech solution. First, voucher privatization proved not to be so inclusive after all. Within a short period of time, investment funds and banks still run largely by the state quickly bought out most of the citizens' vouchers. Formal citizen ownership, in other words, covered for continuing state control. Second, this lack of real private ownership reduced the pressure on firms to restructure. As a result, Czech firms avoided painful restructuring in the early 1990s, only to have to do so in the latter part of the decade, just when neighboring economies were starting to benefit from changes they had made earlier.

Poland began privatization with a law in July 1990 that spelled out several possible paths and set up a ministry of property transformation to oversee the process. Over the next three years, Poland experimented with various privatization strategies. First, it began selling firms on the open market. But there were not enough buyers, and the government usually ended up with majority ownership anyway. Then it began selling firms to single Western buyers, such as a food processing plant to Gerber or a chemical plant to Procter & Gamble. This practice, however, drew stiff opposition. Critics charged that the best firms were being sold at a fraction of their real value, in return for kickbacks or to ingratiate the authorities with the West. Since no one knew what these firms were "really" worth (because

their accounting books were based on the artificial prices of the old system), it was impossible to verify these charges. The fierce criticism, however, required the government to take more care before selling firms to foreigners. All East-Central European countries have had to deal with similar complaints.

Seeking to win popular support, Poland in 1995 introduced a plan known as *general privatization*, in which ownership of several hundred state-owned companies was transferred to private investment firms in which individual citizens could buy shares. Whereas in the Czech plan a buyer purchases shares of the company itself, the Polish plan offers people shares of investment firms that are given ownership of various companies. The Poles chose this indirect method because they felt that what was important was not just privatization but good management. By the end of the 1990s, however, this plan too had run into serious problems, largely because of the poor quality of the firms selected for privatization and the limited capital at the disposal of the investment firms.

In the end, the most common method of privatization in Poland has been to sell or lease firms to their employees. This method was particularly popular with workers, who thereby became formal co-owners of the firm. However, since managers usually put up most of the money, and therefore got most of the shares, workers usually did not get more influence or more money.

This de facto exclusion of labor has been a problem in all the privatization methods. In the original 1990 laws, the government sought to win labor support by reserving a small percentage of shares for the workforce at special prices. But the shares proved unaffordable to many workers even at discount prices, so a 1996 law gave the workforce 15 percent of the shares of a privatized firm for free. Workers therefore got more money, but not necessarily more influence. Privatization in Poland has always been an elite-run affair, despite the powerful role played by the Solidarity trade union.

Finally, we have the many experiences of *bandit privatization*. This term refers to the illegal, semilegal, underhanded, nepotistic, coerced, and just plain criminal ways in which government elites have passed on property to themselves or their friends. All countries have had their share of these. Even Czech privatization, so admired by the West in the early 1990s, turned out by the late 1990s to have been bastions of corruption in which allies of the ruling Civic Democratic Party gained fortunes from plundering state wealth. One of the worst epidemics of bandit privatization occurred in Croatia, whose president tried to put virtually the entire economy in the hands of a few dozen loyal families. One friend of the president was able to "buy" 157 companies with no money of his own.[5] Only after the president's death in 1999 and new elections in 2000 was the public able to learn all this. Dealing with the consequences will not be easy.

Welfare State

Over the past decade, Eastern European governments have radically changed their welfare state profiles. In place of the state socialist tradition of cradle-to-grave services for everyone, their new aim is to mesh with Western Europe's policy of providing assistance chiefly for those whom the market economy leaves behind.

In the Communist era, the main social welfare benefit was provided for all: a guaranteed job. That is definitively over. Table 27.2 shows the rapid increase of unemployment throughout the region. The appearance of unemployment in East-Central Europe has meant the appearance of unemployment insurance. The general pattern is a percentage payment for a set period of time, followed by possible help from the general public assistance fund. In Poland, for example, laid-off workers receive 36 percent of the average national wage for twelve months. If after a year they are still unemployed, they then become eligible for public assistance for the indigent. Public assistance includes long-term welfare assistance for the very poorest (at 28 percent of the average wage, which still leaves the recipient impoverished), as well as one-time-only payments to help buy clothing or pay rent. Active labor market policies such as retraining and public works have also been common ways of fighting unemployment, particularly in the Czech Republic. (The comparatively low rates of unemployment in the Czech Republic can be explained not just by such policies but also by the location of the worst plants in Slovakia and the government's initial resistance to radical enterprise restructuring. When restructuring began in the late 1990s, unemployment began increasing there just when it was declining elsewhere.) In Slovakia, on the other hand, unemployment has been a far greater problem, reaching nearly 20 percent in 2001 and surpassing that level by 2004. Moreover, because of international financial pressure to reduce its budget deficit, the Slovak government in 2004 cut unemployment benefits by 50 percent, producing a spate of street protests and looting, particularly in areas with a heavy Roma population, for whom unemployment has been a particularly painful problem.

Free healthcare constituted another key benefit of the old system. Its scope and quality were deteriorating even before 1989, and they have only gotten worse since then. Governments tried to reform the healthcare sector by imposing hard budget constraints on hospitals and clinics and encouraging better-off individuals to purchase private health insurance. Private doctors now operate everywhere in the region, leading to a situation in which the wealthier have access to care that the poor do not. Of course, the old system had inequalities too. Whereas political connections were the ticket to better healthcare in the past, now money makes the difference. Today, basic healthcare is still nominally free, but many procedures, operations, and medicines are in fact available only when citizens pay.

Higher education has been reformed in a similar way. Formally, it remains free for those who pass the tough entrance exams, but student aid has been substantially reduced, and the imposition of

Table 27.2　Unemployment in the Post-Communist Era

	Registered Unemployment (percentage of labor force)									
	1990	*1994*	*1995*	*1996*	*1997*	*1998*	*1999*	*2000*	*2001*	*2004*[a]
Bulgaria	1.8	12.8	11.1	12.5	13.7	12.2	16.0	17.9	17.3	14.3
Croatia	—	17.3	17.6	15.9	17.6	18.6	20.8	22.6	3.1	19.5
Czech Republic	0.7	3.2	2.9	3.5	5.2	7.5	9.4	8.8	8.9	9.9
Hungary	1.7	10.9	10.4	10.5	10.4	9.1	9.6	8.9	8.4	5.9
Poland	6.5	16.0	14.9	13.2	10.3	10.4	13.1	15.1	17.4	20.0
Romania	1.3	10.9	9.5	6.6	8.8	10.3	11.5	10.5	8.6	7.2
Russia	—	7.8	9.0	10.0	11.2	13.3	12.2	9.8	8.7	8.5
Serbia and Montenegro	—	23.9	24.7	26.1	25.6	27.2	27.4	26.6	27.9	34.5
Slovakia	1.6	14.8	13.1	12.8	12.5	15.6	19.2	17.9	18.6	15.2
Ukraine	—	0.3	0.6	1.5	2.8	4.3	4.3	4.2	3.7	3.7

[a]2004 figures (estimates only) from *CIA World Factbook;* www.cia.gov/cia/publications/factbook/docs/profileguide.html

Source: *Economic Survey of Europe* (New York: United Nations, 2002), no. 2.

fees has become ubiquitous. For those who do not pass the exam, public universities now admit many of those students if they pay their own fees, and private universities also fill the gap. As a result, the number of students in universities has increased substantially in East-Central Europe, but the increase has been almost entirely in the paid sector.

Reforming old-age pensions was one of the key issues in the 1990s throughout Europe. In the West, pension reform was due chiefly to demographic trends showing a growing number of retirees relative to wage earners. In East Europe, it was not demographics but the economic depression of the early 1990s that created a pension crisis. In Hungary, Poland, the Czech Republic, and Slovakia, that depression led to the loss of some 5 million jobs between 1989 and 1996. With millions of near-retirement-age workers allowed early retirement and young people not hired in the first place, the imbalance between wage earners and retirees grew considerably in the early 1990s. In 1997, Hungary and Poland followed an international trend and adopted a new pension system. Instead of paying guaranteed benefits on the sole basis of contributions from current workers, younger workers now place part of their social security contributions into a private investment fund. Subsequent retirement benefits will be based largely on market performance. Given the booming international stock market of the 1990s, most people supported this reform. If, however, markets fail to maintain such spectacular growth rates in the future—and since 2000 there has indeed been a considerable slowdown—the reforms might become much less popular and promote a new crisis in the future.

In sum, East-Central Europe continues to maintain a broad social security network, rivaling that of Western Europe and surpassing that of the United States. In comparison with the Communist era, however, many social benefits have been reduced or even eliminated. In the old system, for example, the enterprise usually subsidized things like housing and vacations, but today citizens have to pay on their own. Even with the social security net, poverty remains high. In Hungary and Poland, two of the more prosperous countries, about 20 percent of the population live below the official poverty level (compared with about 14 percent in the United States). In Bulgaria and Romania, that number is about one-third.

Who is gaining and who is losing in the new Eastern Europe? Those with higher education and relative youth are doing best. Of course, not just any higher education will do. It helps to know foreign languages, particularly English, and also to know business or engineering rather than literature. It also helps to be a man, as a backlash against women in the workplace has resulted in a wave of discrimination. Those doing worst in the new Eastern Europe are the pensioners above all, followed by workers over forty-five years of age who are employed in old state enterprises and have little formal education. Education, class, and gender are paying higher returns in the post-Communist era than they ever did in the past.

Society and Economy

Economic hardship always affects politics. It is commonly accepted, for example, that dissatisfaction with the economy led Americans to vote out both Jimmy Carter and George H. W. Bush after only one term in office for each. But it is also true that economics is far from the only influence on politics. Many political scientists explain the American population's turn away from the Democratic Party in recent years as resulting in large part from an increasing cultural gap between professional, college-educated Democrats and the voters of mainstream America. Where the former cherished the principles of diversity and questioning authority, the latter emphasized the values of order and discipline; where the former emphasized the rights of minorities, the latter defended the demands of majorities; where the former sought environmentally sound growth,

the latter favored old-fashioned economic production above all else. Noneconomic factors are as important as economic ones for understanding a nation's politics.

Are the people of East-Central Europe attached to democracy as a value? Which do they consider more important: individual rights or the rights of the nation? What about the rights of minorities? Do Eastern Europeans believe in capitalism as a legitimate and desirable economic system? Do they believe in the separation of church and state? What do they think is the proper role of women in public life? Answers to these questions can tell us a great deal about how social and political life in East-Central Europe will develop.

Inequality and Minorities

The people of East-Central Europe have had a curious relationship with the problems of minorities. On the one hand, since virtually all of the region was under foreign jurisdiction less than a century ago, people have a sense that they can *all* be considered minorities—that their national identity is inherently fragile. The Czech-French writer Milan Kundera has written that to be a Central European is to be aware that nationhood is not eternal; one's own nation can potentially disappear.[6] We might imagine that such a history makes people sensitive to the problem of national minorities. At the same time, however, it makes people more committed to solidifying their own national identity whenever they have the chance. And it is this that has continually created problems for minority rights in the region.

Most of East-Central Europe's nationalities first had the chance to consolidate their nationhood only after World War I. As the former occupying powers collapsed and the new world powers espoused national self-determination, former minorities now became titular majorities, committed to building a state (government, administration, and military) to serve the interests of their newly dominant national group. The problem, however, was the situation facing citizens of *other* nationalities. With the state now officially promoting the interests of a dominant nationality, members of other nationalities automatically became second-class citizens. As the new states doled out new jobs and leadership positions, they tended to privilege citizens belonging to their "own" national group rather than citizens of "others." The national enmities this created—among both those whose national group had its "own" state nearby (such as Germans and Hungarians) as well as those that were stateless (such as Jews and Ukrainians)—contributed in large part to tearing the new states apart internally even before the Nazi onslaught.

As an ideologically internationalist party, committed to the famous line from *The Communist Manifesto* that "the working class has no nationality," the Communists were seen by many as the answer to the minority problems of the past. And indeed, in Yugoslavia, the Communists succeeded in stemming the fierce ethnic conflicts of the past. Elsewhere, however, it was the war itself, and not the Communist Party, that transformed minority politics. By 1945, most of the region's Jews had been killed, and Germans expelled. In Poland, new borders placed Ukrainians and Lithuanians in the Soviet Union instead. With few of the old minorities left, the new governments prevented the introduction of new minorities by maintaining a closed economy and sharply restricting immigration. As a result, East-Central Europe during the Communist era was more ethnically homogeneous than it had ever been in the past. Communist governments frequently spoke a patriotic-nationalist line in order to boost popularity, but there were few nationalities at hand to persecute. In officially multiethnic countries like Czechoslovakia and Yugoslavia, the government continually preached unity, although material inequalities among the nationalities certainly existed.

Minority problems reemerged powerfully in the post-Communist era. They began when official minority elites in the official multiethnic states (Czechoslovakia, Yugoslavia, and the So-

viet Union) took advantage of the new rules to break away into independent states. In doing so, however, they recreated in miniature the situation after 1918, since these new "nation-states" now had new "minorities" in them whose rights were in jeopardy. Although outside the Baltic republics and the former Yugoslavia, national minorities are still quite few—most prominent are the approximately 10 percent Hungarians in Romania and Slovakia, 9 percent Turks in Bulgaria, and a large Roma population in Hungary and Slovakia—those that are there are increasingly assertive of their identities. At the same time that this renaissance creates a cultural richness that many citizens of the dominant nationality appreciate, it always has the potential of creating tensions, too, especially in the hands of ambitious and unprincipled politicians.

Finally, tensions have begun to arise precisely as the region becomes freer and richer. With the countries of the region either in the European Union or hoping to enter in the future, they have begun to attract refugees from authoritarian countries and immigrant laborers from poor countries, including the nearby lands of the former Soviet Union. Some local residents appreciate being able to provide political and economic refuge to others, remembering that they often sought this themselves during the Communist years. Others, however, and particularly poorer citizens, are susceptible to the view spread by right-wing parties that such immigrants are "taking our jobs." Thus, a host of factors contribute to create new minority problems and inequalities that had not existed before.

Inequality and Women

Another critical noneconomic factor shaping Eastern European politics today is the role of gender. In contrast to the feminism that has transformed Western politics, however, the phenomenon here can best be described as what Peggy Watson calls *masculinism*—the policy of using power to boost men's chances in the world by cutting back the chances for women.[7] It is a peculiar kind of reaction against communism, for one of the first things communism did was to bring women en masse into the workforce. After 1989, as the threat of unemployment has hovered over all of East-Central Europe, some men said it was necessary to "reverse the legacy of communism" and fire women first. And indeed, women were the first to be let go when enterprises started cutting back. In part this was because, owing to educational patterns, women were more likely than men to be unskilled workers. Yet even when such a criterion was irrelevant, women were more likely to be laid off. Men argue that jobs are more important for them than for women, since their role is to support a family (even though many women are also heads of households). Men also contend that they work harder on the job (despite the fact that productivity has traditionally been higher for women, who are less likely to drink on the job).

Besides this, women increasingly are being hired on the basis of their looks. Companies do not even hide this fact; job notices for white-collar jobs often specify a woman under thirty as the desired candidate and require photographs as part of the application. With university education still not widely available, and without the class-based affirmative action policies of the Communist system, working-class women often find that "beauty school" is their best ticket to a good job. What seem to be operating here are not rational economic criteria but old patriarchal stereotypes and old moral and religious norms. In other words, attitudes about gender represent one more way in which noneconomic factors are profoundly shaping post-Communist politics.

The loss of jobs for women has had more dire consequences as well, leading to a boom in prostitution throughout the region and beyond. Police in Western Europe report an alarming rise in the number of Eastern European women being exported to the West to work as prostitutes. Typically the cash-poor woman, with declining opportunities at home, is recruited by a dashing man who promises her a fancy "hostess" job in a chic Western European establishment. The woman flies to the West, hands her documents to her new "employer," and is promptly told that the hostess job is "unavailable" and that she is already in debt for the cost of the airfare and room and board. She is then presented with "another way" to pay back the money. Without her documents, afraid of her "hosts" and the local police, and often unfamiliar with the language of the country she is in, the woman usually finds there is no choice. This international trafficking of women, sparked by the region's economic crisis as well as by a high external "demand" for white-skinned prostitutes (of which East Europe has, since 1989, become the world's largest supplier), now counts as one of the biggest and most nefarious of post-Communist "growth industries."[8]

The Generation Gap

Generational differences have been greatest in the region at the moment of grand systemic change. In the two great social experiments of the last half-century—the building of communism after World War II and the building of capitalism after 1989—young people strongly supported the changes while older citizens had many reservations. Young people tended to be early communism's main bastion of support because of the great social mobility that it promised. Indeed, the system had loads of good jobs for them, too—as managers, experts, policemen, and party officials—jobs that were harder for middle-aged citizens to get, who first had to prove they could be trusted. This generation gap extended itself to the factory line too, where older workers resisted the speedup and high work norms characteristic of Stalinism, which younger workers often embraced as sport. (The state in fact organized "socialist competitions" for young workers to see who could work the hardest, a practice superbly illustrated in Polish director Andrzej Wajda's wonderful film *Man of Marble*.)

In the same way, young people after 1989 gravitated heavily to capitalist democracy, too, for just as Communists did not trust older workers after 1949, capitalists did not trust them after 1989! Many new companies wanted to hire only young people "untainted" by communism, filled with individual ambition rather than collectivist loyalties. This does not mean that all young people have benefited. Education is more highly correlated with success than is age, with highly educated middle-aged people more likely to prosper than poorly educated youth. But young people *thought* they would do better, and had more opportunities to get the training necessary for the new economy. The new system also gave them the chance to travel abroad, an opportunity long denied them in the past. The early twenty-first century still finds many older citizens of the region nostalgic for the security of the past, but young people for the most part never look back.

Culturally the generation gap is not so great, since most of Eastern Europe had its own 1960s, a time of protest against authority and insistence on individual self-expression. East Europe's postwar generation came to embrace rock music and the sexual revolution every bit as much as did those in the West.[9] On issues like feminism and homosexuality, however, people in their twenties are far more open than others. Unlike in the West, where feminist organizations tend to be led by middle-aged women who came of age in the 1970s, those in the East are run mostly by women aged twenty to thirty-five, who became active only after 1989. And the fact that gay and lesbian issues can now be discussed openly is a direct result of the changed attitudes of young people.

Perhaps the major generational difference today is that young people are highly skeptical of politics. More than a decade after 1989, they are tired of hearing about the "heroes" who "overthrew" communism, and they believe that many of the new leaders are as corrupt as the old ones ever were. There are few young people in political parties and even fewer in trade unions. Where they do get involved, it tends to be in nongovernmental organizations and new social movements. At the World Bank meeting in Prague in September 2000 (its first in a former Communist country), or the European Economic Forum in Warsaw in April 2004, the protest demonstrations were led by activists in their twenties, many of whom were involved in the domestic sections of the French-based alter-globalization movement known as ATTAC. Nevertheless, political activism remains quite low among East European youth as a whole, most of whom seem to want to enjoy the freedoms they have rather than struggle for more.

The Dilemmas of European Integration

For Eastern Europe, the year 2004 was the culmination of a dream that until 1989 seemed simply utopian. Poland, Hungary, the Czech Republic, Slovakia, Slovenia, and the three Baltic republics of Estonia, Latvia, and Lithuania became full members of the European Union. Bulgaria and Romania were told they would likely be allowed to join in 2007. European integration has proceeded at a pace unimaginable even a decade ago.

The political benefits of being in the EU are clear. It signals membership in an elite club whose members are committed to the country's political stability as a liberal democracy. The economic benefits, however, are not. Entry into the EU means opening up borders to tariff-free trade, and many East Europeans fear that even with all the preparations, their countries will not be able to compete. Poland and the Czech Republic, for example, have maintained a large machine tool industry, but nothing in comparison to powerful German engineering, which could use the EU's open borders to take over eastern markets. The East might have an advantage in food production, but this is one area in which the old EU members have been highly protectionist. In 1993, the EU maintained tariffs on East European agricultural products even while reducing them on manufactured goods. While that is no longer possible in a single EU, the tough conditions of entering the EU suggest that eastern agriculture will continue to lose out. First, the old members decided that the new members will not receive the same farm subsidies as they do. Although the EU's Common Agricultural Policy (CAP) entails that member states are fully reimbursed for the subsidy payments they make to farmers, the *new* members, despite having many more farmers, will receive only small reimbursement until 2013. This means both that many low-cost farms will be forced to close, and that these already poorer states will have less cash with which to carry out their large restructuring tasks. Second, the East's export possibilities are being cut by the imposition of strict, wide-ranging EU regulatory norms, which most small producers will be unable to meet. Just prior to formal membership, for example, only 150 of Poland's food manufacturers had received licenses to export to the EU. Exactly ten times that many had already been denied.

It is no surprise that rural East Europeans thus tend to be those most worried about EU integration. Besides concerns about their export market, they fear also for their ability to maintain ownership of the land. Since the EU allows all its citizens equal access to real estate, richer westerners are likely to buy up the choice land of the East. (This is one area in which the new members were able to put restrictions on the old: free western access to eastern real estate will not kick in for seven years. In return, eastern laborers will not have free access to the western labor market for seven years.)

Another dilemma of European integration for the East is that while the EU is supposed to make the state and the economy more efficient, the new member states are having a difficult time getting the funds to carry out the restructuring to make this possible. The new members are receiving significantly lower structural adjustment funds from the EU budget than previous new entrants received, despite having many more rules to follow and a tougher environment in which to compete.

There remains much disagreement on why there has been this relatively shabby treatment of the new entrants. Some say it's because the previous fifteen members didn't really want this new round of enlargement. Others say that the old EU business and political elite wanted it, but that they didn't make the case to their citizens. In any case, there is no missing the power disparity in the European integration process. As EU officials have said all along, "The Eastern states are joining us; we're not joining them." And this power disparity clearly derives chiefly from the economic disparity: the combined gross national product of the ten new members is only about 4 percent of the old fifteen members (despite adding about 100 million new people). As one article puts it, "This is roughly the weight of Mexico's economy as compared to that of the United States."[10]

All this does not mean integration is without its benefits. Already in 1990 the EU set up a special agency charged with channeling aid to East European countries. Known as PHARE (an acronym for "Poland, Hungary: Assistance for Restructuring Economies," but whose scope extended to all former Communist countries), the agency provided technical assistance for economic restructuring and privatization policies, as well as for environmental awareness, student exchanges, promoting West European–type labor relations, and other issues of the kind. (Similar assistance was delivered by the U.S. Agency for International Development, or AID.) While some of the assistance came with a high dose of condescension, with Western "specialists" raking in high fees often benefiting them far more than the countries they were supposed to help,[11] the assistance also did help the countries prepare for the market economy. The European Bank for Reconstruction and Development, specially created in 1991 to aid the economic rebuilding of Eastern Europe, offered loans for infrastructural projects like building highways and installing pollution controls. There was also significant debt reduction for East Europe, thus giving it access to new sources of capital.

The major benefits of European integration, however, are supposed to come in the future, which is why East European citizens ultimately voted for accession despite their doubts about the high short-term costs. Whether their hopes prove prophetic or misplaced remains to be seen.

East-Central Europe in the Era of Globalization

Small states cannot shape their environment like large ones can. They must operate in a world where political and economic rule making is dominated by those large states. East-Central Europe has always been aware of its subordinate status, even within the Communist world. The Soviet Union and China may have launched grand development programs based on the notion of national self-sufficiency, but East-Central Europe has always worked together with bigger powers. From 1945 to 1989, it worked closely with the Soviet Union. In the early years, the Soviet Union exercised clear economic control over the region, confiscating raw materials and sometimes even dismantling entire factories for reinstallation in Soviet territory. By the 1970s, terms of trade became favorable for Eastern Europe, which received cheap oil from the Soviets in return for consumer goods of questionable quality. By not having to produce high-quality goods, however, the region suffered in the long run.

Since 1989, East-Central Europe has turned decisively to the West. It tries to sell its goods to the West and coordinates its economic development programs with the West. The change in orientation began after the upheaval of 1989, and intensified following the collapse of the Soviet Union. In 1988, Eastern Europe sent 27.2 percent of its exports to the former Soviet Union and 38.7 percent to all developed market economies. By 2001, the respective figures were 5.0 percent and 74.8 percent.

The chief architect of Eastern Europe's integration into the global economy has been the International Monetary Fund (IMF), whose main role is to be chief enforcer of "good" (i.e., pro-market) behavior. To get grants from Western governments or new loans from banks, East Eu-

ropean countries must get the IMF seal of approval. The IMF seeks to make sure that the loan-seeking government will reduce its budget deficit by cutting subsidies to industries and consumers and pursuing a program of rapid privatization.[12] Aware of the possibility of severe social unrest when these cuts are made, the IMF recommends the establishment of new social welfare programs and unemployment insurance. Nevertheless, it gives its all-important seal of approval only when governments follow its advice on budget reduction policies. Countries must get this approval before either the EU or NATO will consider them for entry.

Western money has also entered East-Central Europe as a result of direct foreign investment. The specific patterns of investment are different in the different countries. Whereas Poland and Hungary have supported full Western ownership, the Czech and Slovak Republics have preferred joint ventures. In the first five years after the fall of communism, Hungary received the most direct foreign investment, followed by the Czech Republic and Poland. This international investment has created new managerial jobs and has helped modernize existing factories. By the mid-1990s, however, direct foreign investment began to generate criticism among some Eastern Europeans as they learned that multinational corporations can change their plans and their investment strategies with remarkable speed. The Czech government in 1990 was delighted to accept Volkswagen's bid to help rebuild the Skoda autoworks, one of the strongest industries in the country. In 1994, however, the Czechs complained bitterly when Volkswagen decided to scale down the size of its investment considerably and move some production to plants in other countries. Hungary, meanwhile, began quarreling with General Electric, which took over Hungary's famous Tungsram light bulb company, and then gutted it. And Poland fell out with the Italian Lucchini concern after the company, having bought majority ownership in the Warsaw steel mill, drastically scaled down its commitment before it even began to invest. On the whole, East-Central Europe has benefited considerably from foreign investment. But people in the region are more critical about it, and more realistic, than they were in 1989.

If incorporation into the global economy brought new possibilities for growth and expansion, it also brought a set of new problems. Immediately after 1989, for example, it brought a major economic depression, the largest in peacetime since the Great Depression of the 1930s. It began as soon as the state decided to free prices, end subsidies and tariffs, and allow goods from abroad to compete with those produced at home. Presented with Western goods and homemade goods at comparable prices and having heard for so long about the superiority of the former, consumers jumped at the chance to feel themselves part of the West by owning its products. Many economists called for stiff tariffs to protect weak domestic industry, but Eastern Europe instead chose greater openness than the West. As a result, domestic production plummeted. Industrial output fell about 30 percent throughout the region in the first year after the fall of communism. Rarely have modern economies seen such dramatic declines. Unemployment, meanwhile, went from zero to well over 10 percent in Poland and Hungary, often reaching 30 percent or more in the small industrial towns where the large factories of the Communist era were grinding to a halt. Only the introduction of unemployment benefits and the growth of small retail trade prevented a complete economic and human catastrophe. As Table 27.2 shows, unemployment remains a serious problem even today, sometimes reaching levels higher than in the early 1990s.

Global integration has contributed to eastern economic woes in other ways too. Let us look briefly at three of them—energy costs, the Iraq wars, and the arms trade.

Energy Costs. Except for Romania, East-Central Europe does not have much in the way of oil reserves. In the past, the Soviet Union took care of this problem, selling its allies plenty of oil at a fraction of its real market value. Freedom has its price, however, and as soon as Eastern Europe broke out of the Soviet bloc, the Soviet Union demanded full global prices, payable in hard currency, to meet the region's oil needs. Whereas the West experienced its own energy-based recession in the aftermath of OPEC price hikes in the 1970s, Eastern Europe began going through a similar experience only in the early 1990s.

Iraq Wars. The West's wars and sanctions against Iraq, beginning in 1991, have taken a big toll on East Europe's economies. In the Communist era, Iraq had been an important trading partner for much of the region—far more so than for any Western member of the anti-Iraq alliance. East European teams worked there on numerous projects, installing modern machinery and receiving high salaries in return. Iraq was one of the few countries with which East Europe ran trade surpluses, and it was willing to pay debts in oil, which East Europe after 1989 needed more than ever. Overnight, however, that relationship ended. East-Central Europe's new location in the global economy made it imperative that it halt all ties with Iraq in 1990, in line with the international embargo that preceded and followed the first Gulf War. Altogether, East-Central Europe lost tens of billions of dollars as a result of the first war against Iraq in 1991. With its support of the subsequent 2003 American invasion, and the thousands of occupation troops it contributed, East Europe hoped it would begin to earn that money back. American commitments on this matter, however, have so far remained unfulfilled, as the Bush administration has chosen to award contracts first of all to its own political allies, such as Vice President Cheney's former Halliburton company. The lack of security in Iraq is another problem. By the middle of 2004, foreign contractors were being increasingly targeted by anti-occupation Iraqi fighters. This makes it difficult to bring new companies into Iraq, and difficult to recruit skilled foreign laborers (as opposed to more unskilled, lower-paid ones). The end result is that East-Central Europe has still not recouped its economic losses of the early 1990s. Indeed, this has been one of the factors for emerging resentment toward America in this traditionally pro-American region. Sanctions against Yugoslavia in the mid-1990s, it should be noted, proved equally costly to Eastern Europe.

Arms Trade. Eastern Europe has had to agree to cut back drastically on its arms manufactures as a condition of receiving Western aid. But what is to replace this revenue producer? Weapons plants can be retooled to produce other goods, but the process takes a lot of time and money. In the meantime, disrupting production in this sector has added to the general economic collapse. It has been especially painful because arms plants were frequently located in small cities far from the capital. When factories die in these areas, nothing takes their place. Perhaps not coincidentally, the United States has used this opportunity to increase its own portion of the world arms trade. The U.S. share of arms sales to Third World countries, for example, increased from 56 percent in 1992 to 73 percent in 1993. By 1997, the United States exported nearly

$11 billion worth of conventional arms, over three times more than second-place Russia. The Czech Republic, meanwhile, once East-Central Europe's most prominent producer, saw its total arms exports drop from $267 million in 1993 to a scant $19 million only four years later.[13]

Altogether, the first decade of transformation was very difficult for East-Central Europe. As Table 27.3 shows, only Poland, Hungary, and just barely the Czech Republic and Slovakia managed by 2001 to regain their gross domestic product (GDP) level of 1989. These countries have seen steady improvement since 1993 or 1994, and in this sense it can be said that life was beginning to get better. The same cannot be said for Bulgaria or Romania, or the former Yugoslavia (with the exception of Slovenia). Ukraine, meanwhile, has suffered a depression of truly historic and painful proportions.

If we look at one classic indication of whether life has gotten better or worse, life expectancy, we see that the situation for the region is mixed (see Figure 27.1). The more industrialized northern countries of the region are clearly doing better than the lesser developed countries in the

Table 27.3   Transformation by Numbers: Real GDP, 1989–2001 (1989 = 100)

	1990	1991	1992	1993	1994	1995	1996	1997	1998	1999	2000	2001
Bulgaria	90.9	83.3	77.2	76.1	77.5	79.7	72.2	68.2	70.9	72.5	76.4	79.5
Croatia	92.9	73.3	64.7	59.5	63.0	67.3	71.3	76.2	78.1	77.4	79.6	82.6
Czech Republic	98.8	87.3	86.9	86.9	88.9	94.1	98.2	97.4	96.4	96.9	100.0	103.3
Hungary	96.5	85.0	82.4	81.9	84.4	85.6	86.8	90.7	95.1	99.1	104.3	108.2
Poland	88.4	82.2	84.4	87.6	92.1	98.6	104.5	111.7	117.1	121.8	126.7	128.0
Romania	94.4	82.2	75.0	76.2	79.2	84.8	88.2	82.8	78.8	77.9	79.3	83.5
Russia	97.0	92.2	78.8	71.9	62.8	60.2	58.2	58.7	55.9	58.9	64.2	67.4
Serbia and Montenegro	92.1	81.4	58.7	40.6	41.7	44.2	46.8	50.3	51.5	42.4	45.1	47.9
Slovakia	97.5	83.3	78.0	75.1	79.0	84.1	89.0	94.0	97.7	99.0	101.2	104.5
Ukraine	96.4	88.0	79.3	68.0	52.4	46.0	41.4	40.2	39.4	39.3	41.6	45.4

Note: Beginning in 1999, figures for Serbia and Montenegro do not include Kosovo.

Source: *Economic Survey of Europe* (New York: United Nations, 2002), no. 2.

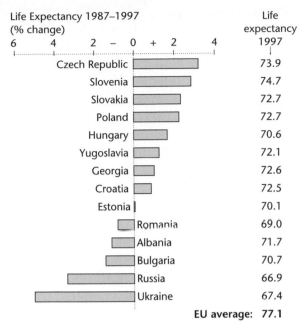

Life Expectancy 1987–1997 (% change)	Life expectancy 1997
Czech Republic	73.9
Slovenia	74.7
Slovakia	72.7
Poland	72.7
Hungary	70.6
Yugoslavia	72.1
Georgia	72.6
Croatia	72.5
Estonia	70.1
Romania	69.0
Albania	71.7
Bulgaria	70.7
Russia	66.9
Ukraine	67.4
EU average:	**77.1**

Figure 27.1   Changes in life expectancy for the region are mixed, roughly reflecting changes in basic economic conditions in the different countries.

south, while even the latter are still doing better than Russia or Ukraine.

With the twenty-first century now fully underway, Eastern Europe has definitively reentered the global economy, although in a very divided way. With the elite countries of the north poised to become full, albeit weak, players in the world around them, the southeastern countries are still, unfairly, treated more as paupers than as players.

Notes

1. Hans-Georg Heinrich, *Hungary: Politics, Economics, and Society* (Boulder, Colo.: Lynne Rienner, 1986), p. 44.

2. Daniel Chirot, "What Happened in Eastern Europe in 1989?" in Daniel Chirot, ed., *The Crisis of Leninism and the Decline of the Left* (Seattle: University of Washington Press, 1991), pp. 5–6.

3. See Roman Laba, *The Roots of Solidarity* (Princeton, N.J.: Princeton University Press, 1991), pp. 15–18.

4. See Cheryl Payer, *The Debt Trap* (New York: Monthly Review Press, 1974).

5. Tim Judah, "Croatia Reborn," *New York Review of Books,* August 10, 2000.

6. Milan Kundera, "What Is Central Europe?" Abridged version available in Gale Stokes, ed., *From Stalinism to Pluralism* (New York: Oxford University Press, 1991).

7. See Peggy Watson, "The Rise of Masculinism in Eastern Europe," *New Left Review,* no. 198 (March–April 1993): 71–82.

8. To follow developments on international trafficking and Eastern Europe, see and subscribe to "Stop-Traffic"; www.stop-traffic.org.

9. On the lure of early rock and roll in Eastern Europe, see the wonderful Hungarian film *Time Stands Still* (directed by Peter Gothar, 1981). Interestingly, recreational drug use never caught on in the East as in the West, both because of supply problems (tight border controls dissuaded potential smugglers, and low Eastern pay levels meant it was hardly worth the effort) and because of demand problems (alcohol has always been the drug of choice).

10. Andrew Moravcsik and Milada Anna Vachudova, "National Interests, State Power, and EU Enlargement," in *East European Politics and Society* 17, no. 1 (Winter 2003): 46.

11. For a powerful critique of Western aid programs to Eastern Europe, see Janine Wedel, *Collision and Collusion: The Strange Case of Western Aid to Eastern Europe, 1989–1998* (New York: St. Martin's Press, 1998).

12. For two critical views on the role of financial institutions in the rebuilding of Eastern Europe, see John Feffer, *Shock Waves: Eastern Europe After the Revolutions* (Boston: South End Press, 1992), and Peter Gowan, *The Global Gamble* (London: Verso, 1999).

13. The 1993 figure is from Eric Schmitt, "US Arms Merchants Fatten Share of Sales to Third World," *New York Times,* August 2, 1994. Other figures from Council for a Living World, Arms Trade Oversight Project; www.clw.org/atop/global_suppliers.html.

CHAPTER

28

Governance and Policymaking

It is one thing to overthrow Communist Party rule. It is something very different to construct a new system to take its place.

The paradox of the Eastern European revolutions of 1989 was that the next day, all the old state officials, save a few at the very top, went to work in the same way and in the same place as before. The police, the mayors, the journalists, the military officers, and the functionaries in the ministries all stayed in place when the Communist Party lost power. There was no violent revolutionary upheaval anywhere in Eastern Europe; even in Romania, street fighting lasted only a few days and did not concern the old bureaucracy, which stayed at its posts. In this sense, every country, not just Czechoslovakia, had a Velvet Revolution.

This institutional continuity could not last indefinitely. One of the first tasks of the former dissidents who came to power in 1989 was to recreate government. This meant rethinking the very structure of the state, creating institutions appropriate to the kind of democracies the creators hoped to build. The new leaders had to create new ways of exercising power, devise rules for the relationships between the president and parliament, the executive and legislature, citizens and the state, parties and the state. Suddenly institutions were important. All the issues of state building—issues that students in the West tend to see as matters settled long ago—had to be confronted as if for the very first time.

It might seem that politicians, in conditions like these, could calmly look around, take stock of the world's political institutions, and choose those that worked best. But in fact the political arrangements that emerged had more to do with the domestic political battles of the day than with considerations of ideal democratic institutions. For example, countries with strong single individuals leading the fight against communism, such as Poland and Russia (with Lech Walesa and Boris Yeltsin, respectively), began to develop presidential systems; those where the struggle was more diffuse, such as Hungary and the former Czechoslovakia, produced parliamentary systems. The rule seems to be applicable to the drafting of constitutions in all countries at all times: the pull of the present is at least as powerful as the lure of the future.

Organization of the State

Contrary to what many Americans believe, there are various types of democratic systems. The U.S. system, in fact, as a strong *presidential system*, is rather unusual, with its popularly elected president as the indisputable political leader who is responsible for forming a government, naming a cabinet, and shaping the legislative agenda. Most democratic systems are *parliamentary systems*, in which a single house of parliament is responsible for electing the country's political leader, who then rules in close cooperation with parliament and can be removed by parliament at any time. Some countries, like France, have a *semipresidential system*, in which executive power is divided between a popularly elected president and a prime minister enjoying the support of the legislature.

In East-Central Europe, the clear preference so far has been for a parliamentary system, not a presidential one. For example, Hungary, the Czech Republic, and Slovakia all have strict parliamentary systems; the deputies, freely elected by the people, choose a prime minister to form a government. In Poland, Solidarity leader Lech Walesa hoped to push through a presidential system, but had to settle for a semipresidential one. The absence of a strong president, however, does not indicate a weak executive branch. On the contrary, *executive authority*—the power to carry out decisions—is strong throughout East-Central Europe, as befits a region undergoing rapid transformations where decisions need to be made fast and there is general agreement on the move to a market economy. There is not much check on the power of the executive either, as the judiciary tends to be weak in former Communist states.

One of the main criticisms heard from democratic activists was that the Communist system led to overcentralization of power. Such overcentralization occurred because Communist states, for the most part, were unitary as opposed to federalist. In a *unitary state*, the country is governed as if it were one giant unit, whereas in a *federal state*, only overarching affairs like defense and monetary policies are centralized; on other matters, local units have considerable autonomy. In the old unitary states of Eastern Europe, power was extremely centralized. Authorities in the capital made all the important decisions. Local leaders were appointed from above and, deprived of their own tax base, had neither the funds nor the authority to take much action on their own. Whether they wanted to build a new school or increase support for local cultural activities, they needed approval from the center. Yugoslavia and Czechoslovakia, as well as the Soviet Union, were exceptions to this rule. The diverse nationalities making up these countries formally had their own local governing bodies. Yet even these were not true federalist arrangements; the central authorities still appointed local leaders and exercised the power of the purse.[1]

One might assume, therefore, that post-Communist politics would entail new federalist structures, in which local regions and communities would take vast responsibility for their own affairs. In fact, that has not been the case. Three factors seem to be responsible for continued centralization. First, the new governments have been anxious to see their broad economic reform plans embrace the entire country, and so have been reluctant to cede power to local regions. Second, local regions themselves often fear the loss of state funds that might result from decentralization. Federalism is good for local political activists looking for a new institution to control, but regular people tend to fear new and costly experiments. When the ex-Communist Democratic Left Alliance won power in Poland in 1993, for example, it cited local fears about the costs of taking over public schools as justification for its abandonment of regional decentralization schemes.

Finally, federalism has not taken hold for the simple reason that regional autonomy has traditionally been one of the area's greatest problems, as evidenced by the breakup of Czechoslovakia and the disintegration into chaos of the former Yugoslavia and Soviet Union. Countries that have already experienced regional division have been the most anxious to maintain strong central control. In the Czech Republic, for example, the Klaus government tried to block the creation of new regional self-governing bodies even after the constitution of December 1992 explicitly required that such bodies be formed. Allowing real decentralization, the government felt, would recreate the kind of administrative dualism that precipitated the breakup of Czechoslovakia in the first place. This episode also serves to remind us that just because a constitution requires a particular arrangement does not mean that such an arrangement actually exists.

In general, relations between the legislature and the executive have not been highly contentious in post-Communist East-Central Europe. The legislatures have generally been supportive of a strong executive office, both because they agree that rapid decisions are necessary in the chaotic post-Communist environment, and because a strong executive is simply the usual European way.

The Executive

Poland was the first East European country to undergo major political transformation. It did so, however, before its politicians were sure just how far change would be allowed to go. The result was initial instability, as institutions were created for a political situation that almost immediately became obsolete. Poland's path to postcommunism began with the 1989 roundtable negotiations between the Communist Party and the opposition Solidarity union, still many months before the fall of the Berlin Wall. Opposition negotiators had a very delicate objective: to ease the Communists out of power and establish a foundation for full parliamentary democracy, while assuring party hard-liners and the Soviet Union that their interests would still be taken into account. The goal was to engineer a stable transition, and that meant offering benefits to all sides.

The two sides worked out an arrangement for partially free elections, in which the Communists would be guaranteed a majority in the lower house, while a newly created upper house would be contested in full. In return for the government's final approval of the deal, Solidarity also agreed to the creation of a presidency. Because the president would be elected by parliament and the first parliament would be dominated by the Communists regardless of how people voted, the roundtable negotiators knew that General Wojciech Jaruzelski, who had imposed martial law banning Solidarity in 1981, would become Poland's president. They debated the powers of the presidency with this in mind. Solidarity originally wanted a weak president—someone to be little more than a reassuring symbol to the Soviet Union and domestic hard-liners. The Communists wanted a strong president who had the right to dissolve parliament and rule by decree. The rules that were finally drafted favored Soli-

darity's vision. As expected, General Jaruzelski was elected by parliament (though with only a one-vote margin) and became essentially a figurehead president who helped keep the hard-liners at bay while allowing democratization to proceed on its own.

The situation was changing so suddenly, however, that this arrangement soon became obsolete. A Solidarity official became prime minister in August. In November, the Berlin Wall came down, followed soon by the downfall of the governments of East Germany, Bulgaria, Czechoslovakia, and Romania. By the end of the year, it was clear that neither the Soviet Union nor local hard-liners would be needing the guarantees Poland's arrangement had left them. At the vanguard of political innovation ever since 1980, Poland now seemed to be lagging, so Lech Walesa decided that he would run for president—even though no elections were scheduled. He explained his decision as follows: "I don't want to, but I have to." Parliament duly changed the law, thus allowing for early presidential elections, and General Jaruzelski duly resigned. In December 1990, Walesa was elected president, this time in general elections open to all.

At this point the old arrangement proved intolerable, for Walesa had taken over a presidency with powers written for Jaruzelski. He wanted to be an activist president—a "president with an axe," he promised during the campaign—but the rules did not allow that. Walesa looked to the new parliament, elected in 1991, to ratify changes giving the presidency more power. But that was not so simple, for Walesa had alienated most of his political supporters by not attacking remnants of the old regime as vigorously as he had promised. The Center Alliance, for example, which had been created to promote Walesa's candidacy, became his fiercest opponent only months into his presidency. So although Solidarity supporters ostensibly won the 1991 parliamentary elections, the new parliament ended up in many ways more antipresidential than before.

For the first six months of 1992, the president was in a virtually constant battle with the prime minister, and the existing constitution was useless in resolving the conflicts. On the contrary, it only made them worse. For example, the constitution implied, but did not explicitly state, that high-level military appointments by the prime minister should have the approval of the president. In fact, Walesa learned of them only from television news accounts. When he sought to maintain his own independent contacts with the military, the truculent defense minister accused Walesa of preparing a presidential coup d'état. Only when the prime minister and cabinet were forced to resign in June 1992 did parliament finally legislate a workable relationship between the president and parliament. The new arrangement, which the new constitution of 1997 formally enshrined, produced a semipresidential system, in which power is distributed between the two authorities. This arrangement is a bit confusing (even for Poles), since it means there are basically two executive branches in Poland, the president and the prime minister, with the latter ultimately more important than the former. The president is weaker than in the United States or France but stronger than almost everywhere else in Eastern Europe except Russia.

In some ways, Poland's system seems to resemble that of the United States. The president is directly elected by the public to a five-year term, has the right to propose legislation, and is in charge of foreign and defense policy. Parliament must pass all laws, but the president has the right to veto them. Parliament can override only by a two-thirds majority. The president can also demand that a constitutional tribunal rule on the constitutionality of legislation. The law is then suspended until the tribunal makes its decision.

Poland remains a parliamentary system, however, in that the chief executive is not the president but the prime minister, who is chosen by a parliamentary majority. The prime minister is responsible for the day-to-day workings of the government, such as drafting a budget or calling on the police to halt a demonstration. He or she can be ousted only if the government loses a parliamentary vote of confidence. Similar to Germany, Poland's system calls for a *constructive vote of no confidence*, meaning that the parliament must propose an alternative prime minister at the same time it votes down the current one. In 2000, for example, the prime minister lost his parliamentary majority during midterm, but because parliament could not agree on a successor, he stayed on as head of a minority government.

Only in the former republics of Yugoslavia do presidents have greater power than in Poland, and that power has been due more to the war legacy than to the constitution. The weakest presidency in Eastern Europe, however, can be found in the Czech Republic, owing both to the Czech constitution and the behavior of its initial occupant, Vaclav Havel. According to the constitution, the president does not even have the power to propose legislation. Elected by parliament, not the public, the president can veto laws passed by the legislature, but the latter can override by a simple majority. Since this is the same number as was needed to pass the law in the first place, such a veto is not very effective. The president can dissolve parliament and call for new elections, but only if the lower house either votes out the prime minister or is incapable of passing legislation for more than three months. The president is not completely powerless. He or she appoints the prime minister, supreme court, and constitutional court and is commander in chief of the armed forces. But for the first years of his presidency, Havel made little avail of the powers he had and did little to intervene in the workings of the government. Instead, his was above all else a moral voice, attempting to guide the country's political as well as existential direction. So ingrained is the notion of a weak president, however, that when Havel intervened during a parliamentary crisis in 1998, this action led a sizable number of deputies to propose new legislation revoking the president's power of appointments. Havel backed down.

Cabinet Government

In addition to the president or prime minister, the executive branch of government consists of the cabinet and the ongoing bureaucracy charged with implementing policy. Cabinet ministers in East European countries, as in other European democracies, are nominated by the prime minister and approved or rejected by parliament. Once approved, they are largely free to pursue policy implementation vigorously in their areas of responsibility. Confrontations with parliament have been rare, as parliaments tend not to keep close tabs on the workings of the bureaucracy and the policies it implements.

This lack of attention is particularly evident in the crucial area of economic policy. The chief role of the legislature is to approve the annual budget proposed by the prime minister. Legislative debates invariably change a few features, but by and large the budget is adopted in the form presented. Day-to-day economic management is also the prerogative of the executive office. Sometimes crucial decisions are made by one minister, without interference even from the prime minister. During the initial periods of post-Communist shock therapy, this practice of concentrating power—in this case, in the office of the Finance Ministry—reached monumental proportions. In Poland, for example, Finance Minister Leszek Balcerowicz ran economic policy virtually as his own private fiefdom. Neither the prime minister nor the president did anything to interfere.[2]

Since 1989, all East European governments have grappled with the question of how to privatize the economy. This policy question has become almost the exclusive domain of the executive branch. Government ministries were created to administer the extensive property transformation, and they have done so with only occasional intervention by the legislature. In Hungary, the State Property Agency decided which firms were to be privatized, to whom, and for how much. In Poland, firms in 1989 were legally governed by enterprise councils elected by the workforce, but once they conceded those rights to the Ministry of Property Transformation, the latter decided on its own how to privatize those firms. In the former East Germany, a West German state agency, Treuhand, ran rough-shod over all other interests in allocating state assets into private hands.

Only on particularly controversial issues is policy initiative ceded to the legislature. This has happened, for example, on the thorny question of *reprivatization*. Are people to be compensated for property taken over by the Communist parties? If so, how, and who decides the price? What form should compensation take, since the property itself, fifty years later, is not likely to exist in the form in which it was confiscated? What about Jewish property seized first by the Nazis, and then taken over by the state when the Jews did not return? These questions have aroused far more emotional disagreement than the issue of mere privatization. For that reason, governments decided that it was best to throw the issue into the legislatures' laps. These issues have still not been resolved satisfactorily.

A major problem facing the executive bureaucracy as a whole is the absence of strict ethical rules, which leads to recurring charges of conflict of interest. Ministers and their underlings, for example, often sit on boards of directors of companies that they deal with in an official capacity. Publicly they explain this practice as a remedy for the shortage of sufficient experts in a given field. No doubt it also results from the comparatively low pay of government officials. They feel they are already sacrificing for the public good by agreeing to serve in government, and they see nothing wrong in earning a little extra on the side. For the public, however, what is going on is personal enrichment at public expense. Much of the time, there may be nothing illegal going on. The practice does, however, lead to popular perceptions of wrongdoing and to much negative opinion about government. Suspicion is not likely to disappear until strict ethical rules are put in place.

Bureaucracy and Civil Service

Below the rank of cabinet minister and vice minister, we enter the ranks of the civil service bureaucracy. The term *bureaucracy* often carries with it a negative connotation, implying crony-ism and routine decision making, but a well-functioning bureaucracy is a vital part of sound government. The classic definition was offered in the early twentieth century by the great German social scientist Max Weber (1864–1920), for whom the ideal type of bureaucracy is the group of neutral, well-trained civil servants who administer state policy continuously regardless of which party or government is in office. In the years since the fall of communism, one of East-Central Europe's main goals has been the construction of just such a bureaucracy. To try to achieve this goal, the new regimes have first had to attack the old system of state service known as *nomenklatura*. In that arrangement, the Communist Party chose people for key positions in the state and economy on the basis of political criteria and loyalty to party leadership. Although the *nomenklatura* system abated over the years as increasing numbers of professionals were trained, it remained a continual source of friction between the Communist state and society, a reminder that high qualifications and good work were not always enough for someone to get ahead.

The post-Communist system is supposed to be based on merit. People are supposed to obtain positions in the bureaucracies because of training or hard work. And for the most part it has worked this way. Many people who could not advance in the past for political reasons have been able to make careers in the post-Communist political, economic, and cultural spheres. The European Union (EU) added its own pressure: all countries hoping to join had to pass a civil service law as a precondition for consideration. Expertise, efficiency, and political neutrality are stressed as the ethos of the new public servant.

Transforming bureaucracies, however, is a slow process. In the first post-Communist years, attempts at change did not seem to be working out the way they should. On the contrary, bureaucrats from the past were holding onto their positions or even moving ahead. The old system was gone, but the same people who had made it

in the old system were making it in the new one. For people at the top levels of the old bureaucracy, such as bankers and diplomats, perseverance was sometimes facilitated by complex personal ties, which created room for blackmail and corruption. For civil servants lower down in the hierarchy, however, the reason for their perseverance was simply their experience and better training. They may have gotten that experience and training for the wrong reasons, but if the new system was to be based on qualifications, these people had them.

Peggy Simpson, an American journalist living in Poland, told me a story that illustrates this scenario well. In one small town, a newly elected mayor, hoping to weed out purely political appointees and put together a staff of competent officials, ordered new civil service exams for the old staff and anyone else who wanted to take them. When the results came in, the old personnel had the best grades. The "democratic" bureaucracy thus came to look almost identical to the "Communist" bureaucracy, despite the abolition of *nomenklatura*. The old elite was managing to become the new elite.

Public and Semipublic Institutions

East-Central Europe emerged from the Communist system in 1989 with tens of thousands of state-owned enterprises (SOEs). Under the old system, and particularly in the early Communist years, the chief goal of SOEs was not to make a profit, and not even to make goods, but to help ensure social and political stability. State factories and enterprises "solved" the unemployment problem by providing jobs for all. They tackled housing problems by building apartment complexes for their employees. Trade unions at the work sites arranged vacations for employees and summer camps for their children, and often they distributed scarce food and appliances to their members. By acting much like social welfare agencies in the West, besides producing goods, SOEs were a crucial part of the entire political system.

Since 1989, the nature of Eastern Europe's state-owned enterprises has changed dramatically. In the first place, each country has embarked on a program of privatization. But even those enterprises that remain state owned have been fundamentally transformed: They are charged with making a profit and threatened with closure if they cannot perform. Consequently, most of them are no longer the social providers they were in the past. They have sold their housing units, closed their vacation bureaus, and stopped procuring scarce consumer goods for employees. Most important, they no longer guarantee citizens a job. Not all SOEs have cut all their services. In cities that are built around a single state enterprise and thus have an inflexible labor market, the enterprise typically maintains more services than in cities where the labor market is more open. Nevertheless, the nature of the firm in East-Central Europe has changed dramatically in recent years.

When enterprises become privately owned and individually managed, the role of regulatory agencies becomes increasingly important. At least it should be. In East Europe, however, the reaction against Communist-era state control led to widespread neglect of working conditions and on-the-job safety. Governments were so anxious to promote private business that they offered not only tax breaks but virtual immunity from regulations. Safety rules, overtime provisions, guaranteed vacations, and other benefits have been violated with impunity, particularly in small, private firms. The situation is somewhat better in larger firms with a higher profile and in state firms where unions are still active. Even there, however, official accounts regularly report routine violations and lax regulation.

Willful neglect is not the only cause. Insufficient budgetary funds are also a key problem, and regulatory agencies tend to be at the bottom of the receiving line. This neglect extends to pollution control agencies. While Eastern Europe has made some strides in fighting pollution, such as installing filters on smokestacks in the giant factories, agencies do not actively combat the dumping of toxic wastes or the lesser but steady polluting practices of small, private firms.

One reason there is little money in the coffers for regulatory agencies is that tax collection does not yet operate efficiently. Under the Communist system, governments got their funds simply by taking the revenues earned by the country's enterprises. The need for separate, elaborate taxation policies appeared only with the privatization of the post-Communist era. Within a few years, most countries in the region introduced a progressive personal income tax, levied through deductions and a year-end reckoning (as in the United States), as well as a host of disparate corporate taxes. The problem is collection. Due to both abuse of the prevalent tax breaks for business and inadequate and underfunded collection agencies, millions of dollars in revenues are lost each year to unpaid taxes. More efficient collection depends on having more efficient bureaucracies, which in turn depends on more state revenues. Poor tax collection is likely to persist for some years to come, as long as governments continue to see the promotion of business activity as the number-one policy goal and turn a blind eye to the private sector's willful tax evasion.

Other State Institutions

In the Communist era, East European citizens had frequent complaints about the police and the judicial system, and objected to the lack of true self-government. Since 1989, these institutions have all undergone thoroughgoing reform, although not always producing the most desirable results.

The Military and the Police

Most nondemocratic countries in the late twentieth century had strong and independent militaries. This was true for Latin America, which saw a succession of military dictatorships, and even for China, where the military has frequently played a more important political role than the Communist Party. It was not the case in Eastern Europe, however. From 1945 until 1989, the military played a secondary, subordinate role in the political system. In fact, it was doubly subordinate—first to the ruling Communist Party and then to the Soviet Red Army.

The party established the principle of civilian rule as soon as it came to power. But the subordination to the Soviet Union was especially painful. Each country's particular military history and doctrines were ignored as the Soviet Union became the model for everything. Officers studied in Soviet schools and prepared plans based on Soviet interests. Overall strategy was determined by the Warsaw Pact, ostensibly a union for regional defense against NATO. In reality, the Warsaw Pact's chief goal was to uphold Soviet domination of the region. This reality was made clear in 1968, when the Soviets invaded Czechoslovakia and used East European troops to assist in the occupation. Only Romania did not participate.

Perhaps because the military was not directly involved in government, it remained a popular institution in Eastern Europe. Even in Poland, when the military declared martial law in 1981, most people recognized that it was simply doing the bidding of the party. This lingering support has helped the military redefine its role in the post-Communist era. The military is still subordinate to the civilian government (in this sense, the Communist past has been helpful for democracy). But it is being repackaged as a vital national institution. It is presented as a symbol of independence, an institution that has always served the nation loyally and will continue to do so in the future. The military is thus helping to legitimate the new political systems by linking them to the pre-Communist past.

Since the mid-1990s, the military has undergone yet another transformation—being incorporated into NATO. To a large extent, this has meant that the previous subordination to the Soviet Union has been exchanged for a similar one to the United States. Officers now study in American schools, their soldiers train with

American troops, and plans are tailored to NATO interests. Membership does, however, ensure that the military does not become too independent, since civilian control over the army is an enshrined NATO principle.

The exception to the story of a weak military is the former Yugoslavia. With the onset of civil war in 1991, the military emerged as a dominant political player in both Serbia and Croatia. That began to change with the death of Croatia's president Franjo Tudjman in 1999 and the coming to power of liberals a year later, and the electoral defeat of Serbia's Slobodan Milosevic in fall 2000. Until all the new borders of all the post-Yugoslav countries have withstood the test of time, however, and the causes of the war are finally eradicated, the military will likely remain stronger than elsewhere in Eastern Europe.

Far more than the military, it was the police that was the feared institution of Communist society. Too often an unchecked power with vast secret networks and large numbers of citizen collaborators frequently blackmailed into service, the police penetrated every aspect of everyday life. This was particularly true in the Stalinist era, although even in the late stages of the Communist period, citizens needed police approval for all kinds of common requests, such as obtaining a passport to travel abroad.

In a very real sense, reforming the police was the first order of business of the post-Communist period. The first task was to impose restraint. New governments gave orders, effective immediately, instructing the police to desist from arresting political activists and to allow basic democratic expression. Comprehensive internal reform, however, has come more slowly. Although some police officials were fired for their previous activities, most, even those engaged in active persecution of the opposition, were judged to have merely been following orders. These have been given new training and allowed to stay on the force. Retention rates are even higher among the top espionage forces, whose services have largely been retained, with orders to redeploy those services against other enemies.

Today most citizens have a very different view of the police than they did in the past and no longer see them as a feared enemy. On the other hand, not everything has changed. When protestors from around the world swarmed on Prague in September 2000 to rally against globalization and the International Monetary Fund, Czech police arrested and held incommunicado thousands of people, denying them food and the right to contact an attorney, and beating many detainees.[3] It is possible that such force was used at the request of the West (Seattle police were equally ruthless in their repression of similar demonstrations in 1999), but clearly much of the old repressive apparatus still remains in place. Old traditions always die hard.

The Judiciary

Citizens often come into conflict with the state, and parliaments and executives often come into conflict with one another. And although constitutions may serve as the ultimate authority, people regularly disagree on just what the constitution actually means. Resolving these conflicts is the task of the third branch of government, to which we now turn.

The judiciary in East-Central Europe is the least powerful of the three branches of government—more likely to accept the decisions of the executive and legislature than to challenge them. This relative weakness is rooted in two factors: the experiences of the Communist era, when the courts too often acted as the arm of the Communist Party, and the region's roots in continental European traditions, in which the judiciary has always been weaker than in the Anglo-American model.

In the United States, the judiciary's role is to make sure not only that the people abide by the laws but also that the government does so. As a check on government, the judiciary plays a much less substantial role in East-Central Europe—as it does, indeed, in all of Europe. Of course, it played an even more pliant role during the Communist era, particularly in the early years, when

the party regularly violated judicial independence and instructed judges how to decide particular cases. The courts have regained their full independence today. As appointed rather than elected officials, judges naturally tend to share the same broad policy orientations as the leading government officials. But they are fully free to decide cases in accord with their consciences and based solely on the rule of law.[4]

Even with this independence, however, the courts still play a less activist role than in the United States. The difference is rooted in the very nature of the legal systems. In most of Europe, law is strictly codified, and the judiciary's responsibility is to apply the law as it is written. In the United States, ever since the early nineteenth century, the judiciary has cast itself as a check on government, an authority charged with deciding whether the other two branches of government have a right to act as they do. The U.S. Supreme Court not only applies the law; its statements *become* the law. This is not the case in Eastern Europe, whose courts share the dominant continental view that lawmaking should be left to legislators rather than judges.

This does not mean there is no check on government. Constitutional courts, charged with assessing the constitutionality of laws, now exist in all East European countries. Typically the president appoints the constitutional court's members, who are confirmed by parliament and serve for a set number of years. This body, however, can only suggest changes in legislation, and its decisions can usually be overturned by a new parliamentary vote. The government is sensitive to the decisions of its constitutional court and usually makes some effort to abide by the court's rulings. But in the end, it is parliament, not the court, that has the ultimate decision on what is and is not the law of the land. It would be wrong, in other words, to equate East-Central Europe's constitutional courts with the U.S. Supreme Court.

Of course, the influence of each constitutional court depends on the specific country. So far, Hungary has had the most active judiciary, with the constitutional court getting involved in political issues that elsewhere are the prerogative of parliament, such as the privatization process. Indeed, one of the reasons de-Communization, or "lustration" (the ousting of former top Communist Party officials), has not gone as far in Hungary as elsewhere is that the constitutional court took action to prevent it. In Czechoslovakia, for example, the *absence* of a strong court allowed lustration fever to flourish in the early post-Communist years, with dangerous consequences. Indeed, this period saw some of the most egregious violations of basic civil liberties in post-Communist East-Central Europe, as in the case of Jan Kavan. Kavan had been one of Czechoslovakia's most important and indefatigable oppositionist activists for over two decades. In exile since the Soviet invasion of 1968, he had founded a publishing house for dissident Czech literature and created one of the best networks for smuggling such literature into the region. Acclaimed as a hero after 1989, Kavan was easily elected to the new parliament in 1990. Then one day in March 1991, the lustration commission charged with rooting out former secret police agents still active on the Czech political scene announced that Kavan had been an informer for the secret police. Kavan vehemently denied this, but he could neither learn the exact charges against him nor see the evidence. Nevertheless, he was soon forced to resign from parliament in disgrace.[5] It looked like a scene from early-twentieth-century Czech writer Franz Kafka's harrowing novel *The Trial*, in which Joseph K. is arrested and tormented without ever knowing why. Things were supposed to be different in these democratic years after 1989, but the Czechoslovak lustration commission had complete control over the process, without judicial oversight.

As it happened, it took a few years before Kavan could exonerate himself. It seemed that the only "evidence" against him was the fact that, as a 1969 student abroad, he met to discuss émigré student matters with a staffer from the Czech embassy who claimed, quite plausibly, to be a supporter of the Prague Spring. In 1996, Ka-

van was officially cleared of all charges. Two years later, he became the Czech Republic's foreign minister. Nevertheless, the episode showed what can happen when the justifiable desire to expose agents from the past occurs without the safeguarding of legal rights. Witch hunts are far more dangerous to democracies than the presence of a few former police agents. Other countries introducing lustration laws have tried to take these unfortunate Czech lessons into account.

One of the most glaring weaknesses of Eastern Europe's judicial system is that it has traditionally been difficult for ordinary citizens to use. In Communist as well as continental traditions, citizens do not have much chance to appeal to the courts against abuses of power by government or by other citizens.* In response to the mass popular protests of 1989, as well as in an effort to create governments more responsive to citizens, the difficulty of legal appeal has recently begun to change. One of the most important innovations has been the introduction of the post of ombudsperson, or civil rights officer. Borrowed from Sweden, this institution was first established in Poland under the Communist system, in 1987, as part of the government's reform program. The ombudsperson is appointed by the president, subject to parliamentary approval, and is a sort of free-floating civil rights troubleshooter. Citizens appeal directly to the ombudsperson when they feel their civil rights have been violated by the government, and the ombudsperson takes up the matter directly with the offending institution or refers it for a binding court decision. At the request of an individual citizen or a government body (or on his or her own), the ombudsperson can identify a law or policy as contrary to the civil rights of a certain group of people and refer it to the constitutional court for a ruling.

---

*The United States is unique in both respects: in the number of lawsuits among citizens and in the ability of individuals to sue the government to force a change in the law, as in the landmark cases that abolished segregated schools (*Brown v. Board of Education*) and legalized abortion (*Roe v. Wade*).

This new institution has been quite successful in making the daunting world of legality more accessible and user friendly. Hungary adopted it in 1993. The Czech Republic stalled but finally passed an ombudsman law in late 1999. The ombudsperson plays an important role in legitimizing the new political systems in the eyes of the population by giving people a sense that their voices can be heard.

Finally, as new members of the European Union, countries in the region have adopted the European Convention on Human Rights and recognize the jurisdiction of the European Court of Human Rights in Strasbourg. Thanks to EU membership, citizens can now appeal their national courts to a Europe-wide body, where the decision is final.

Subnational Government

East-Central Europe does not have a tradition of strong independent local self-government. This fact derives from both the region's long history of foreign occupation and the interwar years of independence, when each state dreamed up grand developmental schemes that could be implemented only by an interventionist central government.

One of the chief accusations against the Communist system was that too much power was concentrated in the center. As a result, post-Communist East-Central Europe has done some experimenting with decentralization. The process, however, is far from complete. For one thing, even the most committed decentralizers in the national governments have not wanted to give up control all at once. They have preferred to institutionalize the new rules and procedures of a market economy and *then* hand over some power to local authorities. In addition, many leaders remain suspicious of local power, citing the Yugoslav, Czechoslovak, and Soviet examples in which regional governments turned into alternative power bases, leading to secession and, in two of the three cases, civil war.

There is an irony in the widespread desire to give local communities more control over their own affairs. Although they could not elect their own leaders in the old system, small communities actually did not fare badly in Communist society. Since investment decisions were made with political stability rather than profits in mind, the central government distributed resources widely. Small cities unlikely to receive investment funds in a private economy (and unable to find them today) had new factories literally thrust on them. Local authorities, rewarded based on how well they administered their areas, had a strong interest in forcefully representing local needs to higher authorities. And the higher authorities, wanting stability, kept doling out funds for factories and cultural activities no matter how uneconomical they were. Small towns thus had clout for two reasons: because they were run by party activists trying to make a career for themselves, and because the government kept putting money into projects to keep people employed and content.

The transition to a market economy has changed this rather congenial arrangement. The new central governments needed to reduce expenditures and cut subsidies in their efforts to balance their budgets and please foreign lenders and potential investors. The first way they did so was by dramatically cutting aid to local communities. In Poland, for example, soon after the first free local elections in May 1990, the central government shifted to local governments the responsibility for funding day care centers, nurseries, cultural institutions, and local utilities. The problem was that the local communities were unable to support these services. Many towns do not even have regular revenues, both because the large enterprises in their areas are closing down and because tax collecting is so irregular. As former Solidarity officials took over local power, they had to make the kinds of tough budget decisions no politician wants to make. In two cities I visited in 1994, two former Solidarity activists who had become elected officials were fighting for their political lives because they had had to close a few sparsely used day care centers. "I didn't fight against communism in order to do this," they both told me. Inevitably, in the 1994 local elections, they were both branded as "antichildren" politicians and were defeated.

Local governments faced similar problems throughout Eastern Europe. Moreover, besides fighting with the central government, local officials also began to fight one another. The first free local elections in Hungary in 1990, for example, produced situations in which opposition parties won a majority in local councils while former Communists won election as mayors. Instead of trying to manage this outcome, quite common in democracies, the local councils in about one hundred small towns and villages made use of loopholes to prevent the mayors from taking office. Such activities would come back to haunt the non-Communist politicians in the form of accusations that they were obstructing stable government.

One of the reasons local affairs often became rather chaotic was the almost complete absence of political parties at the local level. The forty-five-year monopoly of power by the Communist Party, followed by a general dissatisfaction with parties afterward, meant that when Communist rule collapsed, no organized parties were ready to coordinate power anew. The new parties of the anti-Communist opposition were based in large urban centers. In small towns, the new elite consisted of isolated individuals with little experience in working together in complex organizations. The former Communists repeatedly harped on this theme of their opponents' political inexperience, in contrast to their own political seasoning. Opinion polls show that dissatisfaction with quarrelsome new politicians, and appreciation of the former Communists' more level-headed approach, were among the key reasons for the latter's electoral successes beginning in the mid-1990s.

It would be quite wrong, however, to speak only of the negative features of post-Communist local politics. The other side of the coin is that local areas are now free to govern themselves.

Whereas the central party apparatus used to appoint mayors and the city council, now they are elected by the citizens. The new, democratically elected leaders can make decisions about the town that reflect their own interests rather than the interests of planners in Warsaw, Prague, or Budapest. Small cities may no longer have friends in the capital always willing to throw money their way, but at least they are free to devise their own solutions to the problems they face. For a great many people, that is the most important feature of all.

The European Dimension

Even before entering the European Union, the preparation for doing so affected East European politics and governance in numerous ways. First of all, it meant that their parliaments had to spend most of their time passing the EU's rules and laws. The collection of those rules, called the Community *acquis*, runs a gargantuan eighty thousand pages, and East Europe's parliamentarians (or at least their assistants who actually write the legislation) have become familiar with a great many of them.

Right from the start, then, we have here the same theme of *power disparity* that we saw when discussing economic aspects of integration in Chapter 27. Eastern Europe's parliaments have been busy passing laws they had no say in implementing. Even more, because the previous EU had been so lukewarm about admitting the new members, and so many at one time, they monitored the accession process extremely closely—much too closely for East Europeans who resented such intrusive supervision and the implications it carried. This was more than the familiar "democratic deficit" criticized so often in the West: the problem here was not just that citizens played little role in making EU policy but that entire governments were treated as little more than supplicants, forced to pass the bills their overseers asked them to pass.

Scholars trying to characterize the nature of the relationship between the old EU and the Eastern applicants resorted to unflattering analogies: missionary-savage or priest-penitent.[6] In the first version, the old EU plays the role of "civilizer," even colonizer, pushing the witless "natives" to do what's in their best interest, which they do not know themselves. The second version is just a softer variation: the all-knowing "priest," privy to the knowledge of the divine, coaxes the naïve subject in the matters of the truth, administering sanctions when necessary but offering forgiveness when possible (that is, when followed by promises of correcting behavior in the future). These may be harsh characterizations, but the fact is that virtually all the adaptations so far have been made by one side only.

The EU enforced even stricter requirements than it had during previous enlargements, and announced that monitoring would continue after full membership as well. Even more, on some issues such as guaranteeing minority rights, the new countries were "asked to meet standards the EU-15 have never set for themselves."[7]

All this points to the ways in which Western Europe was initially quite unenthusiastic about enlargement. The EU had evolved in the era of a divided Europe and had become quite comfortable with the status quo. In 1989, it had only recently gone through the process of admitting the poorer countries of Spain and Portugal and was not anxious to repeat the experience. Germany's annexation of the former East Germany was already proving to be extraordinarily costly to the EU as a whole. Also, the EU's main concern after 1989 was to maintain good relations with the Soviet Union (which survived until 1991), and it feared that enlargement would endanger those relations.

Yet the EU was in a dilemma. It had bandied about all-European unification as an ultimate goal ever since its foundation. Now that the East was ready to pursue it, the EU could not very easily abandon the idea. Also, the West began to see that the risks of *not* enlarging outweighed the risks of doing so. They had seen in the former Yugoslavia what can happen on European

soil even today when economic crisis intersects with nationalist politics, and feared repeats of this kind of thing if the West didn't provide new hope for the future, in the form of membership in the European Union. They did not want East European citizens demonstrating for EU membership, or illegally emigrating if it was denied. Security thus became a compelling reason for enlargement, and so the West finally offered it in 1998, with the process finalized in 2004. The terms of enlargement, however, have been strictly the West's terms.

Even so, East European citizens overwhelmingly approved. Each country held a national referendum on whether to accept EU membership, and as Table 28.1 shows, people voted strongly in the affirmative. As shown by the relatively low voter turnout—low given the historical significance of the outcome—they generally did not do so enthusiastically. Not even 50 percent of Hungarians bothered to vote. Many observers attribute the low voter frequency precisely to the rather condescending and patronizing way in which the West organized the whole enlargement process.

Yet now that the East European countries are full EU members, they are likely to find they get increased respect as well. For now that they are members, they begin to have some clout. The richer Western countries will need their support to pursue some of their grander ambitions, and will have to offer concessions in return. French president Jacques Chirac could threaten East Europe in 2003 for supporting the U.S. invasion of Iraq, suggesting that this might delay their EU membership, but no one will be able to do this again. East European clout has already been seen on the issue of promulgating an EU Constitution. Talks on the nature of the constitution temporarily broke down when Poland united with Spain in defense of provisions giving influence to countries (such as theirs) with large populations but weak economies. Traditional EU powers France and Germany were forced to make concessions. The new East European entrants will certainly remain weaker players

Table 28.1　EU Accession Referendum Results

Country	Date	Yes (percentage)	No (percentage)	Votes Cast (percentage)
Czech Republic	June 13–14, 2003	**77.33**	22.67	55.18
Estonia	September 14, 2003	**66.92**	33.08	64.02
Hungary	April 12, 2003	**83.76**	16.24	45.59
Latvia	September 20, 2003	**67.00**	32.30	72.53
Lithuania	May 10–11, 2003	**91.04**	8.96	63.30
Poland	June 8, 2003	**77.45**	22.55	58.85
Slovakia	May 16–17, 2003	**93.71**	6.29	52.15
Slovenia	March 23, 2003	**89.61**	10.39	60.23

Source: PriceWaterhouseCoopers; www.pwcglobal.com/extweb/service.nsf/
docid/E987ADD031C18E1A80256D1E004DF2EA.

than their veteran Western counterparts, but they will no doubt be accorded more respect in the future than they have been in the past.

The Policymaking Process

Since the mid-1990s, the countries of East-Central Europe have been engaged in two different types of policymaking decisions: those related to EU accession and those focused on purely domestic policy. Policymaking for EU matters was something special. All applicant countries were required to make deep legal changes in conformity with EU law if they wished to be considered for membership. This led to situations in which special national commissions met with special EU commissions to review national law and see where it needed adaptation, at which point national parliaments then did the job in pretty much a pro forma fashion. This was not very democratic, which is why critics have charged that the EU's famous "democratic deficit" has now been exported to the East. Once again, moreover, it was the executive

branch, not the legislature, that shaped policy outcomes.

Aside from issues related to EU accession, most law is made by national parliaments or state agencies on behalf of national constituencies. Who has influence over these decisions? In the United States, the crucial informal policymaking role is performed by lobbies, which undertake lavish campaigns promoting the interests of specific organizations or individuals and aimed exclusively at winning over a few legislators or regulators. Who tries to organize decision makers in East-Central Europe?

In the early post-Communist period, lobbying had a bad reputation in East-Central Europe, as it once did in the United States. No groups or organizations maintained separate, full-time lobbying organizations like those common in the West. Citizen groups and trade unions also refrained from lobbying because they believed that democratic parliaments would look out for their interests without organized pressure. Corporations or foundations, meanwhile, did not lobby for the simple reason that they were only beginning to function in this period.

The new politicians tended to offer a refreshing though naïve vision of themselves as actors who vote solely according to conscience. The reality was quite different. Many legislators commonly maintained numerous ongoing connections with private businesses. Conflict-of-interest laws are still rare. Politicians and parliamentarians regularly sit on boards of directors of new private companies or have an economic interest in the success of a firm or branch that stands to profit from a specific piece of legislation. In such conditions, lobbies are quite superfluous.

Of course, groups influence policy without having formal lobbies. On concrete policy issues, such as healthcare or education, parliamentarians try to satisfy the wishes of the doctors' association or the teachers' union not because these groups have formal lobbies in Warsaw or Prague or Sofia, but because they have strong organizations that can potentially mobilize their supporters if they want to.

Certainly the most influential lobby in East-Central Europe has been the "lobby of the West," including the international business and financial community (IMF and World Bank), Western governments, and the EU. After 1989, each post-Communist country thought that its best chance for success was to be invited into the West's institutions or to be chosen for investment by a multinational corporation. For this to happen, it had to win a seal of approval from Western banks and governments. Each country sought to convince the West that it, more than its neighbor, was the region's most stable and reform-minded country of all. Consequently, each tried to introduce whatever policies official Western advisory teams recommended.

This kind of influence extends not just to parliaments but to quasi-governmental organizations such as national tripartite councils, where representatives of business, labor, and the government meet to discuss issues of industrial relations. Despite the formal independence of these boards, they tend to limit themselves carefully to what international financial agencies

deem acceptable. As one participant in the Bulgarian tripartite commission wryly put it, the negotiations were "not tripartite but quadripartite, with the main partner [being] the IMF."[8]

Other strong pressures on parliaments come from nationalist groups in the multiethnic countries and from the Catholic Church. These interest groups are able to influence policymaking far out of proportion to their actual numbers. Nationalists came to dominate policy discussion in Yugoslavia in the same way that militarists dominated policy debate in the cold war United States and Soviet Union: by exaggerating the threat from the other side and arguing that it is better to be safe than sorry. As each side began mobilizing against the "other," the "other" mobilized back, thus "proving" to each that the other really was dangerous and setting in motion the vicious circle from which we still have not fully emerged. As for the church, particularly in the strongly Catholic countries of Poland, Slovakia, and Croatia, where political parties are still weak, it exerts power through its direct access every Sunday to millions of citizens and through its control of several media channels. With organization such as this, no groups want to tackle the church. Consequently, despite opinion polls showing strong public support for pro-choice policies in all of these countries, it is the church that has set the tone of the discussion on abortion.

When communism fell, these already organized interests had the most influence on domestic policy. That is now beginning to change, owing to the emergence in the 1990s of many nongovernmental organizations. Working on behalf of civic, environmental, and gender issues, for example, such organizations were widely ignored during the first decade of transformation but have lately become more influential. While politics in post-Communist Eastern Europe has so far been shaped largely by organized elites and foreign actors, social movements may well play a more important role in the future.

Notes

1. On the nature of federalist institutions in former Communist Eastern Europe, see Rogers Brubaker, *Nationalism Reframed* (Cambridge: Cambridge University Press, 1996), and Valerie Bunce, *Subversive Institutions* (Cambridge: Cambridge University Press, 1999).

2. This style of authoritarian imposition has been characteristic of radical capitalist marketization policies, not just in Eastern Europe but in Latin America too. See Bela Greskovits, "The Loneliness of the Economic Reformer," in his *The Political Economy of Protest and Patience* (Budapest: Central European University Press, 1998).

3. See Boris Kagarlitsky, "Prague 2000: The People's Battle," in Eddie Yuen et al., eds., *The Battle of Seattle: The New Challenge to Capitalist Globalization* (New York: Soft Skull Press, 2002).

4. On the post-Communist evolution of Eastern Europe's judiciary, see ongoing accounts in the *East European Constitutional Review,* available on line at www.law.nyu.edu/eecr.

5. For an excellent discussion of the Kavan case and its implications, see Lawrence Weschler, "The Velvet Purge," *New Yorker,* October 19, 1992, pp. 66–96.

6. Andras Sajo, "Corruption, Clientelism, and the Future of the Constitutional State in Eastern Europe," *East European Constitutional Review* 6, no. 1 (Winter 1997), and Wade Jacoby, "Priest and Penitent: The European Union as a Force in the Domestic Politics of Eastern Europe," *East European Constitutional Review* 8, nos. 1/2 (Winter–Spring 1999).

7. Andrew Moravcsik and Milada Anna Vachudova, "National Interests, State Power, and EU Enlargement," *East European Politics and Society* 17, no. 1 (Winter 2003): 46.

8. Grigor Gradev, "Bulgarian Trade Unions in Transition," in Stephen Crowley and David Ost, eds., *Workers After Workers' States: Unions and Politics in Eastern Europe Since the Fall of Communism* (Boulder, Colo.: Rowman & Littlefield, 2001).

CHAPTER

29

Representation and Participation

In this chapter, we are concerned with how East-Central Europe's new systems of political representation actually work and how its citizens affect what happens in the political sphere. We go into considerable detail about the new parliamentary systems, with particular emphasis on Poland and Hungary. We ask how parliaments make the new laws. What kind of people are members of parliament? What are the major parties? What do the parties actually do? Then we look at people's attitudes about politics, and the impact of trade unions, the church, and other social organizations.

The Legislature

In the countries of East-Central Europe, as in most other parliamentary systems, the executive branch tends to shape public policy. Policies devised by cabinet ministries are presented for parliamentary approval. And since the cabinet already has parliamentary support (because such support was necessary for the government to be formed in the first place), the cabinet's proposals are usually approved by the legislature. In a parliamentary system, when one party has a majority, there can be no deadlock: the government passes those laws it wants to pass. When there is no majority party, however, and only a shaky coalition keeps the government in power, then the government either compromises or is removed.

How do Eastern Europeans choose their parliaments? How do the parliaments pass bills? Let us look at these processes in the context of parliament in Poland, since aside from Poland's rel-

atively strong presidency, the process there is similar to what happens elsewhere in the region. The Polish parliament is made up of a lower house (Sejm) with 462 members and a 100-member senate. Elections for the lower house take place by a complex combination of proportional representation and individual selection. Unlike in the United States, districts are not represented by a single individual. Rather, the country is divided into several dozen electoral districts, each of which sends up to a dozen members to the Sejm. Citizens, however, vote for only one individual. The parties in each district put on the ballot as many candidates as will enter the Sejm, and voters put a mark by the name of their preferred candidate, listed under the candidate's party. In this way, the voter casts ballots simultaneously for an individual and a party. Seats are distributed first according to the number of votes received by each party. After that number is calculated, seats are distributed individually to those who received the greatest number of votes on the winning party lists. Elections to the senate are much simpler: candidates in each district are listed on a ballot without their party affiliation, and the two candidates with the most votes in the district win.

The Procedures of Lawmaking

In Poland, as in most other parliamentary systems, parliament discusses chiefly bills submitted by the executive branch, rather than by individual legislators. Bills are first considered by the Sejm, the dominant body. If passed, the bill goes to the senate for possible revision. The revisions stand unless the Sejm overrides them by a vote of at least one more than 50 percent of its total members. As in the United States, the president can veto a law passed by parliament, which can then overturn the veto with a two-thirds majority. (In countries without a senate or a strong presidency, a majority vote by parliament is final.)

When the government has a strong majority in parliament, the outcome of debate is almost never in doubt. Indeed, parliamentary discussion plays a meaningful role, and opposition parties have real clout, only if the government lacks this majority. Hungary has had solid parliamentary majorities since 1990. The Czech Republic has also had strong parliamentary majorities, whereas Slovakia has had fragmented parliaments. Between 1989 and 1993, owing to the large number of political parties, Poland regularly produced governments without a stable majority. As coalitions changed, so did the government; there were four of them during this four-year period. The country managed to produce stable parliamentary majorities only after 1993, when a new electoral law establishing a 5 percent threshold dramatically reduced the number of parties entering parliament.

The only way private citizens can directly influence the legislative process, apart from electing legislators and expressing opinions in the press and elsewhere, is through referenda. For the most part, however, East European countries have discouraged the use of the referendum as a legislative tool. Except for binding plebiscitary votes, such as a yes or no to a new constitution (which is how Poland ratified its constitution in 1997), most referenda that are put on the ballot by civic groups gathering signatures are non-binding on decision makers.

Parliamentarians

Parliaments can be either exciting arenas for passionate and policy-forming debate or boring chambers where deals worked out in the corri-

dors are merely presented for ratification. We see some of each in East-Central Europe. Of the various post-Communist legislatures, the Polish parliament has had the most lively discussions, for several reasons: the large number of parties in parliament; the frequent lack of parliamentary majorities which give smaller parties a real chance to shape legislation; conflict with a president trying to expand his own powers; and a high degree of ideological antipathy between competing groups. Until 1998, the Hungarian legislature, on the other hand, was the most staid and predictable. This was particularly true in the initial post-Communist years, when a deal struck between the two largest parties (by which one held the prime minister's office and the other the presidency) meant that disagreements rarely came to the floor. (A 1997 deal between the two largest parties in the Czech Republic produced a similar lackluster parliament in the late 1990s.) The presence of several dozen youthful deputies from Fidesz, or the Alliance of Young Democrats, made Hungarian parliamentary sessions interesting to watch, but more for entertainment than for genuine insight into policymaking. This situation changed only after 1998, when the same Fidesz, now grown up, itself became the leading coalition partner and provoked a series of noisy fights with the other parties.

Parliaments have not been very well respected in post-Communist countries. Within a few years after the fall of Communist rule, public opinion gave parliament some astonishingly low ratings—less than 10 percent public approval in Poland, Hungary, and the Czech and Slovak Republics. Such ratings reflected a general dissatisfaction with governments imposing painful economic changes. It also reflected the fact that many people who were elected to parliament after 1989 did not know how the institution was supposed to work. East European legislatures in the immediate post-Communist period were top-heavy with writers and historians who could speak plenty about what was wrong with communism but did not know much about parliamentary procedure. For all the ridicule directed at Communist-era parliamentarians, who never had to stand for free elections, it turned out that they had a much better idea how parliamentary rules and procedures worked than did the dissidents who succeeded them. The former Communist deputies may never have voted a bill down, but they did negotiate with party circles on the inside, in corridors and in committees, to get specific clauses changed or have their local interests addressed. Indeed, this was one of the main reasons people began to vote the former Communist parties back into power: voters appreciated the political professionalism that was lacking among the newcomers.

Parliament was also becoming much less attractive to potential newcomers. Highly skilled professionals are reluctant to run for office because of the low pay. Although higher than the average wage, the pay is substantially less than one can make, say, working in the new private sphere or for a multinational corporation. Polish parliamentary deputies in the mid-1990s earned about $500 per month plus a housing allowance, and more if the parliamentarian quit his or her other job (many do not). Low pay and the absence of conflict-of-interest laws have meant that parliamentarians try to supplement their income by being consultants and even members of the board of directors of private corporations. (Naturally, news about these connections leads to even lower popularity ratings for parliament.) By the mid-1990s, as a result of all this, many parties had to go searching for people willing to run on their tickets. (One candidate agreed to run on the Hungarian Socialist Party ticket in 1994 only because he was assured he would lose. Unfortunately, the party did so well that he won. He resigned the next day.) The parties often end up running people who are not even party members, but just upstanding citizens likely to have, or to be able to earn, popular support. This was standard practice in the Communist system, too. Sometimes, parties simply run candidates who pay them for a spot on the ballot.

Parliamentary deputies do not get many benefits. Most do not even have their own offices or their own staffs. The parties they belong to have offices, but the individual representatives do not. Clearly such a situation does not make for strong, effective, self-confident parliamentarians. Unfortunately, it does create incentives for corruption.

Parliament in the new Eastern Europe has also been very much a male organization. Under the old system, women's share in parliament was about 25 to 40 percent. This extraordinarily large number (for its time) was due to the Communist system of "representation," in which the aim was to replicate in parliament the demographics of society. Workers, farmers, enterprise managers, cultural figures, and women all had their formal positions in parliament, even if real power was reserved for the top party officials, almost all of whom were men. In the first free elections after 1989, the share of women parliamentarians dropped dramatically (see Table 29.1). At the same time, however, those women who were in parliament were no longer tokens. Some attained real power, such as Hanna Suchocka, who served as Polish prime minister in 1992-1993. In recent years, the percentage of women in parliament has increased to levels comparable to those in Western Europe, even if still substantially lower than in the Communist era.

Political Parties, the Party System, and Elections

Elsewhere in this book, there are separate sections on parties and elections. Here, we put them together. From the onset of Stalinism in 1949 to the fall of communism forty years later, the only party that existed was the official Communist Party; elections were merely ritualized forms of public participation, not meaningful choices among real alternatives. Since 1989, East-Central Europe has had both real elections and the emergence of real parties. But the two processes have been intrinsically connected: parties have been formed and killed off repeatedly

Table 29.1   Women in National Parliaments, 1991 and 2004

1991 (after first post-Communist election)	*Percentage*
Bulgaria	8.0
Croatia	4.8
Czech Republic	13.0
Hungary	7.3
Poland	9.6
Romania	3.0
Slovakia	12.7
Slovenia	10.0

2004	*Percentage*
Bulgaria	26.2
Croatia	17.8
Czech Republic	17.0
Hungary	9.8
Poland	20.3
Romania	10.7
Slovakia	19.3
Slovenia	12.0

Some Comparative Figures	*Percentage*
France	12.2
Germany	32.2
Italy	11.5
Sweden	45.3
United Kingdom	17.9
United States	14.3

Sources: Nanette Funk and Magda Mueller, eds., *Gender Politics and Post-Communism* (New York: Routledge, 1993), and website of the Inter-Parliamentary Union: www.ipu.org/wmn-e/classif.htm.

as a result of elections. Thus, we talk about these two phenomena together here.

If we look only at the Central European countries of Poland, Hungary, and the Czech Republic, we can divide post-Communist party develop-

ment into two stages. In the first stage, lasting from 1990 to 1993, parties and politics were dominated by anticommunism. Liberal and conservative parties each claimed to be the most anti-Communist, and even the ex-Communist parties took great pains to prove their reformed status. In the second stage, since 1994, anticommunism is no longer sufficient to attract votes, as East Europeans began reacting to the realities of new capitalism rather than the memory of old communism. Social democratic parties won several elections in 1993 and 1994, leading some observers to talk about a "revival of the left." But in the late 1990s, conservative and right-wing parties recaptured power in Poland and Hungary, before new elections in the new century returned the social democrats once again. Ideological divides still remain strong, but politics is becoming "normal" in the sense that parties now win or lose depending on their record (and their campaign strategies), and not just their stated beliefs.

Over the past fifteen years, the party system in Eastern Europe has changed more completely and more thoroughly than in any other part of Europe. The plethora of parties today makes it difficult to recall that these were one-party systems until a short time ago. On the other hand, it is the very fact that new parties had to be created from scratch that accounts for their large number and for the fact that they are still not completely stable. For example, we know that in the next British election, the Labour Party will compete for control of parliament with the Tories while the Liberal Democrats look to achieve an elusive breakthrough, and in Germany the Social Democrats will be pitted against the Christian Democrats while the Greens try to maintain a presence. In Poland, however, in both 2001 and 2004, two different governing parties disintegrated while still in office! Even in Hungary, with the most stable party system in Eastern Europe, the party that governed the country from 1990 to 1994 had been reduced to a humiliating 3 percent of the vote by 1998. In the Czech Republic, meanwhile, the Social Democrats, who stood at the head of the country in 2000, could not even pass the 5 percent minimum threshold for entering parliament in the first post-Communist elections of 1990.

Yet while a continuing party shakeout is likely in the coming decade, some parties have clearly established their record and their identity, and thus their staying power. In this section, we examine the main parties and recent election results in key Central European countries as of 2004 and the ideological tendencies in the elections so far. For shorthand reference, the election results since 1990 in three key countries look roughly as follows: in Hungary, the voting patterns have gone right, left, right, left; in Poland, center, left, right, left; and in the Czech Republic, center, right, left.

Hungary

Hungary is the best place to begin because it entered 1989 with a party system apparently already intact. This was due to the prominence of two parties that seemed able to divide all the non-Communist vote between them: the Alliance of Free Democrats (AFD) and the Hungarian Democratic Forum (HDF). The AFD was formed by the liberal intellectuals who had led Hungary's democratic opposition movement since the 1970s. Maintaining their activities in the difficult years despite constant harassment by the police, AFD activists had accumulated the record, legitimacy, and intellectual firepower to make them the apparently natural successors once the Communist Party left the scene. Indeed, it was precisely this that led conservative intellectuals to form their own counterorganization, the HDF, in 1987. The HDF styled itself as a nationalist and populist movement, opposing communism less on grounds that it was hostile to democracy than that it was contrary to the national and religious identities of Hungary. The liberal and conservative emphases of these two parties seemed to span the ideological divide within the non-Communist camp. The AFD entered the 1990 elections as a classic European liberal party, supporting rapid integration with the West and full individual rights for all citizens regardless of eth-

nicity or religion. The conservative HDF was more cautious about marketization, more focused on protecting ethnic Hungarians, and against substituting a dependence on the West for the old dependence on the East. With its 42 percent of the vote, the HDF came to power, while the AFD's 24 percent made it the leading opposition. Together, with two-thirds of the total 1990 vote, the two parties thoroughly dominated the first post-Communist parliament.

Within ten years, however, both parties had become marginalized. The HDF compromised itself by its four years in power, characterized as a time of scandals, economic decline, and perceived governmental incompetence. By allowing widescale foreign takeover of industry, they lost much of their support on the right. By not severing ties with an extremist anti-Semitic faction in their midst, they lost support among moderates. By 1994, their vote had dropped to 9.5 percent and four years later to 3.1 percent, after which it became a minor partner of Fidesz (see Table 29.2).

The AFD, meanwhile, was eclipsed by the former Communists. The Hungarian Socialist Party (HSP), as they were now called, received only 8.5 percent of the vote in 1990. As the new system developed a record of its own, however, and as the Socialists deftly distanced themselves from their past, their fortunes began to improve. While other parties spoke of the miracles of the market, the HSP noted the high costs of market reform for the majority of the population. While other political leaders proved themselves incompetent politicians, prone to grandstanding for an audience, the Socialists earned respect for knowing the nuts and bolts of lawmaking and parliamentary procedure.

By 1993, the Socialists were already passing the liberals in the public opinion polls. Whereas both supported democratic rights and a market economy, the Socialists exhibited far more social concern than the liberals did. (It is important to keep in mind that in Europe, unlike the United States, *liberalism* implies individualism and pro-market beliefs but not support for state intervention or

Table 29.2   Parliamentary Elections in Hungary, 1994, 1998, 2002

Parliament: The National Assembly has 386 members, elected for a four-year term—176 members in single-seat constituencies, 152 by proportional representation in multiseat constituencies, and 58 members elected to realize proportional representation.

Party	2002 Election (voter turnout, 70.5%)		1998 Election (voter turnout, 57.0%)		1994 Election	
	Percentage of Vote	Seats	Percentage of Vote	Seats	Percentage of Vote	Seats
Hungarian Socialist Party (social democrat)	42.1	178	32.3	134	54.1	209
Fidesz—Hungarian Civic Union (formerlyAlliance of Young Democrats, conservative liberal), running in coalition with Hungarian Democratic Forum	41.1	164	28.2	148	5.1	20
Independent Party of Smallholders, Agrarian Workers and Citizens (agrarian conservative)	0.8	—	13.8	48	6.7	26
Alliance of Free Democrats (liberal)	5.5	20	7.9	24	18.1	70
Hungarian Justice and Life Party (nationalist)	4.4	—	5.5	14	—	—
Workers' Party (Communist)	2.8	—	4.1		—	—
Hungarian Democratic Forum (conservative/Christian-democratic)	(unified slate with Fidesz)	24	3.1	17	9.5	38

Sources: www.electionworld.org/election/hungary.htm; Kesselman et al., *European Politics in Transition,* Fourth Edition (Boston: Houghton Mifflin Company, 2002), p. 582.

strong welfare provisions.) And with class anger growing as a result of the new, inegalitarian capitalism, voters increasingly turned to the HSP as the best political alternative.

The only surprise in the 1994 elections was the extent of the HSP victory. From its miserable showing four years earlier, the party now received an astonishing 54.1 percent of the vote, winning an absolute majority of parliamentary seats all by itself. So thorough was the victory that prominent candidates of other parties found themselves defeated by political unknowns running on the Socialist ticket. Even the highly popular AFD chairman lost a head-to-head race with a little-known actress running as a Socialist. Although voters gave the HSP a convincing vic-

tory, opinion polls showed overwhelming support for a socialist-liberal coalition, and the liberals soon obliged. The AFD moved from being the most anti-Communist party in 1990 to being the governing coalition partner with the former Communists from 1994 to 1998, and again beginning in 2002.

Why a liberal-socialist alliance? The reason has to do with the appearance of religious nationalism in the post-Communist era. As noted before, liberals opposed communism in the name of democracy, not in the name of church or nation. Though cooperating with anti-Communist nationalists before 1989, they always had different views about the future. After 1989, everything changed. When reform Communists no longer opposed democracy, it turned out that liberals had more in common with them than they did with religious nationalists. Both favored a secular rather than religious system and opposed narrow ethnic nationalism. Both sought integration with the West and wanted an educational system teaching scientific know-how rather than moral purity. The liberal-socialist alliance has been one of the most interesting developments in East-Central European politics. Besides Hungary, it has occurred in the Czech Republic and Slovakia, as well as in Slovenia and Croatia.

With the two prominent parties of 1990 marginalized ten years later, who has taken up the slack? The answer is Fidesz—originally known as the Alliance of Young Democrats but now as the Civic Democratic Union. This has been one of the most unusual, and most spectacular, party transformations in recent European history. Having started out as a sort of quirky youth group of the AFD, Fidesz soon remade itself into the premier conservative party in the country. The transformation began in the early 1990s. While other parties were compromising themselves through political infighting, Fidesz attracted support with shrewd political analysis, innovative policy proposals, and one of Hungary's best public speakers in party leader Viktor Orban. When the AFD entered a coalition government with the Socialists and the HDF saw its support evaporate, the right side of the political spectrum suddenly had a huge hole, and Fidesz tried to fill it. Allying with the conservative Smallholders Party, Fidesz rode dissatisfaction with the Socialist government into a stunning electoral victory in 1998, making the thirty-eight-year-old Orban the youngest prime minister in Europe. Though Fidesz increased its vote for the 2002 elections, it lost out to the socialist-liberal alliance in a closely fought race. Indeed, both of the last two elections were very close, and with the same cast of parties. This suggests that despite the wide array of political parties populating the Hungarian scene since 1989, a classic left-right split with two dominant parties has now emerged, as is common elsewhere in

Europe. "Right" here means pro-nationalist more than pro-market, but then that too has become the norm throughout Europe, where even left-wingers no longer seriously try to challenge the dominance of the market.

Poland

Parties had a harder time getting established in Poland than in Hungary, since until 1989 virtually all opposition politics was subordinated to Solidarity, the massive opposition trade union and social movement. When parties began to form after Solidarity started coming apart in 1990, they formed so fast that in the first free elections in 1991, sixty-seven different parties competed, and eighteen won at least one seat. With the subsequent introduction of a 5 percent requirement for representation, the number dropped to six parties entering parliament in 1993, five in 1997, and six again in 2001.

Even with these smaller numbers, Polish party politics has been quite confusing. First, although there has been something of a left-right divide similar to that in Hungary, the meaning of these terms is often unclear. The successor to the old Communist Party calls itself left-wing, and it is now a reformed, social democratic, pro-market and pro-European organization. Because almost all other parties trace their origins to the struggle *against* the old Communist Party, however, all of them tend to call themselves "right-wing," but this includes not just nationalists and Christian fundamentalists but liberals, too. Second, the identities of the parties representing these two tendencies also keep changing. For the first fifteen years after the collapse of the old system it was only the right that kept producing new parties, some more liberal and some more nationalistic. The coalition that won parliamentary elections in 1997, for example, called Solidarity Electoral Action, ceased to exist when the country next went to the polls in 2001. In 2004, however, the previously quite stable Democratic Left Alliance (DLA), which won the elections in 2001, collapsed too, owing to a series of scandals and continually high unemployment. With elections scheduled for spring 2005, the DLA may well be eclipsed by a new left party calling itself Polish Social Democracy.

Nevertheless, if the reader keeps in mind that party formation has not been completed in post-Communist Poland, certain regularities can be detected. Let's begin with the left, focusing on its evolution in the post-Communist era.

The DLA, like Hungary's Socialist Party, was the reformed version of the old ruling Communist Party. It was founded in 1990, just after the collapse of the old system. Despite the old ruling party's role in facilitating a smooth transition to democracy, its successor entered the new era without much popular support. Its presidential candidate won only 8 percent of the vote in 1990, and the party got only 12 percent in parliamentary elections a year later. Yet as in Hungary, the DLA quickly won supporters thanks to its professionalism, the incessant quarreling of its opponents, its clear support for democracy, and its advocacy of better protection for the poor. By the 1993 parliamentary elections, the DLA had emerged as the leading party, with some 20 percent of the vote and 37 percent of the seats (because of electoral rules favoring large parties). It governed the country for the next four years in coalition with the smaller Polish People's Party, representing rural interests. The DLA actually increased its vote total to 27 percent in 1997 but lost parliamentary control because the right-wing parties had in the meantime united themselves. It regained parliament in 2001 with a towering 41 percent of the vote.

Given its large electoral victory and its successful engineering of Poland's entry into the European Union, why did the DLA find itself in such crisis by 2004? The answer seems to be due to the large victory itself, the continuing impact of pre-1989 divides, and the intractable unemployment problem. First, the decisive parliamentary win seemed to give many in the party a sense of untouchability, leading to a series of corruption scandals that sullied the DLA's reputation. Second, even though the DLA pursued policies generally favored by liberals, such as promoting EU accession and aligning closely in international relations with the United States, liberals in parliament refused to support the DLA. Unlike in Hungary, the partisan divide dating from the Communist era has been impossible to overcome. Liberals voted more often with right-wing antiliberals in parliament than with the DLA, even though on policy grounds alone they were closer to the DLA. Perhaps the most important factor for the DLA's decline, however, has been the continuing economic crisis. Most Poles thought that once the economy began to recover in the mid-1990s, dire days would be behind them. But by 1998 unemployment had begun to increase again, and economic growth rates started to decline. By 2004, unemployment reached over 20 percent, a level not reached even during the worst of the post-1989 depression. These three factors contributed to the DLA sinking to single-digit approval ratings even while still exercising power.

The right wing of the Polish political spectrum remains highly fragmented. The dominant group is the moderate Civic Platform (CP), representing anti-Communist liberals. CP emerged only in 1999, as a breakaway faction of the then-dominant Solidarity Electoral Action coalition. (This was a coalition of right-wing parties, led by the political wing of the Solidarity trade union, that came together for the purpose of defeating the DLA. After it defeated the DLA and came to power in 1997, it quickly fragmented, and by 2001 it had essentially ceased to exist.) Civic Platform tries to appeal to young and upwardly mobile voters who support EU expansion and global economic integration, and who do not trust the ex-Communist left. This was not a very successful strategy (as Table 29.3 shows, the Platform won only 12.7 percent of the vote in 2001), *until* the DLA underwent its crisis beginning in 2003, at which point it attracted much of the latter's more prosperous electorate. Opinion polls in 2004 showed CP supported by about 25 to 30 percent of likely voters, making it the favorite to become the governing party after the

Table 29.3   Parliamentary Elections in Poland, 2001

Parliament: Parliament has two chambers. The Sejm (lower house) has 460 members, elected for a four-year term by proportional representation in multiseat constituencies with a 5 percent threshold (8 percent for coalitions, requirement waived for national minorities). The Senate has 100 members selected for a four-year term in forty multiseat constituencies.

Party	*Percentage of Vote*	*Seats (460 total)*
	Results, Polish Sejm Elections (voter turnout, 46.3%)	
Coalition of Democratic Left Alliance, and Union of Labor (social democratic)	41.0	216
Civic Platform (liberal)	12.7	65
Self-Defense (rural conservative)	10.2	53
Law and Justice (urban conservative)	9.5	44
Polish People's Party (agrarian)	9.0	42
League of Polish Families (Christian nationalist)	7.9	38
Solidarity Electoral Action (right—conservative)	5.6	—
Freedom Union (liberal)	3.2	—
German Minority (ethnic minority)	0.4	2

Source: www.electionworld.org/election/poland.htm.

	Results, Polish Senate Elections (voter turnout, 46.3%)
Coalition of DLA and UL	75
Self-Defense	2
Polish People's Party	4
League of Polish Families	2
Senate Bloc 2001 (coalition of Civic Platform, Law and Justice, Freedom Union and others)	15

next elections. (In the June 2004 elections to the European Parliament, often a harbinger for a country's own elections, CP came in first, with 24.1 percent of the votes.) The lack of a clear program besides support for the market, however, means that CP is not a very solid party either. After the next elections, it too could break into smaller subparties very quickly.

The next largest force on the Polish right is the extremist Self-Defense organization. Led by the aggressive, confrontational, yet charismatic farmer Andrzej Lepper, Self-Defense chiefly represents farm interests and the rural poor, but with recent economic downturns has attracted a great deal of angry urban voters as well. Self-Defense emerged as the third-largest party in the 2001 elections. It played a great role in the debate over the EU, and not just because it opposed joining. Because of its fierce criticism of how the EU's original terms of enlargement would hurt rural interests, Poland negotiated some important concessions, such as on foreign purchase of Polish land. As Table 29.4 shows, support for Self-Defense grew steadily in the months just prior to Poland's May 2004 accession to the EU, before beginning to slip soon afterwards. (Indeed, it won only 11 percent of the votes in the 2004 elections to the European Parliament.) Lepper's belligerent style and open disdain for parliamentary procedures has won him support among Poland's most alienated voters, but it also raises enormous questions about what Poland would look like under a Self-Defense government, which may well come about before 2010. Lepper would certainly be a threat to democratic procedures, though Poland's constitution and its integration in the EU would probably prevent any serious attempt to dismantle the democratic system.

Another right-wing challenge to democracy comes from the League of Polish Families, a fundamentalist Christian and nationalist party which vociferously opposed the EU, and has made the fight against abortion and for a government based on (its interpretation of) Catholicism the centerpiece of its program. The League has support chiefly among the elderly poor and the devout. It came in with a surprisingly strong

second-place showing in the 2004 European Parliament elections, with 16 percent of the vote. In a possible alliance with Self-Defense, it could contribute significantly to the emergence of a strong extremist coalition.

Among other parties with durable support, Law and Justice is a moderate right-wing party, focusing chiefly around the issue of crime and corruption. Union of Labor is a social democratic party with roots in the Solidarity movement, and has been closely allied with the DLA. The Polish People's Party was the traditional farmer's party, and had also been allied with the DLA, but has lost much of its support to Self-Defense. The Freedom Union was Poland's dominant liberal party (similar to the Alliance of Free Democrats in Hungary) from 1990 to 1997, until it was eclipsed by the Civic Platform.

As one can see, Polish party politics remains both complex and highly fluid.[1] Despite the identity of the particular parties that govern, however, there will likely remain three dominant tendencies: a social democratic party, a conservative nationalist movement, and a liberal party that moves between the two.

Presidential politics is easier to make sense of, if only because it entails an election for a single person. Lech Walesa easily won the first free

Table 29.4   Polish Party Support in Recent Opinion Polls (in percentage)

	Oct. 2003	Nov. 2003	Dec. 2003	Jan. 2004	Feb. 2004	March 2004	April 2004
Civic Platform	17	22	26	29	31	27	29
Self-Defense	10	14	13	11	18	24	24
Law and Justice	18	14	12	13	10	15	9
Polish Social Democracy	—	—	—	—	—	—	7
Democratic Left Alliance	19	20	17	17	18	10	6
League of Polish Families	10	6	8	10	8	7	6
Union of Labor	5	4	4	4	3	3	4
Polish People's Party	10	6	6	6	5	4	5
Freedom Union	3	4	3	3	2	2	2

Source: Center for the Study of Public Opinion, Warsaw.

presidential election in 1990, but lost in a close election to the forty-one-year-old DLA leader, Aleksander Kwasniewski, in 1995. Although originally a very polarizing figure because of his role in the former ruling party, Kwasniewski proved to be a very adept and astute leader. He withdrew from the DLA to become a "president of all Poles," and has succeeded remarkably. He has maintained good relations with the United States, the European Union, and the Catholic Church, and has gone a long way toward alleviating pre-1989 political divisions. All opinion polls since 2000 report that he is the most popular politician in the country, with over two-thirds of the population in 2004 saying they trust him. Because of the two-term constitutional limit, he will leave his post in 2005, but his popularity is such that there is serious talk about his wife, Jolanta, running to replace him. Other likely candidates for the job are Andrzej Lepper and the Law and Justice leader, Lech Kaczynski, presently mayor of Warsaw.

Czech Republic

Politics in the Czech Republic is also dominated by right- and left-leaning parties, respectively known as the Civic Democratic Party (CDP) and the Social Democratic Party (SDP). The CDP traces its roots to the 1989 Velvet Revolution (though as in Poland, many liberal intellectuals broke away as the party turned increasingly conservative), while the SDP is a party revived from the pre–World War II era. (Unlike elsewhere, therefore, the main left party is *not* the old Communist Party, chiefly because that party never fully converted itself into a democratic organization.) CDP support has stayed fairly stable in the past decade, while the SDP has grown dramatically, attracting support from those who opposed CDP dominance. The CDP stayed in power for a long time by combining tough-talking neoliberal rhetoric with a softer social democratic practice, but when the inegalitarian market elements began prevailing over the inclusive social democratic elements, the SDP grew as an alternative.

Since 1998, the two parties have pretty much divided governmental power between themselves, much to the consternation of smaller parties, who feel increasingly shut out. As Table 29.5 shows, electoral results in 2002 were remarkably similar to those in 1998, with the same parties dividing among themselves the two hundred parliamentary seats. In terms of party politics, Czech politics is quite stable.

Slovakia

Slovak politics has been a bit more complicated, owing to the presence of the authoritarian nationalist and ex-Communist Vladimir Meciar, leader of the Movement for a Democratic Slovakia. His repressive internal policies made Slovakia a pariah in the region, delaying its entry into NATO and the EU and earning the scorn of all committed democrats and socialists. In 1998, a coalition of liberals and reformed ex-Communists won enough seats to oust Meciar and put the country back on a Westernizing path. This allowed Slovakia to move from the second tier of EU accession countries to the forefront, facilitating its entry as a full member in 2004. The new government did much to restore public confidence and improve the economy, but Meciar did not go away. In 2004, for example, he nearly won the presidency, before being defeated by Ivan Gasparovic, an equally nationalist candidate who won in the presidential runoff thanks to voters who wanted anybody but Meciar. (Two nationalists with similar politics and similar backgrounds came to compete in the runoff because the liberals divided their votes in the first round.) As for the current parliamentary makeup (see Table 29.6), we see here a plethora of parties with no single dominant force. There has also been a rapidly changing party scene, as in Poland. The coalition that came together to defeat Meciar in 1998 dissolved into competing parties by 2002. Christian Democratic parties dominate the party system there, but, as the 2004 presidential vote also demonstrated, populist authoritarian candidates continue to

Table 29.5   Parliamentary Elections in the Czech Republic, 1998, 2002

Parliament: The Parliament of the Czech Republic has two chambers. The Chamber of Representatives has 200 members, elected for a four-year term by proportional representation with a 5 percent barrier. The Senate has 81 members, elected for a six-year term in single-seat constituencies, with one-third renewed every two years.

Party	Results in Chamber of Representatives Election, 2002 (voter turnout, 58.8%)		Results in Chamber of Representatives Election, 1998 (voter turnout, 73.8%)	
	Percentage of Vote	Seats (200 total)	Percentage of Vote	Seats (200 total)
Czech Social Democratic Party (social democratic)	30.2	70	32.3	74
Civic Democratic Party (conservative)	24.5	58	27.7	63
Communist Party of Bohemia and Moravia (Communist)	18.5	41	11.0	24
Coalition of Christian and Democratic Union–Czechoslovak People's Party *and* Freedom Union	14.3	31		
Christian and Democratic Union–Czechoslovak People's Party (Christian democratic)			9.0	20
Freedom Union (conservative)			8.6	19
Green Party (ecological)	2.4	—	—	—
Republicans of Miroslav Sladek (right-wing populist)				

Sources: Kesselman et al., *European Politics in Transition,* Fourth Edition (Boston: Houghton Mifflin Company, 2002), p. 586; www.electionworld.org/election/czech.htm.

remain appealing for a good portion of the Slovak electorate.

Comparing East European Party Systems

Since the collapse of the Communist system, new party systems have emerged everywhere in all former Communist countries. Although the identities of particular parties may change, the basic framework appears to be set. We usually see the emergence of two dominant parties representing left- and right-wing tendencies, with "right," as elsewhere in Europe, tending to mean

pro-nationalist more than pro-market. There has been broad general agreement among most parties on the basic issues of the day, such as consolidating a market economy and entering both NATO and the EU, though "Euroskeptics" (mostly on the right) began to gain as integration drew near, and are likely to play an important role in the future. While the different parties that have exercised governmental power have argued against each other quite vociferously, all of them, once in government, have continued to maintain the same basic policies. Focused on taking advantage of the historic op-

Table 29.6   Parliamentary Elections in Slovakia, 2002

Parliament: The National Council of the Slovak Republic has 150 members, elected for a four-year term by proportional representation.

Party	Percentage of Vote	Seats (150 total)
	Results for 2002 (voter turnout, 70.0%)	
Movement for a Democratic Slovakia (authoritarian)	19.5	36
Slovak Democratic and Christian Union (Christian democratic)	15.1	28
Party Direction—Third Way (liberal centrist)	13.5	25
Party of the Hungarian Minority (ethnic minority)	11.2	20
Christian Democratic Movement (Christian democratic)	8.3	15
New Civic Alliance (liberal centrist)	8.0	15
Slovak Communist Party (Communist)	6.3	11
Right Slovak National Party (right-wing authoritarian)	3.7	—
Slovak National Party (xenophobic)	3.3	—
Movement for Democracy (liberal)	3.3	—
Social Democratic Alternative	1.8	—
Party of Democratic Left (social democratic)	1.4	—

Sources: Kesselman et al., *European Politics in Transition*, Fourth Edition (Boston: Houghton Mifflin Company, 2002), p. 587; www.electionworld.org/slovakia.htm.

portunity that opened before them after 1989, each governing party did largely what the EU and international business community have told it to do. Thus, there was policy continuity when left-wing parties came to power in Poland and Hungary in the mid-1990s, continuity when right-wing parties replaced them in the late 1990s, and continuity still when social democratic parties returned in the early 2000s. The identities of the dominant parties may yet change but probably not the basic policy orientations, even if politicians like Lepper in Poland might try. The bottom line is that no party wants to be responsible for squandering this historic opportunity to become part of the European mainstream and to end the centuries-old division of Europe into East and West. Such pressures, and opportunities, explain why extremist

right-wing parties have largely been unable to succeed, as well as why, where they have come to power (Slovakia, Croatia), they have not been able to consolidate their rule. By 2005, basic European principles of liberal democracy and market economy were accepted as dogma by overwhelming majorities in all the countries of the region.

Political Culture, Citizenship, and Identity

The former ruling Communist parties tried to replace people's preexisting loyalties with loyalty to party principles but never came close to succeeding. They certainly influenced people greatly, but alternate identities—according to class, religion, nationality, or political ideology—have always remained prominent. Since 1989, old identities have combined with new ones to create fascinating and unusual concoctions with important implications for the future.

Social Class

Because of the formally Marxist ideologies of the past, the countries of Eastern Europe have a very peculiar relationship to class as an identity. In the early days of the old system, class was an almost obligatory identity. Citizens got credits (or demerits) depending on their class background, and anyone who advanced up the social hierarchy had to swear loyalty to the working class, in whose interests the entire system was said to be run. Over time, the new elite managed to reproduce itself and get its children into good positions, but it was not allowed to develop a class consciousness of its own. Everything it did was still supposedly done for the working class. The impact was that most citizens were unable to think of themselves in terms of class. Since everyone was supposed to be a worker, no explicit class distinctions could arise, despite obvious social and economic inequalities.

This legacy has a strong impact on the post-Communist period. Although the new era is very much about the creation of a class society—building a capitalist system requires creating a capitalist class—class has remained an uncertain identity in the new era. Labor does not explicitly embrace a working-class identity (the very term *working class* is unpopular, conjuring up images of official old men in badly tailored suits) but sees itself as trying to become middle class. The emerging capitalist class meanwhile tries to underplay its wealth and power, conscious of the fact that its right to privilege is not yet accepted by all. The limited scope of class identities is due also to the changing economy. The closing down of the old industrial factories in favor of small-scale service and white-collar jobs (everything from security guard to computer programmer)

led to the erosion of class identities in the West and is now doing the same in the East. As we will see in the next section, this decline of class identity has led to minimal labor unrest despite the steep economic decline.

Citizenship and National Identity

Because of their long experience of foreign domination and the struggle against it—and also because people are generally like this—Eastern Europeans are very attached to their national identities. The Communist parties recognized this and did their best to use national themes to their advantage. The Polish government in the 1960s paid particular attention to playing up nationalist themes, as did the Ceausescu gov-ernment in Romania. Nevertheless, the post-Communist governments now treat communism largely as a foreign imposition. Because the new leaders try to present themselves as the rejuvenators of the nation, they choose not to dwell on the ways in which communism once had popular support, as discussed in Chapter 26. Instead, they use the *post*-Communist era to solidify their national communities. They do so through rituals, ceremonies, and new national holidays. Hungary, for example, has made October 23, the anniversary of the 1956 rebellion against the Soviets, a new national holiday, and Poland, having abolished commemoration of July 22, when the Soviet-supported government took power in 1944, now celebrates May 3 (for the 1791 constitution) and November 11 (for the 1918 declaration of independence) as its key national holidays. In a series of ways, countries have tried to emphasize their links with the pre-Communist past, sometimes acting as if the Communist period never existed. For his 1990 inauguration as president, for example, Lech Walesa received the official trappings of the presidency not from his legal predecessor, General Wojciech Jaruzelski, but from the so-called president-in-exile in London, recognized by no government in the world. Jaruzelski was not even invited.

National and patriotic themes were quite evident in the struggle against communism. They played an especially important role in the Polish Solidarity movement in the 1980s.[2] Solidarity adopted the national anthem as its own union song, and the ever-present pictures of the Polish pope, John Paul II, also symbolized national aspirations. (Many decades of foreign rule made the Polish church the only ongoing sign of national continuity, and so a powerful national as well as religious symbol.) And it was the nationalist revival in the Baltic states of Latvia, Lithuania, and Estonia that led to the final crisis of the Soviet Union.

A strong national identity can be conducive to political freedom, but it can also lead to the breakup of a country and to ruthless war, as we have seen in the former Yugoslavia. Eastern Europeans are quite aware of this dual nature of nationalism. For that reason, we see two competing tendencies coexisting in post-Communist East-Central Europe. The first is a tendency to instill among the population an impregnable sense of national identity. Eastern European countries emphasize this because of their long history of foreign occupations. As the writer Milan Kundera has noted, the people of the region live with the ever-present awareness that statehood has been taken away before and can be taken away again. This awareness leads today's rulers, teachers, and writers to emphasize nationalist themes and national triumphs, even at the cost of historical accuracy. This attitude can certainly lead to abuses, as in the way Serbian historians reinvented the past in the 1980s, turning Croatians into devils and Bosnians into Serbs. (The historians argued that Croatia had always taken advantage of Serbia and that Bosnians were really only Serbs who believed in Islam.) Yet the emphasis on nationalist history is also a necessary process of self-recovery after long years of subordination to the Soviet Union. And the globalization of culture that makes MTV or CNBC available in living rooms throughout Eastern Europe also makes national awareness necessary to guard against the "over-Westernization" of young people.

Along with this nationalistic tendency, however, the other strong tendency today is precisely toward globalism. All Eastern European countries have talked endlessly about "joining Europe." They want their young people to travel to other countries, learn new languages, and think in ways contrary to local national biases. In other words, they are trying to promote a new international identity at the same time they are promoting a new national one. Sometimes the two tendencies are manifested at the very same time, such as when the schoolchild learns of the great contributions made to world history by some obscure (to the West) national hero and is asked to recite the tale of this valiant figure in English.

The nationalist tendency has been strongest where statehood is most tentative: in the Baltic republics. Because these countries were part of the Soviet Union between 1940 and 1991, hundreds of thousands of Russians moved there. They came as party officials and enterprise managers, as engineers or common workers, or simply as retirees. What they had in common was that they usually did not speak the local language, nor did they need to. As these countries have tried to establish statehood, however, they have often made knowledge of the language a condition of citizenship. In local elections in Latvia in the spring of 1994, 40 percent of the country's population and 60 percent of the capital city's (Riga) were not allowed to vote; as Russian speakers, they were not considered citizens of the country. Estonia, deciding that language was not enough, passed laws allowing citizenship only for people able to prove that their lineage in the country extended prior to 1940 (before annexation by the Soviet Union). These rules were attacked by Russian politicians as well as by international human rights organizations, and have since been modified.

Outside of the Baltic republics, no Eastern European country has passed such restrictive regulation of citizenship. Of course, none of them has the same problem of Russian residents either. Until recently, virtually the only people seeking citizenship in the Eastern European countries were ethnic nationals who had lived elsewhere, such as Poles from the Soviet Union or Hungarians from Romania, and these immigrants have been integrated without much difficulty. Same-nationality immigration can be a problem too. The former West Germany had difficulties incorporating former East Germans, and Hungary and Poland may yet face problems if there is mass immigration of ethnic nationals from Serbia and Kazakhstan, respectively. But these will be problems of logistics only. The immigrants will be accepted as citizens; the only problem will be how to accommodate them.

Increasing immigration from other parts of the world, however, means the region will soon have to confront the question of who exactly is a citizen. East-Central Europe's political freedom, relative prosperity, and EU membership have made it an increasingly popular stop among emigrants from Asia, Africa, and the Middle East. In most cases, these people seek to use Eastern Europe only as a transit point. In the past, their main destination was Germany, whose liberal asylum law used to allow anyone who claimed to be politically persecuted to stay in the country until a court could review the case. In 1993, however, Germany changed its law. It now considers for asylum only alleged political refugees who enter Germany directly from the country in which they are being persecuted. Since all of Germany's neighbors are considered "safe," virtually all immigrants without proper visas are turned away at the border. As a result, of the tens of thousands of people who arrive in East-Central Europe hoping to enter Germany, thousands end up staying for months, if not years, in Eastern Europe.

In addition, tens of thousands of former Soviet citizens work illegally in the region, particularly in Poland. Many thousands of Roma, or Gypsies, have also left Romania and Bulgaria for Poland and the former Czechoslovakia, while thousands of refugees from Bosnia are living in neighboring countries.

Countries will define what it means to be a citizen in the light of these realities. For the time being, East-Central Europe, except for the Baltics, has accepted the civic rather than ethnic model of citizenship. The *civic model* accords citizenship to all people living permanently in the territory over which the state rules, whereas the *ethnic model*, as in the Baltic republics, allows only ethnic nationals—those deemed, by virtue of ancestry, as belonging to the dominant nationality—to become citizens. Whether the civic model remains dominant in the future will depend in large part on how immigration patterns develop, which itself depends on the future of the world economy. Of course, much also depends on how the new European Union develops. If people in East-Central Europe experience the EU as truly inclusive for them, too, they are likely to feel secure accepting the civic model. Indeed, the architects of close European integration are counting on this outcome for everyone in the EU. If, however, they feel excluded, the more undemocratic ethnic model of citizenship may well reemerge.

Religion and Politics

During the Communist era, religious affiliation was discouraged but by no means forbidden. The first years of Communist rule saw the greatest pressure against organized religion, including the arrest of clergy and the closing down of houses of worship. By the 1960s, however, the authorities' chief concern was to keep religion out of public life. Schools taught that religion was an unnecessary and reactionary social construct—a myth by which people helped make sense of a prescientific world. People could and did have their own private religious values, transmitted chiefly by family tradition, but those who wanted to enter the political or economic elite had to keep such beliefs to themselves.

Of course, this general truth disguises various national particularities. Albania tried to suppress religion outright, closing down all churches and mosques. Poland, by the 1980s, had reached the other extreme, with the martial law government conciliating the Catholic Church at every opportunity in an effort to co-opt the church as a substitute for Solidarity. Most of the region, however, stood somewhere in the middle, although more on the side of tolerance than proscription.

Religion became more important in the region in the 1980s. The inability to continue the growth rates of earlier times and the increasing self-organization of citizens committed to the expansion of democratic rights were signs of the economic and political crisis of communism, but they also sparked a crisis of identity. Religious feelings grew in this period as a way of holding onto something solid in a world of continuing change. (Only in the highly secular Czech Republic did religion fail to play an important role in recent political and social transformations.)

Because communism has always been officially antireligious, however, religious feelings in the Communist era often reflected a political attitude more than a religious one. As the Polish writer Witold Gombrowicz put it in 1953, "God has become the pistol with which we would like to shoot Marx."[3] People liked what the church stood for, as an institution opposed to communism, but had little intention of living their lives according to church instructions. This attitude was most apparent in Poland. The overwhelming majority of Poles considered themselves believers in the 1980s. Yet few Poles lived by church precepts regarding contraception, extramarital sex, divorce, or abortion. (Contrary to the reputation of Catholics in each country, it is far more common to find Catholic families with eight or ten children in the United States than in Poland.) In public opinion polls, whereas Polish society gave better than 90 percent support to the Catholic Church in the 1980s, that number had dropped almost in half by the mid-1990s. Findings like these suggest that religious identities are often more an expression of political values than of religious convictions.[4]

Religion has played the greatest political role in the historically Catholic countries of Poland,

Slovakia, and Croatia. In each of these countries, Catholicism is intimately associated with national independence. In Poland, the church kept Polish national traditions alive during the long years when Poland was under foreign rule (1795–1918). State and church were also intimately connected in Croatia and Slovakia during the brief periods of World War II when each country attained formal independence under the tutelage of the Third Reich. When people were increasingly dissatisfied with communism, therefore, and identified communism as something alien, something Russian, their longing for a return to national traditions translated into a new attachment to Catholicism. Religious affiliation has expanded elsewhere in the region too—especially Orthodoxy in Serbia (and Russia) and Islam in Bosnia—as people seek new identities in the post-Communist era.

Many observers expected the collapse of communism to mean the rise of religious fundamentalism throughout the region. In fact, this reaction has not occurred. It is true that people needed something else to believe in once communism was officially discredited. But religion and nationalism were not the only contenders for people's hearts and minds. The market was too. One of the most striking aspects of East-Central Europe in the immediate aftermath of the fall of communism was people's almost naïve faith that the new capitalist system would solve all the problems of the past. People looked to capitalism to do the kinds of things that communism promised but could not achieve, such as making everyone equally wealthy. One of the reasons people did not join together politically on the basis of a religious identity is that they believed the market would solve their problems. Only in the mid-1990s did faith in the market begin to erode. Populations then began voting for left-wing parties. That people voted for the left in Poland and Hungary, rather than for the religious parties already available, demonstrates that identity demands based on religion were not yet widespread. But they could still become so in the future. If existing parties prove unable to resolve economic problems and reduce inequalities, fundamentalist groups might succeed in mobilizing people on the basis of religious demands. And when that happens, political democracy is usually the loser. Since identity demands cannot usually be resolved by distributional means, they must be resolved by political means—for example, by establishing an official church and enforcing "religious values" in public life. By compromising on the protection of minority rights, however, such a solution compromises the principles of liberal democracy too.

Ethnicity

The famed ethnic heterogeneity of Eastern Europe has disappeared over the past sixty years in the most catastrophic of circumstances. After the Nazi genocide of the Jews; the forced migrations of Poles, Ukrainians, and Germans in 1945; and the "ethnic cleansing" in the former Yugoslavia in the 1990s, it is no surprise that the countries today have small minority populations. Poland, the most ethnically diverse country before World War II, is the most homogeneous today, with some 98 percent of the population consisting of Poles. In the Czech Republic, 95 percent are Czechs; in Hungary, 90 percent are Hungarians; in Slovakia, 86 percent are Slovaks. The only significant minorities left in the region are Hungarians in Romania and Serbia, Turks in Bulgaria, and Roma, or Gypsies, everywhere, particularly in Hungary, Slovakia, and Romania, where they make up from 5 to 10 percent of the population.

This high degree of homogeneity, combined with the ban on political protest, meant that there was little organizing on the basis of ethnic identity during the Communist era, except for the ethnically diverse and federalist states of Yugoslavia and the Soviet Union. (Even there, ethnic mobilization began in earnest only in the latter stages of the old regime, and was as much about the struggle for democratization as it was for ethnic recognition.[5]) Ethnic nationalism has been more prominent in the region since 1989,

mostly in accordance with Mark Twain's old maxim about patriotism being the last refuge of scoundrels and fools. It has been deployed by elites as a way of protecting their own dominance by diverting the blame for political and economic crisis onto someone else. This was clearly the thinking of the nationalists in the former Yugoslavia, who promoted self-love (and "other-hatred") precisely at a time of great economic downturn. Slovak nationalists meanwhile rode economic dissatisfaction to an electoral victory in 1992 and then gave people an "independent Slovakia" (with the nationalists as its leaders) when all polls showed that people only wanted a better life.[6]

Ethnic identification can of course be a source of pride for economically marginalized people. The Roma, for example, have begun to mobilize around ethnicity as a way of gaining greater political access, and greater autonomy for their way of life. More often, however, ethnic identity has been used since 1989 as a mode of humiliation and exclusion. One defines oneself by excluding others and gains an existential reward instead of a real, material one.

Gender

Gender identities, like class identities, have not come easily to East-Central Europe. It is not that former Communist systems were truly nondiscriminatory, as they claimed to be. On the contrary, women faced the same double burden of job and housework that they do in the West, made even more difficult by the need to stand in long lines to buy basic goods. Nevertheless, women did not feel subordinate to men. Rather, both men and women felt subordinate to the system. This was especially true in the last decades of Communist rule, when opposition movements were already growing. In the context of the struggle against the overarching system, even politicized women did not wish to undercut that unity by talking about gender issues.

But just as labor identities begin to grow in the post-Communist era, so do gender identities.

Gender disparities are quite real in terms of educational possibilities, employment rates, and income—all important issues for would-be professional women trying to move up the hierarchy. By the mid-1990s, such conditions contributed to the emergence of a feminist movement in the region. In new journals, electronic listservs, and public demonstrations, women have begun to protest forcefully against these conditions. This has led to campaigns against abortion restrictions, fights for better birthing conditions in hospitals, demands for gender studies programs in universities, and efforts to stigmatize as well as criminalize domestic violence. One thing that has helped the emergence of gender consciousness is its relative prominence in the West. At a time when Western fashions in politics and economics have been picked up by all, feminism too has a "Western" aura that makes it increasingly acceptable in Eastern Europe. Political parties on the left increasingly emphasize gender issues as a way of winning women's votes.

As in the West, gender identities have also been encouraged by business. Many daily newspapers have created special weekly women's sections, chiefly in order to sell advertising. But since these sections also frequently publish feminist pieces, they inevitably help generate a gender identity that can challenge the "masculinism" that has pervaded the region since 1989.

Interests, Social Movements, and Protests

Given the way the populations of East-Central Europe united so spectacularly in 1989, it was only natural to expect that the new democracies would be marked by a high level of popular participation. We need only recall the images of 1989: the millions of Poles united behind Solidarity; the mass rallies in Leipzig chanting "We are the people!"; the crowds gathered in Prague to hear the dissident (and future president) Vaclav Havel; the ecstatic celebrations in Berlin when the Wall finally fell. The effort to recreate civil society seemed to have succeeded beyond all expectations as it helped topple a regime that had lost public support. Here was a new ethos of participation that it seemed nothing would be able to quell. Postcommunism would be an era of unprecedented popular involvement in politics, as citizens would militantly defend their interests through the same kinds of protests and movements that had worked so well in 1989.

Things have not worked out that way. Instead of being filled with well-organized social groups fighting for the interests of their members, post-Communist public life has been surprisingly quiescent. People have gone to the polls, elected those who initiated the democratic changes, and then largely retreated from public involvement, waiting for the benefits of democracy to pour in. Extrainstitutional protest played a minor role in the first years after 1989. Few rallies and demonstrations challenged government policies, and hardly any politically motivated strikes occurred. There was not even much lobbying activity by the kinds of nongovernmental organizations that help shape so much policy in the West, such as environmental groups, business associations, trade unions, and women's organizations.

Why has there been so little independent civic activity? One of the reasons has to do with the very success of such activity in the past. When the Communist governments were swept away, most former oppositionist activists and organizers themselves became part of the new governments. The outsiders became the insiders, and from their new inside vantage point, they urged citizens to trust the institutions that they used to distrust. The paucity of extrainstitutional protest after 1989 was a result of the long honeymoon period that people were willing to give the new governments as they undertook the difficult work of transformation.

Labor, in particular, was for two reasons widely expected to be very active as an organized force in the post-Communist period. First, working people played a central role in toppling the old regime. This was especially obvious in Poland, where the trade union Solidarity led the successful struggle against Communist rule. But in East Germany and Czechoslovakia, too, it was labor's participation in massive strikes in November 1989 that sealed the fate of the old regime. Second, postcommunism augured poorly for workers. Marketization meant severing the job guarantees and subsidized prices of the past. The labor movement presumably would organize early on to protect itself.

Yet labor was not very active in the first post-Communist years, despite falling living standards. The central reason has to do with ideology: having rejected socialist ideology because of the experience of communism, workers embraced the ideology of their enemy's enemy and entered the new era as believers in free-market capitalism. Of course, workers did not have much experience with capitalism. They looked to Western Europe (rather than, say, Latin America) and saw workers living well. They did not know that they were seeing not so much the results of the market as the results of labor having organized politically to defend itself against the market. West European labor succeeded in taming capitalism by organizing strikes and socialist parties and by mobilizing for elections. But East European workers saw only the end result, without knowing what it took to get there. If this is capitalism, they said, we'll take it. And since, as they were told, building capitalism required time, sacrifice, and a strong managerial class, workers accepted the decline in living standards as well as the declining power of unions at the workplace.

Another reason workers were not very active after 1989 was that they were not sure what the future would bring. To organize in defense of one's interests, one needs to know what one's interests really are, but such things are hard to know in the first years of a new system that promises so much. Workers knew they were losing out, with real wages declining and unemployment increasing. But if these were only short-term setbacks on the road to general pros-

perity, as the market reformers argued, then workers did not want to oppose them. Labor movements were quiescent because workers believed it was in their long-term interests to accept attacks on their short-term interests.

With trade unions disinclined to defend workers' interests, membership plummeted. In Poland in 1981, Solidarity alone had some 9.5 million members. By 1993, total union membership in the country was less than half that, with Solidarity numbering only 1.3 million. Ten years later, Solidarity membership dropped to about 700,000. Throughout Eastern Europe, union membership became concentrated in the old state sector rather than in the new private sector. In part, this concentration developed because wages are often higher in the private sector (although so are violations of work rules and safety provisions). In part, it occurred because private companies regularly fire workers who begin to organize (even though doing so is against the law).

The labor situation began to change in the mid-1990s. Having experienced several years of a new market economy, labor started to learn the lesson Western labor movements had learned much earlier: for wages and working conditions to get better, workers must organize to make them better. Sometimes the unions were simply responding to greater pressure from the rank and file. (Wildcat strikes in Poland, for example, forced unions to take a more militant line.) In Hungary and Poland, the ex-Communist trade unions played a key role in the electoral victories of the ex-Communist parties, and several dozen union officials entered parliament as a result. By 2000, trade unions started organizing even in private firms, from which they had previously stayed away.

New elites have tried to minimize labor input by granting symbolic instead of real representation. This has occurred chiefly through *tripartite councils*, or commissions bringing together labor, business, and government to discuss and decide economic policy. Such institutions have been common in Western Europe, where they have served as the linchpins of the neocorporatist arrangements that have stabilized labor relations and liberal democracy since the 1950s. According to such arrangements, the state guarantees that labor will have input in policymaking in return for labor's promise to limit strike action and exercise wage restraint. By mid-decade, tripartite councils were meeting in virtually every country in Eastern Europe. A big difference with the West European experience, however, is that tripartites in the East are for the most part mere discussion clubs, without the power to decide policy, whereas Western tripartites frequently come up with wage and income agreements binding on all. Because of this largely symbolic role, some have characterized the Eastern European experience as "illusory corporatism" only.[7]

Besides protests around economic issues, there has been some degree of political mobilization in East-Central Europe around gender, religious, and environmental issues. Particularly in the Catholic countries, women have staged rallies in defense of abortion rights and against domestic violence (also against the military violence perpetrated during the wars in the former Yugoslavia). They have begun publishing journals and establishing on-line networks in which to promote their ideas.[8] Partly as a response to this, and in order to promote its own agenda, the Catholic Church has staged counterrallies calling for bans on abortion. Religious fundamentalist groups have also built their own political parties, such as the League of Polish Families or the Hungarian Justice and Life Party.

As for environmental issues, Green parties have arisen everywhere in the region, though they are not yet as well organized or widely supported as in the West. Contrary to the view that people experiencing hard times do not care about such matters, environmental debate has been particularly prominent in the economically depressed and heavily polluted industrial centers of the region, such as Silesia in Poland. In Bulgaria, meanwhile, with its old and weary nuclear plants, an ecological organization was one of the first to be active after 1989.

On the whole, the post-Communist world has seen far less protest than many had anticipated.[9] People have accepted the need for economic reform and have largely left politics to the politicians, hoping that the changes they introduce will make everyone better off. This is not to say that extrainstitutional protest has been absent.[10] Polish farmers have staged a number of actions and protests to publicize their plight, such as blockading roads and dumping potatoes in front of the presidential palace. A 1990 strike by taxi drivers in Hungary played an important role in reminding state leaders about the real social consequences of their economic program. And environmental organizations have scored some successes, such as closing down several particularly toxic industrial polluters, and have used access to the media at election times to keep ecological issues in the public consciousness.

Nevertheless, extrainstitutional protest plays much less of a role in East-Central Europe today than it does in the West. Protest, of course, is an important way in which people become integrated into the political system. Far from threatening democracy, protest is a way of strengthening it. The comparatively low level of protest suggests that many people in East-Central Europe do not yet feel themselves to be full citizens empowered with an array of democratic rights.

Notes

1. For more on the evolution of the party system in Poland, see Marjorie Castle and Ray Taras, *Democracy in Poland* (Boulder, Colo.: Westview, 2002). Also Hubert Tworzecki, *Learning to Choose: Electoral Politics in East-Central Europe* (Stanford: Stanford University Press, 2002).

2. Jan Kubik, *The Power of Symbols Against the Symbols of Power: The Rise of Solidarity and the Fall*

of State Socialism in Poland (State College: Pennsylvania State University Press, 1994).

3. Witold Gombrowicz, *Diary: Volume One*, translated by Lillian Vallee (Evanston, Ill.: Northwestern University Press, 1988), p. 27.

4. For an account of the Polish Catholic Church and its role in politics, see Adam Michnik, *The Church and the Left* (Chicago: University of Chicago Press, 1993), and Maryjane Osa, "Resistance, Persistence and Change: The Transformation of the Catholic Church in Poland," *East European Politics and Societies* 3, no. 2 (Spring 1989): 268–299.

5. See Jane Dawson, *Eco-Nationalism: Anti-Nuclear Movements in Lithuania, Ukraine, and Russia* (Durham, N.C.: Duke University Press, 1996); Mark Beissinger, *Nationalist Mobilization and the Collapse of the Soviet State* (Cambridge: Cambridge University Press, 2002); and Georgi Derluguian, *Bourdieu's Secret Admirer in the Caucuses* (Chicago: University of Chicago Press, 2005).

6. On nationalisms and other hatreds, see Paul Hockenos, *Free to Hate: The Rise of the Right in Post-Communist Eastern Europe* (New York: Routledge, 1993).

7. David Ost, "Illusory Corporatism in Eastern Europe," *Politics and Society* 28, no. 4 (December 2000): 503–530.

8. See (and subscribe to) the Network of East-West Women, www.neww.org.

9. As to why this is so, see Bela Greskovits, *The Political Economy of Protest and Patience* (Budapest: Central European University Press, 1998). Also, Marc Morje Howard, *The Weakness of Civil Society in Postcommunist Europe* (Cambridge: Cambridge University Press, 2003).

10. On protest in the first post-Communist years, see Grzegorz Ekiert and Jan Kubik, "Contentious Politics in New Democracies: East Germany, Hungary, Poland, and Slovakia, 1989–1993," *World Politics* 50, no. 4 (July 1998): 547–581.

CHAPTER

30

East-Central Europe in Transition

This final chapter on East-Central Europe looks more closely at the experiences of the former Yugoslavia—from its violent breakup to its emerging renewal. The story is a mixture of tragedy and perfidy, with elements of democratic durability that hold out hope for the future. A snapshot of Bosnia in 1993 shows the signs of all three.

In the summer and fall of 1993, the embattled republic of Bosnia and its heroic resistance in the capital, Sarajevo, found itself confronted on all sides by forces calling on it to surrender. Serbia, Croatia, and the European Union all urged Bosnia to sign a treaty dividing the republic into three separate ethnoreligious states—one for Orthodox Serbs, one for Catholic Croats, and one for Muslim Bosnians. The war had been raging since the Bosnian declaration of independence in 1991. Poorer Serbs living in the Bosnian countryside, frightened by Serbian nationalists into thinking they would be persecuted by Islamic fundamentalism, declared war against the government in Sarajevo, but their actual fighting was directed not against any Bosnian army but against individual Bosnian Muslims who had been their neighbors for years. The Serbs drove hundreds of thousands of Muslims from their homes, destroyed mosques and other signs of Muslim culture, and raped Muslim women as a way of terrorizing the community so it would vacate the land forever. Then they proclaimed the creation of an independent republic of Serbs in Bosnia. Using a similar ruse about the supposed rise of anti-Christian Muslim fanatics,

Croatia joined in, urging ethnic Croats to carve out a Croatian Bosnia in the western part of the country. By 1993, archenemies Serbia and Croatia had begun to work together, for the first time since the breakup of Yugoslavia, to expel Muslims and divide Bosnia between the two of them.

There was, however, one problem: the Bosnian side was not simply the Muslim side. While Serbia and Croatia sought to root out all Muslim culture and people systematically from the areas they controlled, Bosnia did not respond in kind. The Bosnian president was a Muslim, but the head of the Bosnian parliament was a Serb. Many of the leading officers in the Bosnian army were Croats and Serbs. In Sarajevo, Serbs, Croats, and Muslims saw themselves first as citizens of Bosnia. Bosnia was keeping alive the hope of a multiethnic republic in which different nationalities could live together, just as they had been doing for hundreds of years.[1] By asking them to surrender, the world was asking them to betray the multiethnic principles that had been at the heart of Bosnia—the same multiethnic principles to which the world so often pays homage.

For as long as they could, the Bosnians held firm. Time and again, they rejected plans that would institutionalize the principle of separate countries for different ethnic groups. But in that fall of 1993, with their armies unable to hold out and the world demanding surrender, they finally accepted, grudgingly, the principle of division. Even then, many continued to hope the tide might turn—that the war would shift in Bosnia's favor, that the West would finally intervene on behalf of the multiethnic principles it regularly espouses. In the summer of 1995, the tide did turn. It did so, alas, in a way that only made things worse. First, Serbs took over the eastern Bosnian cities of Srebrenica and Zepa, murdering and raping thousands en route to expelling all Muslims from the areas. Then the Croatian army expelled hundreds of thousands of Serbs from areas around western Bosnia, turning the region into a Croat stronghold. By late 1995, the war had changed population distribution so much that the once unthinkable ethnic partition now seemed all but inevitable. At this point, the United States got involved, directing the North Atlantic Treaty Organization (NATO) to bomb the Serbs as the latter began attacking Bosnian cities. The U.S. did not push for a just settlement, however, but only for partition. In December 1995, a peace accord was signed in Dayton, Ohio, effectively dividing Bosnia-Herzegovina into three separate regions for the three different nationalities.* When U.S. troops entered Bosnia as "peacekeepers" in early 1996, they were enforcing the ethnic partition that Bosnian democrats had tried so hard to avoid. The nationalist fundamentalists had won.

Three years later, in 1999, the war spread to Kosovo. The southern province of Kosovo is the historic heartland of Serbia, but over the last half-century it has become almost completely Albanian. By the mid-1990s, fewer than 10 percent of the population was Serb, although the province formally belonged to Serbia. Unable to win sufficient autonomy, militant Albanian separatists began organizing an armed campaign, which intensified after a governmental breakdown in neighboring Albania made arms easily available. The armed campaign led to even greater Serb repression, and by 1998 it looked to many that Kosovo would be the next Bosnia. In early 1999, the United States called the parties to

a conference in Rambouillet, France, and demanded that Serbia allow NATO troops to monitor Kosovo. When Serbia, unsurprisingly, refused this violation of its sovereignty, NATO, on March 24, began bombing both Serbia and Serb bases in Kosovo. The bombing lasted for six weeks straight, until Serbia agreed to a United Nations occupation of Kosovo. The bombing led to a mass exodus of ethnic Albanians. When the UN (though chiefly, as in Bosnia, the United States) occupied the country and Albanians began to return, ethnic Serbs began fleeing. By 2000, the province had been ethnically divided even more dramatically than Bosnia had.

There is, alas, no moral in the stories of Bosnia and Kosovo. The experience reminds us that brute force often still triumphs over the grandest dreams. By demonstrating the worst possible outcome of the breakup of communism, however, they serve as a model of what must be avoided. Many ex-Yugoslavs recognize this themselves. Even after partition, many citizens in Sarajevo are still trying to hold on to the city's multiethnic character, while a brave few in Kosovo try to do the same there. It will not be easy for them to succeed, but even war does not quench the desire for inclusive democracy. In the years to come, that truth may yet prove to be the real lesson of Bosnia. Indeed, the lesson seems to have been learned even in Serbia, where the Serbian people overcame great odds and in October 2000 pushed President Slobodan Milosevic—the architect of the Yugoslav wars—from office, first in a general election and then in a popular uprising when Milosevic refused to recognize the outcome.

The most hopeful sign has come in the former Yugoslav republic of Macedonia. In 2001, groups of ethnic Albanians, upset at their second-class status and encouraged by the West's recent actions in Kosovo, began an armed conflict against the Macedonian government. Some demanded greater autonomy, while a radical fringe sought to create a greater Albania uniting ethnic Albanians throughout the region. When the government responded with aggressive military action

---

*Formally, the accord speaks of a Bosnian-Croat federation governing both Muslims and Croats. In reality, the Bosnians and Croats have had their own distinct administrations from the very beginning. The formal breakup of the federation may well be only a matter of time.

of its own, the stage seemed set for another Balkan ethnic war, perhaps even bloodier and wider than those in the past. Yet in the end, both sides pulled back from the precipice. In August 2001, the rebels and the government signed a peace agreement stipulating that Albanian would be considered an official language in areas where at least 20 percent of the population is ethnic Albanian, and that over a thousand Albanians would be hired as policemen, assigned chiefly to ethnically Albanian areas. Constitutional amendments in November of that year solidified the arrangement, and it has held well ever since. The historic deal showed that it is still possible to peacefully settle ethnic disputes, provided cool-headed politicians maintain such a will.

Political Challenges and Changing Agendas

In trying to understand the tragedy of Yugoslavia, we must go back to one of the fundamental issues we have been grappling with throughout the chapters on East-Central Europe: how to build a market economy and political democracy at the same time. This central challenge facing all of post-Communist Eastern Europe has been particularly difficult in the former Yugoslavia. Contrary to popular assumptions, the Yugoslav conflict has not revolved solely around nationalism. Rather, elites in Yugoslavia consciously appealed to nationalism in order to divert popular anger away from economic problems. When democracy finally came to Yugoslavia, people were rebelling not just against communism but also against the market reforms that democratic reformers had already introduced to deal with the economic crisis. Local elites won people over with a promise that national independence would bring prosperity.

Yugoslavia began moving to a market economy and political democracy earlier than the other East-Central European states. Cut off from the Soviet bloc, it initiated programs of workplace democracy and began reorienting toward the global economy already in the 1960s. By the late 1980s, with its economic and political system in deep crisis, the country accelerated the pace of reforms.[2] Under the leadership of Prime Minister Anke Markovic, Yugoslavia began experimenting with radical neoliberal market measures. And to secure the public support necessary for painful reforms, it began experimenting with political democracy, too. People now had to determine for themselves a new political identity, and they had to do so at a time of severe economic crisis.

A few new political parties in post-Communist Yugoslavia tried to define themselves on the basis of a commitment to a market economy and universal rights. These parties were committed to building a liberal market democracy throughout the former Yugoslavia. Most of the new parties, however, made nationalism their central theme. These parties talked a great deal about how the economic policies of the Markovic government were hurting the people. And the problem, they said, was that economic policy was being made in the interests of the wrong group of people—in particular, the wrong *nationality*. In the 1990 elections, people tended to vote for the party that promised to make things better for their own nationality. When the democratic elections were over, nationalist parties had won throughout the former Yugoslavia. People had chosen a new post-Communist identity. But it was a nationalist one, not a liberal democratic one. They had used the ballot to vote for parties that blamed one nationality for the problems facing another. Instead of agreeing that all citizens should be free and endowed with inalienable individual rights, people voted to privilege one nationality over those of another. In the former Yugoslavia, in other words, it has so far proved impossible to build a market economy and liberal democracy at the same time. Instead of liberal democracy, there has been ethnic hatred and civil war.

The calamitous problems of the former Yugoslavia have been due to the combination of so many nationalities sharing relatively little space, *and* the fact that each nationality had its own political party and political institutions, whose leaders profited from ethnic conflict. These particular conditions did not exist elsewhere in the region, which is why the destruction and violence of the former Yugoslavia have not occurred elsewhere. Still, ethnic problems remain a major obstacle to stable democratic development elsewhere in the region. Indeed, if the region is to avoid a democratic breakdown in the future, it will have to do something about the dangerous ethnic tensions still prevalent. Much of this is directed at outsiders. There has been an alarming surge in skinhead gang violence against refugees and foreigners. Students and workers from Third World countries have been particularly at risk. This kind of violence, usually committed by young people with little formal education from the most economically marginalized regions, is also frequently directed at homosexuals, and even against centers for children with acquired immune deficiency syndrome (AIDS).

The most significant and chronic ethnic problem in the region, however, is the relationship of the dominant ethnic majority to the Roma, or Gypsies. Of course, anti-Gypsy hostility is widespread even far from Eastern Europe. (It is so ingrained that millions of Americans use the word *gypped* without being aware they are using an ethnic slur.) But the problems are particularly acute here, where most Roma still live. In many ways, the situation got worse after 1989. In the Communist era, governments outlawed Roma nomadic lifestyles, but created the many unskilled industrial jobs that allowed Roma to earn a living without constant migration. Since 1989, most of those jobs have disappeared. Theoretically, Roma are free to be nomadic again. But most no longer know how to survive that way. The result is that Roma now tend to stay in the communities in which they live, but are poorer and more discriminated against than ever before. Paradoxically, the situation is worse in the more developed countries such as Hungary and the Czech Republic, since these were more effective in creating the jobs that changed Roma ways in

the past, and have been more ruthless in cutting those jobs now.

One 1999 event in the Czech Republic symbolized the problem dramatically. In the depressed mining city of Usti nad Labem (Usti on the Labe River), ethnic Czechs as well as Roma had by now lost their jobs, and tensions were getting high. As so often happens, however, instead of joining together to fight for improvements, the two groups turned on each other. Czechs now started seeing Roma as a threat, and got local officials to erect a physical wall in the city, separating Roma from the rest of the population. National politicians protested, but the local politicians were within their legal rights. Shattering the optimistic image of a New Europe in formation, the new millennium thus opened with a Roma ghetto in the heart of Europe. The fall of the Berlin Wall did not spell the end of divisions within Europe.

The protests of the national politicians were not only in vain but also somewhat hypocritical. Official Czech policy has been anti-Roma ever since the new state was founded in 1993. The government did its best to prevent Roma from becoming Czech citizens.[3] A 1969 Czechoslovak law had defined all Roma as citizens of Slovakia regardless of where they lived. This did not mean much at the time, since Czechoslovakia was governed as a single country, but it had great significance after the division of the country in 1993. While citizens were legally entitled to request a new nationality at this time, most Roma residents did not know this. The result was that by 1994, hundreds of thousands of Roma had become foreigners living in the Czech Republic without any legal basis. Policy like this encouraged the racist practices of local officials in Usti. With the recent enlargement of the European Union (EU), East-Central Europe's Roma problems have now become the EU's.

The attacks on Roma are part of the way that "losers" in the post-Communist transition seek to negotiate their fate. The politics of blame is a powerful part of Eastern Europe's post-Communist reality. It is not only Roma who are targeted.

Some people, and parties, have sought to blame economic problems not on other nationalities but on former Communists, and have called for banning such people from public life today. In Latvia, discrimination against ethnic Russians remains the rule. Many who have lived there virtually their whole lives still cannot get citizenship because they do not speak Latvian. Elsewhere, people blame "corrupt" bankers for today's problems, or the corrupting influence of "Western culture." Still others single out "secular humanism" as the problem and propose religious fundamentalism as the answer. In all its guises, this politics of blame is perhaps the chief threat to democratic consolidation in East-Central Europe—indeed, in all of Europe. When one group or way of life is held responsible for all the ills of the present, the danger is that that group or way of life may be banned in the future, or shut up in a ghetto as in Usti nad Labem.

The Challenges of European Integration

Let's look at two particular kinds of challenges that European integration poses to the countries of East-Central Europe: one facing the countries already in the EU, the other facing the Balkan countries still trying to join. The first can be told through the recent example of Slovakia. One of the keys to successful integration into the EU is the attraction of foreign capital. This, obviously, means that Eastern countries must attract Western business. As a late addition to the first group of Eastern countries allowed to join the EU, Slovakia has worked especially hard at doing this. In 2000, it reduced corporate tax rates from 40 percent to 29 percent, and introduced a five-year tax holiday for foreign investors. In 2001, the government committed itself to subsidizing up to 70 percent of the start-up costs of new businesses in certain regions of the country. In 2004, it went even further: jettisoning the advanced industrialized world's long legacy of progressive taxation, according to which those who earn more

pay more, Slovakia became the first country in the region to introduce a flat tax, or a single corporate and income tax rate of 19 percent. (Poland may do the same in 2005.) With bonuses like this, along with a large package of subsidies specifically for the automotive industry, Slovakia beat out its East European rivals and wooed the Hyundai corporation into opening up an automotive plant, following the already large investment of Volkswagen. It is estimated that Slovak subsidies amount to over $100,000 per job created. It is as if the government itself agreed to pay the wages of Hyundai's 2,400 Slovak employees for the next eleven years. The workers, by the way, are paid well in the foreign-owned automotive industry—about twice the national average. Business accepts this because it is still about a fifth of what German workers get for the same work.

If Slovakia thus gets good manufacturing jobs for some of their workers, how is this a "challenge of European integration"? The answer is in how it affects others in the country. For how can the government *pay* for all this largesse offered to business? The flat tax alone cost nearly $600 million in lost revenue. Add in the subsidies offered to the auto companies and it's clear that the budget was in trouble. Slovakia decided to pay for it in an extremely *regressive* way. It levied a high 19 percent sales tax on medicine, added sales tax on basic food, and increased energy prices. It then slashed unemployment benefits in half. The poor, in a word, were made to pay the price. The Roma population was particularly hard hit. Indeed, budget-cutting measures like reducing support for families with more than four children were intended specifically to reduce assistance to Roma, already facing nearly 50 percent unemployment rates.

The direct result of all this came in February 2004, when food riots erupted in numerous small, mostly Roma-populated towns. There was looting of supermarkets, as well as organized demonstrations against the new policies. The government responded with force: special police as well as military units sealed off Roma communities, clashed with protesters for days, and ultimately defeated the uprising after arresting several hundred people.

Eastern Europeans longed to join the EU because they hoped to reap the benefits of the latter. But as the Slovak example shows, the kinds of business that move operations to Eastern Europe tend to be the kinds that do not need a prosperous citizenry. As Dorothee Bohle and Bela Greskovits put it, "The social model has not traveled to the East because [the businesses that go there] are usually the least hospitable to a capital-labor accord."[4] Automakers in Slovakia are trying to export their cars, not sell them on the domestic market. "Trickle-down" does not apply here. Business does not mind making the poor bear the cost of its subsidies, and the government itself sees no other way. In the context of a labor movement already weak because of the Communist experience, the challenge of European integration is thus that the capitalist experience, which incorporation into the EU finally makes real, will only make labor weaker. Instead of Europe becoming one, integration may mean the emergence of two different Europes, with the East remaining at the bottom.

As noted above, East-Central Europe does have some comparative advantage in some areas, particularly agriculture, but these have been the areas in which the western EU has been very protective. Polish hog farmers, for example, initially thought that entry into the EU would be a boon, that their low costs would translate into high profits. But the imposition of tough EU norms and standards has meant that most pork producers could not even get certified. This led to an epidemic of bribe giving to veterinarians in the year before EU entry in 2004, and since this did not always work, a rash of assaults. The EU responded by granting Poland a one-year extension, allowing "un-normed" meat to continue to be sold (though only in the domestic market). Next year, however, it is likely to be more of the same. Thus another challenge of European integration: how to facilitate real participation for East European business?

The Balkan countries of East-Central Europe face different kinds of problems. Only Slovenia is now an EU member. Bulgaria and Romania will likely enter in 2007. The other countries are in limbo. In 1999, the EU offered so-called "Stabilization and Association Agreements with the EU" to Albania and to the four former Yugoslav states of Bosnia, Croatia, Macedonia, and Serbia and Montenegro. But they are not likely to become full members in this decade, or perhaps even in the next. The EU says it's because these countries are not prepared, politically or economically. Some, however, think there are cultural reasons too. The EU, they say, is reluctant to bring in other Orthodox countries (as opposed to Protestant or Catholic), not to mention Islamic Bosnia. (Greece is now the only Orthodox EU member.) In this view, the applications of Bulgaria and Romania have been postponed because they are Orthodox, too. There is no proof that this is so, but the mere fact that many think it is shows that *full* European integration, stretched to include *all* the former Communist countries on the Continent, is still a very iffy proposition, filled with multiple kinds of challenges.

East-Central European Politics, Terrorism, and Its Relation to the United States

In his first major speech after the events of September 11, 2001, President George W. Bush declared that "every nation in every region now has a decision to make: either you are with us or you are with the terrorists." No country in Europe had any trouble deciding where it stood. All had lost citizens in the attack on the World Trade Center. All sympathized with the United States in its moment of tragedy. All had witnessed the catastrophic human costs of inhumane war on their own soil and shared with American citizens their outrage that now it had hit the United States, too. Finally, all knew that those who perpetrated such events were enemies of Europe, too, and of everything Europe in this era of uni-fication was trying to do. And so there was little opposition even when the United States re-sponded by bombing Afghanistan, whose leaders had supported and harbored Al Qaeda. After September 11, all Europe stood united with the United States.

Less than two years later, President Bush told the world that being "with us" meant supporting the planned invasion and occupation of Iraq too. Here Europe balked. Popular opinion, particu-larly in West Europe, turned strongly against the president (and soon against the United States). Iraq, people pointed out, had nothing to do with international terrorism. Occupying a country for no clear reason was just wrong, they felt, and contrary to the principles they had been working for since the end of World War II. But occupying Iraq in particular would be exceed-ingly difficult, they felt, and would likely make the problem of terrorism even greater.

The East European response was quite differ-ent. Public opinion also opposed the war, though not as ardently as in the West. All the govern-ments in the region, however, felt compelled to support President Bush and the war. Indeed, when world pressure against U.S. plans began to grow just before the invasion of Iraq in March 2003, the leaders of thirteen East European countries—Albania, Bulgaria, Croatia, the Czech Republic, Estonia, Hungary, Latvia, Lithuania, Macedonia, Poland, Romania, Slova-kia, and Slovenia—signed statements publicly supporting President Bush and promising to participate in the coalition to disarm Saddam Hussein. Some governments in Western Europe had also gone along—most notably Britain, Spain, and Italy—but the unanimity of the East was on a far different order, as the United States itself understood: thus U.S. Defense Secretary Donald Rumsfeld's famous comment praising the good "new" Europe over the allegedly irrel-evant "old" Europe.

Behind the East European unanimity lay a mixture of authenticity and coercion. On the one hand, East Europeans had strong moral feelings

about the need for decisive action against op-pressive regimes. How governments treated their own citizens, they believed, *should* matter to the world. They also felt that since America had stood beside them during the cold war, of-fering moral support in the fight against dicta-torship, they now had a responsibility to do whatever America and its president asked in return.

Yet as this last point already indicates, East Europeans, unlike their Western counterparts, did not yet see themselves as political actors who *could* say no to the United States. And here was the element of coercion: the power imbalance was so vast that East European leaders felt they had no choice but to do what the United States asked. All but three of these countries were still trying to get into NATO. (The other three had just recently been admitted.) The Bush adminis-tration, moreover, had made it clear on numer-ous occasions that it did not look kindly on critics. In these conditions, no East European government felt it could risk what might happen if it declined to offer its support—particularly once *some* governments in the region an-nounced their intentions to publicly support President Bush. At this point no country felt it could afford to be the one left out. (When the Czech parliament passed a resolution forbidding the government to support the war without a United Nations authorization, the normally weak president took it upon himself to sign the letter instead.) East Europe did feel loyal to West Europe. But they were also upset at its conde-scending and cavalier attitude toward the East in the EU negotiations. This, too, together with the fact that Western Europe was itself divided, pushed it to support President Bush.

As noted in Chapter 26, most countries fol-lowed up on their support by sending at least a token military presence to Iraq. Poland alone sent more than a token force. Its 2,400 troops constituted the fourth-largest military contin-gent in the coalition, after only the United States, Britain, and Italy. (Not surprisingly, the next three largest suppliers of troops came from three countries still hopeful of joining NATO: Bulgaria, Romania, and Ukraine. The first two were in fact admitted the year after the invasion, in 2004.) Poland clearly is trying to set itself up as the Great Britain of the East—in the sense of being America's most dependable ally regardless of the circumstances.

Yet by 2004 some of this support began to wane. In part, this was due to the same reasons support began to wane in the United States: with the strong Iraqi resistance, the war and occupation simply were not going as planned. East Europeans were also outraged by the evidence of American torture of Iraqi prisoners, and wondered whether they didn't bear complicity in this too. There were also more prosaic reasons. East Europeans were upset that they had so far received little in return. Their companies, despite having considerable track records doing business in Iraq, were still waiting for the much-promised supply contracts to be offered to other than American firms. Poles in particular felt their contributions had been taken for granted. They complained that their citizens were still denied visa-free access to the United States, unlike West Europeans. They did not like having to be photographed and fingerprinted upon entry to the United States, while Westerners from countries that opposed the war were not. When Polish president Aleksander Kwasniewski, the United States's closest friend in East-Central Europe, publicly stated in March 2004 that he had been "misled" by America in the run-up to the war, he was indicating that America could not take Polish unconditional support entirely for granted. And indeed, in fall 2004, the Polish government announced that it would begin reducing its Iraqi contingent in 2005.[5]

East Europe's close attachment to the United States has cost it some support in the West. Poland in particular is regarded suspiciously by many West European policymakers, who sometimes refer to it as America's "Trojan horse" in the EU. Most EU leaders, however, recognize the bind Poland and other countries in the region are in. They too, after all, were in a similar position vis-à-vis the United States just after World War II. It takes time to gain real sovereignty.

Fortunately, there has not been a terrorist attack in Eastern Europe at the time of this writing. With its large contingent of troops in Iraq, Poland felt increasingly vulnerable after the terrorist bombing of the Spanish railroads in March 2004, which killed two hundred people. While certainly not impossible, such plots are less likely in Eastern Europe, where there has been little immigration in recent decades and no established Arab communities. Still, police forces have become more vigilant lately and, as in the United States, somewhat less protective of civil liberties. All public demonstrations are now seen by the police as potential terrorist sites. Migrants and visitors from developing countries, particularly Islamic ones, are subject to increased monitoring.

East-Central European Politics in Comparative Perspective

How can we best study East-Central Europe today? Until just a few years ago, students studied the region as little more than an afterthought to the study of the Soviet Union. Experts on contemporary Soviet society were treated as automatic experts on Eastern Europe as well. Introductory courses on European politics usually did not even mention the region, except as "the other" against which "the West" was pitted.

Today there is a danger of going too far in the opposite direction. With virtually the entire region already in NATO (against Russia's strong opposition) and most in the EU as well, scholars are beginning to treat the region as the kidnapped partner of the West finally returned home. European politics courses now regularly deal with democratic and market transition in Eastern Europe (though speaking barely a word about events in Moscow). College students are discovering that a summer trip to Europe demands stops not just in Paris and Rome but in

Prague, Budapest, and Kraków too (and maybe even Riga). In other words, little by little, Eastern Europe is being readmitted to the fold, with Russia and Ukraine carved off as "the other." The East-Central Europe that was once viewed as "belonging" to Russia is increasingly seen as the rightful property of Western Europe instead.

The reality is that East-Central Europe can be understood only in its connections to *both* Western Europe and Russia. It is trying to become more a part of the West today, but the very fact that it must try demonstrates that a chasm still remains. The main streets of downtown Budapest may seem like the main streets of downtown Brussels, but Hungary's or Poland's dying industrial sectors, just moving away from state ownership and Communist Party guidance, are experiencing problems more similar to those facing Russia or China than to the problems facing Belgium or France. We need to understand not only where Eastern Europe hopes to be going, but also where it has been. As we saw in Chapter 26, Eastern Europe was not just "taken over" by communism; numerous internal factors pushed it in that direction. Today, numerous internal factors keep it from simply becoming another part of Western Europe. In some ways, it increasingly resembles not the West but the South, not Western Europe but South America and Southern Europe.[6] We need to be careful about how we "locate" countries or regions, so as not to fall into ideological wishful thinking. In this book, we have tried to highlight East-Central Europe's status as a set of countries in between, with inextricable links to both East and West, both liberalism and communism, both communism and capitalism.

One of the ways to look at these contradictory aspects of East-Central Europe is through the discussion of democratization. How can societies be democratized? How can a newly achieved democracy be consolidated? These questions have been at the center of research in comparative political science over the past two decades. Beginning in the mid-1970s in Latin America and southern Europe, a series of countries that had long been authoritarian or military dictatorships began the transition to democratic forms of government. By the mid-1980s, theorists had speculated on the causes of this transformation, argued about whether the new democratic systems could be consolidated, and suggested how democracy could best be strengthened. Mainstream political scientists, who had considered communism to be unreformable and totalitarian, thought it unimaginable that Eastern Europe would join this new wave of democratization anytime soon.[7] Within a few years, however, journals and conferences worldwide would be devoted to the new study of "comparative democratization," comparing democratic transformations in Latin America and East-Central Europe.

What can such comparisons teach us about how to initiate and consolidate democratic political transitions? What are some of the similarities and differences in transitions to democratic government from right-wing dictatorships and from Communist systems?

One common element is that democratic change is preceded by a revitalization of civil society. Indeed, the very term *civil society*, referring to the public sphere for civic and political interaction outside of government, has reentered the vocabulary of political science because of the experience of democratic transformations, particularly in East-Central Europe.[8] We can now see that one of the main weaknesses of mainstream political science was its focus on elites. Until recently, political scientists tended to have a very thin notion of citizenship. Citizens were considered insufficiently trained in public affairs and were advised to leave governing to the experts. "Acceptance of leadership," wrote Joseph Schumpeter, the influential economist and democratic theorist of the 1950s, "is the true function of the electorate."[9] In Latin America and particularly in East-Central Europe, however, it was precisely those citizens who refused to accept leadership who made democratization possible. Without Solidarity in Poland or the independent political activists in Hungary, the

Communist governments would have had no reason to accept political democracy. Recent democratization movements have returned the study of citizens and civil society to the center of political analysis.

At the same time, comparative analysis also illustrates the importance of *conciliation* and *negotiation*. A mobilized and angry citizenry is not enough. The elites who control the guns must be persuaded that giving up power is in their interests too, or at least that it will not lead to their arrest and prosecution. The authorities need a reliable adversary to negotiate with. And that adversary, representing the citizens in their campaign for democracy, must be prepared to make concessions, even ones most citizens believe to be wrong, in order to persuade the authorities to go along.

What kinds of concessions must democratizers offer? First, they should agree to refrain from locking up the ousted dictator, at least right away. In Chile and in Poland, the respective military leaders Pinochet and Jaruzelski were even able to maintain their positions briefly as head of state after the first free elections. While some former leaders were eventually prosecuted—in Argentina, Bulgaria, and East Germany, for example—the charges and penalties were relatively minor, and all sides understood that the action was more a public relations campaign on the part of the new regime than an attempt to exact vengeance.

Supporters of the old system also remained relatively free from persecution. Nowhere was democratization accompanied by an immediate purge of the bureaucracy, not even the military and police bureaucracies. The leading officials were retired, usually with generous pensions intact, but rank-and-file officials tended to retain their posts, at least for a while, until new recruits were brought in and the old guard could gracefully be retired.*

In Latin America, the need for conciliation of the old elite also meant a favorable attitude to capitalist big business, which had been the main social base of the dictatorships. Here, paths diverge. For in East-Central Europe, there was no capitalist big business. If conciliation is necessary to calm the fears of potential opponents, then in a post-Communist context, conciliation means maintaining policies favorable to the working class. Few other groups are likely to be quite as dissatisfied by the post-Communist system. Certainly not former party officials: most were gracefully retired, quietly retained, or enabled to move on to lucrative careers in business and banking, fields they tended to know better than the old dissidents did. Far from suffering, this group has largely benefited from the building of a capitalist system. Most working people, however, have yet to benefit. That is why they represent a potential threat to democratic consolidation and why they must be conciliated.[10] If workers come to experience democracy as privation, they are likely to be susceptible to the appeals of demagogues and authoritarian nationalists. This was true in Latin America too, but the existence there of a powerful capitalist class, afraid to part with dictatorship because of its fear of labor militance, meant that business-friendly policies were more important in the short run than labor-friendly policies. In East-Central Europe, however, labor-friendly policies are more important as a way of consolidating the new system.[11] Not all supporters of democracy, whether in Eastern Europe or the West, seem to understand this even today.

While working-class support for authoritarianism in Russia shows the importance of winning labor to democracy there, too, we should note that the situations in Russia and China are actually quite different from that in East-Central Europe. Russian and Chinese authori-

---

*The lustration process in Czechoslovakia was an exception, but even here many dismissed individuals were soon able to find good jobs again. More officials were sacked in East Germany, but this is a special case. East Germany was not an example of democratization from within but from without. Instead of confronting its former internal enemies, the East German elite had to confront an external enemy, a previous foreign power, that did not have to worry about unduly angering the old leaders, since the old leaders had simply become the vanquished side, and were thus unable to mobilize resistance to democratization. Significantly, in the year prior to reunification, there was no lustration in East Germany.

tarianism has much stronger roots. Unlike in Eastern Europe, communism was experienced as part of the national tradition, not as something imposed from without. Under communism, both countries became superpowers. As a result, there is far more internal support for the old system than we see in Eastern Europe. Thus, in Russia and China, conciliating potential enemies of democracy requires efforts to change the underlying political culture, not just to reach out to those who may lose economically.

All in all, East-Central Europe's governments must undertake the difficult task of adjusting their systems enough to enter the EU and the global capitalist world while maintaining the support of both regular citizens and foreign elites, of both working people and investors. This does not mean that all policies must be equally acceptable to all social groups. Such consensus is impossible to achieve, and attempting to do so would be a recipe for stagnation. But governments must see themselves as the representatives of all, and make sure that the interests of all groups are at least sometimes addressed in public policy.

To be successful in today's global climate, market reform and EU integration must serve the interests of the business community, whether domestic or foreign investors or international financial agencies. To these groups, East-Central Europe must show continuing commitment to establishing favorable investment climates, as well as an ability to maintain tight budgets. It must establish tax policies that promote investment while also guaranteeing the state sufficient resources to develop infrastructure and maintain social stability. At the same time, there will be no long-term stability without the support of labor. In the heavily industrial world that East-Central Europe remains, the working class still constitutes the largest potentially organized sector of the population. It is the group most affected by systemic transition and the one whose support is crucial if a democratic system is to survive.

Just as the political system must be transformed in a way that is compatible with economic reform, the economy must be trans-formed in a way that maintains support for political democracy. Economic reform, in other words, must be politically sensitive and socially aware. Citizens must come to feel that economic reforms are working for them, and not just for the new or old elite. Creating this environment requires such things as a privatization program with shares for employees and citizens, anticorruption and antimonopoly measures, and strong regulatory agencies safeguarding safety, health, and environmental standards. Such policies are necessary not just to maintain a decent and growing standard of living for citizens, but for maintaining the stability of a democratic system. Eastern Europeans are well aware that change does not come without sacrifice. Indeed, what has been surprising in the years since the fall of communism is not how many strikes and protests there have been but how few. But if the post-Communist world comes to be perceived as being just as immoral and rotten as the old one, many people may lose all hope whatsoever. Society would then be overcome by a crushing sense of despair, giving rise to social pathologies like crime and violence and political pathologies like the emergence of fascist organizations.

So far, most countries in the region have avoided fundamentalist dangers by focusing on real economic issues. For the most part, the parties winning elections have been those that promise to make things better by proposing alternate economic policies, not by singling out one group of people for condemnation. There is, however, no guarantee that this democratic pattern of politics will continue. The emergence of the demagogic and antidemocratic Andrzej Lepper as a real contender for prime minister in Poland demonstrates this all too well. Party affiliation is still unstable in East-Central Europe. No party has succeeded in attracting majority support anywhere in the region. In particular, those who are suffering economically tend to feel left out. They are politically homeless—not yet loyal voters of any party. They are consequently accessible to any party that can win them over. Democracy has been a powerful lure in East-Central Europe. But the struggle for democracy does not end with the toppling of communism. People who lose out economically tend to feel that they still do not live in a "democracy," and they will eventually ally with whatever party seems best able to take their interests into account. If people become thoroughly alienated, governments lose their most precious asset: the goodwill of the citizens.

In Europe, whether Western or Eastern, no country is fully accepted today unless it is formally a democracy. Whether a country can build a democratic system depends on a number of factors, such as its political culture, the nature and duration of its authoritarian experience, the degree of popular mobilization, the internal economic situation, international pressures, and the country's location in the global economy. In some countries, political mobilization from below plays the crucial role; elsewhere, a skilled negotiating strategy is key. In countries with a relatively homogeneous population, nationalism may help attract support for political democracy, whereas in multiethnic societies with a history of conflict, it may only damage chances for democracy. Where a capitalist class is strong, economic policy must be favorable to capital; where capital is weak and workers have historically been deemed the dominant class, economic policy must be favorable to working people.

Western governments do not press all countries to democratize. If a country has a commodity the West wants to buy and a culture the West does not understand, the West does not care if it is a democracy or a dictatorship. (Kuwait, with an authoritarian government able to supply the West with oil, was not compelled to democratize even after the democratic world organized one of the century's greatest military campaigns in its defense in the 1991

Gulf War.) In Europe, however, and particularly in order to get into the EU, countries must be democratic.

But what does this really mean? For there has also been outside pressure on post-Communist countries to restrict civil liberties in the name of fighting terrorism. There is, in the end, no one form of democracy. Democratic countries can have a presidential or a parliamentary system, extensive or limited state intervention, strong or weak local governments, proportional or single-member-district representation, broad or limited social welfare networks. They can allow unfettered capitalist development, or they can empower communities to restrict the privileges of private capital. They can side more with the United States or more with the European Union, and choose to define terrorism as a crime or as a declaration of war.

What makes East-Central Europe so exciting today is that we see so many of these democratic forms in action, and so many of the vital questions for the future laid out on the table. From the civic involvement of the Solidarity movement in Poland to the innovative ideas for involving citizens in economic reforms today, from the resistance of Bosnians against ethnic cleansing to the diverse ways the region is responding to the challenges after September 11, East-Central Europe has much to teach the West about democracy.

Of course, whatever the form of democracy, critics can and will always demand more of it. People can always think of reasons and ways to be more involved in making decisions that affect them. Popular pressure for greater democratization is an inescapable feature of the world as a whole, and particularly of what used to be the Communist world. Democracy is, after all, an eternally unfinished project.

Notes

1. For a majestic account of Bosnia's multiethnic history over the ages, see the great 1945 novel by Bosnian Nobel Prize author Ivo Andric, *The Bridge on the Drina* (Chicago: University of Chicago Press, 1984).

2. For an excellent account of how economic developments led to the outbreak of war, see Susan Woodward, *The Balkan Tragedy* (Washington, D.C.: Brookings Institute, 1995).

3. Jirina Siklova and Marta Miklusakova, "Denying Citizenship to the Czech Roma," *East European Constitutional Review* 7, no. 2 (Spring 1998): 58–64. More information on the East European situation is available on the website of the European Roma Rights Center, www.errc.org.

4. "Capital, Labor, and the Prospects of the European Social Model in the East," Working Paper No. 58 in the Program on Central and Eastern European Working Papers Series, Harvard University, 2004. Available at www.ces.fas.harvard.edu/publications.

5. For more on changing Polish attitudes to America and the Iraqi invasion, see David Ost, "Letter From Poland," *The Nation*, October 4, 2004; available at www.thenation.com/doc.mhtml?i=20041004&s=ost.

6. See Adam Przeworski, *Democracy and the Market: Political and Economic Reforms in Eastern Europe and Latin America* (New York: Cambridge University Press, 1991), esp. pp. 188–191.

7. One prominent scholar went so far as virtually to rule out the possibility of democratic change in the Communist bloc. See Samuel P. Huntington, "Will More Countries Become Democratic?" *Political Science Quarterly* 99, no. 2 (1984): 193–218.

8. See John Keane, ed., *Civil Society and the State* (London: Verso, 1990).

9. Joseph Schumpeter, *Capitalism, Socialism and Democracy*, 3rd ed. (New York: Harper & Row, 1950), p. 273.

10. For more on the importance of labor for democratic outcomes, see David Ost, *The Defeat of Solidarity: Anger and Politics in Postcommunist Europe* (Ithaca, N.Y.: Cornell University Press, 2005).

11. On the importance of the conciliation of workers," see Bela Greskovits, *The Political Economy of Protest and Patience: Eastern European and Latin American Transformations Compared* (Budapest: Central European University Press, 1998).

Part VII Bibliography

Ali, Rabia, and Lawrence Lifschultz. *Why Bosnia?* Stony Creek: Pamphleteer's Press, 1993.

Amsden, Alice, Jacek Kochanowicz, and Lance Taylor. *The Market Meets Its Match: Restructuring the Economies of Eastern Europe.* Cambridge: Cambridge University Press, 1994.

Bozoki, Andras, ed. *Intellectuals and Politics in Central Europe.* Budapest: Central European University Press, 1999.

Bunce, Valerie. *Subversive Institutions: The Design and the Destruction of Socialism and the State.* Cambridge: Cambridge University Press, 1999.

Burawoy, Michael, and Katherine Verdery, eds. *Uncertain Transition: Ethnographies of Change in the Post-Socialist World.* Lanham, Md.: Rowman & Littlefield, 1999.

Callinicos, Alex. *The Revenge of History: Marxism and the East European Revolutions.* University Park: Pennsylvania State University Press, 1991.

Castle, Marjorie, and Ray Taras. *Democracy in Poland.* Boulder, Colo.: Westview Press, 2002.

Chirot, Daniel, ed. *The Crisis of Leninism and the Decline of the Left.* Seattle: University of Washington Press, 1991.

———. *The Origins of Backwardness in Eastern Europe.* Berkeley and Los Angeles: University of California Press, 1989.

Crawford, Beverly, ed. *Markets, States, and Democracy: The Political Economy of Post-Communist Transformation.* Boulder, Colo.: Westview Press, 1995.

Crowley, Stephen, and David Ost, eds. *Workers After Workers' States: Labor and Politics in Eastern Europe After Communism.* Boulder, Colo.: Rowman & Littlefield Press, 2001.

Dunn, Elizabeth. *Privatizing Poland: Baby Food, Big Business, and the Remaking of the Polish Working Class.* Ithaca, N.Y.: Cornell University Press, 2004.

Einhorn, Barbara. *Cinderella Goes to Market: Citizenship, Gender, and Women's Movements in Central Europe.* London: Verso, 1994.

Ekiert, Grzegorz, and Stephen Hanson, eds. *Capitalism and Democracy in Central and Eastern Europe: Assessing the Legacy of Communist Rule.* Cambridge: Cambridge University Press, 2003.

Ekiert, Grzegorz, and Jan Kubik. *Rebellious Civil Society: Popular Protest and Democratic Consolidation in Poland.* Ann Arbor: University of Michigan Press, 1999.

Eyal, Gil, Ivan Szelenyi, and Eleanor Townsley. *Making Capitalism Without Capitalists: Class Formation and Elite Struggles in Post-Communist Central Europe.* London: Verso, 1998.

Falk, Barbara J. *The Dilemmas of Dissidence in East-Central Europe.* Budapest: Central European University Press, 2003.

Feffer, John. *Shock Waves: Eastern Europe After the Revolutions.* Boston: South End Press, 1992.

Funk, Nanette, and Magda Mueller, eds. *Gender Politics and Post-Communism.* New York: Routledge, 1993.

Gagnon, Valere P. *The Yugoslav Wars of the 1990s: A Critical Reexamination of Ethnic Conflict.* Ithaca, N.Y.: Cornell University Press, 2005.

Gardawski, Juliusz. *Poland's Industrial Workers on the Return to Democracy and Market Economy.* Warsaw: Friedrich Ebert Foundation, 1996.

Garton Ash, Timothy. *The Magic Lantern.* New York: Random House, 1990.

Gowan, Peter. *The Global Gamble: Washington's Faustian Bid for World Dominance.* London: Verso, 1999.

Greskovits, Bela. *The Political Economy of Protest and Patience: Eastern European and Latin American Transformations Compared.* Budapest: Central European University Press, 1998.

Grzymala-Busse, Anna M. *Redeeming the Communist Past: The Regeneration of Communist Parties in East-Central Europe.* Cambridge: Cambridge University Press, 2002.

Haney, Lynne A. *Inventing the Needy: Gender and the Politics of Welfare in Hungary.* Berkeley and Los Angeles: University of California Press, 2002.

Hardy, Jane, and Al Rainnie. *Restructuring Krakow: Desperately Seeking Capitalism.* London: Mansell, 1996.

Hockenos, Paul. *Free to Hate: The Rise of the Right in Post-Communist Eastern Europe.* New York: Routledge, 1993.

Howard, Marc Morje. *The Weakness of Civil Society in Postcommunist Europe.* Cambridge: Cambridge University Press, 2003.

Jowitt, Ken. *New World Disorder: The Leninist Extinction.* Berkeley and Los Angeles: University of California Press, 1992.

Kenney, Padraic. *A Carnival of Revolution. Central Europe 1989.* Princeton, N.J.: Princeton University Press, 2003.

Kitschelt, Herbert, et al. *Post-Communist Party Systems: Competition, Representation, and Inter-Party Cooperation.* Cambridge: Cambridge University Press, 1999.

Laba, Roma. *The Roots of Solidarity.* Princeton, N.J.: Princeton University Press, 1991.

Leff, Carol Skalnik. *The Czech and Slovak Republics: Nation versus State.* Boulder, Colo.: Westview Press, 1996.

Legters, Lyman H., ed. *Eastern Europe: Transformation and Revolution, 1945–1991.* Lexington, Mass.: D. C. Heath, 1992.

Meardi, Guglielmo. *Trade Union Activists, East and West.* London: Ashgate, 2000.

Michta, Andrew A. *The Soldier-Citizen: The Political Army After Communism.* New York: Palgrave, 1997.

Offe, Claus. *Varieties of Transition: The Eastern European and East German Experience.* Cambridge: MIT Press, 1997.

Orenstein, Mitchell. *Out of the Red: Building Capitalism and Democracy in Post-Communist Europe.* Ann Arbor: University of Michigan Press, 2000.

Ost, David. *The Defeat of Solidarity: Anger and Politics in Postcommunist Europe.* Ithaca, N.Y.: Cornell University Press, 2005.

———. *Solidarity and the Politics of Anti-Politics.* Philadelphia: Temple University Press, 1990.

Pearson, Raymond. *National Minorities in Eastern Europe, 1849–1945.* London: Macmillan, 1983.

Poznanski, Kazimierz. *Constructing Capitalism: The Reemergence of Civil Society and Liberal Economy in the Post-Communist World.* Boulder, Colo.: Westview Press, 1992.

Ramet, Sabrina. *The Radical Right in Eastern Europe.* State College: Pennsylvania State University Press, 1999.

———. *Balkan Babel: The Disintegration of Yugoslavia from the Death of Tito to the War for Kosovo.* Boulder, Colo.: Westview Press, 1999.

Rothschild, Joseph. *Return to Diversity: A Political History of East Central Europe Since World War II.* New York: Oxford University Press, 1989.

Schopflin, George. *Politics in Eastern Europe*. London: Blackwell, 1993.

Slay, Ben. *The Polish Economy: Crisis, Reform, and Transformation*. Princeton, N.J.: Princeton University Press, 1994.

Stark, David, and Laszlo Bruszt. *Postsocialist Pathways: Transforming Politics and Property in East Central Europe*. Cambridge: Cambridge University Press, 1998.

Stokes, Gale. *The Walls Came Tumbling Down: The Collapse of Communism in Eastern Europe*. New York: Oxford University Press, 1993.

Szacki, Jerzy. *Liberalism After Communism*. Budapest: Central European University Press, 1995.

Tworzecki, Hubert. *Learning to Choose: Electoral Politics in East-Central Europe*. Stanford: Stanford University Press, 2002.

Waller, Michael, and Martin Myant. *Parties, Trade Unions and Society in East-Central Europe*. Essex, England: Frank Cass, 1995.

Wedel, Janine. *Collision and Collusion: The Strange Case of Western Aid to Eastern Europe, 1989–1998*. New York: St. Martin's Press, 1998.

Wheaton, Bernard, and Zdenek Kavan. *The Velvet Revolution: Czechoslovakia, 1988–1991*. Boulder, Colo.: Westview Press, 1992.

Woodward, Susan. *The Balkan Tragedy*. Washington, D.C.: Brookings Institute, 1995.

Websites

For information on women's issues and organizations in Eastern Europe, see the Network of East-West Women: www.neww.org.

For access and links to Eastern European newspapers and journals, in native languages and English, and to other relevant bibliographic material, see the University of Wisconsin–Madison's excellent website: www.wisc.edu/creeca/reeca.

"Transitions Online," an Internet journal covering Central and Eastern Europe: www.tol.cz.

Information on Roma (Gypsy) issues can be found at the European Roma Rights Center: www.errc.org.

For full-text editions of the excellent publication *Eastern European Constitutional Review:* www.law.nyu.edu/eecr.

Daily news from East-Central Europe and Russia is available also at Radio Free Europe's website: www.rferl.org.

Index